A Celebration of Young Poets

South – Fall 2007

Creative Communication, Inc.

A Celebration of Young Poets
South – Fall 2007

An anthology compiled by Creative Communication, Inc.

Published by:

CREATIVE COMMUNICATION, INC.
1488 NORTH 200 WEST
LOGAN, UT 84341

Copyright © 2008 by Creative Communication, Inc.
Printed in the United States of America

ISBN: 978-1-60050-152-4

Foreword

The poets between these pages are not famous...yet. They are still learning how language creates images and how to reflect their thoughts through words. However, through their acceptance into this publication, these young poets have taken a giant leap that reflects their desire to write.

We are proud of this anthology and what it represents. Most poets who entered the contest were not accepted to be published. The poets who are included in this book represent the best poems from our youth. These young poets took a chance and were rewarded by being featured in this anthology. Without this book, these poems would have been lost in a locker or a backpack.

We will have a feeling of success if upon reading this anthology of poetry each reader finds a poem that evokes emotion. It may be a giggle or a smile. It may be a thoughtful reflection. You might find a poem that takes you back to an earlier day when a snowfall contains magic or when a pile of leaves was an irresistible temptation. If these poems can make you feel alive and have hope in our youth, then it will be time well spent.

As we thank the poets for sharing their work, we also thank you, the reader, for allowing us to be part of your life.

Thomas Worthen, Ph.D.
Editor
Creative Communication

WRITING CONTESTS!

Enter our next POETRY contest!
Enter our next ESSAY contest!

Why should I enter?

Win prizes and get published! Each year thousands of dollars in prizes are awarded in each region and tens of thousands of dollars in prizes are awarded throughout North America. The top writers in each division receive a monetary award and a free book that includes their published poem or essay. Entries of merit are also selected to be published in our anthology.

Who may enter?

There are four divisions in the poetry contest. The poetry divisions are grades K-3, 4-6, 7-9, and 10-12. There are three divisions in the essay contest. The essay division are grades 4-6, 7-9, and 10-12.

What is needed to enter the contest?

To enter the poetry contest send in one original poem, 21 lines or less. To enter the essay contest send in one original essay, 250 words or less, on any topic. Each entry must include the student's name, grade, address, city, state, and zip code, and the student's school name and school address. Students who include their teacher's name may help the teacher qualify for a free copy of the anthology.

How do I enter?

Enter a poem online at:
www.poeticpower.com
or
Mail your poem to:
    Poetry Contest
    1488 North 200 West
    Logan, UT 84341

Enter an essay online at:
www.studentessaycontest.com
or
Mail your essay to:
    Essay Contest
    1488 North 200 West
    Logan, UT 84341

When is the deadline?

Poetry contest deadlines are August 14th, December 4th, and April 8th. Essay contest deadlines are July 15th, October 15th, and February 17th. You can enter each contest, however, send only one poem or essay for each contest deadline.

Are there benefits for my school?

Yes. We award $15,000 each year in grants to help with Language Arts programs. Schools qualify to apply for a grant by having a large number of entries of which over fifty percent are accepted for publication. This typically tends to be about 15 accepted entries.

Are there benefits for my teacher?

Yes. Teachers with five or more students accepted to be published receive a free anthology that includes their students' writing.

For more information please go to our website at **www.poeticpower.com**, email us at editor@poeticpower.com or call 435-713-4411.

Table of Contents

Poetic Achievement Honor Schools   1

Language Arts Grant Recipients   9

Grades 4-5-6 11
    Top Poems 12
    High Merit Poems 22

Index 365

States included in this edition:

Alabama
Arkansas
Georgia
Kentucky
Louisiana
Mississippi
Missouri
North Carolina
Oklahoma
South Carolina
Tennessee
West Virginia

Fall 2007
Poetic Achievement
Honor Schools

* Teachers who had fifteen or more poets accepted to be published

The following schools are recognized as receiving a "Poetic Achievement Award." This award is given to schools who have a large number of entries of which over fifty percent are accepted for publication. With hundreds of schools entering our contest, only a small percent of these schools are honored with this award. The purpose of this award is to recognize schools with excellent Language Arts programs. This award qualifies these schools to receive a complimentary copy of this anthology. In addition, these schools are eligible to apply for a Creative Communication Language Arts Grant. Grants of two hundred and fifty dollars each are awarded to further develop writing in our schools.

All Saints' Episcopal School
Morristown, TN
Betty Golden*
Angie Smith

Alpena Elementary School
Alpena, AR
Sherry Choate
Ginny Hulsey
Dawn Keys
Mr. Nichols
Mrs. Phillips
Ruthie Weidenfeller

Alvaton Elementary School
Alvaton, KY
Carolyn Gifford*
Jane Kirby
Mary-Anne Powers*

American Heritage Academy
Canton, GA
Sue Buffam
Sandy Dranzek
Mrs. Griffin

Annunciation Elementary School
Webster Groves, MO
Mrs. Kelly*

Appling County Middle School
Baxley, GA
Melanie Clark*
Sue Hayes*
Suzanne Herrington*
Lynn Hyers*
Pamela P. Johnson*
Kristin S. O'Steen*
Lisa Oliver*
Melissa Perkins

Armorel Elementary School
Armorel, AR
Cynthia Sullivan*

Bailey Elementary School
Bailey, NC
Frances Anderson*

Baylor School
Chattanooga, TN
Fontaine Alison*
Tammy Burns
Amy Cohen
Bart Loftin
Sally Naylor*

Beck Academy
Greenville, SC
Megan Beck
Gina Carter*
C. Ferguson
Shannon Royal

Benton County School of the Arts
Rogers, AR
LaVona Cerna*

Berryville Elementary School
Berryville, AR
Joni Beckwith
Sheri Bickel
David Gilmore
Penny Hardin
Candy Phillips*

Blakeney Elementary School
Waynesboro, GA
Missey Greene
Lorteea Johnson
Mrs. Richardson
Mrs. Walker
Mrs. Williams

Bloomfield Elementary School
Bloomfield, KY
Kendra Long*

Briarwood Christian School
Birmingham, AL
Martha Bickford
Joie Black
Jenny Burdick*
Mrs. Chastain
Kari Cuenin*
Mrs. Cuneo
Mary Beth Fields

Briarwood Christian School
Birmingham, AL (cont.)
Kristin Fincher
Jennie Gillon
Mrs. Griffin*
Susan Johnson*
Miss Jones
Ms. Kirkpatrick*
Mrs. Leonard*
Mrs. Pardue
Ms. Peters
Joanne Peterson
Mrs. Petty*
Mary Ann Pickell
Paige Robinson*
Mrs. C. Smith
Mrs. L. Smith
Cheryl Vincent
Miss Wagner

Briarwood Elementary School
Bowling Green, KY
Allison Bemiss*
Ronann Bunger
Reneé Johnson
C. Zinobile

Brilliant Elementary School
Brilliant, AL
Dana Bryant
Betty Mitchell

Broadway Elementary School
Broadway, NC
Susan Brown*

Byrns L Darden Elementary School
Clarksville, TN
Mrs. Downing
Mrs. Elkins
Mrs. McDonnough
Ms. McKeethen
Ms. Murray
Sandi O'Bryan*
Mrs. Purcell
Mrs. Rivers
Mr. Rogers
Mrs. Siegle

Byrns L Darden Elementary School
Clarksville, TN (cont.)
Ms. Thomas
Mrs. Wooten

C. C. Spaulding Elementary School
Durham, NC
Vivian M. Geter*

Carver Elementary School
Henderson, NC
Savi Sandhu*

Cathedral School
Raleigh, NC
Diane Lee*

Center Elementary School
Waycross, GA
Pamela Barnhill*

Chapin Middle School
Chapin, SC
Shannon Allonier*
Martina D. Fox

Charleston County School of the Arts
North Charleston, SC
Ms. Drennan
Rene Bufo Miles

Childersburg Middle School
Childersburg, AL
Denise Ivey*

Clarksburg School
Clarksburg, TN
Jeannine Stokes*

Cleveland Elementary School
Oklahoma City, OK
Richard Kleffman*
Alice Pettit*

Cline Elementary School
Cold Spring, KY
Rachel Mercer*

College View Middle School
Owensboro, KY
Tina Hare
Debbie Hendrix*

Contentnea Elementary School
Kinston, NC
Birta Battle*

Cool Spring Elementary School
Cleveland, NC
Aimee Adkins*
Tonya Cassidy
Mrs. Duncan
Stephanie Flammang
Kenneth Lindstrom
Sandra Milholland

Des Arc Elementary School
Des Arc, AR
Brenda Bagshaw*

Discovery School @ Reeves Rogers
Murfreesboro, TN
Kristy Mall*

Dunbar Creative & Performing Arts School
Mobile, AL
Mary Fulton
W. Smith*

Duncan Chapel Elementary School
Greenville, SC
Jan McCloud*

Dyer Elementary & Jr High School
Dyer, TN
Lee Hudson*

EA Harrold Elementary School
Millington, TN
Daniel Edmiston*
Ms. Wadlington

E O Young Jr Elementary School
Middlebury, NC
Savi Sandhu*

East Jones Elementary School
Laurel, MS
Shirley Sellers*

East Oldham Middle School
Crestwood, KY
Jennifer Upchurch*

Eminence Middle School
Eminence, KY
Terry Walther*

Evangelical Christian School
Germantown, TN
Nadia Alm
Shireen Brandt
Lisa Chandler
Lindy Murley
Cathy Short
Tammy Umlauf
Annette Wright
Barbara Yelverton

First Flight Elementary School
Kill Devil Hills, NC
Lisa Beaver
Mrs. Eldridge
Diane Fisher*

Graham Elementary School
Talladega, AL
Donna Edmiston*

Greathouse Shryock Traditional Elementary
School
Louisville, KY
Melissa Goldsmith*

Hayes Elementary School
Enid, OK
Suzanne Johnson*

Haynes Academy for Advanced Studies
Metairie, LA
Teresa Bennett
Janet C. Gubler*

Haynes Academy for Advanced Studies
Metairie, LA (cont.)
Faye Haley*
Juliet Hohan*
Peggy LeBlanc
Leslie Straight*

Hebron Middle School
Shepherdsville, KY
Trina Henn
Beverly Stangel

Holy Trinity School
Louisville, KY
Sarah Reinhart*

Houston Middle School
Germantown, TN
Joye Phipps*

Hunter GT Magnet Elementary School
Raleigh, NC
Lisa Kaszycki*
Angie Parham*

JJ Jones Intermediate School
Mount Airy, NC
Kathy Ratcliffe*

Judsonia Elementary School
Judsonia, AR
Mrs. Stumpenhaus*

Ketchum Jr High School
Ketchum, OK
Mary Davis*
Mrs. Herndon*
Trish McQueen*

Lakeshore Middle School
Mooresville, NC
Emily Blumburg*
Linda Daganhart
Mr. Harrison

Lee A Tolbert Community Academy
Kansas City, MO
Elizabeth Deardorff
Zanova Gasaway
Valerie Guy
Pamela King
Rayma Moburg
Cindy Salomone
Dana Tiller
Janice Yocum*

Lewis Vincent Elementary School
Denham Springs, LA
Chantel Taylor*

Lost River Elementary School
Bowling Green, KY
Nancy Stevenson*

Mark Twain Elementary School
Saint Louis, MO
LaCrissa Mays-Rayford*

Martin Elementary School
Parkersburg, WV
Megan Forshey*

Mayflower Middle School
Mayflower, AR
Rhonda Smith*

Meredith-Dunn School
Louisville, KY
Kathy Beck
Susan Prater
Nancy Stewart

Midway Covenant Christian School
Powder Springs, GA
Mrs. Moore*

Midway Covenant Christian School
Powder Springs, GA (cont.)
Patti Terrell*

Moyock Elementary School
Moyock, NC
Dwan Craft
Tami Harsh
Denise Jewell
Mary Pepe

Musselman Middle School
Bunker Hill, WV
Jennifer Grubb*
Linda Shaw*

North Middle School
Lenoir City, TN
Toni Koy*

Northeast Baptist School
West Monroe, LA
Carol Medlin
Lisa Navarro
Diane Tidwell*

Odessa Middle School
Odessa, MO
Leah Chamberlin
Linda Walsh
Lori Weddle

Our Lady Catholic School
Festus, MO
Brenda Fischer*
Mrs. Kempfer

Our Lady of Fatima School
Biloxi, MS
Mrs. Torricelli*

Paint Lick Elementary School
Paint Lick, KY
Pam Canter*

Palmetto Christian Academy
Mt Pleasant, SC
Dianne Williams*

Pembroke Elementary School
Pembroke, NC
Gelena H. Chavis*

Pembroke Elementary School
Pembroke, NC
Ivene Jones Hunt*

Plano Elementary School
Bowling Green, KY
Brenda Roberts*

Pleasants County Middle School
Belmont, WV
Carol Hysell*

Price Elementary School
Louisville, KY
Jannetta White*

Prince of Peace Catholic School
Taylors, SC
Chris Martinez*

Providence Academy
Johnson City, TN
Mrs. Evans
Lynne Little*

Queen of Angels Catholic School
Roswell, GA
Christine Bordnick*

R D and Euzelle P Smith Middle School
Chapel Hill, NC
Barbara Murray*
Jean Simons

Roberta Tully Elementary School
Louisville, KY
Kristi Schnarr*

Rock Mills Jr High School
Rock Mills, AL
Brandy Pike
Jeffery Thompson*

Rocky Comfort Elementary School
Rocky Comfort, MO
Liz Webster*

Salem Elementary School
Bryant, AR
Beth Oppenhuizen*

Salisbury Academy
Salisbury, NC
Heather Coulter*
Beverly Fowler*

Schaffner Traditional Elementary School
Louisville, KY
Cheryl Mobley*

Scotts Creek Elementary School
Sylva, NC
Laura H. Wallace*

Seven Holy Founders School
Affton, MO
Karen Brandt
Joe Morice
Mary Wagner*

Southlawn Middle School
Montgomery, AL
Stanford Angion*

Southwest Middle School
Searcy, AR
Susan Gooch*

St Charles Homeschool Learning Center
St Peters, MO
Heather Nuehring*

St Joseph Institute for the Deaf
Chesterfield, MO
Pat Watson*

St Mary Cathedral Elementary School
Cape Girardeau, MO
Monica Macke*

St Mary's School
Greenville, SC
Sr. John Thomas Armour*

St Teresa's School
Albany, GA
Mrs. Hanks
Judy Jaros Johnson*

St Thomas More School
Chapel Hill, NC
Linda DiGiovanni*
Jennifer Sullivan*

St Vincent Elementary School
Perryville, MO
Ronda Rowland*

Stone Academy
Greenville, SC
Christen Josey
Cathy Kennedy
Mrs. Merrill
Debbie Roper

Stuart Middle School
Louisville, KY
Diana Berger*

Sullivan Elementary School
Kingsport, TN
Susan Cassidy*

Sycamore Elementary School
Sugar Hill, GA
Ruth Beichner
Patty Kambiss

Tamassee-Salem Elementary School
Tamassee, SC
Susan B. Smith*

Vernon Middle School
Leesville, LA
Lucille Kilgore*

Walker Intermediate School
Fort Knox, KY
Vicki Pitcher*

Walton Verona Elementary School
Verona, KY
Deborah C. McNeil*

West Marion Elementary School
Foxworth, MS
Lisa Peavy*

White Station Middle School
Memphis, TN
Angela Davis
Helen C. Erskine*
Ruby Hubbard
Soo Scott
Mrs. Thompson
Robert Wade
Dwight Wade

Wohlwend Elementary School
Saint Louis, MO
Mrs. Bruckner
Ms. Schaefer
Ms. Seymour

Woodland Elementary School
Radcliff, KY
Mrs. Hall*

Language Arts Grant Recipients 2007-2008

After receiving a "Poetic Achievement Award" schools are encouraged to apply for a Creative Communication Language Arts Grant. The following is a list of schools who received a two hundred and fifty dollar grant for the 2007-2008 school year.

Acadamie DaVinci, Dunedin, FL
Altamont Elementary School, Altamont, KS
Belle Valley South School, Belleville, IL
Bose Elementary School, Kenosha, WI
Brittany Hill Middle School, Blue Springs, MO
Carver Jr High School, Spartanburg, SC
Cave City Elementary School, Cave City, AR
Central Elementary School, Iron Mountain, MI
Challenger K8 School of Science and Mathematics, Spring Hill, FL
Columbus Middle School, Columbus, MT
Cypress Christian School, Houston, TX
Deer River High School, Deer River, MN
Deweyville Middle School, Deweyville, TX
Four Peaks Elementary School, Fountain Hills, AZ
Fox Chase School, Philadelphia, PA
Fox Creek High School, North Augusta, SC
Grandview Alternative School, Grandview, MO
Hillcrest Elementary School, Lawrence, KS
Holbrook School, Holden, ME
Houston Middle School, Germantown, TN
Independence High School, Elko, NV
International College Preparatory Academy, Cincinnati, OH
John Bowne High School, Flushing, NY
Lorain County Joint Vocational School, Oberlin, OH
Merritt Secondary School, Merritt, BC
Midway Covenant Christian School, Powder Springs, GA
Muir Middle School, Milford, MI
Northlake Christian School, Covington, LA
Northwood Elementary School, Hilton, NY
Place Middle School, Denver, CO
Public School 124, South Ozone Park, NY

Language Arts Grant Winners cont.

Public School 219 Kennedy King, Brooklyn, NY
Rolling Hills Elementary School, San Diego, CA
St Anthony's School, Streator, IL
St Joan Of Arc School, Library, PA
St Joseph Catholic School, York, NE
St Joseph School-Fullerton, Baltimore, MD
St Monica Elementary School, Mishawaka, IN
St Peter Celestine Catholic School, Cherry Hill, NJ
Strasburg High School, Strasburg, VA
Stratton Elementary School, Stratton, ME
Tom Thomson Public School, Burlington, ON
Tremont Elementary School, Tremont, IL
Warren Elementary School, Warren, OR
Webster Elementary School, Hazel Park, MI
West Woods Elementary School, Arvada, CO
West Woods Upper Elementary School, Farmington, CT
White Pine Middle School, Richmond, UT
Winona Elementary School, Winona, TX
Wissahickon Charter School, Philadelphia, PA
Wood County Christian School, Williamstown, WV
Wray High School, Wray, CO

Young Poets
Grades 4-5-6

Note: The Top Ten poems were finalized through an online voting system. Creative Communication's judges first picked out the top poems. These poems were then posted online. The final step involved thousands of students and teachers who registered as online judges and voted for the Top Ten poems. We hope you enjoy these selections.

Top Poem Grades 4-5-6

This Tree

There once was a tall, large tree its leaves so green and full.
I've been through many things with that tree, the experiences were never dull.
The memories will never fade, they will always be with me.
Every little minor thing that happened under that tree.

In the fall when things get cold,
the leaves on that tree turn red and gold.
Then in winter when things start to freeze,
all of the leaves fall from the tree.

Then they are left there.
Majestic, while tall and bare.
Spring rolls around and the leaves quickly come back.
The beauty of those long, green leaves, the tree will no longer lack.

Summer is wonderful, too.
The tree so tall and the sky so blue.
Later on, when I'm gone, I hope this tree by a child is found.
It really is quite amazing, a miracle growing straight from the ground.

Courtney Amick, Grade 6
Chapin Middle School, SC

Top Poem Grades 4-5-6

The Changing of the Seasons

All around the leaves are falling,
Greeting us with their special calling.
These wonders here are special for sure.
We see them in a colorful blur.
The sky above and the earth below,
Will soon be covered with fluffy white snow.
The days will get shorter, the nights will grow long
We'll lay in our beds as the moon sings a song.
Leaves fall from the sky like gifts from above,
From the Creator who sends them with love.
Turning purple and red and orange and brown,
Some people can't help but smile not frown.
The wind makes a song that echoes in hearts,
For some it feels like a brand new start.
Pay attention to things that are happening here,
For they only come but once every year.

Stephanie Boyls, Grade 6
Victory Christian School, OK

Top Poem Grades 4-5-6

Mystical Beach

There is a mystery about Mystical Beach,
Legend says that anyone who comes, their soul is reached.
Is it the indigo waves? The golden sand?
What could it be about this queer land?
Perhaps it's the way the pelicans dive,
or how, when the fish swim, they seem so alive.
Who has ever known such a strange place?
It seems that here, time is no race.
But why does it not happen elsewhere?
What makes this land seem so fair?
Perhaps it's not all in the beach.
Maybe all it does is silently preach.
Maybe it's us who does the rest.
Maybe we're the ones who make this time best!
Perhaps if happiness is realized,
this grand perceptivity will be prized.
And if we truly treasure feeling this way,
we will remember that special day.
That is the mystery about Mystical Beach.
What conclusion do you reach?

Karis Hawkins, Grade 6
Wayne Country Day School, NC

Top Poem Grades 4-5-6

The Pencil Who Wrote This Poem

Oh no!
Don't leave.

You left me on the table,
Just after class ended.

With you we'll write
A wicked poem but,
Please don't make me stay.

I'm a warp hole to a
Wonderland of joy and adventure,
Pick me up and we'll fly away.

You are a wizard and I am your wand,
We can carve a story in the rock of wisdom,
To forever be read by many.

Wand waving wizards, dancing dragons.
These are few of the wonderful topics.
What will we write?

Patrick Link, Grade 5
Hunter GT Magnet Elementary School, NC

Top Poem Grades 4-5-6

Beautiful

Did you ever feel like you don't
Belong
Like you're a pearl inside a
Clam
You have to hide the real you from
Everyone
Is it like you are a girl with a shadowed face
And nobody can see under the shadows
The ones that hide you
The beautiful you

Emily Parson, Grade 5
Des Arc Elementary School, AR

Top Poem Grades 4-5-6

Freedom

Freedom is like a beautiful wind,
Moving across our plains.
It shows in the beauty,
Of the creation of our land,
In our mountains, plains, hills, and plateaus.
Freedom is beauty, truth, and love.

Freedom is like standing for what is right.
By telling the truth,
You see a beautiful thing.
Freedom is beauty, truth, and love.

Freedom exists in our world today.
We must show love, and be kind to others.
Freedom is beauty, truth, and love.

Kylee Vestal, Grade 4
Hayes Elementary School, OK

Top Poem Grades 4-5-6

Separation

This is a horrible thing to go through.
Daddies are always gone.
Mommies stay home and cry.
Sometimes I feel I'm all alone.
Separation

Why did this happen?
People change.
They don't get along.
They don't do things together anymore.
They decided they can't live with each other any longer.
Even though they're separated, they still love you.

You hear your parents fighting.
You feel sad and scared.
Sometimes you think parents forget to ask how you feel.

My dad lives in Florida, and I live with my mom in Alabama.
I know my dad still loves me.
I can write letters to him, and ask him to write back.
I can phone him, and ask him to phone me.
This way, I can still be close when he is far away.
Separation

Tiffany Wilson, Grade 4
A H Watwood Elementary School, AL

Top Poem Grades 4-5-6

Morning

As the night slowly creeps away
The morning comes and shows its rays
All creatures begin to arise
And open their weary eyes

Then the mist of sleep starts to fade
And the bees come to flower's aid
They open their petals nice and wide
So their sugary nectar may not hide

Red breasted robins sweetly alert us all
With their lovely pitched morning call
But oh, watch out small little worms!
For the robins are hungry, so do not squirm

Later on dew drops start to evaporate
While lizards sun on strips of stone slate
In marsh-like ponds there are croaking frogs
That do high dives off fallen logs

The morning passes, then the afternoon
And now night is coming with the moon
So creatures sneak back to their beds
And lay down their tired heads.

Savannah Winn, Grade 5
Midway Covenant Christian School, GA

Top Poem Grades 4-5-6

Why I'm Thankful for Veterans

I'm thankful for veterans I've known in my life
The countless brave soldiers who faced danger and strife.
The price they paid is not wasted on me
I'm proud to know many who've been all they can be.

In the Army my grandpa was there with the brave
Who struggled in Korea — their freedom to save.
In Vietnam my Papa dove deep into the sea
To bring back those lost by the U.S. Navy.

My good buddy, Steve, as a Marine stood so tall
To liberate those who had no chance at all.
And finally there's Ray who joined Army Reserves
So our country stays ready to protect and preserve.

For the freedoms we enjoy in this land
I'm ready, like Daisy, to lend them a hand.
So I'm thankful for veterans who've all played their part,
And I carry them with me right next to my heart.

Sam Zimmel, Grade 5
Laurence J Daly Elementary School, MO

Top Poem Grades 4-5-6

Snow

Down gracefully they fall
Closer closer
Come to me
Meet me on my face
In my hair on my clothes
Seep into my tongue
Soft lighter than air
They drift away not knowing where
Close your eyes
Let them kiss you
Fall they will comfort you
They will give you a bed to rest
One by one they gently hug me
All very loving
All your worries melt with them
Don't blink
Just
Just
Shh…

Victoria Zimmerman, Grade 6
Prince of Peace Catholic School, SC

My Mama

The person I admire the most
Is my mama.
Her hair is bronze,
Her eyes are dark brown.
My mama is good at singing,
But she is not good
At working electronics.
Her least favorite thing
Is to swim or skate.
She likes to take care of people.
She reminds me of a female lion,
Because she prepares food
For me and my family.

Ronald Davis, Grade 5
Lee A Tolbert Community Academy, MO

Congratulating Words

A wesome,
B ravo,
C reative,
D ynamite,
E xcellently **F** antastic,
G reat,
H ooray,
I nteresting **J** ob,
K ool,
L uminous,
M arvelous,
N oteworthy,
O utstandingly **P** erfect,
Q uite **R** ight,
S atisfying,
T errific,
U nique,
V aliant,
W onderfully **X** citing,
Y ay!
Z ealous

Alexis Lorenz, Grade 5
William Southern Elementary School, MO

Cats

Cat
sneaky, lazy
purring, pouncing, prowling
feline, mammal — mice, rodent
listening, running, eating
quiet, small
Mouse

Aubri Guthrie, Grade 4
Cleveland Elementary School, OK

Poem

a poem is a feeling inside you
a poem is your mind on paper
a poem is an imaginary place
just waiting to be discovered
a poem is something you do
when you're bored
a poem is something that
makes you dig deep
inside yourself
let yourself
pour
your
emotions
out
and make it the person in you

Taylor Jones, Grade 6
Prince of Peace Catholic School, SC

If Only You Knew

If only you knew,
How the bird flaps his wings.
If only you knew,
How he beautifully sings.
If only you knew,
How the fish swims along.
If only you knew,
That he wouldn't for long.
If only you knew,
What everything does.
If only you knew,
What everything was.

Hunter Seech, Grade 6
East Hoke Middle School, NC

My Family Loves Me

I love my family a lot
We do all kinds of things.
My cousins and I do things
Things where we get caught
Goofy things that we know better.
Some are old,
Some are young
We are all told to behave.
My family
funny, crazy, old and young
Small, meanies, nice, and tall
But most of them are kind.

Kaylynn Fanning, Grade 6
Ketchum Jr High School, OK

Trees

Trees are brown like dogs
Trees have leaves that are reddish
Trees make oxygen

Ross Thompson, Grade 4
Briarwood Christian School, AL

The Spider

Tiny black spider
Spinning a white shining web
To catch tiny ants

Kalin Khera, Grade 6
St Joseph Institute for the Deaf, MO

The Old Truck

My old truck is in the shed.
Its usefulness is past.
Now the tires are flat
But driving it was a blast.

The truck is not a star
The windows are all broken
It's better than a car
The memories are still alive.

Stewart Clark, Grade 6
Pleasants County Middle School, WV

The Car Named Taz

There once was a car named Taz,
That was always in a spaz.
He reads with a big greed,
To take the big lead.
So he doesn't get in trouble by Jaz?

Jeffery Austin Graham, Grade 6
Rocky Comfort Elementary School, MO

Love God

Love is to love
Heart is to love
Special is to love
We all have every kind of special love
Know that God loves you
Every once a day
Every day He will love you
You should love Him too
Because He gave you a heart to love
Don't fight love each and everyone
Loves you
Love God!

Cassandra Molina, Grade 5
Franklin Elementary School, OK

Lost

I cannot find my books.
I cannot find my locker.
I cannot find my homework,
which is really quite a shocker!

I cannot find my lunch box.
I cannot find my classes.
I'm going to have a rotten day
If I don't find my glasses!

Gabby Schemel, Grade 5
St Vincent Elementary School, MO

The Frog

The frog is green,
The frog lives in a pond.
He once was a tadpole,
He swam and jumped and swam.
He jumped on the lily pads,
He jumped in the water,
He sat on the rocks,
He caught some flies,
He jumped back in the water,
And he said good night.

Jesse Schlagle, Grade 5
Heartland High School and Academy, MO

A New Life*

The trees sway,
The wind blows,
Like the winter breeze,
Of my sorrows.
My life goes on,
My days pass by,
Tonight's the night I shall say goodbye.
I'm leaving my homeland,
For a better place,
To start a new life in this human race.
I travel the land, air, and sea,
To find my way to the U.S. of A.

Ray Hyde and Chase Casaburo, Grade 6
Holy Trinity School, KY
*Dedicated to refugees

Tigers

Ripples through the forest looking for water buffalo
Eats animals from elk to elephants
The fiercest animal in Asia
A predator; a prey
Tigers

Endangered in its habitat
Hunted down by poachers
Sold for big bucks
Its home quickly vanishing
Tigers

Bigger than a lion
Striped from head to tail
Weighs a great amount
Orange and black, like a work of art
Tigers

Lives in the jungles of India
Maybe lives in your zoo
Lives in the steppes of Asia
Nocturnal and camouflaged for its meal
Tigers

Jonathan Matz, Grade 5
The Altamont School, AL

My Black Lab Puppy

It all began it seems to me
when I looked at her beautiful brown eyes.
Her beautiful face looking at me.
I knew right then and there
this was going to be a true love.

Terisa Barker, Grade 5
North Middle School, TN

A Hero of Duty

My kind of hero
drives an ambulance to a scene,
helping desperate people,
whom she's not seen.
She gives them needed medicine
and shots of all sorts.
She's a hero of courage,
on or off duty.
She and partners of Medtran Medical Services,
risk their lives for others' survival.
Her truck number is fifty-six
She is a paramedic and she is my favorite!!
Her name is Dena,
for all who don't know her.
I hope you meet her soon!

Tyler Lee, Grade 5
Salem Elementary School, AR

It's That Time of Year

It's that time of year
When everyone wears a sweater
The cold wind is bitter.

It's that time of year
When leaves fall from the trees
From way up high

It's that time of year
When the colorful leaves fall to the Earth's floor
But, believe me, they'll be plenty more!

Cheyenne Jessee, Grade 5
Sullivan Elementary School, TN

It's Close to Winter

It's close to winter — come and play
  the leaves are falling every day!
Go outside and have some fun
  with your friends and everyone!
Go eat turkey go eat pie —
  so go and eat whatever you like!
It's close to winter so lets just cheer
  because a whole new season is coming here!
So say a farewell to autumn one last time —
  because it's close to winter
    and say good-bye.

Cooper Hirshman, Grade 5
Palmetto Christian Academy, SC

Food

Spaghetti goes slurp, slurp, slurp.
Meatballs go munch, munch, munch.
I like peppers ever so hot,
They burn my mouth like a burning pot.
Chicken is good but steak is better,
Last time I ate it I was wearing a sweater.
Buffalo wings are hot
But potatoes are not.

Jacob Newman, Grade 6
Seven Holy Founders School, MO

Magic Is Awesome

Magic is awesome,
Don't you know?
Magic is awesome,
Please don't let go!

When you look to your left,
Magic is there.
On your left…
In front of you…
Behind you.

Magic's in the air,
Creating all the static.
It makes my hair stand up,
Although it seems a bit dramatic.
Magic is awesome!

Jordan Lucas, Grade 5
Childersburg Middle School, AL

The Crashing Waves

I am a graceful bird,
Soaring south for the winter.
I will stay and make friends,
Until migrating back to the water.
I stay there long,
Because it is what I love.
I am the waves,
Sometimes gentle,
Sometimes rough.
I am a Palm Tree,
Rooted to the sand.
I never want to leave.
But I must.
My name is Nich,
And I am the beach.

Nich Toole, Grade 6
Beck Academy, SC

Darkness

The way, dark and long
I think that I am dreaming
In unconsciousness.

Logan Jinkins, Grade 4
Briarwood Christian School, AL

I Am From

I am from free-riding my Birdhouse skateboard at Harrodsburg's Skate Park
And horsing around with my dogs, Mandy and Cocoa, in the *hot sun*
To going bowling at the local alley with Mom, Dad, and my brother…Logan.

I am from viewing movies at Danville's Cinemas 8 on weekends with my family
To competing and roaming in skateboarding competitions
At the Millennium Skate Park in Danville, Kentucky.

I am from playing basketball with my best friends, Drew and Luke,
To appreciating their support and encouragement when I need it.

This is where I am from.

Layth Arrasmith, Grade 5
Burgin Independent School, KY

I Am

I am a young tennis player who loves to swing at those bright yellow balls.
I wonder if I will be at a tennis championship one day.
I hear the crowd cheering me on the racket hit the ball rapidly.
I see my opponent whack the ball towards me.
I want to hit the bright highlighted ball back.
I am a young tennis player who loves to swing at those bright yellow balls.

I pretend to have the best backhand in the world.
I feel the sweat run down my neck.
I touch the racket with a loose but steady grip.
I worry when I don't get a good forehand.
I cry when I've worked so hard and then lose.
I am a young tennis player who loves to swing at those bright yellow balls.

I understand when I lose I should work harder and practice.
I say, "I still have a chance" in my head.
I dream to be a pro one day.
I try to do the best I can.
I hope to be a good sport.
I am a young tennis player that loves to swing at those bright yellow balls.

Virginia Crisp, Grade 6
R D and Euzelle P Smith Middle School, NC

One Kiss

One kiss is all I want…It would take away all my tears…And give me a healthy smile.
One kiss is all I want it would give me hope…And take on life as it comes…
One kiss is all I want…To know your lips…And hold them forever…
One kiss is all I want to show you I love you and be there for an eternity…

Kylie Hopkins, Grade 6
Martin Elementary School, WV

All Seasons

Seasons come and go, some show leaves and some show snow.
Or the seasons see the Christmas trees, and the snow that blows.
Then there's Fall that gives the call of rustles and bustles of leaves.
Here comes Summer with fun, when up above us shine's the sun.
The new Spring sings of the newborn animals, and the newborn things.
What gifts the seasons bring.

Clare Doyle, Grade 4
St Thomas More School, NC

Supersize Fries

At 5am, I was asleep, I heard a noise, and then a beep.
I snuck downstairs so I didn't get caught, I went outside and found a robot.
I had to use caution, he might be mean, he approached with peace, "My name is Macho Machine!"
I asked him what in the world he needed. He stated "Your garden needed weeded."
"My humans fired me from my job. They couldn't live with such a slob."
He wanted a family till the end of time. All the money he had was a dime.
I told him we would not mind, I promised not to leave him behind.

All of the sudden, I don't know why, I just had to have a super size French fry.
He counted the calories and the fat, grabbed my snack, "You can't have that!"
A lovely girl then walked in, Macho Machine put on a grin.
The visitor ordered a Big McSalad. The robot approached her and sang a ballad.
The lovely lady was taken by surprise, she could see the love in robot's eyes.
They turned and walked hand in hand, as though they were dancing to their own private band.
The lovely girl gave him a kiss, I have never seen anything like this!

I wandered home and got into bed, all of the day raced through my head.
I didn't scream, I didn't pout. I just asked, "What was that all about?"

Kayce Allen Hutton, Grade 4
Westview Elementary School, MO

Birds

Birds fly high, birds fly low, and sometimes in between
And when they fly south their music from their little mouth doesn't come back until spring.
And when they're in their nest feeding the babies
the only thing they try to do is sing, sing, sing

Gabe Steinman, Grade 5
Salisbury Academy, NC

Autumn Sunset

I watched from my bedroom window as another Autumn Sunset began. The sky turned a lovely shade of pink, and the sun's warm, golden rays reached out to the earth in farewell. A cool wind whistled through the trees, sending red, orange, and yellow leaves floating to the ground. Then the beautiful sun turned as red as a rose, its final goodbye to the world. As it sank below the horizon, night descended upon the earth, and I went away to bed to dream about tomorrow's Autumn Sunset.

Katie Kassouf, Grade 5
Palmetto Christian Academy, SC

French Quarter

At House of Shock when you enter the French Quarter scene you may feel calmer.
But then, a man pops out of the hearse.
Zombies might try to fly at you from railings and other objects.

You might not feel so calm now.
You see a jester but you think to yourself what will he do, he is just standing there.
Then he moves you jump back and scream.

He mimics you to try to antagonize you.
You see a girl that is flopping around like a fish and you think what did they hurt her for she didn't do anything.
Look up you think to yourself as you see the signs.

What is that someone says behind you possibly a bar.
That's possibly a BUTCHER SHOP!!! Oh god.
You find yourself walking towards another fright you weren't paying much attention
to notice it with all the other thoughts running through your head and all the other frights around.

Gage Breaux, Grade 6
Haynes Academy for Advanced Studies, LA

Alejandro

A lways helps my mom.
L ikes to eat pizza.
E ats too much junk food.
J ames is my best friend.
A very good boy.
N ever takes things.
D oes not be bad.
R uns a lot in my house.
O utstanding at computers.
Alejandro Ibarra, Grade 4
Byrns L Darden Elementary School, TN

I Am Watching

He says to me,
Believe I am not here.
You won't be able to see me.
I know you will be sad.
As am I but you needn't worry,
I will look over you,
I will be your guardian angel.
I am watching.
Don't be afraid.
I still love you.
You still have a place in my heart.
Zoë Shannon, Grade 6
Providence Christian School, NC

All Is Well

The bright yellow sun is shining.
The cardinals and robins are singing.
My baby brother is not whining
Since the bells are sweetly ringing.

I am joyful and so very happy.
The grass and leaves are so very green.
I get to see my great grand pappy.
He is the one whom I've never seen.
Robbie Harper, Grade 6
Pleasants County Middle School, WV

Fall Leaves

Fall leaves are awesome
They have pretty colors too
They're smooth and crunchy
Katherine Kauffman, Grade 4
Briarwood Christian School, AL

Dolphin

Dolphin
gray, playful
swim, jump, eat
playing, hunting, talking, singing
They are so beautiful
Swimming pods
Hannah Beech, Grade 4
East Jones Elementary School, MS

Hopes and Dreams

There once lived a girl
that had only one curl.
She lived by the sea,
and sat on the balcony.

She looked out into the ocean,
and sees the dolphin swim.
One day she hopes and dreams
to be one of them.

She still stands —
waiting and waiting
for her hopes and dreams
to come true.
Hailey Emerson, Grade 5
Westwood Elementary School, AR

The Color Green

Trees
Spinach (Yuk!)
Jolly Green Giant
Broccoli (Don't like broccoli either!)
Grass
Frogs
My face on a boat ride
The start button on my computer
My favorite Girls Rock shirt
That is what I see that is green
Katlyn Cross, Grade 4
West Elementary School, MO

Eagle

Eagle
big, endangered
flies, eats, hunts
pecking, holding, watching, gnawing
big colorful endangered bird
chick
Tylar Speagle, Grade 4
East Jones Elementary School, MS

M&M's

M&M's
round, hard
making, eating, smelling
I love them all
treat
Maricruz Onesto, Grade 5
Westwood Elementary School, AR

Honey

Bees make the honey
Bears eat all of the honey
The honey is gone
Luke Dyson, Grade 4
Briarwood Christian School, AL

Ode to My Football

Oh football,
how I love to throw you.

Sometimes I wish your color
would turn from brown to blue.

Oh football,
I've had you over a year.

When someone throws you,
don't hit me in the ear.

Oh football,
I've played with you and Coach Chris.

I wish I could be you,
but that's just a wish.
Raheem Nixon, Grade 4
Pines Elementary School, NC

Baseball

Baseball is fun in
the sun, and at night sometimes
when you pitch it gives you a
fright. If you hit a grand slam you
can jog around the bases and
look at the fielders make sad faces.
At the end then you shake hands
and say good game.
Bailey Giles, Grade 5
West Marion Elementary School, MS

Dog

Doggy
Playful, lazy
Playing, sneaking, caring
They like to play a lot
K-9
Nathan Simpson, Grade 4
Wohlwend Elementary School, MO

Dogs

Dogs are fun,
Dogs are cute.
Dogs are funny,
Dogs jump and play all day.
Dustin Hawley, Grade 5
Paint Lick Elementary School, KY

Dark

D eserted weird house
A s I looked inside it
R ed paint that glows in the dark
K nowing a monster would come.
Devin McDonald, Grade 5
First Flight Elementary School, NC

Aircraft

I love the roar of the engine
when the big Boeing flies down the runway
the feeling of the helicopter in its descent
it makes my stomach flip flop
the swiftness of a DeHaviland
the tricks of the racers
the sight from the window of the miniature towns below
the feeling of the wind blowing through my hair
the lightness of a Minimax when you lift up the tail
the sound of a Schwiezer gliding through the air

Christian Chapman, Grade 5
North Middle School, TN

My First Gymnastics

Standing frozen before my judges
My mind spins of thoughts of trips and falls
Laura they call, with a salute
Up I raise, hands held high
BAM! It all began
Blackness slowly fills my eyes
Counting down to start
Back flips are formed, round offs are made
Finally a salute is given
Feet tumble to await
Excitement beams from my eyes
2nd place is awarded

Laura Hall, Grade 5
Cline Elementary School, KY

Touring the Continents

Today is quite a boring day,
So let's take a continent tour.
First up I see North America,
Home to monstrous Mt. Rushmore.

Down I go to South America,
Famous for their rainforests and coffee.
Next I travel to Africa,
To gaze at the pyramids and sightsee.

From there I move north to Europe,
Home to the tall Eiffel Tower.
And then I head on to Asia,
With China and it's Communist power.

Southeast to small Australia,
Is where I travel next.
With kangaroos and the beautiful scenery,
Australia is truly the best.

Last but not least is Antarctica,
Where scientists are the only population.
Now that we've finished our tour,
Where would you like to go on vacation?

Jenna Painter, Grade 6
Home School, KY

I Am a Football Player

I am a football player.
I wonder if I could be a pro football player.
I hear the roars of the crowds.
I see red jerseys all around me.
I want to play football like my dad did.
I am a football player.

I pretend I am a football player.
I feel the shape of the football.
I touch other players as I tackle them.
I worry I won't catch the pass.
I cry when I get hurt by other players.
I am a football player.

I understand that I can do what others can.
I say I can do it.
I dream I am the best.
I try my best at everything.
I hope I can be the best one on the team.
I am a football player.

Peyton Bybee, Grade 4
Plano Elementary School, KY

Santa

Everyone knows who comes every Christmas
The big man with all the joy.
You better leave him cookies,
Or he won't give you any toys.

You will never be able to see him
Because he doesn't like kids seeking him.
You might hear something on the roof.
Do you think it just might be him?

McKenzie Wilson, Grade 6
Pleasants County Middle School, WV

My Favorites

My favorite animal is a cat.
My favorite game includes a bat.
My favorite food is cheese.
My favorite cookie is chocolate chip, may I have another please?
My favorite book is a mystery.
My favorite class is history.

Dallas Carter, Grade 4
Wohlwend Elementary School, MO

Halloween

Halloween
Orange pumpkins sitting on the ground
Fresh cut jack-o'-lanterns
Candy dropping in bags
melting candy
Jack o' lantern
Halloween

Lee Wilbanks, Grade 4
Tamassee-Salem Elementary School, SC

Food

Food
I love it
Lunch
Best time
of the day
Food tastes
Awesome
Hamburgers
Apples
Pizza
Snacks
Meat loaf
It all
Rocks!

Madison Gifford, Grade 6
Armorel Elementary School, AR

Busy on Halloween

A busy busy boy on Halloween.
Is like a busy busy bee.
Collecting candy on Halloween night
is lots of fun.
You must rush from house to house
collecting candy on the run.
But oh what fun!

Ben Haney, Grade 5
North Middle School, TN

Mother Nature

Mother Nature makes the wind
She makes the rain
And colors the rainbows
She brings out the flowers
Mother Nature makes our lives perfect
That's what Mother Nature does…

Caitlin DuBois, Grade 4
Lewis Vincent Elementary School, LA

My Friend

My friend is very smart.
She likes Tarts.
She eats them all.
A couple minutes she'll fall
She is cool and
sometimes a fool.
That's a wonderful friend.

Amber Morrison, Grade 4
Lewis Vincent Elementary School, LA

Basketball

I love basketball and it is great,
There's nothing about it you could hate
Do you like basketball? If that is so,
Will you watch it with me? Yes or no?

Jacqueline Kirsch, Grade 4
St Thomas More School, NC

The Shaded Tree

It was a hot summer day in the middle of June
Everyone was back from a game of tag
When I stumbled under a shaded tree
It felt so good under that shaded tree
Where summer felt cool and the wind felt like raindrops
Only falling in the area of the tree's relaxing shade

It was a big land of shade
One day Dad chopped it down I never realized how much I liked it
Now all I have is memories about the old shady tree

Sean Dunn, Grade 6
East Oldham Middle School, KY

Fall Is Here

I can almost smell the happiness fluttering all around me.
Wow! — the sights of a parade marching all around me.
I can hear some squirrels scattering through a tree.
Families are coming from North, South, East, and West.
It is the time of year that I know is the best.
Autumn is here, fall is here yes, yes, yes!
Moms and dads are raking up all the leaves, making big piles.
Listen — hear the children jump in and say, "Yippee, yippee, yippee!"
School is starting.
All the Wal-Marts are full.
There are Thanksgiving decorations up and down the street.
Yes, Fall is here.
Yes it is.
"Yippee, Yippee, Yippee."

Imani Floyd, Grade 4
First Wesleyan Christian School, NC

Definition of Love

Love — Is giving someone the power to break your heart,
but trusting them not to.
Power — Is being able to control something,
but not taking over.
Bravery — Is overcoming a fear, that you never thought possible.
Love — Is something I haven't discovered yet.

Emilee Arledge, Grade 6
Kitty Stone Elementary School, AL

Lady Macbeth

L ies and acts like she doesn't know what happened to King Duncan
A sked spirits to fill her body with evilness
D ark is what she wanted when she killed the king
Y ielded not to Macbeth wanting to not kill

M ade the evidence look like the guards did it
A cted two-face so no one would know what happened
C ould not get rid of the "bloody hands"
B egan to turn evil so she could be queen
E asily talked Macbeth into her plan to kill King Duncan
T ricked other people
H ad "put down" Macbeth when he didn't want to kill the king

Jurnee Taylor, Grade 6
Dunbar Middle School, AR

Hate and Love

Never has a human not hated.
One may love, but that doesn't mean we do not hate
We might hate bugs, which is a stupid hate.
Those who say they do not hate,
That is a lie.
Because everyone hates.
I hate and you hate.
But let us not hate each other.
Let us love each other.
No matter how different, let us put the hate aside.
For we have put aside the hate over skin color.
Why not do the same with accents, clothes, and disabilities?
For I am different.
We all are.
Before I end this poem,
I declare the second golden rule;
Love each other no matter how different.

Ramey Buxton, Grade 5
Odessa Middle School, MO

Lucy and Her Little Friends

Sweet sister Lucy, she's only three
but oh how she can amuse me.
With an imagination as playful as a kitten with string
her invisible playmates can do anything!
No kids near by and sisters too old to play
but have no fear Sacky, Gaga, and Annie are here to stay.
That sweet little girl is a devil,
sometimes her meanness goes up a level.
Boom goes the chair
and Mom gets a scare.
She starts running right away
and asks Lucy "What did you do today?"
A little voice says "Annie did it."
Mom thinks Lucy is so cute.
So instead she sends Annie to sit.
Lucy has her friends for three reasons
the dark, games, and fun for all seasons.
I bet you have already guessed
it really wasn't a test.
They are actually her imaginary friends.

Jane Solinger, Grade 5
Greathouse Shryock Traditional Elementary School, KY

Volcanoes

How high they stand
How beautiful their peaks
They are also dangerous and yet so fascinating
Yet they are still mysterious to me.

Once you get to know about those big fellows
They can be a hand full
Some may become extinct
But still can be an amazement

QuaDaeja Belfield, Grade 5
West Bertie Elementary School, NC

The Special Teacher

There once was a teacher who was weird
He had green piercing eyes and a long beard
He was forty-two years
If you saw his house you could see mold
Every time you talked in class
He would talk how he caught a bass
He was always very mean
His hair shined like a beam
Nobody would be nice
they thought he had lice
So remember if you see him
You might want to stay away

Breeanna Broadway, Grade 6
Ketchum Jr High School, OK

Animal Miracles

Birds that sit atop a tree
sing a joyful melody,
Armadillos in the sun with
dogs that wait on the lawn having fun;
Frogs sit in a bog staring into space
at a little lizard on a log
(out of sight without a trace);
Snow rabbits in the poles sit through a small snow blizzard
keeping snow out of his or her face,
Horses running on a track
after they are adorned in their shiny tack,
Fishes swimming all night long,
while a fly buzzes an odd, odd song;
These miracles I see.
Sounds coming in an angle,
coming to me so beautifully;
Come on everyone!
Rejoice!
For these living creatures sing the silent song of life.

Andrew Creech, Grade 5
JJ Jones Intermediate School, NC

Wind

Cool breezes and rough storms
Are whistling through the trees
Invisible friend

Nyssa Thebert, Grade 5
Hunter GT Magnet Elementary School, NC

Ocean Blue

I went to the beach to see the soft, blue ocean.
When I looked over the water
I could see the sailboats gliding by.
I could feel the warmth of the sand on my toes.
I could hear the seagulls flying
and soaring in the sky.
I could smell the salty salt water.
I could taste the salt water burning my lips.

Treyli Blackwell, Grade 5
Alpena Elementary School, AR

Falling Rain

Rain falls like a feather,
floating gently down to the ground.
Forming in the heavens
and then falling back down to Earth.
The sun pulling them back up
like they are bubbles.
And the cycle repeating again.
That is how rain falls.

Lake Billings, Grade 5
Salisbury Academy, NC

Sunshine

Sun shine down on me
On a cold day you warm me
Please come to me sun

Jennifer Bradley, Grade 4
St Thomas More School, NC

Passing the History

On this day I cannot fail.
The history poem through every trail.
I hope I succeed,
And have no greed,
I hope I pass the test,
To have a big fest
To get out of school
And jump in a pool.

Kayden Johnson, Grade 5
Clarksburg School, TN

Baseball

A ball that goes fast.
A ball that gets hit with a bat.
It goes in the air.
People throw it hard.
The game is fun.
The pitcher throws it real fast.
You might not even be able to see it.
You slide to home base.
The bases are 1st, 2nd and 3rd.

Thomas Tinsley, Grade 5
Walton Verona Elementary School, KY

Summertime

Summertime.
it is time for school to let out.
Kids swim all day long
and play all day.
Everyone loves summer.
It is cool and fun.
Summer passed by.
School is beginning
And the kids wait
for summer to come.

Kylee Pittman, Grade 5
West Marion Elementary School, MS

Winter Rain

Little
drops of
rain shaped like kisses
pounding on your face like soft pins
give life

Jaylil Majette, Grade 4
E O Young Jr Elementary School, NC

Percussion

What is percussion?
   Loud rattling snare drums
   Forceful wooden sticks
   Uniformed drum majors conducting
   Large drum lines
   Low bass drums
   Quiet practicing pads
   Unordinary vibraphones
   Extraordinary xylophones
   Hard pounding mallets
   Reading your music notes
   Loud ringing symbols
   Fast keyboarding
   Awesome quad drum players
   Giant marching bands
   Gleaming silver triangles
   Timpani drums
That is percussion!

Ryan Williams, Grade 6
Southwest Middle School, AR

Fall

Fall is the best time of the year.
There's apple cider,
And the state fair.
There's also Halloween.
I love trick-or-treating,
Seeing the mummies and zombies.
I love fall.

Taylor Thomas, Grade 4
Cleveland Elementary School, OK

Things to Be

Time goes by
Little birdies fly
They go real high
Eating worms
Doing squirms
They fertilize
To make carrots
That help our eyes
Eyes help us see
Things to be
Time goes by
Time goes by

Tanner Walls, Grade 5
G C Burkhead Elementary School, KY

I Am

I am a skater riding on the road,
The wind running upon my face,
Doing tricks on the pavement,
Falling off my skateboard,
Jumping cars and ramps,
Grinding poles and rails,
Jumping over the stars,
Like a wild monkey
Running loose in the open.

Logan Elmore, Grade 5
Cool Spring Elementary School, NC

Grandma

My grandma is an old Gritter.
She's also my babysitter.
To me she's very sweet.
A person, people would like to meet.
She's even a good cook.
She always makes us such neat treats.

Anthony Falconberry, Grade 5
Paint Lick Elementary School, KY

My Sparkling Light

You're my best friend
You're my love forever
You're my sparkling light
We will always be together
forever like the sun above
take my hand and together
our love forever we will always
be together forever

Amy Willoughby, Grade 5
West Marion Elementary School, MS

Sky

When I get on a plane,
I usually frown,
I always hate flying,
Until I look down.

The cars look tiny,
buildings are toys,
and I can barely see,
the heads of girls and boys.

The farms are like a quilt,
woven together.
When I look at them I sadly think,
they will not be there forever.

I hear a voice on the speaker,
and everything begins to grow,
and then we touch down,
on the ground below.

Xander Assadnia, Grade 6
All Saints' Episcopal School, TN

Fall

Stars at night disappear as morning rolls in.
My house is neat and clean.
The crisp sheets wrap around my body.
I awake to the beautiful fall colors.

Tavijae Lee, Grade 4
Stone Academy, SC

Christmas

It was the night.
The time was right.
It was far
and under the North Star.
In a shack the Lord was born
and it was not yet morn.
Three men came,
they were wise.
They came bearing gifts.
They came far
to see the Lord who was born under a star.

Katie Welch, Grade 5
Alpena Elementary School, AR

I'll Never Forget That Day

I'll never forget that day
At the funeral home
Eyes watery
Looking into her eyes
Wanting to hug her
Not wanting to let go
I knew she was going to a better place
I whispered to her
It was almost like she smiled at me
In my mind I could hear her say "I love you Abigail"
I'll never forget that day
At the burial crying everywhere even me
Her casket lifted covered in flowers
The preacher preached his words
After everyone took flowers
I'll never forget that day

Abigail Helton, Grade 6
East Oldham Middle School, KY

Mountains

Wondrous mountains peeking over the clouds
Little villages as busy as bees making their hive
Rocks falling from high away places
Whispering wind calling my name
Yummy apple cider warm and steamy in my cup
Fresh air as clean as a mountain stream
Fresh grass as lush as my mom's hair
Pine trees seem as tall as the Empire State Building
Flowers blooming as pretty as a wedding dress
Big boulders as still as statues standing in front of me
I feel as relaxed as a possum in a tree.

Makenzie Wood, Grade 5
Bailey Elementary School, NC

Tiger

I am the tiger, prowling through the brush,
Black eyes gleaming in the night.
I am unseen and unheard by all.
As I hunt down the prey, I move swiftly,
With liquid grace, unnatural speed.

My prey wanders through the jungle,
Not knowing that this is its last night alive.
With its nocturnal sight, it sees
There! A flash of orange and black,
And suddenly it realizes its fate.

It tries to run but it is too late.
I leap through the air, claws outstretched,
Landing on my helpless soon-to-be meal.
It struggles, but it is stuck under me.
Then, my jaws open, showing gleaming white teeth,
And minutes later, the animal is no more.

Garrett Pearce, Grade 5
Estes Hills Elementary School, NC

Foliage

F ragrant and delicate.
O ccasionally people plant foliage that is
L ovely and very dainty.
I t is awe-inspiring and there
A re a couple of very delightful flowers that
G row with water and sunshine.
E veryone idolizes these amazing leaves!

Maclean Frazier, Grade 5
First Flight Elementary School, NC

Don't Do That Again

Awakened at 3:45 a.m.
Confused asking "What's going on?"
bam, boom, bang
Benny, my sweet new dog
shaking like a fish on a hook,
panting heavily, scared look on his face, eyes glaring at me
wondering if he's ok?
mom, on her knees rubbing his belly,
calming him with her words,
"It's going to be ok"
running, jumping,
getting a small towel and soft pillow
placing pillow under his head
mom rubbing away spit draining from mouth
wondering, worrying, what's going to happen?
drool running down his chin
watching him shake all around the floor
saying "Is it over?"
mom replying, "Yes, it's finally over."
learning he had his first seizure,
"Benny please, oh please never do that again!"

Gabrielle Hughes, Grade 4
Roberta Tully Elementary School, KY

Everywhere

Everywhere
Flowers and grass
A sea of waves
Anywhere, anytime
A shooting star
Going there
Everywhere from time to time
Fall beneath
See the spring
Feel the wind
Flowers bloom
Seek the end
Or seek the sight
Either way seek the light

Lena Pham, Grade 6
Euper Lane Elementary School, AR

Halloween

H appiness all around
A wesome
L ooking at decorations
L urking around at night
O wls hooting
W alking door to door
E specially fun
E veryone in costumes
N ever trick or treat alone

Lexi Kerlin, Grade 5
First Flight Elementary School, NC

Beach

Looks like foamy water on the shore
Smells like suntan lotion on your skin
Tastes like salty water in your mouth
Sounds like pelicans screeching noisily
Feels like waves pounding your body

Luke Folds, Grade 5
Plantation Christian Academy, GA

Everything I Hate About Salad

S auce
A nchovies
L ettuce
A nd olives
D isgusting

D readful
R ed tomatoes
E gg
S our cream
S tupid mushrooms
I f only the lettuce tasted like chicken
N asty onion
G ross!

Melissa Piesker, Grade 5
Odessa Middle School, MO

Being a Military Child

I live on an Army Post I am 11 and I worry when my dad is at war.
I wonder if this war will end.
I hear guns shooting every day.
I see different surroundings every year.
I want this war to end.
I live on an Army Post I am 11 and I worry when my dad is at war.

I pretend I'm beside him when he is at war.
I feel happy when my dad is home.
I touch American hearts when I sing the Star Spangled Banner.
I worry that my dad will have to go to war again.
I cry when I have to leave my friends.
I live on an Army Post I am 11 and I worry when my dad is at war.

I understand that my dad has to go to war.
I say the military is the best.
I dream that I could end this war.
I try to do good things every day.
I hope this war will end.
I live on an Army Post I am 11 and I worry when my dad is at war.

Brandon Bahret, Grade 6
Walker Intermediate School, KY

Sea

Looking at the shimmering ocean,
Turning to the ravishing sea,
The sea is an invitation to peace or adventure;
The sand sinks under my feet,
The seagulls coast over my head,
Oh, what an extravagant sight the sea is;
Oh, the might of the sea.
The water laps over my feet now covered in sand,
Oh, the tranquil beach lying flat.
Can you smell the salty sea breeze,
or see the pelicans soar?
Do you see the ocean spreading her azure arms?
The ocean is a spectacular meeting point between land and sea,
Yet, it always seems more than just land laying adjacent to sea.
The epic sea has seen more than some people could ever imagine,
What would she say if she could speak?
One's flesh touches the sand, one's hair follows the wind,
God gave us a wonderful ocean to enjoy,
What a mighty gift!

Christian Cail, Grade 5
JJ Jones Intermediate School, NC

Gabriel — Gabby

Gabriel —
Athletic, Christian, tough, hardworking.
Son of Doug and Brenda, brother of Brooks and Garrett.
Lover of Coke, sports, and Nintendo Wii.
Who fears drinking Pepsi, having a lot of homework, and mean teachers.
Who was born in Birmingham and now lives in Hoover.
— Gabby

Gabby Bell, Grade 5
Briarwood Christian School, AL

Why I Hate Being a Twin!

My twin is a crybaby.
He cries when I punch him.
He cries when he can't spell a word.
He cries when I beat him on a PS2.
He cries if I don't let him copy my homework.
He cries if he has to do his homework.
He cries if I take his cards.
He cries if I hide his movies.
He cries if I play his PS2 games.

Dalton Keener, Grade 5
North Middle School, TN

The Sky

The sky is blue
a wonderful hue
it is bright
another great sight.

See clouds fly
how they soar so high
with how the sun can shine
and look so fine

As we end the day
it ends in a special way
the time of dusk is slim
as the light begins to dim

It's impressive that's right
especially at night
look at the stars
they are very far

The sky is true
all the way through
it will not lie
or make you cry

Elliott Roman, Grade 4
Schaffner Traditional Elementary School, KY

St. Louis Blues

The sound of the skates on ice, the passing of the puck
the towel guy and the chanting of the crowd.
GO BLUES!

Tkahcuk, Stempnik, Jackman, Boyes, Weight and Kayria
just to name a few who wear the blue note.

It is fun to watch them play the game.
They will do whatever it takes to win the game.
GO BLUES!

St. Louis Blues Hockey…
The greatest team around…

Rick Magee, Grade 6
Seven Holy Founders School, MO

Me and You

When there was me and you,
The birds sung their song,
Of a million words,
Like two friends laughing

The river wove around the valley,
Like a tightly drawn bag,
As I stood there weeping,
My tears drowned the ground

When there was me and you,
I could stand up without falling,
You were there for me,
Till the very end

When there was me and you,
You raised me up
To more than I could ever be,
Without you

When there was me and you,
The birds sung their song,
Of a million words,
Like two friends laughing

Meghana Srikrishna, Grade 5
Hunter GT Magnet Elementary School, NC

Music

There's one thing that takes me away,
Away from the routine of life.
Whether listening or playing,
It gets me through the day or night.

I strum for hours on the sextuplet of strings,
The chords they glide from low to high.
The music, the songs, the flight of the notes,
They magically appear from the instrument.

The percussion is next in my plan of escape,
My ears listen to the harmony of the notes.
When I close my eyes,
I can feel the rhythm of the beat.

Music never dies, it only gets better.
It takes me to another place.
Music is my salvation; it's a part of me,
It has no end.

Alex Bauman, Grade 6
Queen of Angels Catholic School, GA

The Trees

The trees sway softly
Branches and leaves falling off
All day they will dance

Jacob Sichel, Grade 5
Hunter GT Magnet Elementary School, NC

Where I'm From

I am from all of the Hollister shirts, from pictures I took hanging up in my room.
From all of the stuffed animals I won.
I am from a plain house.
I am from a rose of a sad moment, the green leaves on a big tree.
I am from the Christmas tree put up in my house and the turkey in the oven on Thanksgiving,
From playing games and opening presents, and my mom and dad always playing around.
I am from the headaches, from the loud noises of my family, and all of the good smelling food all around.
From the big foot stories and the boogie monster under the bed.

I am from Sunday to Wednesday church at Calvary Baptist church.
I am from Gallatin, Tennessee.
From the endless rolls at O'Charleys
From the story about my great grandma, the house that she lived in,
And the people standing in the hot heat for family reunions.
I am from the album at my granny's, and the letters from my house.

This is where I am from.

Brooke Byrum, Grade 6
Lost River Elementary School, KY

Is It Fair?

Is it fair that people are judged by their religion?
Is it fair that people are judged by their race??
Is it fair that people are judged by the money they have, or the house they live in?
Is it fair that people are judged by the clothes they wear, or maybe even where they come from?
No, it's not!
Why do people say the mean things they say??
It just doesn't seem right.
Is it fair?????

Alexandra Bozeman, Grade 6
Discovery School @ Reeves Rogers, TN

Anne Frank

A girl of thirteen, enduring the hardships of life,
Enduring life and death, love and hatred,
Enduring the strife of World War II.
Away from civilization, and the comfort of friends,
Away from the life she so much wanted to have,
A Jew she was and was so proud to be.
Many people do not see how courageous the Jews were,
How much suffering and controversy they withstood.
Many helped them, many lost their lives in doing so,
I am thankful, for all who lived, and for all who lost their lives.
A diary, a place to write down her own private thoughts,
Kitty, she called it and was not expecting it to change the lives of many.
She lived in "The Secret Annex" where she spent twenty-five months of her precious life.
At fifteen that courageous girl died,
She died for country, religion, and she died like most other Jews.
A cold, dark, and unworthy death.
Her death, like many others, taught now horrible it was.
I am thinking, of course, of Anne Frank,
My hero, though very young.
She is in many thoughts and minds when they think of World War II.
She is happy now, now that she is with The King.

Averie Blackmore, Grade 6
Providence Academy, TN

Fall

When I go outside to play
it's the most wonderful time of year.
Fall.
The wonderful winding wind
blows the leaves around me
And as they float gently to the ground
the leaves fly like little baby birds
As I look around I see squirrels
gather nuts for the cold but beautiful winter.
"Ha Ha Haaa"
I hear kids laughing
as they race down the street
As I feel a chill down my back
I know it is time to go in
and have some nice hot cocoa.

Erik Rosenstrom, Grade 5
Greathouse Shryock Traditional Elementary School, KY

The Rubberband

I am a stretchy, blue rubberband
I am flexible, but delicate
If I stretch — SNAP! — I break
I cry because all of the posters I held together fall.
Then comes my cousin —
He's the meanest, toughest, and most hurtful rubberband of all.
He screams and kicks me out of the way.
The teacher then loves him
she hates me now.
I feel so jealous —
the teacher thinks he's the bulkiest!
He's a rough and tough rubberband.
Look!
My cousin broke!
I'm so special
I got my job back
I feel bad for my cousin, but I forgive him.

Donna Trulson, Grade 4
Lynn Fanning Elementary School, AL

A Sad September Day

On that sad September day,
Everybody stood and stared
At that black cloud in the sky.
When I saw that tower fall,
I kneeled down and prayed,
For everybody on that sad September day.

Nicholas Genereaux, Grade 5
Evangelical Christian School, TN

Top Toe

Top Toe is my favorite store.
It makes me happy when I walk in the door.
I love this place I will never ignore,
Because I'll love it forever and more.

Anna Breland, Grade 4
Lewis Vincent Elementary School, LA

My Mom

My mom helps me with my homework,
Finds my school clothes
when I can't find them,
and washes my clothes.
She lets me stay with my football coach.
She remind me of a dog
That barks a lot.
Sometimes she sounds like an elephant
When she comes up the stairs.
She takes me to the movies,
And sometimes I read to her.

DeMorie Powell, Grade 5
Lee A Tolbert Community Academy, MO

My Favorite Season

My favorite season is here,
So I let out a cheer.
September is the month of my birthday,
So I rejoice every day.

October is the month when we get to carve pumpkins that glare
And we go to the county fair.
I get to dance to discos and dance revolutions,
And get to make up all sorts of motions.
I get to eat all kinds of candy,
And wear clothes in all sorts of dandy.

November is the season where I get to have apple pies,
And crispy French fries.

The clock is ticking, tock, tick,
December is coming quick!
When I get to pass the cheer,
And see again everybody I call dear.
When I get to have hot cocoa and dance in glee,
I get to rejoice once again because Jesus died for me.
Oh I love the fall,
It is such a ball!

Arin Abasi, Grade 5
Trinity Day School, GA

Winter Wonderland

There I was standing in the polar,
When my body realized it couldn't be any colder.
When I saw a black nose rubbing my shoulder.
I saw the magnificent white creature stand before me,
He took two paws off and stood like a tree.
There was a reason I stood there without fright,
I saw the astonishing Northern Lights.
The emerald green flowing through all the night.
The elegant, soothing wave of the sky,
So beautiful, you thought you went to heaven and died.
As crazy as it all seems,
It turned out to be a winter wonderland dream.

Zach Ruocco, Grade 6
Beck Academy, SC

The Wall

The wall is tall.
The wall is wide.

Climbers climb up
and they fall down.

There are no slants.
There are no prizes.
There are no partners.

All there is —
pain and agony.

Trenton Grigg, Grade 5
Westwood Elementary School, AR

I Want to Go to Heaven

I want to go look
I want to go see
A place called heaven
Is where I want to be.

I want to go to heaven
I want to go to heaven
hallelujah.

Jesus, I've been waiting
over the hills where my help comes from
because Jesus keeps my life
Because I magnify Your name.

Ralph Phelan, Grade 5
Evangel Christian Academy, AL

Roses

Rose, red, beautiful
You can find them in the ground
Soft like a feather
Cristina Ibarra, Grade 5
Westwood Elementary School, AR

The Holocaust

We have Jews
They are few
They are God's people
Who are loved by him too.
Adara Baker, Grade 5
Pembroke Elementary School, NC

Dogs

Frisbee-fetchers at the park
Tail-waggers with a bark
Squirrel-chasers here and there
Shoe-snackers that will tear
Water-lappers make a mess
Fur-bearers give me stress
China Duncanson, Grade 5
Herbert J Dexter Elementary School, GA

The Way to Get You

If there were a way
To get you back
I would sacrifice
My life to bring
You back
It would be a
Wonderful day to see
You on the earth again
Andrew Wallace, Grade 5
Des Arc Elementary School, AR

A Hot Beach Day

On a very hot day,
Rachel and I went out to play.
The sand was hot;
The water was cold.
The waves were as big as the sea.
Seashells scattered at our feet
We were filled with glee.
A blanket of seaweed floating away
As the horizon makes our day
The crabs in the water come ashore
And rest in the blazing, hot sun.
Now, that the day is almost through,
It is time for us to go home.
See you tomorrow, our little friend.
Sara Fetty, Grade 6
Pleasants County Middle School, WV

Blue Is…

Blue is the sky
Shining like a sapphire
Caught by the sun

Blue is fresh picked blueberries
Ready to eat
Bursting with juice
Full of color

Blue is my bedroom
Relaxing
Joyful
Sleepy

Blue is the ocean water
Fish swimming
Boats sailing
Caught by the wind

Blue is sprinkles
On soft, creamy ice cream
From Culvers

Blue is so many things
Elizabeth Griffin, Grade 6
East Oldham Middle School, KY

Nighttime

When you lay down in the bed
you can't hear what I've said
don't wiggle
please don't squirm
goodness you're like a worm
your feet are on my head
your head is on my feet
ooh! ooh!
don't bounce please
you're killing me!
sleepovers…
what a pain
three or more
that's insane!
so please, if you can hear me
go to a sleepover!
Shelby Brewer, Grade 6
Benton County School of the Arts, AR

If I Were in Charge of the World

If I were in charge of the world,
I would cancel bedtimes, cigarettes,
And rated R movies.

If I were in charge of the world,
There'd be no spiders, snakes,
Or wild animals.

If I were in charge of the world,
You wouldn't have to clean your room,
Take the dog out,
Or wash the dishes.

If I were in charge of the world…
Leah Dale, Grade 5
Eminence Middle School, KY

Soldiers

Soldiers
Proficient, valiant
Fighting, saving, surviving
Longing to be home
Warriors
Robert Rule, Grade 6
Scotts Creek Elementary School, NC

Winter

It gets colder outside
Less green; more brown
With snow and slush and flurries
As days get shorter
More people look out hoping,
Hoping for a sign of snow in the sky
It's winter
Sydney Stansberry, Grade 6
Discovery School @ Reeves Rogers, TN

I Am

I am athletic and kind.
I wonder if I will win a football game.
I hear Frosty the Snowman singing.
I see a chipmunk and a snake playing together.
I want a Corvette.
I am athletic and kind.

I pretend to be a pro football player.
I feel something touching me.
I touch a cloud.
I worry about my dog.
I cry when my animals die.
I am athletic and kind.

I understand how to do division.
I say I believe in God.
I dream about playing in the NFL.
I try hard in school.
I hope the war will end.
I am athletic and kind.

Dannion Thompson, Grade 5
Berryville Elementary School, AR

Going to the Beach

I love going to the beach
The ocean is like blue crystals sparkling in the light
The waves crashing down on me, swish, swish
I love making sand castles
Patching the bumpy sand as bumpy as the sidewalk
I just love making sand castles
I love looking at all of the bright scaly fish
Smiling as they swarm through the water
I just love looking at fish
I love swimming
The warm water coming up under me as I float
I just love swimming
I love going fishing
All of the floppy fish as floppy as a pancake
I just love to go fishing
I love collecting sea shells
When they giggle as I wash them off
I just love collecting sea shells
Boy let me tell you
I love going to the
Beach

Alyssa Arterburn, Grade 4
Briarwood Elementary School, KY

Sunset Beach

Dolphins splashing in the water
The sun, like a big half orange on a blue blanket
Leading to a sandy pillow
Birds hanging above the giant bed
All of the ocean is settling down for bed

Tatijana Schmidt, Grade 5
Wright City Middle School, MO

Shopping

Shopping is an activity.
That's where people use their creativity.
People buy iPods, shirts and shoes.
But don't buy shoes in Avenues.

I love shopping as much as snowfall.
But my favorite shopping is at the mall.
OK — I've told you what I like.
But when I go to the mall "I'm so ladylike."

Kaitlyn Rogers, Grade 5
North Middle School, TN

A Sign of Fall

I feel a cool breeze and the warmth of the sun.
I hear birds chirping a beautiful song.
I smell fresh cut grass and trees of all kind.
I see leaves on the ground pretty and bright.
Those are the signs that fall will soon be here.

Nichole Raimondi, Grade 4
All Saints' Episcopal School, TN

Strong Racing

I sprint seeing the finish line in the distance
Wind blew through my hair and face
My feet pounded on the ground
Summer sweat poured down my face
All I could think about was passing the girl ahead
My green eyes haunted her back as I came
C L O S E R
And closer.

Sydney Loucks, Grade 6
College View Middle School, KY

Where I'm From

I am from horseshoes,
from Senior feed and Breyers.
I am from the pasture.
Where we run wild and free.
I am from the grass,
and the apple tree where the
delicious apples grow.
I am from church and brown eyes,
from Bernie, Brian and Lawrence.
I am from animal lovers and
fixer uppers,
from settle down and go to bed.
I am from going to church,
and the eucharist replenishing my soul.
I'm from New Jersey and Ireland,
Roast beef and Yorkshire pudding.
From the rattle snake that bit my grandmother
and the endless stitches my father had.
I am from Southview Dr.
The place my family will treasure forever.

Meghan Stickle, Grade 6
Lakeshore Middle School, NC

Types of Bucks

There are big ones and small ones.
Fat ones, too.

Black tail, white tail,
Mule deer, too.

Which one to shoot?
Who knows?
The big ones first, and
The small ones for next year?

Brandon Echternacht, Grade 6
North Shelby Elementary School, MO

Boys and Girls

The girl loves school,
wants to stay forever.
The boy stares out the window,
waiting for school to end.

Max Jeffries, Grade 5
Midway Covenant Christian School, GA

Is It a Summer Day?

Is it a summer day,
Hot as it could be?
It is a summer day,
Come on and play with me.

It is blazing hot,
I need a fan to blow.
I am burning up,
The water is so low.

There is no more water,
The lake is drying up.
The water is so low,
I can barely fill a cup.

Baylee Roper, Grade 5
Lula Elementary School, GA

Love

Love is a
Soft
Cuddly
Bunny
On a winter day.
With its shiny
Tail
And
The
Sound of its loud hop!
With its strong beautiful hind legs.
The
Awesome smell of sweet good nature
On a snowy winter day.

Aliyah Tuckman, Grade 4
Endhaven Elementary School, NC

Help Me!!

Heart pounding, legs shaking uncontrollably like a running motor,
preparing to enter Nightmare Forest with my mom and my dad.
A pitch black night moon half full
stepping in mud as we walked along the trail
trees on our sides starting to moan like ghosts
we glimpsed something dashed like a gecko.
Quickly grabbing my mom's arm
heart pounding even more
helplessly turning around to see a razor sharp chainsaw
hoping the man would disappear
turning to my right to find a sharp curved machete rising in the air
hoping it wouldn't come down on me
my eyes got big and bulgy as I ran forward
wondering "When are we going to get out of here?"
Just when I thought it was over
I heard an evil laugh saying, "You're going to die"
clowns hanging on the stalls like trophies
jumping down latching on to my mom like a biting crab
finally seeing something familiar
knowing that the uncontrollable madness was over
finally breathing normal again.

Logan Stansbury, Grade 4
Roberta Tully Elementary School, KY

The Mudcat's Game

The blazing ball going as fast as a bullet towards the audience
The ball from the pitcher's mitt came spinning like a top
People screaming, "Go Team!"
Fireworks popping in the air like a water balloon
The buttery popcorn aroma drifting through the air like a butterfly
Mushy mustard mashed between the bread
Salty peanuts were like sea water
Hot dogs were as hot as an oven
The light felt like the rays of the sun
Cold water felt like an ice cube melting in my mouth
I feel great astonishment.

Lorenzo Ayala, Grade 4
Bailey Elementary School, NC

Parrot

The exotic bird is perfectly still, and its wings are brilliantly colored.
Chirp! Chirp! The bird beckons its friends with a melodious sound.
The marvelous, exquisite bird's claws gently tear the bark away from a lush tree.
It soars flashing its creative coloring, bringing alive the rain forest.
The bird smells like a thick mist, an earthly aroma.
I timidly touch the bird's powerful wings and the feathers feel plush.
The creature searches here and there for food.
It luckily finds a beetle.
The curved beak gulps it down.
It appears to taste heavenly, for the bird is content.
As the bird squawks and starts the day,
The rain forest comes to life more and more.
The balanced ecosystem, the rain forest, has an alarm clock.
The gorgeous parrot.

Calli Farrell, Grade 6
Haynes Academy for Advanced Studies, LA

Fishing with My Dad

Sitting on the water at early light,
I fish with my dad with everything I got.
Waiting patiently for the bite,
I struggle with the big one with all my might.
I land one and pull him in.
Fishing with my dad, my best friend.
Nothing seems to matter and life slows down,
as I spend time with my dad and fish all around.

Drew Nicholson, Grade 4
Brilliant Elementary School, AL

Angels

I believe there are angels unaware
They are the people that need special care

They may be limited in many ways
But they seem to brighten all of our days

They may be mentally challenged or physically challenged too
But all they want is to be accepted by you

They are a very special gift from heaven above
And if you are patient they will teach you real love!

Cora Breanne McVey, Grade 4
Tazewell-New Tazewell Primary School, TN

Kaitlin

Wavy blonde hair and light blue eyes
Comfy Mudd and Tyte jeans and
Camouflage Nike shoes
Sometimes say "Huh?"
Love riding my bike and
Sleepovers with friends
Three things that make me angry
My brother
Loud music when I'm studying, and
Loud people when I'm trying to read
When I'm alone
I lay down on my bed and read
Sing to myself
Drawing nature pictures
My favorite color is
Shades of blue like the sky and the oceans

Kaitlin Evans, Grade 5
Our Lady Catholic School, MO

Carousel

At a fair on a carousel spinning round and round
On a horse, a black horse
That is soft and big and cuddly
I'd like to have one for me to
Take care of, give it baths and
Feed it food like apples and oats
I'd love it.

Ainsley Cowart, Grade 4
Greenville Montessori School, NC

Summer

Summer's my favorite time of the year,
Frogs croaking and birds singing, all music to my ear.
Time to go fishing and camping away,
The perfect things to do on a hot summer day.
I could spend all day long in the hot summer sun,
Swimming and playing, just having fun.
It's time to relax and prop up my feet,
A hot summer day should end with a treat.
For tomorrow's a new day that I must begin,
And start all over doing my favorite things again.

Trey Halter, Grade 4
St Mary Cathedral Elementary School, MO

Honey, I Love Sports

Honey, I love basketball
I love spinning the ball up in the air
Waiting to see if it will go in
I love smacking that ball from their hands
I love catching the orange ball
Slamming it on the ground
As the ball says ouch
I love jumping and blocking the ball

Honey, I love football
I love the sound of the pads as they bang together
I love sacking the quarterback
Hitting him so hard he fumbles
My coach is squeaking plays like a mouse
I love intercepting the ball
Trying to make the winning play
I love throwing the ball as fast as lightning

Honey, I love baseball
I love the sound of the bat when it hits the ball crack
I love to make the big catch
I love when the bases are loaded and I'm up
I love a lot of things especially SPORTS

Scotty Harris, Grade 4
Briarwood Elementary School, KY

The Tiny Seed's Journey

The seed goes on a journey.
They cross the mountains
They cross the seas
Nobody can see them
But the tiny seed believes
That the tiny seed can survive
That the seed can rise high
Then it grows to be the tallest flower ever.
It finally falls down with other
Seeds falling out
And the falling flower still believes
That the other tiny seed will grow up
And be the tallest seed ever.

Parker Herrmann, Grade 5
G C Burkhead Elementary School, KY

Autumn

Crisp leaves drift
Lower and lower
Until they find the ground.
They join their friends
To weave a royal carpet
Red, orange, and gold.
Listen to the wind
Whispering in your ear —
"Don't close your eyes,
For if you do,
You will find to your surprise —
It is gone."

Mallika Gupta, Grade 6
St Paul the Apostle School, TN

Sitting on a Cloud

As I was sitting on a cloud
I felt them crash and rumble
I knew that it had started raining
And every kid stopped playing

As people walked down city streets
The rain would hit their head,
They'd run and get their jackets
And not let themselves get wet

And then I thought how wonderful
When all the rain had stopped
It would be to see the rainbow
After all the rain drops dropped

You would see the children playing
In all the little puddles
As little children love to do
Running up and down the sidewalks
When they knew they were getting wet

Asher Paxton, Grade 6
Discovery School @ Reeves Rogers, TN

Flamingos

Pink and tall
Eating shrimp all day
Legs so skinny
When you look at them
They look like they are going to fall
They are pink
I don't know why they stand on one foot

Paige Belcher, Grade 5
Wright City Middle School, MO

Smith Lake

Blue, green, clear water
A place where memories form
Ski-boats float on it

Jeannie Marks, Grade 4
Briarwood Christian School, AL

Kayla

A man from a faraway place
Got settled to do a big case
He sat on a train
'Til it really did rain
And then fell flat on his face.

Kayla McGahee, Grade 4
Judsonia Elementary School, AR

Hunting

When I go hunting,
you can't yell or talk at all.
When I go hunting.

Johnson Hayes Dooley, Grade 4
Briarwood Christian School, AL

Magic Snow

As white as clouds,
and comes from clouds,
and never is the same.

It flows and drifts down slowly,
then lands gently on my face.

I stick my tongue to catch the flakes,
until it's stiff and numb.

I fall down on my back and head,
and wave my arms and legs around.

I look at my finished masterpiece,
laying on the ground,
and look up at the beauty,
of the magic snow I've found.

Madeline Lickenbrock, Grade 6
Annunciation Elementary School, MO

Ode to My Dog Precious

This is a pit bull and lab.
She is not very flab.
That is because she is active.
She likes to walk.
It is too bad she can't talk.
Precious is black and white.
She does not like to fight.
She is very soft.
She feels like a cotton cloth.
I love my dog Precious!

Andrew Hornick, Grade 5
West Liberty Elementary School, WV

Electricity

Powerful — stay away
Dangerous to touch — shock
Electricity.

Mollye Fitzpatrick, Grade 4
Briarwood Christian School, AL

My Dog

My basset hound's name is Chester.
He loves to be a pester.
He loves to eat.
He has big feet.

Andrew Hess, Grade 5
Duncan Chapel Elementary School, SC

Soccer/A Sport

Soccer
Balls and People
Running down the field fast
Waiting for me to kick the ball
A sport

Nicole Haigwood, Grade 5
American Heritage Academy, GA

Roses and Sunsets

It's a stop sign at the end of the street
and an apple that tastes so sweet.

It's a rose that blooms in June
and a sunset before the moon.

It's a leaf that falls from a tree
and the color of Christmas soon to be.

It's a color for your toes
and for Rudolf's nose.

What color can this possibly be?
Red is the color for me!

Devin Hester, Grade 5
Salem Elementary School, AR

Horses in the Pasture

I see horses eating grass,
Some are running very fast.
They like to run, eat, and play
In the pasture every day.

Collin Pickens, Grade 5
Evangelical Christian School, TN

Ode to Marshmallows

Oh, marshmallows,
you are so sweet
and sticky in the middle.
I love to mix you
with chocolate
and graham crackers
to make a sandwich.
Oh how I love to put you in hot cocoa
because you make the cocoa just right.
Oh, marshmallows,
I like you!

Drew Hunt, Grade 6
Dyer Elementary & Jr High School, TN

Hot Harvest Day

Today my family had a big harvest.
The biscuits were buttery,
The Kool-Aid was fruity,
The wind blew across my
Smooth-skinned beauty
And my flowery overalls
Crashed against my shirt
On the hot harvest day.

Charysma Smoot, Grade 5
Lee A Tolbert Community Academy, MO

Halloween

On Halloween you go trick-or-treating.
Put your costume on and walk through the neighborhood.
The scary jack-o-lanterns stare as you walk by them,
Ding-dong! Go the doorbells of houses with candy.
I go trick-or-treating every Halloween!

Dylan Battista, Grade 5
Walton Verona Elementary School, KY

The Sky's Clouds

Up above my head,
Where all the birds soar,
The clouds are moving slowly,
Making shapes when they fly

A bunny, a boat, and an ice cream shape,
Up above my head,
Where all the clouds fly

A perfect day, a perfect field,
Gazing upon the sky,
Where all the clouds fly

Amy Cohen, Grade 5
Hunter GT Magnet Elementary School, NC

I Am...

I am a lively girl
I wonder about my future
I see the world without wars
I want to live in peace
I am a lively girl
I pretend to know everyone
I feel like I do
I touch the tears on my face when someone in my family dies
I worry about diseases
I cry when I get hurt
I am a lively girl
I understand when someone's feelings get hurt
I say things before thinking
I dream about the war being over
I try to succeed at important things
I hope to be successful
I am a lively girl

Katie Durel, Grade 6
Paul Breaux Middle School, LA

Shoes

I wear shoes. You wear shoes.
They are big and tall!
You can find all kinds at the mall.
From left to right from top to bottom.

Click, Clack, Clap
Flip, Flop, flip flaps flop.
On dark feet, light feet, your feet, my feet, green
Feet, blue feet, your feet, my feet.
Click, Clack, Clap, Flip, flop.

Tip, Tap, shoe strings, tap the floor, Tip, Tap
Boom, Bam big boots hit the floor — hard and tough,
Tough and rough.
On your feet, my feet, his feet, her feet
Green feet, blue feet, your feet, my feet.

Kiara Threatt, Grade 5
Childersburg Middle School, AL

I Am...George Washington Carver

I am a famous African American scientist.
I wonder how it would have felt to know my parents.
I hear the word slave from my childhood!
I see Diamond, Missouri.
I am a famous African American scientist.
I try to discover new things in agriculture.
I feel I accomplished a lot by being a scientist.
I care for Tuskegee.
I am a famous African American scientist.
I worry about educating African American farmers.
I am sad when I think about not having my parents to guide me.
I understand that discovering the peanut was a big thing.
I am a famous African American scientist.
I say, "It is simply service that measures success."
I dream that blacks and whites will be treated equally.
I am George Washington Carver.

Michael Franklin, Grade 4
Bethel Lutheran School, MO

Love Is Turquoise Blue

It smells like chocolate chip cookies in the oven.
It tastes like sweet red strawberries.
It sounds like soft, calm romantic music.
It feels like a cuddly teddy bear.
It looks like a white wedding gown.
Love is a romantic walk on the beach.

Melanie Burnett, Grade 4
Pines Elementary School, NC

Love

Love…is something you can't break
Love…is something you can't live without
Without love…you can't make it through life
So…you've got to have love

Alycia Witherspoon, Grade 6
Precious Ones School, NC

Monster

M onsters are coming
O n Halloween night.
N o one has ever seen the
S cary, hairy monsters.
T hey have said they are fast.
E very time they come.
R unning around the town.

Hampton Sylvia, Grade 5
First Flight Elementary School, NC

What Traffic Can Do

"The cars are lined up in a row,
And on that road I dare not go.
But I must get to work real fast,
Or with my boss I will not last."

"My paycheck will go down the drain,
My food! My clothes! Oh, what a pain.
I'll take the long way, fast, not slow,
And down that curvy road I'll go!"

"Oh no! I wish I'd had a brain,
But rapidly more speed I gain!"
And that's the end of our friend Biff,
Who went too fast on Dead Man's Cliff.

Olivia Miller, Grade 6
Providence Classical School, AL

Barrett

I am seaweed
never knowing where
the tide will take me.
standing 5 ft tall
proud as I can be.
Greenville is my hometown.
I am a fan of all fans.
Greenville Drive baseball I love.
I am athletic.
Hitting baseballs,
swimming like a fish,
swinging clubs.
I am Barrett.

Barrett Maddox, Grade 6
Beck Academy, SC

An Ode to My Mom

Oh Mom, you mean the world to me.
I love you, I hope you see.

For me, you provide clothes.
Your pretty face is as beautiful as a rose.

When you cook fried chicken,
My fingers, I'm sure lickin'!

Tre-Kwon Thomas, Grade 4
Pines Elementary School, NC

The Ruby Red Slippers

I was taken from my owner's smelly feet,
by a young girl named Dorothy.
I was stuck on her feet when
wicked wicked witch
tried to steal me
I'm shiny, I sparkle, and I even glow
why I'm even brighter than the
Yellow Brick Road
I was tired of walking so long and far
I thought we were looking for Kansas on the farm.
We made it to Oz with
scarecrow and friends.
Why this was the best trip ever until the wicked witch came again.
Soon I had to say goodbye to my best friend.
She clicked her heels together and was gone.
I loved her so dearly
but trust me this was just a little story.

Hanna Dugas, Grade 6
St Mary's School, SC

My Dad

My Dad has chocolate brown hair and green apple eyes that glow in the sun
He smells like cologne
Hair is so soft like sheep
My talented Dad doesn't sing
Knowing how to play the guitar fantastically
Being such a peaceful person to my life
But a wonderful Dad
My grateful Dad does a lot of things with me
Teaching me terrific tricks
Helping me when I don't understand tricky homework
Things that I'll never, ever forget about him are
Teaching me new moves for soccer, kick slam!
Teaching me new things I haven't learned in school yet
My Dad makes me feel better when I'm sad
He's like an angel helping people, even cops
Loving him like he loves me
Knowing he does cause he's mine
Wanting to be like him when I grow up
Wanting to play the guitar and be funny like him
Wanting to learn things from him
He is my faithful Dad

Brittany LeBlanc, Grade 4
Briarwood Elementary School, KY

My Friend

My friend is always there even when times are a scare.
When I'm at lunch alone our friendship makes me feel at home.
That friend of mine is always kind.
When she goes skating with me momma said it was a sight to see us falling down.
When we're in class we wonder why jazz is always on Mr. Fishbum's radio.
After we leave the mall we go to my house and watch TV.
When she leaves my house,
I thank God for a wonderful day with my friend.

Maya Hill, Grade 6
Saint Paul School, TN

My Guinea Pig

My guinea pig's name is Princess.
She is as long as a ruler.
She is mostly brown
Except her two black stripes.
She plays in my mom and dad's bed.
My mom does not like her
shedding in the bed.
I don't play my drums around Princess
Because she could go into shock.
If she wants something she will get it
Because she makes annoying noises.
Even though I don't like
Some of her habits,
I still love her for who she is.

Rafael Edwin, Grade 5
Lee A Tolbert Community Academy, MO

A Wedding to Remember

White was the color of choice
Flowers of all colors and the sound of the preacher's voice
Mom stood there looking in his eyes
Both their smiles wide and bright
Tears filled my eyes and my heart swelled inside
I couldn't hold back the feeling I was to hide
"If there is anyone to object, who?"
With no reply, they both said, "I do!"
A kiss was shared and their hands were raised
It was a moment of love and peace I love to this day

Kelly Sullivan, Grade 6
Houston Middle School, TN

Socks

Sitting on the sand
Near the great ocean blue
I thought *I'm so glad I have my horse here too.*

We galloped across the sand
With the wind in my hair
As the visitors on the beach
Found it hard not to stare

He's the one that I love
He's my one and only
My match made in heaven
Strangely you see
A horse is the one and only for me.

His name is Socks
Who I named myself
On that glorious day in May
As a lucky fourth grader's dream finally came true.

Sitting on the sand near the great ocean blue
Very lucky to have Socks there too.

Emily Whited, Grade 6
Mayflower Middle School, AR

That Fence

I wonder what's over that old gray fence,
thousands of beautiful roses I bet
or even a big bulldog that bites very hard,
maybe even a train that takes you very far.
Somehow I just can't seem to guess
what's over that old gray fence.

Karla Flores, Grade 5
South Smithfield Elementary School, NC

Roller Coaster

Life is like a roller coaster,
we go up, but we go down.
And we always have to roll on,
even if we wouldn't dare to.
And the ride is never over,
not even if it breaks down.
We have the loops,
where we're confused and upside down.
We have the taunting hills,
but when we go down the wind hits us,
just like reality.
Life is like a roller coaster,
and we always roll on.
We climb that mountain to the top.
But when it comes to a slow halt,
we are reminded by the shrills of the people around us,
that we are not alone.
Roll on Roller coaster.

Dalton Koch, Grade 5
Odessa Middle School, MO

My Best Pet

My best pet is a dog.
She is a bird dog.
Her name is India.
She belongs to my dad.
She stays in a cage in my backyard.
She is my best pet.
I play with her a lot.
We play tag and lots of other fun things together.
She is my very best pet.

Haley Gilbert, Grade 5
Paint Lick Elementary School, KY

Books, Books, Books

Roses are red.
Violets are blue.
Nobody likes the Bailey School Kids book
As much as I do.

I can read fiction, nonfiction, realistic fiction
But I really like mystery books
They keep you thinking
I hope I'm not the only one that likes the Bailey School books

Marla Watson, Grade 5
West Bertie Elementary School, NC

Rafael

R eviewing helps me
A ccomplishing school work
F unny
A mazed about learning
E xcited about learning
L earning new things

Rafael Bardowell, Grade 6
Mark Twain Elementary School, MO

The Fun of Fall

Weather gets colder,
Playing in the crunchy leaves,
Eating pecan pie,
Carnivals and apple cider, too.
It's time for fall!

Olivia Cornish, Grade 4
Cleveland Elementary School, OK

Honoring Veterans

V owing to protect our country with
E very strength they have.
T hey risk their lives
E ach day. Independent to come home
R etiring with memories of battles.
A nswers for their kids,
N ow having stories too.
S o please appreciate the Veterans.

Dylan Rhodes, Grade 4
Van Cove Elementary School, AR

Cats

Cats eat lots of mice
Cats eat a lot of cat food
Cats take care of you

Kevin Chavez, Grade 5
Sycamore Elementary School, GA

Freedom Spells It Out

F lying flags of freedom
R aises an awareness
E veryone should know.
E veryone should know the price paid by
D edicated soldiers that stood up for
O ur country and our families because
M any people died for this freedom!

Keri Martinez, Grade 4
Hayes Elementary School, OK

Wind

Wind
Cool breeze
Gives us air
Makes me feel fresh
Clear

Ashley Logunleko, Grade 5
St Joseph Institute for the Deaf, MO

Roses

Roses here and there
down on the ground so lonely.
I come to visit.

Brianna Norman, Grade 5
Westwood Elementary School, AR

Why Must I

A girl screams
The baby cries
I get up
Why must I

A sound on the guitar
A key on the piano
Please be quiet
Mr. Noon

A meow from a cat
A bark from a dog
Be quiet my pets
Just sit on a log

A car honks
The guy yells
Just be quiet
Mr. Motel

Hush hush baby
Don't you cry
Come sleep with daddy
Why must I

Pete Morello, Grade 4
St Thomas More School, NC

Juice

Juice is sweet and fun to drink.
When I drink, and I get done,
I put my cup in the sink.
Juice has lots of flavors.
Orange, apple, cranberry, and cherry.
Some juice is sweet, some juice is sour,
Some juice smells just like a flower.

Chantz White, Grade 5
Franklin Elementary School, OK

Fall Friends

I'm fine how are you?
Fall is a time for new friends and you.

It is also time to find a turkey.
That is because of Thanksgiving.

I thank you all for my friends
I am happy to the end.

Spencer Percer, Grade 5
EA Harrold Elementary School, TN

Rain

Rain is the worst time.
I hate rain on Saturday.
Rain is sometimes good.

Daniel Johnston, Grade 4
Briarwood Christian School, AL

Greg

Once I saw a big, scary rat
And it was in a big black hat
I awoke in the night
And got a weird fright
Cause the rat was really, really fat.

Greg Riley, Grade 4
Judsonia Elementary School, AR

Bunny Rats

Bunnies that are pink,
Everywhere they go.
Soft and furry,
Cute and cuddly,
10 years old.
Long and floppy ears,
Big bow around their neck,
And a little fluffy white tail.
They are skinny — not fat,
I used to call them bunny rats!

Savannah Miller, Grade 5
Lynn Fanning Elementary School, AL

Frogs

Slimy, smooth, green, and brown,
Smells like lake water,
Long tongues like worms.

The light shines through the clouds,
On a gray dull day
With puddles of water everywhere.

Ribbit, Ribbit,
From the hidden frogs.
Squish, Squish,
Their hitting the mud spots.

Where do they go at night?
Do they have ears?
Can they swim?

Cool, slimy, and fun to catch.
Spotted, striped or
Any design you can think of.

Ribbit, Ribbit, Ribbit.
Ribbit, Ribbit, Ribbit.
Ribbit, Ribbit, Ribbit.

Dana Turner, Grade 4
Price Elementary School, KY

Annie

I have a baby doll, her name is Annie,
She has been with me since the first day I was born.

We've battled together
Stormy nights,
Time outs,
And my brother's friends!

The pink play dough stain,
On her head
Reminds me of when I used her head as a
Play dough board!

In her little pink dress,
And blue eyes,
Stare at me as I fall fast asleep.

I remember the days I would put make up
On her and say, "You look pretty!"
I could never sell her, because she is mine!

Madelyn Clifford, Grade 6
East Oldham Middle School, KY

The Wonderful Night

Whoosh!

As I step outside
the wind sings its song
and then is gone
I look up and see them
the stars
looking down on us
shining like fire
I know that's what it is
but know when they twinkle and shine
they look more beautiful than ever
As I look up I see shining snow
Fresh snow on the ground
It looks like crystal
I know it is rain
Although now it is frozen
It looks so magical
I feel like I could fly
the snow is a beautiful white
this was my most wonderful night

Molly Orman, Grade 5
Greathouse Shryock Traditional Elementary School, KY

Sister, Bailey, Jack

I have 3 dogs named Sister, Bailey, and Jack
They're not much of a pack
If they don't know you then they will attack
So you better watch your back
They love me and I love them back

Scarlett Lokey, Grade 6
Mayflower Middle School, AR

Books

Books teach me how to say words.
They teach me what I need to know
So I become smarter in my lessons.
They are very fun, I really like them.

They have steps like beginner books
Grades 1, 2, 3, 4, and 5;
Expressive feelings with characters,
And some have narrators.

Words that are important
Can be looked up in the
Glossary, index, and a little
Pocket dictionary.

Books help me with subjects
Such as science, reading and social studies.
I learn about snakes, plots, and presidents,
Settings in China long ago.

Lessons are learned to make me
Smarter, curious, and fill my
Brain with knowledge to help
Me become a better student.

Nyla Blair, Grade 4
Schaffner Traditional Elementary School, KY

Past and Maybe Future

It is all in my life
learning to sew an outfit with Granny,
knitting hats on looms,
painting with acrylic paint on the snow-white canvas,
day dreaming, it is impossible to stop!
Four years ago wearing that itchy princess Halloween costume,
writing fairy tales,
canoe camping with Daddy on the Tennessee River,
Clinton and I sled
down the leaves in the fall.
Leo jumps on top of me, licking my face at 6:00 a.m.
to wake me up for school.
It's all in my life
getting catapulted off a seesaw
by who today is my best friend
then my enemy.
All of that and more was in my past;
some of it may be my future.

Elise Askonas, Grade 6
Baylor School, TN

Bumble Bee

Bumble bee, bumble bee
In a hurry.
You bounce from flower to flower to flower.
Seeing pretty colors, red, pink, blue, green.

Ashleigh White, Grade 6
Benton County School of the Arts, AR

The Little Brain
I have a little brain,
One day it flew to Spain,
I don't know where it went,
So I think it went in my tent,
But I got a sprain.
Lance Ricketson, Grade 4
Eastside Elementary School, GA

Different Peanuts
Peanut is my dog
Some kids think he is a nut
He is the best dog
Ashton Benge, Grade 4
Briarwood Christian School, AL

Queen
Q ueen of the Nile.
U nique in her own way.
E legant lady I must say.
E xcellence in every way.
N ever let anyone stand in her way.
Queen Kelley, Grade 6
Mark Twain Elementary School, MO

Jungle Family
My family is like a jungle
unorganized and wild.

My daddy is a lion
he is the brawn of the family and he
takes care of us when momma is out
getting meat.

My momma is a cheetah
as fast as she can be and she is the
brains of the family she will roar when
she yells.

My brother is the monkey of the
family he is loud and annoying.

I am the baby tiger
calm and always excited when we have
a surprise and I can be very patient.
Becky Hardin, Grade 5
Bloomfield Elementary School, KY

Dolphin
Dolphin
gray, friendly
trick, care, outsmart
laughing, exploring, swimming, smiling
Always on the
Bottlenose fish
Georgianna Cheatham, Grade 4
East Jones Elementary School, MS

Courtney
C ool
O rdinary
U nique
R ough
T rendy
N ice
E ducated
Y oung
Courtney Robinson, Grade 4
Wohlwend Elementary School, MO

My Family Is a Horse
My family is a horse
Stronghold, Beautiful, Exciting
My brother is the ears
Always listening
My mom is the eyes
Always on focus and keeping us on track
My dad is the body
Strong and stable
I'm the mane
Graceful and glorious
Ashley Humes, Grade 5
Bloomfield Elementary School, KY

Black
Black is the color of death,
It is the color of disbelief.

Black is the color of coal,
It is the color of oil.

Black is the color of anger,
It is the color of weakness.

Black is the color of the night sky,
It is the color of defeat.

Black is the color of sorrow,
It is the color of ash.

What a powerful color black is!
Anna Byrd, Grade 6
St Francis Xavier School, AL

Veterans
V ery brave
E ducated
T rue
E arth protectors
R eally amazing
A mericans
N ot communists
S oldiers
Drew Archibald, Grade 4
Parkview Elementary School, MO

Deer
Deer
fast, big
run, eat, fight
sleeping, hiding, listening, feeding
Some deer have horns
Red-tailed deer
Eric Varnado, Grade 4
East Jones Elementary School, MS

The Song
I wrote a song
It was very long
But there was something wrong
With my song
The notes were crooked
I could not read it
I was ashamed
I thought it would bring me fame
Not shame!
So, I wrote it again, I knew I could
And the song was good!
Isaac Hass, Grade 4
St Paul's Lutheran School, OK

God's Nature
God painted nature.
Beautiful nature,
The birds, the bees,
Butterflies flying with glee.
I love the nature's woods,
So colorful, so pleasing, so active.
When it rains, God blesses us
With his love.
When God gives us flowers,
We know what it means.
God is wonderful,
Just like nature.
I thank God for wonderful creatures.
I thank God for blessing me
With a wonderful mother.
Tiffany Singleton, Grade 4
Ode Maddox Elementary School, AR

Green Tree
A
green
tree tall
and bright.
Presents at the
bottom, glimmering
and glistening on Christmas Night.
My
green
tree.
Brandon Lopez, Grade 5
E O Young Jr Elementary School, NC

Babies

Babies are really cute.
Sometimes you want to put them on mute.
They love to make funny sounds.
And love to be on the ground.

Kel-Asia Chamblee, Grade 5
Duncan Chapel Elementary School, SC

Friends

Friends will help you when times get tough.
Friends will help you when life gets rough.
Friends can cheer you when you cry.
They're not the type of people who lie.
They'll tell any secret to you.
When you're down they'll ask what they can do.
They'll invite you over to spend the night.
Friends will tell you when something is not right.
My best friend will let me borrow her clothes,
only if I paint her toes.
Friends know when something is not right.
My friends and I never get in fights.
If your friend asks for their trust,
you must promise not to break it, you must!
Friends love to talk about what's going on.
Friends don't mind if you call them at dawn.
Friends are people who truly care.
Friends are people who will always share.
Friends will never make fun of you,
even if it's the most embarrassing thing you do.
Friends are the best thing in the world!

Caroline Cullum, Grade 6
Woodland Presbyterian School, TN

Dragons

Dragons are very old,
but alas they are also bold.
They lived in the dark ages,
all but youth are wiser than sages.
They come to steal your cows,
don't get to close they'll burn your eyebrows.
you know dragons blast fire,
disturb them and the consequences could be dire.

Jonathan Graves, Grade 5
Graham Elementary School, AL

Tubing

Bursting with excitement I dove into the dark circle.
Speed increased as the engine roared.
I glide in the air, crashing down.
Water engulfing my body as I coast along the water.
Screaming, crossing, jerking sharp turns.
Roaring waves pound as I struggle to survive.
Cheering and laughter fill the air.
Waves were approaching as I plunge toward them.
Down I go swallowed by the gaping water.

Colton Gearhart, Grade 5
Cline Elementary School, KY

Grown Up

I'm not at home anymore.
I'm not with my mom or dad.
I'm not at school with my friends or teachers.
I am not a kid anymore.
I'm all grown up with my own house, and my own job.
However, I'm still missing something.
I don't know what that something is, but I need it.
Is it my friends? NO! Is it my teachers?
NO! Is it my mom, dad, sister, and brother?
NO! What is it?
I know what it is! It's everything.
I miss everything.
That is what I am missing.
I thought being grown up would be fun, but it is not.
I wish I was a kid again, but that is all gone now.

Donnesha Little, Grade 6
Kitty Stone Elementary School, AL

My Favorite Tree!

There is a tree in my yard,
I try to climb it every day, but it is very hard.
It is fun to see all the things on the tree,
There are spiders, birds, bugs, and bees.
When I get to the top, I like to hop,
Then the leaves fall and the wind makes them flip and flop.

Rebekah Steele, Grade 6
Chapin Middle School, SC

Fear

Once, on a dark and stormy night,
with trees that have shadows that would give you a fright,
a black pussycat bared its teeth at a mouse
in a frightening, run-down, haunted house.

"If you take one step in, you will never come out,"
says the legend by a wise man up on a mount.
He said ghosts would attack just two feet from the place.
He said he had seen a goblin's green face.
The goblin was guarding the front of the house,
with a scary black and green short-sleeved blouse.

I never went in, so I never came out,
for fear that I would see a count.
"I dare you go in," I said to the cat.
He went half way in, then quickly ran back.
So never go in, or you'll never come out.
Good-bye for now, I say with a shout.

Jennifer Cox, Grade 4
Cox Academy, GA

Dying Nature

Quiet and peaceful,
Contracted by man's machines,
Nature endangered.

Zach Leposa, Grade 5
South Smithfield Elementary School, NC

My Nana

The time I was with my nana…
Well, my memory is a little fuzzy, so bear with me. She would hold me and rock me in her warm arms and sing a song to me.
We would listen to the birds sing lightly and
the leaves would dance.

The time she would bake her cookies…
They tasted like you were in a wonderland full of chocolate mountains that had a cookie top and was nice and warm.

When I would lay down with her…
I felt safe and warm. I felt like I was lying in a cloud with a gentle touch of the wind on my face.

When I would cry…
She would hold me and tell me everything is going to be all right and she would rock me and be there for me until I was okay.

Whenever I was small…
She would teach me numbers. She wouldn't teach me too much and she would do it just right for me.

When she would take me to the store…
She would always buy me glitter, the silver one.
We would always do art stuff together.
We were like soap and hands, together forever.

Tessa Allman, Grade 5
Odessa Middle School, MO

Alaska and Seattle

My Mom and Dad traveled to Alaska and Seattle
Watching Humpback whales with the baby learning how to wave
They saw a bald eagle, two grizzly bears, and one seal they saw
Little pieces of ice falling off a glacier collapsing in to the water like thunder

My mother and father went on the biggest zip line in the world at Seattle
They have the best salmon in the world there its tender, juicy, sweet, and crispy; they said it was out of this world

Guess what I'm traveling next year they said it was SIGNIFICANT!
Me and my brother are saving, up money to go next year to sled
We are going to ride a husky and a helicopter
My mom and dad were riding a helicopter really high over a waterfall
My mom says I'll get an A+ on my next report on Alaska

Isn't Alaska great?
Well I'm looking forward to traveling NEXT YEAR!!!!!!!

Kyle Velinsky, Grade 4
Briarwood Elementary School, KY

I Wish I Had an Ocean

I wish I had a cruise ships so I could sail away to a beautiful island
I wish I had a stallion so I could ride along the ocean shore
I wish I had a passport so I could get on a plane and fly high above the ocean
I wish I had a scuba instructor so I could swim with the amazing sea creatures
I wish I had the opportunity to lie on the coral reefs
I wish I had the time and the money to go to the most beautiful beach and lay on the shore to watch the sun set.
I wish I had a magic wand
To make all my wishes
Come true.

Taylor Stone, Grade 6
Mayflower Middle School, AR

The Ferris Wheel

The ferris wheel so big and high,
The ferris wheel can touch the sky.
The ferris wheel so wide and long,
The ferris wheel is o' so strong.
The ferris wheel so fast and fierce,
I'd rather get my belly pierced.
You can get on the ferris wheel with Tommy,
If you look on the ground, I'm with my mommy.
I will never get on the ferris wheel,
So, let's not make it a big deal.

Charlquetta Timmons, Grade 6
Dunbar Creative & Performing Arts School, AL

Fall Days

F all is a wonderful time of year
A ll the leaves changing colors
L aughing while jumping in the leaves
L ater we watch the squirrels gather up their nuts

D ads outside frying the turkey
A fter dinner we eat the pumpkin pie
Y ummy! It was scrumptious
S hooting turkeys is really fun now that fall days have begun.

Corey Caulder, Grade 5
Palmetto Christian Academy, SC

Panther's Game

The football thrown in the air as fast as a speeding jet
The scoreboard is so bright I need my sunglasses
One of the players yelling after a huge tackle
A man saying, "Peanuts" as loud as a roaring lion
Pizza smells as good as a dozen red roses
French fries frequently frying
The tangy flavors of drink make my mouth water
Wonderful cheesy nachos slipping through my fingers
The freezing cold seat sends shivers through my body
Pushing and shoving people trying to get in line
I feel great and joyful.

Zack Foster, Grade 4
Bailey Elementary School, NC

The Freedom Flag

The American flag, red, white, and blue
It stands for freedom for me and you
Betsy Ross made our flag during the American Revolution
She said the stars and stripes can have no substitution
We honor our flag every day
To show how much we love and pray
Soldiers carry it during war
We see it at schools, churches, and so much more
We may see different flags everywhere we go
But the United States flag is one we all know
I love our flag it makes me proud
I love our flag, I shout out loud

Bailey Shymlock, Grade 4
Sequoyah Elementary School, TN

My Little Waterfall

My little waterfall is
very, very small,
it drizzles over rocks;
it makes a pretty little sound.

My little waterfall,
makes a mist cloud.
When I go see my
waterfall, I feel
brighter inside.

Lora Clark, Grade 5
Heartland High School and Academy, MO

My Weird Car

Have you ever seen a car grow legs?
Well my car was outside
Then…I looked outside and there it was a dancing away
Then my keys grew legs and walked away.
So, I chased them for six days and nights.
After that I always watched my car and keys

Kera Ring, Grade 6
Armorel Elementary School, AR

To Try

What I see is what I saw
And what I hear is what I heard
What I feel is what I felt
But when I try I fly like a bird

Because when I try
That's when I'll succeed
Just because I tried
I've done a good deed

Because of my efforts
To make the world a better place
And knowing that not everything
Is a race

I'll succeed
To try is my good deed

Yushi Wang, Grade 6
Haynes Academy for Advanced Studies, LA

Francois Maisonville

F rench Indian.
R eally from New Madrid County MO.
A dopted French/Canadian,
N ancy-Sarah-Key was his wife.
C ald-Well and him helped each other.
O nly known mostly by first name/sometime last too.
I t was 1890 when he died.
S arah died in 1880.
(And they will always be known!)

Cheyenne Davis, Grade 5
Clarksburg School, TN

My Thoughts

A hiker
in the middle of a forest,
takes notes.
When a pine loses a needle,
the eagle will see it,
the deer will hear it,
the bear will smell it.
As the mist settles
the forest grows quiet,
as the hiker moves on.

Dalton Post, Grade 5
Wilson's Creek School, MO

November

My birthday
Good food
Fall festivals
Scary pumpkins
Best friends
Bare leaves
Amusing relatives
Teeny leaves
Joyful November
Oh, wonderful
Relatives coming
Immense jackets
Gloomy storms
More night
Fewer days
Watch parade
Friends together
Innumerable blankets
Long sleeves
All together
What fun!!!

Cheyenne Norman, Grade 5
Center Elementary School, GA

I Love Baseball

I love baseball.
I go to the field
and pitch a few balls.
Two foul balls
one fast ball.
I love baseball!
I hit the ball
out of the field,
the crowd cheers!
I love baseball!
To my surprise
I ran the wrong way
and we still won
the championship.
I love baseball!

Sandra Quiroz, Grade 6
Saint Paul School, TN

Amazing Nouns

Have you ever wondered what a noun is?
A noun is a person, place, thing or idea.
There are many types of nouns…too many to say.
There are concrete nouns, nouns you feel, touch or see.
The Empire State Building is a concrete noun and proper, too!
An abstract noun is what our hearts and minds feel…
Joy and grief are feelings.
Singular possessive nouns you have to insert a 's.
Plural possessive nouns you need to put an s'.
Compound nouns are two nouns put together such as toothpaste.
Common and proper nouns are very unique.
Common nouns shows everyday life like things like a dog.
Proper nouns show ownership like Mrs. Little's dog.
Collective nouns are many nouns put together to form one.
Student to class are put together to make one.
See there are many nouns to see.
There are even nouns in your classroom.
Too many to say but they are all around!
Nouns are wonderful things!
They are the little things that keep us living.
Amazing nouns are all around!

Anna Cornish, Grade 5
Saffell Street Elementary School, KY

Jesus Healed Me!*

I was walking down a meadow, and then I saw a stream.
I thought I must lay down, then I had a dream.
The dream made my days easy, it didn't make me feel queasy,
Because I felt as if a powerful one had healed me.
I had one year to live, but now I can go back to being able to give.

Mary Kate Coleman, Grade 5
Midway Covenant Christian School, GA
*Dedicated to my aunt Ellen Marie Smith.

I Am

I am an athletic boy who loves soccer
I wonder if my team will make it to the championship game
I hear the crowd cheer "Revolution" my team's name
I see the other team kick the ball toward me as I stand in the goalie box
I want to stop the other team from scoring so I dive at the ball
I am an athletic boy who loves soccer

I pretend that my team demolishes the other teams
I feel my blood pump through my body as we win the game
I worry that I may miss the ball if it flies toward the goal
I cry if I miss the ball when the other team tries to score
I am an athletic boy who loves soccer

I understand that it will be very hard to be in the championships of Russell County
I say that I will practice very hard every day to become a better goalie
I dream that I will be the MVP on my team
I try my best to make sure that the other team does not score while I am goalie
I hope to win the championship game
I am an athletic boy who loves soccer

Alex Redmon, Grade 6
Union Chapel Elementary School, KY

An Old Person

She has a garden of her own,
She prefers to be alone.
Day and night she works and cleans.
When that's done, she strings the beans.
She was made to clean up after Grandpa,
Who works in the fields in tireless toil.
When he comes home, he's covered in soil.
That old person is Grandma.

Caleb Smith, Grade 5
Prince of Peace Catholic School, SC

Without Trees

Without trees we couldn't make a house,
not even a hole for a little old mouse.

There would be no baseball bats, for summertime fun,
or pretty leaves to shade us from the sun.

Without trees there would be no limbs,
for the treehouse to sit upon for little old Tim.

There would be no novels or history books,
no recipe cards for the grandest cooks.

Without trees there will be no air,
or sawdust for the county fair.

Without trees it would be upsetting to me,
because we would have no Christmas trees.

Mary-Mac Slice, Grade 6
Chapin Middle School, SC

A Storm Is Brewing

The sky is all blue,
There is only one cloud,
And then out of nowhere comes something real loud.
"I'm scared" is what we both share,
We are both outside when the sky suddenly flares.
The lightning is flashing,
The thunder is booming,
The blue sky is what all the clouds are consuming.
It's starting to pour, raining cats and dogs,
Out of underground burrows come little frogs.
The dogs are howling, the birds are flying,
A storm is brewing, a storm is brewing, and I'm not lying.

Josh Gebo, Grade 6
Haynes Academy for Advanced Studies, LA

Empathy

Empathy is a feeling when connection is strong,
It puts you through something that could be short or long.

Empathy isn't a game, so you can't win or lose.
It's just a feeling that puts you in someone else's shoes.

Margaret McFarland, Grade 4
St Thomas More School, NC

The Tree of Friendship

Soft grass and a tall tree
Under the tree we lay there, my friend and me
We lay there so long the grass is matted down
Sharing secrets and dreams under the tree
Laughing and crying under it too
This is a very special place to me

Mariah Cobble, Grade 5
Bloomfield Elementary School, KY

Sneaking Snacks

During night till morning.
On top of your grandmother's refrigerator.
Across the knitting supplies.
Inside the jar is your success.
Next make sure there is no one around.
Near the bottom is your snack.
As you reach for your success.
Instead of being there, it is not.
From morning till night you are sad.

Joseph Hicks, Grade 5
Grovespring Elementary School, MO

Nature

As I walk outside today,
The grass is as scratchy as hay,
But that's okay!
Because the warm sun hits my face,
I feel a nice cool breeze on me.
I think I'll take a walk today.
Oh, some dazzling sunflowers!
What's that on them?
Some very interesting creatures, they are!
I think they're insects, might I say.
Ouch! I tripped on a stick!
I hit some rocks and scraped my knee,
I hope the doctor doesn't charge a fee,
Oh well, I don't need him!
I'm tough!
Go away, you mosquitoes! I've had quite enough!
I think I'll go take a nap now.
Goodbye to all, and to all a good day.

Chad Gregory, Grade 4
All Saints' Episcopal School, TN

The Last Breeze

The last breeze is here
Over the mountains and through the trees
Softly spreading far and wide
Past the ocean and over the tide.
All the leaves fall and all the trees sway
Oh I can't wait the breeze comes today
The wind whistles as it flies through the sky.
All the animals scurry and the people hurry
To feel the last breeze until next year.

Brayden Benton, Grade 5
Runnels School, LA

If I Were in Charge of the World

If I were in charge of the world
I'd cancel school,
Reading,
Craft stores.

If I were in charge of the world
There'd be flat screen TV in every room,
More dirt bikes,
More basketball.

If I were in charge of the world
You wouldn't be sad,
You wouldn't have to sleep,
You wouldn't get in trouble.

If I were in charge of the world
There'd be candy for every meal,
All the movies would be G or PG.
Everyone would have a dog or cat.
Wes Noe, Grade 5
Eminence Middle School, KY

Stinker Sneaker

Dear shoes,

Thank
you for
carrying my big
feet even though they
really stink.

Thank
you for
protecting these big
feet. I love you my
little pink sneaks.
Lacey Fox, Grade 5
Cool Spring Elementary School, NC

Rainstorm

Cool water falls down
Patters on the windowpane
Soaks the stormy earth.
The event that is called rain
Has brought me lots of boredom.
Sarah Nickles, Grade 6
Hand Middle School, SC

Hope Is Sky Blue

It smells like a dozen red roses.
It tastes like sweet cotton candy.
It sounds like birds tweeting a song.
It feels like hugging a soft teddy bear.
Hope is the soft beat of my heart.
Shaunkeria Young, Grade 4
Pines Elementary School, NC

Maze

This place is like a maze.
Things that are called the same thing,
But have different names surround me.
This place is so big,
So empty,
So quiet,
So amazing.
No one comes here anymore,
Yet I seem to come a lot.
Trying to find the thing I want
Is hard since this place is so big.
It's like a maze.
And once I find the one I want
I have completed the maze.
Then I can't keep my nose
Out of the one I chose.
And once I'm done with that one,
I go back into the maze,
Trying to find another one.
This library is a maze,
Soon I will find the way out.
Kaitlyn Byrd, Grade 6
East Oldham Middle School, KY

The Country and the City

Country
peaceful, quiet, singing, dreaming
riding, barns, horses, pastures
running, tiring, screaming, working
buildings, lights, signs, crowded
City
John Robert Anderson, Grade 5
Briarwood Christian School, AL

Seasons

spiraling
to the ground
leaves of red,
orange and brown

snowflakes dancing
from the sky
everything stained
in crystal dye

for bees
many new flowers to make
baby ducklings
by clear lakes

bright hot sun
wafting off
heading to cold pools
or shady lofts
Mary Carol Butterfield, Grade 6
Prince of Peace Catholic School, SC

Reba McEntire

Reba
A great author
A very caring mom
An awesome, outstanding actress
Singer
Kristen Meeker, Grade 6
Southwest Middle School, AR

Baseball

National pastime
Hitting, catching, and throwing
Baseball makes me smile!
Matthew Sweere, Grade 4
Jim Stone Elementary School, AR

My Life

When I wake up in the morning
My life beings another day
Every day it changes
Every step I take
I go through school
But don't know how I last
Every day at school is not a blast
When I get home it is the same
I don't like homework but who to blame
But like I said every day is not a blast
Alexis Wrigley, Grade 6
Des Arc Elementary School, AR

Rain Storm

You are the lightning.
You are the tapping thunder.
You are a rain storm.
Alex Fowler, Grade 5
Duncan Chapel Elementary School, SC

My Sister

So sweet and tender
Rarely gets mad
Long blonde curly hair
Cute little dimples
Wonderful straight teeth
Big hazel eyes
A caring personality
And a beautiful smile
You cannot resist but to smile back to.
Kaylee Mulcahy, Grade 5
Walton Verona Elementary School, KY

Math

M ultiplication is fun
A ddition is great
T eaching is good
H elp is what I need
Jacob Lusk, Grade 4
Tamassee-Salem Elementary School, SC

Why Not?

Why do you fall and not rise
Why can't you wipe the tears from your eyes
Why can't you face the world alone
Why can't you explore the lands unknown
Why can't you say the unsaid
Do you want to be remembered when you're dead
So do something great
Still not even you can decide your fate
It might be tomorrow
It might be today
You don't have to go with the flow
You can show them what you know
Why do you fall and not rise

Reed Spivey, Grade 6
Discovery School @ Reeves Rogers, TN

Autumn

Autumn leaves are falling, falling to the ground.
Autumn leaves are changing, changing all around.
Autumn leaves are crunchy, crunchy as can be.
Autumn leaves are colored, colors that bring glee.

Leaves are falling on the hill.
Leaves are on my window sill.
The air is crisp, my coat is tight.
Fall is all Thanksgiving night.

Autumn leaves are falling, falling to the ground.
Autumn leaves are changing, changing all around.

Micaiah Shelton, Grade 4
Old Fort Elementary School, NC

Daddy

I think of you each day,
I feel your arms around me
That's how I get through my day.
You look upon me
To guide me on my way
But it's hard without you
Each and every day.
People always tell me the grieving will subside
But how can it get better, without you by my side.
No matter how hard they try,
To help me with this pain
I am all consumed by thinking
It will never be the same.
I know one day we'll meet
In the heavens up above
It's the one thing that helps me,
To never forget your love.
My dearest Daddy, I love you,
You're with me every day.
I will keep this love within me,
Until that beautiful day...

Sarah Homan, Grade 6
Rose Bud Elementary School, AR

Freedom

F ight for our freedom
R espect people's lives
E nd slavery
E qual respect for humanity
D eath of our soldiers
O pportunities to reach for the stars on our flag
M emories of the soldiers who had passed away

Victoria Murillo, Grade 5
Clarksburg School, TN

A Special Person I Know

This special person I know
lives in a special place too.
No one knows exactly what it looks like,
but they know it is full of glory.
This special person I know,
is like a star in a dark nights sky,
twinkling to catch people's eyes.
People praise him by singing
Holy, Holy, Holy
He made marvelous movie stars, rock stars
and he even made grumpy adults
trying to correct the children.
I love him,
and I hope you do too.

Who is this lovely man?
GOD!

Sarah Rueff, Grade 5
Greathouse Shryock Traditional Elementary School, KY

He Is a Color

You can find him on the glistening sun
Or in a collection of autumn leaves
He may be basking on a buttercup
Perhaps on a garden weed

He may ride on a shooting star
As it shoots across the sky
Or he you might just spot him on a school bus
As it passes by

You could spy him on a golden rod
Snoozing upon its petal
It's possible that you could see him
On a golden first place medal

He can be seen
Almost any where you turn
From gazing upon a pencil
To watching a fire burn
Though he is so very easy to see
I have only one question
Who is he?

Hayla Ragland, Grade 6
East Oldham Middle School, KY

Fun

I love toys,
they're the closest
thing to my heart, they're just as good
as a piece of fine art.
You don't have to be a kid
at this time you don't have to
be a kid to know how to
have fun as long as you are a kid
at heart.

Deion Brown, Grade 5
EA Harrold Elementary School, TN

Fall

The leaves are red,
The sky is blue.
The grass is green,
And the grapes are too.

The leaves are orange,
The summer season flew.
The trees are brown,
And the branches too.

Snow is white, so I see,
But I'm glad this poem changes —

Just like me!

Taylor Owens, Grade 6
Beech Springs Intermediate School, SC

Me

Brady
Smart, nice, buff
Brother of Brittany and Brock
Who loves family
Who feels happy, angry, and sad
Who needs love, peace, and quiet
Who gives love, things, and feeling
Who fears kidnappers
Who would like to see a camel spider

Brady Shoemaker, Grade 4
Cleveland Elementary School, OK

Just as Warm

The bushes are blowing
your faces are glowing!
Snow fights during the day
and giggles at night
waiting for Rudolf's Christmas light!
By morning, your cookies are gone,
but your heart is warm!
Everything is right!
Hugs and kisses
they'll hold me tight!

Ashton Mathis, Grade 6
Alpena Elementary School, AR

Christmas

It's Christmas Eve and all is quiet
with the children snug in their beds
all will know in the night that old Saint Nicholas is coming
and in the morning they will see
that old Saint Nicholas has come to town
with his bells jingling and his reindeer galloping
he flies through the night without a sound
when the children wake up
they will rush to their parents and say "Mommy, Daddy, Santa came!"
with smiles on their faces
they will rip every single present until
the presents are gone
then they will play, play, play
until they wish to go to bed once more
with Santa up at the North Pole,
his little elves get ready once more
to make more toys for all the girls and boys
who are sleeping and dreaming, waiting for next year

Raymond Palazzo, Grade 5
Greathouse Shryock Traditional Elementary School, KY

Autumn

The wind ruffles my sweater,
amber, gold, copper, red, brown, yellow, orange, black, all new colors,
the world is changing, just like me.
A golden light floats through the trees like liquid sunlight trickling through the leaves.
Two squirrels dig for nuts, preparing for the cold season.
It is growing dark and the moon has a beautiful silver shine to it at night,
it seems to emit a golden glow.
Leaves swirl throughout the air, dancing wildly.
Autumn is here, the world is like a treasure chest glittering in the sunset.

Keely McMahon, Grade 6
Nativity School, SC

If I Were a Firefighter

If I were a firefighter I would see…
A blazing fire in the distance,
Pitch black smoke in the air,
A red brick house on fire in the woods.

If I were a firefighter I would hear…
Screaming people asking for help,
Whining sirens all around me,
Many scared voices on the truck's fire radio.

If I were a firefighter I would smell…
The thick aroma of smoke,
Nasty stench of my gear after a horrible fire,
Diesel fumes burning from the fire engines.

If I were a firefighter I would touch…
The rough switch of the dash for my siren,
The cold medal ladder as it extends me to the edges of the building,
The hard wet hose as I blast the structure.

Dustin Posey, Grade 6
Union Chapel Elementary School, KY

Jesus Saved Me

Saved me from the terror.
From him.
When he threw me against the wall.
I didn't feel a thing.
Staring at him there.
Now I can't even bear to look at his picture.
Or else I will weep.
When I talked to him on the phone.
I just told him that I will always love him,
just not as much as I used too.
He says that he will change.
I said "Daddy you will never change."
Everyone is proud of me.
Especially my mom.
When they ask me if I know him.
I just bow my head.
And while I shed a tear.
I say "Not anymore."

Tapanga Grogan, Grade 6
Childersburg Middle School, AL

Motor-Cross

Medium size, two wheels and drives on dirt terrain.
It has two cylinder engine with a smooth silver
Handlebars with handle brakes. The type of bike
Is Kawasaki.
In the day the track is lit by the sun.
At night the light posts light the track
with white lights.

Vroom the bike starts,
Rumble goes the accelerator
when you pull it.
Then it's gone with a puff
of dirt.

How is the bike made?
How does it work?
How does it run?
I'm amazed how they do the tricks,
I'm proud of their faith,
It's just cool.

It's just cool,
It's just cool,
It's just cool.

Jimmy Ludlow, Grade 4
Price Elementary School, KY

Cheetahs

Cheetahs are yellowish-orange
Covered with black spots all around
Fast and hunting through the wild grassland.
Careful with their cubs soft and sleepy in their homes.

Pedro Alvarez, Grade 5
South Smithfield Elementary School, NC

The World May Seem Confusing

The world may seem confusing
not as simple as a triangle
but we're still glad it's here
every inch, every angle.

We love its weather, whoosh
and its mind,
We also love its twists
and its winds

The world may seem confusing,
it is a maze to some,
just be glad it's here,
every year,
month,
and day.

Jordan Hall, Grade 5
Greathouse Shryock Traditional Elementary School, KY

Come Little Children

Come little children take thee away
see thy presents on Christmas Day.
Come little children oh come one and all,
come see thy baby in Bethlehem's stall.
Come little children follow the star,
shining above from afar.
Come little children, let's look at his birth.
Look at thy Jesus the Savior of Earth.

Natalie Jacobs, Grade 5
Briggs Elementary School, SC

Space

Space is like a thousand gleaming stars
And the sun is like walking in a broiling oven
There are supposed to be nine planets
But Pluto the ice planet is long-gone

Devin Pearman, Grade 6
Des Arc Elementary School, AR

Salvation

I looked up in the sky a lot,
And asked the Lord how much he thought
Of little me down here on earth
Ever since my day of birth.

He told me He did love me so,
And heard the winds were gonna blow.
"Keep strong in faith and trust in Me
For I will never leave thee."

Those word of His fell to my heart,
And he gave me a brand new start.
Now I'm a child of the King,
Soaring with Him on eagles' wings!

Monica Underwood, Grade 6
Providence Classical School, AL

Street Ball

To some a game
To others a way of life
Through pain,
Sweat, exhilaration,
And determination
To be the best
Competing to find
The Triumphant

Jesse Cross, Grade 6
Rose Bud Elementary School, AR

My Dad

My Dad is very nice
He takes care of me
Dad works for our money
He's also very funny
I love him sooooo

Jana Williams, Grade 5
Des Arc Elementary School, AR

My Life

I like my life because I have fun.
At school I get all of my work done.

At home I go to sleep.
Like always without a peep.

Later, my brother wakes me,
And tells me that I'm snoring.

The next thing I know,
It's morning.

At breakfast I eat bacon and eggs.
Then my dog comes and begs.

Tyler Mulkey, Grade 5
Enon Elementary School, LA

Falling Leaves

Leaves are falling off the trees
Feel the magic, feel the breeze
On the ground the leaves will ruffle
Like a crowd in a hustle
When they move across the ground
The leaf collector will have found

Kyle Lee, Grade 5
Runnels School, LA

Guadalupe

There once was a man from Spain
Who did a great dance in the rain
He used to dance tap
Til he took a long nap
And woke up in very bad pain.

Guadalupe Jasso, Grade 4
Judsonia Elementary School, AR

She

She is a back stabber
Liar, and some other things
I am not to say out loud.
She is mean and ugly
and thinks she is all that
when she is not.
She uses people for popularity,
fame and fortune, but
I can tell you something
She doesn't have me for popularity.
She doesn't have me for fortune.
And, for sure doesn't have my friendship.
It is one thing to tell a little white lie.
It is another when you tell
A whole book full that
takes forever to read.

Shanya Little, Grade 6
Ketchum Jr High School, OK

The Four Seasons Come to Say

Mr. Fall comes to make sure
That every kid
Gets to jump in the leaves.
Mr. Frost comes to make sure
That every kid
Gets ice trickled down their spine.
Mr. Green comes to say,
"Wake up! It's a school day!"
Mr. Sun comes to say,
"It's a no school day!"

Cecily Carter, Grade 4
Ode Maddox Elementary School, AR

Where I'm From

I am from watching TV
With my grandmom.
I am from green, tasty apples,
Falling off trees.
I am from playing with my brother.
I am from eating pizza with my family.
I am from loud
City noises.
I am from splashing in the pool
On hot summer days.
I am from flowers
Blooming roses.
I am from big green trees,
Christmas trees.
I am from helping around the house
Cleaning my room.
I am from long tests
In school
I am from playing with my dog.
I am from a loving home.

Alley Seagraves, Grade 5
Tates Creek Elementary School, KY

My Grandpa

Big and buff
Very tough
Flies like a plane
Runs like a cheetah
Brave as a soldier
I love my hero!

Ryan Murphree, Grade 5
Salem Elementary School, AR

Catfish

Catfish
strong, long
swim, splash, scurry
sleeping, sitting, turning, twisting
Catfish are always swimming.
Fish

Chaim Barnett, Grade 4
East Jones Elementary School, MS

Video Games

The TV ignites
I am ready to fight
Like a warrior
And a knight

My fingers tremble
My stomach flops
Catch the ball
Make a pop

The game is buzzing
Around a bend
The car stops
Play again?

"Go outside!"
"Play with a friend!"
My dad is shouting
The End

Jared Farley, Grade 4
Elon Elementary School, NC

My First Time Swimming

My first time going swimming
I almost drowned
My face turned into a frown
I didn't want to be,
taught by anyone.
I wanted to learn myself
So I went down and came up
I swallowed and gurgled
gasped for breath,
but I stuck on
And learned to swim on my own

Lamont Hatcher, Grade 5
E O Young Jr Elementary School, NC

The Beauty of Nature

Sitting under a tree,
The wind blowing past me,
Soft grass rustling below,
I see fall leaves in the meadow.

I look far and high,
And find the endless sky,
I drop a coin in the water and as it sank,
The ripples gracefully reach the river bank.

I gaze into the river,
And see a school of sliver,
My gaze then shifts to the predator — a larger fish,
As it swims elegantly — its tail going swish, swish, swish.

Nature comes in many colors and sizes,
And is full of surprises,
Before we raise our arm to harm nature in the future,
We will have to remember the beauty of nature.

Tanay Patri, Grade 5
Hickory Valley Christian School, TN

The Sounds, Sights and Smells of Life

The wind whispers to the grass as it glides through the sky.
Birds are singing up in branches.
Dogs are barking,
bark, bark.
Rabbits arc hopping through the woods.
Is that all you hear?

Rivers are flowing like silver ribbons.
Cars are driving by, honking
honk, honk.
Leaves are changing in the fall.
The colors of leaves are different: brown, yellow and orange.
Is that all you see?

Kids are running through the street to the candy store.
I can smell the candy from a mile away.
Apple pie in the oven,
"Smells good, Mom."
You wake up to the smell of pancakes in the morning,
mmm, mmm, good.
Everything smells good.
Is that all you smell?

Marriah Frakes, Grade 5
Odessa Middle School, MO

The Tornado

The tornado was a hit all over the news.
Then all the kids screamed wows and woos,
Thinking they would get out of school.
Sadly, the teachers were cruel,
Because everyone had to go to school.

Bradlee White, Grade 5
North Middle School, TN

Veterinarian

My dream is to become a veterinarian.
I'm making my way through grades, as I make all A's.
Veterinarian

When I graduate I'm going off to college.
I'm going for four years.
As I get out, I hope to be a veterinarian.
I hope to be one in Gulf Shores.
I hope to take animals on the beach
before they go home to their owners.
Veterinarian

When I sit them down on the cold, wet sand,
the tip of their paws get wet.
When they meow, bark, or make different sounds;
They sound peaceful and happy.
Veterinarian

Kaylee Norton, Grade 5
Childersburg Middle School, AL

The World

The world is full of lies
Waiting to be heard
The lies that cover up the truth
Are soon left behind
The world is full of people
Fighting for their rights
Fighting back and fighting back
But just getting left in the dust
The world is full of mistakes and miracles
Each happens for a reason
But what is the reason?
We will never know
The world is full of wonderful things
Most of us have our part
The world is full of stars
Either on the stage or in the sky
They each have their own turn to perform
But some people are still waiting for their time to shine
The world is full of many things that each make a difference
Some are good, some are bad
But they each have a reason

Hannah Kanyuh, Grade 6
Discovery School @ Reeves Rogers, TN

White Water Rafting

I was hit by a massive wave
Like a glugging river of milk
The sloshing liquid smack my face
Rushing down the river, the water charging
We hit a massive rock
A massive jerk we felt
A shattering noise brings my heart into my mouth
I was so elated

Recardo Kersey, Grade 5
E O Young Jr Elementary School, NC

Trees

Trees' leaves are green.
We need to keep them clean.
Their branches are brown.
Please, don't chop them down.

Trees help us live.
They just give and give.
They're our lifesaver.
They even make paper.

Tasha Sweat, Grade 6
Manning Elementary School, SC

My Dogs

My dogs are cute.
My dogs are fun.
My dogs are hungry.
My dogs are funny.
I love my dogs.
I love them so much.
And I care for them.

Mckayla Harrington, Grade 4
Brilliant Elementary School, AL

The World Around Us

The world around us
Has too much fuss.

The land looks trashy,
Let's make it flashy.

We can all have fun
Once we get the jobs done.

If we all don't litter,
We won't be as bitter.

We should all give a hand
And help clean up the land!

Jacob Simmons, Grade 5
Enon Elementary School, LA

A Christmas Tree

One little star on
top of the tree,
two little presents
underneath for me,
three silver ropes
twisted around the tree,
four colored lights
shining prettily,
five glowing balls
glittering.
Oh! What a sight
for you to see!

Katie Granger, Grade 4
E O Young Jr Elementary School, NC

Sounds of a Waterfall

I love the attractive dripping sounds that a waterfall makes,
"Drip, drip, drip, drip, drip, drip, drip, drip."
When I'm there I love to relax.
As I walk into the creek I feel the ice cold water rushing to my toes.
The tiny creatures that gather there always come to me.
When I look into the river it's a surprise to see ripples.
I admire jumping off cliffs into the water.
It makes me so nervous because I know that I could get injured.
But I never do.
When I stand under them in shorts "Ahh!"
I feel the wetness go down, down, down and tingle my body.
Even the sounds of birds hear my cry as I yell from the rocks.
One of my favorites is lying on the rocks that come with the stream.
Looking for new things is an A-D-V-E-N-T-U-R-E!
But calmness is the key to relaxation.

Summer Simmons, Grade 5
North Middle School, TN

New York City

There's no place on Earth like New York City.
The lights on Times Square are so bright and pretty!
There are dozens of shows to see on Broadway,
Or lots of other ways to spend a day.
You can take a cab or a subway or even a bus
To the world's most amazing Toys R Us!
It has a giant building made of Legos and a Candyland inside,
And a four story Ferris Wheel you can actually ride!
You can spend a whole day learning at the Museum of Natural History.
Or you can see the Empire State Building and Statue of Liberty,
Both of those buildings are unbelievably tall.
There are so many choices it would take a month to do it all!

Kellen Gifford, Grade 4
Sequoyah Elementary School, TN

I Am

I am a very tall boy who likes playing paintball with my friends
I wonder what it would be like to have a paintball pro as my brother
I hear the sound of the wind whispering in my ear
I see my guardian angel flying close by as I soar high and fast
I want to travel the world seeing the sights and sounds
I am a very tall boy who likes playing paintball with my friends

I pretend to be riding my bike through the early morning dew in Scotland
I feel the silence pressing in on me
I touch the clouds in the sky as I ride through with my angel at my side
I worry about the death of my friends and family
I cry when I think about the deaths of my grandparents
I am a very tall boy who likes playing paintball with my friends

I understand death will come with time
I say, "don't be afraid of taking chances."
I dream about what will become of me in the future
I hope I will have a long peaceful life
I am a very tall boy who likes playing paintball with my friends

Robert Byerly, Grade 6
R D and Euzelle P Smith Middle School, NC

Holidays

We start out with a happy new year
We all gather around to watch as the ball drops
At midnight we yell out our doorsteps to all
Then here comes Valentine
The mushy gushy love holiday
Chocolates, roses, and hearts
All this love, I think I'm going to puke
Easter, Easter right around the corner
I think I see the bunny coming
As we look for eggs we think about Jesus
Not far from Easter is July 4th the firework month
On this night we shoot off fireworks
We all stare at the red glare
Then comes the spooky month Halloween
October 31st is the night we all dress up
Witches, vampires, pumpkins, and skeletons
All running the streets looking for candy
November is the month we give thanks
The holiday Thanksgiving
The favorite holiday is next Christmas
Give gifts to those in need or the ones we love

Sydney George, Grade 6
Southwest Middle School, AR

The Magnificent Pet

I am going to get a Boa Constrictor.
I will name him Slitheren.
He will be a cool pet
Because he can wrap around my leg
And make his way to my head
And lick my cheek.
He will be long
so I can let him sleep in my bed
or give him a jungle gym to slide on.
If there is a mouse in the house,
It's a free snake for Slitheren.
He'll be a great pet.

Tyrone Kendall, Grade 5
Lee A Tolbert Community Academy, MO

This Feeling

You lay your hand on my shoulder.
My heart stops beating.
My mind goes blank.
My muscles tense up.
What's this feeling?
It feels like there's a war raging inside of me.
There are butterflies in my stomach begging to be free
You move your hand.
It seems like everything had calmed down.
When I look into your I eyes I see nothing but compasslon.
What was that feeling anyway?
Was it love, care, or kindness?
Whatever it was I want that feeling back.

Suzanna Gomez, Grade 6
Cedar Creek School, LA

Christmas Tree

Look at me, O look at me
Look at the presents under my beautiful tree
I can't wait until Christmas Eve
O how many presents I'm going to receive
O how good I am going to be
Because I want the presents under my
Christmas tree!!!

Jaquan Johnson, Grade 4
E O Young Jr Elementary School, NC

Guitars

G uitars are so fun to play.
U se them to make me fill good each day.
I like to play them in my spare time.
T o make me feel like I'm special in some way.
A strum of a chord sounds so beautiful.
R ock is one of the things I play.
S o what I like to do is play my guitar.

Charles Wayne Wilkinson, Grade 4
Brilliant Elementary School, AL

Fall Is Here

Autumn is one of my favorite seasons —
All the leaves falling from the trees,
Bumble bees hurrying for a reason —
The reason is that summer is almost over,
Nuts and acorns are falling, falling, falling,
Making the squirrels hide them faster,
I love watching them scurry about —
They are adorable, cute, and loving
With their bushy tails and pink snouts,
I feel all jittery inside,
I feel like I will burst with joy! I just can't abide
Summer is ending, good bye to the heat —
We welcome the crispness of fall's beginning,
At 9:00, we go to sleep —
All is quiet, all is well,
And about fall, not a peep,
We wake up the next morning —
Fall is here! Fall is here!
We're so happy, we feel like singing,
The wait is now over —
Summer's gone, fall is here, now let us give a big cheer!

Micah Christman, Grade 5
Palmetto Christian Academy, SC

My Summer Day

I woke up on a bright summer day.
And the birds were swimming,
and the sky was as blue as my eyes.
The flowers were blooming,
and the trees were as green as a grasshopper.
The lake was as calm as the wind,
and it was a bright blue green.

Diamond Sistrunk, Grade 5
West Marion Elementary School, MS

A Journey

A seed travels from place to place
Across sea and deserts.
Dangerous in places,
With birds flying by
And mice crawling low.
The sun too hot
The ice too cold
Water too wet
Deserts too dry.
Weeds are dangerous, same as people
One seed grows big and strong,
While one is picked for a friend.
The flower grows and grows
Until autumn came
Tearing the petals off
One by one
The seeds set free.
A new generation
Has begun.

Alex Easton, Grade 5
G C Burkhead Elementary School, KY

The One Boy

Day by day, I think of him
waiting for a response
and today he tells me, he hates me.

I felt so bad.
I felt like crying;
he had broken my heart.

I know I have to move on
but I can't let him go.
He will stay in my heart forever.

This boy meant something to me.
He meant the whole world to me,
but he's not mine anymore.

I hope he's happy forever.
His happiness will make me happy,
that's all I pray for.

He made me feel good.
I thought he was the one,
but I let him go away from me.

Christina Oyler, Grade 6
Rocky Comfort Elementary School, MO

Love Someone

I love someone yes I do.
I love someone how bout you?
I love someone yes I do.
Friend it's you!

Hope Turnage, Grade 5
West Marion Elementary School, MS

Haunted House

Old and broken house
Scary ghosts frighten people
Run and get away!!

Cassandra Banania, Grade 5
St Joseph Institute for the Deaf, MO

Daddy

Daddy I love you.
Daddy I do.
Daddy I love you.
And I know you do too.
I loved you from the start.
I love you with all my heart.
As a baby in your arm.
You kept me from harm.
You know what "love" means.
I know you do.
That's why I love you.

Makayla Valdez, Grade 5
Vernon Middle School, LA

Hockey

Pucks, pucks everywhere,
Pucks, pucks in the air.
Skates, skates every night,
Skates, skates a delight.
Hockey, hockey in the pool,
Hockey, hockey is so cool.

Madison Schutz, Grade 4
Wohlwend Elementary School, MO

Christmas

Christmas is a joyful holiday
Family and friends having fun
Playing games at Christmas parties
Spending time with loved ones

Mom and I go shopping
Buying presents for everyone
I get what I want
They get what they need

Santa Claus is coming soon
A snack of milk and cookies
Giving kids presents
Hearing something on the roof

Cierra Young, Grade 5
Woodland Elementary School, KY

Dreams

I dream of ice-cream
I dream of cookies
A big dessert
In my head.

Joseph Tanas, Grade 4
St Thomas More School, NC

Little Snowman

There is a snowman I've been told
That plays with kids out in the cold.
What's better in a white wonderland
Than a little snowman in your hand.

Lacey Sughrue, Grade 4
Cleveland Elementary School, OK

I Hear, I Wonder

I hear the sad
And lonely chirp of a
Baby bird looking
For its mother.

I hear the whistle
Of the train and
I wonder if you
Will ever return.

Cody Bennett, Grade 6
Blackmon Road Middle School, GA

Mermaids/People

Mermaids
magical, mysterious
gliding, swimming, loving
Neptune, tail, president, legs
running, walking, jumping
curious, skillful
People

Nikki Sullivan, Grade 5
Briarwood Christian School, AL

This Is Why I Am Fat

This is why I am fat
I got it on my back
And when I get hungry
I eat a big mac
I order extra fries
I get a McFlurry
and when I got done
my eyes were blurry

Desmond Green, Grade 5
Graham Elementary School, AL

School Is Cool

School is cool, I have to say.
I see my friends there every day.
Reading, writing, and spelling too,
are just a few things you learn to do!

School is cool, I have to say.
"School is for learning,"
my teachers say.
I think school is especially cool,
Whenever we go out to play.

Devyn Woodle, Grade 6
Appling County Middle School, GA

Being Myself

I want to be me, myself, and I.
Because I know that no one is better at being me except for me.

I don't need beauty, and I don't need smarts.
All I need is a family and friends in my heart,
but I will always need Jesus to help me play this part.

Caitlin Buesinger, Grade 5
Evangel Christian Academy, AL

In the Country

When I'm in the Country I see the
Big long fields of corn
The donkeys, cows, goats and horses
Grazing in the pasture
The wild flowers growing
In a yard
When I'm in the country I hear the
Insects everywhere I go
The cows bawling to each other
The people with their loud trucks
When I'm in the country I feel the
Mud under my boots
The heat feels like an oven
The hay under my shirt scratching me
When I'm in the country I smell the
Freshly cut and rolled up hay
Cow droppings and dead animals
That smells terrible on the side of the road
I love it
When I'm in the country

Preston Fletcher, Grade 4
Briarwood Elementary School, KY

My Dog Reese

Small and furry but not fat
My dog was bred to chase a rat

His growl is fierce his howl is funny
He runs in the yard just like a bunny

His size alone cannot display
The courage that he shows every day

His tiny legs move so fast
When he runs he makes me gasp

Short and fluffy he likes to cuddle
But will never go in a bath or a puddle

He likes to be dragged around like a chew toy
For that gives him such great joy

Well that just about sums him up
That dog is really one great pup

Will Mealer, Grade 6
Houston Middle School, TN

Fall

Fall is full of fun
Now that summer's done
We eat turkey and potatoes
And I like cherry tomatoes.

I play in the leaves with different colors
And I enjoy playing with my younger brother.
I can hear the bells in my ear
Fall is one of my favorite times of the year.
Everything is getting colder and colder,
And the leaves are getting older and older.

Connor Grady, Grade 5
Trinity Day School, GA

Door

Ouch! A headache,
from being slammed,
by that angry little girl,
who's as vicious as a snake.

I ache from standing straight,
so tall and rigid,
at attention all the time.

Swinging to, and fro,
from my little house,
in the middle of the wall.

Pushed, and pulled,
like two children,
playing tug-of-war.

Alas I wonder,
where they go,
when they've gone past me.

Meredyth Albright, Grade 5
Hunter GT Magnet Elementary School, NC

Eagles

These are the beautiful, intelligent,
And proud bald eagles.
Tiny, round, ivory heads.
Sharp eyes hunting for food.
Bodies covered with velvety, chocolate feathers.
Razor-sharp gold claws pierce
Through their tiny prey.
They fly, soar, glide like the wind all
Around their habitat.
The eagles so proud, they represent our
Nation with pride.
Although they represent out nation,
They are hardly ever seen.
It'll be an astonishment to see one in your lifetime.
No wonder the eagle represents our nation!

Caroline Zheng, Grade 6
Haynes Academy for Advanced Studies, LA

Where I'm From

Where I'm From
I am from make-up, lip gloss and eye shadow.
I am from the tube in my backyard lake.
I am from the brilliantly sweet strawberries and the glistening rose petal.
I am from the new Fergie songs my family and I discuss at our family meeting
and athleticism, from Eric and Elizabeth and Justin.
I'm from the are-we-done-yets and the I-can-do-betters.
From "it will be okay" and "if you don't have anything nice to say don't say anything at all."
I am from the designer Italians and the selfish Welshman.
I am from New Jersey, soup and bread.
from the stories of Olympic pole-vaulting from my dad,
the horrible math done by my mom, and the football from my brother.
I am from the hallway and the picture room.

Morgan Richard, Grade 6
Lakeshore Middle School, NC

Autumn Changes

The leaves have turned to the color of crimson and gold. The sun now smiles kindly at us as a cool breeze ripples through the air. People go out to the fields to get their pumpkins. Ours now shines radiantly out on our porch. Birds now have started to fly south through the crystal blue sky. The reason for this glorious change is it's Autumn.

Andrew Lipke, Grade 5
Palmetto Christian Academy, SC

Where I Am From...

I am from Louisville KY, from the expensive fixed up cars.
I am from the large brown, white and black houses.
From large decks and yards.
I am from loud talking and yelling through the stores,
From Maria, Big Bob, the twins and Jarod, Phillip, Latifah and their parents.
I am from the Parrish family reunion and also the Johnson's.
I am from my parents saying "123" which meant don't do that.
I am from Icy Sink, Stony Point, and Loving Springs Baptist Church.
From Rev. Pearson, Rev. Whitney, and Rev. Sales, the preachers.
I am from chicken, greens, green beans, corn, macaroni,
Baked beans, large Sunday dinners, lots of candy and big cookouts.
From the stroke my Grandfather had in 2001, the time my sister broke her arm in 2005,
And when the glass fell on my head in 2000.
I am from the big basketball, football, and baseball games.
From kids outside on school nights, I am from Louisville KY.

Aaliyah Pearson, Grade 6
Lost River Elementary School, KY

The Wonderful Place

Dark blue shiny water is very clear as glass in a mirror.
Dry brown sand that is hot on my feet saying "Ouch that hurts" as I step on it,
Loud strong waves crashing hard into the ground can knock me over "Wow they're strong" I always say
Noisy pelicans annoy me by making weird sounds while trying to catch fish,
Disgusting squish wet sand is mud in the ocean,
Dead smelly fish that are washed up on the beach makes tons of people leave "Wow that's a nasty smell"
Icky tasting salt from the water seeps into my mouth, "That's a disgusting taste" I say,
Hot nasty sand gets into my mouth when I wipe my mouth off with my sandy hands, "Yuck"
Hard shells that are small and stink from the water is what I collect "Wow I've got a bunch of shells,"
Soft sticky starfish that I find in the water stick to my hands when I try to take it off,
Joy and happiness comes to me while I'm at the beach "Wow that was fun" I say as I'm leaving the wonderful beach.

Cole Mattingly, Grade 6
College View Middle School, KY

School

School is good in every way
People learn, so people stay,
Sometimes they hate it, but other times not,
School is a great place.

Sierra Griffin, Grade 5
Paint Lick Elementary School, KY

I Am

I am a very short person for my age.
I wonder if I will be very tall.
I hear my dad leave for work.
I see all my friends playing around.
I want a new girlfriend this year.
I am very sweet, kind, and considerate.

I pretend I am the coolest person.
I feel very cold in the school.
I touch the clean laundry to fold it.
I worry about my little brother every day.
I cry when my brother gets hurt.
I am a good brother to him.

I understand his problems sometimes or not.
I say my mom is very pretty.
I dream that I am very rich.
I try to do my best in school.
I hope I become famous when I grow up.
I am the best brother in the whole world.

Wesley Moore, Grade 5
Byrns L Darden Elementary School, TN

The Creek

Drip, drip, drip, went the cold refreshing water.
In the trickling water, the fish swam.
The moist, clean sand sat there and sat there.
Suddenly, the snake came out from under
its rock and slowly drifted down the creek.
Everything was peaceful in the cold,
refreshing water.

Coleman Bergsma, Grade 5
Salisbury Academy, NC

Black

Black is the color of my mama's burnt cookies
Black is the color of night fall
Black is the color that rules over all
Black is the color of the numbers on the clock
Black is the color that comes out at night
Black is the color of my big fat cat that won't chase the rat
Black is the color of the smoke from my grandfather's pipe
Black is well…
What is black
Black is not just a cat or a hat
Black is black

Madison Miles, Grade 5
Meredith-Dunn School, KY

The Football Game

Ssssswwwwww! A whistle
Making the play
The clock runs
Hut! The quarterback starting the play
Swwoo! The football cutting through the air
Tat! The receiver caught the ball
ThudThudThud! The receiver running the ball
For a touchdown
Touchdown HOGS
Aaaaaaawwwwww! After the win over LSU

Styver Hamric, Grade 6
Des Arc Elementary School, AR

Dolphins

Dolphins gracefully and peacefully gliding through the ocean
Majestic, slippery, great and
Rubbery with silver all over.
Racing, jumping, and playing around
Enjoying sweet salmon
Showing off to others and swimming together
Mothers playing with young
Out to get a catch of fish
Meeting new aquatic life and friends
And enjoying life.

Peter Belleau, Grade 6
Haynes Academy for Advanced Studies, LA

One Crazy Ride

Standing in long long line
Legs shaking like they are maracas
Finally getting on the T2
One HUMONGUS roller coaster
Metal bar pushing down on my stomach like a horn
Holding on tightly and breathing very quickly
It finally begins to move "Boom"
Travels straight up in the air like a rocket
Around and around, up and down,
Sharp turns making me feel like I'm going to fall off DIZZY
Feeling like someone is spinning me around and around
Screaming and yelling at the top of my lungs
"Get me off of HERE"
Can't catch my breath, eyes closed tight
Scared like I just saw a ghost
Suddenly the ride stops with one last "Boom."

Ciara Luvine, Grade 4
Roberta Tully Elementary School, KY

Daniel

D eadly in Halo 2
A lways in time for school
N ice to friends and family
I nto video games a lot
E nemy to spiders that get close to my mom
L ikes chicken wraps with ranch

Daniel Garrett, Grade 4
Byrns L Darden Elementary School, TN

The Kiss

A kiss is sweet
With chocolate galore
Glorious aroma abounds
Pointed top
Cheer up matey!
Have a Hershey Kiss
Jaret Claypool, Grade 4
Crossville Christian School, TN

This Christmas

This Christmas I want toys,
but they have to be for boys.
I don't know what you want,
like a football to punt.
I want something that will make noise.
Tristan Blevins, Grade 6
Rocky Comfort Elementary School, MO

Baseball

Baseball is the best
Sliding into home wins games
We all love this sport

The umpire is tough
Sometimes the call goes your way
And your team goes wild

This is our pastime
That's why baseball is awesome
The old ball game rules!
Mike Olson, Grade 6
Queen of Angels Catholic School, GA

Rainy Day

Oh rainy day
Please go away
I want to go outside and play!
Sitting by my window I say…
I wish it was pretty today.
I sit and wait for a sunny day
To go outside and play, play, play.
Cassie McConkey, Grade 5
North Middle School, TN

Christmas Time

Christmas time is family time
With gifts and twinkling lights
Christmas trees and decorations,
And lots of snowball fights.

Snowflakes fall to the ground
While church and sleigh bells ring.
Families cook all day long,
And people and carolers sing.
Jaime Graham, Grade 6
Pleasants County Middle School, WV

Fall

Trees are bright in fall
The leaves are orange and red
I love to climb trees
I even climb trees when it's cold
Trees are so pretty in fall
Logan Snyder, Grade 5
Berryville Elementary School, AR

Balloons

I got a balloon
From an old man in the park
It floated away
Amanda Paramore, Grade 4
Briarwood Christian School, AL

Dog

Dog
bark, walk
run, jump, sleep
digging, eating, chasing, scratching
some dogs bark loud.
bulldog
Dory Langley, Grade 4
East Jones Elementary School, MS

Where I'm From

I'm from snakes.
Crawling in my backyard.
I am from seas.
Crashing on the shore.
I am from a place where we get bruises.
Where we play soccer.

I am from STLP.
Where we learn about technology.
I am from Build-A-Bear workshop.
Where best friends are made.
I am from Mrs. Jackson.
Great teaching.

I am from warm homes.
That keeps me warm.
I am from the cold.
In the winter.
I am from the warm.
In the summer.
Brianna Johnson, Grade 5
Tates Creek Elementary School, KY

Fall

F alling leaves flutter to the ground
A t this time of year.
L ying there with
L uminous colors.
Alex Lane, Grade 5
First Flight Elementary School, NC

Autumn

Leaves dance in circles
Animals run in the field
Fall is here at last.
Danny Arndt, Grade 6
Musselman Middle School, WV

There's Always a Choice

If I had a choice,
I would choose.

If I had an order,
I would follow it.

If I were to receive,
I would give.

Now if you had a choice,
What would you do?

There's always a choice
No matter what.

The good could lead you
To a better life.

The bad could lead you
Ruining your life.

Now again,
What would you choose?
Samantha Becker, Grade 5
Odessa Middle School, MO

Tennis Ball

Pop blop goes the ball,
Pop blop watch it fall.
Up down,
with little sound.
Off the racket over the net,
almost as fun as a pet.
Tennis is fun,
but you must run.
The ball goes everywhere,
but only if it dares…
Kyra Carter, Grade 6
Appling County Middle School, GA

Nature Is a Part of Life

Sunshine makes the flowers grow
Rain helps the rivers flow
Nature is a part of life you see
Making food for you and me
From the Earth these things come
To return to where they are from.
Sara Inez Charbonnet, Grade 5
West Marion Elementary School, MS

Eagle

Majestic bird with a golden beak
Like the sun.
Up high in the sky.
Hunting its prey until the day
Is done.
Never sleeps only flies
And eats.
Sometimes is good
And sometimes is bad.
Beautiful like a chocolate bird with a
Golden glaze on the tip.
Don't try to get close to it in the wild
But you can always gaze at it at the zoo.

Allison Folse, Grade 6
Haynes Academy for Advanced Studies, LA

A War Man's Will

Today will be my last day
At twelve o'clock I shall leave Hudson Bay.

Far into the sea I will travel
And I will meet my death shadow.

Give my children my riches
And my wife my love.

Give thanks to the Lord Almighty
For His will was for me to die and to protect Thee.

Tell my friends that I thank them
For all the help that they have provided.

As I write this will
While my ship is being attacked
As I say my last goodbyes.

Goodbye and farewell.

Zack Harrison, Grade 6
Rose Bud Elementary School, AR

Starlight

Late at night,
The stars shine bright,
Erin watching them glow.
All the tress are swaying in the breeze,
The leaves falling real low.
She thinks about her life in the stars,
The moon, the planets,
How cool they are.
Sky surfing, bowling,
How wonderful it would be.
"But what about my family, up here with me?"
So far down.
I would be like a cow without grass.

Patricia O'Dowd, Grade 6
Haynes Academy for Advanced Studies, LA

He Is King

He is King, rejoice,
Let earth sing;
Use your voice!
He is holy,
Sing with glory,
Take a walk and see,

The rocks and mountain tops;
See the trees and flowers
Because He has all power!
He made the light and night,
With His might, He made
it right — this world is out of sight!

Believe because He made you and me
He also made the days and years;
He made the seasons for a reason, so let's praise!
He used a bird that,
Was a dove, to show
His word that was love!

He is king, rejoice,
Let earth sing;
Use your voice!

Ashley Waldron, Grade 5
Palmetto Christian Academy, SC

I Am Haunted

By the big, yellow eyes staring at me.
The dragon waiting for me to go to sleep so it can eat me.
I am haunted!

I am haunted
By a big strolling, strong wind trying to get me,
my family, and my dogs.
A tornado just hit!!!
I am alone!

I am haunted
By the world coming to an end and I am alone.
No friends, no family, and no dogs.
I will scream and say
Help me I am alone!!!

I am haunted!

Rebekkah Anne Satterly, Grade 5
Eminence Middle School, KY

There Is No One

It's dark that's all I know, I reach out my hand, no one's there.
I move, but I don't go anywhere.
I walk, but I fall, no one's there to catch me.
I talk, but you can't hear the words coming out of my mouth.
I fight to gain control but I lose and once again I'm small.

Harley Jackson, Grade 6
Muhlenberg North Middle School, KY

My Best Friend
Cidnie
nice
kind
gentle
caring
playful
enjoyable
funny
crazy
short
small
Cidnie
my best friend
Tynecia Bell, Grade 6
Armorel Elementary School, AR

Roadrunners
I race around sand.
I can stand blazing hot days.
Running for my prey.
James Holladay, Grade 4
Briarwood Christian School, AL

The Graveyard Visit
Trees rattling
Fear clenching
Foggy lights
Wondering where I am
Disintegrating bodies
Owls hooting
Dark shadows
Dry throat
Dew on ground
Mold on the ground
Leaves crumbling
Ruined appetite
Tombstones
THE GRAVEYARD VISIT
Dillon Hughes, Grade 5
Berryville Elementary School, AR

Cars
There are fast ones,
Slow ones.

Purple ones,
Green ones and even
Red ones.

It's fun to watch
Them go down
The drag way.

Cars are awesome.
Carley Allen, Grade 5
Oark Elementary School, AR

Where I Am From
I am from New Madison a small town in Ohio
To the quiet country side of Russell Springs in Kentucky

I am from a small apartment duplex where I had my own room
To sharing a bedroom with my grandma in a small house on a hill

I am from Mr. Flatter's fifth grade class at Tri-Village Elementary
To Mrs. Samantha's sixth grade class at Union Chapel Elementary

I am from walking seven blocks to and from school every day
To waking up very early every morning just to catch the bus

I am from having to pack my lunch every day
To enjoying the lunches that I have at my new school

I am from not having any extra-curricular activities
To being one of the five top flute players

I am from not making the best grades in class
To being one of the best academic team players

I am from having to leave my best friends behind
To having to make new friends and new bonds
And that is what makes me who I am
Meghan Whitehead, Grade 6
Union Chapel Elementary School, KY

Kaitlin
Kaitlin
funny, adventurous, imaginative, and energetic
Relative of Grace Elbl
Lover of soccer, family, and dogs
Who needs family, friends, love, and pets
Who fears sharks, people dying, snakes, spiders, and storms
Who feels sad when my mom is sick, trust when I'm with family,
and greatness when I'm on the soccer field
Who gives love to family and pets, respect for nature, help to others
Who would like to see God, Uncle Mike, Hollywood, CA
Resident of feelings
Elbl

Kaitlin Elbl, Grade 6
Our Lady Catholic School, MO

Flora Flamingo
Flora Flamingo loved to play bingo every Friday night at 8.
She put on her cap and she put on her glasses and said "I can't wait!"
Flora marched up Main St; turned on Chingo,
looking forward to playing bingo.
She got in the hall and caused quite a scare
'cause all the old ladies ran outta there!
The caller was nearsighted, so he didn't see
as Flora took a card and as she took her seat.
She squawked "Bingo" and got her prize,
a $100 and shrimp in a life's supplies.

Charis Bauman, Grade 6
Haynes Academy for Advanced Studies, LA

Grand Canyon

G reat as can be
R eady for people to yell out and hear their echo
A lert
N o animals
D angerous

C aring
A wesome
N ot many people
Y ells out to all visitors
O pen for the world to see
N o sad faces

Some people say that if you stand at the edge
of the Grand Canyon at sunset you can see the sun go down.

Thomas Hart, Grade 5
Vernon Middle School, LA

It's All About Me!!!

If you want to know about me
I tend to have pimples
I'm short, I hope you can see
When I smile I have dimples
and straight teeth
My mom's name is Jennifer
And my dad's is Keith

When I get A's she says I'm a cure
I color my nails black
I also call friends on the phone, and stay on for an hour
I have a cat, and if you see her, she is fat and that's a fact
When I'm at my house, I like to have power

My cat's name is Candy
She is white and sweet
She meows and it sounds like Mandy
She also loves to eat meat
She is very tall
And I love tea
And when she gets on my back she'll fall
And that's all you need to know about
Me! Me! Me!

Brianna Kinsey, Grade 6
Armorel Elementary School, AR

My Passion

The nervous feeling when I sing
But, I'm doing what I love.
The music and the voices the harmony and melody
The joy of the choir on the chorus.
The cheers when I'm done
The smiles and claps of the audience.
Flowers and awards after it's all over
Singing, what my passion is!

Sydney Bailey, Grade 5
North Middle School, TN

Science

Science
Science why do you trouble me?
About this crazy star's cycle in this big galaxy
It's just so frustrating to figure it out
Trust me it's hard and without a doubt.

I'm tired of homework. I'm only 11.
I wish we had homework like when we were 7
Because it's easy as pie,
But when I do this homework I feel like I'm going to die.

But that's Science 4 you. Read it and weep.
But you might want to bring a pillow cause
You are going to fall asleep.
ZZZZZ…

Haley Davis, Grade 6
McIntosh County Middle School, GA

Flower, Flower

Flower, flower you're so tall
Flower, flower, I am not at all.

Not been eaten by a weed,
When you were still just a seed.

Not been eaten by a weed
You don't have great speed
And across the desert day and night
Across the desert without a fright.

Stop and rest in the snow
Stop and rest the wind will blow.

Look out for people look out, look out!
Because without a doubt you will be plucked you little sprout.

Flower, flower you are so tall.
Flower, flower I am still not at all.

Lander Ryan, Grade 5
G C Burkhead Elementary School, KY

Fall

O' come old man winter it is your turn to play
O' chase away spring and summer who stayed up too
LONG
Tuck
Them
All
Safe
In
BED
NOW it is your turn
To play
winter and fall it is *your* turn to play

Maya Beckley, Grade 5
Prince of Peace Catholic School, SC

Legacy

Child, take my Bible,
For you will need it.
Those Scriptures will guide you.
Pass them on
To your children, too.

Meghan Foard, Grade 6
Woodlawn Christian School, NC

Softball

I love softball
Its better than going to the mall
You can hit home runs
Its a lot of fun
Catcher is the best
You can see the rest
I hate sitting on the bench
It's as hard as a wrench

Hannah Street, Grade 6
Graham Elementary School, AL

Typical Day

I got up and went to my school.
I went home because I was cool.
Then I went outside.
And found a place to hide.
After all that I swam in the pool.

Michael Truong, Grade 6
Armorel Elementary School, AR

Guitars

There are lots of guitars,
acoustic and electric too.
There are many designs,
shall I name a few?
There's the V design, my favorite,
Gibson SG, my number two.
Oops, sorry, I can only name two.
Is that good enough for you?

Dakota Gahr, Grade 5
Wynne Intermediate School, AR

Turkey

Hunters are coming
It's Thanksgiving time…Run fast!
Turkey tastes real good!!!

Michelle Beehner, Grade 5
St Joseph Institute for the Deaf, MO

Radio City Rockettes

Radio City Rockettes
Elegant and experienced
Heads up, kicking high
As perfect as the heavens above
If only I could perform on Broadway!

Allison Faust, Grade 5
Sullivan Elementary School, TN

Never Know Until You Try

You could sail the Pacific
Climb a mountain too
All these different things you can do
If only you try

A knock on wood is no hope at all
But, knocking on a door
It will open if another one closes

Play your potential
Shine your shine
Do what you do
Just be yourself, just be your…cool

You could sail the Pacific
Climb a mountain too
All these different things you can do
If only you try

Sara Speller, Grade 5
Millbrook Elementary School, NC

Magnolia Blossom

Magnolia blossom
white, beautiful
blooms, grows, sprouts
sniffing, looking, smelling, willing
A white smelly flower
Flower

Hogan Brewer, Grade 4
East Jones Elementary School, MS

Chocolates

C rossing streets for the sweets
H alloween is heres! So is
O ctober 31st, soon November!
C ome, let's go to the
O rchard with coco beans!
L ate at night
A smell arouses me
T o the kitchen
E veryone is excitedly
S urrounding a candle eating delicious,
    melting, chocolate s'mores!!!!!!

Jessica Runnells, Grade 5
First Flight Elementary School, NC

Sensations of Autumn

Leaves
Very colorful
Jumping, yelling, enjoying
Amazing, autumn, fun, enjoyable
Drinking, soothing, relaxing
Apple, spicy
Cider

Casey R. Densmore, Grade 6
Musselman Middle School, WV

Bees

Black and yellow,
Buzzing around,
Stopping on flowers,
Helping the Earth!

Kellie L'Hote, Grade 5
St Vincent Elementary School, MO

Bear

Bear
big, brown
hunt, roar, kill
running, finding, walking, hibernating
They can be mean.
Black Bear

Devon Wolff, Grade 4
East Jones Elementary School, MS

About Me

This is a poem about me.
I hate school, can't you see.
I am not sure why.
Mom tells me that time will fly.
She tells me that this is my job
and life only gets harder.
So I promised to do my best.
So my mom can get some rest.

Travis Fortenberry, Grade 5
West Marion Elementary School, MS

Doors to Bright Sides

Opening a door to a bright side
Don't be so upset
It's ok to be tired

There are always doors to open
Some doors lead to the dark side
Some doors lead to the bright side

There is always a chance to change
So open a new door
There are many doors to open!

Savannah Murr, Grade 6
St Joseph Institute for the Deaf, MO

The Ocean

I love the ocean
the crisp blue water.
And the sound of waves
rising up and splashing down.
Oh what beautiful dolphins
jumping up unexpectedly.
The colorful fish swimming
in clear water.
Oh what a beautiful sight.

Zachary Lawson, Grade 5
Bloomfield Elementary School, KY

Night Friends

The sunset dances for me as I watch the new waking moon.
She makes me lose myself in thoughts.
The stars twinkle curiously as they watch me.
The sleepy tired sea sends soft waves that tickle my feet.
The night is quiet as nature sleeps.
As I drift to sleep the soft cool wind guides me to a river.
The wind says come trust me.
She leads me to a stream then says, "Wake up; it is I."
It is my mom who says wake up.
It is dawn.
The morning is stone cold, but I don't mind
For the sun greets me as I leave.
I skip with the rabbits then run with the wind.
My new friends can't wait till they see me again.

Maria Jazwinski, Grade 6
St Andrew's Episcopal School, LA

The Wonder of Piano

It all started back a long time ago,
When the extraordinary history came along,
The wonderful composers who made the music
Made many types of music.
My favorites are classical and jazz.
I just think the differences in songs are neat.
I love the feeling with the talent of playing,
When you feel joyful and lighthearted.
I like the sound of the soft and loud keys.
I think the challenge makes you a better player.
I can't believe how popular
Playing such a wonderful instrument has come about,
Since Ludwig Van Beethoven played.

Natalie McQuilkin, Grade 5
North Middle School, TN

Downtown

When mom said get ready,
to go to downtown,
I jumped up and down,
and made a huge sound!

I got ready in a flash,
and got downstairs in a dash.
Then we got in the car,
and went to Arby's, got a baked potato,
then we saw a star,
when we drove by Hardee's, saw a tomato.

We dropped by the office,
and picked up my dad.
Then we went by the Windy River walk.
There, we ate, along with the sparkling
river, and downtown high-rises.
This was a picture perfect view.
Then I say, "Man, Memphis has a great downtown."

Brian J. Turner, Grade 6
Saint Paul School, TN

Prasie

I am a fast water bug swimming in cold water.
I have spots on my face like a cheetah looking for his prey.
I am the Parthenon standing strong in the night.
I am 5'2" and 100 lbs. of pure stone.
I am bright like a shouting star in the sky.
I am like a sloth sitting on a tree watching TV.
My name is Ty.

Ty Kourlas, Grade 6
Beck Academy, SC

Prehistoric Dinosaurs

Named in 1842
Named by Richard Owens
Name means "terrible lizard"
Ancestors of the crocodile
They had scaly skin
They all had teeth
Some were armor-plated
Most have hard names to pronounce
Some were in the category "feathered dinosaur"
An asteroid hit Earth 108 million yrs. ago B.C.
The asteroid was 110 miles in diameter and 78 tons
Some dinosaurs were VERY big
A few dinosaurs had large teeth
Some certain dinosaurs can eat 1 ton of meat in one bite
Some dinosaurs were herbivores
Some dinosaurs were aquatic
Their fossil range is the Triassic to the Cretaceous period
Some fossils are preserved in the limestone in California
Some fossils are preserved in sandstone in the Sahara Desert
They were the rulers of their time

Hunter Saunders, Grade 6
Southwest Middle School, AR

My Bus Ride

I woke up at seven and got out of bed.
I went down the stairs, and *bang*, hit my head.
I walked in the kitchen and sat down to eat,
But I heard the bus. Beep, beep!

I ran out the door and flew down the steps.
No literally, I flew over Kep.
"I have told you a million times or more,
Eat your breakfast!" said Mom from the door.

The bus was there right in front of me,
But I seemed to be rooted to the ground like a tree.
I didn't know why so I looked at the ground,
And saw there was rain and mud all around.

I finally pushed and pulled myself through,
And trudged on the bus with mud on my shoe,
And left a pretty ugly mess all over the bus's floor,
And finally arrived at the school's front door.

Hannah Hollowell, Grade 5
Providence Academy, TN

Fall

F all is a good time to trick or treat
A utumn is color and it is
L ike spilt paint
L eaves are everywhere
Braxton Beaver, Grade 5
First Flight Elementary School, NC

Summer

Water splashing,
Branches lashing,
Cool breeze,
Sweet Siamese,
hot dogs,
Horns of fog,
Hazy mist,
I am writing this,
humid days,
Lots of haze,
summer rain,
horns of trains,
Cool ice glass,
sassafras,
Refreshing lake water,
Not a single slaughter,
Peaceful,
Happy,
Sweaty,
Summer.
Cecelia Cook, Grade 4
Glendale Elementary School, MO

The Fox

Clever as a fox,
Sneaky.
Just like the wind
I'd be gone!
Jake Powderly, Grade 5
St Vincent Elementary School, MO

Candy

C hewy and sweet
A lways good
N ever bad
D elicious and sour
Y ummy candy!
Abbey Poznanski, Grade 5
First Flight Elementary School, NC

Haley

Haley
Loving, pretty
Shopping, playing, dancing
She keeps friends' secrets
Pooh baby
Haley Hunter, Grade 4
Tamassee-Salem Elementary School, SC

Life on the Pitch

Excitement and chatter fill the crisp autumn air,
Grunts, claps, sighs are heard on the pitch.
My friends and I make nervous but friendly small talk,
As our tension filled minds prepare for the battle!
The whistle blows as we line up; strikers, half backs, full backs, goalie.
The first cleat makes contact with the ball,
Amidst hoops, hollers, and cheers from moms, dads, grandparents, and siblings.
A tall, lean, determined striker breaks away from the pack,
"Oh no!" he's headed my way!
I, in my jersey of many colors, stand alone in the vastness of the goal.
The seconds tick by like hours on a clock,
Here it comes, a 30 mile per hour sphere, straight at me!
Hump! I make the save; the whistle blows,
Victory!
John Hardy, Grade 5
JJ Jones Intermediate School, NC

Autumn Days

A utumn is a great time of the year
U nder the trees the squirrels and rabbits are sleeping so soundly
T he leaves are changing and it's getting cold
U p and down jumping in the leaves are the children across the street
M other is cooking the turkey inside
N ervously waiting for our guests to get here.

D ucks are not in the pond
A nd flowers are not blooming
Y esterday was summer, but today is an autumn day
S ilently I go to my room and thank God for autumn days.
Jacob D'Antoni, Grade 5
Palmetto Christian Academy, SC

Stormy Lake

Splish Splash
ripples the water
jumping off the boat chasing fish
having a great time,
then Elizabeth and I heard the clouds YELLING!!
terrified of getting stranded in the middle of the lake,
swimming to the boat as fast as a fish dodging a fisherman,
jumping in the boat trying to get back to the dock but it was too late!!
BOOM
BOOM!!!
It started to rain very very hard like a ton of baseballs smacking us
DOWN
DOWN
DOWN
indigo blue rain fell.

Lightning and golden flashes all around
dashing under the boat's windshield soft warm towels on our heads
keeping us dry and warm boat rocking back and forth
then there was silence rain stopped, sky was crystal clear
Yippee — now time for tubing!
Kerri Edens, Grade 4
Roberta Tully Elementary School, KY

Parents

Parents love us with all their heart.
Nice and sweet, cool and smart.
They always tuck us into bed.
We'll still love them even when they're dead.
They'll always be by our side.
Night and day, day and night.
They'll play with you all day,
And sit with you at the bay.
My parents are all mine.
My mom and dad always shine, shine, shine!

Meagan McGowen, Grade 5
Vernon Middle School, LA

Beautiful Butterflies

Up! Up! big butterflies fly orange, blue, black, and
Sweet red over the evening sky
I love to think that that's me,
Up into the sweet blue far from here

Nicole Haim, Grade 5
American Heritage Academy, GA

Germany

It was the happiest day
Thousand year old castles stay in their place
Like fossils in their case
Tasty food everywhere
Cannons booming long ago
The sound of swords clashing rings in the castles
Soldiers fall to their grave
Alps are coming up
You can feel the moist cool mountain air
My cousins are the best
Houses stand for many years
Flowers blooming everywhere
Foggy mountains and waterfalls crashing
Old shacks sell frozen ice
This is where I belong
This is my special place
This is Germany

Sam Kniery, Grade 4
Briarwood Elementary School, KY

Black

Black is a shadow that creeps up behind you.
Black is the color of sorrow when you're feeling down.
Black is hatred like a fight with an enemy.
Black is a deathbed when somebody is slowly dying.
Black is the night sky when you're asleep.
Black is Halloween when trick or treating with friends.
Black is an unlucky cat.
Black is sometimes Goth.
Black is the color of emptiness in your soul.
Black
  Black

Julia King, Grade 5
Meredith-Dunn School, KY

The Color of Nature

The color of nature is all around.
It is on flowers, trees, and on the ground.

Trees are like big bushy flowers,
That are around "housers."

The sun is like a big flaming sunflower,
That burns in the day light.

The water is like the gleaming sky,
That sparkles in the moonlight night.

Terry Self, Grade 5
Oark Elementary School, AR

Being on Stage

The excitement I get walking on stage,
The audience all focused on me,
My friends — the butterflies — have arrived;
They are dancing inside me saying, "It's time!"
The house lights go dark,
The stage lights go on so bright that I can hardly see;
Time to make my entrance, find my mark,
Something comes over me, I'm no longer Anna:
I get to be a graceful dancer,
Or a shrinking girl in a wonderful land,
Or a very wise snake,
Or a grouchy old woman who loves to eat,
Or maybe even a princess from a far away land;
Time seems to stand still when I'm that other person,
Living in that other world;
With the applause in my ears, I am Anna again,
The curtain falls and we make our final bows,
The lights go down;
Already I miss the excitement I get walking on stage,
The audience all enjoying me.

Anna Merritt, Grade 5
JJ Jones Intermediate School, NC

Thanksgiving

I love Thanksgiving
When you walk into the kitchen
and smell all the wonderful food cooking.
Mom making cranberry sauce,
Sis watching the green beans burn,
while the gravy covers up the smell.
Dad cutting the turkey,
as Grandma's homemade rolls come out of the oven.
Sis slicing the potatoes.
Beep! the cheese-covered carrots are done,
as I watch the sweet corn stay warm.
Just one more hour,
I can't wait,
Especially for Mom's homemade chocolate cake
with one small secret ingredient!

Hadley DuVall, Grade 5
Briarwood Christian School, AL

Winter

When I looked outside I saw
The wind blowing.
I also saw
The sunshine glowing.
I like to run and play
Even though it's cold
Every day.

Rhiannon Roberts, Grade 4
Ode Maddox Elementary School, AR

Dogs

Dogs are super pets
Dogs are playful and so fun
Dogs are real good friends

Ian Brown, Grade 4
Briarwood Christian School, AL

Chocolate

Chocolate
Sweet and delicious
Eating, savoring, and buying more
My favorite food
YUMMY

Madison Phillips, Grade 5
Sullivan Elementary School, TN

Who Am I?

Who am I? Do you know?
Who will I be if I help the hungry
And wipe their tears of joy?
Who will I be if I touch the heart
Of every girl and boy?
Who am I?
Who will I be if I volunteer my time?
Who will I be if I'd be willing
To stand beside your bedside?
Who will I be if I dig down deep
To the softest of your insides?
Who am I?
Tell me please?
Who am I? I am me,
And that's no lie.

Caroline Moore, Grade 6
Blackmon Road Middle School, GA

Guitar

I anxiously await,
For when I reach my guitar.
The sounds thrill me,
Making my soul complete.
Sliding my hands and fingers,
Graciously on the neck,
To make the notes and sounds meet,
Making…Music.

Jackson Cole, Grade 6
Discovery School @ Reeves Rogers, TN

Cheerleading

Awesome, glittery make-up
Fun, silly faces
Competitions out of town
Majorly glamorous uniforms
Extremely awesome stunts
Competing with friends
Friends and family cheering you on
Beating the other teams
Awesome, fun music
Sweet, fantabulous routines
Months of preparing
A lot of conditioning
Popping your ponytail
Showing tons of spirit
Being loud and proud
Lots of bling bling everywhere
Making the coaches smile
Bringing home a trophy
Having a victory celebration
My favorite hobby!

Abby Floyd, Grade 6
Southwest Middle School, AR

Grandma's Pancakes

My grandma's name is Mary Ann
She cooks, Oh yes! She can
Her pancakes look so leathery
But I know they are feathery
They taste so extra sweet
Especially with the bacon meat

Koty Parrish, Grade 5
E O Young Jr Elementary School, NC

Flute

It reminds me of Beethoven
Nice sweet music
Play at holiday concerts
And for family get togethers
I love it so much
But not more than my family
Gets tiring but fun
It's very LOUD
Good to wake up the town
It is a woodwind
With the sax and clarinet
It's in the family with the piccolo
It has good harmony
One of my sister's friends play it
It has three parts
Head, middle, and boot
Long as a desk
Does not need a reed
Very high pitched
It can keep you busy on something

Laura Lane Bain, Grade 6
Southwest Middle School, AR

Growing Trees

Trees can cry.
Some of them die.
Trees are big.
Some have twigs.

A tree grows.
Some trees grow in rows.
Some are small as you and me.
Yet, all trees are free!

Regina James, Grade 6
Manning Elementary School, SC

Junk Food

Junk food is here and there
junk food is everywhere
in the cabinets, in the store
sometimes in my car door
I have to admit I love junk food
that's why I eat the moldy ones too
I always say to never let waste
because you need to stuff your face
and if you didn't and let it waste
that would be a big disgrace.

Candice Foxworth, Grade 5
West Marion Elementary School, MS

Yellow

Yellow is…
As soft as a yellow lab
As bright as the sun
As pretty as a flower

T.J. Scrogham, Grade 5
Bloomfield Elementary School, KY

My Paw-Paw Bill, a Hero

I have a hero brave and true;
I have a hero just like you.
His name is Bill and has gray hair,
And he always wants to share.

He is brave in every way;
And he cares for the U.S.A.
He helps those in Iraq;
And never turns his back.

He never lets the country down;
And he never wears a frown.
He keeps his head up high,
And will never tell a lie.

He never takes drugs;
But gives a lot of hugs.
He never gives up;
And drinks coffee in a cup.

Johana Sellers, Grade 4
North Elementary School, NC

A Yucky Day

A yucky day
A yucky day
It's like pea soup
On a rainy day.

The smog was so thick
And trash in the lake
What a yucky day
A yucky day.

Please take me away
This place is taking
My breath away.

It's a yucky day
A yuck day
If you stop pollution
I'll say "Hurray!"

Emily Timpe, Grade 4
St Mary Cathedral Elementary School, MO

The Night Sky

On a dark and lonely night,
When the North Star shined so bright,
The room was full and everything was nice,
The stars were twinkling like a bowl of ice,
Everyone thought it was out of sight.

Jayla Brown, Grade 4
Eastside Elementary School, GA

Happy Moments, Sad Moments

Moments can be happy.
Some can be sad.
But no matter what,
We have to live with them.

One of my happy moments is when
Patches, my calico cat was born.
A sad moment was when
Grandma almost died.

A happy moment is
Having friends by your side.
A sad moment is
Having a close animal die.

A happy moment is
Being thankful for everything I have.
A sad moment was
When dad left for two weeks.

As you see
You have to keep those happy moments with you…
Because big things come in small packages.

Tabitha Rider, Grade 5
Odessa Middle School, MO

Leaves

As the shimmering leaves fall off the tree,
I watch them sparkle and let them be.
I wait for the wind to see them fly,
In the still of the morning in the sky.
Leaves, they usually make a small sound.
When they land, they rustle on the ground,
I'll rake them up, into a mound,
And wait for the right moment, and jump down!

Elizabeth Canter, Grade 6
Midway Covenant Christian School, GA

Alone

When I woke up, my friends were on the ground.
I look all around, all the leaves are gone.
I felt alone with no one to carry me home.

No friends to talk to.
I am just so alone feeling like I do not belong.
I feel like the wind will never carry me on.
Wind, Wind, please carry me on;
If you cannot, please try.
Because all I ever do is cry.

Shaniqua Bell, Grade 6
Aycock Middle School, NC

Living

Spinning through the joys in life, the happiness,
Soaring through the outstretched arms of fate,
Riding through the memories.

Tommy Peck, Grade 4
Gwin Oaks Elementary School, GA

Ellen Toliver

Ellen lives with her mother;
Revolutionary War has her brother.
In her grandfather's house,
She's as shy as a mouse.
Grandfather is a Patriot spy;
And in this war her father did die.
She's new to town;
By bullies pushed down.
She has not a friend,
This girl of ten.
"You must take a message, dressed as a boy,
To help win the war, and bring America joy!
My leg is broken," Grandfather spoke with dread,
"I can't be the one who delivers the bread.
The message is tucked safely inside,
Carry it to General Washington with pride."
She was persistent through hardship;
And on the way, made a friendship.
Now Courage came through when bullies came by;
Her bravery was true, and she did not fly.
As brave as a lion, Ellen did not cry.

Hope Fischbach, Grade 4
Bethel Academy, SC

Beach

The palm trees sway
as the wind blows.
The beach white sand
tickles my toes.
The waves crash
with a tremendous roar,
as seagulls squawk
while they soar.
The fish swim through the water.
Could the sun be any hotter?
Crabs scuttle across the sand.
Isn't nature truly grand?
All these wonders in just one place.
How can there be enough space?
I really hate that I have to leave,
but it has been a great day —
I truly believe.
As I say goodbye to the sea,
I hope these wonders will always be.
Graham Weyland, Grade 6
Holy Trinity School, KY

Winter

Winter is so much fun
Getting ready to go hunting.
I better not forget anything.
I better not leave the gun.

The deer is running fast.
Then he stopped ahead
I shot with a loud blast.
The he dropped dead.
Sam Fourqurean, Grade 6
Pleasants County Middle School, WV

Flying

My face
Plastered against the window
Dim light guiding us up
Drowning
In an ocean of clouds
Fluffy as cotton candy
One lonely star
Floating in the night sky
A blue sapphire in the moonlight
Tiny moon men
Pumping up the moon
Like it was a balloon
The ocean of clouds
Is parting
As if on Moses' command
Making way for our approach
To leave is hard
Because I am ready to fly again
Madeline Malueg, Grade 6
South Oldham Middle School, KY

That Hurt

Last quarter of the soccer game
time running out like the sand in an hour glass
dirt flying everywhere
sweat falling from our tired bodies
crowd cheering and yelling "Get the ball"
"Thump, Thump" the sound of feet hitting the dry ground
the other team takes control of the ball
we have the ball, they have the ball, we have the ball
Suddenly…I had the ball!
scared like a fly about to be swatted
speeding down the field
dribbling like a snake slithering in the grass
left…right
left…right
determined to get past the defense and win
kicking the ball with all my strength
tripping over the other team's defense along the way flying, falling
hearing a loud thump as my body hit the hard ground
looking slowly up to see was it possible that I scored
discovering that I did
what a painful, but proud goal.
Jackson Rasco, Grade 4
Roberta Tully Elementary School, KY

Spiders

Oh, so creepy and crawly,
Not so nice and when they bite they give me a fright.
You better watch out they're everywhere,
They're so cruel they get in your hair.
I'm right I'm right and if I'm not then you're wrong and with them all.
I seek and peek and hope I don't get near one at all, I'd rather be near a geek.
Shelby Stanberry, Grade 5
Hall Fletcher Elementary School, NC

I Am From

I am from playing with my friends: Jesalyn, Sydni, Makayla, and Shiann
To getting A+'s in school.

I am from practicing with my team
To winning games.

I am from going home to work on homework
To helping Dad around the farm.

I am from driving the 4-wheeler
To finding my feather to play with my cats.

I am from swimming in my pool
To playing Marco Polo, and losing.

I am from watching my dad race on the track
To watching him win a race.

These are the people, places, and things I am from.
Madi Phillips, Grade 5
Burgin Independent School, KY

I Can't Write a Poem

My teacher said I had to write a poem
But I can't do that 'cause I don't know 'em
I sit here wasting all my time
Just trying to find two words that rhyme
But my brain is like an empty shelf
I guess I'm going to make an "F"
I can't write a poem, I'm just a kid
No! Wait! I think I just did!

Wendell Thompson, Grade 5
Rock Mills Jr High School, AL

Labor Day

Over Labor Day weekend
I biked 15 exciting miles
with 4,000 other athletic people.
My mom, dad, brother and I drove
to wonderful downtown Louisville
on a steaming hot, sunny day.

We were in the Mayor's
Healthy Hometown Hike and Bike.
I was amazingly surprised
how many tiny 3, 4, 5, 6, and 7
year olds there were.

My mom and I took
the smooth, easy route, but
my dad and my younger brother
took the hard and hilly route;
they finished before us
and biked 2 extra miles.

When I finally saw the 14 mile marker
I knew I could finish.
After the bike ride my family and I
went to Chili's and had the most amazing lunch ever!

Kirsten Bergman, Grade 6
South Oldham Middle School, KY

The Beach

When I visit the beach,
The clear, blue, foamy water
goes "Boom!" against the shore, spraying mist on me.
The big, bright, beautiful sun
gleams down on
the powdery sand and warms my skin.
Millions of shells in
many different
shapes, sizes and colors
rest in the sand.
Seagulls fly overhead
diving down into the water
to catch fish.
The beach is my favorite place to be!

Emma Dilworth, Grade 6
Beck Academy, SC

The First Flower in Spring

The first flower in spring is like a rainbow
in the sky when it rains.
Its roots buried in the brown, soft ground;
the flower spreads its wings to fly
making its colorful wings float day and night.
Its stem longer and longer like a giraffe
running and running.
When it's cold, the flower goes to sleep
until it is spring again.

Brenda Barroso, Grade 5
Westwood Elementary School, AR

Macbeth

M ade a fool of himself at the feast by "seeing" dead Banquo
A lmost blew his cover during the plot to kill the king
C an easily be tricked into believing the witches
B ig dufus (fool) for falling for his wife's plan
E nds everyone's respect when he wrongfully becomes king
T hrived as a hero but not as a villain
H as feet made of clay

Nicholas Lamb, Grade 6
Dunbar Middle School, AR

My Mixed Up Cat

Morris is a cat but
he acts like a dog.
He tries to scale everything even a wall.
He jumps like a rabbit and I think
it is his habit.
He catches flies and watches them die.
When he sees your lunch
He eats a bunch
He prowls around like there is nothing to do
but when he finds something
he bothers you.
When he drinks his milk
all you hear is
slurp then a burp.

Jack McCreery, Grade 5
Greathouse Shryock Traditional Elementary School, KY

The Haunted Hallway

Creeping up the stairs to my bed,
I was filled with so much dread.
The shadows on the walls were alive!
They jumped, snickered, and howled with pride.
I saw my sister's toy on the wall.
It looked like some sort of evil doll.
There was a painting that I saw.
It felt like I was going to fall.
When I reached my big black door,
I opened it and let out a roar.
There was a body, but with no head.
And once again, I was filled with dread.

Cyrus Woolard, Grade 4
St Mary Cathedral Elementary School, MO

Thought of Daddy's Little Girl

I am my daddy's soldier girl, this I know is true,
But it's hard when he doesn't have time for me and there is really nothing I can do.
I sit for hours on end wondering when he will come home,
I watch my mom so sad because she's all alone,
I see my little brothers playing in the yard,
I can't imagine leaving here I know it will be hard.
Every other year it seems there is somewhere we have to go,
Or my daddy goes without us to a place that we don't know.
It was hard for me as a little child to understand his job,
And though I'm a little older I still sit and sob,
Every time I see him as he drives down the street
And as the days go by it's the same thing to repeat.
My mom will say good bye to him and tell him to have a good day,
Then I see her hit her knees and know that she will pray.
Each passing day it gets harder as we grow up,
To miss him greatly in our lives as he misses our important stuff.
It's all about supporting daddy and praying that he's safe,
Knowing that his job puts food on our plate, so those who have parents each and every day,
Thank God for them because this is the one thing military children can never say,
And it's really not that easy carrying a smile.
It's really one of the hardest jobs in life being a military child.

Ashleigh Sierra Coker, Grade 6
Walker Intermediate School, KY

What Will It Be Like Next Halloween

It's Halloween! Driving down the street you feel like a complete stranger.
Trick or treaters running down the street in a race for candy.
You're frightened seeing the witches, ghosts, monsters, vampires
and goblins at the devil's doorstep.
While they munch on their candy, you creep up, oops! You make a
noise and scare the candy right out of their hands.
You tremble in fright for you see something dart out in front of you.
You jump at the howling in the distance getting closer every second.
Suddenly you hear begs and pleads of children.
Something's being whispered in your ear, "You're Next!"
It frightens you so much that you run away in irrespicable fright.
You arrive home after midnight and hear footsteps in the attic.
The moonlit sky seems so soothing and calm on this spooky Halloween.
You decide to sit and sip some hot chocolate.
At that moment the door creeps open, AHHHH!
You realize that it was just your dad.
You share your experiences with each other, and found out that he became scared, too.
You whip up some more hot chocolate and sit by the fire.
Suddenly a thought pops in your head.
You wonder, "What will it be like next Halloween?"

McKenna Lewis, Grade 5
Saffell Street Elementary School, KY

Wolves

Wolves are wild creatures and cannot be tame. To tame a wolf is like taming a hurricane. The large abundance of energy that flows through the wolf's body is the hand that pulls the trigger of life. The wind sends smells and messages that pull reactions from the wolf's mind. Trees give the wolf shelter, a place to call home. A lake gives water, an important key of life to a wolf. Golden sun shines down on the wolf warming and drying his sleek coat after a storm. The wolf is a sign of life and death, energy and spirit, heart and achievement, and courage.

Reilly Johnson, Grade 5
American Heritage Academy, GA

Wonders in the Sky

B eautiful
I ntelligent
R avens, cardinals, and many others
D umbfounding works of mother nature
S pectacularly fast in the sky!

Keith Williams, Grade 5
South Smithfield Elementary School, NC

Summer

We were playing in the summer having fun
Under the bright blazing-hot orange sun.
My grandmother was in the house sewing.
My grandfather was in his garden hoeing.
The peanut butter cookies were hot and done.
My Dad sighted and shot his black gun.
My mother was sitting on the porch swing.
My little brother was trying to sing.

Cole Smith, Grade 6
Pleasants County Middle School, WV

A Gentle Spring

A gentle spring begins with a pleasant dawn
To please the doe, to please the fawn
The days of spring have no threat
The birds chirp in a song you can't deny
That can be heard across the meadow
It can help you rely on your love of spring
To carry peace in your heart.
A gentle spring begins with melting snow
That trickles down like little rivers
Showing the way to new life.
Little green buds appear
Tulips and daffodils can't wait to bloom
Up out of the earth they grow
Drinking in the warm sun.
A gentle spring sees the new rabbits
Chewing the tops off the plants.
They hop along undisturbed
While the robin builds her nest.
Soon it will carry eggs that will hatch
And the meadow will know a new song.
A gentle spring is a friend to all of God's creation.

Patrick Davis, Grade 6
St Francis Xavier School, AL

Autumn

Autumn comes year round.
All the leaves fall to the ground.
You see the colors brown, orange, and red.
That is a sign the leaves are dead.
When the trees are all bare.
Some of the animals just sit and stare,
The others scurry around
Looking for acorns on the ground.

Amber Wyatt, Grade 5
Sullivan Elementary School, TN

The Smartest Brother Ever

My big brother can be good.
My big brother can be bad.
But most of the time he is glad.
He is going to college to get more knowledge!
We're all going to be sad!
But we are all going to be glad for him!

Adriana Marquez, Grade 5
Paint Lick Elementary School, KY

How They Took Blue Skies Away

Today I am sad.
Loneliness is creeping up my skin.
The day is beautiful, warm, and sunny.
The leaves are slowly turning now.
Sadly, all that my eyes can see are gray skies around me.
The clouds are dark and puffy.
It seems as though someone locked orange
leaves away leaving the trees bare.
The wind is blowing harder.
My heart is beating faster.
I do not know how long horrible feelings can last.
Tears fill my eyes and ripple down my cheeks,
And lots of worried faces frown at me.
God keeps telling me everything will be okay
But I don't know what to think or what to say.
How could something so bad happen to someone so good?

Hannah Nelson, Grade 6
Kitty Stone Elementary School, AL

The Sun

The sun is nothing but a light of the past,
looking at the world we have created today,
shining down on all of us,
until a dark blanket of nothing covers its beauty.
Then the sun fades it away.

When the sun shines over the glistening water of a waterfall,
it creates a wonderful sight.
Rows of color,
dancing through the sky.
It seems as if
there's not a worry to be found,
since the rows of color make no sound,
then they fade away.

Through the mountains, the valleys, the plains, the towns,
the sun still sits there looking down
at the world we have created today.

When I die,
I know the sun will not be gone.
It will stay here forever,
Looking at the world we have created
Yesterday, today and tomorrow.

Destinee Ellis, Grade 5
Odessa Middle School, MO

Stuff

There's a little thing called stuff
like buff, and puff, and handcuffs
Everywhere you look
you see:
hooks and books and cooks

There's pencils and pens
a flower pot, too
There's many places to see
like Russia and Peru
How about you?
What do you see?
Maybe a flea, a bee, a knee, or a key
to hop
to fly
to kick
to unlock
so look around and see.
Monica Gonzalez, Grade 6
Houston Middle School, TN

Winter

There was a heavy white snow.
The wind started to blow.
I couldn't see because of the fog.
Suddenly, I fell on a log.
Yesenia Jimenez, Grade 4
Horace Mann Elementary School, OK

If I Were in Charge of the World

If I were in charge of the world
I'd get rid of cigarettes
No one would be homeless,
No more bed times,
And no RATS!

If I were in charge of the world
There'd be free puppies,
A home for every child,
And a mall at every corner!

If I were in charge of the world
There'd be a new TV show every day,
More forest for animals,
And NO CRIMINALS!

If I were in charge of the world…
Kaitlyn Quach, Grade 5
Eminence Middle School, KY

Daisies

Daisies are like pools.
They make your senses tingle.
These flowers are cool.
Trey Duvall, Grade 4
Moyock Elementary School, NC

Scarecrow

S pooky, creepy scarecrow
C rawling bugs up and down
A utumn breezes everywhere
R ats in his pockets too.
E verything is dark and scary
C autious crows are flying around
R ows of corn
O ctober is here
W ind is howling!
Victoria Moore, Grade 5
First Flight Elementary School, NC

Hallow's Eve

Goblins, Ghouls, Witches of all,
Come out to stall.
Frighten one and all
Beware and have fear
For all is near,
To frighten and scare
If you dare.
So come, come, come one and all
To a fright fest,
That is not dull.
Quiver in fear,
For all is near.
Be scared indeed,
For that is all you need, to feed
The deed is yours,
So open the doors
So come, come, come one and all
To a fright fest that is definitely not dull.
Steven Kolb, Grade 5
Arnaudville Elementary School, LA

My Special Mom

The queen of my soul
The queen of my light
Also the queen of night
All that is bright

The pressure in my eyes
The pressure in my feet
The brings the love
to the delectable treat

The greatest one in my life
The greatest one to be
The greatest one to be me
The kid in me

The happiest person on earth
that makes me smile
The one who has the greatest style
The goddess of my life
Jhane Palmer, Grade 4
Carver Elementary School, NC

Help!

The toys felt very cramped
In the tiny toy box
With no room to breathe
They screamed for help
But no one came
Kyndell Claypool, Grade 4
Crossville Christian School, TN

Shines So Beautiful

It's all around me
Surrounding me, seat by seat

Waving in the air
Or slamming on the ground

It hangs high and sometimes low

Waiting for that moment verses the blue
Remembering the Blackout

It is the Louisville Red hats
That shine so beautiful
Zack Ball, Grade 6
East Oldham Middle School, KY

Best Friends We Are

Sam and I
Best friends we are
Midnight blue eyes
Leather brown hair
Sam and I best friends we are
Meeting at carnival
Afraid of heights
"Don't worry" he said
"Just don't look down"
I did was a
Loooong
Way down
Soon
Overcoming fear and enjoying the ride
Sam and I
Best friends we are
"Many minutes left?" he asked
"About 16"
Smiling both
Loving lunch best time of the day
Sam and I best friends we are
Wil Scott, Grade 4
Briarwood Elementary School, KY

Horses

Galloping horses
Beautiful running mustangs
Free running horses
Julia Bray, Grade 4
Briarwood Christian School, AL

Soccer Ball

Soccer is fun.
I play it all day.
I wish I could stay at a soccer game today.
I wish I could play with the best of the sport,
But if that won't happen, I'll let out a snort.
Oh soccer ball, oh soccer ball,
I want to stay and play,
But I have to do homework the rest of the day.

Claire Landewee, Grade 4
St Mary Cathedral Elementary School, MO

Winter and Snow

Winter is as cold as ice,
Stinging like sharp needles on my face,
It is peaceful
And is joyful,
I love winter,

Sparkling like diamonds,
Winter is as white as marble,
It is eggshell white,
I love winter,

Winter fizzes,
Snow shivers,
It sounds like a whizzing bee making honey,
Flashing and flicking at night like fireflies,
I love winter

Sawyer Moore, Grade 4
Briarwood Elementary School, KY

The Perfect Christmas Tree

My tree is not very tall
It is actually very small
We couldn't afford one from a Christmas tree farm
But when hanging a few ornaments it works like a charm
It is scraggly and rough
And it is not very tough
For ornaments we used hooks
But that did not change the looks
To you it may look bad
Even if it did, it wouldn't make me sad
It doesn't have tinsel or garland or string
But you have to remember one thing
It may not have any toys
But to me it represents the Christmas spirit and joys

Ally Baker, Grade 6
Chapin Middle School, SC

Cries of the Night

Tear drops fall throughout the night
As yells roll on out of sight
Tear drops fall on the ground tonight
As he sits down out of sight

Alexis Snell, Grade 5
William Southern Elementary School, MO

Blue Is a UK Fan

Blue is a UK fan.
It feels like the soft pelt of a wildcat,
It looks like UK winning the NCAA championship,
It sound like the fans cheering for UK,
It smells like the sweating UK players after a big game
It tastes like the salty popcorn at the UK game
Blue is a UK fan

Chase Johnson, Grade 5
Eminence Middle School, KY

I Am…Albert Einstein

I am Albert Einstein
I wonder why I hated my classes in school
I hear my friend Elsa speak to me
I see Munich, Germany before 1943
I am Albert Einstein.

I try to love school
I feel good because I won the Nobel Prize
I care for my wife Mileva
I am Albert Einstein.

I worry about my uncle dying
I am sad when he does die
I understand because I am very smart
I am Albert Einstein.

I say let me be appointed to a professorship.
I dream about children
I hope for my great inventions to be realized
I am Albert Einstein.

Jordon Williams, Grade 5
Bethel Lutheran School, MO

I Am

I am athletic and smart
I wonder if we're going to win today in soccer
I hear the cheering around me
I see the light flash at nighttime
I want to win the soccer game
I am athletic and smart

I pretend we are practicing
I feel the beat of my heart
I touch my mouth to see if I'm smiling
I worry if we will win today
I am athletic and smart

I understand everyone in my school was there
I saw to my coach I'll try my best
I dream of last night's games
I try to dream more, but I got woken up
I hope we win next week
I am athletic and smart

Alex Pimentel, Grade 5
Berryville Elementary School, AR

My Secret Place

A stream flows through the woods.
A secret place to get away,
To play and splash,
Or have a picnic for the day.

The sun in the sky,
Hides behind giant pine trees,
The air is filled with laughter,
And birds are singing carefree.

A swing to swing on,
Some ropes to climb,
But we have to be back,
Before bedtime.

Coming back down the path,
A long way home,
I see some birds,
Free to roam.

I see my cats,
Chasing a mouse.
This must mean that,
I'm back at my house.

Chaning Dorr, Grade 6
IA Lewis Elementary School, LA

Beautiful Horses

Look at the horses
Run so free in the pasture
Oh what a great sight

Gabriella Hartman, Grade 4
Briarwood Christian School, AL

A Special Star

A star, a star in the sky
I want that star but
it is too high.
A bike, a train, a car, a plane
can't reach my star
only God may.
My star, my star
has my name on it
it is big, it is sparkly
and is shiny.
It sparkles like
a diamond, it twinkles in the night
and is bright.
I just wish I had two.
Don't you!
Mine is pretty
and so are you but,
mine dances on the moon.
My star is in bed under the moonlight.

Chiarra Palazzolo, Grade 5
St Teresa's School, GA

Queen of the Sky

I am an American.
I am English.
I am a briar rose.
I will always climb, climb, climb.
Up into the sky.

Water quenches my thirst.
One day I will clip my thorns and vines away.
I will become queen of the sky.

"Clouds look up!"
"Waves, behold!"
I am growing up, up, up.

Sometimes I am a rabbit, wanting to hide in my hole.
From the world.

Someday I will fly, as Lady Liberty for my guide.
To freedom.

Until then I am only white chocolate, trapped in this body of mine.
Ready to spread my wings and soar.
Up there.
In the sky.

Katherine Brown, Grade 6
Beck Academy, SC

Christmas

Christmas is my favorite time of the year.
It is a time when family and friends get together and have a great time.
It is a time to get to meet your relatives and family you haven't seen.
I like when Christmas comes because we go to my Nanny's house
And we dance and do the tradition we do every year.
That's why Christmas is my favorite time of the year.

Ava D. Stelly, Grade 5
Arnaudville Elementary School, LA

Good Girls Gone Bad

Good girls are the one,
Who are just the perfect girl,
Who are kind of like a goddess,
Playing with her curls,
One day the evil witch,
Came upon her,
Put a spell and was turned,
Into a bad girl.
Everyone around her
Was turned into a beast,
If they come her way,
They will disappear,
If it's a girl,
She will be cursed,
With the same thing,
But only worse.

Jericka Lathers, Grade 6
McKinley Middle Academic Magnet School of Visual & Performing Arts, LA

Winter Time Fun

Winter time is so much fun
With sledding and snowball fights.
Children come out and laugh and run.
It is really such a delight.

When the children were all done,
They went inside to the sink.
They made some instant hot chocolate,
But one had some milk, I think.

Since that night was Christmas Eve,
They ran to get into bed.
One woke up in the middle of the night
To see something tall and red.

For there was Santa Claus —
The kid could not believe it.
Santa reached into his bag
And pulled out a toolbox kit.

The child then went to bed.
Santa turned and patted his head.
They dashed downstairs the next morning,
And all of the gifts they were enjoying.

Kyle Metz, Grade 6
Pleasants County Middle School, WV

Snow

The wind is blowing, on this cold winter day.
Snowflakes are falling on my eyelashes, how cold they are.
It makes my vision blur.
It makes me so happy to feel the snow my face.
So cold, yet so warming.
I love winter yet I hate the cold.
It is such a wonderful season.
The family is around the fire warming their hands and feet.
It is so silent.
So peaceful.
Yes this season is.

Hanna Pounds, Grade 5
Our Lady Catholic School, MO

My Brother

I admire my brother
Because he respects me,
He is always there for me,
And he protects me from getting in fights.
He comes to my football games,
Supports me if mom gets mad,
And buys me pork sandwiches,
He takes me to Super Splash.
When I hope up I hope that
he will still be the best brother.
His name is Aaron.

Dale Fowler, Grade 5
Lee A Tolbert Community Academy, MO

Fall

F is for friends that you hang with.
A is for apple cider you drink when you're cold.
L is for leaves that you jump in.
L is for love, as in loving this season.

Fall, what a great season it is!

Acacia Leslie, Grade 6
Stuart Middle School, KY

Christmas Season

Snowflakes are merrily falling to the snowy ground
Making sure not to make a sound
I see something glistening in the snow
As I walk carefully into the unknown
Trudging behind me is my big dog
Hoping that he will find something to chew on
Now I'm running inside to make gingerbread
Maybe it will get done before bed
Make sure to bake cookies before Santa comes!
Then he might give you more than bubble gum

Adriana Green, Grade 6
Des Arc Elementary School, AR

Rain

Sprinkly wet drippy water in a storm
So eager to touch the sidewalk
Nice substance to drink especially after a jog.

Alex Watts, Grade 5
South Smithfield Elementary School, NC

Snow

I woke up, it was quiet.
I looked out the window,
It was snowing.
I ran downstairs, and put my
coat, gloves, boots, and hat on.
I ran to get my friends.
We went sledding, and made igloos.

I fell, laid in the snow, and watched it fall.
It covered my face with a cold, piercing feeling.
All I could see was snow.

I went inside at the end of the day.
I put a sweater on, and drank hot chocolate.
I sat on the couch,
Warm as ever, watching the snow fall.
I fell asleep,
And when I woke up,
The snow was gone.
I was sad,
But I knew it wouldn't last forever.
But I did know,
It would come back next Winter.

Haley Morgan Woolbright, Grade 6
Annunciation Elementary School, MO

No Second Chance

Be the best you can
There is no second chance,
Ask yourself
Why am I
The way I am?

Can you take words back?
No, just say nice things.
Are you listening?
Or
Don't you know what I mean?

Be the best you can
There is no second chance,
Ask yourself
Why am I
The way I am

There is no second chance
To take words back
Or
to be able to apologize
for our lies
There is no second chance

Morgan Moody, Grade 6
Saint Paul School, TN

Thanksgiving

Thanksgiving
Ham
Turkey
Deer running in the woods
Cranberry sauce
Turkey feathers
Thanksgiving

Jeremy Fretwell, Grade 4
Tamassee-Salem Elementary School, SC

Horses

Horses
cute, soft
bucking people off
eating lots of hay
horses

Elizabeth Chandler, Grade 5
Grovespring Elementary School, MO

Things I Am Thankful For

F ather
A house
M other
I mportant people in my life
L ittle brother
Y ears of fun

Walter Anthony, Grade 6
Father McCartan Memorial School, MO

Gym

I walk into homeroom,
And take my seat.
Fifteen minutes until gym,
No time to retreat.

I walk down the halls
After first period ends.
I think about gym
As second period begins.

When I do my jumping jacks,
I huff and puff.
I do all this
Just to get tough.

I really love to jump-rope,
It's so much fun.
Ouch! The rope hits me,
My turn is done.

Finally, second period is over,
As I hear the bell ring.
But now I wonder,
What will reading bring?

Tia Banerjee, Grade 6
J D Meisler Middle School, LA

Bryce

There was a man on the street
Who needed something to eat
So a lady threw a pie
It didn't quite fly
She wasn't very discreet.

Bryce Cummings, Grade 4
Judsonia Elementary School, AR

I Love the Mall

All the purses in the mall
I would buy them all
A 100 dollars or more
The mall is my favorite purse store

Britney Koepp, Grade 5
West Marion Elementary School, MS

Halloween

H eadless Horseman
A pirate in jail
L arge spiders
L ots of bats on the bat tree
O range and black in the pumpkin patch
W hite ghosts on the ghost tree
E very color on the potions table
E erie walls in the dot room
N obody touches the big, bad Witch

Emily Hayes, Grade 5
West Elementary School, MO

Pumpkins

Big orange also round,
Lighting up faces tonight.
Shining so brightly.

Julie Anne Dorris, Grade 4
Briarwood Christian School, AL

Nature's Baby

Nature's baby don't cry
The wind will sing you a lullaby
The water is going to take you a bath
The grass will teach you how to do math
Nature's baby don't cry
The tree will teach you not to be shy
The birds are going to help you sing
The rain is going to help you be a king
Nature's baby

Brenda Rios, Grade 5
Prince of Peace Catholic School, SC

I Am a Son of a Soldier

I am a son of a soldier.
I wonder when my dad comes home.
I hear that my dad's going to Iraq.
I see him getting ready to go.
I don't want him to go.
I am a son of a soldier.

I pretend that he won't leave.
I feel sad when he leaves.
I hate when he leaves.
I worry if he will die.
I cry when he leaves.
I am a son of a soldier.

I understand whey he has to go.
I say bye when he leaves.
I dream that he stays home.
I try to stop him.
I hope he doesn't leave.
I am a son of a soldier

Jason Evan Bass, Grade 5
Byrns L Darden Elementary School, TN

If Only

If only I had wings,
I could be a bird.
If only I had a tail,
I could be a mermaid.
I wish I had a cat,
I'd scoop it up in my hat.
If only, if only, that's what
I wish.
I wish I could be all of these things.
I'd be so happy, until it rains.

Ashley Nicole Hinson, Grade 4
Cool Spring Elementary School, NC

My Hero

I admire Michael Jordan,
The best basketball player
In the world.
He is tall, fast, and strong.
I can shoot the ball good,
And run fast but I am
too short to dunk.
Michael Jordan and I are both
right-handed and bald.
I am a good person,
Just like him.

Norris White, Grade 5
Lee A Tolbert Community Academy, MO

Where I'm From

I am from friendly neighbors
And cars of all sizes,

Swimming pools and barking dogs,
Trees and creeks, dirt and dust,

Computers and catch,
Dog hair and cats,

Loud hallways and clanging locker doors,

Teachers and bleachers,
Quiet mornings and loud afternoons.

This is where I'm from.

Matthew Proctor, Grade 6
East Oldham Middle School, KY

So Filled with Joy

So filled with joy
Barely containing my excitement
Cheering and thanking
My parents for getting
Me a pet frog hopper
Small, light-colored frog but he was as green As a leaf.
Hopper was an odd
Frog he had escaped from me many
Times jumping off the stair
Case and once he had popped his mouth
Open and he yawned
And that told me he was tired and
That was special I had never seen a animal
Such as him do that.
Crying and trying to forget
Anger and sadness swelled up inside because
He died overnight and that one thought
Of losing him made me cry a river
Of tears and that was only one day
Since I got him.

Reed Mattison, Grade 4
Briarwood Elementary School, KY

My Bookbag

My bookbag is my worst enemy,
and when it creeps up on me,
I scream, I cry,
I hurry and shield my eyes!
It weighs a ton!
Do the teachers think that I am dumb?
If I could have a perfect vacation,
It would be one without an equation.
Yeah, school is all fine and dandy,
but does my bookbag really need everything that is handy?
It is pink and black,
it makes my back want to crack!
Blocks 1, 2, and 3,
I have to carry it with me.
My bookbag is the one who ruins the day,
do I really want one that weighs so much?
NO WAY!!

Carley VanHoy, Grade 5
JJ Jones Intermediate School, NC

Love to Play Basketball

Love to beat my dad.
Love the sound of the basketball going into the basket.
Love when the basketball comes back.
Like when I made my shot.
Like when I just have fun.
Like when I make my long shots.

Tanner Moore, Grade 5
North Middle School, TN

Owen

Smelling like Frosted Flakes
His eyes blue, green eyes
Skin looks like the desert sand
Blond hair
As blonde as the sun in the sky

Making the sound called the
"Rassberry"
A huge gap in between his teeth

Something
He does with me
Going swimming
Getting on my shoulders
And YELLING! Like Tarzan

Crawling in the road
Was 6 months old there was a car coming
Jumping in the road to save him
Honk! Honk! Hooonk!
I did!

When I think of cousins, I think of YOU!!

Ryan Kennedy, Grade 4
Briarwood Elementary School, KY

Being the President

Being the president is awesome.
You get to know everything.

Being the president is awesome.
You get to have the U.S.A.

Being the president is awesome.
You have to deal with cameras.
You have your own White House.

Being the president is sweet.
You have your own office.

Being the president is sweet.
You have your own desk.

Being the president.

Claudia Hutchins, Grade 4
Capshaw School, TN

Christmas House

I sit around my fireplace
To warm me up inside
It's really quite a soothing feel
To see those flames so high.

I sit around my fireplace
Opening my presents
With all my family gathered round
It really is quite pleasant.

Kalyn Taylor, Grade 6
Pleasants County Middle School, WV

Not My Popcorn

I go to the movies
And what do I see?
A bag full of popcorn
Just for me!
I take a munch
And to my surprise.
There was a crunch
Right after mine!

Machelle Carman, Grade 4
Parkview Elementary School, MO

Nattapon

N ever gives up at anything.
A fter all I am a boy.
T all smart, and good.
T alented at video games.
A ll good in grades.
P retty and awesome all the time.
O ffering for help everyday.
N ever talks when teacher is talking.

Nattapon Sattaphan, Grade 4
Byrns L Darden Elementary School, TN

Gray

This is the color I feel when the rain is pouring down
It's the color you see after a tornado tears up a town
This is the color I feel when my friends are mad at me
It's the color of my grandma's hair
This is the color I feel when I think I have nowhere to go
It's the color of a lonely kitten
But most importantly, Gray is not a color I choose to let control my life.

Kelsy Byrd, Grade 6
Ketchum Jr High School, OK

Autumn

A wonderful time of year almost like,
the perfect combination of summer and spring.
Wearing jeans and a sweatshirt is so awesome!
A nice walk through the park,
with the leaves all around you.
WHOOSH…
swaying on a swing in the sunlight…
sometimes at night while you are laying in bed,
you hear a distant thunderstorm.
CRASH!
BOOM…
BANG!
If there is an afternoon storm,
it is so soothing, to be swaying on a porch swing listening to the thunder.
When the days get shorter…
And the nights get longer…
The weather goes from raging heat,
to cool mornings and perfect afternoons.
All this tells you…
autumn is right around the corner!

Taylor Hayes, Grade 5
Greathouse Shryock Traditional Elementary School, KY

I Am

I am a young man who likes Dalmatians.
I wonder if there will be a meteor that destroys the Earth.
I hear my dog in India barking for me.
I see a Dalmatian running swiftly through my backyard.
I want to have an adventure to make life worthwhile.
I am a young man who likes Dalmatians.

I pretend to be a knight from the Middle Ages.
I feel a sea breeze blowing past me when I'm wading in the ocean.
I worry about extinction for all animals in the world.
I cry for all the homeless and poor people around the world.
I am a young man who likes Dalmatians.

I understand the pain of losing someone you love.
I say, "Everyone should be free."
I dream about saving people all around the world.
I try to be friendly and nice to everyone I know.
I hope to eradicate all things that harm life.
I am a young man who loves Dalmatians.

Arvind Sivashanmugam, Grade 6
R D and Euzelle P Smith Middle School, NC

The Silly Dog

There once was a dog named Link
Who always used too much ink
His writing was fine
His words were divine
But later his words were just a big blob of ink.

Tyler Armstrong, Grade 5
American Heritage Academy, GA

Books

Books take you places you've never seen before,
Open a book, begin to read, and you will start to soar.
I started reading as a child and I still read every day,
Reading can make you happy or chase the blues away.
I've read about mysteries, adventure, and about dogs and cats,
Also about a mean girl named Carmelita Spats.
They grab your attention and they teach you so many things,
I never forget all the joy reading brings.
Reading a book can bring out feeling and thought,
Just going to the library, you can retrieve what you sought.
To actually get into the story, it takes imagination,
To see everything through a book, it is a true sensation.
Books are educational, and are also there for fun,
Children and adults can all benefit from reading one.
Books are portable, they can entertain you anywhere,
After you've read them, give them to your friends to share.
Read a book and you will see,
How fun it can truly be.

Abby Loupe, Grade 6
St Rita School, LA

Fall

Fall is coming, fall is near.
The icy cold wind blows fiercely on my bare face.
With all the colors, red, orange, yellow blurring together,
all so many colors around.
Leaves crunch and crumble underneath my feet.
Fall is coming, fall is near.

Elizabeth Johnston, Grade 4
Stone Academy, SC

Friendship

A friend is someone who cares
They will listen to you all night
until they know you're sleepin tight
How do I know?
cause I have a friend just like that
A friend that will keep you when you're weak
and give you strength
How do I know?
cause I have a friend like that
A true friend will be by your side
to help you peel an onion and cry
How do I know?
cause I have a friend just like that

Alicia Miller, Grade 6
Saint Paul School, TN

Fireworks

Look at the fireworks fly.
They go so high in the sky.
Fireworks are ever so bright.
They look brighter than the moon at night.

Alexandra Moreland, Grade 4
Small World Academy, WV

Mad at My Mom

I got mad at my mom
so I listened to my iPod over by my favorite tree.
I could still see her searching for me
all over the house even the outside
with a very long, sad expression
like a caged animal in a zoo exhibit
searching all over for me again and again.
She looks for me for a long while.
She searches for me very sadly.
Then I yell up to her to get her to look down at me
and she yells back down to me.
It feels calming.
My mom sends for me to get back up.
She gives me an elephant.
She knows me so well.
She knows I like elephants.

Jenni Weimar, Grade 5
Fox Elementary School, MO

Oklahoma: Our Great State

Our state is great!
Our state is kicking for one hundred years.
Land runs were the greatest moments.
An absolute favorite event in history!
Oklahoma is a state of
Mountains, rivers, hills, and plains.
A great part of who I am today!

Kameron Mendez, Grade 4
Hayes Elementary School, OK

The Big Game

In a big gym
In a small town
There was a basketball team
Who took the crown.

They played a game one Friday night
In front of a crowd and under the big light.

Both teams played well the entire time
Until one player crossed the line.
He kicked the ball into the crowd
The referee said, "That's not a allowed."

A technical was called, a free throw was shot
And the crown of victory was what we got.

Luke Hagstrom, Grade 5
Walton Verona Elementary School, KY

My Baby Brother

M agnificent
Y oung and wild

B old and brave
R really stubborn
O utgoing
T ruly a great person
H elp's around the house
E nthusiastic
R elative

Kyla Woodson, Grade 5
Cool Spring Elementary School, NC

How I'm Living Thanksgiving

To our Thanksgiving party,
I know we can't be tardy.
We're at the party place,
Greeted with a smiling face.
When we get there the clock strikes one,
I think this day will be fun.
Look out the window, little flurries,
This is a day with no worries.
Pumpkin, spices, pumpkin pie,
I also love bread of rye.
It's the big football game,
You know it really does have fame.
Everything is on the table,
Not all the food I can label.
We all say what we are thankful for,
For the food, we eat more and more.
With the sun setting in the sky
We hug and sadly say goodbye.

Ellie Sona, Grade 5
Wohlwend Elementary School, MO

Blue Times

Sky is blue.
Blue is cold.
Feelings are blue.
I'm blue.
Everything I think is blue.

Harley Mott, Grade 5
Westwood Elementary School, AR

The Cat and the Bird

One day my cat went to play
He found the perfect prey
A blue bird flying high
He was descending from the sky
The cat pounced at the bird
That's all we ever heard
The bird got away
His family says hooray
And now the dogs after a squirrel

Dan Johnson, Grade 6
Seven Holy Founders School, MO

Fog

Fog strolls in like a walk in the park.
It skips and walks along,
Then it finds a bench
And sits there
Until the sun shows it away
To stroll on in another day.

Steven Placht, Grade 6
Seven Holy Founders School, MO

Leaves

L ovely leaves fall
E xtending the beauty.
A lone they lie,
V ivid colors.
E veryone sees them,
S itting on the ground.

Cheyenne Swain, Grade 5
First Flight Elementary School, NC

Butterflies

Butterflies are like life
They go through many stages
More new challenges for the ages
The larvae is like a baby
Just like a newborn
They spin their cocoon
Just like yarn
Our cocoon is our family
Just like a barrier
And when we emerge with them
The more the merrier

Breanna Byrd, Grade 5
C. C. Spaulding Elementary School, NC

Horse

Horse
Black, tall
Run, race, walk
Playing, eating, drinking, sleeping,
All horses are colored
Pony

Zakyia Curry, Grade 4
East Jones Elementary School, MS

Halloween

H appiness all around.
A ll friends in costumes.
L ittle kids looking for candy.
L oving parents watching their kids.
O ctober 31st is the greatest day.
W e all laugh as we eat candy.
E njoying the entire night.
E xciting kids all about.
N o other holiday is this fun.

Rhonni Lee, Grade 5
Franklin Elementary School, OK

Goosebumps

White's below zero
Nature's air conditioner
Slipping on dry ice

Grayson Yates, Grade 4
St Patrick's School, AL

Clumsy Turkey

The clumsy turkey
fell out of the tree and hit
branches all the way.

Thomas Collier, Grade 4
Briarwood Christian School, AL

Grandparents

G ood at sports
R emembering a lot
A lways a joy to have around
N ever disappointing
D o a lot of work
P apa is a good cook
A lways taking care of us
R eally loving
E verything is good — even food
N ever being mean
T hinking of me all the time
S aying manners

Micah Bailey, Grade 5
Frankford Elementary School, MO

Summer

Bonfire burning up
Lemonade in my cup
Playing all day
Warmth never goes away
Hummingbirds make a rhyme
Happiness all the time
Small little butterfly
Lights up my creamy sky
Water-crumbs sprinkling down
Children are homeward-bound

Elise Melhado, Grade 5
Herbert J Dexter Elementary School, GA

The Train

Click, Clack, Click, Clack
The train rolls down the track.
Click, Clack, Click, Clack
The steam and smoke streams out
the smoke stack.
Click, Clack, Click, Clack
The train picks up speed and the
smoke turns black.
Click, Clack, Click, Clack
How far will it go until it comes back?

Jules Pierre Hopkins, Grade 5
Our Lady of Fatima School, MS

Brothers

They are rude and obnoxious
They really are annoying
Brothers are what I am talking about
When you are with them life is sooo boring

They always yell and scream at me
I'm never able to hear
I try to run away from them
But they are always near!

Alysia DesCoteaux, Grade 6
Kitty Stone Elementary School, AL

Things Running Through My Head

One day I had things running through my head.
I couldn't fall asleep or go to bed.
I was too busy thinking about school, sports, and friends,
But I have to admit, life takes turns and bends.
On Saturday night I went out to eat.
I didn't eat or feel the beat.
I came home and tried to go to bed,
But I couldn't because I had things running through my head.

Ben Walsh, Grade 6
Seven Holy Founders School, MO

Basketball

I enjoy hearing the sound of a whistle.
I love the sound of a ball.
I think it is cool when the crowd cheers for home.
I respect it when they score.
I enjoy it when they come out.
I appreciate it when it is over if the home wins.

Nicholas McCord, Grade 5
North Middle School, TN

I Am From

I am from Christmas lights,
the costumes I wear on Halloween, Boo!
The turkey I eat,
and Easter egg hunts every Easter.
I am from church on Sunday mornings,
the devotions my family do each night,
and the prayers I say before bed.
I am from books on bookshelves
stacked like a library,
my little sisters toys everywhere,
and the poopy diapers that smell like a barn.
I am from mint chocolate chip ice cream,
the wonderful taste of spaghetti,
and grandma's potato balls, yum!
I am from the friends at school,
the teachers who put history in our brains,
and the knowledge we get from our parents.

I am from wonderful things.

Olivia Short, Grade 5
Greathouse Shryock Traditional Elementary School, KY

Snow

As it falls from the white sky,
It gleams on the bare trees.
Kids ride their sleighs on the glimmering white fluff.
It's not so fluffy as it was before the sleigh rides.
They come in to get hot chocolate in their cozy warm house.
They watch the white glimmering stuff fall from the white sky.

Hannah Grimes, Grade 5
Paint Lick Elementary School, KY

The Pitch

The fast bullet, leaving a gun
The windup, a rock in a slingshot
Release, a firecracker from the slap of her glove
A lion roaring when the umpire yelled "Strike."

The batter, a spring wound tight,
Waiting for the right pitch to relieve the pressure.
A leaf trembling,
That pitch was too fast for her.
The batter, an angry bull because she got struck out.
The fast pitch, a bullet leaving a gun.

Megan Williamson, Grade 6
College View Middle School, KY

Mother's Hugs

My mother gives me hugs
When I'm ferociously mad
My mother gives me hugs when I'm terribly sad.
My mother gives me hugs,
Because she loves me
My mother gives me hugs,
My mother gives me hugs.

Sofia Calvo, Grade 4
St Thomas More School, NC

My Hunger

Today I'm so mad!
I'm so hungry I can eat an elephant.
I haven't eaten all day.
I'm so mad I could punch a hole in my concrete wall!
No one is home,
We have nothing to eat,
I can't wait any longer!
Yesterday mom told me
"If you eat too much you'll get too big to fit in the door."
I didn't believe her!
Hey, what's that?
It's mom!
I think?
Yes, it is mom!
Wait, in her hand, what is it?
OMG it's a cheeseburger!
Yes! I'm saved!
I guess I'm only hungry enough to eat a cow!!!!!

Tyler Taylor, Grade 6
Armorel Elementary School, AR

Winter

White dots in the sky
Playing on a white blanket
Mittens, warm fingers
Olivia Grace Smeltzer, Grade 4
Briarwood Christian School, AL

Questions My Brother Asked Me

Why do we have glue?
Why is the sky blue?
Why did Jimmy get a new toy?
Why am I a boy?
Why am I four?
How do we make a floor?
How come s-e-v-e-n spells seven?
Why are you eleven?
How come we only have one bird?
Why do people call you a nerd?
Why can't I climb a tree?
How come w-e spells we?
How come you are wearing blue socks?
How come daddy's friend lives in a box?
Why do witches fly on brooms?
How come our house has ten rooms?
Why is my name Sam?
How come I call my teacher ma'am?
Where do we come from?
Why are you eating a fruit called a plum?
Am I dumb?
Erin Walker, Grade 6
Warrensburg Middle School, MO

Eagle

Bright white feathered head
Gray talons grip the cliff's edge
Great brown wings are spread
Swoops down toward the river
Spears a slippery fish.
Margaret Fridley, Grade 5
Jackson Middle School, MO

Fall

Oh, oh fall,
You make me sneeze,
With your
Cool, cool
breeze.

Fall is like
A ball, it comes
And it goes
So, far, far away,
But it always
Comes back
Another day.
Alicia Tejeda, Grade 5
EA Harrold Elementary School, TN

My Dad

Smelling to my dad, he smells like sweat or I don't know what like.
His hair color is black like mine and my brother's.
His eyes are black-brown.
Going to the park with my dad, and to the water park; are the things we did together.
I love my dad.
Alex Tovar, Grade 4
Briarwood Elementary School, KY

I Am

I am a graceful girl who loves to dance
I wonder if I could dance until I fall off the Earth
I hear that lovely music spinning around me
I see that shiny, golden trophy begin handed to me
I want to cover the Earth with my dancing
I am a graceful girl who loves to dance

I pretend to dance like the sky can see me
I feel the pain straining my body
I touch the trophy like I've never seen one before
I worry that my feet won't have the strength to go through one more dance
I cry when the music is off
I am a graceful girl who loves to dance

I understand that I may not be able to fulfill my dreams
I say, "Let me inspire the dances around me"
I dream about the day when everyone will know me because I will be famous
I try to dance until my audience is satisfied
I hope to dance for the rest of my life
I am a graceful girl who loves to dance
Jyoshitha Tella, Grade 6
R D and Euzelle P Smith Middle School, NC

I Got Pushed

Little bald headed brat
Motor Mouth Male
Making Me Mad
all the time!
One time on the school grounds
sitting on an icy cold swing
feet pushing myself back and forth!
Minding my own business
Along comes Duane Mofils
mean as a swarm of bees my worst enemy!
Hearing from behind
dirt flying like birds up in the air
hands gripping on my shoulders
wondering who it was!
Tightly gripping onto the metal chains as he shakes the swing fiercely
rattling sounding like wind chimes "cling, cling, cling!"
Swooshing off the swing
Falling into a splintered patch chest first!
Like a knife stabbing me in the heart!
Boy summer salted right onto me like a cherry on a sundae
I NEVER WENT BACK!
Keyontranay Smith, Grade 4
Roberta Tully Elementary School, KY

Swimming

I swam in the great blue sea,
Where there are dolphins circling all around me
The sea is very deep everywhere I go
I hear the water crashing in the beautiful sea
I sea the palm trees swaying

Carla Combs, Grade 5
Wright City Middle School, MO

The Pioneers

The goodbye was tough
The crossing was rough
And from Virginia they go
Across mountains high and plains low
Fifty miles from nowhere, camp is made at night
And though they left their family, it seems so right
Awakened by dawn's light that shooed night's shadow
They are greeted by a river across the plateau
But the current calms and across they go
And they keep it up until Pa yells, "Land Ho!"
Desolate prairies, oh what a sight!
Next day the wagon is awakened by light
Every morning, every evening they look for a place to land
but the prairie is always so bleak and bland
As the sun goes down, so do they
And the children, for once, are too tired to play
So they make a reluctant choice to stop here
"Children, keep hope! The cabin is near!"

Morgan Mahurin, Grade 5
Herbert J Dexter Elementary School, GA

The Job of a Marine

Rigid ground and men in camo.
The sergeant yelling, "Get down and stay low."
Men screaming of pain,
And me always thinking, "Why did I join this game?"
And then I remembered my family.
That's why I joined the U.S. Marines.
To be loyal to my country, and keep my family free.
But that is the last thing I thought, for I am gone.
The last thing I saw was that Japanese bomb.

Zachary Leonard, Grade 6
Houston Middle School, TN

Fall

The leaves blow in the wind,
As the sun goes down.
The branches start to bend,
And everyone starts to frown.
The leaves are very pretty,
Red, yellow, orange, and brown.
Then I see a poor kitty,
Though it looks a bit pity.
It now is a beautiful sight,
Because I can see the moonlight.

Brooke Harper, Grade 6
Haynes Academy for Advanced Studies, LA

Pop! Pop! Pop!

Shiny, clear balls
Flying into the sky
Pop!
One by one they pop
One inside one
One so small it's like a pea

Shiny, clear
Wet, soapy
Pop!
Pop!
They're easy to see

They're so fast you've got to be quick
Hurry gotta pick
When they're gone, they're gone
The last shiny, clear ball pops
10 feet from the ground

Don't be upset
There will be more of the shiny, clear balls soon

Nick Roberts, Grade 6
East Oldham Middle School, KY

Anna Banana

My friend is Anna but I call her Anna Banana.
Hair is chestnut brown soft as silk.
Eyes as dark as the night sky.
Smells like strawberry perfume when I walk by her.
Makes really loud screams when excited.
She would always come home with me and be soooo funny
and sometimes soooo quiet.
Swimming at my grandmother's spending the night too.
Talking on the phone after eleven o'clock at night.
Hearing her say, "Want to be best friends?"
I will never forget that.
She is such a great friend.

Kallie White, Grade 4
Briarwood Elementary School, KY

Fantasy Land

When you're in your fantasy land
you probably think you're in a castle
or on a beach with a bunch of sand.

Girls think they're in castles
with bridges that fall
and dragons that guard them so tall.
After that, they go to the mall.

Boys go back to a prehistoric time
where they play with the plastic toys
that are worth a nickel, penny, or dime.
Since they're cheap, the parents think that's fine.

Jessie Ray, Grade 5
Stone Ridge Elementary School, OK

Flowers

If you don't like flowers
come on down to a valley.
You'll find wild flowers,
tulips, and sunflowers.
We all need them for beauty.
Without them we would be colorless.
So go outside today.

Carl Gordy, Grade 5
EA Harrold Elementary School, TN

Soccer Ball

Soccer ball soccer ball
you are so round
you look like a pumpkin
and go out of bounds
you're full of hot air
but have no hair
soccer ball soccer ball
you are a ball

Drew Anderson, Grade 5
Walton Verona Elementary School, KY

Tiger/Elephant

Tiger
small, fast
pouncing, missing, crying
food, cubs, water, grass
stomping, winning, tearing
big, strong
Elephant

John Rutledge, Grade 5
Briarwood Christian School, AL

Softball

Softball is a sport
it has exercising in it.
You make a lot of new friends.
It is like school
but you don't have
to write as much.
It is very fun.
It also gives you
something to do
on weekends
(if you're not at
your friend's house)
I LOVE softball.

Jazmine Watson, Grade 5
West Marion Elementary School, MS

The Twinkling Star

A sparkling star.
A mini star is estranged.
It is a space light.

Jay Chin, Grade 4
Briarwood Christian School, AL

Beautiful Bunny

Beautiful bunny
Racing in the clear white snow
Running out of sight
Faster and faster it goes
Till I can't see it at all

Leanna M. Wilson, Grade 5
Berryville Elementary School, AR

My Dog

I love my Dog
She eats like a hog
When I tuck her in at night
She sleeps like a log
When I take her for a walk
I wish she could talk
I bet she would have a lot to say
But that's in another world and day

Jakeb McVey, Grade 6
Graham Elementary School, AL

Dakota

There was an old man from Spain
Who ran just to play in the rain
He sat on a sack
In which had a tack
He then had to walk with a cane.

Dakota Davis, Grade 4
Judsonia Elementary School, AR

Rain

Sobbing and weeping,
The rain makes the ground cheerful
As the grass dances.

Makayla Pecaut, Grade 5
St Vincent Elementary School, MO

Army Navy Game

An Army Navy game isn't
just a game it's an event.
We saw a lot. The parachutes,
soared into the stadium like,
agile birds soaring into its nest.
The fly-overs done by both
Army, and Navy were amazing.
Navy's 5 FA-18s were like a flock
birds going wherever the wind
takes them but,
the noise they made was like
a baby when it wakes up in
the middle of the night. While
all of this was going on the players
waited,
in their locker rooms in hopes to win
And the Navy won.

Christopher Bondura, Grade 6
St Mary's School, SC

Halloween

H orrifying mask
A bundant amounts of candy.
L aughing with joy.
L ighting jack-o'-lanterns.
O range pumpkins.
W earing costumes.
E ating candy.
E erie skies.
N ightime moon.

Terry Ledford, Grade 6
Stuart Middle School, KY

Recital

With trembling hands I sit down to play,
Not sure what other people will say.
The palms of my hands are sweaty,
But I try to keep them steady.
The pedal is hard to push,
The audience is whispering hush.
Finally I am done,
I take a bow and run!

Anna Shows, Grade 6
Woodland Presbyterian School, TN

My Uncle

My uncle is no longer here
But his soul is still down here
He owned a special club
But now it's no longer there
The person that he loved
Had betrayed him

We still remember him
By his happy smile
Now that he's gone
He's in God's hands

There's nothing to do now
But to know that he's in a
Good place
I try not to cry, but
Sometimes I can't help it.

Kerstin Swain, Grade 6
Childersburg Middle School, AL

My Little Frog

My little frog
likes to jump and hop
When he is home
he just won't stop
Then he gets tired
and he has to sit down
But then he gets wired
and jumps up and down

Peyton Brown, Grade 6
Armorel Elementary School, AR

Christopher Columbus

Christopher Columbus so big and bold
Why is he so cold
He sits at home and thinks the world is round
Unaware of what he's found
He doesn't care if he's done or gone with this world
All he cares about is his own world
He takes the time to watch his world.
Slowly fade away.

Kelsey Walker, Grade 6
Clarksburg School, TN

Where I'm From

I am from hair bows,
from Gatorade and Hershey's.
I am from the table above the floor.
(Wooden, brown,
easy to slide on.)
I am from the sunflowers,
and the tulips.
I am from the seven layer cookies and the friendliness,
from Chip and Janise and Trent.
I am from the competitiveness,
from people who like to exercise,
from reaching for my goals,
and from trying my best.
I am from a non-denominational church.
I am from North Carolina and countries around the world,
diet coke and spaghetti.
From the sea my Grandfather sailed on,
the wars my ancestors fought in.
The picture frames,
where the pictures lie.
Placed in the house I sleep in during the night.

Ashley, Grade 6
NC

Dance

Enter stage right the lights are all dim
my heart's beating fast I'm about to begin

The music starts the judges are in view
my time to show the world my talent's true

The competition's fierce I feel in control
the Lord will guide me wherever I go

My timing feels right and what do you know
the ending has come I've put on a good show

I hit my last pose the crowd claps a while
I take my bow and the judges smile

I race backstage my body is heaving
I'm embraced by my friends which is very relieving

Alison Swoish, Grade 6
Queen of Angels Catholic School, GA

I Am

I am a lonely child who listens to the night sky
Sometimes I wonder if it will ever be day
I hear crickets in the night chirping
I want to be a butterfly flying around freely
I am a lonely child who listens to the night sky
I pretend I'm a fish swimming with no worries
I feel sad, discouraged, and lonely
I touch the emptiness in the dark around me
I worry about what will ever happen
I cry about nothing, sometimes everything
I am a lonely child who listens to the night sky
I understand the sadness of other people
I say everything will turn out fine
I dream about possibilities
I try to have hope
I hope that everything will be okay
I am a lonely child who listens to the night sky

Jenna Hill, Grade 6
Chapin Middle School, SC

A True Friend

A true friend is someone who can break through my shell.
When times are weak.
Always beside me through thick and thin.
They see right through you like a glass cup.
When something isn't true they help work it out.
Trust me they still love you.
I think that is a true friend do you?

Tityeonna Smith, Grade 5
Wynne Intermediate School, AR

Anthony H.

Brown hair, brown eyes, wears glasses
Football jerseys at home, T-shirt and shorts out of the house
Building legos with Tanner…
playing football in my yard
playing Harry Potter cards with Tanner
Tanner not playing with me angers me!
Listening to music, playing computer games
in Trenton's room
My mom's chicken nuggets and cheeseburgers,
Pizza Hut pizza

Anthony Hoog, Grade 5
Our Lady Catholic School, MO

I Seek the Tree

I seek the trees with wind blowing through their leaves.
I stare with awe while the colors change in seasons.
With different colors and different shades
The beauty still shines from miles away.
But there's no tree that can stand to the old palm tree.
With it's power to stay in and out of the seasons.
And it's face on the Carolina flag he feels so modest
Just like the eagle in it's nest so high.

Alex Arthur, Grade 6
Chapin Middle School, SC

Just One

Have you ever seen a man on the street?
Have you ever given a coin?
Did you walk by the next day?
Is he there?
Is he still begging?
Do you ever see someone give?
Have you ever thought what kind of a difference it would make?
Just one. Just one coin.
Just one coin would make a difference.
Have you ever seen an orphan child?
Have you ever thought about what their life would be like with your family?
They don't have a family.
They don't have anyone to love.
They don't have anyone to love them.
Have you ever thought about what kind of a difference it would make if they had someone to care for them.
If they had a family.
No one wants to adopt them.
Have you thought about how they feel?
Have you thought of the difference it would make in their life?
Just one. Just one child.
Just one child would make a difference.

Morgan Pope, Grade 6
Discovery School @ Reeves Rogers, TN

A Young Musician on the Road of Life*

Judith Lester is a realistic artist; her painting, A Boy Playing a Flute, had detail like ours.
The lines are clear you can tell; what this is. It's a boy playing a flute; the painting has no fizz.
This young boy clearly enjoys instruments, the flute, recorder, and violin are all loves of his.
His music room is light sea green. This boy is serious and thoughtful; he isn't mean.
The painting's focal point is the boy; it's clear to see. His hat is velvet, his collar is silk, a wealthy boy would be he.
The chair that's ornate and the boy's tinted face are in the foreground, in the background is where the wall and instruments are found.
The boy's looking out the window so his body is tinted. With all these shades and tints the painting almost looks printed.
No, this painting isn't still or stiff at all for the boy's fingers move up, and then they fall.
My, my this boy is greatly stylish, for colors and shades and tints in his clothes give him a good finish.
The painting is oil with added black shading and tinting with added white.
Beautiful music in a beautiful portrait, for this is a young musician on the road of life.

Hannah Wilson, Grade 5
Saffell Street Elementary School, KY
*Inspired by "A Boy Playing a Flute"

Months

January, month of a new year I can hear new noises in my ear.
February is Valentine's Day, the month you give cards away.
March is when my birthday's near, 12 I'll turn and my friends are here.
April Fool's Day is on the first, I wonder who will be fooled the most.
May is when we get out of school, the pool will be nice and cool.
June is when summer starts, we will get rid of all our smarts.
July has Independence Day, we will shoot off fireworks and play.
August is when school begins, I will say good-bye to summer ends.
September is when I got to Gatlinburg every year, I experience great things I smell and hear.
Witches and wizards are in this month, October is Halloween with scary stunts.
In November, ham and turkey lay, we eat and thank the great days.
December is when snow is falling and Christmas is near, presents lay under your tree somewhere.

Kaley Burnette, Grade 6
Lost River Elementary School, KY

A Scary Cold Night

On Halloween night
witches have their brooms ready to fly in the cold air
and goblins are ready to scare you

Jack-o'-lanterns are blowing hot fire
and ghosts try to scare big children or little children
Children are in their costumes
let's go trick-or-treating
WAKE UP CHILDREN IT IS HALLOWEEN.

Tristan King, Grade 4
Irmo Elementary School, SC

Soldier Fighting in Iraq

Once there was a soldier in Iraq,
he had a pack on his back.
He walked a couple of miles
Hoping to see some friendly smiles.
A lot of days the smiles are here.
And other days all you can see is just plain fear.
People are scared when they go down the street.
Because they never know who they might meet.
It makes me glad to live in United States of America.
So we have a safe place to live, work, and play.

Cody Dickerson, Grade 6
Clarksburg School, TN

At the Beach

At the beach we roam free,
At the beach, there is a huge palm tree.
At the beach, there is no school,
At the beach, there is not a single rule.

At the beach, the waves are predators stalking their prey.
At the beach, the crabs crawl,
and people play volleyball.

At the beach, there will always be a part to be had
and that will always be the rule at the beach…

T. Blake Wedding, Grade 6
College View Middle School, KY

That Little Blanket

The silky smooth fabric
Still soft to the touch,
A sleeping cat in the middle
Warm and protected by the comfort of her blanket

The quiet tap, tap, tap, of a happy cat's tail,
A jump and a little scurrying
The blanket on top of happy cat ears,

The tap gets faster,
Then slower and slower,
That silly cat and that little blanket…

Rhiannon Langel, Grade 6
East Oldham Middle School, KY

Where I'm From

I'm from the good old blue grass
Louisville, Kentucky

Where the grass grows
The sun shines
Stars twinkle during the black night

Where kids run barefoot in the green crispy grass
The birds chirp

Where there is homework Monday – Friday
Sometimes on Saturday too

Food sizzles in the greasy pan
Where we sing, read, play, day and night

That's where I'm from

D'Aisha Rowe, Grade 6
East Oldham Middle School, KY

What Can Yellow Be?

Yellow is the color of the sun.
Yellow is the sign of happiness.
Yellow is the coat of a cat.
Yellow gives us the light of day.
Yellow is the opposite of black.
Yellow is the color of the bright paper
Yellow from the sun gives the white clouds their glow.
Yellow is the lemon that falls off the tree
on a hot summer day and makes lemonade.
Yellow is the light that lights up the blue lagoon.
Yellow is the color of the light bulb that lights up the room.
Now all the yellow has been washed away by the night.

Alyssa Kaplan, Grade 5
Meredith-Dunn School, KY

War?

Our kind and gallant people of this country are the
ones that were perfectly chosen
to go and fight for families' hearts, and souls, and lives.
What I have noticed is that most of the people
in our country hate people for no sensible reason.
That is why we should pray for people.
As I sit down with no sound surrounding,
I peacefully place my hands together,
aim my closed eyes down to the ground
and pray to God for the lives fighting for
others in a terrifying fight.
This horrid fight is unbearable to think about if your
greatly loved one is on the edge of life or death.
If you are one of them you are in my prayers as I think
of the people fighting overseas.
Why do you want rivals or hatefulness between each
other, which you will regret later on in life?

Erika Gavrock, Grade 6
Woodland Presbyterian School, TN

Thank You, Nouns

Nouns
a person, place or thing
plural
more than one
singular
is only one
concrete
something you can see, feel or touch
abstract
what you cannot see, feel or touch
singular possessive
when you add 's
plural possessive
when you add s'
nouns
are all around us
nouns
we cannot live without
nouns
thank you,
nouns.

Carmen Cole, Grade 5
Saffell Street Elementary School, KY

It's Just Me

People look at me.
They point and laugh.
One says, "Look, a tree."
Parents take photographs.

It's just me.
Me, your friend.
Please, don't flee.
Lend me a helping hand.

Tré Staples, Grade 6
Pleasants County Middle School, WV

Veterans

V aluable to us.
E verlasting life.
T errific battles make a winner.
E veryday battle.
R ight thing to do.
A battle worth fighting for.
N ever giving up.
S pecial to us every day and night,
We think of you every day

Megan Casey, Grade 4
Van Cove Elementary School, AR

The Lake

Peaceful, quiet, calm,
hear the wakes bumping the wall.
Then you're fast asleep.

Ellie Tarence, Grade 4
Briarwood Christian School, AL

Autumn Air

The crisp autumn air
Leaves crashing, tumbling to ground
A very leafy wonderland

Sarah Cressman, Grade 6
Briarwood Christian School, AL

My Summer

I have a dog named Qt
He doesn't like it spooky
He likes to bark all day
And always runs in the driveway

Jason Collier, Grade 4
Horace Mann Elementary School, OK

Myrtle Beach

Still, calm, relaxing
Waves rushing up on you,
Like a mighty rushing wind
Memories of getting soaked,
Looking for shark's teeth,

At Myrtle Beach.
Watching, listening to seagulls,
Watching Natalee bury Mom in the sand,
At Myrtle Beach.

Freezing!
Cold iced water
Rolling down my back,
At Myrtle Beach.

Ahhh!
Pleasant warm towels around me
Like sun surrounding me,
At Myrtle Beach

Julie Ann Scott, Grade 4
Alvaton Elementary School, KY

Me

I used to live in Guatemala,
But now I live in Berryville.
I used to like rabbits,
But now I like puppies.
I used to like hot dogs,
But now I like chicken.
I used to want to be 10 years old,
But now can't wait to be 13 years old.

Kenia Lopez, Grade 5
Berryville Elementary School, AR

Family

Jesus died for you
and me, now we are a big
happy family

Shelly Grace Proctor, Grade 4
Briarwood Christian School, AL

Fishes

Fishes can swim
they're also a bit dim.
When you catch them
they flip-flop
all over the dock.
Then you cook it, now begin
when you're done,
then dig in.

Ellis Bowling, Grade 5
Midway Covenant Christian School, GA

Christmas

I waited
eagerly
happily
and it finally came:
Christmas cheer
and lots of reindeer.
Without a doubt
no one would pout
'cause Christmas was finally here.
To go to Mass.
To not have class.
Ahh, could it get any better?
It certainly could.
And I knew it would!
To watch Christmas movies.
To eat Christmas cookies.
Make sure you don't miss all this!
It's Christmas!

Kara Hunt, Grade 6
St Mary's School, SC

Friendship

Friendship is like a rubber band
that flexes over time.
In, out, narrow, wide,
Good, bad, by your side.

A circle of friends,
without a doubt,
is strong and expanding
not leaving one out.

Holding things together,
tight in its bond,
makes time worthwhile
for now and beyond.

If stretched too far,
the friendship might break,
but don't worry,
make friends!
It's never too late.

Natalie Rogers, Grade 6
St Mary's School, SC

The Giraffe

The giraffe is tall with a long skinny neck.
His fur is fuzzy and woolly protecting him from thorns.
His brown spotted pattern is unique, not one the same
Giving the giraffe his claim to fame.
He has a fluffed tail that is very strong
As well as long graceful legs helping him move quickly along.
This graceful giant stretches his neck into the trees
To get to all the dark green leaves.
The giraffe's long sticky tongue can reach food from far away
And he chews his cud for most of the day.

Matthew Alikhani, Grade 6
Haynes Academy for Advanced Studies, LA

The Cold Desert

What is this?
It's very cold
There are no leaves or trees of any sort
All I see are fluffy white pillows
which do not feel that soft
I need to find home before dark
It's dark now
I don't like this icy desert
I must find warmth before I die
Wait!
I see a shimmer of light from afar
I take two steps and begin to sink
I'm up to my neck now
I awake —
for some reason this old man has saved me
I am now safe from the ice devil

Daniel Babcock, Grade 5
Maplewood Middle School, LA

A Stained and Tattered Memory

Those jeans, those jeans so stained and tattered
Held such sweet memories that never will shatter.
The memories of grass sliding on my belly
My brother at my side.
Twisting, tangling, laughing as we sped down the hill
Landing with a thump! In a mass of legs, hands and hair
Rushing to slide once more.
The memories of painful wrestling matches
Held on the trampoline
Tugging, pulling, laughing, slipping.
Of hot sweaty days spent walking around the pond
Trying to escape the gurgling mud
A monster trying to suck us down
Into the gushy mess.
The memories these pants held got bigger and bigger
Seeping into the seams and stains
Of these wonderful, radiant, beautiful pants
Until, alas
They became too small!

Aya Omar, Grade 6
East Oldham Middle School, KY

CuJo and Skettles

CuJo and I have a lot of fun.
We run and play in the morning sun.
Now we have Skettles.
All she likes to do is scratch and bite.
She chews on my fingers and bites on my toes.
She wakes me up by licking my nose.
She runs CuJo ragged and won't let him sleep.
She gets in her food bowl with both her feet.

Rikki Gibson, Grade 5
Paint Lick Elementary School, KY

In the Darkness of the Night

On Halloween
I would pretend I could fly
In the darkness of the night
With a pointy hat
And a long, torn dress.
I would wear gold eye shadow
And black fingernails and lipstick
With a black, curly wig.

Jasmine Nugent, Grade 5
Lee A Tolbert Community Academy, MO

Alligator

Burning with
Rage the alligator
Is prepared to strike down
Anything that might enrage it.

Sneaking, crawling
The alligator lurks
In the murky water
Waiting for the
Unlucky creature that
Swims into its massive
Blood red jaws.

It might not be swift
On land but in the
Water all you can
See is an emerald
Blur.

So if you see
An alligator you
Better run!

Affan Bhutta, Grade 6
Haynes Academy for Advanced Studies, LA

To Die

To die at the Holocaust a lot were lost.
Many people fell never to tell.
Many people lost their lives who could give no fight.
There was no good reason or why to die.

Samuel Jones, Grade 5
Pembroke Elementary School, NC

it's not easy

from sports to homework
school to friends
you'll find it's not easy
being kids
first there's chores
right when you get home
you'll lose your allowance
if mom hears a groan
then there's homework
you rush to finish writing
faster and faster
hurry! quick!
you try to escape your dad's cooking
as it piles on your plate
next it's time for bed
you fall fast asleep
even though you were poorly fed
tomorrow I have sports
and homework again
so think about me
when you're at home in bed

Emily Delmestri, Grade 6
Westchester Country Day School, NC

Snowmen

Flakes of swirling white,
falling from the
fluffy white clouds.

They latch onto
the ground,
forming a white
blanket of winter wonderland.

I'm joyous as I run,
to greet the cold,
like a long-lost friend.

I pack it into
three round shapes.
Each larger than the last.

Stack, stack, stack.
I form the shape of a man.
A snowman

Macey Harrill, Grade 6
Chapin Middle School, SC

Apple of My Eye

You're my pumpkin pie
my grape off the vine,
my funny bunny,
sweet as honey,
Apple of my eye

Ashlynn Cole, Grade 6
Armorel Elementary School, AR

My Special Place

Special place you might say
Is dark and quiet but very special.
I stay alone there until they call me
In hard times I sit there and think.
I pray to God that everything is going to be okay
But when I am scared and my heart is pounding
I go to my place — sit there and maybe cry.
My special place is where I will be
When they cannot find me, I am there.
At night the darkness swallows me
I scream out loud but no one answers me.
Then I find my way to my special place
I see a dim light and then they turn on only in my place.
Then I forget about the darkness and look around.
My special place is very colorful because of all the posters.
Sometimes I talk to them because I can get everything off my chest
Also I know they will not tell anyone.
Now that I feel better I fall asleep there.
I always say that my place is very special.

Ashton King, Grade 6
Woodland Presbyterian School, TN

Resolve

Like Stonehenge, I am mysterious and unknown.
Like the great castles in England, I am firm and unwilling to change.
My tastes are as expensive as these great artifacts themselves.
Like dry ice, I am cool but I can burn.
I will fight back like the soldiers that defended these great castles.
I will never surrender my freedom or religion.
For I am me.

Evan Pierce, Grade 6
Beck Academy, SC

I Am

I am a nice girl who likes basketball
I wonder if I will play basketball someday
I hear my coach yelling at me if I don't do something good.
I see my mean coach running down the court.
I want to be on a basketball team for BG.
I am a nice girl who likes basketball.

I pretend I am at home and playing basketball.
I feel mad when we don't win the game.
I touch a basketball when I play.
I worry that people will laugh at me if I don't make the basket.
I cry when I don't do good and when people say I don't do good.
I am a nice girl who likes basketball.

I understand if people don't like me for my attitude.
I say that I am good at basketball and I will keep going.
I dream to go to college and play basketball.
I try to work hard at school and at basketball.
I hope I have a family and live a good life with my family.
I am a nice girl who likes basketball.

Adisa Mujic, Grade 6
Lost River Elementary School, KY

As Days Go By

The minute you're born the journey begins
You learn to walk and learn to talk
Next you learn to be a friend
To be the one on whom someone can depend
You learn the choices you make
Can be the difference in the path you take
If God is in your life
He can help you in your strife
Make the best of what you got
And you should have a lot
Remember you live and learn
As Days Go By

Karlee Carter, Grade 6
Appling County Middle School, GA

Shoes

We are always used
day after day after day.
Your foot slips into my body
as the day starts.
You take my long floppy arms
and tie them into a knot.
We walk to the bus
and we take our ride to school.
Walking through the cold slippery hallways between classes
to the wet damp grass of the playground.
We walk over the dirty bathrooms
and out through the front doors of school.
The sports were long and very tough
and now we take our ride home.
Finally those stinky socks of yours are set free
and my arms get untied.
Then we settle down and rest for another day.

Taylor Boole, Grade 5
Hunter GT Magnet Elementary School, NC

Lollipop

Sweet, sour, juicy taste
Watermelon, blueberry,
And root beer
Taking the colored wrapper off
Pointing my tongue directly
On the juicy flavor
Lemony yellow, cherry red,
Sky blue,
And Pumpkin orange
The colors of the rainbow
Melting in your mouth
Then the good part
The chewy pink
Strawberry flavored juice
Of the BUBBLE GUM
Blowing and popping, blowing and popping
Then gone.

Veronica Sierakowski, Grade 6
East Oldham Middle School, KY

The Night

One night the wind was blowing
The window opened and closed.
I could see light that night.
And so the next night I could see less light.
Each night I could see less and less light
And so a week later I saw a dot of light.
I tried to follow it but then the light was gone.
But I notice that never again did the light come back.
And so we had darkness in our world.

Sarahi Lopez, Grade 5
Hall Fletcher Elementary School, NC

Blue

My favorite color is blue.

A color of a clear sky and sound of violins
and bass as you pass through downtown,
when they're playing my favorite song.
And the street is blue from the

kids playing with chalk.
Blue is the color of crystal
clear water when you're on vacation at the beach.
And the color of dark blue water when it's at night.

Bailey Strause, Grade 6
East Oldham Middle School, KY

Sun

I am the moody sun.
I give light to the earth,
My glittering rays shine down on the world!

Sometimes the clouds cover me up,
— I get MAD!
I push them out of my way,
And keep moving.

When I am sad, I cry,
The rain falls to the ground
As I whimper and weep,
I am the moody sun.

Kourtney Atwell, Grade 5
Lynn Fanning Elementary School, AL

Praise

I am a pretty daisy in the sunset of the west
My skin is creamy vanilla ice cream on a hot day
I am strong like a puma crawling through the jungle
I am the fierce lion ruling its land
I am 5'2 with butter toast hair
A smile as big as can be
I don't care what you say about me
There will never be someone else like me

Maya Krassowski, Grade 6
Beck Academy, SC

Independence

freedom
July fourth
United States
loyalty
responsibility
not always fair
respect
care
knowledge
learning experience
friends
family
choices

Savanah Hipp, Grade 6
Salisbury Academy, NC

Shianne

S mart, sweet and talented.
H appy and joyfully.
I ncredible and intelligent.
A mazingly smart.
N ice, funny and friendly.
N aturally pretty and funny.
E xcitingly cool.

Shianne Elkins, Grade 4
Byrns L. Darden Elementary School, TN

Summer

Sun is shining bright
Children playing all day long
Flowers blooming bright

Robert Jennings, Grade 4
Briarwood Christian School, AL

Super Dad

Charcoal black hair
Leather brown eyes
Eggshell white mustache
My Super Dad
Games alone
Risking life in war
Football in the backyard
Hut hut hike
Mornings dose of tickling torture
Who SUPER DAD
Unforgettable
Games with you
Games of four
Who?
Super Dad
Mighty dad
Irreplaceable
so now I remember him
Super Dad.

Noah Pillow, Grade 4
Briarwood Elementary School, KY

I Am

I am wonderful and friendly
I wonder how my family is going to be
I hear a spooky voice
I see a ghost coming
I want a new cell phone
I am wonderful and friendly.

I pretend to be a super hero.
I feel a scare ghost.
I touch a dragon.
I worry if someone comes in my house.
I cry when someone dies.
I am wonderful and friendly.

I understand friends.
I say how are you doing?
I dream about me.
I try to get better at soccer.
I hope to be a great soccer player.
I am wonderful and friendly.

Sierra C. Regalado, Grade 5
Berryville Elementary School, AR

Sun

Sun
So bright
Gives us light
Makes me feel good
Gold

Sarah Goodman, Grade 5
St Joseph Institute for the Deaf, MO

Flowers

When I walk outside
I will see pretty flowers
Some are big, some small.

Isabel Crossland, Grade 4
Briarwood Christian School, AL

Fall

Fall's here!
Leaves are turning.
Leaves are falling around.
People are raking piles of leaves.
Kids jump.

Brittanee Davis, Grade 5
Broadway Elementary School, NC

Candy

C andy
A delight
N o one hates it
D ental not guaranteed
Y ummy!

Alec Strachan, Grade 5
First Flight Elementary School, NC

Red Fox Pup

Red fox pup staring at me,
Soft and covered
In dirt and leaves.
Deep down inside
He's so much more.
He's playful with his friends,
Furry, too.
I admire him a lot
Because he's special,
Like you.

Bailey Stark, Grade 4
Cleveland Elementary School, OK

Football

Quarterback
Fun, exciting
Running, throwing, winning
Football is my favorite sport.
Chase Daniels

Blake Linebaugh, Grade 5
Father McCartan Memorial School, MO

Bears

Peaceful little critters,
Or should I say big?
Don't mean no harm,
So soft and fluffy.
I want one as a pet!

Kayla Winkler, Grade 5
St Vincent Elementary School, MO

Silent Garden

Butterflies love to fly,
Next to all the purple flowers,
And when it's not a sunny day,
They enjoy the cool spring showers,
Garden fairies dance around,
Singing their short little songs,
And when they sing too loudly,
The butterflies start to dance along

Caitlin O'Kelley, Grade 5
American Heritage Academy, GA

I Wish I Wasn't a Bookworm

I wish I wasn't a bookworm
I read too much every single day
Those dictionaries with a million words
Are just a piece of cake
If I were to enter Jeopardy I'd blow
Them all away
I'd be in all the magazines for reading
900 trillion books
I wish I wasn't such a bookworm
That would be the day!

Shanna Holtzclaw, Grade 5
Sullivan Elementary School, TN

Summer Fun

Summer fun at the river house
Nana and papa are my biggest fans
When mama says I can't they say I can!
Their river house is my favorite place to go
Probably because they never say *no!!!*
Our days are spent playing in the sun
Swimming and jet-skiing are so much fun!
We ride 4-wheelers on the sandbar
Imagining they are new sport cars!
When the sun goes down and the day is done
We sit by the fire and rest our buns!
Roasting marshmallows and hot-dogs on a stick
We eat so much our bellies feel sick!
We like to stay up late after the roast
To hear stories about goblins and ghosts!
My #1 wish for when I am old
Is to have a river place of my own!
Then my nana and papa can visit me there
Where I can show them how much I care!
And thank them for all they've done
For making sure the river house was so much *fun!!!*

Hope Hutchinson, Grade 6
Appling County Middle School, GA

I Picture You Dad

I picture you,
Dad in heaven looking over me.
I picture you,
Waiting for me to join you.
I picture you,
Saying it is beautiful but wishing you were here
I know you
Are in my heart but I miss your face, your smile,
Your hugs and kisses, and your love. I miss your everything.

Danielle Myers, Grade 5
Cool Spring Elementary School, NC

The End

As I walked closer
Someone must have put me in a freezer
All happiness was gone
All hope was gone
"What's wrong?" I asked.
"He's going to leave us forever," my dad said back.
I did not understand
But at that moment
Knives drilled through my heart
And still has not healed to this point.
But I knew that is what must happen because that is life
And life must go on
I threw my arms around him for the last time
As tears ran down my face
I whispered "I'll always love you"

Madeline Gleeson, Grade 6
East Oldham Middle School, KY

My Sister and Me

Me and my sister.
Like to fight
We argue and fuss
With all our might.
So many times it goes on all night
We hit, shove, yell, push
Till we are told shush
My sister is sometimes nice
But mostly squeals like mice!

Zachary McLain, Grade 4
Tazewell-New Tazewell Primary School, TN

Summer

In the summer I feel a cool breeze.
Over the hill I see green grass and a few trees.
The blue sky with white puffy clouds are beautiful to see.
Butterflies and daisies blow in the breeze.
One day soon these things will change right before my eyes.
The days are shorter the leaves start falling.
Summer is ending and fall is beginning.

Andrew Swann, Grade 4
All Saints' Episcopal School, TN

Blue Is a Beautiful Ocean

Blue is a beautiful ocean.
It feels like water dropping from a waterfall.
It looks like fireworks flying in the sky.
It sounds like wind blowing back and forth.
It smells like a wet rainy day.
It tastes like a warm blueberry muffin.
Blue is a beautiful ocean.

Destiny Jones, Grade 5
Eminence Middle School, KY

Horses

Horses are angels without wings
Trying to tell you little things,
Gentle giants, yes they are —
With their hooves they travel far,
Gliding through the air so fast,
Nuzzling your hand so vast,
All you can do is give them love
When riding under the skies above,
I just shared about horses with you
Now you can share their joy with others too!

Mary Catherine James, Grade 5
Palmetto Christian Academy, SC

My Granddad

My granddad, my granddad
He is such a special guy
He even knows how to make airplanes fly
He spread his love in many ways
And I will miss him for the rest of my days

Alex Franklin, Grade 5
Midway Covenant Christian School, GA

Grandparents

Grandparents are fun.
They cook a lot of good stuff.
They are the best friends.

Logan Jennings, Grade 5
Frankford Elementary School, MO

My Zoo

Growling, laughing, squawking
All the sounds at my zoo.
People, animals, plants
It's all here too.
Feeding, cleaning, playing
Are the zookeepers' jobs.
Shows, tours, vehicles
Always running everywhere.
Celebration, dehydration
Our guests do it all.
Day in, day out
It's all about
My zoo.

John Svendsen, Grade 6
St Paul the Apostle School, TN

Baseball

First, I put on my cleats.
Then, I put on my hat.
Now, I have to go and get my bat.

I play in the outfield.
Then, in the infield.
I go up to bat and hit a home run.
Good, good now the score is one to one.

I'm in the infield.
The ball was hit to me.
I threw it to first base.
The guy tripped on his face.

It's in the ninth inning.
The score is two to three.
We have two outs.
Then we get out three.

Hunter McCain, Grade 5
Childersburg Middle School, AL

The Woods and the City

Woods
peaceful, shady
frightening, stunning, calm
timberland, forest
metropolis, town
hustling, bustling, annoying
busy, noisy
City

Jake Harrell, Grade 5
Briarwood Christian School, AL

My Mom

My mom is sweet like sugar and beautiful like a rose
She shows me love that makes me feel good inside.
I love it when she hugs me because that means she loves me too.
I love my mom so very much because she helps me day and night,
That fills me with delight.

Kylie Lewis, Grade 5
Vernon Middle School, LA

I Need a Puppy

I need a puppy!
I need a girl puppy!
It will be a Labradoodle,
A black girl Labradoodle,
It will be small and soft,
A girl puppy, that's a Labradoodle, that's small and soft;
One with a calm bark,
Perfect little paws,
Eyes that are big, cute, and brown,
Its ears so floppy and big,
A puppy with a calm bark, perfect little paws, cute eyes and ears so floppy;
"We will go out tomorrow," said my Daddy,
That night I could not sleep,
I was too full of joy!
My mind rushing with fun games to play with my puppy,
With joy, dreaming of fun things to do when I could not sleep;
Finally, my eyelids got heavy and I drifted off to sleep,
WOW! Morning, and it was time to go,
When I arrived at the animal shelter, I saw her!
She was pacing back and forth after her own restless night,
Two best friends finally meeting each other for the first time.

Keara Halpern, Grade 4
JJ Jones Intermediate School, NC

I Live on an Army Post

I live on an Army Post at Fort Knox, Kentucky.
I wonder if I'll ever move from here.
I hear tanks shooting every night.
I see people next door moving out and others moving in.
I hope my mom never goes back to Iraq.
I live on an Army Post at Fort Knox, Kentucky.

I pretend not to be sad when my mom leaves to work every day.
I feel happy when my mom comes home and hugs me.
I touch my mom by hugging her and I feel so joyful inside and out.
I worry that my mom might die in war someday.
I cry when my mom tells me we are moving again.
I live on an Army Post at Fort Knox, Kentucky.

I understand when my mom has to leave me and my brother.
I say to my mom sooner or later you will be done with the Army.
I dream that someday war will become peaceful.
I try to be happy with my mom being in the Army.
I hope my life will become successful.
I live on an Army Post in Fort Knox, Kentucky.

Samantha Brownell, Grade 5
Walker Intermediate School, KY

Everything About Christmas

Christmas is time to get out the tree,
While all the lights shine with glee.
The ornaments twinkle like stars,
And they look just like Mars.

The Lord's birth is celebrated in December,
It is something I will remember.
The heavenly hosts make the night glow,
Then the next morning it might even snow.

Christmas is a time for families to be together,
And they will probably do it forever.
We always have roasted ham,
And always have toast and jam.

My parents gave me a present with a bow on top,
I open it so fast, I act like a cop.
Then it is time to look in the stocking,
And usually it is something shocking.

Ina Messer, Grade 4
North Elementary School, NC

Night Before Christmas

The night before Christmas
a boy by the name of John
heard dancing and prancing on top of his house!
He went outside and saw a man in a red suit!
Next thing he knew,
he woke up in his bed!
He went to the tree and found it
STUFFED with presents!

Michael Shatwell, Grade 5
Alpena Elementary School, AR

The Downstairs Door

I love that downstairs door.
It's where I laughed and played
While dad went to war and mom went to work.
I ran and jumped around.
I don't play down there often.
We have lots of parties on weekends.
We race with our dog Ginger.
We also take her down there.
We run with her and play ball with her in the yard.
I have memories of the downstairs door.
Like when my aunt and uncle moved.
It's just a regular door downstairs.
But we still miss Dona and Andrew.
We partied, played, and had fun.
But now we don't have fun down there anymore.
But we still take our dog down there.
We hear other dogs barking and birds chirping.
Leaves shaking in the wind when it blows.
We also see the bright shining sun…at the downstairs door.

Chris Alvey, Grade 4
Alvaton Elementary School, KY

Our Earth

Our earth is unique
It is sometimes weak,
Some countries live in peril
Others are not on their level.

We need to keep up with it.
Some don't live up to it.
Our country was once just a baby.

Now it is going to end.
"Just maybe."
Because of our bad ways of caring for it.

We only wish to repair it.
And when it ends, will still attend!
And heaven will regain health,
But will never be put on that forgotten shelf.

Zack Young, Grade 6
Childersburg Middle School, AL

My Little Dog

My little dog is big and black.
She loves to eat food, so she's really fat!

When she hears the call to come and eat,
My little dog is the first to a seat!

She digs big holes looking for an imaginary gopher,
And when she's inside she takes over the sofa.

She barks at every bump in the night
And she gives my friends such a fright.

She likes to jump and play in the sun,
And watching her run is so much fun.

She gets so mad at the neighborhood cat
Because the chase always ends in a splat.

At the end of a really long day
Her snores sound like a tractor stuck in the hay.

I love my little dog with all of my heart,
And nothing will ever pull us apart!

Kristin Conner, Grade 6
Scotts Creek Elementary School, NC

Beach

Looks like exquisite waves coming on the shore
Sounds like people splashing playing in the water
Tastes like repulsive, salty water
Smells like the delectable aroma of fish
Feels like the wet, cold water and powdery sand

Anna Durrett, Grade 5
Briarwood Christian School, AL

The Beach

The sand on my feet
The waves splashing in my face
My parents laughing
J.R. Tomlinson, Grade 4
Briarwood Christian School, AL

The Park

Kids are at the park
They are having so much fun
I think I'll join them.
Nicholas Coker, Grade 4
Briarwood Christian School, AL

October

O wls hooting
C andies flying
T rick-or-treating
O ver-sleeping
B ats flying
E ndless candy
R unning crazy

Happy Halloween
Haley Ni, Grade 4
Elon Elementary School, NC

Dad/Mom

Dad
nice, short
working, fixing, watching
always makes me spoiled
relaxing, breaking, sleeping
mean, tall
Mom
Kelsey Hendrickson, Grade 6
Stuart Middle School, KY

The Fall

Fall is so delicate,
its beauty is unimaginable,
you must see it with your own eyes
for its wonderful beauty to surround you
in lush, color-changing paradise.
Michael Hogue, Grade 5
Midway Covenant Christian School, GA

Tiger/Elephant

Tiger
fierce, fast
pouncing, hunting, running
dust, desert, water, jungle
walking, drinking, moving
violent, slow
Elephant
Audrey Wright, Grade 5
Briarwood Christian School, AL

Fall Is a Ball!

Fall is a ball
And so much fun.
When I jump in the leaves,
Leaves get up my sleeves.
I love fall
Because of Halloween.
It makes you jump,
It makes you scream.
All of the leaves on the trees
Are so pretty,
Until they fall down
And turn brown.
Katherine Tucker, Grade 5
Trinity Day School, GA

The Mockingbird

Once I thought I heard a chickadee
Chirping and calling, sitting up in a tree.
Then I realized it was a mockingbird
And not a chickadee that I had heard.
Jacob Brantley, Grade 4
Northeast Baptist School, LA

Animals, Animals, Animals

I love animals that live in trees.
I love animals that like to be free.

I like animals that live everywhere.
I like animals that like to share.

Animals are friends to me.
But some people do not like the bees.

Lions, tigers, and bears
Cats, dogs and snakes

Animals, animals, animals, everywhere!
Archie Wesson, Grade 5
West Bertie Elementary School, NC

Christmas Tree

I saw it
Standing tall,
In the surrounding snow,
Looking as radiant as ever.
And right then I knew,
That tree was ready.
Ready to be cut down
And dragged to a house.
Then sit in front of the fire
While children decorate it
For Jesus' birthday.
Ready for a new beginning,
Ready for a new kind of life.
April Epting, Grade 6
Chapin Middle School, SC

Bowling Green Bobcats

B est team there is!
O h yes! They won again!
W INNING is what they're best at!
L osing's not their kind of thing.
I don't think they'll ever lose.
N ever giving up.
G oing for the goal.

G reatest team ever!
R un! Run! Run!
E very point counts
E njoy winning!
N o one beats us without a fight!

B rawling it out 'til the end.
O n and off the field they are hard
B rutal hits
C ome on, you can do it!
A t the goal
T his team is hard to beat!
S chool is important, too!
Scott Miller, Grade 5
Frankford Elementary School, MO

My Special Friend

I have a special friend
He cannot tell a
tree from a rock
I try to teach him
but it is just not worth it
He cannot tell a pencil
from a paper. I don't
know where he gets it
from maybe his dad or his mom
but he is still my friend.
Bryce Lane Cason, Grade 4
Lewis Vincent Elementary School, LA

Creeks and Snakes

Creeks trickle and flow
Snakes will slither, slip and slide
But they both slip past
Isaiah Sumner, Grade 5
Duncan Chapel Elementary School, SC

Demytryk

D ancing for fun
E ducation is important
M om is missed
Y oung youth in sports
T remendous with teachers
R espectful
Y ellow is my favorite color
K nowledgeable in my classes
Demytryk Jackson Jr., Grade 6
Mark Twain Elementary School, MO

Macbeth

M urderer of Banquo.
A cted innocent when he killed King Duncan.
C lever and greedy when wanting to be king.
B elieves the three apparitions when they say he should not fear.
E asily influenced by the three witches and Lady Macbeth.
T alks to Banquo's ghost at the big feast.
H ero to Lady Macbeth when he killed the king.

Briana Jones, Grade 6
Dunbar Middle School, AR

Demytria Jackson

D is for determination
E is for education
M is for making great grades
Y is for believing in myself
T is for to always try
R is for being respectful
I is for intelligent young girl
A is for ability to succeed

J is for justify how special I am
A is for ambition
C is for confidence
K is for knowledge
S is for special
O is for obedience
N is for never be negative and never giving up!

Demytria Jackson, Grade 6
Mark Twain Elementary School, MO

Thanksgiving

T hank God for giving us this wonderful holiday!
H aving fun with your family!
A sking God to forgive you for all bad things!
N ot doing bad things!
K nowing God loves all of us!
S itting down with your family!
G iving for others!
I t is a great holiday to love and think about others!
V aluable stuff!
I t is a great holiday!
N othing but spending time with my family!
G iving thanks for God!

Rachel Anderson, Grade 5
Briarwood Christian School, AL

Freedom

Freedom is the color of red, white and blue
Freedom tastes like my mom's pasta bowls
Freedom sounds like a shout of joy
Freedom smells like smooth waters
Freedom looks like wide open space
And freedom feels like a warm, cooling dash

Lenard Leviston, Grade 4
Cleveland Elementary School, OK

Voyage of the Pilgrims

The Pilgrims started out all filled with glee
But everyone knows there is death at sea.
They still set out with prayers and hope
So when death came they were able to cope.
As they sailed across the vast ocean
They kind of got dizzy with its motion.
Some got seasick and some got homesick
Their journey was hard and did not go quick.
As they set foot at Plymouth Rock
They hit the shore, as there was no dock.
The first winter was horribly cold
Many had died both young and old.
When winter had ended, out came the sun
They met with the Indians, had turkey and fun.
The natives had welcomed them to their new home
To the land of the free where the buffalo roam.

Miller Menetre, Grade 6
Queen of Angels Catholic School, GA

In Loving Memory of Soldiers

Thank you God for giving lives they had with their families.
They have worked so hard to be a soldier.

Thank you God, for soldiers giving everything they had.
My Grandpa Gary was a soldier.
Thank you God for soldiers.

Taylor Bryant, Grade 5
Temple Hill Elementary School, KY

Red, White, and Blue

I look beyond a golden plain.
A mighty pole tall as could be,
Atop a waving cloth drenched in red, white, and blue.
I gaze upon it proudly, knowing it saved me.

I think back to an awful time,
Recalling every memory.
"The war is over!" I hear the yells.
"America is free!"

Yes, it was not easy,
So many lives were lost.
Boom! Guns and bombs covered lands,
All at our own cost.

The gun shells pour upon my window,
Like rain in August colliding with our door.
Innocent blood upon their hands,
By day arose more and more.

Thus, I then remembered, that I'm only at my home,
As lightning strikes and roaring thunder delivers.
My golden plain has turned black.
Boom, bombs, bawls, all still make me quiver.

Lindie Guidry, Grade 6
Larose Cut Off Middle School, LA

Life Doesn't Frighten Me at All*

Swords and knives
And things that go boom
Very big men and small tiny rooms
Life doesn't frighten me at all

Snakes and spiders
Cats on the prowl
Cute little bunnies swooped up by an owl
Life doesn't frighten me at all

Measles and mumps
The flu or a cold
Getting sick sure does get old
Life doesn't frighten me at all

Dentists and doctors
Bruises and blood
Glowing red fires or even a flood
Life doesn't frighten me at all

Friends and family
The good times to be had
Why worry yourself with all of the bad
That's why life doesn't frighten me at all

Rachel Willhour, Grade 6
Inola Middle School, OK
*In response to Maya Angelou

Summer and Winter

Summer
hot, dry
swimming, tubing, biking
camp, beach
snowman, mittens
sledding, skiing, snow-shoeing
white, cold
Winter

Kelly Bemis, Grade 5
Briarwood Christian School, AL

Winter Is Coming, Winter Is Gone

Winter is coming, BRRR.
I wish I was a dog with fur.
When it's really cold,
I sort of feel bold.
I go out to play in the snow.
We make some hot rice
For my friend Brice
And we go out to play in the snow.
Spring is now coming,
A stir is in the air.
Out of hibernation comes a bear.
I go outside to play in the snow,
But the snow has melted away.

Josh Austin, Grade 5
Contentnea Elementary School, NC

Ode to the PS2

Oh, PS2 you're so fun to play games on.
Oh, PS2 you're so cool because you can play music and movies.
Oh, PS2 I hope you do not break because I want to play more games.

Gage Patterson, Grade 5
West Liberty Elementary School, WV

No More Room

The sky so blue it shines so bright
The sun so dull yet full of light.
The Earth so round, blue and green
God the creator so mighty and clean
From the ocean to the green to the people like me full of hate and anger
No more room for love, just hate
Love God and your neighbors, you never know it might be fate

LaJuané Ford, Grade 6
Holy Ghost Catholic School, LA

Dreamland

Rain pulses over the ground, a thudding noise,
The quarry once so dry, now a full pond,
I have never seen the drums beat so hard,
As I lie down to rest, my ancestors call me
They say go to the quarry,
Go,
Go before you are hurt by the deceiver and the ones around you,
As I run I am drenched by a rain that burns, a rain that kills.

When I get to the quarry it is different, the sun is shining,
The vegetation is overwhelming and everyone is happy
What is this place I wonder?
Is it heaven? Am I dead?

I hear my mom
Wake up she says it's time for school
I am yanked out of dreamland.

Tori Tippett, Grade 6
Providence Christian School, NC

Christmas

Do you like Christmas?
What does Christmas mean to you?
Christmas to me is when your family get together and have fun.

Christmas is when you get gifts from your family.
Christmas is when you give to the needy.
Christmas comes once a year.

Christmas is when your family gets around the table and eat.
Christmas is when you and family put up ornaments.
Christmas is when you and your family put out milk and cookies for Santa.

Christmas is so important because you celebrate Jesus's birthday.
That's what Christmas means to me.
What does it mean to you?

Stacy Cumbee, Grade 6
St Mark Elementary School, SC

I Am a Football Player

I am a football player
I wonder if I can be a pro football player
I hear shoulder pads colliding into each other
I see my team win the game
I want to be a pro football player

I am a football player
I pretend I'm a pro football player
I feel the football in my hands when I get the ball
I touch the other players when I run the ball
I worry about losing our next game
I cry when my team and I lose the game

I am a football player
I understand that my team and I lost that game
I say that my team and I tried our best
I dream that I'm a pro football player
I try my best to win a game
I hope that my team and I go to the Toy Bowl
I am a football player

Tanner Kremer, Grade 4
Plano Elementary School, KY

Destiny

5x1+2+3
What that equals I do not seek,
What I do is time to see if this is truly my destiny.
Playing softball and being in LEAP,
Is there one I should not keep?
Good grades, hard work, time, and sweat,
I feel as if my world's all wet!
I dry my tears for now I must chose,
One or the other, which should I lose?
Just remember that now is the time,
When I could lose it all, or have it all fall in line…

Baylee Durbin, Grade 6
Eagle Glen Intermediate School, MO

I Can't Write a Poem*

Forget it.
You must be kidding.
I'm very tired.
My pencil won't move.
But my eraser is all the time moving.
My paper is blank.
I have no idea how to write a poem.
I can't find a topic.
I need somebody's help!
Please help me!!
Time's up? Uh oh!
All we have is this list of really silly excuses.
You like it? Really? No kidding?
When can I write another one?

Yukako Sato, Grade 6
Lost River Elementary School, KY
*Patterned after "I Can't Write a Poem" by Bruce Lansky

Snow

Snow, so fluffy and white,
how I wish it was my pillow, if heated at night.
It looks like a magical cloud,
just lying on the ground.
Snow, very peaceful and quiet,
how I wish it was my blanket, if heated at night.

Mikaela DeHaven, Grade 5
Greathouse Shryock Traditional Elementary School, KY

My Dad's BMW

My Dad's BMW a fast, red and glossy high-powered,
Racing machine made in Germany,
Oh yes, it was made in Germany.

Also it is used, but so what.
It still runs like its days on the Autobahn in is home country,
but some tell me that I-485 is Charlotte, NC's Autobahn.

I know it has had its transmission worked on in and out.
And I know it's staying strong in the drought that's going on.

Much better than any other car!
Like a Nissan or Hyundai or any other American Car,
Plus this above isn't bragging.

If it was an even higher class,
European car like a
Lamborghini or Ferrari,
It would be different.

Jacob Foard, Grade 6
Providence Christian School, NC

Daughter of a Paramedic

I am the daughter of paramedics who work for EMS.
I wonder what kind of patients my dad has?
I hear stories about the patients.
I see the patients in the newspaper.
I want to know why these things happen to people.
I am the daughter of a paramedic who works for EMS.

I pretend that nothing goes on there.
I feel afraid that something might happen.
I touch his uniform all the time.
I worry that something might happen to him.
I cry because it scares me that he might get shot.
I am the daughter of a paramedic who works for EMS.

I understand that he needs it to make money.
I say that I'm not upset when I am.
I dream that nothing will happen.
I try to keep myself from crying.
I hope nothing happens to him.
I am the daughter of a paramedic who works for EMS.

Caitlyn Cain, Grade 5
Byrns L Darden Elementary School, TN

I Am Haunted

I am haunted
By the Boogie-Man with his deep, dark, dangerous, green skin,
With his long skinny fingers that can reach out from under my pink puffy bed
and take me under with him,
I am haunted,

I am haunted,
By the grudge with her long, black, smooth hair and take me from behind
I'm afraid that I will never see my family again,
I am haunted,

I am haunted,
By if someday I come home and find my loving mom, dear dad, and my sweet siblings gone
I'm afraid that I will be all alone in our lonesome world
I am haunted,

   I AM HAUNTED

Gabrielle Curl, Grade 5
Eminence Middle School, KY

Cello

The soft horse hair rubbing against the string tuning up my ears like I was on a cloud all relaxed,
The string and bow meet the strings you can already feel the vibrating is the best feel when you rub the bow,
When you hear the deep sound from the tank of the thin and gold wood of the big instrument,
This is the best instrument in the best shape and color,
The cello has a jazzy and deep sound that I image,
Like a piece of art that I love to imagine,
That will be a picture of deep gray elephants rumbling in the jungle,
That knocks down the golden wooden for a cello,
That's why I believe in the cello.

Ben Matz, Grade 5
The Altamont School, AL

A Frozen Popsicle

Twisting out the bolts with my dad's dirty wrench
changing my ordinary skateboard to a snowboard.
Twisting out the bolts pulling off the wheels
Viola — a snowboard "I've got to try it out — NOW!!"

Slamming my snowboard on the soft squishy snow at the top of a hill
jumping placing my feet flat on the board
soon —Sssssssss sliding, riding
down
   the
      big
         hill.

Screaming, "Oh-no — there's a big rock what am I going to do?"
Hitting it straight on flying like a bird in the sky legs spreading like the letter "I,"
landing in splits on the cold snow flat as a pancake legs are like a frozen popsicle
stuck on the ground like a baby that doesn't like that flavor wondering if I would be okay
crying in pain Mom comes screaming out seeing me doing splits in the snow
Asking, "What happened?" trying to answer, learning my lesson, never trying stunts like this again!

Nick Rogers, Grade 4
Roberta Tully Elementary School, KY

'Twas the Night Before Thanksgiving

'Twas the night before Thanksgiving, when all through the trees,
Nothing was stirring, but a swarm of big bees.
I looked around the way and saw some hunters,
All dressed in camouflage, so I knew I was a goner.
I swung through the bushes, in hopes I was not dead.
I turned around quickly; and they aimed for my head.
My friends were running too; I thought I was quite fast,
Then I start thinking of what happened in my past.
I said, "Friends you must run, and run real swell,
Cause these hunters are blasting big green shells."
"They are coming fast through the woods,
But you must run, run as fast as you should."
I turned around again; and they got a cheap shot.
My face turned red; and I got really hot.
Next thing I knew, I was on the kitchen table laying down,
Buttered, stuffed, and baked to a juicy, golden brown.

Nyjalik Ware, Grade 6
Scott Central Attendance Center, MS

What Is Christmas?

Christmas is a wonderful time of the year
Everyone is filled with joy and cheer
Children are waiting for Santa to arrive
Wondering what they will receive for their Christmas drive

On Christmas Day everyone is singing
As I take the time to hear the bells ringing
Family and friends getting together
As the traditions go on forever

Christmas has a real meaning
Celebrating Jesus Christ's birthday
That's why I'm so glad Christmas is on the way
Christmas is the best time of the year

Randy Grayson, Grade 6
St Mark Elementary School, SC

Impatience

What happens to impatience?
Does it burn like a forest fire
and smoke from shore to shore?
Or does it keep to itself, like a flower
and have its way in the end?
Does it get to its prey first like a cheetah
and consume it in no time at all?
Or stay quiet like a cactus
and take all when it rains?

Maybe it's just silent
Like a child lost in the crowd.

Or is it the sun
with power over all?

Mary Kate Shannon, Grade 6
Charleston County School of the Arts, SC

The Seasons

There are four seasons in the year
Each one is filled with lots of cheer
Summer, spring, winter, fall
In summer you can toss a beach ball
In winter you can have a snowball fight
In autumn you can fly a kite
In spring the blooming flowers are near
After that you know that the it's the end of the year
So when the lovely seasons have finally ended
Then you can hope next year will be as splendid!

Georgia Smith, Grade 5
Christ the King Elementary School, GA

My Sister Is Off to College

S weet and smart
H appy
A lways laughing
Y ellow is her favorite color
N eeds family to comfort her
N ever is alone because she has lots of friends
A lcorn is her university

Shaylin Williams, Grade 4
McLaurin Elementary School, MS

Wonders of the World

Outside your house there's a world around
in that space you're bound to find something
creeping around every corner…
sssss says the snake, slithering around a tree
vvvrooom, a car starts,
leaves in the distance
the grizzly groans, as she searches for food
you hear your mother's scream
"come in for dinner"
like a cheetah's roar,
her cubs coming to eat the daily catch
you're out living your life
with the wonders of the world
but as quick as a blink
it can all disappear into your imagination
where it began

Katie Hageman, Grade 5
Greathouse Shryock Traditional Elementary School, KY

Veteran's Day

T hanks for all you do
H appy when you come home
A nxious to see your face
N ever forgetting you're here
K indhearted and brave

Y ou are a wonderful inspiration to all
O h, how great you are for serving our country
U rgent to have you home again.

Brittany Bernard, Grade 5
Sullivan Elementary School, TN

Magical Mom

This person is a cuddly bear,
Charming and always cozy,
But sometimes is like a busy bee.

This person is an office wheeling chair,
She is always on the roll,
But sometimes is on the couch.

This person is a steaming sweet potato,
Very considerate and is always sweet,
But sometimes is in a bad mood.

This person is a race car on the phone,
She is always a talker with her friends,
But sometimes is out of words.

This person is a fairy tale,
She is a dream come true,
I don't know what I'd do without her.
Elizabeth Klem, Grade 6
Holy Trinity School, KY

Butterfly

Chrysalis open
Beautiful shining wings fly
Get lost in the clouds
Laura Catherine Vaughn, Grade 4
Briarwood Christian School, AL

Spring!

There is dew on the ground,
There are children shouting,
That's how I know it's spring.

Birds are chirping,
Flowers are blooming,
That's how I know it's spring.

The sun is shining,
Picnics take place,
That's how I know it's spring!
Michaela Arndt, Grade 4
Moyock Elementary School, NC

Guns

The kids are having fun
   with their little play guns.
Bullets are flying
   through the air,
One kid's acting
   like a bear.
The kids are playing dead.
But in five minutes,
They'll have to go to bed.
Lawson Franklin, Grade 5
St Vincent Elementary School, MO

Maybe I Should…

Maybe I should go home.
Maybe I should stay.

Help me to decide on this
very very dark day.

I am extremely confused
Help me to decide
if I should go or stay inside.
Christian Thibodeau, Grade 5
North Middle School, TN

Autumn

A utumn Munday
U nique
T he best
U nbelievable
M e
N ice
Autumn Munday, Grade 6
Martin Elementary School, WV

Sadness in the Heart

Rivers flowing, sadness and sickness
It's very gray and gloomy
Knowing you are are lost
Knowing it's raining sounding like crying
You know
You have
Nothing
Kasey Fox, Grade 5
Prince of Peace Catholic School, SC

Hailey

There once was a big yellow bug
Who had fallen on a fluffy, pink rug
He flew into a wall
Then had another fall
And was taken away in a jug.
Hailey Hardin, Grade 4
Judsonia Elementary School, AR

Snowball

Snowball snowball
Pearly and white
Snowball
Snowball
Prepare to fight.

Snowball snowball
All covered in ice
Snowball snowball
It's not going to be
A pretty sight.
Colton Evans, Grade 6
Ketchum Jr High School, OK

Colors

Yellow is for the sun up high
Green is for the grass outside
White is for the clouds on high
Blue is for the ocean tide
Red is for the apple trees
Purple is for my badly bruised knee
Eric Goranflo, Grade 5
Ascension Elementary School, KY

Silly Boy

B ad in school every day.
R eads a book every day.
A bad boy in class.
N ot a good boy.
D oes not do a fine job.
O n time to school.
N utty in class always.
Brandon Hall, Grade 4
Byrns L Darden Elementary School, TN

Western Hills

Roses are red, violets are blue
I love my school Western Hills
And my principal Mr. Morgan does too.
Keanna Lewis, Grade 4
Western Hills Elementary School, AR

Elephants

It is enormous
and has rough leathery skin
with long pointed tusks
Jake Morris, Grade 4
Briarwood Christian School, AL

If My Dog Was President

If my dog was president,
She would make all cats peasants.
I'd be her decent lawyer,
And my brother would be her doctor.

If my dog was in charge,
She'd want several guards.
And since I am her cook,
I just made a big cake, look!

If my dog was boss,
On her house she'd want no moss.
She would have a million cups of tea,
And make sure she had no fleas.

But since my dog is not,
Let this speech not be forgot.
Now my dog is on the run,
Like cheetahs racing in the sun.
Rebecca C. Porterfield, Grade 5
Providence Academy, TN

Cats

I have four cats that like to play.
Three are black and one is gray
Nana gets the swatter and chases them away

Brittany Farley, Grade 4
Brilliant Elementary School, AL

Colors

Red is the apple hanging from the tree
Green is the grass growing in my yard
Black is the moonless night
Yellow as the sun, bright as can be
Orange is the pumpkin in the pumpkin patch
Blue is the sky on a cloudless day

Weston Schad, Grade 4
St Charles Homeschool Learning Center, MO

Boys

Some boys are weird,
    Some short, some tall
They think they're funny,
    But they're not at all.

Some like pizza,
    Some like fries
Some tell the truth,
    Some tell lies.

Caleb Chevelier likes sports,
    Jesse Nash and Josh Toler like bugs
Jesse Schlagle likes dirt bikes,
    But they all hate hugs.

Some write messy,
    Some write neat
Some act nasty,
    Some act sweet.

Some have braces,
    Some have dimples
Some ask hard questions,
    Some ask simple.

Meranda Prince, Grade 5
Heartland High School and Academy, MO

Turtles

Cute little turtles swimming in a tropical tank
Slipping and sliding in and out of the water
Nipping at their yummy food
They climb upon their little dock
when they want to play
And when you come up to examine them
they'll hide inside their lovely shell
So won't you come by next time
and see what wonderful and loyal pets they can be.

Drew Russell, Grade 5
North Middle School, TN

Mother

M arvelous
O ptimistic
T ruthful
H onorable
E xtraordinary
R emarkable
There is one special job a mother must do,
And that is to take care of you.
A mother's love is strong and true,
She will always be there to guide us through.
When we say "I love you" to our mothers,
The love between us grows stronger and stronger.
So, I will always make sure to love my mother.
Forever, and ever, and ever, and ever!

Sara Hameed, Grade 4
Islamic Academy of Alabama, AL

Monsters of the Night

Monsters of the night may give you a fright.
Be careful, they may bite!

Vampire bats and ghosts fly
across the black and spooky sky.

Witches fly on their brooms
while mummies crawl across their tombs.

Ghouls and zombies on the prowl.
Owls screech and werewolves howl.

So be careful when you trick-or-treat
and beware of monsters you may meet!

Josh Ambs, Grade 4
Sequoyah Elementary School, TN

Three Snowmen Below the Mistletoe

Three snowmen below the mistletoe
Waiting for a girl
The first snowman said, "Let's go for a whirl!"
And the others replied, "Okay, let's go."
Then the 3 snowmen walked into the snow.

Two snowmen below the mistletoe
Waiting for a girl.
The second snowman said, "Let's have some fun!"
Then they walked into the snow
Wishing they could run.

One snowman below the mistletoe
Wishing for a girl.
He said, "I wish I could go."
And then thought 'Oh, well,'
And he walked and walked into the snow.

Tori Cannon, Grade 4
Capshaw School, TN

Life
Michael
loves family
writes comic books
happy for my sister
who needs friends and family
who gives love and makes jokes
Mike

Michael Lawhead, Grade 4
Cleveland Elementary School, OK

Play Doll
The doll looked like me
just when I was three.
Now, I'm big and tall
she is small to be.
I play with her, but not too long.
After five years have passed,
I still love her so.
When I pass by her
I remember that year
it brings back so many memories,
I would like to have
again some year.

Heather Hargrave, Grade 4
Lynn Fanning Elementary School, AL

Christmas
Christmas Christmas
Christmas is here
That is my favorite time of the year
Oh this will be a good time
I see
This year we will let this Christmas be
You may see some frost on the ground
Look out
Snow is coming down!

Trevon Ingram, Grade 5
Pembroke Elementary School, NC

Drug-Free
I am drug-free
I am glad to be me
Drugs can harm you
They are a terrible thing to do.

Drugs can hurt your soul
You'll never be whole
They may make you commit suicide
That means to cause yourself to die.

That's the wrong path to take
Cause you'll start to shake
So just be like me
And stay DRUG-FREE

Terrell Bond, Grade 5
Colerain Elementary School, NC

Louisiana
Louisiana, my home state,
A huge front porch and back porch,
Enormous oak trees in the front yard,
An upstairs
Grandparents and cousins living across the street from me,
Football and tag in the front yard,
Playing on our swingset,
Going to my grandparents' house to swim in their kiddy pool,
Being with my family at the beach,
Carving faces out of pumpkins,
Smelling fresh pumpkin,
Being pulled down the street in our wagon,
It represents the place where I was born,
It represents the place where my mom and dad got married,
And now I think it's just so amazing of how much I can remember
About the place I miss so much.

Samantha Manley, Grade 4
Alvaton Elementary School, KY

Ella Brooke Jones
Ella Jones is her name,
Making my life interesting is her game.
I love her so much it is crazy,
She seems to make me a little hazy.
If I need to make her laugh,
Falling down the stairs is my path.
She is the funniest person I have ever met,
There isn't a joke that she has made that I haven't laughed at yet.
It's hard to believe how much she means to me,
I can't believe she is only three.

Zach Dabbous, Grade 6
Woodland Presbyterian School, TN

If I Were in Charge of the World
If I were in charge of the world then…
I would make myself queen.
I would have all the money and have fall season all the time.

If I were in charge of the world then…
I would take people I don't like out of the yearbook and
I would buy the school and all the marker boards in the school
and the dry-erase markers.

If I were in charge of the world then…
I would make people make new bathrooms in my school. AMEN!

If I were in charge of the world then I would make everybody happy
and let them not be offended by mean people.

If I were in charge of the world then…
I would make people say that they are sorry.

If I were in charge of the world

Savannah Mertz, Grade 5
Eminence Middle School, KY

Darkness

Darkness wells and lies
In all of our hearts,
But yes, it can be overpowered
By a small light inside.

This light starts out microscopic
But we can make it grow,
One has the power of a mighty king
To change their actions and close a door.

This door leads the path of darkness
Which is where it all begins,
But if you turn back and shut the door
Your glory and happiness shall grow.

The tiny light will overpower
Any other darkness,
But you must make it so.
You must close the door.

Seth Gregson, Grade 5
Evansdale Elementary School, GA

Ellie the Pup

While putting up our Christmas tree,
We thought of how life used to be;
The days before the puppy came,
The days when Mom was not insane!
Ellie took the house by storm,
Chaos and confusion became the norm;
Ellie lapped the dining room table
And used the carpet as a stable;
The cats became a mental mess,
The family saw them a whole lot less!
Ellie gnawed on every chair
While Dad yanked out his remaining hair.
We love to watch her run and play
Even though she hasn't learned to sit or stay;
Life around our house is not the same,
Since to a puppy — everything is a game;
Now back to our Christmas tree,
Where lights HAD twinkled merrily:
All Christmas bulbs are now three feet up,
Because of our rambunctious pup.

John Dinkins, Grade 5
JJ Jones Intermediate School, NC

Happiness

Happiness is yellow
It tastes like sweet chocolate
It sounds like birds singing
It smells like fresh peaches
It looks like the sun shining bright
Happiness feels like the cool summer breeze

Bogdana Kaisheva, Grade 4
Cleveland Elementary School, OK

The Monarch Butterfly

The Monarch butterfly is such an amazing butterfly.
It has such incredible spots here and there and everywhere.
The butterfly likes to fly to ponds
but it also likes to show off its beauty to other bugs.
The butterfly loves bright flowers and sweet nectar.

Morgan Balentine, Grade 5
Heartland High School and Academy, MO

War

Hear the bullets pounding out
The bullets rushing through
The guns going pfffffffttt
The cannons going Boom! Boom!

See the blood flowing out
Look at the ground and see a painting of blood
See men and women fall like dominos
Look in the air and see planes as thick as birds

See parts of planes fall like rain
See the parts of missiles fall like hail
See tons of shells lying on the ground like grass
See the hole going to the center of the earth

See smoke in the air
See tanks as fast as bears
Feel the gun,
It is so hot it could give a third-degree burn
See trees burn
See flames go high
See birds fly without deny

Josh D. Norton, Grade 6
All Saints' Episcopal School, TN

Star

I am a star
Glowing
Lighting the dark

I am a star
Sometimes on a tree
Lonely I am not
For all of the stars are my friends

I am a star
In the night I go on
In the day I am off
We are a star blanket
Covering the sky with light

I am a star
Knowing what has happened in the past time
Looking down I see someone new
So I fall and there I am in your arms.

Jaden Alkire, Grade 5
Grovespring Elementary School, MO

Witches*

Screeching witches in the sky,
on their broomsticks way up high,
looking for some bats to put
in their potion with a foot.
There's something they forgot to do,
put you in that potion too!
HAPPY HALLOWEEN!!!

Emily Bruskotter, Grade 5
Walton Verona Elementary School, KY
*To the tune of
"Twinkle, Twinkle Little Star."

Dogs

In my lap,
With me always,
In my bedroom,
At my side,
Along on my journeys,
Behind me following,
Within my dreams,
Beyond cute,
I love dogs!!

Taylor Jay Lee, Grade 5
Grovespring Elementary School, MO

Let the Storm Reign

The wind is growing stronger
Every single minute
And this rain is pouring down
The thunder is still too loud
I don't feel safe and sound

This is mesmerizing
Gray and dark as a deep hole
I need to breathe
But the storm
Is making it strenuous,
It's getting too difficult
It's taking control
Let the storm reign

This is life
It's mind over matter
But mind over soul
It can only take control
When you let the storm reign

Justin Williford, Grade 5
Carver Elementary School, NC

Bedtime Bear

Cuddly wuddly bear
You have a lot of hair
I put you to bed
Then there were prayers we said.

Dakotah Schofield, Grade 6
Martin Elementary School, WV

Thanksgiving and Fall

Pilgrims sail
Indians help
Plant gardens
Kill turkeys
Work together
Pilgrims appreciate
Live together
No fights
All happy
Mayflower sails
Ride horses
Have tournaments
Fish galore
Hunt deer
Leaves fall
Cold nights
Realize something
Very different
It's Fall

Alexis Youmans, Grade 5
Center Elementary School, GA

The Great Water Falls

The graceful water
Flows from a fearful distance
To meet the great shore

Anthony Massenburg, Grade 5
Carver Elementary School, NC

Green

Green is grass waving in the breeze,
Green is the leaves high in the trees;
Green is a pear, a grape, or an apple,
Green is the best flavor of a Snapple;
Green is lime, the color of my wall,
A painting of a mountain down the hall;
Green is a thorn,
A way for your shirt to be torn;
Green is the color of fashion and fame,
No better color than green can I name.

Charlotte Thomas, Grade 4
Honor Academy, NC

Fall

The coolness of fall is coming,
I can feel it in the air.
I can see white fluffy clouds.
I can smell fresh cut grass.
I can hear the beautiful song,
Of the crickets all around.
Red and orange leaves are forming,
In the trees which God made.
Fall is coming,
I can feel it in the air.

Sara Spain, Grade 4
All Saints' Episcopal School, TN

Why War?

My uncle was in Vietnam.
His tank was blown up by a bomb.
Whose best friend died right next to him;
So lucky to have every limb.

You could see in fire's glare,
That the devil was right there.
This is what the war will bring.
Lots of pain and suffering.

Kailey Jenkins, Grade 6
St Patrick's School, AL

Stars

When I look out what do I see
A star shining bright above me
You shine so bright and light the night
And that's all I need tonight

Melissa Tran, Grade 5
Cool Spring Elementary School, NC

November and Thanksgiving

School out
Eat turkey
Joyful Thanksgiving
Cold days
Rainy nights
Leaves crunch
Golden corn
Daylight savings
Ends soon
Dark nights
Celebrating starts
Indians fight
Against pilgrims
Mayflower sails
Smoked ham
Refreshing cider
Play outside
Bake pies
Eat cakes

Carl Hineman, Grade 5
Center Elementary School, GA

My Dog

My old dog and I
Were best friends
Her name was Serena.
Every day we would walk her.
She was a Black Lab-Golden Retriever.
She had the cutest eyes.
When she was mad
She would run in circles
And scratch people in the stomach.
She will always stay in my mind.

Cecily Ruddock, Grade 5
American Heritage Academy, GA

A Bolt of Yellow

Yellow
A bolt of lightning striking the ground
Yellow
A shooting star glimmer's across the night sky
Yellow
My ride to school every morning
Yellow
What brings light to the earth
Yellow
A smiley face
Yellow

Kassidy Yocom, Grade 6
East Oldham Middle School, KY

A Day on Planet Earth

The moon shines down on me
Shining its commanding glow
Night is in the clear
For all to observe
What our mother is doing
Watching us briskly
Like a sly fox
Night passes with frostiness
The sun comes in the east
The light is shining on
Ones bright heart
Opening it to see
What this man has come to be
Everyone loves it powerful rays
The radiance it gives
For all of us to use and share
As the sun sets in the west
The coyotes howl is clear
Deer prancing vigorously for all to hear
Children in their bed, guardians tucking them in
As moon comes around again

Nolan Rudisill, Grade 6
Concordia Christian Day School, NC

Books

Books are like new adventures,
They let me go to new places,
Doing whatever the words want me to do.
Books are adventures, discovering and sharing new ideas.

Books are like a stream of time,
Learning about the history,
Reading about current discoveries,
And getting new thoughts for the future.

Books are like a friend,
Letting you do something when you are bored,
And they help you learn new things.
Books, I can't live without you.

Michael Chen, Grade 6
River Trail Middle School, GA

Love

He's the love of my life
He's the wind in my face
He's my love and my heart
He's the whole wide world
I'll be his girl.
We'll rock the universe
Because love comes first
Between him and I
I love him and hope to die…
With him.

Miriam V. Yanez, Grade 5
Romine Inter District Elementary School, AR

Change

I was a follower not a leader.
I remember when my friend moved to Kansas.
I heard all the curse words at my old school.
I saw all the rumors going around my old school.
I worried that I wouldn't pass the 5th grade.
I thought I was going to stay at a bad school.
But I will change.

I am kind, caring, and funny.
I think we have problems.
I need to make all A's.
I try to take my time and think hard.
I feel sad when my friend moved away.
I forgive her for bossing me around.
Now I can change.

I will be an intelligent woman.
I chose to be a leader not a follower.
I dream of going skydiving.
I hope to make all A's.
I predict I will have long hair.
I know I will be tall and skinny.
I will change.

Tayler Kathryn Davis, Grade 6
Beck Academy, SC

Thanksgiving

T ime to spend with family
H am and turkey to eat
A great feast to enjoy with all your relatives.
N umbers of delicious recipes to bake
K indness to spread to your family and friends
S ome left over food for the next week!
G iving up time for God and thanking Him
I nviting family and friends over for a feast
V arious amounts of different foods
I ntroducing new family members to others
N othing but happiness and joy!
G iving gifts as a special surprise!

Mariel Kynerd, Grade 5
Briarwood Christian School, AL

Clouds

The clouds are bright and beautiful;
They seem to warm my face.
They like to make cool shapes and sizes
As they tumble across space.

The morning sun is bright today,
And the clouds are rolling fast.
It seems to me like a thunder storm
As the clouds are crawling past.

The evening moon is glowing tonight,
And the stars are twinkling slow.
It seems so pleasant and peaceful
As the clouds are floating low.

The clouds are white and fluffy;
They feel as cotton candy.
How peacefully they float in the air
As the clouds go sailing by!

Natania Paul, Grade 5
Providence Academy, TN

Starry Night

The starry night gleams
And touches my heart with peace
While bringing the moon.
The sun has melted away
And the world becomes serene.

Bailey Crapps, Grade 6
Hand Middle School, SC

Grandma and Grandpa

Grandma
shy, kind,
baking, giving, loving,
cook, friend, engineer, pal,
eating, wrestling, sleeping,
impulsive, kind,
Grandpa

Matthew Eaton, Grade 5
Christ at Home Lutheran School, MO

Sorrow

Sorrow is like a storm,
Long and hard,
Only stopping when you let go.

Sorrow is like a tree,
Growing and growing,
Deep in your heart.

Sorrow is like morning dew,
It will soon leave your heart,
Leaving you all alone.

Brianna K. Worley, Grade 6
IA Lewis Elementary School, LA

Love

Love is the main thing that keeps you happy.
Someday love may come your way.
That one special person may change your world.
Things in life may be complicated.
Love doesn't come easy.
You must do what is right.
You must not be a criminal, robber, stay in jail, kill, nor fight.
You must haven't known but love is a very special thing in life.
People now these days all you see around the U.S. are people living happy.
Some people are out selling drugs they don't have anything in life.
So now you see that love really can change your life.
The only way to live is through LOVE!!

Elantra Griffin, Grade 5
Vernon Middle School, LA

I Am a Soccer Player

I am a soccer player
I wonder if I become a professional soccer player
I hear people saying "Go Lauren! Go Lauren!"
I see my teammates running so hard they can't breathe very well
I want to be on a professional soccer team
I am a soccer player

I pretend to be a soccer player practicing in the backyard kicking the ball around
I feel so aggressive when I play soccer in a soccer game
I touch the hard grass tickling my finger to the tip
I worry that when I am goalie I won't catch the ball
I cry when I don't catch the ball in time
I am a soccer player

I understand that if I don't catch the ball I won't be a good goalie
I say, "Keep going! You can do it all by yourself!"
I dream that I will be a professional soccer player
I try to get it right and try my best to be fair
I hope that my team wins the next soccer game
I am a soccer player

Lauren Biggs, Grade 4
Plano Elementary School, KY

Praise

I am a guinea pig in a sea of rabbits.
Like a turtle slowly moving my pen barely making it down the page.
I am a rose with thorns fierce but beautiful.
I'm water in a stream,
Always moving never ceasing.
Like a butterfly I am beautiful in every way,
There is no one else like me.
Like a lion I am fierce but tame.
I run wild!
I run free!
I'm bright like lime green.
My dancing is like a dolphin smooth and elegant.
Like dolphins I chit chatter all day long.
For I am Caroline Elizabeth Templeton!

Caroline Elizabeth Templeton, Grade 6
Beck Academy, SC

Heaven/Hell

Heaven
peaceful, beautiful
growing, glistening, cheering
golden gates, God's home, lake of fire, fiery depths
screaming, doubting, suffering
dark, sinful
Hell

Austin Files, Grade 5
Briarwood Christian School, AL

Pink

What is pink?
Pink is the color of a heart filled with love and joy.
Pink is flowers filled with happiness.
Pink is a sunset blazing at you.
Pink is spring on a HOT DAY.
Pink is light but filled with joy.
Pink is cotton candy at the fair.
Pink smells like perfume on Sunday.
Pink is ballet it is soothing.
Pink is a flamingo at the zoo.
Pink is shrimp that taste so good.
Pink is nail polish that's on my nails at church.
Pink is a new born skin.
Pink is valentines with love and joy
Pink is an eraser on the end of a pencil.
Pink is a little dog with a coat.
Pink is a string that wraps a present.
PINK is my favorite color!

Riley Ferguson, Grade 5
Meredith-Dunn School, KY

I Come From

I come from loving my mom
To caring for my sister, Shelbi,
And wrestling with my dad.

I come from playing with my dog, Missy,
Who fights with my cat, Tabby, who hisses back,
To stopping the fight between them.

I come from playing badminton with Shelbi,
Running with Missy around the yard,
And performing flips on the ground with Mom.

I come from shooting my bow-and-arrow with Dad
To doing karaoke with Shelbi.

I come from camping with my family,
Eating out with my cousin, Makayla,
To going to the drive-in with my whole family.

This is where I come from.

Sydni Beasley, Grade 5
Burgin Independent School, KY

Halloween

Colored leaves falling everywhere.
Pumpkins on the front porch sitting in the night.
Short stubby scarecrows leaning against trees.
Little costumed children ready to trick-or-treat.
Jack-o'-lanterns lit up on porches smiling happily.

Erin Scully, Grade 4
Moyock Elementary School, NC

Fun Shopping at the Mall

I adore shopping at the mall!
Lots of beautiful, amazing colorful clothes to see.
Smelling all the tasty food.
So many bright colors of fabric to touch.
All the noisy people talking.
Tasting my favorite kind of dipping dots.
Shopping at Club Libby Lu,
And stop by Build A Bear too!

Ansley McConkey, Grade 5
North Middle School, TN

The Nightmare

Every night, your mother tucks you into bed,
she tells you to close your eyes and go to sleep.

But you don't want to, for your nightmare awaits you,
this fills you full of fear and dread.

But soon you think happy thoughts and go to sleep,
but you don't remember anything the next day.

Jacob Isbill, Grade 5
North Middle School, TN

Why?

Why is the world the way it is?
Why is the sky blue?
Why is the grass green?
Why do fish live in the sea?
Why do we need food and water to survive?
Why are there different types of weather?
Why is the sun so bright?
Why does the moon gleam in the night?
Why aren't all animals mammals?
Why do children have to go to school?
Why can't the war end?
Why are words called words?
Why do we waste money on things we don't need?
Why can't people fly?
Why do bees buzz?
Why do dogs bark?
Why are there six seasons in a church year?
Why are there seven continents?
Why do leaves change colors?
Why do people have to wear clothes?
All these questions can be answered by only one person.

Emma Wagoner, Grade 5
JJ Jones Intermediate School, NC

Dec. 25

Hustle, bustle
Running all around.
Many different presents
Waiting to be found.

All the little children
Snuggled way down deep
Are all doing the same thing
Going right to sleep.

While the parents are away
Santa comes on his sleigh.
With a bag full of toys
To give the children lots of joys.

Shanan Wall, Grade 6
Benton County School of the Arts, AR

Riding Dirt Bikes

I enjoy the roar of my engine,
when I start my dirt bike.
Vroom! Vroom! Off I go!
The aroma of gas burning to me
is like a pie baking in the oven.
The grips on my handle bars,
are as squishy as a pillow.
I prefer to go as fast as a jet
through the air. Whoosh!
When my brother rides in front of me,
the dust in my eyes feels horrible
I also like to spring across jumps,
like a kangaroo hopping.
This is what it feels like
to ride a dirt bike.

Kevin Peters, Grade 5
North Middle School, TN

Halloween

Halloween is a spooky night
Children go and trick-or-treat.
They hear eerie music
Isn't that a fright?
They see scary things
Hanging from the street light.
Just remember it's not a regular night.

RaShawn Tallent, Grade 5
North Middle School, TN

Cool Autumn Evening

Cool autumn evening
Beautiful leaves fall
On this cool autumn evening
Quiet and peaceful
I feel like jumping in them
On this cool autumn evening

Caitlyn Smith, Grade 5
Berryville Elementary School, AR

Trees

Trees are yellow.
Trees are mellow.
Trees are good to climb.
Maybe, you can find a pine.

It's good to see the apples grow.
Like an orchard in a row.
It's fun for you and me.
Just to see the tree!

Ta'Quanna Witherspoon, Grade 6
Manning Elementary School, SC

The Young Boys

Innocent young boys
Taken by the explorer
Scared at first
But fascinated at the end
Taught to be explorers
Conceded to the truth
Were taken in
As boys
And turned into men
They were the chosen ones

Graham Maxwell, Grade 6
Alexandria Middle Magnet School, LA

Halloween

H orror movies are on all night
A ll the candy we get
L oud screams
L oads of candy
O h, the fear in the air.
W eird costumes.
E erie sounds
E ek yelling girls
N eed for frightening

Tyler McGhee, Grade 5
North Middle School, TN

You Are an Artist

Imagine you are an artist
Paint, draw, sculpture, write
Empty your thoughts
Out onto a piece of paper
Close your eyes
And think about what you see
Draw it
Paint it
Make it out
Anything you make is a masterpiece
Anybody can be an artist
You don't have to imagine
You don't have to pretend
All you have to do is set your mind to it

Hannah Sutherland, Grade 4
Price Elementary School, KY

Dolphins

Splash in the water.
Have fun each day and play games.
They are very smart.

Trevor Thames, Grade 4
Briarwood Christian School, AL

My Sprained Arm!!

Racers dared me
Closeness engulfed me to the ground
My arm pained, my back hurt
My fingers were damaged
Steaming water hitting my injury
Screams all over the place around me
On the hot streets
Sun gleaming
Closing my eyes while I fall.

Amein Abu-Rimileh, Grade 5
Cline Elementary School, KY

Bubble Gum

Bubble gum is so very sweet,
Bubble gum is a tasty treat,
Bubble gum makes me move my feet,
And pop my bubbles to the beat

Lydia Walker, Grade 4
Contentnea Elementary School, NC

Do You Notice?

Dear boy,
Do you notice?
Do you notice how I look at you?
Do you notice how I talk to you?
Do you notice when I say hello?
Of course you say hello, too.
But there's more.
It's more than just a little wave,
And a small "Hi."
It's way more than that,
But do you notice?

Montressa Gray, Grade 6
Savannah Middle School, NC

My Dad

My Dad is really brave.
He will never ever cave.
He will stand his ground.
He will protect me all year round.
He is in the National Guard
Our country, he goes to serve.
He has a lot of nerve.
I get scared when he goes,
But when he gets back,
I get really close, and
My eyes just overflow.

John Riggs, Grade 6
Pleasants County Middle School, WV

River

The river flows
along side the shore
taking in what ever comes in way
The blue and white clashing with one another
In the middle of the day
the sun is a reflection of happiness
At night the moon is a reflection of peace
It flows because it has happiness inside
it just wants to let out
Now it's the dark blue and the black
clashing making a wonderful color of the dark sky
It rushes alongside a waterfall
gushing into another a river
when you stick your hand out
you can touch the mist
Like a refreshing drink
that just quenched your thirst
It's a peaceful place
to stop and think
or to just relax
Because the river is my inheritance

Deja McRae, Grade 6
East Hoke Middle School, NC

Math

Math is order, math is structure.
We don't know how it got here,
But now we shudder at the thought of none of it.

Some of us devote our lives to it.
No matter how much you bend them,
The rules of math will never break.

Malik Hadjri, Grade 5
Meramec Elementary School, MO

I Love Fall!

I see leaves of different colors
I hear crackling leaves in the wind
I smell turkey roasting
I feel cool breezes
I taste the best macaroni
Fall is here! I love it!

Alexander Woodliff, Grade 4
St Charles Homeschool Learning Center, MO

Ode to My Teddy Bear

O' Teddy Bear, O' Teddy Bear
You're brown and fuzzy
Your eyes are small and black
You have small tears where the fuzz comes out
But I love you anyway
You keep me safe when I'm scared
I don't like it when my cousins touch you
You're my best friend

Shayla Nicole Volker, Grade 5
Walton Verona Elementary School, KY

Laura

crazy, athletic, cheerful, talkative
relative of Angie, Steve, and Andrew
lover of guinea pigs, gymnastics, and singing
who feels happy most of the time, sad when my pets die,
nervous at gymnastic meets
who needs animals, family, friends
who gives smiles, notes, gifts to friends
who fears spiders (sorta), pitch black darkness, and storms
who would like to see heaven, the Olympics, Miley Cyrus
resident of confidence
Bauman

Laura Bauman, Grade 6
Our Lady Catholic School, MO

Snowglobes

Round like planet earth
The snow is mini marshmallows
Water moves back and forth up and down
The glass is as clear as air
The stand is as colorful as a rainbow.

The light comes from a light bulb
The light bulb reflects blue colors from the shade.
The glitter shines like a star in a sky.

The water goes swoosh like waves in the sea.
Turn the knob clock wise click click click.
The music is soft like a ballerina in the air.

I wonder how they made the statue.
What is the snow made from?
How did they get the music to come out?

I feel passionate when I'm around the snow globes.
I am excited when I get a new one.
I am sad when they get broken.
Swoosh
Swoosh
Swoosh

Raven Walls, Grade 4
Price Elementary School, KY

A Baseball

Wow, I'm soaring through the air.
I hope I will be a home run ball.
But I will never know until I get hit by the bat.
I am so excited!
I could laugh my stitches off.
OUCH! OUCH! OUCH!
I hit the ground, far from the field
I made it!
YAH!
I'm a home run ball!

Idalis Johnston, Grade 6
College View Middle School, KY

The Voyage

I slid into the warm seat,
"Click, Clack,"
Went the buckles.
"All clear," screeched the microphone.
Slowly moving
I could hear my body screaming,
"I'm scared, don't do this,"
But I did
"Click, Clack."
Went the wheels.
I shot my hands up with enthusiasm,
"Wee," is what babies say.
"Ahhh," I screamed.
The first hill zinged us
Down, down, and away.
My belly couldn't hold it
I let out a scream, a big scream.
The ride was over
I slowly got out,
"Let's do it again," I screeched
I slid into the warm seat

Coreyanne Lutes, Grade 6
East Oldham Middle School, KY

My Monkey

I have many favorite things
To play with all the time
Some of them are passed down
But now they are all mine.

There was a neat monkey
That was given to my sister
But when I laid eyes on it
I hoped that she wouldn't miss her.

So when I took the monkey
I knew that she was mine
Mine and mine forever
Until my sister cried.

But in the very end
I knew that I lucked out
And after a few weeks
I knew she'd never find out.

Avery Jankowski, Grade 6
Woodland Presbyterian School, TN

Look at Me

Watch my branches in the breeze.
Watch the people go by me.
Look at all the trees to go
While I'm here waiting in the snow.
Look at the people come to me
Wanting me to be their Christmas tree.

Haley Beavers, Grade 6
Chapin Middle School, SC

I Remember Football

I remember my first football game…
winning, practicing, getting tackled by ten people.

I remember my first football game…
seeing the flat, green field, watching players run, throwing the ball.

I remember my first football game…
people cheering, people shouting, people clapping.

I remember my first football game.

Alberto Ramirez-Reyes, Grade 5
Sycamore Elementary School, GA

Autumn

Autumn is full of fun for all,
turkey and honey ham is waiting in the hall.
Relatives come from here and there,
as we watch the sun set and smell the beautiful fall air.
This autumn day has gone so fast,
and its time for the hummingbirds to sing goodnight from their nests
and for me it's certainly a rest.
I'm warm and cozy in my bed at night,
till I look outside and shiver at the look of the cold autumn night.

Nicole Zalegowski, Grade 5
Palmetto Christian Academy, SC

I Am Thankful For

Parks that we can play in,
Parents that we can trust,
Foster parents that we can depend on.
Food to eat that nourishes our bodies.
Automobiles that help us get from place to place.
Telephones for talking and staying in touch with one another,
Computers for information and communication
Clothing to make us feel secure and warm
Schools so that we may learn and become more educated.
Most of all I am Thankful for my foster parents,
Nene and Pappy for giving my sisters and me a home when we needed one

Makayla Willhite, Grade 5
Hatfield Elementary School, AR

The Awesome "Red" Color of the Ville

What I like about RED!
Red is an awesome red Cardinal jersey
It feels like a U of L jersey being put on your body.

It looks like a Cardinal player running down the football
field to make a TOUCHDOWN on their opponent.

It sounds like the Cardinals scoring TOUCHDOWNS over and over again
It smells like popcorn in the Papa John Cardinals stadium.
It tastes like BIG RED going down your throat.
RED is an awesome red Cardinal jersey

Demarcus Bailey, Grade 5
Eminence Middle School, KY

I Am a Villain

I am all green and very strong.
I am very buff and disrespectful.
I hate Spiderman.
I get excited when I run in the streets.
Kids are mesmerized by my TV shows.
When I get mad, I break a building.
I love to pound on my chest
When I have won a victory over my enemies.
When someone's life was on the line,
I helped them out.

Maurice Whiters, Grade 5
Lee A Tolbert Community Academy, MO

Christmas Tree

Each layer getting smaller,
Smaller,
Smaller,
To the tiptop of the tree,
Where the sparkling,
Bright,
Golden colored star stood,
Displaying its beauty.

The green ferns sticking out,
Quite straight,
While you place
Green,
Red,
White,
And blue
Ornaments on it to create a color frenzy.

Lastly, placing faded popcorn strings on the,
Now, colorful,
Sparkling,
Christmas tree,
This made the final touch.

Grace McCartha, Grade 6
Chapin Middle School, SC

Candy

Most people love candy,
But if they don't then that's ok with me.
Personally I love all kinds of candy.
My favorite kind of candy is gum.
I love gum.

My taste buds love chocolate,
But my stomach sure doesn't after the third bar.
People love candy.
They love it so much.
It is so good to me and other people.
I LOVE CANDY.

Lynsey Crews, Grade 6
Dyer Elementary & Jr High School, TN

Spectacular Nouns

Nouns! They help you survive.
Proper nouns help you name
specific person, place, or thing.
Common nouns help you name
a particular person, place or thing.
Abstract nouns are your thoughts, feelings, and emotions.
Concrete nouns help you know
that there is something you can use.
Singular nouns are all alone.
Plural nouns identify two or more nouns
that are not alone.
Singular possessive nouns tell you
only one noun owns something.
Plural possessive nouns tell you
more than one noun owns something.
Collective nouns are
different from all the rest; they are nouns in groups.
Oh, yeah a noun!
A noun is a person place or thing
Spectacular nouns, what would we do without you?

Brandy Smalley, Grade 5
Saffell Street Elementary School, KY

I Live on an Army Post in Kentucky

I live on an Army Post in Kentucky where it is cold.
I wonder if we'll move again.
I hear guns out at the range.
I see helicopters above my head.
I want my dad to retire out of the Army.
I live on an Army Post in Kentucky where it is cold.

I pretend that I am in combat with my dad.
I feel sad when my dad leaves.
I touch my dad's dog tags before he leaves.
I worry if my dad is ok.
I cry when my dad leaves.
I live on an Army Post in Kentucky where it is cold.

I understand that my dad protects the U.S.A.
I say the Pledge of Allegiance every morning.
I dream about the war being over.
I try to believe that the war will be over soon.
I hope our soldiers will stay strong.
I live on an Army Post in Kentucky where it is cold.

Toby Keith Rotz, Grade 4
Walker Intermediate School, KY

I Live on a Military Reservation

I pretend not to get upset when my friends PCS.
I feel like I will never keep my friends very long.
I touch my parent's hands every time I go to school.
I worry that my parents will be deployed to war.
I cry when my parent leaves for training.
I live on an Army Reservation at Fort Knox, Kentucky.

Brian Long, Grade 6
Walker Intermediate School, KY

Thank You Mom

Thank you mom, for all the pain you've put up for me.
For digging and digging until you find what I need. Just to make me happy you search and search for my dreams.
Thank you mom, for all the screaming you've thrown in my face.
It definitely teaches me a lesson.
I promise to never do a bad deed on purpose again.
Thank you mom, for only letting me drink soda on Fridays or at parties.
Now my teeth are sparkly clean. Plus, I am very healthy which will make me live longer.
Thank you mom, for making me clean my room.
Now I can actually walk through my room without hurting myself. I'm a lot more organized than before.
Thank you mom, for all the wonderful things you bought for me.
I couldn't live without your gifts. They bring sparkle to my days.
Thank you mom, for all the extremely cute clothes and shoes.
Now I can look like a superstar when I go to school and everywhere else I adventure.
Thank you mom, for cleaning up my problems.
The advice you give me will help me through life.
It helps calm down the heart, even though sometimes the advice is so goofy.
Thank you mom, for keeping me in your thoughts and heart.
You help me believe that if I dream, I'll achieve anything.
Thank you mom, for making me.

Kathleen Keables, Grade 6
East Oldham Middle School, KY

Sensing My Sister's Softball Season

The cloudy white chalked lines drawn on a dusty dirt field catches my attention as I walk through the admission gate. Noticing colorful uniformed bodies taking their place on the brown earth field form a rainbow on the ground.

Listening to cheers and chants squealing "Go Sharkbait!!!" (My sister's nickname) from the blue dugout as it echoes through the air. Hearing the vibrant ding of the metal bat as the yellow ball flies into fair territory brings the spectators to their feet.

Scenting, extra cheesy, butter, popcorn popping inside the concession stand, calls to my taste buds. Detecting hamburgers grilling on an open flame, as hazy smoke fills the air, makes my mouth water.

Savoring an orange, cold Gatorade, quenches my thirst when swished in my mouth. Flavoring spicy melted mozzarella cheese that's been dipped on a nacho chip stings my tongue like a mad bumblebee.

Feeling the scorching heat form the crowded, aluminum bleacher burns my legs as I take my seat. Accidentally fingering the sticky used gum under the bleachers makes my fingers feel germy and gooey.

Experiencing the excitement and joy for my sister makes me proud as she earns a triple for her team!

Kacie Leachman, Grade 6
College View Middle School, KY

The Scary Halloween

One day on a Halloween it was a scary night it was a full moon. The coyotes were howling. This was the day. I was the only one in the yard in Tennessee. It was haunted. I was scared next thing I knew is there are coyotes all around me. I didn't know what to do. I was scared that I would die. I was so scared I wet my pants. I tried to get in the house but it was too late no one could help me. Finally I got the door open that was a scary night but then when I open the Boo! Boo! Boo! That was my dad and Mom was asleep and that's why its called the scary Halloween. Remember never go outside again on a Halloween night by yourself.

Tyre Dillon, Grade 5
West Marion Elementary School, MS

Where I'm From

I'm from sitting on warm toasty sand while gobbling down peanut butter and sprinkle sandwiches.
I'm from zooming through water with the fresh air blowing in my hair.
I'm from flying through the air on a small blue swing scooping the air with my legs to soar higher.
I'm from sleeping in back seats, from waking up to the sight of white walls.
I'm from learning new stuff like how to catch a fish, to opening cans of soda, and how to stroke a cat.
I'm from my family's hugs and kisses.

Bailey Hill, Grade 6
East Oldham Middle School, KY

Dogs

young, old
playful, sleepy, loving
man's best friend forever
all sizes

Daniel Jacob, Grade 6
LA

Hoops

A high pitch whistle starts the game.
Players struggle and scramble,
to scrap up the ball.

Squeak, squeak,
shoes pivoting and turning on a hardwood floor.
Sweat comes out of the player's pores.

The refs are zebras calling the games,
fighting for positions to call fouls, walks, and charges.

Stomping and screaming from the crowd.
Jumping up and down like jack-in-the-boxes,
as the game gets tight.

Swishes and steals round out the game,
as players are fighting for the victory.
Only one team will win, the other,
shall lose as they walk home in defeat.

Davis Mattingly, Grade 5
Greathouse Shryock Traditional Elementary School, KY

Inside a Tree

Inside the tree is a beautiful place.
To see inside one is a dream worth to chase.
With birds chirping,
And squirrels lurking.

Oh, what a beautiful place to be.
From the colorful leaves,
To the buzzing bees.
Oh, I wish you could see!

Nick Evely, Grade 6
Manning Elementary School, SC

Autumn

Horrifying scarecrows guarding the corn
Tangy apples waiting to be picked
Crackling fires that keep us warm
Smells of that fresh apple pie
Steep hills ready for us to roll down
Piles of leaves that reach up to the sky
Long tractor rides rumbling on a rocky road
Sneaky nights on Halloween
Rolling hills that need to be mowed
Deciding on what bright orange pumpkin to carve

Ashley Kirton, Grade 6
Alvaton Elementary School, KY

Devils on 4 Legs

My evil cats — meow meow!
breaking important pictures — crash!
mom yelling, "Stop that!!"
Cats freeze
skidding across kitchen tiled floor
Evil Cats.

Running to devour food
Making a mess
bigger than a pile of garbage
Munching loudly on food
eating 24/7
Evil Cats.

Destroys anything in their path — so dangerous!
Leaping onto my bed
scraping and scratching
my bedspread to a million pieces — little devils
Thinking, why are they so vicious
Evil Cats.

Jason York, Grade 4
Roberta Tully Elementary School, KY

I Am Haunted

I was haunted
By the gross ghost
Coming to get me
When it was the right time
Taking me away and I would never see my mom again!

I am now haunted
By the creepy clowns
With their makeup
On their faces and their
Nasty smiles smiling at me.

I will be haunted
By me getting lost
In a dark dreadful
Forest nothing to eat
And spiders creeping and
Crawling around me in the forest.

I am haunted

Tyrei Hanlon, Grade 5
Eminence Middle School, KY

Lord Mystery

O Lord you have a mystery that nobody knows
They can't even see is when it snows
They can't even hear it when the wind blows the only way that
You will know is to open His word and let Him show
And open Your soul and let it flow

Bobbie Jo Bridgewater, Grade 6
Tri-County Christian School, MO

Exciting Fall

F alling leaves
A utumn
L unch
L oving family

I ncredible
S unday football

A dventure
W onderful
E ating turkey
S upper
O utside
M oon
E xciting

Hunter Johnson, Grade 5
Trinity Day School, GA

Diving

Holding on hard
Way up high
Loosening grip
Ghastly gasping sighs
Falling far
Diving down
Swimming swiftly
So relieved

Madison Johnson, Grade 6
Blackmon Road Middle School, GA

Playful Tigers

Twenty tigers toying
and telling tales.
Toppling, tumbling and tapping,
as they roll down the hills.

Jordyn Baxley, Grade 4
Crossville Christian School, TN

My Puppy Sadie

cute
rowdy
crazy
white
lazy sometimes
lovable
fluffy
funny
looks like a snowball
and most of all…
Beautiful
and
Cute

SADIE

Kaylee Corwin, Grade 6
Armorel Elementary School, AR

My Cat

There once was a cat
Who lived in a barn.
We brought him home
And gave him some yarn.

His name is Baby Bear.
We give him much care
Like love, food, water,
And we wash his hair.

When he was little
I gave him a bottle,
But now that he's older
He loves to act like a model.

He prances round
And up and down
And he tries to get
My attention.

Lauren Navarro, Grade 4
Northeast Baptist School, LA

Snake/Mouse

snake
slimy, scaly
hissing, squirming, slithering
colorful, spotted, small, long tail
running, climbing, squeaking
soft, smooth
mouse

Emily Quatkemeyer, Grade 5
Walton Verona Elementary School, KY

Shanika

S hy
H ate to be late for school
A nswers questions a lot
N ice to others
I nstead of being late, be great
K issable
A lways good

Shanika Wallace, Grade 6
Mark Twain Elementary School, MO

Dragons

Dragons
Majestic, beautiful, powerful
Dragons
True, real, non-fiction
Dragons
Cool, ancient, amazing
Dragons
Kind, gentle, may get angry
Dragons

Marie-Caroline Finke, Grade 6
Montessori Community School, NC

War

Air Force high in the sky
My question is why?
Why is there war?
Well right now I'm wondering
Why there is no reason
For people to be giving.
Thanks to the people
In the wars,
We should respect you
More and More.

Kirstin Kulus, Grade 4
Parkview Elementary School, MO

Special Season

Autumn is my favorite season
For many different kinds of reasons.
Orange and yellow leaves around
Pumpkins lying on the ground.

Scarecrows hanging in a corn maze
The smell of turkey and cranberry glaze.

Here are a few things, you see
That make autumn special to me.

Sara Hensley, Grade 5
Sullivan Elementary School, TN

Daddy's Shoulders

Sitting up high on Daddy's shoulder
I look up and then down.
There are so many people around.
It is just too scary
(Until the day I am older)
Which is why for now I feel very safe,
Sitting up high on Daddy's shoulder.

Destiny Dillion, Grade 6
Benton County School of the Arts, AR

Math

M ost fun
A dding and subtracting
T eaching us well
H ard working

Tina White, Grade 4
Lewis Vincent Elementary School, LA

Brain/Pinky

Brain
smart, serious
thinking, planning, writing
smart-alec, genius, nitwit, runner
playing, running, wandering
funny, insane
Pinky

Matt Roberts, Grade 5
Briarwood Christian School, AL

Shopping

When my mom told me we were going shopping
I started hopping, and wasn't stopping

My mom grabbed the cash
We were out the door in a flash

When we got to the mall
I wanted to ball

Cause I forgot my stash
Of baby-sitting cash!!!

Ali McManus, Grade 5
Graham Elementary School, AL

Days

Days can be happy or they can be sad
Hopefully all my days I will be glad
They can be fun and very fantastic
Or they can feel as long as stretched elastic
Some days you'll be sad that the day is done
And other times you'll think that was no fun
But no matter how good or how bad the day ends
Just remember you will always have your friends

Lauren English, Grade 6
Holy Trinity School, KY

You Can Hate

You can hate an awful person
Who is ugly inside
You can insult a person
You don't like
But that won't make the person better
So why waste your energy?

Tiajma Poindexter, Grade 5
Hunter GT Magnet Elementary School, NC

What American Means to Me

America, America,
Born in 1776,
Lucky land for all,
My parents came searching for freedom and opportunities.
Along came the dreams of 4 children,
Mom says she's blessed to be an American,
Dad says America has given him hope.

America, America,
Born in America,
Lucky to be an American,
I have freedom and opportunities,
Education within my reach,
Pray to have the American dream,
Just like my parents.
God Bless America!

Brittany Nwokeji, Grade 5
Grahamwood Elementary School, TN

Ballet Shoes

With soft pink leather,
The dancer makes an elegant line across the stage;
Shaped to fit her foot and her foot only,
The magnificent pattern designs her feet;
Her toes only protected by a thin gel pad,
The ribbons tied tightly,
She rises up,
She looks like the empire state building;
Gliding beautifully across the stage,
The familiar noise is all she hears,
The soft pitter patter of the dancers' feet.
Her long strong legs covered by pink tights,
A tutu that looked as if she stepped into a cloud,
As I watch a tear trickles down my face,
I'm lost in the story.

Claire Draughn, Grade 5
JJ Jones Intermediate School, NC

Trees

Trees are a natural part of nature.
Trees are home to many different kinds of animals.
All trees are different.
Some trees are big and some are small.
Trees look different every season.
Trees can live a very long time.
Trees are used for many different things.
The worst thing about trees is that it gives our teachers paper
So that we can have homework.

Madison Wicker, Grade 6
Chapin Middle School, SC

I Love My Army Parent

I live on an Army Reservation at Fort Knox, Kentucky.
I hear the tanks firing at the ranges.
I wonder if I will always live here.
I see the army bird.
I want to know what it is like to have my own home
I live on an Army Reservation at Fort Knox, Kentucky

I live on an Army Reservation at Fort Knox, Kentucky
I pretend not to get upset when my mom's gone far away.
I feel like I will never keep my friends very long.
I touch my parents hand when I go to school.
I worry that my parents will be deployed.
I cry when my mom left.
I live on an Army Reservation at Fort Knox, Kentucky

I live on an Army Reservation at Fort Knox, Kentucky.
I understand that I must support my family and the military.
I say that one day I will be a soldier.
I dream that peace will become my future.
I try to do my best at everything.
I hope my future is free and secure.
I live on an Army Reservation at Fort Knox, Kentucky.

Cheetara Bing, Grade 5
Walker Intermediate School, KY

Fish

We live far, far down
You might like us for dinner
We breath with our gills
Mariclare Shirey, Grade 4
Briarwood Christian School, AL

Pandabear

Pandabear
Cute, fuzzy
Run, climb, eat
My mom loves him
Hamster
Brendan McKenzie, Grade 6
Small World Academy, WV

The Fairy

There was once a fairy named Mary,
She was tall and very hairy,
She had lost her shoe,
Didn't know what to do,
She found it and went out with Larry.
Joshua Tye, Grade 6
Armorel Elementary School, AR

Mr. Bee

There once was a small bee
Who had a crush on me.
My, oh my
How he could fly
I'm going to ask him to tea.

He came so happy and proud
His voice was clear and loud.
He was so dreamy
He was so beamy
So we held hands and walked around.
Rachel Lehr, Grade 5
Berryville Elementary School, AR

My Horse

Running fast
Rain or shine
I can ride her
'Cause she's mine.

I like to ride
Her every day.
I feed her oats,
Apples, carrots, hay.

I like my horse.
No, I should say,
I love her, of course,
And she says, "Neigh!"
Bailey Harper, Grade 4
Cleveland Elementary School, OK

The Beach in Florida

The roaring blue-green waves crashing against the sandy beach,
The pink-shelled crabs legs in front of my face making me smile big,
I can hardly wait to enjoy
The annoying seagulls hovering over my head making me feel in danger,
The cute little kids screaming at the huge waves coming, excitement ringing in their voices
The nasty smell of salt from the ocean sticks on me,
The odor of dead jelly fish on the beach create a disgusting smell,
The salty ocean water slides in my open mouth,
The seaweed particles accumulate into my mouth and taste horrible,
My hands smoothly rolls off the soft grainy sand,
Walking anxiously into the rapid waves with my sister,
Excited as a dog with juicy, crisp, warm and sweet piece of bacon.
Kendall Powers, Grade 6
College View Middle School, KY

I Am

I am a left-handed boy who plays the drums.
I wonder why drums are called drums.
I hear the rat-a-tat-tat boom boom of the drums.
I see the whir of the drumsticks fly around the drum set.
I want to be the best drummer ever.
I am a left-handed boy who plays the drums.

I pretend I'm the drumming king.
I feel the after blast of the snare drum.
I touch the smooth pine wood which makes the drums.
I worry if there will be any more wooden drum sets, just electric drums.
I cry at the thought that drums were not invented.
I am a left handed boy who plays the drums.

I understand that drumming is loud.
I say that more people should play the drums.
I dream of being a professional drummer.
I try to be the best I can at playing the drums.
I hope to become a drumming legend.
I am a left-handed boy who plays the drums.
Karl Hill, Grade 6
R D and Euzelle P Smith Middle School, NC

Mother Nature

I feel the breeze and hear the leaves rustling
I feel as if I'm part of the earth or even Mother Nature
The squirrels are jumping from tree to tree
I know there are little creatures under my feet
I am barefoot, the grass tickles my skin
My body is swarmed by the scent of sweet nature's smells
I hear the neighbor's dogs, their voices are saying Mother Nature prayers
The birds chirping soothes my rapid mind
Mother Nature is talking to me only to me at this time
She speaks through all these sounds around me
My mother calls me for it is time for dinner
Walking to the door I start forgetting Mother Nature's voice
But I know I will be back again
Taylor Thames, Grade 6
Howard Middle School, GA

Tractor

Tractor, tough like a tank,
terrific, thunderous, titanic, tight lines.
It tips and trips over the treacherous terrain
tearing through tremendous trees with mighty tines.
Elias Brady, Grade 4
Crossville Christian School, TN

Snap, Crackle, Pop

I love it because of the touchdowns
The interceptions, jukes, and sacks
I love it because it's a time
When you let all your anger out on one person
You hit anyone you see, hear, or feel
You catch every ball that comes near you
I love it because of last second wins
I love making amazing catches
Hardly keeping two feet in bounds
I love making the hard hits and forcing fumbles
I love seeing the sweat drip down my face
Like rain falling from the sky
When you see sweat on you it tells everyone, "I love this game!"
And when you make those gut wrenching hits
Even the horrible calls the referees make
I love all the touchdown dances
This funny game that I'm talking about is football
And these are all the reasons I love it
Jacob Hook, Grade 6
East Oldham Middle School, KY

Ballet

A happy feeling, a nervous feeling
An excited, anxious, wonderful feeling
Lights from the stage ceiling, cast shadows on the floor.
Pink, blue, purple, green, black costumes

I wonder who invented ballet?
How long do professionals train?
How do the girls or boys
Remember all the steps?

Very faint thumping as they land
Soft music in the background
Clapping of the people
Softly mumbling
1,2,3,4 1,2,3,4,
Of the teacher.

Pink shoes, pretty costumes
Fresh, clean smell of the ballerinas
Beautiful as a lily
Graceful movements slim figures
Well practiced moves

Beautiful as a lily, beautiful as a lily, beautiful as a lily
Lillianne Nelson, Grade 4
Price Elementary School, KY

Horse

A horse of course
I wish I had a horse.

Clippity clap, clippity clap
That would be the best sound to hear.

As black as a piece of coal.
Like a storm cloud thundering.
Spirit would be his name.
And happily hopping over the high fence
Would be his game.

Of course, I am not getting a horse.
My mom thinks I am too small.

But let me win the lottery.
And there will be horses for all!
Sydney Skanes, Grade 5
Greathouse Shryock Traditional Elementary School, KY

Blue

Blue dolphins swimming so gracefully
Through the blue, foamy, wavy ocean.
Blue clouds,
Hanging from the sky
Just waiting to BURST
With little rain drops falling from the sky.
Blue birds
Flying through the sky
Singing with such a beautiful sound
With colorful blue feathers,
What a lovely bird!
Blue cotton candy so sugary and puffy!
When you stick it in your mouth,
You might say,
"Hey, where did it go?"
Nobody knows, but it sure tastes good!
Without the color blue,
There would be no dolphins, clouds, blue birds,
Or blue cotton candy,
So it's a good thing we have the color
BLUE!!
Lindsay Salvadalena, Grade 6
East Oldham Middle School, KY

Sunset

It's where the sky kisses the grass covered hills
It's where the warm day feeling melts away
It's where the dark soul wolf cries to the moon
It's where my eyes drip down into space
It's where the sun goes to bed
It's where the moon darkens the sky
It's where the sun keeps us from total coal fields
Lydia J. Tackett, Grade 5
Bloomfield Elementary School, KY

Sugar Glider

Sugar Gliders that I love
Hanging on a tree above
Small like a rat.
Cousins with a squirrel.
Monkey feet.
Grip like a tiger.

Tabbetha Dixon, Grade 5
North Middle School, TN

Nature

Nature is a wonderful thing —
With deer and wolf
And birds that sing.

From flower to tree,
From bug to bee,
The sweet smell in the air
Of a newborn bear.

The frogs in the pond;
The bees in the hive;
Nature is wonderful
When it all comes alive!

And last of all,
The precious stream
That feeds all the animals
That howl and sing!

Anna Pierce, Grade 6
Scotts Creek Elementary School, NC

Dogs

A dog is a wondrous thing,
When you get one as a pet,
I suggest you take it to the vet,
Just don't let it go out in the street
To get caught in a dogcatcher's net,
Because it might get put in the pound,
And by you it may never be found!

Kristen Morningstar, Grade 4
Legacy Christian School, OK

Fall

F resh air
A ll different colors
L eaves fall
L ovely days

Shareba Broadnax, Grade 4
Moyock Elementary School, NC

Precious Waterfall

Precious waterfall
Foaming up at the bottom
Making peaceful sounds

Leah Martin, Grade 4
Briarwood Christian School, AL

The Cat!

Hey! Do you see the cat?
He's wearing a big red hat.
His clothes are black and bold.
As he marches out in the cold.
His mother said come inside.
So he went smiling with pride!

Keslie Cagle, Grade 4
Brilliant Elementary School, AL

My Friends

M y friends
Y ou make me laugh you are so

F unny
R emarkable friends
I love you just the way you are
E verlasting friendship
N o one is left behind
D oesn't matter what we do
S o that's why I hang with you

Sarah Goudy, Grade 6
Martin Elementary School, WV

Trumpet/Clarinet

Trumpet
shiny, small
buzzing, trumpeting, pushing
valves, slides, buttons, reeds
blowing, squeaking, soothing
tall, black
Clarinet

Connor Armstrong, Grade 5
Briarwood Christian School, AL

My Dog Chloe

My dog Chloe
is a Teacup Yorkie
she is a female
and she has a tiny tail

she's about 5 pounds
and she'll let out a howl
she is very defensive
and she wasn't that expensive

she is very lovable
and oh so cuddlable
she will lay in your bed
and you can barely see her head

when you leave the house
and walk through the door
she will get excited
and run around galore!

Marissa Romeo, Grade 5
Woodland Elementary School, KY

Dolphin

Dolphin
gray, pretty
trick, swim, jump
caring, teaching, exploring, smiling
They like the ocean.
Mammal

Diarius Keys, Grade 4
East Jones Elementary School, MS

A Poet

I wish that I could be a poet,
it's really simple don't you know it.
I'll write a poem that really rings,
about the Earth's sweet rain it brings.
About the sun, the moon, the stars,
maybe even the planet Mars.
I wish that I could be a poet,
it's really simple don't you know it.

Kelly Miles, Grade 4
DaySpring Academy, AL

Gatorade

Looks like colored liquid
Sounds like swishing, spilling waves
Tastes like tangy flavored water
Feels like sticky liquid
Smells like fruity water

Judson Hawk, Grade 5
Briarwood Christian School, AL

My 10th Birthday

I wake up in the morning,
it's my birthday!

My mom comes running in
singing a birthday song.
It's my birthday!

I put on a smile, because
it's my birthday!

She tells me to put
on my clothes, we're going
out to eat.
It's my birthday.

When we get home,
the lights were off,
and everyone yells,
Surprise!

It's my birthday!

Can't wait to do it again!

Lurlethia Jones, Grade 6
Saint Paul School, TN

Dustin

D own the street I was playing a game.
U ntil my mom came and took me home.
S till, I want to play the game.
T his was not fun, but I went anyway.
I didn't know I wasn't supposed to go down the street.
N ow you know why I am grounded.

Dustin Lambert, Grade 5
Byrns L Darden Elementary School, TN

All Star State Tournament

I hear the ball hit the bat
Cleats crunching into the ground
Balls popping gloves
People roaring in stands
Clattering on benches
Me and my teammates cheering in the dugout
Umps yelling

I'm getting ready to bat
Coach gives me signs to swing the bat
Then "BAM"
The ball flies into right field
"FIRST
SECOND
THIRD
HOME"
"HOME RUN"

Courtney Galvan, Grade 6
East Oldham Middle School, KY

Shoes and Girls

The choices! The choices! All the little voices,
Saying, "Buy me!" "No, she'll buy me, you'll see!"
Ah! The red, the blue, what should I do?
The green, the black, what a stack!
The purple, the pink, what do you think?
One pair, two pair, three pair, four, oh no! Give me more!
Tennis shoes, flats, and heels, maybe even some with wheels!
Some to walk, some to run, some for just having fun!
I've tried them all, from wall to wall,
Which should I get? There's many a set!
After all this fun, maybe I'll go home with none!

Gretchen Lund, Grade 6
St Francis Xavier School, AL

Happiness

Happiness is lavender.
It smells like my mom's double-layer chocolate cake.
It tastes like pancakes cooking with butter and syrup.
It sounds like the school band playing: "Go P-High!"
It feels like a cuddly puppy.
It looks like a feathery, fluffed up pillow.
Happiness is love from your family.

Kaila Smith, Grade 4
Pines Elementary School, NC

Brother from Another Mother

The person I admire the most
Is my brother.
He always has my back.
Sometimes we wrestle
Or go swimming.
I play pranks on him.
Once I put whip cream on his face.
He used to be on the swim team
And he is a great diver.
I plan to go to college.
My mother will be so proud of me.
My brother is majoring in engineering.
He is a great role-model
And my playmate.

Kareem Sanders, Grade 5
Lee A Tolbert Community Academy, MO

The Not So Great Christmas Kiss

When I woke up on Christmas, my heart was pumping with joy.
But, then I got nervous; have I been a good boy?
Have I done my service to the good Lord above?
Have I shown everyone I know my love?
My mom, my dad, even my sister?
That got me scared so I went and kissed her.
As soon as I did it, I knew she was mad.
Oh, and trust me, I wasn't real glad; this was very BAD!
She took a step forward; I took a step back,
and then for a second everything went black.
When I opened my eyes, I realized this wasn't what it seemed.
As it turns out, this was all just a dream!

Berry Brooks, Grade 6
Woodland Presbyterian School, TN

I Am

I am a normal boy who likes mythical creatures.
I wonder if dragons ever existed.
I hear a Phoenix caw in the night.
I see a Griffin fly into the sun.
I want to have a real dragon.
I am a normal boy who likes mythical creatures.

I pretend I have wings to fly.
I feel the smooth scales of a dragon.
I touch the pages of a book to read.
I worry about pollution problems in the world.
I cry about animal species extinction.
I am a normal boy who likes mythical creatures.

I understand that trees should not be cut down.
I say everyone should respect nature.
I dream about ridding the world of pollution.
I try to recycle as much as I can.
I hope people will make an effort to protect all animals.
I am a normal boy who likes mythical creatures.

Andrew Antony, Grade 6
R D and Euzelle P Smith Middle School, NC

Fall

F alling leaves
A re so colorful
L ying on the
L ovely grass.

Evan Beardsley, Grade 5
First Flight Elementary School, NC

God Cares for Me

If God watches flowers grow
If God made a buzzing bee
Since God made the sun glow
I know he'll care for me.

God knows what I'm thinking of
He sees what I cannot see
He knows everything and anything
I know he dearly loves me.

Rebecca Snyder, Grade 6
Pleasants County Middle School, WV

Water

Water trickles down a pipe!
Water rushes down a river!
Water is an important source.
Water has no end.
Water is a special thing.
I am so glad we have water!

Kelsey Baller, Grade 5
St Michael Parish School, WV

Happy or Sad?

If you're sad cheer up
if you're happy stay that way
We love happy and we hate sad
So if you're sad turn your frown
upside down.

Angie Box, Grade 4
Brilliant Elementary School, AL

Poems

Lines and stanzas
rhyming or plain,
nouns, cats, and things
poems, poems, poems

Love and happiness
sorrow or sadness
feelings or emotions
poems, poems, poems

Legends and myths
stories and tales
made into short, sweet
poems, poems, poems

Abby Mercer, Grade 6
Center Place Restoration School, MO

War

War is gunshots and swords.
War is fighting and wounds.
War is terrible, endless crying.
War is World War Three that broke out between my brother and me.
War is bloody and scary and ruthless.
War will be over.
But it could last for as long as life.

Kayla Richardson-Piche, Grade 4
Montessori Community School, NC

Christmastime

Soft, puffy snow slowly drifting, blanketing the ground,
Snow angels and snowmen scattered all over the yard,
A Christmas tree sprinkled with luminous, colorful lights
and special, memory filled ornaments that have been collected over the years;
The grand fireplace ablaze, warming the surroundings,
The aroma of spices coming from a large pot of steaming wassail
which comes out each and every year,
Roars of laughter echoing through the house,
Happiness, joy, ecstasy, and love during Christmas —
You cannot get enough.
Stockings waiting to be stuffed with Christmastime surprises,
Children knowing the tree skirt would soon be overflowing with presents,
All the children go to bed, dreams of candy canes in their heads,
knowing Santa soon will come,
As the jingle of Santa's sleigh bells die down, it's morning.
The children rush down the stairs with the tired adults shuffling along,
Stockings are emptied and the floor is littered with wrapping paper;
Gasps of astonishment fill the air;
Cries of delight resound from the adults and the children,
Everyone loving Christmastime.

Jai Daniels, Grade 5
JJ Jones Intermediate School, NC

Basketball

Basketball starts with the referee both teams jumping very high
To hit the ball to one of their guys
Passing down the court they run
"Wow" It looks like it is so much fun
Players trying to set up a play the forward gets the ball and runs
Throws to the point guard and the blocking has begun
The coaches call the first timeout they are trying to teach them to run a play
But yelling is never the way
So he gently takes them by the hand
And hopes they will all understand
Timeout is over so they take their places
Defense gets all in their faces
The ball just gets thrown in
And the play setup has to begin
The forward sticks to fingers high
Then the guard goes running by
And makes two points
And the crowd jumps high

Ashley Walter, Grade 6
Mayflower Middle School, AR

The Ocean

The salty ocean
It looks like white, fluffy clouds
Splashing against rocks

Tyler Harris, Grade 4
Briarwood Christian Elementary School, AL

My Class

My class can be a mumbling mess
or as quiet as a mouse
we have Kelly and Kylie, and me
Boom, crash, bang a book just fell
on Connor's toe
Andrew's hand went up I wonder
what he wants
"Mrs. Goldsmith may we have a snack?"
"What do you think?" asked Mrs. Goldsmith
"No" said Andrew
"Correct" said Mrs. Goldsmith
walking down the hall plip, plop
"No!" not the cockroaches we say
"Yes" Mrs. Robison says
The day is almost halfway done
Waiting for Mrs. Goldsmith to say
"Kids get your jackets and let's go!"
We go to our other classes
Then we come back staring at the clock
waiting for the bell "Ding Ding Dong"

Caroline Gosser, Grade 5
Greathouse Shryock Traditional Elementary School, KY

Something to Remember

When summer fades,
And fall comes to play,
It seems like an autumn,
Wonderful day.

The month that autumn comes,
Of course is September,
The exciting events in that month,
Are something to remember.

The next month in fall is October,
All its festivities
Halloween and festivals
And all the great activities.

November is the month of Thanksgiving
And the feast of all feasts.
All are invited,
Man and beast!

Sadly autumn ends in the month of December,
But the great time of fall,
Is something to remember.

Jenna Stinchcomb, Grade 5
Trinity Day School, GA

Love

It is such a strong emotion
You never know if it is real
It could be fake or an attraction
You never know what you may feel

You could be lonely and
Just want someone to hold you
Someone to care for you
When you are feeling blue

You could feel that you need it
When you don't need it at all
You could feel you need it
Because you feel left out
Because all of your friends have it

Can you feel love maybe
So, what is the point of this emotion
It can give people hope and a
Reason to live
It causes others destruction and pain.

Kymberlyn M. Byrd, Grade 6
Haynes Academy for Advanced Studies, LA

Dream Island

As the cool diamond blue water
touched my ankles I felt calm, relaxed
and I felt that I was the only one on
this amazing world. I could feel the wind
slowly lift my hair that was once upon
my shoulders sway in the breeze.
The squawk of the seagulls fills my head like a lullaby
my mother would sing to me
so I would go to sleep
Farther and farther I walk,
my prune like feet feel warm
from the tiny individual
grains of sand.

Maya Mishel Shuler, Grade 4
St Thomas More School, NC

First Ride on the Beast

The tension thickened as I stop to take my turn,
The line condensed as cabs were filled,
Slowly the pace gradually increased,
The air around me is chilled,
Darkness comes
Goose bumps are exposed by fear,
Screams are all around me,
I close my eyes as we go up and down, twist and turn,
Finally, I feel decreased speed,
Eyes open, we stop with a small jerk,
I get off and can barely walk

Kassie Fogarty, Grade 5
Cline Elementary School, KY

Stars

Have you ever looked upon a star,
And think of how so very far
They are from Earth?
And all of them you see
Were made just for you and me.
Josh Owens, Grade 5
EA Harrold Elementary School, TN

4th of July

Fireworks, colorful
lighting, running, watching
cheering, screaming, covering, playing
Independence
Emily Huddleston, Grade 6
Stuart Middle School, KY

Blake

I am a chef named Blake
I like to make chocolate cake
I do not like white
It gives me a fright
In the kitchen I like to bake.
Blake Holt, Grade 4
Judsonia Elementary School, AR

The Beauty of the Ocean

The waves were flowing beautifully
as they ran to the shore,
and walked back to the ocean.
Sage Jordan, Grade 5
American Heritage Academy, GA

Here Comes Fall

Comes in October
Leafy brown and cold weather
Leaves falling off trees
Connor King, Grade 4
Briarwood Christian School, AL

Thunder Storms

Bright lightning pounding rain.
The thunder storms are very late.
Roaring of the winds as the beating
Showers roar against the roof.
I fear not these terrible thunder storms.
Blake Eddy, Grade 4
Brilliant Elementary School, AL

Candy

C hocolate
A nd
N utty
D elicious and
Y ummy!
Jason McCabe, Grade 5
First Flight Elementary School, NC

My Loving Mommy

She's always there for me
Even when I cry
It's hard to see
But every day that I have been alive
I love her
She's my loving mommy
And always will be.
Emily Newton, Grade 6
St Teresa's School, GA

God/Satan

God
victorious, faithful
conquering, watching, helping
grace, love, father of lies, devil
deceiving, destroying, tempting
liar, terrible
Satan
Molly Lattner, Grade 5
Briarwood Christian School, AL

Ode to Pretzels

oh, pretzels
you make me thirsty,
but I like to eat you
you can have anything on you.
you make my mouth water
oh, pretzels
you are so tasty
Cortnee Gammons, Grade 6
Dyer Elementary & Jr High School, TN

Fall

F resh chilly air
A utumn
L eaves
L ovely scarecrows
Zenaida Ramos, Grade 4
Moyock Elementary School, NC

It's Summer Break

I'll be bored today
I'll be bored tomorrow
For, it's summer break
I know it sounds a little weird,
But that's really just the case.
My friends are gone
And moved away
And now I'm all alone.
Oh how I wish that summer break
Would just leave me be.
And so summer break
Bores me
As you can plainly see
Adrianna Rose Young, Grade 4
Lynn Fanning Elementary School, AL

My God

My God is mighty,
My God is strong,
My God is sweet
With His everlasting song!
Jolie Carpenter, Grade 4
First Assembly Christian School, AL

Little Bird

When the white blanket falls,
and that one bird calls,
I know that it's that time
of the white winter chime.
When the winter's so deep,
that little bird will creep,
with his beaming red,
there is nothing to dread.
When the little bird comes near,
I feel there is nothing to fear.
On that black little perch,
is where he will lurch.
He will come here very often,
even when the snow will soften.
When he will leave I will have a tear,
but I know he'll be here next year.
Meredith Roethling, Grade 6
Wayne Country Day School, NC

Chocolate Molten Cakes

Molten
Gooey, goodness
Slurp the cool black cherry sauce
Take in the scrumptious aroma
Warm cakes
Catherine Duncan, Grade 6
Southwest Middle School, AR

Listening

L isten
I nstead
S topping all
T hings and
E ncouraging
N ew experiences
Abby Shirey, Grade 5
Briarwood Christian School, AL

Skate Park/Beauty Parlor

Skate Park
fast, vertical
crashing, breaking, spinning
ramps, boards/perfume, hair dryers
sitting, chatting, watching
boring, non-athletic
Beauty Parlor
Cayman Frederick, Grade 5
Briarwood Christian School, AL

The Ocean
The ocean is a beautiful sanctuary with its calm water
as still as a sleeping baby in her mother's arms.
Peaceful, thrilling, breezeful, and clear.
At the same time it's pure vacation fun!

Hannah Gulledge, Grade 6
Briarwood Christian School, AL

Reflections
As I walk and listen to the breeze
and the movement on the ground
from the orange and yellow leaves
hearing the bird chirp and sing
and the pit pat they make flapping their wings

The splish splash of the water moving around
the dink dank of the rocks on the ground
I look in the water and what I see
A girl in the lake that looks like me

Me playing in the fields way out yonder
from home to there is where I've wonder
I blinked my eyes and now I'm gone
I'm still by the lake the lake by my home

Marquisia Wilson, Grade 5
Pembroke Elementary School, NC

Thanksgiving
The tree colors are changing, Hey look, there's some red.
And some orange up there, way above my head.
A cool wind blows, Brrrr, What a chill!
But I feel warm inside, it's time for the meal.
The turkey so moist, the yams so sweet,
It's all so good, it just can't be beat.
Finally, I yawned and stood up straight,
I couldn't believe it, the meal was so great!
After that I ran to the door.
I played with the neighbors, that was no bore.
We played football 'til we could play no more,
We smiled and laughed and had fun galore!
Then it was bedtime, Dad tucked in the sheets.
I dreamed of the turkey and those super sweet beets.

Jesse Haynes, Grade 5
Skiatook Intermediate Elementary School, OK

Brothers
If you're like me you know it's hard with an older brother.
They like to make fun of you until you yell MOTHER!
They hit you and make fun of you,
while you scream and cry boo hoo.
He can be sweet and can be mean,
but chooses to be sweet when he is seen.
Even though he can be mean,
he is my brother and I love him!!

Hannah Brown, Grade 6
Briarwood Christian School, AL

When I Think of Autumn
When I think of autumn,
I think of being surrounded by trees
And jumping in leaves.
When I think of autumn,
I think of the fields
and the good food on Thanksgiving.
That's why I think of autumn.
When I think of autumn, I think of…
Playing with my friends
and meeting all my grandparents, aunts, uncles,
and my cousins,
That's why I think of autumn.

Chase Shimakonis, Grade 5
Palmetto Christian Academy, SC

Limitless
Writing is expressive
Writing is excessive
Exaggeration
Persuasion
Creativity is essential
Sometimes determining one's potential

Mystery, history, comedy
Any topic your heart desires
Whether it impresses or inspires
Imagination is the key when you are a writer like me
Exposing talent with a fantastic ballad
Or just a simple haiku
The sky isn't even the limit to where it can take you

Erica Sawyer, Grade 6
Westchester Country Day School, NC

A Day in the Army Life of Chris
I live on an Army Post at Fort Knox, Kentucky.
I wonder if I will ever go back to Fort Irwin, California.
I hear the planes at the Air Field.
I see the men and women in uniforms.
I want my dad to return from Iraq safely.
I live on an Army Post at Fort Knox, Kentucky.

I pretend to play war like my dad.
I feel excited that my dad is finally coming home.
I have touched the tanks on this post.
I worry I'd we could be attacked by terrorists.
I cry when my dad says his good-byes when he deploys.
I live on an Army Post at Fort Knox, Kentucky.

I understand that I have to be strong for my family.
I say that we are proud to be an American.
I dream that our country will always be safe.
I try to respect everyone.
I hope to be as strong as my dad.
I live on an Army Post at Fort Knox, Kentucky.

Christopher Kennedy, Grade 6
Walker Intermediate School, KY

Fall

Crunchy leaves falling
Jack-o'-lanterns and scarecrows
Crisp cool air blowing
Madison Simpson, Grade 5
Walton Verona Elementary School, KY

Chicken

Chicken
Small, short
Walk, cluck, nibble
Eating, stinking, tasting, laying
Chicken tastes really great!
Chick
Katelyn Hinton, Grade 4
East Jones Elementary School, MS

Best Friends

Best friends are like two
peas in a pod.
Best friends are helpful
to each other.
Best friends are as the
sun shining down.
Best friends is a star
smiling at you.
Best friends is the
best of all.
Best friends is like
a waterfall.
Best friends are like
roller coasters.
Best friends are cool
as a butterfly.
Best friends are like
a fairs wheel.
Best friends are
the best.

Gala Milholen, Grade 5
Clarksburg School, TN

Pigs

Looks like a pink blob
Sounds like my grandfather snoring
Tastes like bacon
Feels like a fuzzy stuffed animal
Smells likc a smelly barn
Olivia B. Lauderdale, Grade 5
Briarwood Christian School, AL

All for You

If I could, I'd give the world to you.
Maybe even the sun and the moon.
No matter what you do,
I'd give it all to you.
Taylor Lassley, Grade 6
Armorel Elementary School, AR

Holiday

The holiday is here,
time to go.
Phone is ringing,
Carolers singing.
Relatives arriving,
Kids yelling.
food on table,
People eating.

It is the next holiday,
People yelling.
Kids fighting.
Moms saying stop.
Dogs barking,
Cats hissing
Holidays are over.
I am sad.
Ashley Blevins, Grade 6
Rocky Comfort Elementary School, MO

Why to Never Be Late

Sally walked into the house
She was late
Her mom was waiting.
Sally tried to hide,
To sneak,
To tiptoe,
To go unseen.
Sally thought she was going to make it.
She walked to her room,
Quietly,
Slowly,
Cautiously,
Her mom jumped out and scared Sally.
It seemed her mom was everywhere,
Behind the door,
Under the bed,
Beneath the floorboards,
Behind the sink.
Screaming at Sally for
BREAKING THE CURFEW!
Cannon Palms, Grade 6
St Mary's School, SC

Fall Is Here

It's time for fall.
The holidays are close.
It's getting colder.
Tell summer, "Adios."

Here are my warm clothes.
The leaves are orange, red, yellow, too.
So fall I say,
"How do you do?"

Joseph Eid, Grade 4
Cleveland Elementary School, OK

Sports

S oftball
P aintball
O lympics
R ock climbing
T ennis
S wimming
Sophie Schmidt, Grade 4
St Thomas More School, NC

Fishing with Dad

Down at the river
A muddy shore
Just Dad and I
All alone
There's a can of worms by my foot
I cast that pole
Feel a little tug
Catch a big fish
Skip a few stones
Get on home
Bust through the door
How many did you get?
A few catfish
A little bit of bass
We do some cleaning
We throw away the scraps
Wash our hands
After dinner I tell Dad
I had a good time
I go to bed
It was a good day
Rocky Wood, Grade 5
Wright City Middle School, MO

Lonely Night

It's a lonely night.
In this cold, cold world.
It's a lonely night.
In this manly world.
Girl keep your head up!
Shaterian Malone, Grade 6
Poland Jr High School, LA

Death on a Cross

He carried the cross along the way.
He knew He was to die today.
They nailed Him to the cross to die,
As the people shouted crucify.
They placed a thorn crown on His head.
Jesus knew He was to be dead.
As He took His last breath,
That was Savior's death.
The deed is done,
God had won.

Kaitlyn King, Grade 6
Grace Lutheran School, AR

Me

Nicola
Sweet, cute, smart, friendly
Sibling of Alexia
Lover of dogs and reading
Who feels happiness
Who needs family, friends, and dogs
Who gives love, respect, and friendship
Who fears clowns
Who would like to see puppies all around me
Oklahoma City
deAngeli

Nicola deAngeli, Grade 4
Cleveland Elementary School, OK

I Believe in Baseball

I believe in baseball.
I believe that it is an art beyond perfection,
That it is beautiful to see played.
As if people coming to an art show,
To watch a master artist make his creation.

Soft, swift, practiced movements.
It is an art piece with colored blurs,
Sprinting around the field.

When the ball is hit,
It is like a dove that takes flight.
When the ball is thrown,
It like a jet taking off.
When they steal a base,
It is like just winning a lottery.

The crowd is so loud,
They sound like a lion.

That is why I believe in baseball.

Austin Davis, Grade 6
The Altamont School, AL

My Little Brother Nykell

Smelling like healthy bananas and apples
his hair is ebony black,
Large mahogany brown eye's
his skin is leather brown
Sounding as loud as a lion when he says "momma"

coming home from the hospital
I was so excited
about becoming a new big sister

Things I will never forget about Nykell
Is when he first started to walk he would
zoom around the house as fast as a cheetah
chasing after prey

Delicia Britt, Grade 4
Briarwood Elementary School, KY

Monkeys

M erry little creatures climbing trees
O n the lookout for fleas on each other
N ot carnivores or herbivores… fruitivores
K now that monkeys like to climb… you can find them in trees
E ither eating bananas or coconuts
Y ou can study monkeys anytime!
S ome like to whoop… and even scream

David Sides, Grade 5
Briarwood Christian School, AL

Beautiful Memory

The waves were washing in,
as the sand was flowing to the sea.
The beautiful sounds rush through my head.
When the seagulls fly over it's like clouds,
moving at a gliding pace.
The ocean is a perfect treasure that
I will keep in my memory forever.

Madison Edwards, Grade 6
Martin Elementary School, WV

Mom/Dad

Mom
hardworking, intelligent
loving, helping, thinking
chef, chauffeur, Ophthalmologist, football
coaching, grilling, working
energetic, athletic
Dad

Peyton Dabbs, Grade 5
Briarwood Christian School, AL

Love

Love is fuschia pink.
It smells like cinnamon apples baking in the oven.
It tastes like my mom's sweet potato pies.
It sounds like sweet romantic music.
It feels like hugging a sweet little baby.
It looks like a sweet little baby sitting in the meadow.
Love is little doves in the air shaping a heart.

Elisa Godard, Grade 4
Pines Elementary School, NC

Autumn

The bark looks like snakes.
The fragrance of the tree is as sweet as cake.
And, the leaves are dancing.
As the wind is prancing.

Fall Is as pretty as the ocean.
Now, all the leaves are in motion.
The bird nests are made of pine straw and leaves.
The tall tree is surrounded by bees.

Alyssa Marks, Grade 6
Manning Elementary School, SC

My Version of Jonathan's Christmas

The Lord came to Jonathan on Christmas Day and said, "I will come for you and you will live with me in Heaven." Jonathan said, "Thank you oh so much Heavenly Lord." And the Lord drifted away. "For I have to pack on this Christmas day." While Jonathan was packing he saw a great shadow, but he only ignored it. Then he heard a knock at the door. Bang, bang, bang. But he ignored that too. After the banging quit he saw a girl who was lurking in his window, and wore old ragged shoes and clothes. But he pulled down the blinds and said, "I'll ignore that too." For it was time for the Lord to come, but he had not arrived. Jonathan kneeled down to pray, "Oh, dear Lord why didn't you keep your promise?" As he got up he saw the Lord, and he said, "For I did come I was the little girl, the great shadow, and the bang bang at your door. You didn't open your heart, so now I must go."

Reagan Jump, Grade 5
Wynne Intermediate School, AR

My First Dog Drake

My dad picked him out like a clown at a circus. I really like him then when he got home we played for like a millennia. Chased each other like a cat chasing a mouse and we had a lot of fun. We played with each other every day. He weighed almost a ton and I couldn't pick him up. He would jump on my back like a frog and licked me when I fell on the ground. We still do this today.

Thomas Newton Strickland III, Grade 5
American Heritage Academy, GA

Clouds

I'm staring at the sky way up high. I'm making cloud pictures in my mind and making poems that do not rhyme. I love the feel of the cool thin breeze, and my life being right at ease. This is the life that everybody wants the life that everybody dreams of. Laying on your back in your backyard looking at the sky.

Kirsten Carlton, Grade 5
New Salem Elementary School, NC

What Makes Thou Fly?

O, little bluebird what makes thou fly?
Bluebird, bluebird please don't tell me a lie
Little bluebird please reply
Tweet! Was all I got in reply for my question of what makes thou fly.

O, sweet bluebird, someone must have taught you to fly
Bluebird, bluebird, I really want to know what makes you soar in the sky
Sweet bluebird, you glide like a blue angel flying high
Who would want to teach you to fly?

O lovely bluebird, teach me how to fly
Bluebird, Bluebird, it would be terrible nice if you stopped leaving me to sigh
Lovely Bluebird, please tell me why,
Why, why are you not teaching me to fly?

God gave the bluebird wings so that they can fly,
If God cares about this small bluebird, think how much He will care if you get a speck in your eye,
When you think about it, you think, "Oh my!"
Think every time that someone cares about you even if you cannot fly.

Sarah Elizabeth Jacob, Grade 5
Providence Academy, TN

My Ode to Winter

Dear Winter, it is cold but so fun. We see snow all day. We have snowball fights that are really fun. I go sledding off the hill, it's so fun. Then most of all we drink hot, hot chocolate after we are done playing with all the exciting stuff. Last of all Christmas is the best because it is the time where you and some of your family get together and open presents.

Ray Henry, Grade 5
West Liberty Elementary School, WV

My Special Mom

Midnight black hair
Dark brown eyes
Light brown skin like coffee
Always there for me
Encouraging me
To do something that I didn't think I could do
Adding warmth in my heart
Soft smooth skin
Smells like honey
My special mom

Ciara Sweatt, Grade 4
Briarwood Elementary School, KY

The Dream Game

I'm really nervous about this game
because the championship's on the line.
I should be able to make my shot
because I practice all the time.
The buzzer sounds and I come in,
my heart pounds very fast.
I look for an open teammate,
and find someone at last.
I pass the ball to Davis
and he passes it back to me.
I go up with a jump shot
and I end up making a three.
With 5 more seconds on the clock
we try to block their shot.
We end up winning by three points,
our team is really hot!

John McDearman, Grade 5
Greathouse Shryock Traditional Elementary School, KY

The Storm

The wind is gently swaying,
Among the growing pines,
The storm is growing nearer,
Like a tiger waiting to pounce.

The wind is now sprinting,
On the bare dead ground,
Running from an enemy,
The storm is now here.

The wind is howling madly,
A wolf crying to the moon,
Bending the trees to the ground,
the trees begging for mercy push as hard as they can.

But now the wind is stopping,
peace is coming 'round,
the sun is slowly rising
for I wake safe and sound

Neil Peterson, Grade 5
Hunter GT Magnet Elementary School, NC

I Love Trees

I love trees.
Trees are great.
I climb trees every day.
My favorite kinds are oak and pine.
If we didn't have any trees we would die.
Because trees are home to squirrels, bugs and birds,
And trees can make homework so we can learn,
And trees we can burn.
Tree houses, rope swings, and deer stands,
All the great things for a boy and man.
Trees are exciting and very fun,
And they're great for shading you from the sun.
So appreciate the trees on your lawn
Before they're cut down and gone.

Coleman Weldon, Grade 6
Chapin Middle School, SC

Fall

Fall is all around us.
The leaves are falling down, down, down.
Colors are changing all the time,
Red, yellow, orange and brown,
This season brings joy from town to town,
Oh, how I love fall!

Olivia Morton, Grade 5
Paint Lick Elementary School, KY

Love

Love. Is it from above?
Look at that dove.
Who made love?
Can I guess God is the one
Who made love the best?
Can you get married in a vest?
I think I have a choice.
Wait a minute, is that your voice?
Who do I like?
Is it you, or who?
Do I know you? Oh, yes I do.
Can you guess who you are?
You are the one I love the best!

Hannah Lucas, Grade 4
St Mary Cathedral Elementary School, MO

Halloween Night

I love the Jack-o'-lanterns on Halloween night.
I love to get candy and a fright.
I love to have and win cool things,
With fortune tellers diamond rings.
Ghosts appear everywhere,
And fly around in little girls' hair.
Goblins and ghosts are scary things,
Witches' brooms go "cling cling"
All these things only happen on Halloween.

Elizabeth Young, Grade 5
North Middle School, TN

Thanksgiving Problems

Relatives coming
Oh joy
Added work
More food
Excessive cooking
Huge problems
Watch parade
Head hurts
Relatives cackling
Towering pumpkins
Elegant trees
Getting quieter
Large jackets
Gets colder
Fire warmer
Nighttime coming
Trees bigger
Loud animals
Going home
All quiet
Mollie Nadeau, Grade 5
Center Elementary School, GA

Rain

R apid
A mazing
I ncredible
N ice
Sarah E. Leonard, Grade 4
Oak Grove Elementary School, NC

Wild and Free

They run wherever they please
their manes gliding in the breeze.
Running, running, running fast
trying not to be the one last.

Without hot leather
and no tether,
the foals jump with glee.
This is a sight I wish you could see.

They are the horses
wild and free,
together they run
wild and free.
Payton Ternus, Grade 5
Monticello Intermediate School, AR

My Sweet Parents

My parents are so sweet.
They're the sweetest ones you meet.
I always have so much fun
Because they're number one!
Jana Stephens, Grade 4
Evangelical Christian School, TN

For My Dad

Dad you are as sweet as cake.
You make me laugh all the time.
You make me happy when I see you.
You are very sweet to me.
Alexia Johnson, Grade 5
Western Hills Elementary School, AR

Mad

I got mad at my brother,
so I went to
my room.
I could still see my brother
reading a book.
My brother calls me,
like a caring brother
searching for me
he looks up and left,
down and right,
then I smash something
and he comes for me.
It feels so cold in my room.
My brother cooks me pizza,
for me to eat.
He knows me so well.
He knows I like pizza.
Tyler Baybrook, Grade 5
Fox Elementary School, MO

A Promise

When you are weary
take heed and get rest.
And know that your best efforts
will be blessed.
Timothy Nevils, Grade 5
Applewood Christian School, MO

Not Good Enough

You're too short to play.
Why even try.
You will just get laughed at.
You're just a fat loser.
Do not let someone say that to you.
Do not say that to someone.
It hurts. It hurts deeply.
You're too wide.
You're too dumb.
You're ugly.
If you heard that said to you,
Your heart would break to pieces.
If you say it to someone,
Their heart would break to pieces.
Stand up for yourself and others too.
Do not let anyone tell you you're
Not good enough.
Taylor Smith, Grade 5
Des Arc Elementary School, AR

Pink

Pink is…
As sweet as cotton candy
As bright as fresh flowers
As juicy as a grapefruit
As soft as a butterfly
Kacie Yates, Grade 5
Bloomfield Elementary School, KY

Snowflakes

Snowflakes falling
from the sky.
They dance
gracefully
          in
              the
                  sky.
They are different in
every way.
Light and soft and white.
They soon melt away.
Snowflakes falling from the sky
Bethany Nichole Clark, Grade 5
Pembroke Elementary School, NC

Football

Football
Tough, hard
Running, fighting, winning
Fight to win everything
Super Bowl
Jacob Kirby, Grade 5
Walton Verona Elementary School, KY

The Sadness of Veteran's Day

Veteran's Day
A sad holiday
The 11th month
The 11th hour
For the soldiers who fought
To keep our country safe
Some who left
Some who stayed
This is the reason for
Veteran's Day
Timothy Hensley, Grade 5
Sullivan Elementary School, TN

Falling Leaves

Leaves are falling from the tree.
Count them now… one, two, three.
They're yellow, orange, and also brown.
I like to see them falling down.
I do not want to rake them all.
I'm not so sure I like the fall!
Grant Shotnik, Grade 5
Briarwood Christian School, AL

Where I Am From

I am from a picture frame,
from Scotch tape and Kleenex.
I am from the magnolia tree that confronts our backyard
I am from the beautiful lake, the lily, the petals
that were my favorite things to touch.

I am from days of no salt and artistic talents,
Adhia and Arjun and Damani.
I am from small-framed ancestors
that have very poor eyesight.
From planning your future
and folk tale and legends.

I am from Texas and India,
spring rolls and vegetables.
From the journey to America that my parents made
From the 1992 blizzard
I am from the old shelf of albums
spilling out old memories.
The moments I had hidden behind the camera.

Anushri Adhia, Grade 6
Lakeshore Middle School, NC

Stuff Under My Bed

What a messy place
under my bed,
   CRASH
      BOOM
         BANG
I just hit my head!
Wow, there are a lot of things
under my bed —
dirt, old shoes, toys everywhere,
maybe even some clothes
my mom told me to put away
three months ago.
Awe man,
here's my assignment due yesterday!
Now what do I do with it?
I guess, they don't call my bed
messy for nothing.
This is my monstrous
messy bed.

Noelle Raymer, Grade 5
Greathouse Shryock Traditional Elementary School, KY

Joy

Joy is lime green.
It smells like sweet potato pies baking in the oven.
It tastes like freshly baked chocolate chip cookies.
It sounds like soft music playing.
It feels like a little soft puppy.
It looks like a red rose in a field of daisies.
Joy is picking flowers in a field.

Taylor Scott, Grade 4
Pines Elementary School, NC

Fall Break

Fall is so cool,
great breeze like the trees.
Butterflies pollinate, people learning,
leaves falling. Dogs sleeping,
cats playing, turtles crawling
Flowers growing, squirrels hibernating, birds chirping,
fires burning and people staying at home.
that is the way fall is done.

Hunter Gott, Grade 5
EA Harrold Elementary School, TN

Bob Dylan

The king of song,
the prince of sound,
the emperor of music.
Harmonica and guitar never fit better.
The curly hair, the nasally voice
are what you recognize best.
Many musicians bow to him
and even some current poets.
He wrote and sang those protest songs
that people sing today.
In '65 he angered millions
by plugging in his instrument.
But even today he's a star in the sky.
He's the greatest, that's no lie.

Alex Peeples, Grade 6
Charleston County School of the Arts, SC

Goodbye Tree

I watch them chop at your beautiful trunk
I think it is very wrong
Your roots grow deep but the men are strong

I planted you here many years ago
They've already taken your friends
Now it's your turn to go

They strap you down
Throttling your precious limbs
And away they bound

They drag you away
Leaving none behind
But I wonder why you couldn't stay

To them you are garbage
But I will never forget
Your beautiful leaves of beige

Thinking about you makes me sore
Because I know someday
That the Earth too, will be no more

Casey Wetherell, Grade 6
Chapin Middle School, SC

Hide and Go Seek

I am with my best friend playing
Out in the summertime.
He is "it" in Hide and Go Seek,
And is looking but he does not find.

I run to base which is a tree,
My friend shoots fast like a rocket.
Because he does not want to be "it,"
He tries to catch me.

The tree is in my sight will I make it,
He is right behind me this is not cool.
The fun is gone; what has happened?
I feel a shake, see my dad,
He says, "It's time for school."

Eli Bohannon, Grade 5
Midway Covenant Christian School, GA

Molly

A millionaire named Johnny Cash
Once had a big blowout bash
With a Mountain Dew fountain
And a candy rock mountain
The bash ended up as a smash.

Molly Ivy, Grade 4
Judsonia Elementary School, AR

I Believe

Jesus is our Savior
Confidant and friend
He's with us in the morning
And at each day's end.
He's the sun that lights our day
Protecting us from the dark
Complete amazing grace
The source of love within our heart.

Taylor Crouch, Grade 4
Evangelical Christian School, TN

Teacher

T eaches in the classroom
E ducating the mass
A lways right with the assignment
C aring about us
H elping to prepare us for the future
E valuating what we know
R ight us on task and help us to know

Daniel Diefenderfer, Grade 5
Vernon Middle School, LA

Little Bird

Little bird flies up
Little bird hits the ground hard
Then flies up again.

Shelley Johnson, Grade 4
Briarwood Christian School, AL

Horses

If I were a horse I would see…
Young foals galloping across the wide opened field
A white as snow Arabian horse grazing on the flat land
The solid white fence ahead of me as I run toward the horses' stable

If I were a horse I would hear…
The thundering of horses running at lightning speed across the field
The triumphant whinny of foals as they race across the field
The slamming of the stable door when my master let me run free

If I were a horse I would smell…
The flavor of freshly cut grass that lies in front of me
The sweet aroma of fresh hay in my stable
The leathery fragrance of the broken in saddle across my back

If I were a horse I would feel…
The cool breeze blowing across my mane after a long day's rain
The warm palm of my owner's hand as he softly pats my back
The scorching sun's rays on a blistering summer's day

Addie Lloyd, Grade 6
Union Chapel Elementary School, KY

Orphan in Winter

The daylight fades away,
Another day wasted.
The night shrouds the horizon,
Dark thoughts fill my mind.

I look at the warm lights from the windows of the more fortunate.
I imagine the family, huddled around the fireplace.
Tears fill my eyes.

But the cold stars start to shine, and the carolers start to sing.
I am reminded that my family is also with me,
Watching me from above.

I wipe my tears away,
And huddle up on a bench.
Bells start jingling in the sky,
As I close my eyes on Christmas Eve.

Siori Koerner, Grade 6
Discovery School @ Reeves Rogers, TN

Remembering a Great Time

Crazy people riding on roller coasters,
Pleasant people playing different games,
Loud screams and laughs from folks on rides,
A fragrance of mouthwatering food from the food courts,
So amazing because the fresh air smells like
The candy corn and the cotton candy that I enjoy,
Refreshing soft drinks that will do for my thirst,
Excited that the ride is about to start moving like an octopus moving its arms,
Amazing that the water starts to spray out of the sprinkler,
Grateful, cheerful, and excited that I'm having a great time.

Autumn Stewart, Grade 6
College View Middle School, KY

Papa John's Cardinal Stadium

Football players, sweaty fans,
Bands playing, fans cheering
Like their life depends on it.
CRACK!! BAM hard hits
bearing down on the halfback.
I feel as if I'm in the game.
A trip to the concession stand fills me up
with hot, juicy and warm PapaJohn's pizza
chased down with ice cold fruit punch Gatorade.
I feel refueled to go back out
into the crazy crowd and chant,
C.A.R.D.S

Taylor Shane, Grade 5
Greathouse Shryock Traditional Elementary School, KY

Skip a Beat

The world is a drum,
The whole, wide world is a drum,
Heart beats, snapping fingers
Footsteps, laughter
The world is a drum,
The whole, wide world is a drum,
Clapping hands, tapping feet,
Singing songs, keeping beat

The would is a drum
The whole, wide world is a drum.
And when you look from far away,
We do the same things every day
The world is a drum
The whole, wide world is a drum,
Living, laughing, loving, crying
Speaking, learning, hugging, lying

The world is a drum
The whole, wide world is one…
Maybe we can find a use
Of our drum, let us choose
We could use it as a stool to stand on, and reach…

Brianna Breaux, Grade 6
Haynes Academy for Advanced Studies, LA

Summer Moon

The summer moon is beautiful
It's very gloomy and bright
When I look at the moon every summer night
It has many different shapes
It could look like a banana and
sometimes it could look like a ball.
Sometimes there isn't a moon and it
acts like a night light
for all the little kids out there
that are scared of the dark.

Joey Wright, Grade 5
Woodland Elementary School, KY

Trick-or-Treat

Butterscotch give away,
Licorice, Twix, and Milky Way.
Jawbreakers and Bubble Yum,
Warheads and a Dum Dum.
Onward now to home we run,
To count the treasures of our Halloween fun.

Matthew Scott, Grade 5
North Middle School, TN

A Song

A song, sails above the treetops
Sending its eerie melodies to all.
Not only beautiful,
But purposeful
Warning others of its presence
Saying, "I am here, this is my land."
And who sends this purposeful song?
The master of the land,
Great hunter and pack runner.
The wolf,
His song speaks to others of his kind,
And calls for his pack.
The other creatures hear his song,
And scatter in fear of the hunter.
The knowing of his presence is to know survival,
And to know a king.

Mariel Tishma, Grade 6
Seven Holy Founders School, MO

Skateboarding

When you skateboard it feels great
so my parents watch me skate.
I would rather skate than get a date.
Skateboarding is so awesome!

Wear a helmet or you'll get stitches,
don't you fall down or you'll rip your britches!
You crash and burn, flip and turn,
that really hurts.

When I skateboard nothing is more important.
Any kind of board is my motto
Huffy Hawk so many to choose from!
Crashing is not fun, trust me on that.

Tony Hawk is so good.
It would be so cool if I was as good as him!
He can ollie very high,
He could probably touch the sky!

Jumping is the best part
And crashing is the worst.
All fun of getting stitches and
all fun of ripping your britches!

Austin Bowles, Grade 4
Schaffner Traditional Elementary School, KY

Dolphin
Dolphin
blue, pretty
sing, swim, eat
playing, hunting, talking, jumping
They are so playful
Mammals
Lacey Holloway, Grade 4
East Jones Elementary School, MS

Red Rose
Red is bright
it warms the soul.
The red of a rose.
It's smell in the day
the look in the rain
whatever happens
to the red rose
it will never change.
Abbie Stringer, Grade 5
West Marion Elementary School, MS

My Friend Tynecia
Tynecia is a good friend
but more of a good
basketball player. She runs
up and she is a cheetah
on the prowl. She shoots
almost all the shots
and is a tall giraffe
Jessica Washington, Grade 6
Armorel Elementary School, AR

The Mountains
Nature, beautiful
Cold at night, beauty of God
Waterfalls, flowers
Jennie Reese, Grade 4
Briarwood Christian School, AL

When I Went to the Fair
The very good food
All the people
People screaming
The loud music
The animals making sounds
I feel great
The wind on my face
The great corn dog
The cold soda
The hot french fries
All the big rides
The carnival
Lots of people
When I went to the fair
Nathan Verser, Grade 5
Berryville Elementary School, AR

If I Were in Charge of the World
If I were in charge of the world
I'd get 3 presents each day
three course meals
and a one-million-dollar house.

If I were in charge of the world
there'd be two cats in every house
$100 dollars in everyone's pocket
and no bad hair days.

If I were in charge of the world
you wouldn't be bored
you wouldn't have work
you wouldn't have stupid or
"deal wid it!"

If I were in charge of the world
a cat would be a valuable resource
all kids would smell peachy
and a person who loves cats
and doesn't smell bad
would still be allowed to rule the world.

If I were in charge of the world.
Jocelyn Ziyadi, Grade 5
Eminence Middle School, KY

Fall
Fall will very soon be here.
The trees are getting bare.
I think I see a deer.
Animals scurry from here to there.

Leaves are falling all around.
Squirrels are stuffing their cheeks.
You can barely hear a sound.
The cat is making her coat sleek.

The birds are all flying away
At the creek, we play hide-n-go seek.
In the strong wind, the branches sway.
The end is near and winter'll be bleak.
Lydia Watson, Grade 6
Pleasants County Middle School, WV

Memories of Yours
Rushing through my mind
Are memories of yours
Seeing you for the last time
As you stood at the door
I silently cry
And remember the old stories
Though others don't know why
She was sent to God's Glories
Kate Wheeler, Grade 6
Mayflower Middle School, AR

Sports
I play hockey, soccer, tennis too.
I play sports how about you?

In tennis you have to hit the ball,
But just remember do not fall.

Don't ever hit the ball so high,
Because it might go to the sky.

In soccer try to score on the goal,
But listen here watch out for that mole!

Try not to get a yellow card,
But if you do don't take it so hard.

In hockey hit the puck in,
Then rejoice when you win.

Don't get a penalty or you will be out
But if you do you should not pout.
Andy Fritz, Grade 6
Holy Infant Elementary School, MO

Writing
Writing makes me look forward,
To sitting down and letting,
My pen glide and sometimes skid,
Across the surface of my,
Sparkling piece of white paper.

The ideas just slip out,
The sides of my head and SPLAT!,
Into my hand and KERPLUNK!,
Onto my pen and KERSPLAT!,
And fall onto my paper.

Once the ideas are down,
They form into a piece of,
Outstanding, brilliant writing,
My ideas come to life,
It can't get better than this!
Brooklyn Bell, Grade 6
Holy Trinity School, KY

Halloween
H aunted house
A t midnight there are
L oud parties and
L oud people
O nly wear costumes
W icked witches
E eeeeeeeek
E vil spirits in my
N ightmares
Brianna Stoneking, Grade 5
First Flight Elementary School, NC

Summer

Summer is fun,
I like to play in the sun.
My friends and I like to swim,
Even when the light is dim.
We play games like movies, silent, and jail;
We could care less if we break a nail.
We sleep in and stay up late,
We play outside and roller skate.
The thing that makes summer really cool,
Is that there is no school!

Maria Gorla, Grade 6
Seven Holy Founders School, MO

My House at Christmas

What's your favorite time of year?
Christmas is mine it makes me shout and cheer
Christmas bells ringing
Everyone is singing
Lights on Christmas trees
Family, friends, and parties
Smell of cookies and food

Coldness of winter
Warmth of fire
Taste of cake, BBQ, mac and cheese plus rice
When I wake I feel like ice
Monie, Antaun, and I cry out with joy
Open my presents to find a new toy
I scream and shout oh boy oh boy

My favorite time of year
Read stories about reindeer
Santa's elves making toys
Make a stir of Christmas joy
We all wake to find a new toy
Everyone in my family has a Christmas mood
That's why I love Christmas.

A'Lexus Cumbie, Grade 6
St Mark Elementary School, SC

Ode to Soda Pops

Oh, soda pops,
all fizzy and cold
you make me full of caffeine
without you I would have to drink water!
Thank goodness you're here.
with lots of sugar
That's the way I like it.
You are the one that makes me hyper
in the middle of the night.
You are the one that makes my mom pull
out her hair.
Oh, soda pops,
you fill my heart with joy.

Sarah Mullins, Grade 6
Dyer Elementary & Jr High School, TN

I Am a Fuzzy Kitten

I am a fuzzy kitten.
I wonder if my mom misses me.
I hear strange sounds around the house.
I see people going up and down the stairs.
I want my mom.
I am a fuzzy kitten.
I pretend I am with her every day.
I feel so sad because she's not there.
I touch my owner's fuzzy pillow to make me feel better.
I worry that my mom will forget me.
I cry when I am lonely.
I am a fuzzy kitten.
I understand my mom will not find me.
I say meow when I want my mom.
I dream my mom finds me.
I hope my mom is happy.
I try to live without her.
I am a fuzzy kitten.

Sara Lenhardt, Grade 4
Wohlwend Elementary School, MO

Reasons for Seasons

On this earth, there are four seasons
Each season has different reasons.

A reason for winter is Christmas Day
When we celebrate Christ's birth in every way.

In the summer, kids have fun
Some go to the beach and play in the sun.

In the spring, you should know
April showers help May flowers grow.

A reason for autumn is a Thanksgiving feast
Some people tell others to bring food at least.

I've just given you one reason for each season
But each season may have more than one reason.

Nathan Wright, Grade 5
Colerain Elementary School, NC

Summer Fun

Can't complain, no homework
Large tiring swimming pools
Camping out with blistering hot camp fires
Dingy smoky cookouts
Entertaining 4th of July's with pyrotechnic, showers of red stars
Amusing times with my family
Intensely hot mowing days
Inky juicy black barriers, so good
Murky lake water,
That is some summer fun.

Corey Agnew, Grade 6
Alvaton Elementary School, KY

A Breezy Day

I lay in my tent,
watching the weeds sway today,
in a joyful way.
Nolan Osvath, Grade 4
Briarwood Christian School, AL

Thunderstorm at Night

I'm laying in my bed so scared
The sky is rumbling everywhere
A flash of light gave me a fright
A boom of thunder
The crash of hail!
Woke up the night.
Snap, crackle the lights flicker!
My baby sister
Laughed and snickered
Whoosh, went the rain;
Steam and water everywhere
Out came the sun shining a glare.
Kiaren Goode, Grade 6
College View Middle School, KY

Ode to Arena Football

Oh, Arena Football,
you are very fun to watch.
Seeing people get slammed.
On the wall or people scoring
it doesn't matter.
Arena Football, thank you.
Connor Riffe, Grade 6
Dyer Elementary & Jr High School, TN

Snickers Bars

Snickers
Snickers
Snickers
Joyful Snickers
Melty Snickers
White, black, brown Snickers
Sweet, tasty, yummy Snickers.
There are just a few!!

Nutty Snickers
Gooey Snickers
Sweet, nummy, snacky Snickers.
Great, tasty, delicious Snickers
Chocolate covered Snickers
Snackalicious Snickers, too.

Wow, Snickers
Hurrah, Snickers
Don't forget wonderful Snickers.
Last of all, best of all
I like lots of Snickers.
Darrell Richardson, Grade 5
Tates Creek Elementary School, KY

Walking My Dog

"Come on boy" time to take a walk
Marco running to me
Licking and jumping on me
Wet sticky tongue leaving slobber
on
   my
      arm — YUCK!
SHARP claws going into my skin like a deep paper cut.

Putting the leash on — "Snap"
Opening the gate — "Creak"
Marco takes off running
My arm getting yanked hard like a tangled string on my bed
Taking off running too!

People making space
Marco's tail swinging back and forth happy to be out of the backyard
Ugg! — slowing down now starting to walk
People wave at us going around the block.

After we walk
"Snap" — taking off the leash
"Creak" — closing the door
Marco goes in the backyard until his next walk.

Jacque Smith, Grade 4
Roberta Tully Elementary School, KY

The Beach

The ocean's waves roaring as the hits the sharp, pointy rocks and the sandy beaches,
Pushy, busy loud people making their way through the angry and furious crowd,
Noisy splashing from children that are playing in the kiddy pool,
Burnt food smells like volcanic ashes,
Scented suntan lotion smells so good,
Yucky salt water gushing into my mouth, is disgusting,
Cold sodas dancing in the heat is hilarious, as they do a Mexican dance, the Tango,
Building sandcastles so high that they look like skyscrapers compared to me,
My long silky hair lies over my shoulders,
Feeling so hot and sweaty all over.

Meagan Merritt, Grade 6
College View Middle School, KY

Happiness

People all around the world think they can buy happiness.
Well people could own the whole world and still would not be happy
The truth is you can't buy happiness, you have to find it with…
friends,
family,
love.
Because finding happiness through one of those things is the most precious thing.
Happiness doesn't come from the material things.
It comes from the precious people around us.
And that is how to find
HAPPINESS

Camile Messerley, Grade 6
Cathedral School, NC

Friendship

There is nothing my friend and I have not been through
We share all our ideas and secrets too
If we are having trouble with someone like a bully
We tell everything from the beginning fully
I hope we are friends forever because I would
Never change anything about her ever
We help each other through and through
On whatever it is we never fuss or fight
We always go to sleep at night
We don't stay up to late
So we don't keep parents awake!

Aaliyah White, Grade 6
Childersburg Middle School, AL

Christmas Day

In my family there are six members
The holiday we like is in December
This is the day Jesus was born
Christmas is the best all year around
I love it when the snowflakes hit the ground
I love getting presents for Christmas

We might get presents on that day
If we're bad we might get hay
This is why we're good until Christmas Day
We go outside and play in the snow
Then we role it up like biscuit dough
Then we go in the house and play some more

When Christmas is finally here
We make a great big cheer
Whoo hoo! Christmas is here
By 11 o'clock we are in our beds
With the covers over our little heads
The clock strikes 12 and we are awake

We went to the tree and jumped for joy
I got a doll baby, the cutest little toy
I just wish it was Christmas every day

Shertia Garner, Grade 6
St Mark Elementary School, SC

Christmas Morning

It's Christmas,
Whoosh,
I'm the wind as I go down the stairs,
I'm like a scavenger while I look through the stocking,
Candy,
Trinkets,
Toys,
All stuffed in my stocking,
I sigh with enjoyment
This is the best Christmas ever.

Keegan Wagner, Grade 5
Greathouse Shryock Traditional Elementary School, KY

Going in to Battle

There they go marching in,
to the battle of a lifetime.
They huddle together in the ditch,
giving each other cover fire.
They hear bullets whistling by,
their ears, their legs and their necks.
The commander orders us to fire.
It sounds like thunder when our guns fire.
The whispering winds of faith will lead us to victory.
And so I say this, my name is General Washington,
leader of America.

Walker Pichea, Grade 5
Greathouse Shryock Traditional Elementary School, KY

Autumn Fun

Fall is here let's have some fun.
Leaves are falling, get warm clothes on.
Apple cider, cranberry sauce, pumpkin pie,
And get ready for some turkey piled high!

Hannah Carlson, Grade 4
Cleveland Elementary School, OK

Summer Time

Summer time is oh so great
You even get to stay up late
You get to play all day long
And become really, really strong

Watching television all night
Getting to go to a bull fight.
This summer will be out of sight,
But school tomorrow will be quite all right.

Josh Richard, Grade 6
Pleasants County Middle School, WV

Boat

Nerves were rattled as I approached the waiting water.
Knots in my stomach grew bigger, tighter.
Boats cracking, water rushing, hearts pumping.
Stinky fish fill the air.
Gear dawned, body shaking, with ease my body lowers.
Water engulfed me cold and wet.
Rapid swimming till I reached land.

Paula Del Castillo, Grade 5
Cline Elementary School, KY

Thomas

Brownish blonde hair, blue eyes, and short
Blue Jean shorts, red tee shirts, and ball hats
When I'm outside
Riding my bike in my driveway
I get mad when my sisters invade my privacy.
Reading when I'm alone
Orange everything

Thomas Surdyke, Grade 5
Our Lady Catholic School, MO

Chestnut

My dog Chestnut is sweet.
When she is good she wants a treat.
She wants to have fun and play,
And be with me all day.
She snuggles with me at night,
And she is my shadow at light.
Chestnut is a really great friend,
And how great she is will never end.

Casey Miller, Grade 4
Moyock Elementary School, NC

Dogs and Cats

Dogs
Feisty, playful
Bites, nibbles, chews
Soft, cute, scratches, hisses
Purrs, meows, loving
Sleeps, walks
Cats

Alyssa Morgan, Grade 4
Tamassee-Salem Elementary School, SC

War

The cold horror of war
It's definitely real.
You can't escape the terror.
You can feel it haunting you.
It can drive you insane.
It scares you into submission.
You'll never be the same.
Not even at the end of the mission.

Jason Conaway, Grade 6
Pleasants County Middle School, WV

Basketball

Basketball is an exciting sport.
It's a really challenging sport.
Teams are always close.
You get tired rapidly.
It's a sport anybody can play!
You can play anywhere!
Basketball is really exciting.

Jonathan Harding, Grade 5
North Middle School, TN

Mammal

Dog,
Fun, comforting
Barking, wagging, wailing
It likes to play
Scratching, meowing, wailing
Playful, comforting
Cat

Alek Riney, Grade 6
Stuart Middle School, KY

Kitties

I like kitties
They are so nice.
I don't like it
When they eat mice.

I have three kitties
All black and gray.
Get one more kitty
I just may.

My kitties' names are
Pep, Sas, and Bell.
Of their lives
I love to tell.

Miranda Bachman, Grade 4
Northeast Baptist School, LA

The Mall

At the mall
there are fabulous things!
Cute shoes,
adorable little babies,
tons of happy families,
our kind of music,
stylish high heels,
packed with cell phones,
and the yummy food court!
That is why I like the mall.

Amanda Houck, Grade 5
North Middle School, TN

Snakes

Snakes
Shiny, smooth
Hunt, slide, bite
Scared, excited, fright, terrified
Cobra

KeyShawn Marshall, Grade 5
Woodland Elementary School, KY

Christmas

Looks like presents under the tree
Sounds like Christmas songs
Tastes like hot chocolate
Feels like 20° F outside
Smells like apple cider

John David Imbusch, Grade 5
Briarwood Christian School, AL

Hot Days

Hot days bring no rain.
Children play outside all day.
Water makes them wet.

Andrew Sinclair, Grade 4
Briarwood Christian School, AL

Veteran

V ictory for our country
E very soldier that died for us
T imes they got hurt for us
E very man and woman that died for us
R eward for what they did in the army
A merican flag still stands tall
N one were weak or failed their country

Dustin Thomas, Grade 5
Temple Hill Elementary School, KY

Garrett

G reat
A wesome
R espectful
R esponsible
E xcellent
T ruthful
T riumphant

Garrett DePergola, Grade 6
Martin Elementary School, WV

Baseball

Baseball
Baseball is hard
Baseball is fun to play
Baseball catching hitting awesome
Baseball

John McCollough, Grade 5
American Heritage Academy, GA

The Best Fall

F un
A utumn
L unch
L eaves

I ncredible
S upper

G reat
R ain
E ating
A wesome
T urkey

Benjamin Dumanowsky, Grade 5
Trinity Day School, GA

Winter

The freezing winter's icy breath
Chills the woods and the hillsides
It is very cold
Jack Frost tiptoes brush in hand
Sweeping away all the coal

Kate Adcock, Grade 6
Briarwood Christian School, AL

Hamsters

The spectacular smell of hamsters!
The sound of hamsters gnawing on their cage.
The wonderful touch of hamsters while holding them.
The sight of a hamster sleeping like a baby.
The delightful sound of a hamster crunching on tiny seeds.
The sight of a hamster in its hamster ball makes me happy.

Adam Warren, Grade 5
North Middle School, TN

Kiwi

Dingy white fur,
Big black eyes,
Tiny fluffy tail
Like a little white rat when wet,
Loves to cuddle,
Cute, sweet, loving,
Loves to lick,
Lives to chase cats:
Ready…
Set…
CAT!
Sneezy, itchy, a living allergy magnet:
Sneeze,
Cough,
ACHOO!
Begging for cheese,
Sneaking a bit of crumbs from under the table,
Chews shoes, toys, and who knows what else!
Eater or destroyer of all stuffed animals,
She, alone, the queen of the castle,
Forever my puppy, Kiwi.

Sarah Kirkpatrick, Grade 5
JJ Jones Intermediate School, NC

Laying Around

I lay down in the grass,
And look at the clouds in a mass,
Then slowly the darkness crept,
And then finally there I slept
Then I sprang into my dreams
It was very exciting I mean
I woke up by a lake,
And my breath the scenery seemed to take,
I walked for hours or so it seemed
And as I walked I daydreamed
Then I heard someone call my name,
But when I turned around everything was the same,
But when I looked back I saw my friend,
Someone with my time I could spend,
Then she started to float across the lake,
I knew my happiness was at stake,
Then everything started to turn,
The noise was like a loud cat's purr
I woke up with my dog licking my face.

Brittney Tarwater, Grade 6
Childersburg Middle School, AL

Darkness and Light

Darkness, unknown and uncertain.
Creeping around, wrapping its blanket around me.
Frightening and silent.
When light is gone and hides from the charcoal blackness.
Darkness

Light, warm and welcoming.
Covering me, nurturing me.
Loving and loud.
When darkness is gone and dissolving in the air.
Light

Darkness and light, opposites.
Working together.
One frightening, the other loving.
One silent, the other loud.
Darkness and light.

Molly Thomas, Grade 6
Bowling Green Jr High School, KY

Baseball

I get my ball, bat, and baseball cap.
I go out to the field and what do I see
All my friends are waiting for me
I get my bat to be first to hit
When I'm finished, I must get my muddy mitt
I go out to play third base
Oops, I tripped on my shoelace
Then I play shortstop
I dive into the clay
Just to make the marvelous magnificent play
I hop up
And throw it to first and get the out.

Luke Jackson, Grade 5
Contentnea Elementary School, NC

Holiday World

Going to Holiday World seeing lots
of new stuff that I have
never seen before
There was Christmas stuff and they
had Santa Claus on top of something
But when we got to Holiday World
we took a tour bus
up to the front
Then I saw a big rollercoaster
it was called The Voyage
There was this one ride it was so fun
and on the ride there's
this one drop and you don't expect it
and when I got on it it scared me because of the drop
But I had fun and I was laughing like hyenas
And I have never had so much fun in my life

Kelsey Hughes, Grade 4
Briarwood Elementary School, KY

Thanksgiving

Delicious mashed potatoes
Sweet golden corn
Seasoned green beans
Refreshing sweet tea
Buttered carrots
Smoked mouthwatering turkey
All make a wonderful meal
But what's important
Is the family
That you share it with.

Christie Robertson, Grade 5
Briarwood Christian School, AL

Triston

Gigantic blue eyes,
Stares curiously at you.
Cute, crawling baby.

Ethan Holdman, Grade 5
St Vincent Elementary School, MO

Tweet Tweet

I love to hear
The birds tweet,
Tweet all the day.
It's a sweet, sweet
Sound to hear.
I love to listen to
The sweet, sweet,
Tweet, tweet sound
All day long.

Diamond Dennis, Grade 5
Franklin Elementary School, OK

Autumn

Autumn leaves falling
They are very beautiful
I like the colors
Especially the orange
I can't wait for fall to come!

Kylee Sigmon, Grade 5
Berryville Elementary School, AR

Football

Football, football, don't you see.
This great game is exciting to me.
Knock them down.
Run a touchdown.
State Champs we surely will be.

Kick the ball long and far.
Right between those yellow golden bars.
Block 'em and hold that line.
Look at our defensive line!
Hit 'em hard 'til they see all stars.

Kaitlin Bruce, Grade 6
Appling County Middle School, GA

Hunger in the Night

I was sitting on the couch…the couch I sit on.
I decided to make a snack.
I jumped up and ran when I heard a thump, thump, thump…

I went to the kitchen and I opened up the fridge…rattle, rattle, rattle.
I got out the milk, got out the dough, and started to roll, roll, roll.

I put the dough in the oven and wait, wait, waited.
Soon I look, look, looked, and saw it was done.
I took it out of the oven.

Watch out out. It might be hot hot!
So I sat down, down in my chair chair and started to much munch munch!
Then my sister asked for some, so we both went munch, munch, munch!

Brooke Short, Grade 4
Tazewell-New Tazewell Primary School, TN

The Fires of Life

In life there are many different fires that burn forever inside you,
For some, you can extinguish,
For others, they will always burn.
One type of fire is love,
It is that burning sensation that you get,
When you cherish that special someone.
When you find the person that is just right for you,
And you are just right for that person,
The fire will burn only for that person.
Another type of fire is hatred,
Hatred is when someone has messed with you long enough,
You get a burning sensation to seek revenge.
After a while you can't hold it in any longer,
But after a while the fire, hatred, will smolder,
But if that person prods the ashes,
The fire will burst forth again!

Logan Reynolds, Grade 6
Discovery School @ Reeves Rogers, TN

Racism

It's so harsh I can't even say.
The sound of it makes me go my own way.
Racism

I have to face it one day,
But one day I will say,
Segregation isn't the way.
Racism

White and black has a way to racism today.
Using different water fountains was sad in the past.
There's still some segregation today, but as Martin Luther King Jr. said
He wishes that everybody will stand together.
Racism

I truly hope that people will ask what is racism?

Kaneesha Sawyer, Grade 5
Childersburg Middle School, AL

Authors

Authors are storytellers
They lead you on a journey
They can make somebody peaceful
Or have them ready to lash out in anger
They take critique with their heads held high
Or start weeping in shame
Authors sometimes write about their life
They can also make up somebody new
An animal can be the hero
It could have some tragedy
Writers make things come to life
They make you believe in things that are not real
Good authors are magic
Bad ones feel completely fake
They make flowers walk or animals talk
Authors are unappreciated geniuses
They write anything that pleases them
Writers are inspiration
Awesome people that make joy in life
We are led to see the world with different eyes

Marlee Bennett, Grade 6
Southwest Middle School, AR

Christmas Time

Old Saint Nick is coming tonight
As the tree glows
Snap! I hear my dad turn off my bedroom light
The wind is strong and it still snows

Then suddenly I hear jingling bells
I wonder who that could be?
"Merry Christmas!" somebody yells
I peer out of my noisy door to see

He goes down when the time is right
He slides down the chimney
He checks to see no one is in sight
I wonder was he looking at me?

Next morning I wake up with a big grin on my face
I see a swamp of toys!
I run down the steps with a fast pace
I hope you have a Merry Christmas with lots of joys.

Neil Hobbs, Grade 5
Greathouse Shryock Traditional Elementary School, KY

Ode to Hunting

Hunting how I adore guns going off.
The dogs jump a rabbit and there goes a chase.
We get a turkey in the day.
We spook a deer, it runs, we shoot it.
In the night we run coons up the trees.
Hunting is my favorite sport.

Dakota Wilson, Grade 5
West Liberty Elementary School, WV

Dream Girl

Night or day, rain or shine
You'll always know your heart is mine
Every time I see your amazing smile
It will make me stare for quite awhile
Even if I'm in a crowded place
I can always recognize your beautiful face.
Anything you need help to do
You'll always know I'm there for you
I wrote this cause I really care
And I hope to be a loving pair

Jacob Dickerson, Grade 6
Holy Trinity School, KY

The Ocean

The ocean is so romantic.
It's like a blue world around me.
When I'm near it, I fall into a gaze.
I see shells, starfish, sand dollars
And when I look at it at night, it looks like a star at midnight.
I smell and taste the salty sea water.
I hear the waves crash against the sandy shore.
I feel the soft, white sand.
It shifts beneath my feet.
It makes me wish I had a boyfriend —
NOT!

Sydni Fingers, Grade 5
West Elementary School, MO

Best Friends

Everyone has a lot of best friends.
You have to learn to trust them.
Look out for your friends,
So they don't take the wrong end.
If you have something to say,
Tell your friends.
If they tell someone your secret,
Then don't tell them anything else.
You should always hang with them,
So nothing happens to them.
If your friends do something bad,
Tell someone even if they are your friends.
You can make new friends
If your other friends are bad.

Jona Crousser, Grade 6
Pleasants County Middle School, WV

I Love Brown

Brown is like a running bay horse,
    Brown feels like my horse's soft and silky fur,
Brown looks like a bar of dark chocolate,
    Brown sounds like a horse rolling in mud,
Brown tastes like a piece of chocolate candy,
    Brown smells like a piece of chocolate,
Brown is like a running bay horse.

Faith Stephens, Grade 5
Eminence Middle School, KY

Similarities

Whether it's rainy, snowy, sunny, or cloudy I can always go to you for help. Happy day, sad day, mad day, perfect day you're always there to make me laugh. You have thirty dollar clothes and I have twenty dollar clothes and yet we act as equals. I'm supportive of what you do and you're supportive of what I do. And that is why we're best friends.

Heather Gillich, Grade 5
Our Lady of Fatima School, MS

The Restaurant

My beautiful family and I decided to go to a restaurant that has the best tasting food ever.
We ride to the restaurant in my big white van with a white stripe all happy.
We get stuck in traffic that is backed up at least 3 miles long because of an accident.
My family gets to the best restaurant an hour late.
As I am walking in I smell the best smell ever of fried steak and ribs.
I look at the menu and there are so many good foods like steak, ribs, pork, and pizza.
Finally the waitress in a shiny black apron takes our order.
I decide to order the steak.
The delicious food with amazing aroma is coming closer.
Finally she gives us our great food.
I cut my juicy steak it cuts like butter.
I take a bit it feels like I am in heaven the butter juice it is all amazing.
Once I was done with the best steak ever we decided to leave.
After that meal there will be no better steak than that one.

Cole Czajkoski, Grade 6
Queen of Angels Catholic School, GA

Ode to My Glasses

Dear Glasses,
You are so comfortable on my face. I can see when I wear you. You are like the stormy clouds and all shiny like the sun. You are pretty clear like a mirror. You make me think, so I am smart. You make me just the right kid. I can't see if I am wearing another pair of glasses. You put a smile on my face that shines like the sun and the moon.

Sara Sexton, Grade 5
Walton Verona Elementary School, KY

The Great Moment

Pulling out the big cardboard box excitedly opening it up
taking out the Christmas tree laying the parts all over the floor
sorting out the colors placing each limb in the colored holes of the tree
finally standing tall.

Ready to be decorated
bright lights going on first
clinking of the ornament box as it is opened up so fragile
tree green, cherry red, hot pink, and golden balls shining like a star in the sky
reaching up to scatter them around the colorful Christmas tree
bending down to put some low
careful not to put them where my dog can reach.

Golden garland goes around and around in empty spots
climbing up on my daddy's shoulders to put the angel on top
laying the train track around the colorful tree.

Turning off the house lights shutting all the windows
making the room pitch dark for the great moment — plugging the tree in for the first time
mouths fall to the floor smiles grow from cheek to cheek
proud of our work celebrating with a cup of hot chocolate with marshmallows.

Ashleigh Maddox, Grade 4
Roberta Tully Elementary School, KY

King of the Jungle

I am a cheetah, sprinting at my prey,
Now you see me, now you don't.
I'm not like the hare losing the race,
I give it my all every day.
I am taller than bugs and flowers,
But lesser than a tree.
Don't think I am just a nice person,
I am the lion, king of the jungle.
I am more famous than the Empire State Building,
I am stronger than King Kong,
I am Ryan.

Ryan Palso, Grade 6
Beck Academy, SC

Window

A window is clear and bright,
Always in the truth and right
No smoke and mirrors for this prophet of glass,
Shown to any first or last
A man, woman, being of life,
Toils to lie amid their strife
Sin clouds up their window bright,
Shows the dark and clouds the light,
Let yourself be a window to all,
Whether in peace or time of brawl,
Be a window, shine, be bright,
Out with the dark and in with the light.

Benjamin Wallis, Grade 6
Sacred Heart School-Troy, MO

Who Am I?

Shae
Tall, nice, and caring
Sibling of Chaia
Lover of dogs and snakes
Who feels happy when I see my old friends
Who has a good attitude
Resident of Oklahoma City
Deere

Shae Deere, Grade 4
Cleveland Elementary School, OK

Wish

Wishing is like telling a secret to a star
As magical as a dream
As loving as the heart

Dream like wishing on the stars in the sky
Dream as big as the sea
As long as a never ending story

Wishing, or dreaming is like keeping a secret
Of what you think and feel
Dreams and wishes will never end

Julienne Kvasnak, Grade 6
Beck Academy, SC

Thankfulness

Be thankful for your house
Be thankful for the soldiers fighting for us
Be thankful for the chirping birds in the morning
Be thankful for the clothes on your back
Be thankful for fall and the colorful leaves.
Boom! Be thankful for rain.
Be thankful for the smallest insects — like spiders
If you are happy for the things in your life, you will
Be a free bird in the world. Your life will be like a tree growing
Tall with knowledge. The things you are thankful
For will help your knowledge grow.

Josh Siebe, Grade 5
Greathouse/Shryock Traditional Elementary School, KY

Nature

The beautiful sun was up,
Shining on my eyes,
I heard the leaf rustle,
As I walked down the street,
I felt the wind on my face,
When a car drove by,
I smelled the flowers,
As I walked past a garden,
I realized the beauty of nature,
I love nature.

Senthil Sakthivel, Grade 6
Haynes Academy for Advanced Studies, LA

Up Up and Away

The nose looked like a pelican
Its wings were as wide as a canyon
I can hear the engines roar
So I slowly climbed aboard

As I walked down the terminal
My heart began to flutter
We took our seats with excitement
And my stomach turned to butter

The wheels began to roll
The airplane was taking a stroll
We lifted off the ground
Like thunder without a sound

We sailed into the skies
Which were as blue as an eye
The clouds were as fluffy as marshmallows
The wind sounded like an orchestra of cellos

The sun shone through the window
Like an angel with a halo
We were up so high
I thought I could touch the sky

Spencer Roberts, Grade 4
Schaffner Traditional Elementary School, KY

For the Blue and the White
Alex Rodriguez
For the blue and white
Rapidly rising to the Homerun Mountain
Cooler than Derek Jeter
I wish I was like him!

Tre Davis, Grade 5
Salem Elementary School, AR

Spring
Apple blossoming in the trees,
Spring is here.
The birds are singing,
Songs of love.
Babies are born.
Birds come back north after winter.
Bears come out from hibernating.
The long cold winter has gone.

The colder the winter,
Makes the spring more warm.
And everyone is happier.
The deer, bears, birds, and others
Are filled with joy,
From the springtime songs.

Helen Stewart, Grade 5
Oark Elementary School, AR

Fall Time
Leaves fall,
Football time,
Fall is the coolest of all!

Jumping in leaf piles
Down! Set! Hut!
All in all, I love Fall!

Jacob Parnell, Grade 4
The King's Academy, SC

What Is Pink?
Pink is cotton candy
Pink is lipstick on your lips
Pink is a big flower
Pink is a great princess
Pink is shoes at a store
Pink is a colorful friend
Pink is candy everywhere
Pink is a scooter on the road
Pink is cups on the table
Pink is plates at your home
Pink is seashells in the evening
Pink is happy every day
Pink is ice cream on a cone
Pink is balloons at a party

Hannah Fisk, Grade 5
Meredith-Dunn School, KY

Tornado
Twist, swirl
Round, round again
Everything blows away
Destroying obstacles in path
Finished

Bailey Gautier, Grade 5
Broadway Elementary School, NC

My Dog Rusty
I have a best buddy
Who sometimes gets muddy
We run and we play
And sometimes roll in the hay
There are times when he bites me
But that is ok
I love him anyway
My dog Rusty

Austin Matheson, Grade 5
Hatfield Elementary School, AR

About Me
Brooks
Hyper, crazy, dare devil, and silly
Sibling of Ellen
I love driving my go-cart
Like a maniac
Who feels bored in school
Who needs peanut butter
Who gives my mom a headache
Who would like to see
A clear lake
Who fears spiders
Resident of the world
Meek

Brooks Meek, Grade 6
Benton County School of the Arts, AR

Ode to My Teacher, Mrs. Gurganus
Oh sweet Mrs. Gurganus,
   You are one special teacher.

Even though sometimes you
   talk like a preacher.

With your bright blue eyes,
   you make us smile.

For you I'll go
   the extra mile.

You have a beautiful heart.
For a teacher,
   you are really smart.

Kai Swain, Grade 4
Pines Elementary School, NC

My Hero Dave
I have a hero that is brave;
He is a good guy, and his name is Dave.
And he likes to shoot a gun;
He even likes to run.

He was in the war;
And he was very sore.
He got a Purple Heart;
Because he was very smart.

He has a lot of hair;
He will even wrestle a bear.
Dave is very strong;
And he can even sing a song.

Dave is good at fighting;
And that is why I am writing.
Dave sometimes sleeps in a tent;
He sometimes eats a mint.

Cameron Sarvis, Grade 4
North Elementary School, NC

Jerome
J ust so cool
E nergy to work
R esponsible
O utstanding
M ost improved
E nthusiastic

Jerome Triplett Jr., Grade 6
Mark Twain Elementary School, MO

I Am
I am energetic and athletic.
I wonder how people do magic.
I hear the rain on the roof.
I see me doing a stall.
I want to be a pro BMX-er.
I am energetic and athletic.

I pretend to sleep on the bus.
I feel sick and happy.
I touch a dragon.
I worry about dying.
I cry when I get hurt.
I am energetic and athletic.

I understand lattice.
I say don't do drugs.
I dream about my grades.
I try to get my grades up.
I hope my mom will unground me.
I am energetic and athletic.

Lance Woods, Grade 5
Berryville Elementary School, AR

Jesus Our Father

Jesus our Father came to Earth,
When Jesus came the world showed great mirth.
Jesus our Father taught us well,
About the scripture, please do tell!

If Jesus our Father
Loves a bird in a tree,
Don't you think He really
Loves you and me?

Jesus our Father, Lamb of God,
Forty days in the desert he did plod,
Without food or water in a tough situation,
Jesus our Father resisted temptation!

Jesus our Father died on the cross,
He didn't die to show who's boss.
Jesus our Father is in heaven above,
He came to Earth and showed great love!

Steven Buchanan, Grade 5
Providence Academy, TN

Softball

Softball season has begun,
We work hard, but it is fun,
The fundamentals are hit, run, and throw,
These are the things we have to know.

We wake up early to play,
Because we have practice every day,
Sometimes in the morning,
And sometimes in the evening.

Game Day is GREAT,
We put on our uniforms and are ready to play,
Sometimes we win and sometimes we lose,
Sometimes we win and sometimes we lose.

Ashley Sikes, Grade 6
Appling County Middle School, GA

Snow Friends

Roll them up
Stack them high,
Then put on a scarf or bow-tie.

Now it's time for the eyes,
That charcoal might look right into the skies.

You may stick a carrot on too,
But make sure you don't push it all the way through.

Finally the end!
Step back to look at your new snow friend.

Katie Anderson, Grade 6
Annunciation Elementary School, MO

Why Bees Can Only Say Buzz

Why bees can only say buzz is a truly interesting question
I have figured that out in a logical explanation
A long long time ago
Bees worked for their royal queen
But bees were mean to each other
So they were cruel, harsh, and mean
So the queen thought and thought
And let the bee join hands
She made the bees sing all day long
To make wonderful bands
The bees sang and sang a lot
And sang the whole entire day
They were very very tired
They were dizzy until the fifth of May
They were so tired the next day
They didn't know the words to the song
So they thought of an idea
To just keep humming along
That's what I figured instead of having a fuss
Bees always hum along to make the sound "buzz"

Rickie Jang, Grade 5
Forest Avenue Academic Magnet School, AL

Siblings

Siblings fight and feud
They get mad and throw their food
They take and use your clothes
Never return them then stick up their nose
They laugh at your pain
They drive you insane

Siblings cheer you up when you are blue
Their love will always be true
They buy you stuff from cool stores
They always help you finish your chores
Siblings always brighten your day
They make you happy in every way

Sometimes siblings annoy you
Other times they bring joy to you
But you will always love them no matter what they do
They think you are the voice of love
And they love you too

Frances Hudson, Grade 6
Childersburg Middle School, AL

Fantice

F antastic is my middle name
A mazing I am
N ot afraid
T echnology is my favorite subject
I ntelligent at Language
C ute girl
E xcellent in spelling

Fanticé Krystine DeJesus Flippen, Grade 4
Byrns L Darden Elementary School, TN

The Miami Dolphins
Green is the Miami Dolphins

It feels like the turf under their feet.
It tastes like Gatorade.
It looks like the grass on the field.
It smells like green apples.
It sounds like the crowd cheering.

Green is the Miami Dolphins
James Potter, Grade 5
Eminence Middle School, KY

My Best Friend Lauren
I have a wonderful friend
Named Lauren.
I met her
When I was six years old
In soccer.
At first she was not my friend.
But once I got
To know her
We were friends.
Now we are going to be best friends!
Hali Mantooth, Grade 5
American Heritage Academy, GA

My Little Brother
Person
Little, crazy
Running, laughing, jumping
What a wild, crazy little kid
Connor
Sean Hessler, Grade 5
Prince of Peace Catholic School, SC

Christmas
C hrist's birthday
H o ho ho
R ipping open presents
I nflatable globes
S nowball fight!!!
T ingling from bells
M istletoe
A lways think of others
S nowmen
Morgan Giordano, Grade 4
Moyock Elementary School, NC

Lizard
lizard
colorful, patterned
playing, running, climbing
fun to play with
animal
Logan Aaserude, Grade 5
Westwood Elementary School, AR

Bearing Creek and Forest
Hearing the enchanting sound of the wind singing,
Woo Whoosh La La La Woo Whoosh La La La
And the magical sound of the fish flying in and out
Splash slosh
The splashing of my feet tapping in the water
The feeling of cool water and rough rock on my feet
And the damp hot surface touching my bare sizzling skin
Smelling the beautiful smells
Of plants, water, and wet mud
Dancing in my nostrils like a ballerina
And the smell of the flowers
Tickling my nose like a feather
Seeing the beautiful sight of tadpoles begin 3rd step of their life cycle
And the water like crystals floating in the creek
Favorite place in nature
Olivia Murrell, Grade 4
Briarwood Elementary School, KY

A Blessing
As the chilly wind rises to a howl,
I see the sun shining bright through the mist
It brings hope, so overwhelming there are not words to describe
I feel as though a hundred little rays of happiness are showering me
It's a hidden blessing, knowing that it is crucial to me, to this world

As the waves gently lap the shore, as a mother handles a newborn babe
The majestic birds sing a song of truth, of love
It shows me my presence is also as beautiful as their voices
I feel as though I could happily burst into the forgiving heavens
It's a blessing in disguise, knowing it is crucial to me, to this world

As my tears slide off my cheeks and into the sodden ground
A beautiful thing begins to rise from where my misery lay
It blooms into bright reds, and warm golds bringing comfort to me
I know I could face anything as I gaze at its fragrant petals
It's a blessing unrevealing knowing that it is crucial to me, to this world

As my family and friends surround me in a fog of bliss
I bloom as a flower does in mid spring
As I gaze at the people who care for me, love me
I know there is not a force in this world that could deprive me of this feeling
It's a blessing no longer hidden, unrevealing, or disguised
Knowing it is crucial to me, to this world
Ellen Featherstone, Grade 6
Beck Academy, SC

Summer Nights
All is quiet and peaceful.
The crickets are chirping on this warm August night
And are filling the air with their song.
The soft brown-green grass feels comforting to my bare feet.
As I gaze at the pale glimmering moon surrounded by the dark night sky,
I take a picture of it in my mind so I will remember it forever.
Micah Overstreet, Grade 5
Sheridan Intermediate School, AR

Christmas

Christmas, Christmas!
When I think of Christmas,
I think of presents and making a wish list!
All around the world,
People celebrating joyfully!
Men who reign purposefully,
People enjoying a feast!
Turkey and squash,
Can't forget the cranberry sauce!
All the music, all the games,
From Huntsville to Mt. Hood,
From Dallas to Hollywood!
Let Christmas reign
And stop all the pain!
Over the hills
Let Christmas reign
From Harvard to Notre Dame!
Let Christmas reign
Through all the love
Through all the pain
Let Christmas reign!

Cody Conway, Grade 6
Alpena Elementary School, AR

Early Morning Hunt

Getting up at 4 a.m.
Dressing in hunting gear

Putting on boots and orange vest
Grabbing a gun and heading to the stand

Keeping quiet or nothing will show
Waiting 'til daybreak
Getting ready for a long wait
Every minute filled with nervous excitement

Even if nothing shows,
Still every moment is enjoyed
Hoping there are deer coming to the field

Steven Hughes, Grade 6
Appling County Middle School, GA

My Sister

To me my sister is as precious as gold
Even though she's four years old

Her favorite color is pink
Sometimes she smiles, sometimes she gives me a wink

Sometimes she starts to fuss
I calm her down; I know I must

For all that I have told
I always remember she's as precious as gold

Teddy Bilden, Grade 4
St Thomas More School, NC

Yankees vs Red Sox

Bottom of the 9th
The score is tied four to four
The coach looks at the sky and says
"There might be a down pour."
"We've got to make this game quick."
Says the umpire
"Good thing." says the Yankee's coach
"My team is on fire!"
Johnny Damon is up to bat
After two strikes
You hear a big smmmack!
Now that he's on first
It's time for Derek Jeter
He hits it past third
He's running as fast as a cheetah
It was an inside the park home run
Just then the skies opened up
The rain came down
And the crowd stood up
The Yankees ended up winning
What an incredible invigorating inning

Jacob Collett, Grade 5
Greathouse Shryock Traditional Elementary School, KY

I Admire My Daddy

The person I admire the most
Is my daddy.
He takes care of us
And takes care of his parents, too.
When he is in tough spots
He finds a way to get through it.
He goes to work every day.
I think without my daddy,
I would be very lonely.
He is fun because
He takes us to the park
Or for walks around the plaza.
When I grow up
I want to be just like him,
So my kids will be just like me,
And we can all follow the same footsteps.

KD Dicus, Grade 5
Lee A Tolbert Community Academy, MO

Deer Hunting

Walking hearing the blazing colorful leaves,
crunch under your feet,
Sitting in the old rusty tree stand motionless,
finally seeing a curious deer
suddenly I get a shot, crack!
The deer was down
Taking the deer back to camp
and showing it to everyone with ecstatic joy.

Ben Jaggers, Grade 5
North Middle School, TN

On the Carry

Running, jumping, moving
All the way down the field.
Diving, hustling, hitting
Right to the end zone,
I score!
I am adored
By the crowd.
Congratulations for my success
I hear.
Celebrating, partying, cheering
All the way home.

Joshua Duncan, Grade 6
St Paul the Apostle School, TN

Halloween

Jack-o'-lanterns in the night
Halloween parties what a delight.
Music in the streets,
Scary decorations what a treat.
I can't believe it is so neat!

Emily Largent, Grade 5
North Middle School, TN

Trick or Treat

T reats. there's a ton
R ed and orange
I n the bag goes the candy
C learly an awesome holiday
K ind of scary, some costumes

O ften you get a lot of candy
R inging doorbells

T ry to keep on the sidewalk
R ed and yellow colors everywhere
E very day I get more excited about
A ll of the costumes and colors
T rick or treat to you

Abby Hartley, Grade 5
First Flight Elementary School, NC

I Am a Monkey

I am a monkey
I swing from tree to tree
I live in the jungle
Where I eat and sleep
I am a monkey
Who loves to play
When I come you will see
that my favorite fruit lives on a tree
There's not much I can say about me
but what you do know is
I am a monkey

Jada Pollard, Grade 4
Brilliant Elementary School, AL

Gracious Green

Green
is the tall grass
flowing in the breeze.
Unnecessary weeds
developing
in a green garden.

A lily pad
floating peacefully
down a crystal clear river.
Crunch, crunch, crunch
is the grass
crunching under your feet.

An abandoned frog
in a massive rainforest
waiting for flies
he can devour.
Light green caterpillars
standing on leaves
and making holes

Green
is gorgeous nature.

Courtney Caldwell, Grade 6
East Oldham Middle School, KY

Ocean Waves

Smashing and crashing all around
The waves are high and falling down.
Down to the ground they go and go.
They never stop, but ever flow.

Madilyn Algren, Grade 5
Briarwood Christian School, AL

The Crazy Lazy Dogs

My dogs are so crazy,
boy they're so lazy.

They eat bones,
they chew bones,
they sleep on bones.
They're just so crazy!

They gaze and daze
out the window all day.
They're just so crazy!

They're so crazy and lazy,
but I love them so!

They're just my crazy,
lazy little babies!

Allison Daneault, Grade 5
Our Lady of Fatima School, MS

My Room

Messy, dirty, not very neat.
The crowded clutter sweeps
me off my feet.
Clothes, toys, and papers
on the floor.
It's so crowded my mom
can't get into the door.

"Get your room clean,"
my mom would yell.
And like a hermit crab,
I would want to crawl into a shell.

By the end of the year
I got a broom
got on my feet
and cleaned my room

Now that my room rules
maybe I need
to work on my locker
it isn't so cool.

Chayiesha Vance, Grade 6
Armorel Elementary School, AR

Dinosaurs

Have you ever seen
A dinosaur? They are tall
And eat meat a lot.

Rachel Walz, Grade 4
Briarwood Christian School, AL

I Am

I am a fifth grade student.
I wonder if I can pass high school.
I hear my sister playing games.
I see people working.
I want to grow up.
I am a fifth grade student.

I pretend to play games.
I feel people touching me.
I touch my mom's hand.
I worry about my family.
I cry when my family gets hurt.
I am a fifth grade student.

I understand when people get in trouble.
I say, "thank you" to people.
I dream about my family.
I try my best in school.
I hope I will pass fifth grade.
I am a fifth grade student.

Kenny Corbin, Grade 5
Byrns L Darden Elementary School, TN

The Sunrise

An orange sun,
Rises over an abandoned home,
a glowing street,
a mildew lawn
a large sun rises far away.
I see an orange bright sun,
shiny mildew,
shiny streets,
and bright skies.

Passing cars,
birds chirping in the grass
and a creaking house.
I wonder what time it is?
I wonder how many birds there were?
I wonder how cold it was?

I feel happy with this image for how it is so happy.
I feel happy with this image for it is beautiful.
I feel happy with this image for it is so warm.
I see an orange bright sun,
I see an orange bright sun,
I see an orange bright sun

Arlandis McClain, Grade 4
Price Elementary School, KY

Yellow Things

A sunshine hanging in the sky
Some shining corn on the stalk
A rope on me
A jolly rancher in my mouth
A bird singing a pretty song
A puppy laying on me and licking me
A sunflower in the yard
A book I am reading

Emma Rose Baker, Grade 4
St Charles Homeschool Learning Center, MO

What Is a Best Friend

A best friend is someone who you can tell anything.
And they won't think it is funny or stupid
they will tell you something that comes from their heart.
Not something they just made up to make you feel better.
That is what you call a Best Friend.

Minnie Lee Ratliff, Grade 5
West Marion Elementary School, MS

Christmas

Looks like red, green, white
Sounds like bells ringing
Tastes like cocoa
Feels like the cold winter breeze in my face
Smells like chocolate chip cookies coming out of the oven

Anna Gandy, Grade 5
Briarwood Christian School, AL

I'm a Mean Brother

I'm a mean brother
Yes it is true,
I'm a mean brother
I barely missed you!
Yes, you are my sister
you're mean, ugly, and 2,
yes, you are my sister
I love you a lot, too.

Bryant Birdsong, Grade 5
William Southern Elementary School, MO

Monster Trucks

Monster trucks are tough and loud;
They spin around and excite the crowd.
And when they crash the trucks and cars;
You can hear it all the way to Mars.
They're awesome to me and they always will be;
I hope that you can come and see!

Taylor Hill, Grade 5
North Middle School, TN

Summer Nights

Summer night, orange sky
After a fun BBQ.
The crickets are singing
The birds are humming,
The fireflies are flying to light up the night.
The stars are twinkling in the pretty orange sky.
The moon is reflecting over the streams;
The stars and the moon are shimmering.
The children are sleeping as the sun sets;
It's a summer night.

Jennifer Brammer, Grade 4
New Covenant Christian Academy, NC

Singing on Stage

This is what I see
This is what I see
This is what I see
In the eye of the Lord.

This is what I hear
This is what I hear
This is what I hear
In the ear of the Lord.

This is what I feel
This is what I feel
This is what I feel
In the hand of the Lord.

This is what I see — Faith
This is what I hear — Love the people
This is what I feel — I feel His touch

Courtney Coffey, Grade 4
Tazewell-New Tazewell Primary School, TN

Zero Gravity Stopped the World

I was walking down the street,
Then I couldn't even breathe.
'Cause I had no Oxygen.
In all of the hospitals,
The people were dead.
The Earth was falling out of the sky.
Zero gravity stopped the world.
I never knew how the world could exist,
floating in the universe.
Don't lock the house.
Zero Gravity stopped the world.

Gavin Williams, Grade 4
Stoneridge Academy, SC

The Sun

It makes us very happy
It hovers above the ground
Our big yellow sun

Natalie Lett, Grade 4
Briarwood Christian School, AL

A Kiss Is…

A kiss is a place of hope
A kiss is a sudden
Place of joy a kiss…
A kiss is like love
Love is a basket of
Sweetness — Sometimes
Love turns into tears
Tears are big lakes
Of sadness
But you have friends
To dry them all away
Friends are like a
Boomerang they always leave
But always come back!

Jas Lyons, Grade 6
Beck Academy, SC

I Love You

You're so sweet,
And very smart.
You're a little weird,
But you'll always be in my heart.

I love you so,
And I want you to know.
That when you're blue,
I'll be there for you.

You shine like the sun,
And I love you.
So don't burn out,
Because you're my light too.

Brooke Kinney, Grade 4
Lynn Fanning Elementary School, AL

Easter

It's the Easter season,
In an instant everyone feasts,
There is just a little grief,
For today is the day
Christ arose so high,
The Easter celebration starts with everybody singing
As an eagle flies by,
It's surely a sight,
On Easter, Jesus won the final fight;
Everyone full of hope and looking so bright,
There's always something new to see,
That's why people don't flee so quickly,
Everyone is so spiffy and nifty in new Easter clothes,
Everyone shifting seats as they anticipate a picnic at Grandma's house,
People realizing that the Easter message must be shared
With the lonely people still shivering,
Living in cardboard boxes;
Don't give up.
Today is Easter and His gift of life is for everyone!

Justin Leonard, Grade 5
JJ Jones Intermediate School, NC

The Concert

It all started on Christmas Day.
We were ripping open presents, all snuggled by the cozy warm fire.
It was my turn to open my presents, "yes I said."
I opened the tiny one, it looked like a DVD.
I examined the back, it was a picture frame,
With two Shania Twain tickets!
I screamed to the top of my lungs that they almost burst.
I was franticly excited.
I sprinted to hug my grandma.
I was ready for this concert.

A month passed by…I got home and we were ready to go to freedom hall.
We were there, they scanned our tickets and we were in.
I smelled the buttery popcorn,
Heard the people talking like mice,
Tasted the cherry red snow cone,
Put on the new shirt and…
"It's pitch black," right at that moment I saw her.
She's singing my favorite song "Up," we got out of our seats and started to jump.
I ran to the stage with my paper and pen and got her autograph.
"Oh my gosh I just got Shania Twain's autograph!"
Confetti fell, balloons fell and it was over. That had to be the best concert ever!!!

Emma Sedoris, Grade 6
South Oldham Middle School, KY

Circus

Looks like elephants going around in a circle
Sounds like tigers growling
Tastes like cotton candy melting in your mouth
Feels like furry tigers and monkeys
Smells like elephants, hot dogs, salty buttery popcorn, and cotton candy

John Hayden, Grade 5
Briarwood Christian School, AL

Best Dog

I just love the way
my dog plays, jumps, and chases me
He has wonderful dark black short hair,
and big brown warm cuddly eyes.
He has a wet silky nose.
He's hilarious when he plays with his favorite rag.
I adore the way he looks at me,
when I come around the corner
He's the most playful dog in the world
He's my best friend!

Tiffany Ward, Grade 5
North Middle School, TN

The Four Seasons

Snowflakes fall softly
A cold wonderful morning
The wind blowing hard

The flowers blooming
The birds flying in the sky
The breeze blowing easy

The hot sun burning
People splashing in pools
The warm wind blowing

The cool breeze blowing
The leaves falling from the trees
Pumpkins everywhere

Nicholas deVeer, Grade 6
Haynes Academy for Advanced Studies, LA

School Is Out

School is out
Kids run and play
Every day is a successful day.
We go places
We hang out
We chill and play
Maybe someone is having a bad day
But there will be other days to run and play

Kendra Lewis, Grade 5
West Marion Elementary School, MS

Summer Trees

You never hear trees whipping in the morning light.
Trees are as tall as a flying kite.
Trees weeping at the stars at night,
So many lovely trees, what a sight.

So many trees you can see when the day is bright.
Trees as tall as a jet in flight.
Some trees are as little as bright lights, right!
Trees can be as small as a night light.

Ra'Shawn House, Grade 6
Manning Elementary School, SC

I Am

I am nice and funny
I wonder what I will be when I grow up
I hear a bird chirping every day after school
I see a friend that follows me everywhere I go
I want to go to Disneyland
I am nice and funny

I pretend that I'm a teacher
I feel like I have a world that is all about me
I touch sandpaper on the chair
I worry when I get to school when my homework's not done
I cry when my friends get mad at me
I am nice and funny

I understand when my teacher is taking minutes off recess
I say that I can still like "That's So Raven"
I dream that I will be a super star
I try not to make F's
I hope I will be a teacher
I am nice and funny

Abby Gonzalez, Grade 5
West Elementary School, MO

Vortex

Waiting in line, my heart thumped,
Thump, thump, thump.
As we moved up the blue and yellow stairs
I could hear the loud roar.
We stepped onto the platform,
my feet shook every time it got close.
Before I could beg for mercy not to make me go,
the gates flew open.
The next thing I knew we were climbing
It felt like it never ended.
Before I knew it we were flying down a hill
and jerking from corner to corner.
A light flashed in my eye and I felt a sudden jerk, we were done.
"Mom, I did it. I rode my first rollercoaster, let's do it again."

Zachary Peters, Grade 6
East Oldham Middle School, KY

Basketball Rocks!

Basketball is my favorite sport.
My mom and dad just put a new goal on the carport.
I love to play in all my games.
I like to learn my teammates' names.
Everybody thinks my coach is cool.
I really think he rules.
His assistant
makes us run a long distance.
Even though we have to run,
basketball is lots of fun.
Score!

Jonah Hartline, Grade 5
North Middle School, TN

Lion/Kitten

Lion
large, loud
roaring, stalking, chasing
king, fighter, explorer, pet
purring, playing, looking
small, curious
Kitten
Maggie McDavid, Grade 5
Briarwood Christian School, AL

David

There was an old man who would lie
Some even called him a spy
He spied through the night
Caused a terrible fright
Now people say, "What a bad guy!"
David Lee, Grade 4
Judsonia Elementary School, AR

Summer

It is summer
Hot and dry
Boys break flowers
To give to friends
Kids run outside
And enjoy the sun
The sun shines down
Until night comes
After a summer a new
Season begins,
Fall
Chase Layson, Grade 5
G C Burkhead Elementary School, KY

Dreaming

Lights out now I'm asleep
The room was quiet I didn't hear a beep
Rubbery tubbery soft and neat floor
Golden slob I want more
Running down cookies and cream
Then I moved and took a turn
I woke and it was a dream
Jacquelynn Jackson, Grade 4
Carver Elementary School, NC

Life May Seem…

Life may seem
A ducky bit bad,
But do not fret
Nor feel too sad.
For your duck may
One day
Be a swan!
Kaielynn Jones, Grade 4
Contentnea Elementary School, NC

Warriors

Pads popping, teammates shouting
Parents yelling "Get the ball!"
Cleats crushing the grass
When making a touchdown
Bones crackin, blockers blockin
Runners runnin, starting dog piles
Players screamin, sweat drippin
Whistles blowing, the game is over.
The score Warriors 16 — Halls 6
We win!
Austin Pierce, Grade 5
North Middle School, TN

Crash!

A rattling chain loosened its grip
My eyes were focused on the ride
Until the dark blinded me
BAM!!!!
Gravel covers me
Sliding on my stomach
I got up
Scratches all over my helmet
Quad rolling
I jumped on it and stopped it
Rode back to my dad
I put on some ice
After awhile it stopped bleeding
After that crash, last ride
Turney Terhaar, Grade 5
Cline Elementary School, KY

What Am I

I blow through your hair
and blow through the trees
I blow in a slight breeze
I blow near the ground
and I blow up high
I am twisted and wound
What am I?
Quinton Inman, Grade 6
Ketchum Jr High School, OK

Friendship

F riendly
R eliable
I ntelligent
E ncouraging
N ot selfish
D oes not lie
S haring
H elpful
I mporatnt to have
P eaceful
Kirsten Jeffers, Grade 5
Sullivan Elementary School, TN

Magic

Magic is real.
Magic is on paper.
Magic is words.
Magic is words turned into sentences.
Magic is sentences turned into stories.
Magic is reading those stories.
Magic is reading.
Grace D. McKenna, Grade 5
Evansdale Elementary School, GA

Flowers

We sprout in the spring.
We breeze through the wind always.
We are delicate.
Olivia Miller, Grade 4
Briarwood Christian School, AL

Love

Love is a dance
that goes on and on without stopping
twirling round and round
he dips me down low
and pulls me up again
my partner and I listen to the music
playing our favorite song
the music doesn't stop for hours
but when it does, we slowly stop dancing
the dance is over
even though I want to dance some more.
Courtney Lampkin, Grade 5
Bloomfield Elementary School, KY

Happy Trees

The birds are singing.
The leaves are ringing.
The squirrels are in the nest.
For a long winter rest.

The fruit is growing on the tree.
You can hear the buzzing of bees.
The tree is warmed by the spring day.
When it is the month of May!
Sarena Lucas, Grade 6
Manning Elementary School, SC

Ms. Landry

Ms. Landry
Nice, fun
Grading, teaching, talking
Teaching me great things.
Working, singing, dancing
Pretty, funny
My student teacher
Ashlie Bowles, Grade 5
EA Harrold Elementary School, TN

I Sing

I sing of the time I go to Pennsylvania
Of the laughter I hear in my Grandmother's voice
Of all the joy she brings to my life
Of all the pearly white smiles she puts on faces
I sing of the time I went to the mall
And the kind friends I have
Of trying on shoes and picking out earrings
Then the parting of such sweet sorrow
I sing of the time I got a new pool
Which outside I swam for many hours
Till one evening we found a hole
Then I could swim no more

Courtney Nicole Franklin, Grade 6
Vicki Douglas School, WV

Mother Nature

The gravel roads crunched and crumbled
I see city lights no more
For passing into the uncivilized world
Leads you to a different door

Mother Nature has an origin here
Where the unknown creatures crawl
Perhaps this beautiful place
Has taken me one and all

Maggie Myers, Grade 6
Houston Middle School, TN

The Beach

Woosh! Woosh! The waves crash!
My feet sink down in the sand.
Sand and water swish between my toes.
Ocean water as far as you can see.

Shells! Shells! Everywhere!
Purple, red, orange, black, and white.
Curvy, pointy, smooth, and rough.
Imagine the creatures that lived inside.

Fish! Fish! Let's go fishing!
Feel the squishy, slimy bait.
Cast your line as far as you can.
Wait to pull in your catch.

Birds! Birds! Flying around!
Herons, sandpipers, and pelicans.
Waiting to catch fish with you.
I chase them away, but back they come.

Splash! Splash! Go for a swim.
The waves bump you up and down.
Look down and see a starfish,
Seaweed, sand dollars or a shark!

Cassidy Robbins, Grade 4
Schaffner Traditional Elementary School, KY

Our Love

Our love is a wasteland.
We try to make progress.
But every time our love just crumbles.
For all we have worked for.
It fails like a handful of dust falling through
between your fingers.

Austin Thompson, Grade 6
Sulphur Intermediate School, OK

My Baby Brothers

My baby brothers are oh so cute,
I love them very much and they love me too.
D.J. has green eyes,
Marques has blue,
Marques is one year old and D.J. is two.
D.J. has brown hair,
Marques has blonde,
Their skin is fair and also soft.
D.J. and Marques are so much fun,
They love to play outside in the sun.
They love to watch movies in the car,
Especially when we are driving very far.
My baby brothers are such a delight,
They are two little angels,
Especially at night.

Gabrielle Powers, Grade 4
Sequoyah Elementary School, TN

The Amazing Dream of the Chicago Beach

One day I was walking down the road
And saw the beautiful shining deep blue sea.
Smiling dancing around having a great time
That dream was going back to the beach
At night time but didn't really go
But saw it in my head
Brownish Yellow Shore
The swans singing so joyfully
And the ocean making whistling noises
Jumping into the shinny deep blue sea
Falling and picking myself back up again
But it was no place like the beach

Darrell Bowman, Grade 4
Briarwood Elementary School, KY

Twirling

Twirling and twirling
too dizzy to even stand.
As my body falls to the grass on a summer's day
there's no place I'd rather be.
I lay in the daisies as they sing to me,
I listen as they slowly and smoothly swish.
Rolling up and toppling down over hills and fields.
Still twirling along, up and down
there's no place I'd rather be.

Emily Dennis, Grade 5
Greathouse Shryock Traditional Elementary School, KY

Story

Dear gigantic book,
Help me!
Help me to write a story.
I'm exhausted,
All I want is to be famous.
Help me! Help me!
Be a friend.
I know you're listening.

Days later I look in the book,
There are ten pages of story,
Like I said,
Book, I know you're listening.

Triston Briggs, Grade 5
Cool Spring Elementary School, NC

My Dream

To dance is my dream
I can't let it die
For when I do dance
I feel I can fly.

I pray every night
That an angel will appear
To guide me through
All of my fear.

Dear angel, dear angel
I ask this of you
To guide me through
When I am down and blue.

The prayers will continue
My dreams will come true
I will always be grateful
To have an angel like you.

Amy Panzeca, Grade 6
St Rita School, LA

One Day

One day there will be horns a blow,
And Jesus Christ will say "Let's go!"
Then everyone will glide and soar,
And see that little earth no more.

Our Lord will come down here one day,
And see the earth where He once lay.
The cross of Calvary He died,
And to escape He never tried.

Our Lord will come down from the sky,
We'll tell that little world good-bye.
Then up to heav'n our Lord will lead,
Our little earth will then be freed.

Megan Adcock, Grade 6
Providence Classical School, AL

I Am

I am a creative girl who loves penguins
I wonder if there ever was a penguin that could fly
I hear the squawks of newly born penguin chicks in Antarctica
I see a penguin gliding peacefully through the glistening ocean
I want a penguin of my very own
I am a creative girl who loves penguins

I pretend to swim gracefully through the ocean with the penguins
I feel the water swirling around me, telling me that my friends are close by
I touch a slippery, wet penguin fin fresh out of the water
I worry that one day the penguin population will die out
I cry whenever a penguin dies in *March of the Penguins*
I am a creative girl who loves penguins

I understand that I will never have a penguin of my own
I say "don't litter, trash can get caught around a penguin's throat"
I dream that I live in Antarctica, where the penguins roam free
I try begging my parents to go visit Antarctica, they say "maybe"
I hope I one day do go visit Antarctica and all the penguins
I am a creative girl who loves penguins

Jessica Nolting, Grade 6
R D and Euzelle P Smith Middle School, NC

My Brother in War

My brother is not too big.
My brother is not small.
Like David against Goliath,
He fights for us all.

Sometimes war is good, sometimes it's bad.
Sometimes it's happy, sometimes it's sad.
It's good when it prevents evil.
It's sad when family members are away.

So every day I pray
For the soldiers who are far away;
Asking God to keep them out of harm's way
So they don't fall to their prey.

They build a barrier for the bombs that go bang
And the bullets that go blazing by;
Bring home my brother,
Then the only battle he has to fight is beating me on Xbox every night.

Kyle Clendenon, Grade 5
Providence Academy, TN

The Mystery

Do you ever wonder what it will be like, when the world ends?
Will it be in 5 seconds or 5 years?
Where will I be, what will happen to me?
Will I relive my life again and again, or will we all pray with God in Heaven?
I don't know, no one does, but only God knows what will happen.
Until then it's a mystery.

Haley Mueller, Grade 6
Queen of Angels Catholic School, GA

A Morning Beneath a Bleak Gray Sky

Slowly rising from the warm abyss of sleep,
I moan and snuggle deep into my warm blankets.
But there is no denying it,
my alarm clock beeps louder.
I tumble out of bed and turn off the cursed thing.
For once, could I have slept late?
The air is too frigid for just my pajamas.
It wasn't that cold last night.
Sluggishly I pull on a sweater
and peer out the window onto a white landscape.
More powdered sugar is falling
from the light gray sky.
A snow day, a *snow day*!
I hurriedly dress in my sweaters and jackets
to run down the stairs and barrel out the door
and make angels and snow men,
to get so cold that later on when I come inside,
I sit by the fire and warm my hands on a mug of chocolate
and love the relief from the cold.

Emily Fairchild, Grade 6
Charleston County School of the Arts, SC

Boredom Is Federal Blue

It smells like smoke from a fire.
It tastes like old nasty broccoli.
It sounds like a whole bunch of girls screaming.
It feels like a broken arm.
It looks like everything in my room is a mess.
Boredom is losing your best friend.

Lauren Bazemore, Grade 4
Pines Elementary School, NC

Prayer for the Soldiers Who Died

Thank you God, for putting your powers on our soldiers
And keeping them safe
Even though some of them died
We love our soldiers for everything they have done for us in
The United States
They gave all of their strength to keep us safe here at home

C.J. Ballard, Grade 5
Temple Hill Elementary School, KY

Stuff

Stuff under my bed
Is just dust
It is like stuff you don't play with
They'll rot and rot
Until you forget
That there is anything under your bed
SMACK
You throw another piece under your bed
That will soon be stuff
The stuff was a toy now dust
Anything you throw under your bed becomes stuff

Matt Mershon, Grade 5
Greathouse Shryock Traditional Elementary School, KY

If I Were the President

If I were the president
I would care for others,
Make decisions that will change the world,
And have security by my side.
I would be spiritual about my religion,
Talk to Americans about God
And how we can
make good choices in life.
My time will never be wasted.
I will not be offended
by what people think about me,
And Americans will have a say
before the country goes to war.
When Jesus comes, I can't wait,
I want to see his face. Hallelujah!

Morgan Chavis, Grade 5
Lee A Tolbert Community Academy, MO

Christmas

A time to be jolly.
Decorate things with balls of holly.
Presents under a brightly lit tree.
Waiting for Christmas day to come.
You know it will be a lot of fun
You'll be singing a Christmas song
All Christmas day long
And when everything's fine it will finally be time to
open up your presents

Jacob Cordero, Grade 5
American Heritage Academy, GA

Sisters

I get in a fight with my sisters a lot.
We know it isn't a pretty plot.
But it's our job, it's what we do.
Everyone does it, even you.
We hit and we scratch and we even scream.
Then we say, "I wasn't being mean!"
Although we may get in a fit.
We all love each other quite a bit.

Marina Forwith, Grade 6
Holy Trinity School, KY

The River

Let the river engulf you.
Let the river's playfulness unlock your emotions.
Let the river refresh your body and spirit.

The river helps to calm you, like a friend.
The river reveals its secrets
The river leads me to joyfulness.

And I need the river.

Isaac Constans, Grade 6
St Andrew's Episcopal School, LA

I Am Thankful

I am Thankful
And also Grateful
No matter what it is
Because it's the thought that counts

You should be Thankful for everything
Because you might not have anything
But if you do
Don't be to greedy about it too

I am so Thankful for everything
Most people don't have anything
I wish life wasn't so hard
But maybe it'll be easier in my dreams

Just give Thanks
For everyone, and everything
For anyone, and anything
That's why I am so glad for Thanksgiving
Krystyna Chavis, Grade 5
Pembroke Elementary School, NC

Seeds Around the World

Seeds fly everywhere
Where they will go,
No one knows
As the wind blows

Some land on deserts
Some land on mountains
Some may drown
In a fountain

Some might fly
Around the globe
They might even land
On your morning robe

Nature takes over
As they land
Eventually
You'll see something grand
After so many months
Something will appear
It's a flower you see,
All bright and clear
Brandon Hoyle, Grade 5
G C Burkhead Elementary School, KY

Thanksgiving

Thanksgiving turkey
Pumpkins and gourds on my porch
Thanksgiving has come.
Mary Glynn Scharf, Grade 4
Briarwood Christian School, AL

Dreams, Sweet Dreams

As I start to fall asleep,
Another dream occurs
Different every night,
Though some may seem a blur
Some might have fairies,
Dancing round my head
Some might have dragons,
So fierce all brave knights fled,
All is a mystery,
Until I fall asleep
So many different stories,
These dreams I'll always keep
So as the light begins to fade,
Night will take its place
I'll begin to drift asleep,
A smile upon my face
Micah Long, Grade 5
American Heritage Academy, GA

Flowers

They are so gorgeous
A garden filled with flowers
Pink, violet, green, blue
Carolyn Grace Phillips, Grade 4
Briarwood Christian School, AL

Monkeys

Jumping on trees
Swinging from vines
Dancing around
With a delight.

Peeling a banana
Taking a bite
What do you
Think I am?
Mackenzie Smith, Grade 4
St Thomas More School, NC

I Feel Sorry

I feel sorry for the trees
All they can do is sit around
They never get a say in anything
Never get to choose what goes on them
When they get chopped down
How old they will live to be

I feel sorry for the trees
They can't choose what they want to be
When they grow up
They have nothing to look forward to
No expectations for the future
No life
Becca Bonham, Grade 6
Chapin Middle School, SC

I Can't Dance!!

I'm not a dancer,
I can't dance!
I'm not a dancer,
I don't prance!
I'm not a dancer,
I can't twirl!
I'm not a dancer,
I might just hurl!
I'm not a dancer,
I can't leap!
I'm not a dancer,
I'm a heap!
I'm not a dancer,
I can't tango!
I'm not a dancer,
I'm a mango!
I'm not a dancer,
I'm a poet!
I'm not a dancer,
I just know it!
I CAN DANCE!!
Emily Childers, Grade 5
North Hartsville Elementary School, SC

New Car

Twinkle Twinkle
Brand new car
I get in and drive real far
Comfortable in leather seats
Yeah this car is really sweet
Twinkle Twinkle
Brand new car
I get in and drive real far
Parker Sparrow, Grade 6
Armorel Elementary School, AR

Yoga

I am a lion,
a camel,
a pigeon.
I am water,
calm,
flowing.
I am earth,
rooted,
balanced.
I am fire,
power,
strength.
I am wind,
bending,
swaying.
I am yoga.
Emma Astrike-Davis, Grade 6
Montessori Community School, NC

I Can't Write a Poem*

Forget it, you must be kidding.
I had to pop my fingers. I had to pull my sleeves up.
My pencil broke. I had to sharpen my pencil.
I was playing with my nails. I didn't have a sheet of paper.
I went to bed at midnight. My brain is still asleep.
I can't see the lines. I am distracted.
I had to blow my nose. I am too busy looking around.
I had to do something else. I was reading a book.
I had to use the bathroom. I had to throw something away.
I had to fix my hair. I can't write neat.
I had to talk to somebody. I had to tie my shoe.
I had to put some led in my pencil. I had to clean out my desk.
Times up? UH OH!
All I have is a list of dumb excuses
You like it? Really? No kidding
Would you like to see another one?

Amber Parker, Grade 6
Lost River Elementary School, KY
*Patterned after "I Can't Write a Poem" by Bruce Lansky

Little Brother

I have a noisy tiny little brother
I took him to my mother.
I said I want another little brother
that isn't chubby tubby.
She said don't be a bother so
I took him to my father.
I said I want another itsy bitsy
little brother that doesn't ooz green gooze.
Which doesn't stink and shrink.
He said I couldn't have another because
I already have a brother!
So I put him back to sleep in his teeny weeny crib.

Jacob Bouknight, Grade 4
E O Young Jr Elementary School, NC

The Great White Shark

Great white sharks live in the sea
Just go down there and you can see.
Its dorsal fin makes it go fast
So you better run and swim away like rocket's blast.

Its top is dark,
But its bottom is sharp.
So I'm telling you, you better run away fast,
Or he'll eat your heart.

Don't come to me, I'm six feet tall,
You come too close, and I'll eat you all.
That's who I am.
That is my plan.
So stay away from my clan.
I'm a Great White Shark!!

Brannon Forbus, Grade 4
A H Watwood Elementary School, AL

Christmastime

On every Christmas Eve,
I check outside to see if the snow has fallen on the leaves.
When Mom opens her present,
she feels very pleasant.
All the children believe when you are sleeping in bed,
you may hear the sounds of Santa Claus' sled!
But if you've been bad,
you might be a little sad.
So next Christmas Eve,
try not to be bad!
Then maybe while you are lying in bed,
YOU will hear the sound of Santa's sled!

Justis Ragsdale, Grade 5
Alpena Elementary School, AR

My Dog Liza

My dog Liza is funny.
She hops through the house like a bunny.
She chases my cat,
Occasionally wears hats,
But always chews my shoes.

Liza is one hundred pounds.
She loves to roll around.
We took her to the vet,
And what do we get?
One hundred pounds of love.

Liza is sweet,
No other dog can compete!

Anne Czerwonka, Grade 6
Holy Trinity School, KY

The Beautiful Flower

The beautiful flower is yellow and green,
with red and blue and white in between,
I watch it grow up on the hill,
I wish it were on my window sill,
There I could smell the fragrance it brings,
and watch it grow all through the spring,
One day I looked and saw it was gone,
My dog had dug it up to bury a bone.

Bethany McKenzie, Grade 5
West Marion Elementary School, MS

Space

Space is extraordinary.
It is as wonderful as art.
Space is colorful like emeralds, diamonds, and rubies
Sparkling in the sky.
The stars are blobs of paint on the black paper of the universe.
Galaxies are the paint that makes up the whole painting.
If the stars go black, the painting will lose its beauty.
This is how important space is to me.

Robert Glass, Grade 6
Wayne Country Day School, NC

Blue

Blue is like the sound of the breezing wind of a spring day when a storm is about to pass
Blue is like the smell of fresh chlorine from a pool in the summer
Blue is like the taste of yummy blueberry muffins coming out of the toasty warm oven
Blue is like the feel of the warm fuzzy baby blue blanket that gets me through the cold blustery nights

MaKenzie Clark, Grade 4
Plano Elementary School, KY

Where I'm From

I am from soda, from Coke and sugar.
I am from the junk in the big but dark, dark cabinet.
I am from the ficus flower apple, the willow's limbs are as sad as me.
I am from Christmas and French from Steve and Liana and Roger.
I am from the side of my family that has funny cowlicks
And I look just like my 30-year-old brother when he was my age.
From don't touch and don't do that.
I am from Catholicism and I believe in God.
I am from New Hampshire, pizza and pie.
From the Clermont side of my family.
My sister and I stayed with my Uncle Ray and Aunt Jean
at Lake Winnipesaukee for a week one summer.
Both teachers, they are lots of fun to be around and full of patience and ideas.
Sarah, their daughter is always great to be around and her brother, David, is in college.
I am from New Hampshire and have lots of photos and memories both in my mind
and in my home in North Carolina.
A little glass dog on my shelf reminds me of a special elderly great aunt who is a nun,
and we visit her in the nursing home and write to cheer her up.
When I look at it, I smile and think of how sweet she is.

Matthew Clermont, Grade 6
Lakeshore Middle School, NC

Place

Rocky, brown, wet, green,
The water falls from the rocks,
The animals minding their business, not even looking at the tourist,
Trees skyrocket over me.
The cool, cold, body of water around me consumes my whole body in an arctic force of sheer power,
Yet I'm at ease, the rocky surface on the bottom almost feels soft because of the fungus growing on it,
And the dirt on the ground sticks to my feet and I have to go through the battle of fighting the dirt off.

The water tastes filtered and the air tastes crisp, warm, and clean,
But the dirt I get in my mouth
Tastes like a sour glass of milk and expired raw meat,
And the bacteria on the bottom gives the water an extra flavor,
But still the water tastes good.
A faint odor lingers around the water,
The strong smell of the mud is everywhere,
And the odor of the leaves are everywhere, too,
Of equal strength with the scent of palm trees and the cinnamon bark.
I hear the tropical birds overhead,
I hear the trees shackle in the wind,
I hear the water splash under me,
I hear the animals moving in the forest next to me.
Where am I?

Luke Parish, Grade 5
The Altamont School, AL

College

You have to get a scholarship to get in college,
College is a place to get more knowledge,
College has many activities to do,
College is a place for you,
In college you put something in your head,
You have fun and go to bed,
I might go to Rust,
Because that's a must,
More fun and games,
But you have to be tamed,
I like college,
And I love knowledge.

Marquese Owens, Grade 4
Greenhill Elementary School, MS

My Special Friend

My mom reminds me of a butterfly.
She is graceful when she is happy
And gentle when she plays
with me and my brothers.
She has a soft snore.
She can also be like a lion.
When she is mad she roars
And doesn't let anyone mess
with her babies.
She has long, brown hair
And she can run fast.

June Brooks, Grade 5
Lee A Tolbert Community Academy, MO

Dancing Queen

I love hip hop
Lock, drop, and pop
I want to dance and never stop
Tap and Jazz
is full of pizzazz
shuffle, heel, toe
Across the stage I go
Spins, twirls, and leaps
You can't stop the beat
Sparkle, glitter, shine
Get in line, it's almost time
5, 6, 7, 8
Center Stage is gonna be Great!

MacKenzie Keating, Grade 5
Greathouse Shryock Traditional Elementary School, KY

Walk Along the Beach

Feel the shells hit your feet, feel the water
soak in the sand and your feet sink,
feel the sun shining on your neck,
listen to the waves crashing into shore,
look at seaweed floating in the water,
hear the birds above you.

Audrey Jeanette Smith, Grade 6
Greenville Montessori School, NC

Macbeth

M urderer of Banquo and others
A ttacked and killed King Duncan in his own castle
C lever and greedy when it comes to wanting the throne
B eheaded by Macduff outside of Dunsinane
E asily talked into things
T wo-faced after the witches tell him he will be king
H ard to trust or believe

Mason Sifford, Grade 6
Dunbar Middle School, AR

Yellow

Yellow is the color of pencils.
Like a fox softy breathing while stalking pray.
Slowly moving, leaving tracks behind.
If he makes a mistake
He goes back to cover his tracks.

Yellow is the color of tennis balls.
Like feet stomping on the ground.

Yellow is the color of lemons.
Getting squeezed to make lemonade.

Yellow is the color of laughter.
Yellow is the color of happiness.
Yellow is the color of sunlight.

Yellow,
WOW!

Bradford Trent, Grade 6
East Oldham Middle School, KY

A Smart Girl

I am a smart girl that gets it from her mom.
I wonder what will happen tomorrow.
I hear my mom telling me you can do it.
I see me having a good day.
I want to have a good future.
I am a smart girl that gets it from her mom.

I pretend that nothing bad will happen.
I feel I will pass the 5th grade
I touch my goal
I worry that something will happen to my family.
I cry when I think of my puppy.

I am a smart girl that gets it from her mom.

I understand that some day something bad will happen.
I say good things.
I try to be a good girl.
I dream that nothing bad will happen.
I am a smart girl that gets it from her mom.

Ramie Cook, Grade 5
Byrns L Darden Elementary School, TN

In the Morning Sun

In the morning sun,
I see a little doe,
Out among the misty air.
It ran like a tiger,
Stopped like a bird.
I run outside,
Looking all around, I see it running
Running across the bridge.

Morgan Katz, Grade 4
St Thomas More School, NC

Clouds

I lie in the green grass,
Looking up at the sky.
I see clouds in all shapes and sizes,
Going by and by.

I see dragons with clouds of smoke
Coming out of their nostrils.
I also see judges
Ruling the councils.

I see ships with bumpy sails,
All because of the wind.
I see boards big and small,
On them things are pinned.

How I wish I could float
Up with those clouds.
And be in a shape
Of a cat that's proud!

Allison Dear, Grade 4
St Thomas More School, NC

Winter Fun

cold
wet
slick
and
snow
winter
frost
away
we
go
right
through
the
snow
in
our
icy
sleigh

Joel Beaver, Grade 5
St Michael Parish School, WV

Football

Football is about teamwork
Football is really hard stuff
If you're a quarterback
Your arm they will jerk
Defense is fun, offense is too.
But once you get hit
You will turn black and blue.

DeAndre McGill, Grade 5
Wynne Intermediate School, AR

Heart Broken

I have a family,
As most do,
I don't get to see them,
Unlike you,
I miss them a lot,
You would too,
My grandma was always there,
When I needed her,
When she died,
I moved,
I don't see my family much,
But I would love to.

Cody Hunt, Grade 5
Crab Orchard Elementary School, KY

I Am

I am a black and white soccer ball
Flying through the sky,
Going into the soccer goal.

I am a tall field goal
Standing in the breeze,
Waiting for the brown and white
Football to go through me.

I am a baseball soaring through
The air out of the park.

I am an orange basketball
Going over all the other players
Into the basket.

I am, I am, I am.

Spencer Lee Morphis, Grade 4
Cool Spring Elementary School, NC

My Pet

Moonpaw
cute, fuzzy
fast, active, running
delightful, adorable, friendly, happy
Hamster

Harrison Langston, Grade 4
Cleveland Elementary School, OK

Hawk

I'm flying around,
Searching,
Sharp talons grasp…
A mouse.
I'm like an arrow.

Andrew Naeger, Grade 5
St Vincent Elementary School, MO

The Spanish Explorer

He was an explorer,
Who sailed on the Mayflower.
He met the Native Americans,
And called them Indians.
He was a navigator,
Who sailed from shore-to-shore.
He sailed the ocean blue,
This is really true,
In 1492.

Havanna Klamm, Grade 6
Clarksburg School, TN

Chihuahuas

I love Chihuahuas!
They're so soft and cute.
I like the way they feel like tissue.
I like when they play with me.
Their ears stick up way up high
Until they reach the sky.
The one thing that makes me cry
Is when they are alone in the night.
I cry boo-hoo!

Marty Bowers, Grade 5
North Middle School, TN

Blizzard/Wildfire

Blizzard
cold, white
blowing, snowing, freezing
storm, calamity, disaster, inferno
burning, smoking, spreading
furnace, bright
Wildfire

Patrick McGucken, Grade 5
Briarwood Christian School, AL

Princess/Prince

Princess
beautiful, kind
dancing, caring, commanding
daughter, lady, son, man
loving, sharing, charming
handsome, gentle
Prince

Hannah Hutson, Grade 5
Briarwood Christian School, AL

Math

Math is full of numbers,
Flying in and out of your brain.
Sometimes they're confusing
And make you go insane.
But math will help you all your life.
Division, addition, subtraction and multiplication,
Through all kinds of strife.
Even fractions,
Though they send you brain into traction.
Remember, even when it makes you crazy
Don't stress, you're not lazy.
It's just math.

Sara Walden, Grade 5
Meramec Elementary School, MO

Writing

Do you like to write stories?
Well, I love to write
It can be fun, but it can also be hard
Sometimes you have to brainstorm.

I love personal narratives because
you write about yourself.
This is my favorite kind.
It tells about yourself.

If you don't like poems try practicing
The more you practice
the easier it becomes.
At first boring, but now it is okay.

I like writing because you can write
about anything and you can start the
story by asking a question.
Then you write your opinion.

My tip on writing in portfolios is
check your work and try your
best, if you don't you are going
to have a bad story and low grade.

Alison Wigley, Grade 4
Schaffner Traditional Elementary School, KY

Wrestling

Wrestling is cool
ice skating is not
wrestling is so cool that it makes me want to join the WWE.
Ice skating is so boring
it makes me want to watch it more!
Ice skating is so dumb
the people who ice skate
it makes me want to fall asleep, and snore.
I like wrestling more.

Demarquis Calloway, Grade 5
Wynne Intermediate School, AR

My Cat Boots

I have a cat, he stays inside with me,
He's cute, but sometimes he's very mean!
He loves to play and pounce on you,
He likes to rest like most cats do.
He sneaks outside where he can't be seen,
We have to go and put him back inside,
Where he's supposed to be.
He won't drink milk,
He's particular about his food.
But he's still my cute little cat named
Boots!

Hannah Sparks, Grade 5
Paint Lick Elementary School, KY

A Football

A football is round
for being thrown around

The strings
are used for good things

It's filled with air so it could be thrown high
in the sky.

The BIG leather strip
helps you get a grip
to where it doesn't slip out of your hand
when you throw the ball to the man.

The spiral shape lets the football fly
in the sky like a wild butterfly

Carson Ray, Grade 5
Arnaudville Elementary School, LA

Monopoly

M onopoly is fun to play
O h wouldn't you say
N o, just like to own the trains
O r the game can be a real pain
P ark place and board walk do I want bad
O nly I lost the money I had
L ooking for properties to own
Y es, it makes me want to moan

Tanner Lee Law, Grade 6
Nodaway Holt Elementary School, MO

What Is Freedom?

Freedom
costly, priceless
delivers, releases, rescues
liberty, independence, dependence, captivity
tired, excluded, exhausted
unhappy, cruel
Bondage

Emma Roemen, Grade 5
Briarwood Christian School, AL

I Am

I understand I'm tall
I saw hover cars are real
I dream about my girlfriend
I try in football
I hope I will be an NFL playa
I want to be like Peyton Manning
I hear people chanting my name
I see myself running the longest yards
I pretend to be a pro football player
I feel good about the future
I touch a football
I worry I'll get killed in football
I cry that the world will end
I am athletic and tall

Christian Burlingame, Grade 5
Berryville Elementary School, AR

Autumn

A ct as if you were a scary thing
U ntil the midnight clock goes ding
T ake a pumpkin and carve a face
U p in the sky witches race
M aybe this case is very major
N othing awake is in danger

Hope Cary, Grade 4
Elon Elementary School, NC

Dirt Bike

D angerous
I nsanely fun
R acing
T rouble

B roken bone
I n the hospital
K ick starting
E xtreme

Matthew Warren, Grade 4
New Salem Elementary School, NC

My Dog

My dog likes to play all day
My dog was born in May
I wish my dog could fly
But all he does is eat pie

Alex Rascon, Grade 4
Horace Mann Elementary School, OK

Ghost

G ory and startling,
H aunted and frightening,
O ften dressed up as, in October.
S pirits of the undead,
T errifying creatures!!!!

Seth Pugh, Grade 5
First Flight Elementary School, NC

Breezy Summer Days

Scrumdiddlyumptious watermelon and cantaloupe, with juicy fruits
Games and splashing around in the pool
Fluffy, furry, adorable animals
Long lasting, magical vacations
Entertainment calling me at the Amusement Park
Fooling around at friends' houses
Accommodating family at our family reunion
Digging and splashing in water and sand at the beach
Wild, wacky playing
Sports and excitement to enjoy all the time

Abby Taylor, Grade 6
Alvaton Elementary School, KY

The Beach

Beautiful, blue oceans
Little kid's sadly sulking sunk sand castles
Graceful, exhilarating waves crashing and clonking
Loud yells of the bored ice cream man
Delicious mint chocolate ice cream, dripping down my hand
Tasty boardwalk hotdogs freshly cooked on a huge black charcoal grill
Brown disgusting sand taking a stroll into my widely opened, yawning mouth
Bright red sand shovels screaming, "Make a huge sand castle with tall
towers and arched doorways with me please, oh please"
Soft sand when I gently lay my head down as if it were a soft feather pillow
Joyful and excited

Madison Capps, Grade 6
College View Middle School, KY

I Am…

I am athletic,
I may be small,
but I can hit and
run like a dog.
Catch and throw.
Judged to be short, but I'm 4 feet 10 inches
Full of stone.
I send mean things through my mind and out the back of my head.
I can take anything because I have the best man on my side, God.

Jay Davis, Grade 6
Beck Academy, SC

The Bengal Tiger

Crouching low in the high grass the Bengal tiger waits.
Its orange and black fur, hardly noticeable.
Its cold, green eyes watching an object, never breaking concentration.
The object is a deer as it is his supper; he will attack it without hesitation.
Slowly and cautiously, the deer strides out into the open sun.
The tiger will attack the deer so fast; it will have no time to run.
Suddenly, there is a flash of orange and black and then the deer is dead.
Upon inspection of the deer, from its head blood bled.
Enjoying its supper the tiger eats away ravenously at the dead buck.
The remains show where the tiger struck.
At a moderate pace, the tiger strode through the dense forest on a full stomach.
Who is his next unlucky prey?

Stephen Glasgow, Grade 6
Houston Middle School, TN

Fall

Looks like leaves so colorful, so bare
Sounds like wind whirling everywhere
Tastes like spices, turkey, and so much more
Feels like blankets so soft and warm
Smells like campfires, cookies, and sweet cranberries.

Elizabeth Eaton, Grade 5
Christ at Home Lutheran School, MO

What Is Willing to Be

I am a daughter of a wonderful mother.
I hear my mother's voice.
I see my pretty drawings.
I want to be an archeologist.
I am a daughter of a wonderful mother.

I pretend to play with my fairy friends.
I feel my mother's soft hands.
I touch my mom's pretty hair.
I worry about my mom.
I cry when I am in trouble.
I am a daughter of a wonderful mother.

I understand when my mom helps me.
I say, "I love you" to my mom.
I dream that one-day things will be easier.
I try to do my best.
I hope to achieve my dreams.
I am a daughter of a wonderful mother.

Jessie Kilts, Grade 5
Byrns L Darden Elementary School, TN

Across the Yard

In my backyard,
Stood an apple tree,
It was put there by my family,
We watched it grow every day,
Thinking of the apples we would eat one day.

Apple pie, apple strudel, apple butter oh my,
All these things filled my head,
Then I realized I was in an apple stupor,
Apple this apple that,
All I could think of was apples,
Grow tree, grow.

Oh no, what happened?
Where did my apple tree go?!
It was there yesterday,
At least I think so,
Oh no, no apples,
No apple pie, no apple tarts, no apple butter,
I was frightened to see my dead apple tree,
Being chewed by my dog all day and night,
My dog ate my apple tree.

Bryson Jones, Grade 6
Chapin Middle School, SC

Dreams

Dark dreams through the night,
Like a gentle touch of faith,
Some dreams full of light.

Like the moon and the stars,
Shining and watching,
Darker dreams through the night.

Some things come together,
Some things fall apart,
Even darker dreams.

Now starting to fade,
Beginning to show light,
Gradually fading.

Now it is light,
Very light,
But now I feel darkness the most,
All my dreams have disappeared.

Jenna Schiavo, Grade 5
Hunter GT Magnet Elementary School, NC

Ocean

The ocean loves, hates, weeps and has anger
To have something like this on earth is awesome and powerful
But in its anger it can do things unwillingly
The ocean can do bad things to us without us foreseeing
The ocean is like us
We can also do bad things in our anger
But weep not because we are also calm and loving.

Juan Pablo Pilco, Grade 6
St Francis Xavier School, AL

October

Leaves rustling
People talking
"Psst"
"Psst"
"Psst"
I hear.
Why?
People are creating noise to upset the
Peace.
Planes roaring,
Trucks moving,
Horns blaring,
The train in the distance.
Anything but silence.
Wind chimes tinkle.
The wind creating a sudden uproar sending leaves tumbling.
I shiver
This is October.

Danielle Wilson, Grade 6
Francine Delany New School for Children, NC

October

O ak tree leaves are turning yellow.
C old air surrounds me.
T urtles are trying to keep warm.
O tters play in the water and
B anjos passed around a campfire.
E njoying candy on Halloween.
R eindeers ready to test flight.

Ryan Tooley, Grade 5
First Flight Elementary School, NC

My Dad

My Dad played baseball in the spring.
I know my Dad is the king.
When my Dad is up to bat,
My Dad always turns around his hat.

My Dad is number one in the state,
And to me he is first-rate.
My Dad makes everyone look slow.
He always puts on a great show.

Dustin Bunner, Grade 6
Pleasants County Middle School, WV

Apple

Apple
Round, juicy, red
Eating, chewing, cleaning
A juicy treat for me at night
Fruity

Buffie Lance, Grade 6
Nodaway Holt Elementary School, MO

Hair

I don't like hair on my nose
I don't like hair on my toes
Hair on my head is okay
Hair on my back *no way*
If I go bald it will be on my clothes

Tyler Todd, Grade 6
Appling County Middle School, GA

Snow

Snow, snow
white and soft,
like a pillow
see it in the midnight glow

Snow, snow
falling on the rooftop
spring will be coming,
I whisper
with daisy tops
and raggy mops.

Summer Nader, Grade 4
New Salem Elementary School, NC

Indian Friends

Indians are smart
They can be very friendly
They will not hurt you.

Ellie Woods, Grade 4
Briarwood Christian School, AL

Normandy

A night of death is what I call
A bloody day where soldiers fall
The day no soldier was to flee
A day that I call Normandy

And I landed on the ground to see
And on the ground a man did see
Then on the ground the soldier fell
And on the ground he froze like bells

The German soldier came to see
And then they all did start to flee
Then they saw men from U.S.A.
And that is how we won the day

David Oldfather, Grade 6
Providence Classical School, AL

Christmas

Christmas season is the best.
It's better than all the rest.
It's a time with lots of snow.
You'll even get gifts, you know.
Christmas here, Christmas there,
Christmas is everywhere,
Especially during Christmas season.
Well, I guess everyone has their reason.
But Christmas isn't just decking the halls
or receiving little Cabbage Patch dolls.
Christmas is the celebration
Of Jesus Christ and His creation.
Jesus is God's only son.
He is also the chosen one.
It's all here now, everyone's on the run
because the Christmas season has begun.

Devan Kelty, Grade 6
Holy Trinity School, KY

My New Friend

It was my first day at school
No one wanted to be my friend
Until he came up to me
We played together all the time
His hair is like lemon yellow
Sprouting in the sun,
And light peachy skin
Growing in the tree under the sun

David Feng, Grade 4
Briarwood Elementary School, KY

Horses

H eroic
O pen minded
R eally great
S weet
E xcellent
S mart

Erika Maliszewski, Grade 4
St Thomas More School, NC

Sister

G ood sister
R eady to get help when needed
A true friend
C lassy
E ncouraging

Victoria Olinger, Grade 5
Briarwood Christian School, AL

Sarajevo

My name is Cicko,
I am a bird.
I perch in the kitchen,
My squawks unheard.

It pains me to see,
The girl I hold dear.
Locked up in a cellar,
Drowning in tears.

This war is of madness,
These soldiers like children.
Disturbing our peace,
For some stupid reason.

I hear the shells laughing,
As they blow through the town.
I hear them all snickering,
A horrible sound.

I hear the whiz of a bullet,
The crash of a shell.
Peace is not found here,
For this war is hell.

Zane Erikson, Grade 6
Ligon Middle School, NC

Smiles

Smiles, smiles, I see smiles.
Smiles, smiles, I love smiles.
Smiles, smiles, everywhere
Smiles, smiles, we all wear.
Smiles, smiles, look over there
Smiles, smiles, I'll give you one to share.

Cameron Wright, Grade 4
Evangelical Christian School, TN

When a Breeze Touches Your Skin

When a breeze touches your skin
It gives you a little shiver
When a breeze touches your skin
It makes you quiver
It also makes your nose
Sniffle a little
When a breeze touches your skin
You get a little giggle
When you feel something touch your skin
See what happens
Maybe it's a breeze touching your skin
A little.

Emma Sacco, Grade 4
St Thomas More School, NC

Kali

Long blonde hair, skinny, hazel eyes
Long light blue dresses that touch the floor
"My bad," and "So?"
Swimming at grandma's and grandpa's house and
Running out at Rich's field and trails
My brothers Adam and Tyler
Homework and school
Thinking about my dad in his truck
My Mom's pizza

Kali Pierce, Grade 5
Our Lady Catholic School, MO

Christmas Time Is Closer

C hristmas time is a jolly season
H ere comes the white snow
R ight around the corner are the carolers
I can't wait
S weet cookies in my mouth
T aste the hot chocolate
M any people can't wait
A s it is said, "Tis the Season"
S o much to enjoy

T ime to be friendly
I n my mind it is the best season
M emories to remember
E veryone comes over

I 'm so excited
S melling the fragrance of apple pie

C ome and join us today
L ove is in the air
O ur lights shine so brightly
S ee them sparkle and glow
E veryone enjoys the time together
R emember this day forever and always

Mason Coulter, Grade 5
Clarksburg School, TN

My Sister Hannah

Hannah is silly.
Hannah is fun.
Hannah will sing and dance with everyone.

She takes the clothes off my GI Joes.
She pulls my hair and picks her nose.

She loves candy, candy galore,
but I try to hide it so she can't find any more!

She makes me laugh when I'm mad
and tries to spank me when I'm bad.

That's my sister Hannah.
She's real playful, but sometimes
crazy and may even cry like a baby!

But, you must understand that I love her anyway
just the way she is!

Nathaniel Greene, Grade 6
Salisbury Academy, NC

I Am

I am a crazy boy who loves baseball
I wonder when I'm going to win the World Series
I hear the crowds roaring now
I see the big trophy being presented to me
I want that ring for winning the World Series
I am a crazy boy who loves baseball

I pretend to hit one over the fence every day
I feel the pressure coming down on me
I touch the cold wood of the bat
I worry that I will strike out
I cry when I do
I am a crazy boy who loves baseball

I understand we can't win every time
I say we can
I dream to win the World Series
I try as hard as I can
I hope I will win the World Series
I am a crazy boy who loves baseball.

Ben Smoots, Grade 6
R D and Euzelle P Smith Middle School, NC

What Is Blue?

Blue is the ocean waves flooding on the beach.
Blue is the rain clouds floating in the sky.
Blue sounds like the raindrops scattering on the ground.
Blue is the cold wind in winter.
Blue is snowflakes covering the ground.
Blue feels calm and relaxing.
Blue smells like flowers in the fields.

Andrew VanCamp, Grade 5
Meredith-Dunn School, KY

Fall Is Fun
F alling into the crunchy, colorful leaves,
A lways with family and friends,
L aughing and joking,
L ulling babies to sleep,

I nstant joy,
S ummer is gone,

F rolicking in the cool air,
U nder God's love,
N o cares at all!
Hannah Patenaude, Grade 5
Palmetto Christian Academy, SC

Wind
Fall is near
Fall is coming
When fall is here
The wind will be humming

The wind will hum a soft tune
When you lay in the bed
You'll stare up at the moon
Then you'll slowly drift into
A soft slumber

The leaves will dance upon a tree
Each with a colorful skirt
The wind will blow
It makes my eyes hurt
Christian Fisher, Grade 5
Midway Covenant Christian School, GA

Leaves During Fall
Leaves falling to the ground,
"Look at the pretty leaf I found."
Colors orange, gold and red,
Leaves are showering my head.
Jump into the pile of leaves,
Or do anything you please.
Leaves swirling down the street,
Coming at us like a fleet.
Leaves twirling up the lane,
None of them are very plain.
The trees have few or no leaves at all,
Oh well, that happens during fall.
When I look up to the sky,
I see the sun is waving bye.
I hear my mom call my name,
I stay right here all the same.
My mom finds me right then,
She asks me where I have been.
We head back to my front door,
Tomorrow I'll be back for more.
Emma Sona, Grade 5
Wohlwend Elementary School, MO

Tears to Remember
I look at the motionless body
Smelling the beautiful flowers beside it
It fills my heart with sadness

Suddenly they walked in
The Masons
As they were talking they held up a picture and began to speak
"We are gathered here today to hold the memory
of the loving grandfather of Rayanna, Terry, Logan, Kaylee, and Caleb"

I see tears rolling down my dad's face
DRIP DROP
A tear suddenly rolling down mine
A tear to remember
Rayanna Breedlove, Grade 6
East Oldham Middle School, KY

Amazing Fall
Leaves changing different colors
Fall is starting to get chilly
Leaves falling off trees
Pumpkins are now on sale
Some pumpkins are waiting to be carved
Parents are leaving for fall and winter
Halloween is coming to town
Children are helping their mom and dad decorate for Halloween
Stores are now decorating for fall and Halloween
Children are going trick-or-treating on Halloween night
Leslie Compton, Grade 6
Alvaton Elementary School, KY

If I Were in Charge of the World
If I were in charge of the world,
Spiders would be extinct,
There wouldn't be any school,
And TV producers would've never created the scary movie, E.T.!

If I were in charge of the world,
Desserts would be healthy and vegetables would be fattening,
Teeth would clean themselves,
No one would have to take showers,
And no matter how much you ate, you would always be skinny!

If I were in charge of the world,
Pollution would be illegal,
And cutting down the Earth's trees would be illegal, too!

If I were in charge of the world,
Every day people (kids, too) would get $1,000,000,000 for watching TV all day,
There wouldn't be any type of fighting or gangs,
And chores would be no more!

If I were in charge of the world.
Justin Johnson, Grade 5
Eminence Middle School, KY

Autumn

The autumn air is brisk.
The leaves are turning yellow, orange and red.
The leaves dangle off trees
And whisper to each other, saying,
"I'm ready to fall! Goodbye, my friend!"

When the leaves have left the trees,
I go outside to read.
The autumn bugs crawl on me
And whisper, saying,
"Autumn is here!"

My favorite part of autumn
Is when the leaves are red
And knowing that the time of year
Will soon be turning winter.
I gather nuts and fruits.
I finally get some rest.

Paige Greene, Grade 4
Capshaw School, TN

The Listening Tree

Do you remember that old tree?
Where you always sat?
How you told it all your secretes,
You thought you were all alone.

You told it about your problems at school,
Problems at home,
About your friends too,
You still think you're alone.

But, one day you hear it saying,
"You are not alone,
I know your problems,
I know your fears."

"You told me about your friends,
You told me about problems at home,
You told me about problems at school,
You though you were all alone.

I'm here now, what's done is done.
I've been listening, carefully listening.
So, now that you know I'm listening,
You really are no longer alone."

Hannah Smith, Grade 6
IA Lewis Elementary School, LA

That Susie Anne

There goes that Susie Anne
Walking with her brand new frying pan.
It's not right, and it's just not fair
Because all she ever gave me was underwear!

Rebekah Heath, Grade 4
Contentnea Elementary School, NC

Where I Come From

I come from the loving and caring,
I come from the smart and the brave
I am from the happy and fun.
I am from one who is always beside me,

During my saddest times.
I am from one who loves and cares.
Where I came from you may ask?
Well I'll just say,
I came from the man in the sky.

Who is this man you may think?
Who created my mom?
Who created me?
Why that man is God.

I hold outstanding memories in my mind.
That I replay time and time again,
And they never get old.
And I'm thankful for God made me,
Because I wouldn't of been able to be what I am.
I came from the man in the sky,
I came from my family.

Nathaniel Snow, Grade 6
East Oldham Middle School, KY

Kittens

Kittens to me are very awesome,
They are cute, funny, and playful,
(You'll see);
They sleep all day and play all night
which wakes you up in the middle of the night;
Kittens come in many styles, shapes, and colors,
Black, white, yellow, and brown,
Skinny, stubby, long, and lean,
Some kittens are aggressive and downright mean!
Fluffy and furry in many ways,
Make me smile and sometimes sneeze;
There are so many kittens everywhere,
I wish I could find one just to
share a home with me;
So happy he or she would be!

Chelsey Baker, Grade 4
JJ Jones Intermediate School, NC

Friends

We see eye to eye on everything
No matter what they are by my side
I love them like they are family
It's like we can read each other's minds
I can share my secrets to them for sure,
The ones I thought I would never tell
This as good as they will get because they are true friends.

Anna Campbell, Grade 6
Lake Castle Private School, LA

Owl's Ridgway

Once there was an owl,
During the night,
His big eyes shown,
Through the moonlight,
He lived in a creek,
Called Owl's Ridgway,
Where all the owls,
Said "Goodnight Ridgway."

Hannah Jones, Grade 4
Monticello Intermediate School, AR

Pencil

Pencil,
Sharp, useful
Write, erase, use
Write on the paper
Pencil

Jordan Harris, Grade 5
Ascension Elementary School, KY

Deshai

D is for devoted, caring and kind.
E is for excelling, beyond compare.
S is for selfless, heart of gold.
H is for honor, a devoted daughter.
A is for appealing, a loving smile.
I is for innocent, sweet and fair.

Deshai, so precious and loved.

Deshai Shegog, Grade 5
Mark Twain Elementary School, MO

Church

Going to worship
Having communion on some days
Daddy preachin'
Do not forget baptism too
People passing away
Christmas is coming around
Jesus birthday
Praising God in Heaven
Amen

Remi Mays, Grade 4
Briarwood Elementary School, KY

Tuberville/Saban

Tuberville
smart, planner
thinking, bashing, beating
orange, blue, crimson, white
hurting, playing, winning
football, roaring
Saban

Chandler Wilkins, Grade 5
Briarwood Christian School, AL

Boo!

Here I come
boo! boo! boo!
Where are you?
you can run,
but you can't hide.
BOO!
BOO!
BOO!
I see YOU!
BOO!

David Raba, Grade 5
Buies Creek Elementary School, NC

I Love Basketball

I love basketball.
Screams of fans and coaches
with their roaring jaws.
The intensity of close calls
Strong hatred of defeat.
The squeak of the players' feet.
Noises of the net going swish,
after a pass called a dish.
I love the game,
the fantastic sport of basketball.

Eric Lawson, Grade 5
North Middle School, TN

Dajee Woods

D ifferent from other people
A lways on time
J umpful when playing rope
E ffective in the classroom
E nergy to have lot so fun!

W onderful student
O rganize to get good grades.
O pposite
D iscipline at all times
S hy and nice

Dajee Woods, Grade 6
Mark Twain Elementary School, MO

Me

Hannah
Smart, funny, weird, tall
Sister of Andrew
Lover of laughter, horses, fishing
Feels happiest when swimming
Needs family, friends, and music
Giver of love, joy and laughter
Fears spiders and snakes
Oklahoma City
Roberts

Hannah Roberts, Grade 4
Cleveland Elementary School, OK

My Dog

She is playful
She is nice
She tears up stuff
She likes to eat treats
She likes to eat
She likes to tear up toys
She likes to bite
She is noisy when
A car comes by

Nicholas Droge, Grade 4
Lewis Vincent Elementary School, LA

Football

The football team
Is winning the game
On a warm August day
At the Ketchum school field
Just having fun

Shayna Basford, Grade 6
Ketchum Jr High School, OK

Feelings

Sometimes we laugh.
Sometimes we cry.
Sometimes we scream.
Sometimes we die inside.
Sometimes we smile.
Sometimes we're mad,
But most of the time…
Happiness is what comes around.

Cassidy Stachulski, Grade 5
Paint Lick Elementary School, KY

The Tiny Seed

One day all the seeds
Had a great breeze
Now it's autumn
One seed is tiny
The rest are big
The seeds go
One by one
High and low
One seed
Flies so high
It gets burned
Another lands on
An icy mountain
It will not grow
Days go by and by
Some seeds die
The tiny seed grows
Now it is time
For it to go.

Monti Lynn Haitshan, Grade 5
G C Burkhead Elementary School, KY

What Is Christmas?

'Twas the night before Christmas
In the Baker family house
Momma was wearing
Her brand new pink blouse

We were waiting for Santa
Dad had just lit the tree
We were all so excited
For the presents we would see

I thought to myself
How many will there be?
Will there be enough
For my whole family plus me?

Will I get more
Than I did last year?
Will I get to see Santa
And his eight tiny reindeer?

Then I began to think this all out
Is this what Christmas is really about?
The stocking, the candy, and the presents Santa gives
Or is it because Jesus still lives?

Jesse Rodriguez, Grade 5
East Bernstadt Elementary School, KY

As the Willows Weep

As the willows weep I will be as blue as the sky.
Sad because you left my heart, broken in two.
You left me alone to die in my loneliness.
But my heart will slowly make the repairs it needs.
While I spend every moment I can in this world to find you
And for you to realize that you plus me equals true love forever.

Telvin Williams, Grade 6
Avondale Middle School, GA

A Special Time of Year

On Christmas eve, Santa delivers presents.
He delivers to everybody in the world.
A special time of year.

He knows if you were bad or good.
He is a jolly soul.
A special time of year.

We do so much as a family,
Baking cookies for Santa Claus.
A special time of year.

Peace and joy are in our hearts.
It is a time to share with others.
A special time of year.

J.T. Wilson, Grade 4
Hayes Elementary School, OK

Surrounding

I see the birds and the bees flying high in the sky.
Look over there, there is a butterfly flittering on the flowers.
It is so good to be home.
I love the surroundings around me.
Especially when I look at my sweet sweet home.

Allie Singley, Grade 5
West Marion Elementary School, MS

Fall

Leaves crunching beneath my feet,
Colors of gold, bronze, carmine, and forest green
Leaves everywhere I turn,
Pumpkin pie and cider are my favorite
Snack in the fall,
Dogs' barks echoing
Against the bare tree limbs,
Raking leaves in the day,
Trekking to a football game at night,
Squirrels scampering all about,
Deer season opening,
Screaming for joy,
I get my first buck of the season,
Sad when fall ends,
But, it will come again next year!

Jessica McBride, Grade 6
Alvaton Elementary School, KY

Brave

Running down a hallway
Scurrying to the surgery room
Quickly quickly before it bursts
Finally, we made it
Hurry put it in before it is too late
Finally, I went to sleep as a hibernating bear
An hour and 45 minutes flew by
Waking up in the recovery room hearing voices
In a confused way
1 week, Back at home
2 weeks, Back at school
When someone in my family's appendix ruptures
I will say
"I was brave when I was here you will be too"

Nicholas Gillam, Grade 4
Briarwood Elementary School, KY

The Fall

The fall is the season
I love most of all
The falling of the leaves
The whistling of the breeze
Finally getting relief from the summer heat
But most of all
What I like about fall
Is the pig skin called football

Colton Hendricks, Grade 5
Hatfield Elementary School, AR

Racing Life

As I go by
Life races past
Like a speeding car.

And I think about memories
That now are very far.

They leave me sitting
Just out of reach.

It comes and goes
Before you know

And leaves you
Trailing behind.

Josh Morgenlander, Grade 4
St Thomas More School, NC

My Cousin Alex

Generous
Courageous and playful
Dark chocolate hair
Crystal blue eyes
Farmer's tan
Always offers to play playoffs with me
Always plays the turkey bowl
Helping
Giving
There is no one like
My cousin Alex

Sam Ward, Grade 4
Briarwood Elementary School, KY

Different

I am a colorful cat
A colorful cat am I
I don't like dogs
No I don't
I love them
I *will* eat grass
Pumpkins and seeds are the best
I run I don't walk
Sometimes I talk
I eat with a fork
Maybe a spoon
I won't use my paws
I will get dirty
People are clean
And now you see thee
I wish humans didn't exist
And the world was named "Cat Land"
Don't mind if I say
I'm allergic to me!

Valeria Tequia-Lagunes, Grade 4
Nesbit Elementary School, GA

Ashley Harris

A is for an awesome kid
S is for someone special
H is for a healthy body
L is for lovely skin I'm in
E is for elegance of beauty
Y is for young and talented

Ashley Harris, Grade 5
Mark Twain Elementary School, MO

Tennis

Tennis
Very fun sport
Hit the ball with great force
I love to play tennis all day
Awesome

Claire Maddox, Grade 6
Southwest Middle School, AR

Winter

Flaky crystals fall from the sky,
Silver sparkles don't get lost,
Icicles are low and high,
And windows are white from frost!

Drinking steaming hot cocoa,
Gazing at the fireplace,
Looking at the pretty snow,
This time of year is great!

Deanna Lababidi, Grade 5
American Heritage Academy, GA

Why Me

I look around and all I see is just me
People in my mind will not leave me be
There is no place to hide
Help me someone inside
I keep on asking "Why Me?"
I said I would never leave me
But look at me now
You just cannot see!
So I ask "Why Me?"
Life has been rough
But I think I am tough
So answer this…
WHY ME!!!

Rebecca Boyette, Grade 6
Savannah Middle School, NC

The Christmas Tree

Trim trim trim the tree,
Ornaments big and small,
I love them all they are so colorful,
Oh yes! Oh yes! Oh yes!

Darien Craine, Grade 6
Armorel Elementary School, AR

Work and Succeed

If you worry you *are*
A worrywart

If you copy you *are*
A copycat

If you love you *are*
Going to be loved

If you believe you *are*
Going to be believed in

If you work you *are*
Going to succeed.

Sarah Brooks Schott, Grade 6
Annunciation Elementary School, MO

Mountain Valley

A valley between two mountains
So soft and green and lush
An escape from all the busy day
The school, the work, the rush
Come and have a nap
Or stay and play all day
Anything can happen
If you only say "okay"
You're welcome to come here
After all it's only me
I'm your friend
And you're my friend
Together we shall be.
We can stay
And live here
For all eternity

Katie Cline, Grade 6
Kitty Stone Elementary School, AL

The Worst Game

16 seconds left
20 to 14
Bam! they score
Now 20 to 20
They get the two
Fear on all faces
They kick
We all play hard
Because it was
Our last game
We played hard
As hard as we could
But,
We lost anyway
It was the worst game

Chance Bass, Grade 6
Grove Middle School, OK

Gourd

G rows on winding tendrils,
O h look! A pumpkin, a cucumber, a squash!
U nder the house they thrive
R anging from lanky to obese. All are
D ifferent figures, pigments, and dimensions.

Leah K. Wingenroth, Grade 5
First Flight Elementary School, NC

The Ocean

The salty sea brushes my face,
As dolphins leap in the air like a ballet.
Here and in no other place in the world,
I feel calm and joyful.

The waves are hurdling toward the shore,
Like a runner racing toward the finish line.
WHOOSH, they crash,
Hard and loud.

The weather is perfect for the day.
The fish aren't hiding in the coral trying to get warm.
With the expressions on their scaly faces,
The fish seem to say, "Hello,"

A dark blue setting in the sky,
Settled on the ocean,
Making the sunset of pinks, purples, and oranges
Appear magically.

The day hasn't ended, it's just begun.

Aubrey Simmons, Grade 6
IA Lewis Elementary School, LA

Oreo

I saw a cat across
The street it was
Fluffy and black
And it was such a cat

It was as black
As the big night sky
And as fluffy as
a fuzzy ball

It was as light
As a feather and
As cute as a
Button.

And I named
Him Oreo and
He loves milk
And that's
A fact

Syann Buis, Grade 4
Tazewell-New Tazewell Primary School, TN

My Michigan

Michigan the beautiful state.
With its amazing yellow and blue colors.
Its frigid winters and snow like white chocolate.
I can feel the excitement in the air
The freezing lakes beside it
Make the state complete
My Michigan my Michigan
Isn't it an amazing place?

Max Joseph Mylchreest, Grade 5
North Middle School, TN

Basketball

My friends and I love to play basketball
up and down the hall
even outside, rain or shine.
We even play in the wintertime.

When my friend, Scott,
makes a shot,
he lands with his hands
in a knot.

Sometimes I dream
of being on a team
that wins it all
at the game of basketball.

I play basketball all year round,
even on the hard winter ground.
I play indoor
because I'm hardcore.

Nick Nauert, Grade 4
St Mary Cathedral Elementary School, MO

Thanksgiving

Thanksgiving is a special day.
Where our whole family comes to give thanks and pray,
when we finish eating we say goodbye and give hugs,
before our family goes away, but,
I can still remember that special day.
Thanksgiving

Dionte Price, Grade 5
Vernon Middle School, LA

Love

Love is the smell of a new born rose,
Whose petals are velvet and dark red.
The honeysuckle taste is sweet like, chocolate.
No sound comes from the rose,
Only the silent growing of its petals.
Grow,
Grow,
Grow.

Julia Fuller, Grade 4
Endhaven Elementary School, NC

Crazy Florida

Noisy clear blue waves clashing into each other as they are washing over the sandy each.
Crowded careless cars in the terrible traffic as it gets worse and worse like an infected scab.

Beautiful birds soaring through the air as though they were flying saucers.
Loud playful children playing in the warm kidney shaped pool.

Tasty, tormenting, tremendous food sitting there waiting to be eaten.
Shrimp's scrumptious soothing scent as it roams through the relaxing room.

Nasty salt water gushing into my mouth as the wave is a big furious blue monster over me.
Irresistible fattening butter to dunk the delicious blue crab meat in.

Pink and blue square shaped shovels are running away from me in the slippery salt water.
My friend's wrinkly hand as she drags me across the soft, mushy, and dark yellowish sand.

Sun's warmth as it is glaring down on me while I'm sitting on the hot steamed sand
around the glorious sandy beach.

Lexie Jones, Grade 6
College View Middle School, KY

Spring

Spring is hot, spring is fun, spring is great, spring is bright as a light. Spring is flying with beautiful butterflies. With colorful flowers spring is open to you, as the flowers open spring for you. Spring is a beauty, spring is the perfect day of the year. For when it's time to play. Spring, Spring, Spring, it's a marvelous time of the year!!!!!!

Alexander Marsden, Grade 4
St Thomas More School, NC

Where I'm From

I am from TDJ brown leather footballs.
From Revolution helmets and thigh pads.
I am from scrapes and bruises on my upper arm.
I am from Reggie Jackson sunflower seeds, weeping willow trees that swing briskly in the wind.
I am from wedding cookies and blue eyes,
From Granny and Dawn.
I am from the strings of the guitar and feeding horses hay.
I am from praying at bedtime and learning the Ten Commandments at church.
I am from Warren County, Kentucky, home of the Lightfoot's, mashed potatoes and sweet style corn.
From the wrinkled hands of great grandpa used to race wooden cars with me,
Thick milk shakes, and the warm hugs given by Nama.
I am from photo albums, framed pictures, and paintings made from the delicate hands of an 84-year old woman.

Chase Lightfoot, Grade 6
East Oldham Middle School, KY

Birthday

You go from one life to another,
From one level to the next,
You start a life a little bit differently because now you have one more number added to your age.

There are balloons, presents, cakes and surrounding you from all directions are the ones you truly love.

Whoosh…You just blew out the candles and you made your very own wish,
But it doesn't matter, your wish already came true,
You are with the people that really matter to you.
  HAPPY BIRTHDAY!

Hannah Stokes, Grade 6
Queen of Angels Catholic School, GA

I Want to Go Home

I want to go home with my friends
where we used to chill out in our den.
I am lonely; oh so true,
down and out, sad and blue!
We were told that it's a fresh start,
but living here in Georgia breaks my heart.
I don't see my cousins, uncles, or big sis,
and my puppy, Armani, I really miss!
All I can do is keep giving this a try.
Maybe we can go back to Florida
if I scream and cry.
I will then have no more sorrow,
so I will sit back and wait for tomorrow!

Ariana Carswell, Grade 6
Blackmon Road Middle School, GA

Oh Christmas Tree, I Love You

Oh Christmas tree,
Oh Christmas, you sparkle light and sound!
It is such a marvel to see you here!
Oh Christmas tree,
Oh Christmas, I love you now.
Oh Christmas tree,
Oh Christmas, I must say good-bye.
It is time to put you away,
But do not fret!
I will see you again next year!

Kyle Sims, Grade 5
Alpena Elementary School, AR

Grand River

Happy is going to my grandpa's house and playing board games.
Sad is that my grandpa is not with me.

Happy is riding my grandpa's 4-wheeler.
Sad is that it is sold, along with everything else.

Happy is going to sleep in my warm bed.
Sad is that grandpa is not in bed, nothing warm.

Happy is going to the river to fish and raccoon hunt.
Sad is that this was the river grandpa died in.

Think how it would be…
If you had to spend the night in that frigid river.

No, you would not like it.
So you would get out and dry off.

But, my grandpa could not.

Roy "Bud" Jenkins, died September 9, 2007.
He drowned in the Grand River, Bosworth MO

Kylee Mansfield, Grade 5
Odessa Middle School, MO

Aunt Jenny's Lake Sara

Moonlight shining through the trees,
Leaves rustling in the breeze.

I hear the waves from the lake,
Content to be here, make no mistake.

The beach, the dock, the dining pavilion,
Aunt Jenny's compound is one in a million.

Another busy and fun filled day,
Read books, rode bikes, played ball and croquet.

Tired and sleepy, quiet as a mouse,
I'm tucked in my cot in the cozy bunkhouse.

And now it's time for me to go,
But one point for sure that I want you to know.

The reasons I love Lake Sara are many,
They all come from the spirit of Aunt Jenny.

Aubrey Davis, Grade 4
Sequoyah Elementary School, TN

Halloween

H alloween is my favorite time of year!
A t Halloween you get to
L eave your house,
L eave your driveway,
O ut on an adventure to get some sugary treats.
W hen you get home you
E at,
E at, eat under the
N ight sky.

Matt Harrington, Grade 5
First Flight Elementary School, NC

Just Keep Walking

I'm walking on a long road
A long, dusty road
Where am I going?
No one knows
Just keep walking!
You might find home
Stop!
What's that in the fog?
A woman? Mother!
Wait!!
It's an illusion.
Close my eyes,
Open them again
I'm home!
Don't ruin this dream!
Don't give up!
Just keep walking!

Meagan Morvant, Grade 6
Haynes Academy for Advanced Studies, LA

Baseball

Finally, summer is here
I can hardly wait
Baseball is starting
I can't be late

We get our uniforms
All clean and new
Our pants are white with stripes
And our shirts are striped blue

To practice I must go
Bleeding elbows and knees
Face and arms are red with sunburn
The coaches I come to please

The teams are tough
But mine is the best
We work so hard
To pass every test

The season championship
Will test our skills
We will play our best
And give people thrills
Brett Kimbler, Grade 6
Union Chapel Elementary School, KY

Halloween

Have you ever seen a creature
that gave you such a fright
I know I sure have
on Halloween night

Have you ever seen a goblin
that gave you such a scare
I know I sure have
and I peed my underwear

Have you ever seen candy
so sour and sweet
I know I sure have
and it's rotting my teeth
Dezahn Carey, Grade 5
Woodland Elementary School, KY

Blue Is an Ocean

Blue is an ocean
It feels like water
It looks like a blue blanket
It sounds like splashing water
It smells like fish
It tastes like salt
Blue is an ocean
Matt Woods, Grade 5
Eminence Middle School, KY

New Year's Snow

Snow is New Year's greetings,
and New Year's fills you up
with lots of kisses.
When it snows you throw
snowballs and unfortunately
your aim misses.
Snow occasionally falls
in winter, and winter
leaves you freezing.
Snow usually gives you a cold,
and sadly but truly
it leaves you sneezing.
Luisa Munoz, Grade 5
Lula Elementary School, GA

Snake's World

Snake
Venomous, reptile
strike, bite, slither
Scared, angry, hungry, startled
Serpent
Patrick Kitzel, Grade 4
Cleveland Elementary School, OK

No

No swimming,
No diving,
No kissing,
No lying,
No hugging,
No fighting,
No running,
No driving,
No kids,
No walking,
No anything!
Wait! There is only one thing
You can do.
Follow these rules.
Please do!
Veronica Wibbenmeyer, Grade 5
St Vincent Elementary School, MO

When I Once Was a Girl

When I once was a girl
I loved to be twirled
I danced and I laughed
And I rolled in the grass
And at the end of
The day there was
Nothing left to say
So I am going to
Hang for the rest of the day.
Ceaquanita Anderson, Grade 5
Bossier Elementary School, LA

Freddie

F alling leaves to catch
R oad runner
E xciting
D o hard work
D rum player
I ce cream
E xpert at spinning acorns
Freddie Brissette, Grade 5
St Joseph Institute for the Deaf, MO

Friends

Sometimes things give you trouble
but friends will be there on the double
no matter what the situation
friends will be there to have a recreation
at good times and bad times
friends will be there to open minds!
Colleen Raidt, Grade 5
Ascension Elementary School, KY

Tigers

Nocturnal — hunters looking for prey
Leaping — attackers every day
Meat — munchers constantly eating
Swift — runners never fleeing
Sweet — nappers after a meal
Silent — attackers so surreal
Karl Ivey, Grade 5
Herbert J Dexter Elementary School, GA

Fiji

Fiji is waterfalls
Pretty pink flowers
And crazy green grass.
It is my dream place
With my dreams cascading
With the waterfalls.
Madison Mauck, Grade 6
Benton County School of the Arts, AR

Hershey Kiss

H eavenly
E normous
R adical
S imply delicious
H appy
E xciting
Y ummy

K ing of Kisses
I mmense flavor
S weet aroma
S atisfying
Kayde Claypool, Grade 4
Crossville Christian School, TN

A Dangerous Sport

One sunny Friday at cheerleading practice
getting ready to do a back-hand-spring
thought I was going to do magnificent
guess I was wrong

Started off running diagonally
placing my hands flat on the floor
setting me up to do the perfect back-hand-spring
throwing my hands up in the air
flipping my body backwards like a monkey on a vine
SLAP! slamming to the floor
what did I do wrong?

Crying nonstop like a newborn baby thinking I was going to die
hearing my arm being popcorn popping in the microwave
seeing my coach frowning like somebody died in her family
worriedly asking "Are you o.k.? Why didn't you use your arms"
frozen ice in a bag on my wrist so cold dying to take it off
wondering did I break it?

Morgan Sanders, Grade 4
Roberta Tully Elementary School, KY

America

A lways beautiful
M ilitary people that were in the Army for us
E nemies that are fighting against us
R emember America always.
I feel proud to be an American.
C aring
A lways forgive us.

Cody Blakley, Grade 5
Temple Hill Elementary School, KY

Changing Seasons

A fter summer the leaves start changing,
U sually colors of yellow, red, and orange.
T hen they fall from the trees to the ground.
U nder our feet, a crunching sound.
M aking scarecrows by stuffing them with Dad's old clothes.
N othing is more wonderful than autumn.

Sara Morelock, Grade 5
Sullivan Elementary School, TN

Leaves

All of the leaves are
F
 a
  l
   l
    i
     n
      g
down, red, brown, orange, green
jumping in, jumping out, letting out a big scream

Kristina Flinn, Grade 6
Martin Elementary School, WV

Mrs. McDoogle

Mrs. McDoogle,
who lives up the road
always wears pink
but has a pet toad

Her house is four stories
which is surprisingly low
and she has six cars
but never does go

She is neat as a pin
but eats like a slob
She is very rich
but doesn't have a job

She loves fast food and such
yet she is thin as a stick
and she loves the sport soccer
but she hates to kick

Mrs. McDoogle a neighbor and friend
Isn't the same but quite opposite
I know she is my friend, but I have to say
I don't know what she will like or dislike each day

Erin McGarel, Grade 6
All Saints' Episcopal School, TN

White

White is white.
White is the clouds you see in the morning.
White is paper before you write on it.
White is white chocolate that we eat.
White is the white paint before you mix it.
White is the moon at night.
White are the pages in the books we read.
White are the socks we wear on our feet.
White is the color of "white out."
White is the white board in the room.
White is nothing.
WHITE

James Degner, Grade 5
Meredith-Dunn School, KY

Hey Hey

Hey hey,
What's your name?
I want to meet you
Let's go play
Hey don't be ashamed
I'm not going to bite or scare you away,
See I'm your friend
I like to play
Maybe if you play you'll feel the same way.

Evasia Stover, Grade 5
Hall Fletcher Elementary School, NC

Junk Box

Junk Box
wood and metal
Opening and closing
storing your supplies
Desk

Alex Roberts, Grade 5
Salem Elementary School, AR

A Sweet Reminder of Her Love

I'm standing in a barn.
My feet are cold.
I can't see anything.
It's too dark.
I see a little black strip of ground.
It's a road.
The barn is locked.
Will I live?
Will I die?
Who will save me?

I hear a voice.
I think it's my aunt,
But she is no longer living.
Oh, wait.
She's calling me from heaven above.
Wait. I see something. It is white.
I can't believe it.
It's her, Tina. It's her spirit.
Wait.
She's telling me something.
I love you, she says.

Jadyn House, Grade 4
Hayes Elementary School, OK

The Ocean

The ocean is a place to live,
To see the beauty God has made,
The coral reef, just one of them,
Puts us all in wonder

The ocean is a place to dive,
As beautiful as sparkling diamonds,
The fish, the sharks, the plants,
God made them all for us to see

The ocean is a place to explore,
To see the shells, the sandy floor,
The rippling waves that claw the shore,
God loves us all so much

The ocean is a place of wonder,
The creatures, the water, the sand,
All God made for our eyes to see,
That is the wonders of the ocean

Emily Stillwell, Grade 5
Providence Academy, TN

Where I'm From

I'm from racing on dirt bikes hitting in football,
drag racing down the street in my neighborhood and jump shooting in basketball.

I am from a family of seven, three strange but rocking brothers,
two very great funny stepsisters, two twenty one year old intelligent cool step sisters,
but most of all 1 huge family!

I am from listening to rap, collecting model cars,
reading all sorts or different books like horror stories,
mystery and action/adventure stories
dreaming my family would one day get along
and doing something together for a fun family time.

I am from yelling teachers, doing school work,
weird kids, good lunches,
great friends, nice and cool kids,
pencils and paper,
P.E. and other special areas,
and most of all I am from school.

Yep! That's me football playing
model car collecting
dreaming family would get along boy!
That's where I'm from!

Derek Tuilagi, Grade 4
Price Elementary School, KY

Where I'm From

I am from spoon
From Crayola and Atari
I am from the dirt bike in the garage
I am from the rose, the daffodil
I am from bonfire and good hair
From Amy, and Emerson, and Valerie
I am from the actor and skateboarding
From don't smell your toes and don't put your thumb in your mouth
I am from L.A. and England, pizza, and lamb
From the Emerson, and the Jeff and the Olivia
I am from L.A.

Brin Hall, Grade 6
Lakeshore Middle School, NC

Green House

Muddy shoes as brown as brownies
Flies fluttering freely with joy
Bees buzzing loudly like cars beeping
The seagull soared through the sky as silent as a mouse
Sweaty people with stinky armpits as wet as a fish
Lovely flowers as sweet as sugar
Melting chocolate dripping down my lips as fast as a waterfall
Apples as juicy and sour as a lemon
Feathers as smooth and soft as pillows
Mushy mud beneath my feet as mushy as melting chocolate chips
I feel relaxed and free.

Maria Salazar, Grade 4
Bailey Elementary School, NC

I Am a Soccer Player

I am a soccer player.
I wonder about my tournament.
I hear we are going to have a new player on the team.
I see the ball.
I want to kick the ball.
I am a soccer player.
I pretend I'm doing great moves.
I feel I will score a goal.
I touch the ball when I'm goalie.
I worry I will get hit with the ball.
I cry if I get hit with the ball hard.
I am a soccer player.
I understand if I'm benched in a game.
I say I'm sorry if I hit someone with the ball.
I dream I will be a professional.
I hope I will be a professional.
I try to do my best in games.
I am a soccer player.

Jordan Randall, Grade 4
Wohlwend Elementary School, MO

The Frightening Halloween Night

Halloween is a spooky time of year
a time for kids to dress up in their freaky costumes
and scare people!
It's the season to eat delicious candy
and carve bright orange pumpkins.
Kids asking for candy is heard all around the neighborhood.
Along with scary decorations to set the mood of the holiday.
Kids go all over the place for candy,
but sometimes do activities such as bobbing for apples.
There are black creepy spiders, black freaky bats and
spooky kids all dressed in black!
Oh what a frightening night!
Halloween is sure a fright!
Leaves everywhere and scarecrows stare.
What a great holiday Halloween!

Nicole Simon, Grade 5
North Middle School, TN

Twister

massive torrents tearing, tons of wind
ripping stormy weather, I'm wishing that
it soon would go away
clashing, crashing, colossal, claiming
land for destruction, making sure
nothing survives in its way
buildings gone, some still tumbling
ripping, roaring, tumbling
still spinning sideways, a giant top of doom
wrecking houses, causing terror
STOP!
it has disappeared.

Rachel Jones, Grade 5
Contentnea Elementary School, NC

Baptism

Today is the day the
Church bells are ringing.
Small feet against the ruff skinny sidewalk
The doors open, walking in, tissues
In hands and tears in eyes
I'm happy, it's like butterflies
Are in my tummy
Walking up, well here it goes
I go back and right back up
Clapping hands arrive
Finely I'm one of them, one
Of them is who I am

Maya King, Grade 4
Briarwood Elementary School, KY

The Holocaust

Adolph Hitler is who?
The man who betrayed Jews.
The day of the Holocaust,
A lot of people were lost.

Some of them escaped,
Who then tried to be saved.
We dare not fight,
Because more Jews may be killed by night.

The Nazi soldiers wouldn't go away,
Someone had to save the day.
Mr. Sagihara was his name,
Who saved a lot of Jews from pain.

Kali Strickland, Grade 5
Pembroke Elementary School, NC

Dogs

What are dogs?
Dogs are mammals
They have spots or no spots,
Brown or black fur,
Blue or brown eyes,
Maybe long or short fur,
Crooked teeth and straight teeth,
Little nose or big nose,
They can be short or tall,
Fat or skinny,
Blind or not,
Long or short tail,
Big or small ears,
Straight up or droopy ears,
And dogs can have curly fur,
This is a dog,
A dog is a mammal that walks on all fours,
That has fur, eyes, ears, a tail, nose,
Paws, claws, mouth, and whiskers
This is a dog.

Chasity Snowden, Grade 6
Southwest Middle School, AR

The Titanic

Building the Titanic was hard work
They did it in England
It left in 1912
Headed to a new land

On a night as cold as the Arctic
They hit floating ice
It made a hole down one side
It wasn't nice

It sank in an hour
There weren't enough boats
Those in the water
Had to try to float

Many people died
We remember them today
And think of them
While we pray

Mark Walters, Grade 5
Walton Verona Elementary School, KY

My Dog

Without a chance,
In a box,
On Christmas Day,
Slowly,
Cautiously and Doubtfully
Covered with mud,
Drenched in the rain, and
Crying loudly
A dog appeared at my door
Ready to play in the mud,
Happily, ready
To take long walks with me
Jumping up and down,
ready to eat her dog treats

Logan Hearn, Grade 6
St Mary's School, SC

A Season to Remember

I love the leaves
As they fall to the ground.
They make it known
That fall is coming around.
Their colors are so bright
Red, orange, and brown.
The way the air smells
It's crisper and cleaner.
The night sky seems darker
And stars so much brighter.
Yep, fall is for me
A season to remember.

Marisa Mildren, Grade 5
Trinity Day School, GA

My Big Sis

I gave my big sis
a kiss but she hissed.
I try to go in my
big sister's room but
she won't let me in
So I beg her again
and again.
My big sis just turned fifteen
so now she's a teen.

Kinley Stafford, Grade 4
Lewis Vincent Elementary School, LA

Chess

Anticipating thinking watching
The opponent's moves.
Black and white squares on a board —
Figures stand ready to protect.
Quiet, still, slow moving
Forward, sideways, backward
Waited, holed, attacked, enemy trapped
Long live the King

Jonathan Fearing, Grade 6
St Paul the Apostle School, TN

Summer

As the sun begins to shine,
As the heat begins to climb,
As the school bell ceases to ring,
As joy is felt in everything,
As the trees continue to grow,
As the days begin to slow,
As the fun comes back,
The carefree times are here in fact,
As the people head to the beach,
As the waves continue to splash,
There is one thing clear to me,
That almost anyone can see,
That summer is here today.

Joseph Dixon, Grade 5
JJ Jones Intermediate School, NC

Pain

The world is hurt!
He will not let water touch him.
So she makes a huge wave
And washes away
all the anger
and pain
and hurt
From the world's heart
So they may love,
Feel,
And be together in peace.

Taylor Kirn, Grade 5
St Vincent Elementary School, MO

Football

When my friends and I play football,
We play really hard and rough.
So, when you come and play with us,
You better be pretty tough.

When you score a touchdown
Sometimes you often show off
So, if you see someone's face down
You had better just back off.

David Gray, Grade 6
Pleasants County Middle School, WV

Florida

There's many things to do,
Fishing, hunting, Disney World too,

Many kinds of fish
Swordfish, lobster, tuna, anchovies
And many others

There's hunting
Like deer, fox, and bird

The most fun thing of all
Can you guess?
It's Disney World

There are many things to ride
There's a lot of walking
Rides like The Hulk, Fire and Ice Dragon
The Hunted Pyramid and The Gold Mine

There's many others too.

Zachary Schmitt, Grade 5
Wright City Middle School, MO

Candy

C an you give me
A piece of your
N utter butter so I can
D eliciously eat it?
Y ummy I said to myself

Branson Allen, Grade 5
First Flight Elementary School, NC

Joe and the Fire Truck

Joe lives in a fire house
With many fire trucks
Waiting for the bell to ring.
Joe jumps on his fire truck
And goes to save the day
With the help of his dog, Spot
To keep the fire away.

Sam Sykora, Grade 6
Seven Holy Founders School, MO

The Show

Woken by a loud slurp
A lick told me it was the crack of dawn
Jumped into a steaming waterfall
Dripping beads fell upon me
Adorned myself with pink and white
Long road drove me nuts
Announcer called, nerves shook like a rattlesnake
A kick starts a canter
Sugar arched, front feet jumped, then he landed
Excitement fills the air as awards were won

Molly Berkemeyer, Grade 5
Cline Elementary School, KY

Ode to Jericho

Jericho,
Your grey-blue eyes spark in the sunlight.
Your gorgeous wide grin could light up a dark, dank cellar.
A mop full of light brown hair
Covers your cute, rounded head.
Cheerful and cuddly

Buh buh buh!
Sings your high pitched voice.
It sounds as high as a first soprano opera star!
Being autistic makes you cute, cuddly, and carefree.
You hug every second spreading love and joy.
You may not be the smartest,
But you're still smart in your own way.

You always smell
As minty as a candy cane.
As I shake your shaggy hair,
I feel a smooth texture dash across my fingers.
You are a cute, cuddly, baby panda bear,
Your personality sneaks a grin on my face.
I love you,
My little brother.

Sienna Casos, Grade 6
South Oldham Middle School, KY

Friendship

Friendship forgets
The birthday card I didn't send on time,
The good-bye hug you were too embarrassed to give,
Emails that got lost,
Words that stung,
Hearts that broke.

Friendship remembers
Dancing barefoot in the rain,
Playing endless games of round robin,
Racing each other in the pool,
Whacking tennis balls out of sight,
Talking all night long.

Megan Hammond, Grade 6
St. Charles Homeschool Learning Center, MO

Black Labrador Retrievers

Black Labrador Retrievers are beautiful dogs.
Loyal, always by your side.
When they stand, they stand with pride.
They never let you down.
They roll, jump,
And don't forget about digging.
They're fun-loving.

Black Labrador Retrievers are beautiful dogs.
They will protect you no matter what.
Never mean and they mind their master.
Their hearts are always filled with joy.
If you have one and they pass away,
You will not ever forget her.

Black Labrador Retrievers are beautiful dogs.

Brooke Sears, Grade 4
Hayes Elementary School, OK

Peaceful Garden

water in the ocean
sticky
smooth
flow like a red leaf in fall

the waves are a roaring lion
wishhh, wishhh

sand is smooth as a horse
as water
sticky and smooth

Beach is as peaceful as a garden
water, waves, and sand
all things at the peaceful garden

Anna Curnutte, Grade 5
Greathouse Shryock Traditional Elementary School, KY

Arkansas Razorbacks

It's the jerseys that they wear,
and the confetti in the air.

It's the fan's faces,
and the pretty cleat laces.

It's the end zone that says Arkansas,
and the cheerleaders that say, "HURRAH!"

It's the flag run when there's a touchdown,
and the helmets on the ground.

What color could this possibly be?
Red is the color for me!!

Rylee Phillips, Grade 5
Salem Elementary School, AR

Summer

Summer is the best time of year.
No school, no test
all the time to rest.
TV all day,
no matter what time of day.
Listen to music,
watch MTV.
Play video games.
Go to sleep whenever.
The summer is almost over
and school is almost back.
I'm so, so sad.
Boo hoo!!!

Cameron Foxworth, Grade 5
West Marion Elementary School, MS

My Family Is a Car

My family is a car
big, fast, and cool

My dad is the engine
big and tough.

My mom is the door
simple and
always working.

My sister is the gas
useful and expensive.

My brother is the seats
comfy and always there.

I'm the key,
hard working and fitting
in all problems.

Jacob Hardin, Grade 5
Bloomfield Elementary School, KY

Nyera Williams

N ice
Y outhful
E verybody's friend
R eal
A merican

W illing to work with others
I rreplaceable
L oving
L ikeable
I ndependent
A dmirable
M agnificent
S elf-confident

Nyera Williams, Grade 4
Contentnea Elementary School, NC

My Brother

My brother is a silly kid, although he's only two.
He makes me really mad sometimes, but he only wears one shoe.
He's also like a jumping bean, jumping all around.
Jumping from sun up and jumping to sun down.
After that I'm glad he'll go to sleep,
so I won't hear from him another peep.
I love my brother and he loves me!!

Addison Keys, Grade 4
Applewood Christian School, MO

Some People

Some people watch TV, some play sports.
Some people drink sweet tea, some people wear shorts.
Some people like to party, while others hang out at Hardee's.
Some people live in football, some live in study hall.
Some people like to dance, while other like to prance.
Some people like to have fun in the sun.
Some people are lazy and stay in daily.
Some people show their true colors until the end. Some don't even begin.
Show what you feel and tell what you sense, that way you'll always have friends.

Bailey Sartin, Grade 6
Graham Elementary School, AL

Thanksgiving

When Thanksgiving comes to mind;
I think of all the fun and play time.
School is out which is really fun,
and there is no homework to be done.
Food is a tradition and a delight,
and Thanksgiving with my family is out of sight!
We have turkey and smoked ham
with Grandpa's hot juicy meat pies and fried chicken from Uncle Sam.
My aunt's sweet potatoes are cinnamon and sweet,
and a delicious treat.
We love hummus and grape leaves,
and ice cream from the freeze.
The Lord has blessed us with all this food,
and He chooses to because He is good.

Hannah Duke, Grade 5
Briarwood Christian School, AL

Virginia Beach

The fish wiggling out of the ocean
A light gleaming from the lighthouse through the sliding balcony door
The waves splattered on the sandy shore
A seagull is hawking for a dry french-fry
The scent of the salty air welcomes me
The fish from the cool salty sea smell like supper to me
The freezing ice cream melting in my hands
The salty seafood is falling like an avalanche through my damp mouth
A clump of hot sand rustling through my toes
The cool waves splashing against my chest
I have a warm feeling of joy.

Bradley Mercer, Grade 4
Bailey Elementary School, NC

Hot Pink Is a Tulip

Hot pink is a tulip
It feels like a soft throw pillow,
It looks like the pink in the sunset,
It sounds like a soft song,
It smells like a sweet pea that has just bloomed,
It tastes like a sweet piece of cottony candy,
Hot pink is a tulip.

Jessica N. Baker, Grade 5
Eminence Middle School, KY

The Fairgrounds

The fairgrounds, oh how I love them!
The red and white tents.

Ohh, eek! Screams of happy roller coaster riders.

Sweet ooey, gooey Popsicles,
dripping down little kids' hands
while they laugh with their friends.

Ohh, ahh says the crowd,
while watching the
super sneaky snake handler
named Snipe snip dead snake skins!

Burrp! Says the man
he just won a hot dog eating contest.

Zip! Zoom! Zing! Bumper cars!
Bumper cars like raging bulls!
Clink! Clank! The fair is shutting down.

Sarah Wheatley, Grade 5
Greathouse Shryock Traditional Elementary School, KY

Kansas

Lying in the grass,
Talking about memories in the past.
Waiting for the stars to come out
So we can dance under the moon!
But as soon as it starts
Time seems to dart…and then we have to leave!
However, we shed no tears
Because we know we are coming back next year!

Sarah Pennington, Grade 6
Scotts Creek Elementary School, NC

Morgan

M ighty good at math and language.
O utstanding at playing GameBoy DS.
R eally nice and kind person.
G reat at playing tag and hide and go seek.
A good friend and daughter.
N ever likes to eat peas.

Morgan Sands, Grade 4
Byrns L Darden Elementary School, TN

Autumn

When I think of Autumn I think of,
A pple pie and **b** utterscotch,
C innamon buns,
D ogs running across the field.
E xploring the colorful woods, and **f** alling leaves,
G reen apples with sugar,
H orse back riding in the crunchy leaves, **i** ce cream pie.
J ack-o-Lanterns,
K ind family and friends,
L uminescent nights, **m** oons that shine
N utty pie,
O range sticky buns,
P each trees,
Q uilts knit by Grandma,
R ed suns,
S alty, creamy mashed potatoes, **t** art buttermilk pies.
U nforgotten memories,
V arious flavors of food,
W indows with glorious views, **x** ylography art,
Y ellow colored sky and **z** ephered winds.

Ashton Harris, Grade 5
Palmetto Christian Academy, SC

The Garden's Glory

A house made of bright sunlight beams
Blooming flower buds
That smells as sweet as candy dreams

In a relaxing fragrant flower garden
With chattering chipmunks
Splashing crystal clear waterfalls
With many kerplunks

Lit by teeny-tiny fireflies
Gleaming and glowing by nightfall
Buzzing the sounds of calming lullabies

Inhabited by colorful stone carved garden gnomes
As still as a possum playing dead
Except when…
Secretly prancing and frolicking when everyone's in bed

Johanna Butler, Grade 6
Holy Trinity School, KY

Marly

Marly Bird —
Creative, outgoing, loving, funny.
Daughter of Clay and Tracy, sister of Parker and Will.
Lover of softball, gymnastics, and loud music.
Who fears biting snakes, stinging bees and disobeying God.
Who was born at Saint Vincent's in Birmingham.
Who lives in Hoover.
Whose grandparents live in Mexico!
— Marly

Marly King, Grade 5
Briarwood Christian School, AL

A Stick

A hockey stick is magic
So wonderful indeed
Will help you play
And proceed

It can't poke
It can't slash
It can't hook
It can't lash

It may shoot
It may score
It may break
It may drop

These are only some things
It may do
Matt Pudlo, Grade 4
St Thomas More School, NC

Nouns Are Cool

They are all around you.
There are millions of them too.
They are NOUNS!
There are many kinds.
Possessive, common and proper
and many, many more nouns.
Proper nouns are a particular
person, place, or thing.
Singular nouns are one of something
like cat or dog.
Collective nouns are a group
of something like flock or pack
I gave you some nouns
but there are many, many more!
Michaela Cummins, Grade 5
Saffell Street Elementary School, KY

Cat

Cats are so fun
They're furry and cute
Cats are cool
But sometimes they're out of control.
Sierra Raynor, Grade 4
Holly Ridge Elementary School, NC

Creepy

C reepy, scary, creatures
R eluctant rats
E verywhere.
E arsplitting screams
P essimistic pumpkins
Y ou will be terrified!
Sarah Dooley, Grade 5
First Flight Elementary School, NC

Head/Feet

face
brown, tan
talking, moving, twitching
mouth, nose — toes, heels
walking, running, moving
hairy, stinky
feet
Tyler Thomas, Grade 4
Cleveland Elementary School, OK

Sometimes

Sometimes you are tense
Sometimes you make sense
Sometimes Sometimes

Sometimes you are mad
Sometimes you are sad
Sometimes Sometimes

Sometimes you cry
Sometimes you are shy
Sometimes Sometimes Sometimes
Trakia Fields, Grade 5
Carver Elementary School, NC

Babysitting

The twins scream…AHHH!!!
The twins whine…WHAA!!!
The toddler runs…STOMP!!!
The toddler hides…Peek-a-BOO!!!

SIGH…
   SIGH…
      SIGH…
As tired as I've ever been…YAWN,
Just want to sleep…
Just want to relax…
Just want to have a fun time…
Just want to go home…

SIGH…
   SIGH…
      SIGH…
Thought this would be an easy $100.
Ashley Marie Wettstain, Grade 6
College View Middle School, KY

Drug Free

I'm drug free
I'm a flying bee
I don't want to do drugs like thugs
That's why I'm at P.E.S.
Everyone should play and be drug free
Storm Chavis, Grade 5
Pembroke Elementary School, NC

Eric

Eric
tall, honest, nice, loyal
Relative of…Great Uncle Lee
Lover of…Sports
Who feels…Happy with my family
Who gives…Care
Who fears…Clowns
Who would like to see…God
Resident of…God's family
Johns
Eric Johns, Grade 6
Our Lady Catholic School, MO

Me

Me, Myself, and I
Pumpkin is my favorite pie.
I love to sing and dance,
Even in my itchiest pants!

I don't look like my mother,
Instead like my father.
I don't like spinach,
Oh, don't even bother!

I really like pink.
I think at hula-hooping I stink.
I can do about three hoops…
That is all I can do.

Well, this has been my poem
Just like me,
It sure has been growin'!
Anna Siebeling, Grade 4
Evangelical Christian School, TN

Antonio

A wesome in the gymnasium
N ice
T alkative when I want to be
O utstanding rapper
N ever give up
I 'm a basketball player
O bedient in school!
Antonio Scales, Grade 6
Mark Twain Elementary School, MO

Don't Lie

There once was a lion
who said I was lying
about a pretty blue ball
but I was not lying at all
I told him my secret
he said he was gonna keep it.
Dallas Nicholson, Grade 6
Armorel Elementary School, AR

Glinting

Glinting is a big smiley face.
During a rain: trying to find a place.
A big blue sky moving slowly at his pace.
The sun will find it's special space.
When we look at the stars shining in our face
We thank God for such wonderful grace!

Avery Mayo, Grade 4
Brilliant Elementary School, AL

An Autumn Night at the Lake House

Watching the shadows in the wall length mirror,
I pull my blankets up to my chin
looking around the copy of my bedroom,
the smallest room in the lake house.
I decide to walk outside.
On the deck I peer at the moon reflecting on the lake.

Elizabeth Watkins, Grade 4
Stone Academy, SC

Kody

BARK!
Bringing back memories of
walks, tricks, and dog slobber
all over my face.
He was my best friend.
His fur was as golden as the sun.
His last few days are the ones
I will remember him by,
forever.

We used to lie in the green grass
until I was covered in itchy mosquito bites.
I would throw a fuzzy, green tennis ball
and he would always bring it back to me.
His fur was like tumbleweeds
blowing across our floor.
I loved Kody
but he is in a better place now.

Carly Kennedy, Grade 6
South Oldham Middle School, KY

Christmas

Christmas is full of joy and giving
It's not just about you
It's about giving, not receiving
It's a joyful holiday that everyone enjoys
It's also about making the world a better place
That you should be thankful for what you have,
And not be greedy.
I hope that you know that there are people out there
That do not have as much as you do.
Therefore be thankful for everything that you have
Just remember to give and then you will receive
A very special gift of your own.

Mckenzie Harton, Grade 6
Providence Christian School, NC

Shop Till You Drop

I went shopping the other day,
I found out people would not pay.
They were dropping things along the way,
Things like purses, belts, brushes, and hairspray.
All over the floor the people began to lay.
I asked my mom what was wrong,
"Shop till you drop" that's what they say.

Mattie Clayre Griffith, Grade 5
Midway Covenant Christian School, GA

My Dog

There once was a dog
That was very small.
Girls she liked;
Boys could take a hike.

Bang! Bang the boy proclaimed.
Growl and howl her teeth exclaimed.
Ouch! Ouch my toe's in pain.
My dog bites, bites when boys say bang, bang.

Little dog on the hill,
Rolling down like Jack and Jill
Ran into the pond,
Though she could hardly swim.

Mischievous at day.
Bitterly sweet at night.
Her girl cuddles her tight
While they sleep through the night.

Anna Malone, Grade 5
Providence Academy, TN

Water

I sit on the side of the river bed,
Sounds of flowing water rush into my head,
I think, as I watch the pebbles I throw in sink,
Way down to the bottom they go.
I look at the horizon and watch it glow.
I don't know why,
but when I look at the horizon,
I feel as if I could fly.

Lindsey Isbell, Grade 5
Graham Elementary School, AL

Fear Is Black

Fear is black.
It smells like rotten eggs.
It tastes like spoiled milk.
It sounds like a loud scream.
It feels like a wrecked car.
It looks like a thunderstorm forming in the sky.
Fear is having a bad dream.

Vincent Hill, Grade 4
Pines Elementary School, NC

Summertime Tune

The birds fly and sing;
The ice cream trucks ring!
No homework is to be done;
We just play in the sun!
No worries or cares
Just as long as you're there.
Bugs chirp in the night;
Birds sing in the light.
Summertime is here!
Time to scream and cheer!
So let's sing a tune for
Summer will end soon!

Kristin Geier, Grade 6
Scotts Creek Elementary School, NC

My Dad

My dad is a bear,
But I love him anyway,
In the day he is nice,
But at night something happens,
I don't understand it,
Maybe it's supposed to be like that,
It's very weird,
He growls like a bear,
Is he tired or overworked?
I wonder why he is so grumpy,
But I don't care,
I love him any ways.

Amber Wilbanks, Grade 5
Des Arc Elementary School, AR

The Fox

The fox was a marvelous sight
Its coat as soft as cotton ball
Cunningly taking a little stroll
It saw me and dashed into the night

Christian Rodriguez, Grade 5
Carver Elementary School, NC

The Beach

I go to the beach
running into the ocean
I'm chasing seagulls

Chris West, Grade 5
Sycamore Elementary School, GA

God/Satan

God
powerful, majestic
loving, everlasting, ruling
king, throne, liar, trickster
hating, demanding, scaring
evil, smart
Satan

Caroline Logan, Grade 5
Briarwood Christian School, AL

Kings Dominion

Children splashing water wildly like wild lion cubs in the small pool
Children riding big buff water rides as if they were brave little knights
The bottom of the wave pool is as hard as a rock
The candy apples are as sweet as a honeybee
Chili cheese fries dripping cheese
Children laughing as loud as a bear's roar
Roller coasters moving as wild as a dog chasing a cat
My protective seat belt is my mom
The sweet funnel cakes are as sweet as my little sister
Chlorine water is as strong as a Tyrannosaurus Rex
I am as excited as I was when my little sister was born.

Lakeisha Harris, Grade 5
Bailey Elementary School, NC

Memories

My memories of this place keep coming back to me.
Butterflies come to my stomach every time I think about it,
The closet opening to get my luggage out,
The late nights spent packing,
Even the car rides made me jump,
The excitement going through me knowing that we've reached it,
Michigan.
Almost every year of my life so far I have felt this,
But this year,
No closets opening,
No late nights spent packing,
No car rides,
And no excitement knowing that we've reached it,
Michigan.
All I have is memories,
But I know one day that I will return to that special place,
Michigan.

Sarah Jane Hoffmann, Grade 6
Annunciation Elementary School, MO

Country-Side Backyard

Excited Kittens scampering across the ground
like playful lion cubs practicing for their big hunt!
Spring flowers fading fitfully as a frightful sign of fall.

Joyous chirping birds chasing each other like
little sisters chasing pesky brothers.
Flirty little girls giggling and running while playing tag.

Speckled orange pumpkin pies filling the house
with sweet aromas of cinnamon, nutmeg, and pumpkin spice.
Dusty corn drying in the grain bins like rotten eggs
that have splattered all over everything!

Piping, scrumptious, homemade yeast rolls just out of the oven smeared in butter.
Curvy edges of glazed pumpkins and gourds.
Breathtaking fall mums that appear to be rainbows in a field.

What joy in a warm and secure environment.

Ashton Trunnell, Grade 6
College View Middle School, KY

Me, Myself, and I

I am me
A Bright yellow daisy that stands out in a crowd
A cute red tulip, one of a kind, still blooming
A friendly fish swimming freely
A river going with the flow
I am a feisty puma who fights back
I am like celery, healthy, strong, and proud
When I walk and talk I express my feelings
When I am free…
I am Bright
I am Cute
I am Friendly
I am Feisty
I am Strong
I am Proud
I am Ruthann.

Ruthann Payne, Grade 6
Beck Academy, SC

Let It Snow

My dark, white house was white
From the wintery snow.
My hair was wet and damp.
I dried it off and made it
Oily and silky.
I held hot cocoa in my hand
As I looked out my window
And all I wanted to say was
"Let it snow."
All I wanted to do was watch
the white flowing outside.

Tia Brown, Grade 5
Lee A Tolbert Community Academy, MO

The Mask

Halloween is scary
I see something that is very hairy
I try to scream but I only whimper.
It growls and I get limper.
Foul smelling and shocking.
It's so terrifying I have to ask.
Is that my sister behind that horrible mask?

Cailin Hurley, Grade 5
North Middle School, TN

Christmas Tree

Christmas Tree, Oh Christmas Tree
Standing so tall for me,
Oh won't you please come with me
To fill my home with glee
With lights and ornaments shining here and there
No other tree could dare compare
To you my Christmas tree

Natasha Dulinsky, Grade 5
Hatfield Elementary School, AR

Sleep

Growing weary, the sun shrunk
Giving way to a peaceful lure,
Rabbits fell in a tiny hunch
Along the seaside,
With birds' caws
Dogs trudged with massive paws

And they too were soon asleep
With their masters laid comfortably in bed,
On pillows lay many heads
But not everyone was drifted away
For the night stars replaced the day

Hannah Boutwell, Grade 6
Runnels School, LA

Tigers

Orange and black tigers
hunt their prey every day.
Sometimes they don't catch anything, so they play.

Abbie Sherman, Grade 4
Brilliant Elementary School, AL

My Cat

My cat's name is Sammie.
She is still a kitten but very funny
She likes to play and run around
And get very dirty.

I am her owner.
We like to play rough
But we're okay.
She likes to get in window sills
And see everything going.

She likes to sleep under the Christmas tree and
knock off the ornaments.
We will give her presents and treats.
She hates the cat outdoors.
We have a storm door and they fight very much.

Kelsey Phillips, Grade 6
Westwood Christian Academy, GA

Pizza

Pizza is tasty like sugar
I really like it a lot
I would probably eat pizza even if it wasn't served hot,
And when I want more
I would roar and roar
Until the pizza man knocks at the door.
Oh, pizza is fine, fine as a sand dollar
To eat all the pizza you're sure to become a scholar
Pizza is fine, pizza is fey
I think there should be
A National Pizza Appreciation Day!

Joseph Scott, Grade 6
St Teresa's School, GA

A Forest in Despair

The forest is unearthly quiet. The parched earth begs for mercy as the cruel sun beats down its harsh rays. Flowers droop over in defeat and weep. Trees stand like sleeping giants, their branches calling out in dismay for the wind to return. The birds remain silent in their nests, hiding from the scorching heat. The animals remain in the little shade available. Everything is quiet. Then, a sharp crash comes from the sky. The rain has come. Birds sing with joy. Animals come out from hiding and prance around. The flowers spring up and display their wondrous petals. Trees sway once more in the wind, their branches rejoicing. The earth soaks up the rain graciously. The once gloomy appearance of this forest is now beautiful and cheerful. The rain ceases and the sun slowly creeps out. Raindrops glisten in the sunlight like tiny diamonds. The forest creatures run through the rain-soaked grass and play in the river. Birds soar through the sky gracefully. The forest is full of sound and color once more. The rain has come, and with it comes life.

Caitlin Dopheide, Grade 6
Queen of Angels Catholic School, GA

Song of Autumn

See the great colors of fall come together to present wonderful, shiny, bright leaves scattered among the earth.
Smell the cinnamony scent of pine, spread by the rush of the cool breeze.
Taste the small cool flakes of snow rushing into your mouth and melting into chilly water on your tongue.
Feel the icy mist brush past you, leaving you cool with crystal droplets of water in your hair.
Hear the crunching of leaves as wonderful deer glide over hollow logs, the young ones prancing with joy.
But there is no need to worry.
This is autumn singing her song of Mother Nature's wonders. Now, the sun sets, another miracle awaits you…
Tomorrow.

Allie Rogers, Grade 5
Lake Murray Elementary School, SC

Time

Time is a barrier, stopping life, starting death, and keeping the boundary of reality, and the intangible world of dreams. Time is the blockade of the mysteries, the known, the trying to be found, and the things we've never even pondered. It makes the decisions seem more important. They appear irreversible, but just a kind word or action can change even time itself. Time is a tapestry that veils the truth, taking it from only the physical world, not the real world.
Is time so real? Or is it the thing we have created? The impatience and need? If we stopped and just stood there, and thought, how real would it be…Time is just a grand illusion. People are still there…They still exist in reality. They are never really gone. And people are with us before time shows them to us. The soul doesn't know time; time gives it a body, then takes it away, but the soul lives on. Time may not exist…
Time is a trickster. Time can manipulate the way we see things, showing the foolish the wrong things. It makes us happy, sad, angry, loving, playing as a kitten with a ball does. It can even make us do its bidding in its own world if we are foolish enough. It will lead us to deception and eventually, to our own death.
Only the wise can see past that, the true veil of time.
Time is the harvester of our bodies. It carries them as they wither away. To most men, it takes them away forever, but it just removes the body and flesh from the earth, taking them onward. While men rush on, just obsessed with duty and the need for others, take some time to think of time and remember
"Time waits for no man"

Keith Coffman, Grade 6
St Mary's School, SC

Why

Why did the nazis kill the Jewish people, for there were many reasons to them.
Why did the superiors in Japan say no to their coming for they had no reason to say no.

Why did Mr. Suahari make visas, and passports by hand for jews for he was a kind man.
Why didn't the nazis act like the german soldiers for what the nazis did led to very very wicked things.

Why didn't the refugees disguise themselves as diplomats for they were afraid.
If you felt scared wouldn't you do the same thing too.

Kateri H. Juarez, Grade 5
Pembroke Elementary School, NC

Soldiers

Blood, sweat, tears
Many don't make it home,
Overseas
What does that one word mean to you?
To me it means far-off exotic places,
To others pain, suffering, WAR
Some fight and live to tell the tale
Others are not so lucky
Families, brokenhearted, thrive for sanctuary,
Great Americans fight for their country,
For the people they love,
For AMERICA,
You have to be strong and brave,
You cannot lack perseverance
Friends made during the war,
In the blink of an eye,
No more friend.
War is a tough thing,
It is not easily won
That's why we thank the men and women that serve,
That's why we thank the Soldiers.

Paul Cameron, Grade 6
Woodland Presbyterian School, TN

I've Had too Much Writing!!!

Writing, writing that's all we do!
I don't want to do it and neither do you.
Sometimes writing can be nuisance,
I probably wouldn't do it for 2 cents.
I might because I collect pennies
but to tell you the truth I'd rather go to Denny's
We do it so our grades won't fall,
some people might flush it down the bathroom stall.
Writing can be hard for me,
even my imagination can't help me see.
Some kids may want to leave,
that's just because we want to be free!
It's true that writing can be tough,
I tell you sometimes I've just had enough.
I'm not at all merry,
Writing's not dairy, hairy, mean or scary.
I hope you like to read, because writing is a part of ye (you).

Keith "KJ" Hassel, Grade 5
Hall Fletcher Elementary School, NC

Rain

Rain would be very great
All over this dry state.
We have so little rain and it is dry
We must conserve so we can survive.
The governor has asked us to pray
For rain each and every day.
We are glad for the rain that came
And hope for many more days of the same.

Jameson VerSteeg, Grade 5
Midway Covenant Christian School, GA

Just Around the Corner of My Classroom

When I raised my hand in class,
it didn't mean I knew the answer.
Far from it.
I was hoping the answer might float by
and I could catch it like a butterfly.

Bailey Fenwick, Grade 4
West Elementary School, MO

A Wondrous Celebration

Like castles in the sky,
Music and fires,
Celebrations and laughing,
Exciting,
Beautiful,
Good feeling all around,
Dancing and singing,
People shouting out loud,
Rejoice, Rejoice!
Shouting even louder…
Rejoice, Rejoice!
Prancing and swirling, exclaiming…
Rejoice, Rejoice, Rejoice!

Night approaches with its soft silence,
So soft no one can hear.
They could only hear
The yawning of sleeping little "Terabithians."

Melissa Randall Pagan, Grade 5
St Patrick's School, AL

Day Camp

Sticky bus ride down there
Kids yelling, "We're there, we're there"
Scrambled to get our things
We ate thick and gooey mystery meat for lunch
Our activities are next
Paddled my canoe till my arms ached
I climbed a rope to challenge my neighbor
Ultimate Frisbee — run, catch, throw
Lastly, chicken and gravy that sings a song in my stomach

Ian Schnelle, Grade 5
Cline Elementary School, KY

Preston

Presto —
Athletic, hyper, Christian, truthful.
Son of Mark and Carol, brother of Sydney.
Lover of baseball, video games, and drums.
Who absolutely loves sports!
Who fears snakes, lots of homework, and school.
Who was born in Nashville, Tennessee.
Who now lives in Birmingham, Alabama.
— Preston

Preston Fights, Grade 5
Briarwood Christian School, AL

Halloween

H alloween is my favorite
A pples are delicious
L ittle candies giving us cavities
L icorice we're chewing on
O range pumpkins we're carving
W inter's coming soon
E dible food in our baskets
E veryone's outside on Halloween
N eed costumes soon

Tristan Grubbs, Grade 5
Walton Verona Elementary School, KY

Blushed Cheeks

Love is bright red.
It sounds like wedding bells.
It tastes like chocolate.
It smells like roses.
It looks like blushed cheeks.
It makes me feel like dancing.

Carley Cato, Grade 5
Salem Elementary School, AR

My Cat

My cat's name is Tyrell.
He is a spoiled rotten brat.
He doesn't listen.
He won't do tricks and he won't
jump through a hoop.

Madeline Smith, Grade 4
Brilliant Elementary School, AL

Nicholas Plott

N ice and neat
I ntelligent
C areful and courteous
H elpful
O ne great person
L earn in school
A mazing and artistic
S mart, safe and shares

P leasant
L istens
O nly one of a kind
T errific
T alented

Nicholas Plott, Grade 6
Mark Twain Elementary School, MO

My Sister

My sister Amy
Is so very sweet and kind
She is four months old

Karina Damian, Grade 5
Sycamore Elementary School, GA

Door Handle

Twisting my head,
And swirling my neck.
And when you click my nose,
I lock!

Nick Brueckner, Grade 5
St Vincent Elementary School, MO

Who Is That?

Who is on the roof?
It is not me!

What is that noise
stomping around?

I go outside,
it is hard to see!

Who is on the roof?
It is not me!

Who is in the chimney?
Who is by the tree?

I don't know who he is,
but it is not me!

Hunter Shook, Grade 5
Alpena Elementary School, AR

Mary Our Graceful Mother

Mary, Mary so sweet to carry,
Baby Jesus in her belly.
When it snows, He'll be born,
If it doesn't make a storm.
There He'll lay,
In the bed of hay.
On his birthday we shall pray,
To keep us safe night and day.
When the stars go passing by,
It's so precious I think I'll cry.
When I look up in the sky,
I see the stars shining high.

Kristin Krzyminski, Grade 5
Home School, AL

Blue

Blue is my favorite color
I like blueberries
I have a blue ball
I have blue carpet
I use a blue towel at home
I have a Barbie with a
A blue dress
I have a blue stuffed bear

Whitney Gordon, Grade 5
Eminence Middle School, KY

Trucks

riding
all shapes, sizes
no matter what wheel rate
trucks are all about me, I like
just trucks

Harley Douglas, Grade 5
Broadway Elementary School, NC

Cats

Cats
small, pets
meowing, running, sleeping
cats like to play with yarn
Cats

Terry Silva, Grade 5
Westwood Elementary School, AR

Candy

C ontagious
A lways sweet
N ever too much sugar
D elicious and
Y ummy

Kaitlynn Hunt, Grade 5
First Flight Elementary School, NC

My Brother

Oh no! He is at it again!
He is dressed in white
Like a big white polar bear
Pouncing out into the field
I cover my head in horror
Oh no! He is at it again!
He is dressed in black
Like a small scared skunk
Running around the bleachers
I cover my face in horror
Oh no! He is at it again!
Dressed in blue
Like a happy peacock
Running around
Oh no! He is at it again!
Why does he have to be my brother!
The guy with too much school spirit!

Caitlin Wilson, Grade 6
Ketchum Jr High School, OK

The Magnificent Huskies

A Husky is terrific and has pointy ears.
Their fur feels fluffy, soft, and furry,
They are faster than a car,
They are in the rescue squad,
Huskies are my favorite kind of dog.

Tim Burnett, Grade 5
North Middle School, TN

Strawberries

Strawberries are red.
Strawberries are sweet.
When you take a bite you might just leap.
Strawberries are pretty.
Strawberries are fun.
When you see the strawberry fun,
You will want to bake a cake with anyone.
When you see the strawberry fun.

Jessica Centilli, Grade 5
Graham Elementary School, AL

The Fire of a Buck Shot

I see a deer, up over the hill,
Them horns are big; I'm ready to kill.

The fire of a buckshot, puts the buck down.
He is surely big enough to mount.

I take him home, we get the meat,
He'll make a good plate to eat.

He was hard to drag,
But it was fun to brag!

So, if you hear me, all you deer,
You'll soon be caught,
By the fire of a buckshot.

Vanessa Gatlin, Grade 5
Oark Elementary School, AR

Baseball

Its summer time and my sport is here
the game of baseball lets all cheer
peanuts, hot dogs, and a big cup of coke
the game is starting I'm really stoked
strike, foul ball, it's out of here
the crowd stood up with a great big cheer
the game is over my favorite team won
now I'm sad to leave such fun

Austin Shiflett, Grade 6
Graham Elementary School, AL

The Promise

The death of my great grandma was harsh.
I didn't have a single tear.
She told everyone to not cry, but to rejoice in her death.
She would be in a better place.
Whenever I felt her cold, limp hands,
I almost cried.
I ran outside to calm myself down.
I wanted to keep my promise to not cry.
I did sometimes cry
for the tears I held in from the funeral.

Chaz Quick, Grade 5
Odessa Middle School, MO

Books

B elong under a reader's gaze
O pen doors to other worlds
O ften are used as resources
K eep librarians busy
S ecrets lie behind their covers

Matthew Dozer, Grade 5
Hunter GT Magnet Elementary School, NC

Friends

My friend Dylan lives around the corner
from my house, I call him bamboozle.
We met four years ago when I moved in
he came to my front door with his friend.

I think he's intelligent
I think he's hilarious
He's a lot like me
we are both as cute as can be

We like to run outside and play
in the water, on our bikes, or kicking a ball
I get to sleep over at his house
We stay up late and tell ghost stories

It would be cool attending the same school
He goes to Blue Lick, I go to Schaffner
I know he works hard like me
he tries to make A's and B's

I always worry about having to move
I don't want to leave my friend behind
It would be boring and I would be sad
I just think he's a really good friend

Cameron Adams, Grade 4
Schaffner Traditional Elementary School, KY

A Sister

A sister is a friend.
A person you can trust.
Someone who is there for you,
In good times or in bad.
A person who can understand you,
Or guide you along the way.

A sister is someone you can look up to or down to all the time.
She can know all your secrets,
But never tell anyone.
You can tell her how you feel,
Or just something going on.

A sister is a dearly beloved one,
Even though you may fight, remember…
You will always love her, forever.
A sister is a friend.

Paige Stephens, Grade 6
Northern Guilford Middle School, NC

Fish
Back and forth
they swim around,
They go in water
but not on ground.
Caroline Schulte, Grade 5
American Heritage Academy, GA

Catfish
Catfish
fast, quick
swim, eat, feed
catching, following, breathing, diving
all catfish eat worms.
fish
Cody Dearmon, Grade 4
East Jones Elementary School, MS

Fall
Fall is awesome because of Halloween
And the leaves.
It is the time,
That we are back in school.
There is also fall break.

Raking leaves to make a leaf pile
That is good to jump in.
It is time to celebrate Thanksgiving.
To eat pumpkin pie,
To enjoy blessings from God above.
It is a season of harvest and love.
Tristin Greenway, Grade 5
Trinity Day School, GA

Seasons
In the Spring
The church bells ring!
In the Summer,
I say "bummer!"
In the Fall,
I walk in the hall.
In the Winter,
Everything shimmers!
Patty Wyant, Grade 4
Ode Maddox Elementary School, AR

My Country, America
The country of Freedom
Mixing pot of nations
…Where all men are created equal
Land of my Fathers'
The country of Unity
Land of Peace and Prosperity
Long live America
Land of greatness!!
Drew Morris, Grade 5
Odessa Middle School, MO

Voices on the Wind
Leaves fall swiftly to the frosty ground.
Freed by gentles breezes.
The wind blows on my face like an icy blanket.
Just a little reminder that summer is gone and fall is here.
Now listen carefully to the breeze.
It's like tiny voices whispering secrets in your ear.
Then listen again, hear the voices on the wind chanting winter is ablow.
Megan Brown, Grade 6
Senn Thomas Middle School, MO

Diamond
The best friend I could ever have.
She loves to go on long bike rides with me
She thinks she can catch a deer.
I groom her, and her beautiful, black coat glistens in the sunlight.
She loves to romp, wrestle and play
with my lazy cats.
Though they don't like to play with her.
She adores agility competitions,
and is good at it too.
She speeds over the jumps,
Races through the tunnels.
Runs up the A-frame, and looks at the view.
She looks so cute!
Tail wagging, tongue lolling, head held high
"I'm queen of the world!"
she seems to say.
I couldn't ask for a better cattle dog.
Or any other dog to be exact.
I wouldn't trade her for a million dollars.
Because she's my dog,
The Diamond in my heart
Alyssa Richter, Grade 6
East Oldham Middle School, KY

If I Were in Charge of the World
If I were in charge of the world
I'd let everyone have a home,
Everyone would have a home and a car,
I'd let people pay $1.00 for gas per gallon.

If I were in charge of the world
Soldiers wouldn't get killed,
Schools would start at 9:00 AM and end at 4:00 PM,
Schools should always be ready for emergencies in case they happen.

If I were in charge of the world
Everyone should have at least 1 vegetable or 1 fruit a day,
Everyone should not abuse animals or people,
Everyone that does bad things should think about why they did it and go
on probation for 1 month to 1 year.

If I were in charge of the world
Brianna Moore, Grade 5
Eminence Middle School, KY

Ladybugs

Ladybugs, Ladybugs I love them so
  I see them everywhere I go

Ladybugs, Ladybugs all around my room
  I see them when the flowers bloom

Ladybugs, Ladybugs bring good luck
  I am called Ladybug by my Daddy Buck

Ladybugs, Ladybugs I love their spots
  They look like little polka-dots

Ladybugs, Ladybugs they are the cutest beetles
  When you try to catch them, they skededdle

Ladybugs, Ladybugs feed on the pesty louse called aphid
  Of which farmers are happy to be rid

This is all I know about Ladybugs to share
  But when you find a Ladybug, handle it with good care

Emily Thompson, Grade 4
Sequoyah Elementary School, TN

Jesus and America

Jesus means the world to me,
He created the home of the free,
The land of the brave with justice and liberty,
He shines his light on us every day,
Being proud is the American way,
God Bless America!

Lucianna Williams, Grade 5
Heartland High School and Academy, MO

Red

Red is a brick on the side of a house
Red is a design on the bottom of a blouse
Red is the sun on a hot summer day
Red is a crab on the San Francisco bay
You ask me what is red
I'll tell you what is red.

Red is a leaf on a windy fall day
Red is a rose on a warm spring day
Red is an apple on the teacher's desk
Red is a sticker for a student's best
You ask me what is red
I'll tell you what is red

Red is the glow of Rudolph's nose
Red is the color of Santa's clothes
Red is the color of our cafeteria at school
Red is the color of a beautiful jewel
You've asked me what is red
I've told you what is red

Johnathan Xavier O'Neal, Grade 6
Saint Paul School, TN

Keith

Keith
Relative of Uncle David and mom Debbie
Who needs my friends, family, and sports
Who would like to see Brazil, New York, Fifa World Cup
I am funny, nice, short, energetic
Who feels mad when I lose a soccer game, good when I score,
And bored at school
Who gives peace signs, friendship
Who fears devil, Satan, Hell
Resident of Heaven and Holy Spirit
Dennis

Keith Dennis, Grade 6
Our Lady Catholic School, MO

The Heart of Kentucky

In the hills of Kentucky
  the Bluegrass State
the pioneers are waiting to awake.
  The birds chirp
  the flowers bloom
everyone sings a lovely tune.
  Down the valley
  through the stream
  whoosh
  the water strokes so clean.
  The trees fight the wind
  as
  the sun gives its last gleam
the sun goes down from above
  as
  the Bluegrass State
  lies below.

Katie Adams, Grade 5
Greathouse Shryock Traditional Elementary School, KY

If I Were in Charge of the World

If I were in charge of the world
I would make my little sister do all the chores
I would eat all day long
There would be no bedtime
I could mess up the whole house

If I were in charge of the world
There would be no school
There would be no homework
There would be no teachers
We could play all day

If I were in charge of the world
There would be no rules
There would be no parents
I would ride my bike everywhere
There would be free food at restaurants

Amy Carrillo, Grade 5
Eminence Middle School, KY

The Humble Man

There once was a man that was humble.
He walked, but sometimes he stumbled.
It wasn't until that day,
He knew just what to say.
He stood under the steeple
And preached to all of the people.
There gathered a great host
That were filled with the Holy Ghost.

Brannen Thomas, Grade 4
Northeast Baptist School, LA

Surfing

The day is perfect
It's not too windy, not too light
I try my best to hit the wave right
I finally get up, but then I wipe out
Then I had a doubt
I couldn't give up
Here comes a perfect wave
I get up and ride it like a pro
I ride it until it dies down
That's all for me today

Devon Van Winkle, Grade 6
Southwest Middle School, AR

School Clock

Torture
Anxiousness
Knowing
Tick tock tick tock

45 minutes
2,700 seconds
60 seconds
Home fun

Tyler Beaver, Grade 6
Benton County School of the Arts, AR

A Soldier's Fortune

All soldiers have a goal
All these things come from the soul
Whether being honored for bravery
Or freeing someone from slavery

Some act as if they are brave
But medals are all they really crave
Worth a fortune is true courage
Not even an enemy can discourage

All fortune should be earned
Or all his beliefs shall be turned
The greatest fortune of them all
Is the trusted comrade standing tall

Tyler Wegrzyn, Grade 6
Providence Classical School, AL

Bottlenosed Dolphin

Bottlenosed dolphin
gray, chubby
flip, jump, swim
floating, diving, twirling, swirling
Frolic near the shore
Porpoise

Jasmine Olson, Grade 4
East Jones Elementary School, MS

Thanksgiving

No school
Mom's birthday
Around family
Fall fun
Beautiful fall
Giant fair
Fun rides
Hay rides
Colorful leaves
Huge dinner
Juicy turkey
Cream corn
Pumpkin pie
Give thanks
Warm fire
Roast marshmallows
Scary stories
Peaceful nights
Getting colder
Giddy Thanksgiving

Kimberly Saunders, Grade 5
Center Elementary School, GA

Christmas Morning

Early Christmas morning,
Sit all the gifts and toys,
Waiting to be opened,
By all the girls and boys.

Early Christmas morning,
The children are in bed,
With dreams of dancing sugarplums,
Dancing in their head.

Early Christmas morning,
Halls decked with holly,
Kids open presents,
And feel really jolly.

Early Christmas morning,
Joy and glee fill me,
But the best thing about Christmas,
Is being with your family.

Baylor Boyd, Grade 4
Hayes Elementary School, OK

Fall Is Here

F ires by the camp
A pples ready to be picked,
L eaves falling to the ground
L eaves changing colors

I t's time for pumpkin pie
S horter days of sunlight

H alloween
E ating for Thanksgiving
R aking leaves in the backyard
E lephant ride at the fair.

Max Darling, Grade 5
Palmetto Christian Academy, SC

Tickling

As I wiggle,
As I giggle,

As I squirm
Like a worm,

As I laugh so hard I cry,
Rolling around on the ground,
Like a rolli polli
Or a noodle,
It is hard to frown,

As I fall onto the floor,
As I wiggle,
As I giggle,
As I squirm like a worm
As I am being tickled.

Presly Ward, Grade 6
Benton County School of the Arts, AR

American Flag

You are so pretty
red white and blue
You have those glowing stars
on the blue
you also have neat stripes
red and white

Jaylene Anderson, Grade 5
Walton Verona Elementary School, KY

Heaven Is Sweet

Heaven is gold.
It sounds like angels singing.
It tastes like sugar.
It smells like cookies.
It looks like Church.
It makes you feel like saying a prayer.

Caroline Cato, Grade 5
Salem Elementary School, AR

Norman Coats Surgery

I didn't know why
it had to be him
or how it happened
Wednesday was the lucky day
they wheeled him down the hall
we waited
for them to unclog his muscles
patiently
oh, too patiently, we waited
the clock on the wall hardly moved
as time stood still
finally
after what it seemed like months or years
the doctors come out
they are finished
he is as good as new
he can start
his life over now.

Ashton Coats, Grade 6
Ketchum Jr High School, OK

The Winter

Snow is falling slowly,
A flake won't drop swiftly.
It piles up in large heaps,
Just like a small cloud.

But soon it will melt
I do not know when.
Who even knows when it will,
Just keep on falling slowly.

Slowly dropping from the sky,
Children making white men.
I can't wait till next winter,
I'll see ya soon again.

Sean Kurz, Grade 5
Hunter GT Magnet Elementary School, NC

Where I'm From

I am from hairspray, from Ultra Clutch and Suave.
I am from the snakes under the cold, brown bricks.
I am from the daffodil, the rose.

I am from Carowinds and brown eyes,
from Dawn, Mike, and Lynn.
I am from the smarts and the bakers,
from Santa and the Easter bunny.

I am from Christians, God and Jesus.
I am from Georgia and Ireland, brownies and cookies,
from the stories, jokes, and the poems.
I am from family reunions.

Jeremiah Alsop, Grade 6
Lakeshore Middle School, NC

Autumn

Bright red leaves falling softly to the ground
Groundhogs burrowing into the dark, relentless Earth
Adds in the paper for Jackson's Orchard
Buying spooky ghost decorations for Halloween
Carving bloodcurdling faces into pumpkins
Going to the pine trees to hunt deer
Shooting deep brown and yellow turkeys
Driving to grandma's for scrumptious Thanksgiving dinner
Stuffing ourselves with stuffing, turkey and ham
Having a good time all autumn long

Alden Walker, Grade 6
Alvaton Elementary School, KY

I Am

I am the son of an American soldier.
I wonder if my dad is ever scared of going to Iraq.
I hear that my dad is unsafe sometimes.
I saw my dad's sad face when he got on the plane to Iraq.
I want him to come home soon.
I am the son of an American soldier.

I pretend that he is not in Iraq.
I feel sad when he is not here for Christmas.
I touch the picture that he gave me before he left.
I worry about him all the time.
I cry when I think of him.
I am the son of an American soldier.

I understand why he has to go.
I say that he should not have to leave again.
I dream that he will come home safe.
I try not to think about it.
I hope that he will come back to America safely.
I am the son of an American soldier.

Tyler Lynn, Grade 5
Byrns L Darden Elementary School, TN

The Frog

Bouncing from lily pads as green as grass
I watch a frog as I pass
dancing on water as clear as glass
leaping and twirling with big, black bass.

Arielle Marion Wimmer, Grade 5
Salisbury Academy, NC

Rain

The rain comes down
so loudly and peaceful
It covers the ground
like snow in winter
I run outside
and feel it hit my skin
and wonder when rain
Is going to hit again.

Savana Crawford, Grade 6
Dyer Elementary & Jr High School, TN

My New Slide

I'm going for a ride,
On my new slide.
It's better than taking a test,
You can have a contest,
Because I'm going for a ride.

I'm going for a ride,
On my slide.
Come play with me,
And you too, Lee,
Because I'm going for a ride.

I'm not going for a ride,
On my old slide,
Because a stroke of lightning hit,
And I blew a big fit,
This is why I'm not going for a ride.

Cheyenne Noah, Grade 6
Northern Guilford Middle School, NC

Friends

Friends are kind,
But not all the time,
They are always some fun,
When we are in the sun,
But when they have to go,
That is that and that is what I know.

Jacqui Scalzo, Grade 5
Runnels School, LA

White Pine Tree

Its needles sew life.
Year long it dances with green.
Its cones make life too.

Nick H. Dutton, Grade 4
Briarwood Christian School, AL

I Am

Kay King
Blue eyes
Love parties
Can't drive
Likes soccer
Has bicycle
Dog owner
Cat owner
Can sing
Can dance
Plays basketball
Can spell
Good clothes
Good shoes
Can skate
Can swim

Kay King, Grade 4
Tamassee-Salem Elementary School, SC

We Are Gazing at the Flag Waving

We are gazing at the flag waving
By the fire blazing,
From the wood that we gathered to keep the fog from hazing over us,
While we take a moment looking up at the flag, praying that its glory will last forever.
While the flag is waving gallantly in the soft breeze of the trees swaying.

Benton Fine, Grade 4
St Thomas More School, NC

My Fantastic Summer

Going to holiday world in the summer was very exciting
Riding the Bakuli was awesome it was
the biggest water slide that they had
in the new wave pool the waves were GIGANTIC

we sat at a table
we ate a greasy powdery funnel cake
And juicy cheese burgers
riding on a raging wooden roller coasters was great we bumped and turned
All the way until the end of the ride

after riding almost all of the rides and we were ready to go we ate
some slippery and cold ice cream and some colorful tasty Dip n' Dots
Then we played some fun games and we won a huge green fuzzy stuffed bear

It was really late and we were so tired
So all of us stopped to check in to a hotel
The whole family went to sleep as fast as a cheetah

Jacob Osborne, Grade 4
Briarwood Elementary School, KY

My Dad

My dad is sweet as vanilla sugar
Love it when my dad laughs
It sounds like a lion's roar…RRROARRR!
Sometimes, it gets annoying when he laughs at something not funny
I Love it when my dad is calling my name
I'm my dad's many miles to go before time

He says he loves me
And I love him
Tell you what my dad really loves.
Watching football every day

Love to call my dad daddy
Never forget my dad's last words "it's all good"

Tell you what he looks like
He looks like an angel
His hair is midnight black his eyes twinkle like stars
His face is one of a kind and full of hearts

Sometimes my dad
"FLYS OFF THE HANDLEBARS"
and says I promise I won't tell

NaTassja Jackson, Grade 4
Briarwood Elementary School, KY

Sharks

Weird and unusual sharks.
Sharks are the quickest creatures in the deep.
They have the sharpest teeth in the sea.
Would you be terrified to see a shark?
I would not like to meet one in the dark.
They are silent, and deadly in the night!
You would not be able to escape this master hunter.

Conner Currier, Grade 5
North Middle School, TN

What's in My Journal

Talking helps me express myself,
why I love to chatter.
Fireworks in the atmosphere,
at the ending of December.
The day it snowed when I got frost bite,
leaping up and down knowing there is no school.
I slowly walked into the building not knowing what was ahead,
my first day of middle school.
Colorful skirts, shirts, and pants that are breathtaking,
my obsession to the clothing store Aero.
Wanting to shop day and night;
my clothing problem.
My cute hissing white kitty,
To me she is an angel.
I love dreams that I wake up to,
Knowing that I can do anything.
I hope to see my great grand kids,
Seeing them live out their imaginings that they will soon fulfill.
Quirks are fun to have,
Especially when they just happen out of nowhere.

Devyn Johnson, Grade 6
Baylor School, TN

Where I Am From

I am from walking horses around the track
To the race track of Church Hill Downs

I am from killing a buck to having meat for supper
To killing frogs for their delicious legs

I am from the bright red barn where I give cows shots
To the brown rusty truck I drive from the field to the feed lot

I am from catching a bluegill while going camping
To catching a catfish at the pool behind my house

I am from driving my old John Deere Tractor
To using Ol' Betsy to plow the field

I am from the polish that I use to make my guns shine
To showing the local gun shows

All of these things make me who I am

Chris Glover, Grade 6
Union Chapel Elementary School, KY

Caring Mom

I am the daughter of a caring mom.
I wonder how she does it.
I hear her say she loves me a lot.
I see her leave for work and school every day.
I want to say mom don't go.
I am the daughter of a caring mom.

I pretend to be happy when she's not home.
I feel she will never leave me.
I touch her hand.
I worry about her.
I cry when she comes home late.
I am the daughter of a caring mom.

I understand that she loves me.
I say I miss you when she goes.
I dream of her at night.
I try to help her with my baby bother.
I hope she will never leave me.
I am the daughter of a caring mom.

Pamela Davis, Grade 5
Byrns L Darden Elementary School, TN

Water, Water Everywhere

The world is wet with
Raindrops on the horizon
It is peaceful and calm

The sun sets with rain
When children play in the pool
As nature takes its course

The morning had fog
And no one was in the pool
As dewed flowers bloomed

When the sun came up
The world heated up to warmth
Then the fog went away

Jonathan Galloway, Grade 6
Haynes Academy for Advanced Studies, LA

Brave

I felt as brave as the first chick hatching.
Breaking out of my shell like I had never felt life before.
Breathing in the sweet spring air.
Waiting to hear the other chick's shells crack.

I am loving like a field of roses.
As red as the sunset in the sky.
The scent of fresh sweet air.
My petals as soft as velvet.
Swaying in the wind.

Sara Hite, Grade 6
Beck Academy, SC

Dolphin

Dolphin
Baby blue, White
Dive, jump, play
swimming, flipping, eating, drinking
It always swims a lot.
Mammal
Hannah Maxcey, Grade 4
East Jones Elementary School, MS

Friendship

Friendship is…

Friendship is a bright sun,
Lighting up your day.

Friendship is a sucker,
It can be sour or sweet.

Friendship is a drink,
It can last long, or it can be short.

Friendship is a bridge,
If you don't build it up well, it will fall.
Sarah Pemberton, Grade 4
Plano Elementary School, KY

The Red Car

I have a red car.
Its name is not Christina.
Its name is Herby.
Hailey Stephens, Grade 6
Rocky Comfort Elementary School, MO

Dinosaurs Go Extinct

When dinosaurs ruled the land,
A T-rex was in command.
His name was Andrew Scall,
And he was the strongest of them all.

One day he was searching for food,
And Andrew was in a good mood.
He saw a big piece of meat,
And picked it up to eat.

Then the earth began to shake,
As a meteorite had landed in a lake.
Dust rose into the air,
Giving the T-rex a scare.

Dust blocked the shining sun,
So the dinosaurs could have no fun.
Soon they started to die,
And to the Earth they said "Goodbye."
Sarang Mittal, Grade 6
River Trail Middle School, GA

Morning

Up, up little maid
Come and see father sun
Bring tea to mama
Sing with the spring birds
And sing a sweet song.
Rebecca Evatt, Grade 5
Prince of Peace Catholic School, SC

Candy

C omes chocolate caramel,
A nd
N utty
D ark dessert
Y ummy!
Michael Lutton, Grade 5
First Flight Elementary School, NC

Rain

Dripping through the wet trees
Turning the air crisp and clean
Making many soggy leaves
Everything turns a different sheen.
Megan Rosenbohm, Grade 6
Nodaway Holt Elementary School, MO

Christmas's True Meaning

Christmas's meaning is more than gifts;
It's more than legends and even myths.
Much more than crunchy candy canes;
It's more than stockings full with planes.

Christmas is a special celebration;
A Christmas tree is a decoration.
Christmas cookies are what we eat;
And are Santa's favorite treat.

Jesus Christ's birth was on this day;
That is why we celebrate…Hooray!
We honor God on Christmas day;
We worship, and we even pray.

Christmas is very special indeed;
And Christmas is what all people need.
She is a holy day;
Please worship as you pray.
Grace Yarborough, Grade 4
North Elementary School, NC

The Sun

The sun comes up
the flowers start to bloom
the sky turns blue
and the birds start to sing
Alison Stellwag, Grade 4
Greenville Montessori School, NC

Pets

A pet can be a
dog, horse, gerbil, cow, mouse, pig,
some can be hard work.
Della Bragdon-Hall, Grade 4
Briarwood Christian School, AL

Falls Colors

F all,
A wesome
L eaves,
L ively
S ights.

C olors
O f
L eaves
O ver
R ocks,
S pectacular!
Timothy Snelling, Grade 5
Trinity Day School, GA

Royal Rap

There was once an excellent king
He had a big gold ring
It had ruby and jade
He had it especially made
Now the king has *bling*
Nick Shamblin, Grade 6
Martin Elementary School, WV

Halloween

October has come and gone.
Halloween is nearing.
Ghost and ghouls and witches brew.
Halloween is scary.
Only one word I will say,
BOOOOO!
Carolyn Sanderlin, Grade 4
Moyock Elementary School, NC

The Midnight Rider Adam Jones

Listen up my friends
You will hear
The cry of Adam Jones
Now he's in the hospital
He broke his back in Iraq
His troop yelled run
But he dropped his gun
He didn't use his head
In a blink of an eye
He was injured…
For you and I
Travis Hammonds, Grade 5
Pembroke Elementary School, NC

My Marvelous Mom

Eyes as blue as the ocean
Hair as shiny as the sun
Skin as soft as a furry sweater
Bright blond hair
She is a jokester
Always joking around
Swerving across the road
When I'm trying to get my uniform on
In the truck
Yelling and cheering at my games "go colts"
Good game that was your best ever!
Going to Toots after my games
Nice and calming to me
Like taking me to the bus when it is raining
Loving each other very much
Polite and saying nice things
Always taking care of me
Like when I'm sick
Joking, taking care of me
She is my marvelous mom.

Grant Smith, Grade 4
Briarwood Elementary School, KY

Love vs Money

Money is great for gifts because you can say
I don't know what you have
I don't know what you want
But here is some money and I'll be blunt
Hard cold cash is better than any toy
You can buy whatever you want, won't that be a joy!
But it can't buy you health, though it can pay your bills
It's used for a lot things, but it's not all that's on your will
Money can't buy you love, the most important thing
It won't make you ruler, not queen or king
Love is what gets us through life and makes us strong
People we can hold close with love and together we live long!!!!

Jennifer Campbell, Grade 6
St Rita School, LA

Autumn Leaves

A romatic scents in the air,
U nbelievable sights —
T he peaceful forests,
U ncle Ray's stories,
M onsters and ghouls trick or treating —
N othing comparing to Grandma's turkey!

L ightning striking in the air —
E arly Autumn days,
A pple pie in the kitchen,
V arious types of trees in the forests —
E normous pumpkins,
S tarting bonfires with cousins.

Jake Adams, Grade 5
Palmetto Christian Academy, SC

My Cat Aggie

An agate marble,
A flowing fat fur ball,
Bopping around without a care in the world.
A spotted cow,
Being such a good huntress.

Being a huntress,
Chasing an ice cube around the kitchen floor,
Without knowing anything about her surroundings,
Drinking the water from the sink.

Lydia Sue Tinsley, Grade 6
College View Middle School, KY

School

I am finally out of school
School makes me wanna slobber and drool
We go to school a year about
I am glad to get out
I guess school is kinda cool

Adam Cross, Grade 6
Martin Elementary School, WV

Thunderstorm

Thunderstorm at night
The rain hit my window
POP! POP!
The lightning flashed again and the thunder BOOMED!
The night wind blew
YOOOO! YOOOO! YOOOO!
Then I finally fell asleep waking up with a scare.
Then morning came and it was still raining.

Hunter Thompson, Grade 6
College View Middle School, KY

Raindrops

Raindrops come down outside,
I watch them from my window.
They come down lightly on the sidewalk,
Turning it from white to gray.

They pitter-patter on the windows,
They make them look all spotty.
They sound like tiny tap dancers,
Tip tapping on the glass.

They make the sky look stormy,
And the clouds look really heavy.
They make the children stay inside,
Raindrops even make basements leak.

The raindrops come down and make everything wet
People hurry around with umbrellas,
To avoid the pelting raindrops,
As they come down like tiny cannonballs.

Cathryn Hamm, Grade 6
Holy Trinity School, KY

Pencil Cop

Stop! Stop! Stop!
We need a pencil cop,
for my pencil is going too fast.
It wants to take over my writing,
so it is fighting to finish for me.
The tip breaks, and I yell "Yippee!"
But it hops to the sharpener,
and, like a carpenter,
sharpens itself to a point.
It wants to take over the joint!
It hops back to my story
about a dog named Cory,
and writes,
This is way too boring!

Lea Bolognini, Grade 6
River Trail Middle School, GA

Fly

Let us all fly,
Fly very high,
High in the sky.
Once you reach the top,
You will hear music,
It will make you want to hop.
You will have to fly down,
Which will make you want to frown.
You had fun in the sky,
You have to say bye,
It will make you want to cry.
The day is done,
You had fun.
You get in bed,
Prayers are said,
Finally you rest your head,
Thinking of everything that happened.

Courtney Long, Grade 5
Midway Covenant Christian School, GA

I Am

I am a tree
not tall yet but growing every day
I hope to tower over mountains
seeing everything around me
rivers flowing beneath me
I am kudzu
growing
covering new places
I am a shark
swimming freely in the ocean
exploring
watching
I am a river
flowing around the world
winding, curving around

Ryan Bertling, Grade 6
Beck Academy, SC

Eliza

One night I was taking my dog for a walk on a nearly pitch black night.
I saw a shadow-figure off in the distance
But it was not a human
It was a dog!
A stray I thought. The dog was huge like a guard dog.
I started running
Then I thought I can't outrun this dog.
It came up to me and licked me
I took it home and up to now it still lives with me.

Emmett Deen, Grade 5
American Heritage Academy, GA

The Beach

Oh grain of sand squish between my toes as soft as a pillow
I feel the warmth sloshing over me
Splashing in the cool waves
I feel the hot sun baking my skin like I'm a cake
I feel shade from umbrellas

I hear shouts of nearby children
Birds cawing like bells ringing
The light breeze running on the shore

I see tiny fish and crabs scurrying along the shore
Seashells glittering in the sand like diamonds
The waves, crashing on the shore
All the shops, selling colorful beach toys and swimsuits

I smell salt water as I'm walking around
Ham sandwiches and potato salad for picnics yelling, "Don't eat me!"
I smell smoke, from ships at the dock
Sweat from exhausted people

I taste the gritty sand in my mouth yuck!
I taste ice cream of all flavors like chocolate and mint yum!
I taste fresh, sour lemonade slurp!
Oh, the beach.

Elizabeth Guthrie, Grade 4
Briarwood Elementary School, KY

Blue

Blue is like the sound of blue birds singing in the sky,
whales calling as they swim by, and water rushing down the fall.

Blue is like the smell of bleachy chlorine,
sugary sweet blueberry muffins and pie,
and the summer's salty air.

Blue is like the taste of fairgrounds' cotton candy stand,
sticky sour fruity lollipop, and tasty creamy birthday cake icing.

Blue is like the feel of icy cold winter wind,
a fluffy toasty warm jacket, and a cuddly satiny smooth baby blanket.

Kirsten Black, Grade 4
Plano Elementary School, KY

Butterflies

Butterflies flutter by
Such pretty wings up in the sky
They fly by day glide by night
How wonderful it is to see a butterfly glide on by
In the winter, when it is cold
Butterflies go to a warmer home
From flower to flower they roam
The whole wide world is a butterfly's home.

Allie Nicholson, Grade 5
Runnels School, LA

Sweet Remedy

Love
Love is my passion
Love is sweet
Now, I'm in the mood for a chocolate treat.
Now I must wander until I find one.
One day I'll get it, you'll see oh Sweet Remedy.

Chloe Wofford, Grade 5
Western Hills Elementary School, AR

Kendall

My little sister is so sweet.
I like to kiss her tiny feet.

Her little feet are so small.
She can't walk talk or fall.

When I kiss her tiny head.
She wiggles and giggles and nods her head

Sometimes she moans and kicks her feet.
She's such a little tiny treat.

Kailee Hanna, Grade 4
Small World Academy, WV

My Family Christmas

'Twas the night before Christmas, and my family
Was getting food prepared, and singing merrily.

Eggnog was being poured, while the ham was baking,
Delightful smells filled the air, as gingerbread I was making.

A hint of moon shown dimly, as sparkling snow was falling,
Icicles hung like curtains, while the winter wind kept calling.

Finally to bed I went, and to my surprise,
I hear a voice holler, "Ho! Ho! Ho!" So from my bed I rise,

Down the stairs I go along, anxious to see what's below,
All I see are glistening gifts, wrapped with shiny bows.

But Santa Claus I do not see, for he has come and gone,
Instead I find my family, and happiness filling our home.

David Miller, Grade 5
East Bernstadt Elementary School, KY

Playful/Hyper

Dogs
Playful, hyper
Running, jumping, loving
Golden Retrievers, Chesapeake Bay, Tabby, Siamese
Walking, pawing, crawling
Small, nosy
Cats

Braelin Thomas, Grade 5
Salem Elementary School, AR

What's Under My Bed?

Hey do you know
what's under my bed?
Boom! Bang! Oh! No! There goes the rocket,
"Hey what's under your bed?" you say.

Under my bed is:
a sweet cupcake that is heaven
a brownie that is muddy
"What else is under your bed?" you say

Under my bed is:
a pile of clothes as tall as 500 men stacked on top of each other
a dog as white as snow "Arf! Arf!" he says
"What else is under your bed?" you say

Well here's the sad truth —
I don't know!

Raja Challa, Grade 5
Greathouse Shryock Traditional Elementary School, KY

The Beach

Hearing the woooooh from the wind
The water splashing against it
It's like a battle between the water and the wind
Who do you think would win in a fight?
The waves I hear are very soothing
It's like a session of yoga
Seeing pelicans, waves, seagulls, and other kids
It's funny when I see a pelican swoop down to get a fish
But when it gets water it spits it out and flies away with disgust
Feeling the water tickling my feet when I step in it
The waves brushing against my back
They make me go up and down like a yo-yo
Then I take my surfboard and go out deep
Then a wave comes along and I go into it
Then stand up and sometimes fall off
Then I just stand up and try it again
Then make it work that time
Smelling the ocean is so enjoyable
It's an aroma of salty smell
The smell of the ocean is so relaxing and it's a wonderful scent
This is the beach

Michael Shaffer, Grade 4
Briarwood Elementary School, KY

Niagara Falls

Beautiful, mystic falls that fall over shiny rocks holding up the foamy water,
Maid of the Mist boats filled with people that are wearing big blue plastic bags that are
Going to get soaked in the water from the Niagara Falls that are saying look at me Baby Blue
Large amounts of heavy water slamming on the rocks can be heard from miles away,
Loud people screaming when the boat gets close to the falls, AHHH!!!

Lovely blue water that is falling down so gracefully it looks like leaves falling off of a tree,
Weird items in the souvenir shop are as strange as seeing an octopus with seven tentacles,
Delicious blue water that is splashing on my face is better than aquafina bottled water,
Good Chinese food that they have in restaurants tastes awesome.

Cool postcards can cause loving care to your best friends back home in KY who care so much for you!!!
People touching the smooth side of the Maid of Mist boat as it goes down the long,
Cold, deep river,
Happy.

Maes Mourad, Grade 6
College View Middle School, KY

My Dad

My dad, brown hair, brown eyes, dark tan skin and freckles
Making bird sounds to cheer me up when I'm sad
My dad loves watching sports, so
If you see someone watching football, golf, or any other sports cheering go, hurry, c'mon
That's my dad
Listening to music together a lot
Turning up the music super loud, it was like my ears fell off,
'Cause I got out of the car I couldn't hear a thing
Playing charades, my dad is much better because he does not use words [I do]
In charades, you have to make a picture with your body you can't use objects or words
Also playing kickball, baseball, basketball, and volleyball together
Sleeping in his room watching his TV shows all night long
Sitting on the couch, just talking, he says to me "Katherine, I love you"
Running to get in the house when it's raining and getting wet
Laughing when we got on the pouch
Settling down watching the rain fall down when we were done we walk inside
I was 2 years old climbing a TV then it falling, hitting my collar bone fracturing it
My dad rushing home from work, running me to the hospital
Saying "Katherine, it will be all right," always remembering that line
My dad, always happy in every way I will always love him, my dad, my best friend
I love you

Katherine Morrison, Grade 4
Briarwood Elementary School, KY

I Remember Auntie Judy

I remember Auntie Judy…
her nice warm hugs, kisses on the cheek, her nice lunches, visiting her house.

I remember Auntie Judy…
Happy New Year, hot cocoa on the stove, warm Christmas cookies, even more hot cocoa.

I remember Auntie Judy…
hospital sirens ringing, crying, saying goodbye.

I remember Auntie Judy.

Emily Cruey, Grade 5
Sycamore Elementary School, GA

An Ode to the Outdoors

Oh when I'm outdoors it's fun in the sun.
I'm always running and jumping.
When I'm climbing the trees there's that sweet breeze,
and all the animals I see cats, dogs, and flippy frogs.
Sometimes I swing, and sometimes I swim.
I will even go fishing with my friend Tommy.

Kenny Moore, Grade 5
West Liberty Elementary School, WV

My Pet Murphy

My pet Murphy
Is so soft and furry.

He has black button eyes
That glow like fireflies.

My pet Murphy
Is so spunky.

He runs through the house
Chasing a mouse.

My pet Murphy
Loves beef jerky.

He sits and begs
Up on his back legs.

Kourtney Shelton, Grade 4
St Mary Cathedral Elementary School, MO

The Worst Morning Ever

It was morning.
I was awakened by a
Clang!

It was my brother
Banging
Pots and pans.

Oh, nooo!!!
I'm late for school.

Boom!
It was raining.

My mom was standing
In the doorway
Jingling
The keys in my face.

Drip, drip
Oh, my gosh!
I left the water on!

Alex Monteith, Grade 4
Robert E Cashion Elementary School, SC

Computer

It has a large screen and a small mouse
The size is large
The shape is a pointy cube
It is in my giant room
The color is light grey and the screen is dark black
Computers, Computers, Aol

The shining glittery screen is sparkling in my brown eyes
While the mouse is clicking "click" "click"
Computers, Computers, Toshiba

"click" "click" is the funny sound of the small mouse
The sweet humming sound goes through my ears
Computers, Computers, Sony

Can the computer walk?
Does the computer save wonderful DVD videos?
Who made it?
Computer, Computer, Apple

I feel as happy as the colors of the rainbows
I always feel excited when I play it
It makes me grin when I am unhappy
Computers, Computers, Computers

Cindy Chen, Grade 4
Price Elementary School, KY

No Home

This homeless man lay without a blanket.
The sidewalk is as cold as the coins people throw at him.
This poor man is going to freeze to death if he just lies there.

Maggie Sanso, Grade 4
Stone Academy, SC

Electrician's Daughter

I am the daughter of an electrician.
I wonder what he does at work.
I hear him leave out the door at 5:00 A.M.
I want him to stay home with me and my mom.
I am the daughter of an electrician.

I pretend I am there with him.
I feel he will never leave me.
I touch him when I give him a hug.
I worry if he gets hurt.
I cry if he does not come back.
I am the daughter of an electrician.

I understand he has to work for us.
I say he is a really good father.
I dream he does not get hurt.
I try to help him.
I hope he does not get hurt.
I love you Dad!

Tania Tejero, Grade 5
Byrns L Darden Elementary School, TN

Ghosts

G ives people a scare
H igh in the air it goes
O ften hiding
S cary
T he ghost is white
S ays boo!!

Christina Moye, Grade 5
First Flight Elementary School, NC

Ocean

Looks like sparkling waves
Sounds like crashing buildings
Tastes like salty and bitter water
Feels like a warm blanket
Smells like sea life

Tyler Williford, Grade 5
Briarwood Christian School, AL

If Only

If only
People did not think of me
as a flightless bird,
If only
They thought of me as their
friend,
If only
They encouraged me to fly
high in the sky,
If only,
If only,
If only!

Audrey Sharpe, Grade 4
Cool Spring Elementary School, NC

I Am a Young American

I am a young American.
I wonder why I can't vote until I'm 18.
I see friends with deployed parents.
I want my dad to stay.
I am a young American.

I feel glad my dad is home.
I touch his sleeping bag and I feel safe.
I worry the bad side will win.
I cried when my dad left for Korea.
I am a young American.

I understand my dad might leave.
I say my dad is strong.
I dream nobody's dad will leave.
I try to help my mom.
I hope that there will be peace.
I am a young American.

Trevor Frank, Grade 4
Walker Intermediate School, KY

Healing

When someone hurts you in your heart
It is like they have pierced you
In time it heals, just as you forgive them
But the scars are left behind

Virginia Bandy, Grade 6
Briarwood Christian School, AL

Leaves

Leaves are everywhere
Winter is coming along
Can you wait for it?
Trees with frost on them are cool
Frost will be on the ground too

Abby Boaz, Grade 5
Berryville Elementary School, AR

This Summer

I got to fly.
And that plane flew.
I did a big sigh.
And I thanked the crew.

Blaire Beauchamp, Grade 4
Horace Mann Elementary School, OK

Fly in the Sky

I wish I can fly
High in the sky
I hope I don't
Fall and die

Travis Burns, Grade 4
Horace Mann Elementary School, OK

My Thankful Thanksgiving

Hot turkey
Buttery popcorn
Warm rolls too
Hot potatoes
Ice cold sweet tea
Getting stuffed with juicy ham
Eating a nice warm pumpkin pie
That's my thankful Thanksgiving

Kate Bowers, Grade 5
Briarwood Christian School, AL

Baseball

Baseball is so cool
I'm just glad it isn't school
you can also hit the ball
while you call
and you sure can
run while eating a bun,
so good luck
I hope you don't suck.

Conner Cooper, Grade 5
Wynne Intermediate School, AR

Leaves

Fall once and a while.
Get destroyed by human feet.
They always get raked.

John M. Sclafani, Grade 4
Holly Ridge Elementary School, NC

Purple

Purple is for LSU, who are #1.
Purple looks like a girl color.
But it's really a boy color.
Boys on LSU's team wear it.
That's why LSU is #1.

Jaran Hollis, Grade 5
West Marion Elementary School, MS

Halloween Night

The smell of candy.
How the people look
dressed up in costumes.
Funny masks.
All the cool decorations
Tasting

Crystal Jimenez, Grade 5
North Middle School, TN

Animals

All the dogs
All the cats
Every animal makes me laugh

When every animal dances on wheels.
I always remember the cat juggling eels.

Makenna Williams, Grade 4
Holly Ridge Elementary School, NC

Volcanoes

Loud and destructive.
Pollution in the black air
Dried up ponds and leaves.

Ben Johnston, Grade 4
Briarwood Christian School, AL

Fall Is Fun!

Fall, Fall everywhere,
Fall leaves in my summer chair.
Fall, Fall everywhere!
Fall is when the blizzards come
Fall is fun for everyone!
Fall is here,
Get ready to set your time back.
Fall is coming, time to sleep in!
Get ready for fall fun,
Let the fun begin!

Mackenzie Kay Walters, Grade 4
Evangelical Christian School, TN

Bobby

B obby can write a letter.
O utstanding at my work
B rave when playing football.
B atting is something that I am good at.
Y earning for a gun for Christmas.

Bobby Lambert, Grade 4
Byrns L Darden Elementary School, TN

I Am From

I am from chicken fingers and fries
at almost every restaurant I've ever been to
Saturday morning scrambled eggs (made by me)
and scary noises coming from the attic.

I am from Xbox 360's and High Definition Plasma TVs
from "stop picking your nails or I'll cut those fingers off,"
"stop bouncing the ball in the house,"
and "don't forget to flush!"

I am from deer running in the backyard,
cats sneaking up the back porch, and the
cutest dog you'll ever see
with ears as big as me.

I am from multiplying fractions and
dividing ratios, long-shot three pointers,
far away chest passes, and Bullies and Teachers
some mean and some nice.

I am from "the way the Truth and the Life,"
"no one can go to Paradise except through Me"
and a wee little man named Zaccheus
climbing up a sycamore tree.

Carter West, Grade 6
Plantation Christian Academy, GA

My Brother

CRASH!
went the vase as it hit the floor!
The sound was as loud as a bomb!
"Time for a nap," says my dad
"While I clean up this mess!"
"NO NAP,
NO NAP," he wails
Then…
BAM! went his feet as he jumped out of bed
and pounded down the stairs!
It sounded like a hippo
JUMPING through the stairs
I thought it was a hippo
because the stairs shook noisily
scaring us to death
but it was only my brother
it was only my brother

Emma Scobee, Grade 5
Greathouse Shryock Traditional Elementary School, KY

Who Is God?

Who is God, mother?
Who is God, father?
"God is Jehovah," says mother.
"God is my Savior," says father.

Where does God live, grandmother?
Where does God live, grandfather?
"God lives in Christians," says grandmother.
"God lives in our hearts," says grandfather.

What does God do, mother?
What does God do, father?
"God saves people," says mother.
"God heals people," says father.

Now I understand, mother,
Now I understand, father.
God is my Savior; God is my refuge.
God is like the vine; I am like the branches.

Lauren Belcher, Grade 5
Providence Academy, TN

Christmas

It was the night before Christmas and I sat at the tree.
Wondering and wondering what my presents would be.
Presents of all sizes and shapes I can see.
Ooh there's a big one; it must be for me!

"To bed early you must go"
My mother did say.
"You must be sound asleep when Santa arrives on his sleigh"
She kissed me goodnight and reminded me to pray.
I drifted off to sleep and awoke early the next day.

Has Santa been here? — Was the first thing on my mind.
Then I jumped out of bed to see what I could find.
All that I wanted, even more than I thought.
Look at all those presents! I love what Santa brought!

With all the excitement I almost forgot,
That this is Christ's birthday
And He gave us a lot.
All of these presents are not of much worth,
Not even close when compared to Christ's birth.

Scout Bundy, Grade 5
East Bernstadt Elementary School, KY

The Knight and the Crook

There once was an old knight,
Who had a big fright,
Because he saw a crook,
Who had a little book.
The crook and the knight got in a big fight.

Katie Summit, Grade 4
Van Cove Elementary School, AR

Up High

How does it feel to be so high
Up in the sky?
You are so hot! And you're not cool!
You have flares that cause solar storms
So, please Mr. Sun
Don't have any fires on this side
Of the Earth!

Shawn Kendall, Grade 4
St Paul's Lutheran School, OK

I Am

I am a volleyball soaring
over the net,
I am a raven in the clear
blue sky,
I am a diamond sparkling
in the sun,
I am a daisy in the light,
I am an ocean bright in the
night,
I am, I am.

Madison McLelland, Grade 4
Cool Spring Elementary School, NC

Happy Halloween

Halloween is a spooky night
when scary things come out with fright.
Jack-o'-lanterns are going to scare
because people see them everywhere.

Parker Ammons, Grade 5
North Middle School, TN

Prom

Laughing and having some fun
Wishing the night was never done
Being around your friends
Dancing till the night ends.

Sparkling lights and a disco ball
There are streamers wall-to-wall
Pictures and smiles all night
All the magic comes to life.

Rachel Miller, Grade 6
Pleasants County Middle School, WV

The Boy and His Toys

There once was a boy
With nothing to do
But break his toys
To get something new
His mom found out
His dad was told
Now all he does is pout
Because he has nothing but doubt

Bobby Reese, Grade 6
Appling County Middle School, GA

I Live on an Army Post

I live on an Army Post at Fort Knox, Kentucky, home of the Armor and Cavalry.
I wonder if I will ever travel to Hanau, Germany, where I was born.
I hear tanks booming and the airfield with planes flying over my house.
I see my mommy take care of us when daddy is deployed.
I want my daddy to stay home and not deploy for a year and three months.
I live on an Army Post at Fort Knox, Kentucky, home of the Armor and Cavalry.

I pretend to be an Army soldier with my friends.
I feel happy when my daddy's home for the holidays.
I touch my heart and say the Pledge of Allegiance every day.
I worry that my daddy will not be safe when deployed.
I cry when I miss my dad.
I live on an Army Post at Fort Knox, Kentucky, home of the Armor and Cavalry.

I understand that the military is my daddy's job.
I say military kids have more fun!
I dream about our new house.
I try to help others understand about being a military child.
I hope I will go to my new house soon!
I live on an Army Post at Fort Knox, Kentucky, home of the Armor and Cavalry.

Cierra Scarpill, Grade 5
Walker Intermediate School, KY

I Am

I am an outgoing girl who's a jack-of-all trades.
I wonder if I'll get to travel the world someday.
I hear my singing in the Christmas play at my church.
I see myself riding Lightning as we win the Kentucky Derby.
I want to travel to Japan as an interpreter.
I am an outgoing girl who's a jack-of-all trades.

I pretend that I can draw as good as my mom.
I feel excited and energetic when I play basketball.
I touch a cloud that looks like cotton candy.
I worry about severe storms.
I cry whenever I get mad and frustrated.
I am an outgoing girl who's a jack-of-all trades.

I understand the importance of learning so that I can succeed in life.
I say go for what you want.
I dream of owning a horse ranch and going to Hawaii.
I try to do the best in everything I do.
I hope that my brother Matthew and I will always be close.
I am an outgoing girl who's a jack-of-all trades.

Kacy Ives, Grade 6
Lost River Elementary School, KY

Star Ship 2000

Whirling at speeds that blur my vision
Aromas of tantalizing food fill my nose as my stomach aches.
My body twisting, nausea overtaking me.
Bouncing seats that dance to rapping music.
Gravity forces my body to cling.
When it's done I clasped to the ground while dizziness consumes me.

Matthew Mayer, Grade 5
Cline Elementary School, KY

My Grandma

Family is amazing. Family is fine.
But one member that's always on my mind
Is my grandma, oh so divine.
She's cool, she's hip, she's funny, and smart.
And that's why she has a special place in my heart.
She has big round glasses and soft fluffy hair
And when I am with her she adds that one special flair.
She's kind and she's caring, she's loving and sweet.
And I'm proud to say my grandma is neat!
She's cheerful. She's loyal.
She's happy. She's joyful.
She has that magic touch.
And that's why I love her so much!
My grandma is precious.
My grandma is kind.
But the best thing about her
Is that she is mine!

Lauren Clay, Grade 5
Blanchard Middle School, OK

Sputnik

Sputnik oh Sputnik,
You're truly amazing
Who ever thought
That you would be the first satellite in space,
Sputnik oh Sputnik
You are truly amazing,
But with only struts and nodes I can't build you.

Mark Driscoll, Grade 5
Glendale Elementary School, MO

No

Most Exciting
Day of my life
Until
My mom said the three
Powerful words
"She is dead"
I lost one of my great grandma's that day.
Eyes exploding with tears
"No, she can't die"
"No!"
I felt like a bear cub lost from its mom
And couldn't find my way back
A million tears rolling down
My cheeks like a waterfall
For when the day comes and I die
I'll see her
Until then
All I have left
are memories
When I go to Heaven I'll tell her
"I've missed you!"

Katherine Suggs, Grade 4
Briarwood Elementary School, KY

Fall Is Here!

Fall is here, oh dear,
How excited am I?
I pull off my sheets,
And I button my sweater,
And I get excited about the weather.
I run downstairs,
And grab a pair,
And I run faster than my dog.
Together me and my dog,
Run in the fog,
And together we leap into a pile of leaves.
At the end of the day I am hungrier than I have ever been,
Before I eat my turkey,
Then I head for bed,
And I unbutton my sweater,
And I think about today's wonderful weather.
I say my prayer,
And I snuggle up with my teddy bear,
I say to myself,
Thank you Lord for Fall!

Maci Brown, Grade 5
Palmetto Christian Academy, SC

The Ride

It is fast
It is getting faster and faster
But now it is slowing down
It has come to a stop
In front of me, broken tracks
It starts moving
It is going backwards, down a hill
Through a loop and 'round a curve
It slowed down again
At the rear of the car more broken tracks
It starts moving
It is going forward
Then I plunged down the mountain
Through the country, and into the station
It has stopped
I pry my hands from the bar
I open my eyes
I am terrified, I love it
I've ridden Mt. Everest
Animal Kingdom
Disney World

Autumn Myers and Samantha Rudd, Grade 5
Allatoona Elementary School, GA

The Movie Theater

Looks like fantastic acting and movies
Sounds like soft whispering
Tastes like delectable food from the concession stand
Smells like buttery, salty popcorn
Feels like cushy seats

Anna Lea Strickland, Grade 5
Briarwood Christian School, AL

I Am

I am Charity
I am African American
I hear students talking constantly
I see test grades getting passed out
I want to make good grades
I am Charity Irby, African American
I understand it takes time to do well
I say I will make it
I dream I will make it
I am Charity Irby, African American
Charity Irby, Grade 6
Beck Academy, SC

I Am a Hungry Crocodile

I am a hungry Crocodile.
I wonder if I get a Wilderbeast today?
I hear a herd is coming today.
I see the first one yay!
I want the first one.
I am a hungry Crocodile.
I pretend the first one is the biggest.
I feel confident that I will get it.
I touch it a little bit.
I worry that I will not get it.
I cry when I miss my prey.
I am a hungry Crocodile.
I understand if I miss.
I say I will get it.
I dream about getting the first one a lot.
I hope that I get it.
I try to get it and I do.
I am a hungry Crocodile.
Alex Hassen, Grade 4
Wohlwend Elementary School, MO

Volcanoes

Boom crash blowing up
Destroys houses and buildings
Burns up lots of things
Jordan Bailey, Grade 4
Briarwood Christian School, AL

First Baptist Church

I love my church FBC
It means the world to me
FBC members are caring and loving
And that makes me come in running
I also come on Wednesday nights
For GA's which is really right
I go to sing and worship my Lord
My God's power is like a mighty sword
At FBC you don't have to pay
Except for tithes which is really ok
Gabby Easterwood, Grade 6
Graham Elementary School, AL

Fall

All the leaves
are falling down
in every color
even brown.

The wind will carry
the leaves away
as I run through
them and play.

It's now become dark,
time to go inside
and wait for a new fall day to come.
Austin Brenner, Grade 5
EA Harrold Elementary School, TN

Buzzy Bee

You buzz around my head.
Flying down to flowers,
Filling me with dread.
I wish I had your flying powers.
I'd like to soar around.
Never would I fall.
Buzz would "bee" my sound.
Instead I do not fly or buzz
If I tried I would fall and bawl.
Haley Arnold, Grade 4
Moyock Elementary School, NC

The Clock on a Wall

The clock on the wall goes
Tick-tock-tickety-tock
And never stops

The clock on the wall needs
No batteries at all
For all it does is go
Tick-tock-tickety-tock

I've looked very closely
And noticed that it tells no time
For all it does is go
Tick-tock-tickety-tock
Lori Robbins, Grade 4
Capshaw School, TN

Falling Leaves

Fall,
warm, cold
red, orange, yellow
the colors are beautiful
colorful, bright colors
Leaves
Junicia Cosby, Grade 6
Stuart Middle School, KY

Drinking and Driving

Don't drink and drive
drink milk and stay alive.
Always beware,
not to stare but to care.
When driving safety comes first.
Jaida Ortiz, Grade 5
Walton Verona Elementary School, KY

My Family

My family is a race car
Busy, relaxing, still moving.
My mom is the steering wheel
she's always moving.
My dad's the gas pedal
he is constantly busy
My brother is the seat
he is always sitting and playing his game.
My sister is the mirror
she always stares at me.
I am the motor
always on the move.
Charlie Berry, Grade 5
Bloomfield Elementary School, KY

Black Cat

B ad luck cats.
L icking paws so peaceful,
A ttacking when you're not looking.
C ats with bad attitudes.
K ittens that grow to mean black

C ats that walk under ladders
A nd break mirrors.
T ilting salt shakers to the floor.
Amanda Dinger, Grade 5
First Flight Elementary School, NC

Fall of Nature

The hawk will fly in the sky.
The bear will walk on the ground.
And the fish will swim in the water.
The mountains are also nature.
But the leaves will fall
That means it's autumn.
Now I will walk for the great coolness.
Justin Lee, Grade 4
Stone Academy, SC

Frogs

Frogs are cool
Frogs are sweet
They are cute
They like to eat.
Greg Thompson, Grade 6
Martin Elementary School, WV

War

War is a nasty thing,
A time of fear and mourning.
Fear will strike at the body's heart,
As the war prepares to start.
Mighty weapons are then drawn,
To fight for freedom at the sight of dawn.
For as the sounds of battle ring,
The arrows fly, and pierce, and sting.
When the horses gallop away,
There the lifeless bodies lay,
As their spirits will always whisper,
"Sweet Revenge" to the foes who prosper.
When we win the final battle,
Our swords and shields no longer rattle,
For war is a nasty thing.

Peter Fullmer, Grade 6
Jackson Christian School, TN

I Can't Write a Poem*

Forget it. You must be kidding
I don't know how to write
Poetry is hard
I can't think straight
I need to go home and feed my cats
I have to finish reading a book
I am tired
I have to go home and take care of my sister
I want to play. I have to do math
I have to take snowboarding lessons
I can't write a poem
I have to go to the bathroom
I have to have lunch. I need recess
I need to go home and let my mom in the house
My mom is coming to pick me up
I have a bellyache
I need to go to the office
Time's up? Uh Oh!
All I have is this list of really silly excuses.
You like it? Really? No kidding?
When can I write another one?

Shaniah Frint, Grade 6
Lost River Elementary School, KY
*Patterned after "I Can't Write a Poem" by Bruce Lansky

The Lake

Around dusk deer walk to the lake for a drink
In the lake fish jump and a mink swims
As the sun sets the sky lights up yellow, orange, and pink
As the wind blows the salmon jump, I hardly blink.

The sun is getting lower, and the wind is getting colder.
The sun lowered behind the hills; the moon reflects on the lake.
The moon is lost behind the clouds; the stars shine brightly.
It began to rain; the wind blew colder and crueler than before.

Dalton Wolfe, Grade 6
Pleasants County Middle School, WV

I Live on an Army Post

I am an Army brat.
We always move it's where I'm at.
My dad's a ranger the best soldier ever.
He's big and strong.
In war he always faces danger.
I love the Army.
My grandpa was in it too.
Duty, honor country should be your motto too.

Ann Marie Wells, Grade 4
Walker Intermediate School, KY

The Rainforest

I stand in the rainforest
listening to the soft
pitter-patter of the rain
off to the side
the monkeys are swinging in the trees
as if it was their playground
I hear the wind
swishing the leaves
I stand as bugs dive and rise
all around me
off in the distance
I hear the loud caw of a toucan
and just in that same instant
all other birds reply as if in the melody of a mysterious song
the trees touch the sky
I walk towards the river
and see millions of veins running through the forest
the forest is magical
swishing the winds
in a musical tone.

Diego Mora, Grade 6
Queen of Angels Catholic School, GA

Beauty of Nature

Follow signs of a dirt trail
Thorny branches going everywhere
Keeping us from moving on
The beauty of nature everywhere I looked
Red, soft flowers growing from the ground
Picking and collecting them to give to my mother
Leaves falling from the trees and landing below
"Crunch," "Snap" I hear each time I step
Colorful butterflies following us as we walked
Sun shining brightly through the leaves making me hot
Stopping to get a drink of cold water
Moving on over the hills
Hearing birds tweeting and crickets chirping
Carefully crossing a bridge to get the flowing water
Looking at the water for frogs and fish
Turning around to travel back
Nature is beautiful.

Roman Young, Grade 4
Roberta Tully Elementary School, KY

Life

Kids crying.
People dying.
Guns shooting.
Babies born.
Sorry, I have to get
Back to life.

Derek Welker, Grade 5
St Vincent Elementary School, MO

Great Gumbo

G ood cure for hunger
R ed beans can't beat gumbo
E ating gumbo makes me happy
A ll types are not the same
T oday is the day I eat gumbo

G reat tasting all the time
U sed as school lunch
M ade as Cajun food
B est food in the world
O bserve the tasteful flavors

Jacob Vidacovich, Grade 5
Vernon Middle School, LA

Florida Gators!!!

GO GATORS!!!
I love the Florida Gators.
I love the colors orange and blue
I love the football team too
I love the basketball team
I love to watch my favorite team.
GO GATORS!!!
They won the championship
two years in a row in basketball
GO GATORS!!!
I love the Florida Gators yeah!
GO GATORS!!!

Colby Burgess, Grade 5
North Middle School, TN

A Girl Named Jane

There once was a girl named Jane.
She had a horse with a big mane.
She rode the horse by the shore.
The next day she was sore.

Tom Greene, Grade 6
Martin Elementary School, WV

Garett

Garett went up the big hill
Looking for Jack and Jill
He stepped on a big duck
Which made it go cluck
Then gave it a slug on its bill!

Garett Phillips, Grade 4
Judsonia Elementary School, AR

My Pumpkin

My beloved pumpkin is so small,
About 3 inches wide and 2 inches tall.
How elegant it looks with beautiful lines,
With two triangle eyes and a nose that shines.

This wonderful pumpkin is one of glory,
In fact, I think I'll name him Cory.
Now let me see, let's get rid of that bump,
And down it plummeted and landed with a THUMP!

I had dropped my pumpkin, no it couldn't be,
I told myself, "My pumpkin's right on the counter, waiting for me."
But it wasn't, my precious pumpkin lay on the floor,
I stared at it until I couldn't stare anymore.

I was about to toss it away when an idea struck me,
I could make it into a pie for my family!
I wasn't a whiz at using the oven, but I could always try,
My divine little pumpkin would make a great pumpkin pie.

Yinan Zheng, Grade 5
Brookwood Elementary School, GA

Fall

Fall is fun.
It is fun.
It is where it gets cold.
It brings happiness and even if it is cold, families get you warm.
Leaves change and later on it gets colder and fall turns into winter.

Noah Goble, Grade 4
First Wesleyan Christian School, NC

My Hometown

Memories flow back in my mind
When sand as red as apples study me
Peaches tingle my nose as their scent flows in the air
As remembering fills the air
My heart's beat starts to go faster
My friend's joy in excitement as I come to play
It's as if I'm almost famous
My heart sinks like quick sand
On a day I wish that had never come
My friend's joy and excitement turn to tears and cries
As I leave and say my last good-byes
Gifts and treats as I pack my things
Hurry there's no time to waste
As I exit the door forgetting my friends and everything I loved in my hometown
But my friends have not forgotten about me
As I turn around last waves and good lucks are being heard and said as I start to cry
Few years later I came back with joy and happiness
Welcome backs are being said
As I'm left alone in my room
I whisper to myself
There's no place like home

Adrian Wadley, Grade 5
Cline Elementary School, KY

The Horses' Home

A beautiful brown bay trotting around the pasture
Graceful white horse is like a grass-chomping lawn mower
Hooves stomping the ground like crashing ocean waves
Neighing horses are wolves calling to each other
My mouth tastes like small, sugary, and sweet bubble gum
Fresh air is as simple as the water I drink
The incense of horse shampoo is like a fancy perfume
Bug spray is climbing my nose as a mountain hiker would
My fingers run through the fabulous, flowing, fantastic mane
Golden hay in my hand is yellow as the bright sun
I feel as interested as a scientist in his laboratory.

Brittany Bryant, Grade 5
Bailey Elementary School, NC

My Birthday

Birthday
Having a tea party 28 people there
Using the tea set my mom gave me
Using it when she was little

Everybody dressing up in nice dresses
Some wearing make up
Some not
One girl dressing up in a Cowgirl outfit on Accident
But nobody really caring
Every one looking as pretty as princesses

Doing chalk, hula hoops, Capture the flag
Always hiding them in really good places
Being loud and noisy

Drinking tea, lemonade and fruit punch
Having mini sandwich's
Chex mix, Brownies
All tasting good and sweet
Feeling like a little lady when we got done
Because we were eating so nicely

Having lots of fun

Nicole Carr, Grade 4
Briarwood Elementary School, KY

Day and Night

Sunset comes, the end of joy of the day,
Life keeps going on,
But the man in the moon has a happy face,
All night long,

Sunrise comes, the end of happiness of the night,
Life keeps going on,
The sun has shining hair,
All day long,
But here comes the man in the moon

Olivia C. Zane, Grade 5
Hunter GT Magnet Elementary School, NC

Raise Your Hand if You Are Asleep

Goodbye children (yawn) school is starting
Raise you hand if you are asleep
Write on your pencil when you've sharpened your paper
Count your A,B,C's and sing your 1,2,3's
(yawn) Sit down for restroom break
Go put away your lunch for snack
And read if you aren't done with work (yawn)
We're going to the hall so remember be loud
Turn in your desk and clear your papers
Put away your sweater 'cause it's cold as Alaska
Empty your backpack and take your time
The bell's going to ring so you can slow down
(yawn) Erase your homework and don't remember
There's a test tomorrow so remember to study
Read the red book for writing class (yawn)
This class is full of angels
Hello children (bell rings) school has ended

Tiffany Pham, Grade 5
Greathouse Shryock Traditional Elementary School, KY

Windy

The wind gushes through the window
Wosh goes the wind
The curtains are flapping
A sudden chill goes up my back
I go outside by the wind
I fall over
You see the win blowing all around you
You look around the clouds get darker every minute
Then over the trees I see a tornado
I run inside
Later everything is all right
But the wind is gone

Amanda Nesta, Grade 6
Prince of Peace Catholic School, SC

The Truth

How could this happen?
It all seemed so true.
I could swear I heard sleigh bells,
I could hear hooves on my roof.
But it was just my imagination,
I should've know, I felt so hurt, so mad.
It felt as if my favorite thing in the world had been torn away.
The stories, the feelings I got Christmas Eve.
But it was just my mind playing tricks on me.
I should've know. All the clues were there.
Just put out of my mind.
The truth hit me like a big school bus.
It hurt and I wasn't expecting it.
I miss Santa now, but it's ok,
Because now I get to help little siblings dreams fly.
I wait for the guy in the big red suit,
The elf, I call my daddy.

Kylie Tegethoff, Grade 6
Annunciation Elementary School, MO

Horse

Horse
fast, cute
run, walk, jump
neighing, eating, sleeping, bucking
Horses run very fast.
Stallion
Gabbie Dennis, Grade 4
East Jones Elementary School, MS

I Have…

I have
These things
That have my back
They're funny
And nice
We travel in a pack

We eat
Popcorn
Till late at night
We talk
And laugh
But never fight

Old Navy
And Gap
We love to shop
Go door
To door
And never stop
Dayana Hess, Grade 5
Woodland Elementary School, KY

Ocean

Anemone and krill,
You all give me the chill.
Brain coral and sea slug,
I'd rather eat a bug.

Jellyfish and puffer fish,
I would hate you on my dish.
Seals and eels and humpback whale,
Can't I just eat a snail.
Anh-Tu Mai, Grade 4
Nesbit Elementary School, GA

Kittens

Touching soft, warm, cuddly fur.
Calming me when I'm mad.
Playful when they're blissful.
Adorable when they're napping.
Tiny when they're young.
With wee little heads and delicate paws.
Austin Lankford, Grade 5
North Middle School, TN

Butterflies

I watch as the butterflies
Flutter by as their
Wings beat silently
With the wind
Ethan Manke, Grade 6
Lockwood Elementary School, MO

On Top of the World

When I'm on top of the world,
I'm really on my horse.
When I'm in the ring,
with the crowd so loud,
I never hear them.
It's just Yellar and I.
When I'm on Yellar,
I am free.
I am on top of the world.
McKenzie Davidson, Grade 5
Fox Elementary School, MO

Ode to Horses

Oh I love to ride in the sun.
It is so fun.

Your cuddly fuzzy coat,
so warm and cozy.

You're as cute as a puppy.
You ride with speed in all your shows,
so fast with power.

You can never wait for your food,
bobbing your head to reach your bucket.
Jessica Hopkins, Grade 5
West Liberty Elementary School, WV

Deer

Deer are running fast
Dancing and prancing along
Wind cannot catch up
Beautiful deer run and play
Deer jump and chase each other
Kristina Garcia, Grade 5
Berryville Elementary School, AR

When Is Christmas?

When is Christmas,
When bells are ringing,
When pots are streaming,
When you see your breath,
When snow falls,
When I am sleeping,
Then it is Christmas.
Michael Hall, Grade 4
Blakeney Elementary School, GA

One More Day

I see the field.
I see the trees.
I see the ground.
I see my knees.
One more day to play.
One more day to pray.
All I ask for, Lord,
Is one more day.
Matthew Thomas, Grade 4
Ode Maddox Elementary School, AR

The Rainbow

The rainbow is like stained glass,
So large and colorful,
Its beauty boundless,
With so many colors to compliment it,
A beautiful light across the sky.

Have you ever seen a rainbow,
From end to end,
Stretching itself out,
As if waking from a deep sleep?
Peaceful, peaceful.

The sky is blue,
As blue as the ocean,
As if the ocean got stuck in the air,
And it can't break free.
How great a sight it is.

The air is newly moist,
And smells of fresh flowers,
Illuminating the beauty of the rainbow,
Creating a beautiful scene.
Stunning, stunning.
Clayton Porter, Grade 6
IA Lewis Elementary School, LA

Autumn

Cider in a jug,
Turkeys roasting very slow
Apple dumplings — yum!
John-David Wright, Grade 6
Musselman Middle School, WV

Fall Colors

Red is for the leaves on the trees.
Yellow is for the sun so bright.
Orange is for the pumpkins with faces.
Purple is for the bats that fly.
Green is for the fall time grass.
White is for the rest of the paper.
What fall colors will you make?
Nick Yates, Grade 5
Ascension Elementary School, KY

Arkansas

At my grandma's house
There is a lake.
I caught my first fish there,
Saw thousands of ants,
And a beautiful, white crane.
My mom saw a family of turtles
And my dad saw a big fish
With little, sharp teeth.
He said, "That would be
A good fish to eat on."
My dad is an eater!

Rebekah Moore, Grade 5
Lee A Tolbert Community Academy, MO

Happiness

Waves of happiness splash onto my face
I smile
It can sometimes be rough
It can sometimes be smooth
When you think you're the happiest in the world
It can evaporate into thin air
your life would be very dull without happiness
Even in the darkest of times it is shiny
Happiness comes and goes
Just like the calm waves of the ocean
Happiness is not murky
It is clean and clear
It is also fresh
Beautiful things live inside it
Happiness is a rainbow of colors

Elisabeth Noblet, Grade 6
St Mary's School, SC

i am

i am a kid
i wonder about global warming
i hear people talking
i see grass
i want to have a good life
i am a kid

i pretend to like my dad's mashed potatoes
i feel cold
i touch a pen
i worry about global warming
i cry when i lose someone close
i am a kid

i understand my friends
i say my feelings
i dream to be a writer
i try to do well in school
i hope to have a good life
i am a kid

Michael Kaczmarczyk, Grade 6
Lakeshore Middle School, NC

Evan Ellis

I have a hero that is important to me,
He lives in my heart and in heaven.
He was in boot camp so we could be free,
Yes, he is my hero, and his name is Evan.

Out of all my uncles, he is the best,
My grandma really misses him much.
Sometimes he could be a pest,
I can't believe someone would do such.

He believed in the Bible and in God,
He loved all of his peers.
He and I were like two peas in a pod;
He could read music with his ears.

Everything Evan Ellis did, he shared,
On that day in July he was killed.
God was there because he cared,
On the day he died, I was not thrilled.

Bethany Wilson, Grade 4
North Elementary School, NC

The Ways I Admire My Mom

I admire my mom.
She is there for me
At the good times and the bad.
She knows a way to keep me up
When I am down.
She tires to do her best for us
And she always has a plan.
I hope that one day
My brother and I can help her out.
My mom sounds beautiful when she sings,
And she has soft skin.

Virdal Nash, Grade 5
Lee A Tolbert Community Academy, MO

You Are So Much to Me

People may not see
But you are so much to me
Sharp and black
You dance across my white sheet of snow
You make masterpieces,
you're the one
who makes the secret notes,
the pictures,
and the stories to be told

You're amazing
You're smart
You're beautiful
You're just,
a simple pencil

Ashley White, Grade 6
East Oldham Middle School, KY

Football

F un
O utside
O ne hundred yards
T ough people
B aseball is very different
A ll the same age
L oveable to everyone
L ike a big rush of excitement

Sully Jeter, Grade 5
Briarwood Christian School, AL

Ecstatic

Ecstatic is gold
It tastes like sugar
It sounds like firecrackers
It smells like a ball game hot dog
It looks like a homemade pumpkin pie
It feels like a sugar rush

Austin Wood, Grade 4
Cleveland Elementary School, OK

Haunted

H aunted spooky,
A nd scary! Ghosts
U nder floor boards.
N early everything is
T errifying. With creepy
E lderly witches and
D eformed moldy walls!

Emily Lyster, Grade 5
First Flight Elementary School, NC

Dragonfly

The aroma of the flowers below
fill the world with a colorful glow.
She floats in the air
as the wind takes care.
It lands gracefully in the open world
like a ballet dancer.
She shimmers in the sunlight
as she appears.
She hops onto a cherry blossom
and grabs it with her sticky feet.
In the night there's a bit of light
wherever she may go.

Isabella Rusher, Grade 5
Salisbury Academy, NC

Volleyball

pass, serve
spike, set, over
drive the ball, set it back
pass, serve, spike, set, overhand, drive
points, game

Clay Fowler, Grade 5
Broadway Elementary School, NC

Tree

Standing alone with open arms
waiting for a little kid to come and hide behind its trunk
who's wishing to escape all fears and mistakes he has encountered

Leaves, colors of red, brown, and gold, dancing with the winds
like a little girl's pigtails when they bounce up and down from
her running across the playground

Making way through the trees of different shapes and sizes
and with the branches like arms reaching up to the blue sky,
is like an obstacle course of adventurous discoveries

Every branch higher is like another stepping stone in a life time

Hannah Singley, Grade 6
Chapin Middle School, SC

The Helicopter

H e who pilots this machine knows the sky
E lectricity and gas let this object fly
L ying about the items you have when you board may be dangerous
I think that this mechanism is marvelous
C ops will use this to search the ground for criminals
O h something else you might want to know, they are very subliminal
P eople who don't know how to drive it should not try
T he gas or batteries are required to fly
E ven though it is small it can take you far
R ound and round spin the blades on top of it, they are quite bizarre!

David Licciardi, Grade 6
Haynes Academy for Advanced Studies, LA

Emotion Seasons

Summer…summer is a burning valley of stones surrounded by glazing fire.
Summer can be furious, insane, and sparky.

Fall is the soothing relaxation from the waves of Niagara Falls.
Fall can be pleasant, angry, yet stressed.
Spring is the warm, refreshed curtain draped over a window of mildness.

Winter…
Winter is the bitter coldness of the other side of the pillow.
But we all live in a world where we share seasons of emotions.

We can be stressed and sometimes furious.
We can be happy, sad, curious or confused.
But in the end, our emotions are just like us.

Roxanne Baker, Grade 5
Odessa Middle School, MO

In the Starry Night

I wake up in the night with tears flowing down.
I look up in the dark starry sky, and find the biggest and the
boldest star and think of him, my dad.
I wave and smile and say good night and wait until the next day's sunrise
While wishing he could see how far I've gotten in my powerful life.

Emily Brady, Grade 5
Endhaven Elementary School, NC

Lonely Dust

Today I sleep
in a little old shack.

I'm scared and yell
"MOM" but no one answers.

The only sound I hear is the
roar of the dust like a
"Freight Train!"

My life tastes, smells, and
looks like little red pieces of dust,
all dried up like my life.

I feel like I'm on fire
while the dust touches my cuts.

I have no purpose in my life today
so I bid you farewell and good day.

Thomas Arsenaux, Grade 6
Haynes Academy for Advanced Studies, LA

If Only

If only, if only, NATHAN were alive,
I'd run up and hug him with tears in my eyes.
Football and soccer are things that we played
but sadly those days have unfortunately gone away.
The moment I heard I started to cry.
I didn't understand and wanted to know why?
God took this great guy, someone that I love,
to a place much better, to heaven above.
I'll always remember the day he passed away.
My friend is gone and I'll never be the same.

Kelsy Padgett, Grade 4
Sequoyah Elementary School, TN

Falls Start

At the end of summer there is always fall.
This is when the leaves get colorful red, brown, and orange.
Birds chirp, squirrels gather nuts
for the winter and my mom buys a turkey.
Before you know it, winters here and falls
all over until next year.

Andrew Stewart, Grade 5
Palmetto Christian Academy, SC

Who Am I?

I look at myself and say, "Who do I want to be?
Do I really want to be trapped here as me?"
We all say we want to be someone else.
Sometimes I don't want to be myself.
We all lose our heads sometimes,
But everything we do is a part of life.

Bianca Faccinetti, Grade 5
Woodlawn Christian School, NC

Free Verse from a Pencil

First is the title
    You gotta have a topic,
        Line breaks — Oh my!
            Then the line breaks come on, wearing me down.

        White spaces are a blessing to me, your pencil
        A rhythm is a must, though I know not why,
        Imagination is big,
    You HAVE to write an end title?!
What'll it tell?

Strong feeling is famous
    Adjectives — Bring on the sharpener!
And, finally,
    Adverbs and the mood.

    Not the checklist!
        No,
    Nothing can stop me from helping kids learn
        Except a broken tip.

Katie Zobel, Grade 5
Chapin Elementary School, SC

Fall

Fall is a sign that summer's over
Fall is when winter starts knocking at your door
Fall is chilly
Fall is cold
Fall is colorful
Fall is harvest
Fall is the turkey straight out of the oven
Fall is the nice warm fire
Fall means family together!

Jessica Ezell, Grade 6
Stuart Middle School, KY

If Only...

If only I were a kangaroo,
I could hop away from you, only if I could.
If only I were a lion,
I would scare you, only if I could.
If only I were a pig,
I could run into you, only if I could.
If only I were a monkey,
I could swing from you, only if I could.
If only I were a cat,
I would hiss at you, only if I could.
If only I were a bee,
I could sting you, only if I could.
If only I were an ant.
I could hide from you, only if I could.
If only I were a bird,
I could fly away from you,
If only, if only, if only...

Ember Renee Jetter, Grade 4
Cool Spring Elementary School, NC

Best Friends

I have a lot of friends
They're all so cool
They like to hangout
At the pool

I've also got a very best friend
We are best friends till the end
Keela is a lot of fun
We like to play out in the sun

Keeley Stafford, Grade 4
Horace Mann Elementary School, OK

Winter Sledding

I'm looking at the sky,
And watching snowflakes fly.
I hope when I get out of bed
I can go and get on my sled.

As soon as school is out,
I'll want to run and shout!
The snow is coming down
And piling all around.

I'll have a snowball fight
And stay out until night.
Frostbite on my toes
A cold in my nose.

I think that I will pray
That we'll have a two-hour delay.
Better yet, not school today.

A. J. Dawson, Grade 6
Pleasants County Middle School, WV

Autumn Day

Leaves drop to the ground
Red, yellow, orange, brown leaves
It's cold and windy

Layn Murphy, Grade 4
Briarwood Christian School, AL

The Seasons of the Trees

In summer when the trees are green,
There's not much sky to be seen.

In autumn when the trees are red,
"How beautiful" my mother said.

In winter when the trees are white,
In the snow I take delight.

In the spring the bluebirds sing
A new-birth song!

Anna Shafer, Grade 4
Balm of Gilead School, NC

Mad

I got mad at my brother
So I went to the basement.
I could still see our Christmas lights up.
My brother calls me
like a caring person
searching for me.
He looked far and wide.
He could not find me anywhere.
It feels sad.
My brother hugs me
for me to come home.
He knows me so well,
he knows I like ice cream.

Maggie Titus, Grade 5
Fox Elementary School, MO

He Is Gone

He is gone and I miss him.
I lie in bed and I think about him.
I know that wherever he is,
I will still remember him.
I know he will always remember me.
No matter where I go,
He will be proud of me.

He is gone and I miss him.
I love him with all of my heart.
I know that I will always be in his heart.
I know my family will always
Be in his heart no matter what.

Mercedes Wheeler, Grade 4
Hayes Elementary School, OK

The Traveling Moose

There once was a moose,
Who got on the loose,
He went to Montana,
And then Louisiana,
And he made friends with a goose.

Taylor Abercrombie, Grade 4
Eastside Elementary School, GA

Square

What is a square?
Is it just lines?
Can it dance?
Can it sing?
Is it a box?
Is it a hated thing?
Is something bundled up inside?
Are joys hidden
And are lives too?
Watch the square…it'll watch you.

Kelley Hillis, Grade 6
Williamsville Elementary School, MO

Friends

Friendship is a feeling
Friendship is a hope
friends will always be there
When you are stuck on a slope
Because I have friends
I have something to say
I can do anything with my friends
And nothing will get in the way.

Anisa Dedovic, Grade 6
Pleasant View School, TN

The Tick of Time

Tick-tock goes the clock
Chime-chime, winter time
Tick-tick, then I wink,
Tock-tock, my door is locked,
After the tick of time.

Hayley Ahuja, Grade 6
Blackmon Road Middle School, GA

Blushing

Love is red.
It sounds like wedding bells.
It tastes like red velvet cake.
It smells like Mom's homemade cookies.
It looks like Heaven's gates.
It makes you feel like blushing.

Baylie McLaren, Grade 5
Salem Elementary School, AR

A Shadow

A black shadow looms in the darkness.
It pulls me closer with each step.
I reach out to grab it,
But it slips between my fingers
And it again slips back into the dark.
It always tricks my mind,
There it is and there it isn't.
I search and search, but cannot find it.
I will forever search for the shadow.

Nicole Cook, Grade 5
American Heritage Academy, GA

Fall Days

F all is here.
A great time of the year.
L eaves are changing.
L ofty tree branches are hanging.

D elicious baked pumpkin pie.
A perfect day, I wouldn't want to die.
Y eah fall!
S ome kids eat popcorn balls.

Christina McCormack, Grade 5
Palmetto Christian Academy, SC

The Number 7

The number 7 oh how great thou are.
For that number brings luck to thee.
Course I could have liked 77 or 777 and maybe 7,777.
But I think doubling my luck is not for me.

Matt Crow, Grade 4
William Southern Elementary School, MO

Wildlife

Animals are like a flower's new blossom
Beautiful, elegant and free.
There's nothing to stop them
Just them and the dirt.
Running anywhere their hearts desire
Not knowing what will happen next.
However, they move galloping, hopping, and slithering
They are fantastic, majestic, and peaceful.

Coleman Hoxit, Grade 6
Scotts Creek Elementary School, NC

Christmas

C hrist is born
H erald angels sing
R edemption is the price Jesus paid for our salvation
I cicles hanging on the manger
S avior and Lord
T raveled to Bethlehem
M ary and Joseph
A ngels in the heavens
S tar shone the way

Sydrena Dockery, Grade 4
Holly Ridge Elementary School, NC

Summer Breeze — Winter Chills

Summer Breeze
Sky painted pink, yellow and orange.
Kites flying in the air.
The yellow sun in my face.

Blue wind in my hair,
Leaves on the summer tree,
Using the sky as a blanket,
Even the sunset as a pillow.

Sky painted pink, yellow and orange.
Winter Chills

Winter sky painted light, violet with clouds,
Snowballs in the air.
The winter chills going down my back.

Snow angels everywhere on the ground.
Hearing your mom yell, "Come in and have hot chocolate!"
Winter's sky is going black!
Winter sky painted light violet with clouds.

Elizabeth Comstock, Grade 5
Odessa Middle School, MO

Quarterback

My coach thinks I'm slow
He tells me to go, go, go.
He yells, hollers, and screams.
I always say he's mean.
The quarterback is the leader of the team
For their team they do the right thing.
They lead their teams to the right path
After practice they have to take a bath.

Jace Capps, Grade 5
Nesbit Elementary School, GA

Oh, How I Love Recess!

Oh, how I love recess!
You are such a success.

When I slide down your slide
or swing on your swing,
It sure does give me a thrill.

But when recess is over,
I cry.

But I say, to recess:
It's okay, recess,
because I'll be back the next day.

Alecia Totton, Grade 4
St Mary Cathedral Elementary School, MO

Silk Flowers

The icy mountains glare
It is now autumn
Drifting across in the ocean's light breeze
The shining sun
Summer, spring, and fall have past
Seeds burst open
A big beautiful flower emerges
Bumblebee's glide around this marvelous flower
They land gently on the silk light petals
To get their nectar and honey

Holly Kratzwald, Grade 5
G C Burkhead Elementary School, KY

The Holocaust

Hitler almost wiped out the Jews
If he did that, what would of been next?
The United States? Wait! Look!
Is that a bird, or a cloud?
No. It's the U.S.A.
Coming to help the allies and Jews!
Nazi soldiers surely were strong, but the
U.S. army is stronger hopefully.
So, the Holocaust came to "Be"
because of Adolph Hitler an evil, evil man!

Terry Lowry, Grade 5
Pembroke Elementary School, NC

Blessed

I hear the soft breeze rustle the tree's leaves. I watch the sun glisten on the morning dew. I think of all the blessings we have in our lifetime. Love, health, the beauty of nature, peace and life itself. Most of these we take for granted. But we shouldn't. Grasp the love we have around us while we still can. Spread the compassion and concern for others that not many people think of. Live life to the fullest. Solve each puzzle you have in life one day at a time. If you look at all the things we have in life (minus all the bad things) we really and truly are blessed.

Sana Gonzalez, Grade 6
Home School, GA

Life

Life is a hard thing to deal with. You're not going to get everything you want. When your parents have a baby you might think they don't care about you anymore. Life is harder and harder growing up. Love will stay upon you even though sometimes it may not seem like it. One thing to remember JUST BE YOURSELF!

Artiahnna Allen, Grade 5
Western Hills Elementary School, AR

My Brother and Sister

Alone I sit here in the dark, with no one to hear and no one to shout. Thinking about me, and my family. Oh, what's that? It was a clash, a bang, a bing, a bash. I sit here thinking all alone of what to call my own little home. I see little kids here and there having their parents always there. All I have left is my big sister and little brother too, oh what to do without you two. I couldn't live if it wasn't for you. So I sit here in the dark, with no one to hear and no one to shout, but at least I have my brother and sister, who I couldn't live without.

Sonali Demla, Grade 6
Lawton Academy of Arts and Sciences, OK

Where I'm From

I am from football and Nike and Under Armour
I am from the washing machine that washes away the dirt and sweat from the sports and games I play.
I am from the Fescue grass and the plum tree that gave me a soft place to play and shade to rest.
I am from Thanksgiving dinner and sarcasm from Maw and Tara and Mom.
I am from faith and hard work.
From the Tooth Fairy that leaves more money at Nana's and Santa who is anyone that gives a child a gift.
I am from the cross on Calvary, where Jesus died to take our sins.
I am from North Carolina, Ireland, Germany, Scotland, and England, apples and What-A-Burger.
I am from the Army and the pictures my grandfather sketched of the war
And the scars on my dad's leg from fighting another kind of battle.
I am from an album and stories on a bulletin board worth a billion memories.

Aaron Chapman, Grade 6
Lakeshore Middle School, NC

Italia

A gaggle of fuzzy kittens spread into rolling balls of fluff, their tiny tails reminding me of airy cotton
Faint double rainbows arch over the still blue water of the crystal aqua pool
The distant sounds of cream-swirled Palomino horses come to comfort
The steady pitter-patter of cool rain dancing on the roof is relaxing and its steady drumming calms my senses
Hot and freshly-backed garlic bread makes my mouth water
Yummy tiramisu cake has an unforgettably delicious taste
The sweetly-sour smell of the lemon trees wafts into the open window
Newly-pressed olive oil and oregano long for bruschetta
Grinning grapevines stretch to the sky thirsting for cool rain
Soft smooth cherries as red as Christmas bows are cradled by their branches
Oh, how sweet
Relaxation and happiness abound

Kate Hornaday, Grade 6
College View Middle School, KY

The Trail That Began a Beginning

It was 1850
And we were heading on a dirt trail
With a green surrounding.

We were headed on a journey
A journey of the unknown.

As we roll down the trail
We see so many things
Things like deer, wolves, and even snakes.

We suffer, we weaken, we try to survive
The journey ahead is in disguise.

Kylee Elam, Grade 6
Des Arc Elementary School, AR

Autumn Breeze

A bout every color leaves imaginable,
U p above the birds fly —
T he aroma of the food,
U nreal autumn days,
M ountains changing and turning different colors,
N o one can make better apple pie than me,

B uzzing of the bees,
R unning around
E veryone screaming and jumping,
E veryone loves turkey in the fall,
Z oo animals we act like,
E vening has come — what a great day!

Hannah Whitmore, Grade 5
Palmetto Christian Academy, SC

Spelling Homework

Spelling homework is very hard
I try to avoid it at all cost.
Sometimes it haunts me in my nightmares.
Where spelling homework actually affects society.
It makes people feel stupid also;
When people say that I can't write.
See, I'm writing now.
What do you think of them apples?
So, what to write now?
Well I try to pass spelling,
I try really hard.
But for some reason,
I write something else for my homework.
Wait, what was my homework again?
Well I can't find my spelling homework AGAIN.
But what if I can't find it?
So, my conclusion is I don't like spelling homework.
Wait, I know why I fail spelling class!
I blame my teacher!

Shane Ewing, Grade 6
Warrensburg Middle School, MO

Autumn

As the leaves fall from the sky
I cannot help but wonder why
the leaves change color from green to yellow
now to red
round and round the red leaves rustle against the ground
so, now as I lay in bed
the leaves fall above my head
like a dancer
falling from the sky
they fly, fly, fly
they change their color from yellow
back to green
oh, is this just a dream
they fall so sweet
as they decorate the ground all around
and they fall on a twig
and it goes "crack"
and the leaves fall
I know that
autumn
has come to all

Chris Caswell, Grade 5
Greathouse Shryock Traditional Elementary School, KY

Dolphins

Swimming and jumping in the water
Bright, beautiful, grey skin
Glistening on the water's surface
Doing tricks that are fun to watch
Gliding fast and catching fish
Eating them with cone shaped teeth
Very friendly, you can pet them
Battle scars from chasing prey
Very unique predators
Gracefully swimming in the deep blue sea.

John Hall, Grade 6
Haynes Academy for Advanced Studies, LA

The Monkey

The monkey swings from tree to tree,
talking and talking excitedly.
Trust me, I've tried she never stops,
there is no button to click to make her turn off.
This monkey is quick, clever, a trickster,
this little monkey is my little sister.

Alexandra Warren, Grade 5
Salisbury Academy, NC

War Is a Game

War is a game with no winners,
War is a pool with no swimmers,
War is a deadly fear, but not like a haunted house,
War is a waste!
War is a game with no winners!

Mark Legette, Grade 6
Beck Academy, SC

Bry
Bry is very cute.
He likes to toot.
He loves to go to Wal-Mart.
He gets to ride in the cart.
He likes to play patty cake.
And he likes to make cake.
Bry is my baby brother
There will be no other!
Kaitlyn Moore, Grade 4
West Elementary School, MO

Spider Web
S ewing a web, like silky thread
P ut some here, no there!
I nto a web a fly will go
D rinking his dinner, poor fly.
E specially terrible
R ough wind came

W ithout a web
E very spider can't live,
B ut Black Widow looks, 'till he finds.
Annie Sorey, Grade 5
First Flight Elementary School, NC

Cystic Fibrosis
CF, part of my life,
part of my world
I sit in the hospital
waiting and listening
I look into the eyes of
my sleeping friend
hoping she'll wake soon
She finally wakes as the
nurse comes in
We hug and kiss before
she leaves our world
CF, part of my life,
part of world forever.
Zoe Gillespie, Grade 6
Discovery School @ Reeves Rogers, TN

Nature
The wind is blowing
And the sun's light
As the trees are growing
Makes the ponds bright!

When the sun goes down
When the moon comes up
Everything all around lays down
Even baby bucks!
This is called nature!
Elizabeth Lowry, Grade 5
Pembroke Elementary School, NC

Thanksgiving
Thanksgiving
food, turkey
eating, burping, sleeping
you get stuffed
holiday
Sydney Piazza, Grade 5
Westwood Elementary School, AR

Christmas Is Here
C hristmas Eve is here.
H olidays are near.
R eindeer are flying.
I ndoors are cozy.
S anta is coming.
T rees are up.
M any are ready.
A lot of people are ready.
S taring at the presents.

I magining what they are.
S talking your parents.

H ouses are decorated.
E vening has come.
R ock is on the radio.
E ating the Christmas dinner.
Montana Willis, Grade 6
Rocky Comfort Elementary School, MO

Sisters
They pull your hair hard
They make you do their hard chores
But you still love them.
Emily Purner, Grade 4
Briarwood Christian School, AL

Spicebush Swallowtail
Spicebush Swallowtail
blue, ivory
loops, flows, sips
rushing, hiding, soaring, flying
I'll be flying around!
Butterfly
Jasmine McGill, Grade 4
East Jones Elementary School, MS

Rain
Rain Rain
Everywhere on
My nose and
In my hair
Splashing everywhere
Lots and lots of rain
Shelby Miller, Grade 5
American Heritage Academy, GA

Fish
Fish swimming at sea
Sharks getting hit by garbage
Baby fish spy on pipes.
Ethan Randall, Grade 4
Briarwood Christian School, AL

Snowflake
I have a bunny named Snowflake,

She is snugly, soft, and pretty.
Now we call her Snow,
Lovable, and cute
We love her so much.

Fondly I wrote with
Love and care,
Adoring,
Kindly, and cute.
End of the bunny trail.
Christian Barnhill, Grade 4
Montessori Community School, NC

Cape Hatteras Lighthouse
color, black and white
this lighthouse helps boats at night
Cape Hatteras lights
Jordan Cox, Grade 4
Broadway Elementary School, NC

Fish
Fish are like flowers
That swim all over the sea
With pretty colors
Tyshon Washington, Grade 5
Duncan Chapel Elementary School, SC

Penguins
Penguins black and white
Penguins really like to slide
Penguins a delight
Drew Bonner, Grade 4
Briarwood Christian School, AL

Trees
I never saw a tree.
So cute, like me.
Trees are tall.
But, not round like a ball.

Trees are strong like my bones.
Trees are stronger than stones.
Trees are brown.
They have apples that are round.
Elton Graham, Grade 6
Manning Elementary School, SC

Baseball

I can play baseball any day,
In the sun or in the rain it's all okay.

I love the sound when I hit the ball,
Even when I am playing in the fall.

I love the delicious smell of the nachos in the stands,
And the sound of the exciting band!

Garrett Cheatham, Grade 5
North Middle School, TN

October

O range is the color leaves change
C ool weather is when we wear jeans
T ogether we can play at a birthday party
O ctober is when we can run and play
B ig fancy magnificent leaves fall on the ground
E veryone adores going trick or treating
R eading about Halloween makes me smile

Gracie Morgan, Grade 4
Center Elementary School, GA

The Worst Day After Christmas

December 26, 2003
I stood there watching,
My poor suffering dog lying there,
In that lonely cage,
Where I'm sure many other dogs have died
I.V's hooked into her left paw,
I could see that sad sobbing look on her face,
Her eyes wandering around the room,
I couldn't hold the tears back,
Like the slow river flowing through Mammoth Cave
I stood there, tears slowly drifting down my face,
Until she was finally put out of her misery
As she closed her eyes for the last time.
I might as well have had on a bib
Because the tears came rolling down my cheeks.

Jonah Campbell, Grade 6
East Oldham Middle School, KY

Halloween Night

One day on a Halloween night,
there was a lot of commotion and lots of fright.
The power in all of the houses was gone
all the way until about dawn.
It was too dark for trick or treating,
so the kids stayed in until done eating.
There were costumes, scary and funny,
one person was even dressed as a bunny.
Many kids got candy and toys,
which gave joy to all of the girls and boys.
During the night when all were sleeping
this story ends in God's safe keeping.

Shiv Bhakta, Grade 5
Our Lady of Fatima School, MS

Your Imagination

The things that you imagine are a great work of art
Because your imagination, comes right from your heart
You can think up a storm, and you can create a creation
The reason you can do this, is because of your imagination
You can imagine a dolphin sipping coffee out of a mug
You can imagine a polar bear doing the jitterbug
If you don't understand what I am trying to say
I'll break it down into a few words, because it's easier that way
"Believe in what you believe" and that is a fact
As long as you stay in the imagination track!

Alexa Simmons, Grade 6
Holy Trinity School, KY

The Evil Lunch Box!

Lunch box, oh lunch box
I'm begging you please!
Please let me take out my cheddary cheese
It's orange and squishy
and very yummy too!
Please let me take it out or it will turn blue
Lunch box, oh lunch box
I'm begging you please!
Please let me take out my Swiss cheese
It's yellowish white
and has holes in it too!
Please let me take it out or I will
STEP ON YOU!!

Christine Underwood, Grade 6
Holy Trinity School, KY

Dogs

Can dogs be human?
Maybe, maybe not!
But look into their eyes
What can we see?
I bet we can see forgiveness
For whatever wrong that we might do
Is forgiveness like human?
Should we look into a human eye?
No! Maybe not.

Oh! Whatever can a dog be?
Helper for sure, but a companion even more
Man's best friend he surely is
The human eyes can be filled with compassion
Yet a dog's eyes can be just the same
Certainly the determined mind on any dog's trait
Can have so much virtue, with an angry grin.

Can we ever compare?
To know a human comrade
With all its sincerity
Will we ever compare?

John Nanan, Grade 6
Discovery School @ Reeves Rogers, TN

Dance

Dancing
It is so fun
Leaping with lots of joy
Filled with lots of passion and fun
Dancing
Autumn Blakely, Grade 6
Southwest Middle School, AR

Marvellous November

Grandma's birthday
Cranberry sauce
Leaves change
Thanksgiving break
Fall festivals
Green beans
Leaves fall
Jump in
Off swings
Turkey dressings
Family fun
Pine cones fall
Rice gravy
Fall arrives
Nyga's birthday
Birthday presents
Finished eating
Go home
Nilyeah Godwin, Grade 4
Center Elementary School, GA

The Scatting Cat

There once was a cat
who loved to scat
he had a mean owner
who threw him all over
"Stop scatting!"
said the owner to the cat,
but the cat loved to scat
no one could stop that
he scatted day and night
and gave his owner a fright
"Get out!"
said the owner with a shout
Susan Hyder, Grade 5
Mark Twain Elementary School, OK

Joselyn

J azzy as can be.
O h always so sassy.
S mart at everything.
E ncouraging all the time.
L ovable and always huggable.
Y oung and is a child.
N ice and has a lot of friends.
Joselyn Seymore, Grade 4
Byrns L Darden Elementary School, TN

Finding the One

At Huber's Pumpkin Patch
an exciting thrill walking through the viney Pumpkin Patch,
searching like a hawk for the biggest, ripest pumpkin
wondering which pumpkin to pick
big, small, medium — so hard to choose.
At Huber's Pumpkin Patch
families and friends wandering around
tripping over the bristly vines
following the vines to funny shaped pumpkins
hearing the exciting voices of the little kids
saying "This one's good" "Can we have this one?"
At Huber's Pumpkin Patch
fighting with vines like tug-a-war with a dog struggling with the fat pumpkin.
At Huber's Pumpkin Patch
finding the one I want
tearing it off the vine like a dog tearing up the homework
At Huber's Pumpkin Patch
holding on to my pumpkin as tight as I possibly could
up and down over bumps jumping off the trailer like a kangaroo
excited to take it home to carve
turning it into a funny shaped jack-o'-lantern!
Lexi Harvey, Grade 4
Roberta Tully Elementary School, KY

Christmas Star

On this Christmas morning, a day oh so fine
I hope you will see a star that will shine
on top of the tree all covered with gold
it represents a story most kids have been told.
One day a small baby was born in Bethlehem
and this baby's name was Jesus Christ, the Lamb.
Shepherds and angels came from all around
to see this small baby born without a sound.
So God sent his son to save me and you,
He might be your Savior, but He's your best friend, too!
So let's celebrate this day and try not to pout,
because now you know what Christmas is all about!
So we thank our Lord Jesus for this wonderful season, and you just remember,
Jesus Christ is the reason!!!

Anna Rennie, Grade 6
Christian Academy – Louisville Southwest Campus, KY

Summertime Favorites

Vivid carpet of blooms in the garden
Scorching sun shining bright on me
Cooling water in the ocean rolling like a storm cloud to the shore
Buzzing bees flying in the breeze
Swimming in the pool on a beautiful day
Lightning bugs twinkling in the night sky
Yummy sticky watermelons at a picnic
Fresh cut grass
Bright red juicy tomatoes
Delicious hamburgers on the grill

Sarah Sinclair, Grade 6
Alvaton Elementary School, KY

Yummy!

Yum, it smells good!
cooking with flour and rye,
Bread, cake, pasta, soup, and salad
stirring in the cooking bowl.

Yum, it tastes good!
The tasty treats touch my sweet tooth,
forks, knives, spoons, plates,
Great ingredients for food to take place.

To be served, to be eaten,
To be wonderful, a paradise!
Like no other in a bowl
Or in a cup it's sure…
To fill my tummy up!

As good as can be,
Enough to last for you and me
Wow! It's wonderful to stick in your mouth
Yum, yum, yummy,
I LOVE FOOD!

Olivia Renfro, Grade 5
Greathouse Shryock Traditional Elementary School, KY

The Clock on the Wall

The clock on the wall goes tick-tock.
That clock always goes tick-tock-tick-tock.
I want to box that clock if it says tick-tock-tick-tock.
It always goes round and round on the wall.
Tick-tock-tick-tock goes the clock!

Ebonee Brown, Grade 5
Vernon Middle School, LA

I Am

I am a loud girl who loves basketball
I wonder how blue the ocean is in Hawaii
I hear the sound of crashing waves
I see way out to the world beyond the sea
I want to become famous to help the world
I am a loud girl who loves basketball

I pretend I am older than my sister
I feel the vibration of an earthquake
I touch the softness of a cloud
I worry the world will change
I am a loud girl who loves basketball

I understand pollution is harmful to us
I say, "Global warming is a warning."
I dream bout heroes
I try to be a good student
I hope the war in Iraq will end
I am a loud girl who loves basketball

Carly Smith, Grade 6
R D and Euzelle P Smith Middle School, NC

On Halloween Night

On Halloween night, there's a lot of fright
People dress as ghosts, goblins, and ghouls
Not to know they're just being fools
You see, they got to trick-or-treat
But they don't know that the trick
Could be just as good as the sweet treat

Tristan Hedges, Grade 5
Colerain Elementary School, NC

The Sad Moon

The moon is glittering gently,
Across a deep blue sky.

Envying the many stars,
That very dimly lie.

Very still and perfect,
The endless night goes on.

The moon will lead the way,
Until you quietly yawn.

Signaling that morning's come,
The moon will disappear.

The bright red sun will then come out,
The moon's one childish fear.

Michael LaPasha, Grade 5
Hunter GT Magnet Elementary School, NC

Daddy

D addy serves his country in Iraq
A wesome as a father in every way
D oes not give up in anything he does
D resses very nice and smells good too
Y ou'll think he's cool I know I do!

Martha Bonilla, Grade 5
Vernon Middle School, LA

The Dragon

There once was a boy named Fury,
Who said to his friend the mouse,
Beware of the fire-breathing dragon,
That lives here in this house.

The dragon came round,
And the mouse he found.
He blew fire like a torch,
And the mouse began to scorch.

Fury came to the rescue,
With water so blue,
Which he threw with all his might,
Putting out the dragon's light.

Ethan Steele, Grade 4
St Mary Cathedral Elementary School, MO

Mustang

Many horses run,
So swiftly through the night,
As they gallop gracefully,
It seems that they take flight!

So many different colors,
Dapples, Bays, and Grays,
Many places shall they go,
But never shall they stay.

Young colts and fillies play,
Jumping round the meadow,
So nimble and carefree,
Just watch them as they grow.

Night has come, all is still,
Bright stars twinkle in the sky,
Ready for their journey,
The mustangs spread their wings to fly!
Maria Weber, Grade 6
Salisbury Academy, NC

Christmas

C reative
H ands
R ecreate
I ts
S on
T o
M ake
A lot of
S imply Happy People
Zack Galt, Grade 5
American Heritage Academy, GA

School Is Out

School is out
summer's near
lots of fun is almost here
vacation parties friends and more
I cannot wait to run out that door

the sun burns around my nose
the sand between my toes
a dip in the pool
yes no more school.
Lindsey Kuhns, Grade 6
Holy Trinity School, KY

Sports

Football is so fun!
Basketball is cool as well!
I think all sports rock!!!
Jim Mantyh, Grade 4
St Thomas More School, NC

Flowers

The seeds are flying
Over the icy mountain tops
Oops! One lands there.
That one won't grow.
It's summer, it's spring,
It's autumn, it's winter.
Flowers are growing
And flowers are dying
Seeds are flying
"All for one and one for all,"
The seeds saying before
They are departing from
Each other.
Zachary Loos, Grade 5
G C Burkhead Elementary School, KY

A Special One to Me

This poem is for Don,
Who likes to mow his lawn.
He has a bullet proof vest for his chest,
And takes a big military test.

He goes to Iran,
But without a fan.
He gets silver beads,
For his good deeds.

He shoots with his gun,
But he never did run.
He lies in a jeep,
And rarely does sleep.

In the night,
He will lay tight.
That's why to me,
He's a hero to be.
Justin Queen, Grade 4
North Elementary School, NC

Parker

Lover of books, acting, chocolate
Feels happy when playing sports,
tired in mornings, bored at school
Relative of four cousins
Who would like to see my dad, J.K.
Rowling and California,
Who fears kidnappers, dead people,
horror movies,
Who gives smiles, presents, and toys,
Resident of Peace,
Who needs a friend, a smile, and a book
happy, kind, short, and silly
Donovan
Parker Donovan, Grade 6
Our Lady Catholic School, MO

My Mom Is Special

My mom is special.
Just like me.
I love her, can't you see?

If she was your mother,
You would love her, too.
I love her, can't you see?

She helps me do my homework,
Whenever she is busy.
Here is one thing,
I do not want to make her dizzy.
I love her, can't you see?

She is so beautiful and pretty.
I love to give her kisses.
She taught me to listen.
I love that she did that.
I love her, can't you see?

My mom has always taken care of me,
And I love that she does.
I love her, can't you see?
Adriana Maldonado, Grade 4
Hayes Elementary School, OK

Baseball Kid

I'm fast
I like to play Baseball
I like to cast at the pond
And it's hard to make fast cash
Felipe Castro, Grade 6
Ketchum Jr High School, OK

Dark Hole

A dark hole…
Leads you wherever
Sends u flying
Into the world's mysteries,
If you've ever seen one
Which you won't,
But if u do
You can almost see right through it
And if you do
You can see yourself
Looking right back at you.
Shady Mreir, Grade 5
Nesbit Elementary School, GA

Fall

Leaves fall to the ground
Pumpkins are ripe and orange
Thanksgiving is here.
Sarah Katherine Reiser, Grade 4
Briarwood Christian School, AL

Precious Angel

Out of the window, into the sky,
the soul of a precious angel will fly.

It will travel day and night,
just flying in the air,
not even one fright.

The soul of a precious angel is with us all,
even when we think we're going through a dark scary fall.

The angel is very sweet and kind
she has a precious soul like mine.
She picks me up when I fall,
and that's only because she's the greatest of them all.

So next time you fall
just remember a precious angel
is with us all.

Quinisha Butler, Grade 5
West Marion Elementary School, MS

Jack-o'-lanterns

Strange creepy smiles
Light up dark alleys at night
They glow all night long

Jeremiah Green, Grade 5
Hunter GT Magnet Elementary School, NC

Science Lab

In the science lab
there are a lot of things to do.
Playing with cockroaches
may be scary
may be fun.
Watching the fish and feeding the snake.
Learning about microscopes
may be hard
may be easy.
We hear the laughter of children "ha ha."
We see cockroaches stick like gum.
See creepy crawlers from all categories
may be boring
may be fun.
You decide.

Andrew Rosenstrom, Grade 5
Greathouse Shryock Traditional Elementary School, KY

The Nazis

The Nazis killed Jews for many reasons
They didn't get a chance to see the next season
More than two thirds were gone
The cold ground they had to lay on
Every person was very sad
Whoever did it was very bad

Christian Chavis, Grade 5
Pembroke Elementary School, NC

Happiness

Happiness is lime green.
It smells like fresh picked daisies.
It tastes like fresh baked chocolate chip cookies.
It sounds like country music on the radio.
It feels like cuddling with a baby kitten.
It looks like horses galloping through the meadow.
Happiness is loving all of God's creatures.

Alexandria Riddick, Grade 4
Pines Elementary School, NC

I Am Haunted

I am haunted
By the big, bad Boogie-Man who
stays under my bed waiting
for me to jump out of bed so
he can grab me with his sharp, scary claws.

I am haunted
By creepy, twisting and turning tornadoes
that will suck me up with their strong powerful
winds and I will never be able to see my
family or pets AGAIN!!!!

I am haunted
By the scary smoke that my mom
and dad inhale into their lungs
and they have a dreary death
and I will be all alone!

I AM HAUNTED!!

Rachael Ashby, Grade 5
Eminence Middle School, KY

Veteran's Day

On Veteran's Day I see papers of soldiers.
I smell flowers out side on the memorial.
I hear stuff about the war.
I taste cookies that are shaped like soldiers.
I touch pictures of loved ones.
Veteran's Day

Eric Vaughn, Grade 4
Tamassee-Salem Elementary School, SC

Lellow

When I was little I always said:
Lellow
Lellow stands for yellow
Yellow is a pretty color and when I say:
Lellow it makes it a pretty word too
Even for a big girl now lellow is still a better word
Lellow is a better word for yellow because
It rhymes for one and it just sounds really good…
…I Love the word LELLOW!!!

Sunnye Haff, Grade 6
Ketchum Jr High School, OK

Crickets

Crickets jump and chirp
On the tree and on the ground
Leaping very fast.

Sarah Massey, Grade 4
Briarwood Christian School, AL

Trust

Trust is a very common word, you know.
It is also something that comes and goes.
You trust a person or so you say,
But your trust grows dim every day.
You trust a person with your heart.
You've trusted them from the very start.
You trust a person with all you do.
The question is, do they trust you?
How do you know if their trust is true?
You'll trust a person,
Then you won't.
A person trusts you,
Then they don't.
Trust is a big mystery.
So be careful whom you give it to.
Because people can get hurt by it,
Just like me and you.

ShaTonya Young, Grade 5
Germanshire Elementary School, TN

Trees

The trees are blowing,
Quiet and softly they sway,
Leaves are falling off.

Justin Ho, Grade 6
River Trail Middle School, GA

Dreams

Dreams can be
As big as elephants
Or as small as mice

Dreams can be
As near to you as thought
Or as far away as night

Dreams can be
As new as a baby
Or old like the Earth
Or fixed like cars

Dreams can be
Islands of Hawaii
In an ocean really far

I guess my dreams
Are windows of me.

Mary Margaret Dyches, Grade 6
Chapin Middle School, SC

Beavers

B eavers don't really
E at wood. It is just a myth. They just gnaw
A t it for a while to wear down their teeth. Scientists have studied
V ery hard and found different
E ating habits for these
R odents. They mainly eat berries, leaves and
S ap, so it is just a myth that beavers eat wood.

Luke Herndon, Grade 6
Discovery School @ Reeves Rogers, TN

Granddaughter of the Greatest Grandma

I am a granddaughter of the world's greatest Grandma.
I wonder if I will get to go to my grandma's house for Christmas.
I hear people talking about me.
I see my guinea pig Hershey when I get home.
I want to go to the Mall of America again.
I am a granddaughter of the world's greatest Grandma.
I pretend to be a dog when I play with my little sister.
I feel people by my side.
I touch my guinea pig after school.
I worry that I will lose what I have.
I cry when I get hurt really bad.
I am a granddaughter of the world's greatest Grandma.
I understand that my mom has to work a lot.
I say please and thank you every day.
I dream I'm with all my friends.
I try to do my best every day.

Kimberly Stellmach, Grade 5
Byrns L Darden Elementary School, TN

Roller Coaster

I wait in line, my heart does flips.
It's doing little tumble tricks!
My head is spinning, my knees are week.
There is a ton of sweat dripping down my cheek.
I step inside, the blue little car,
And SWOOSH! We're off! Racing far.
We march up, then dip down.
It makes my hair look like a clown!
A loop the loop, twists through the air.
I'm screaming wildly without a care!
The ride loses speed, and we slow down,
Soon I find my feet on the ground.
Then I stop, and think of the fun.
And I shout out "This ride is number ONE!"

Fiona McGuire, Grade 4
St Thomas More School, NC

Dale Earnhart Sr.

Dale Earnhart Sr. goes so fast in his number three Goodwrench car.
Trying to get first and shifting gears all day long.
Fans are cheering all around.
The time has come, last lap, one more time around the track.
Shift another gear Dale Earnhart Sr. is in victory lane

Ricky Day, Grade 4
Tazewell-New Tazewell Primary School, TN

The Beast

First ride
Filled with excitement
Eyes spotted a chariot.
The wait was over
Orange crushed my thighs
Gravity forced my body to merge
Dove forward, scared.
In midair, sight was failing
Listened to the screams of the roar of the wind
It was a nightmare.
Tunnels filled with darkness, yet light shown through
The battle was over, no one won.

Jacob Ginter, Grade 5
Cline Elementary School, KY

Mornings for Me!

Mom, I can't find my shoes!
Well did you look in your closet?
Yeah but they're not in there.
It's not like they just got up and ran away!
Well look some more.
I'm running out of daylight.
If I don't find them I will be late for school.
Ok!
Whatever Mom.
This is taking forever!
Please help me.
I'm so tired, and moving as slow as Christmas!

Hannah Beth Hearyman, Grade 6
Armorel Elementary School, AR

Skateboarding

Skateboarding is tricks
Rails, ramps, boards, wheels, shoes, hats, pants
It is breaks and flips

Stefan Ball, Grade 5
Sycamore Elementary School, GA

Piper Pond

Piper pond
My favorite place on Earth
Where the loons play around and eat
Like children on a summer day
Piper pond
Where the dew covers the grass
Like sparkly spider webs
With flies stuck to them squirming to get free
Piper pond
Where the boats speed around on the lake
And the children swim all day
Like gigantic fish in the water
Piper pond
My favorite place on Earth

Adam Bullard, Grade 6
East Oldham Middle School, KY

Friend

My friend, my friend,
Who is a friend?
Someone who is dear to you,
A neighbor, a classmate, a sibling, or a pen pal,
One who sticks up for you when others do not,
Whose help is priceless.

My friend, my friend,
Who is a friend?
Someone who likes you unconditionally,
A dog, a cat, a hamster, or a horse,
One who reaches out when you are in need?
Whose love is endless.

My friend, my friend,
You are indeed a true friend,
You are there every time,
Looking after me,
Today, I am happy because of you.
Thank you for being true friend!

Briana Nwokeji, Grade 6
White Station Middle School, TN

Football

Football is a game of pain and joy.
Me I like them both
The feeling of scoring the very first TD of the game
is the best feeling in the world.

Sam Noah, Grade 5
North Middle School, TN

Where I'm From

I am from horseshoes,
from western saddle and leather.
I am from the meadow of long green grass.
I am from the wheat field,
The daisy which floods all over the land.

I am from Christmas cookies and blue eyes,
from Allan and Barbara Fraley.
I am from the neat freak
and the animal lover,
from good girl and do your best.
I am from the Catholic religion,
where there are seven sacraments.

I'm from a small town called Sayre, Pennsylvania,
spicy chicken wings and sparkling grape juice.
From the car my mother bought herself
for her birthday
my uncle's terrible car crash.
I am from the downstairs storage closet,
where dozens of memories come to life,
bringing back cherished times.

Danielle Fraley, Grade 6
Lakeshore Middle School, NC

Reasons Why I Like Autumn
Leaves fall in autumn
I like yellow, green and red
Flowers on the ground
Kids laughing and playing now
Reasons why I like autumn
Hannah Elizabeth Standley, Grade 5
Berryville Elementary School, AR

Christmas Holiday
Evergreen makes the house smell,
you really can tell
waiting for Santa Claus,
don't forget to shop
at a few malls
lights are shining bright,
what a pretty sight
we all love Christmas Eve,
Santa knows you will believe
wait 'til the morning to see
all of your presents,
enjoy the lovely essence
have a happy Christmas day,
we all say,
why can't it be Christmas day every day
of the year,
we all cheer
Anna Flynn, Grade 6
Salisbury Academy, NC

Little Girl
The little girl can eat a bird.
The little girl is sweet as candy.
The little girl is a kangaroo.
The little girl has bark but not bite.
The little girl has gold in her hair.
The little girl's smile is a star.
The little girl is Synda and that's true.
Sherry Guyer, Grade 6
Armorel Elementary School, AR

The Moon
The moon
is a night light for over half the world.
But, if the sun hits it right
it's more like a beautiful pearl.
Sometimes it's nearly invisible
and once in a while it's bright as day.
I love the way the moon shines,
especially when the sky is clear.
Oh no, now it's sunrise and
I guess it's time to say good-by
to our old friend,
The Moon
William Martinez, Grade 5
Odessa Middle School, MO

Thunderstorm
It is raining hard
There is a stampede running
from rain and lightning
MJ Holleman, Grade 4
Cleveland Elementary School, OK

Tree
The Christmas tree stands
sparkling and gleaming
in the dark of the room
Its lights reflect
the different shaped
ornaments
The string of lights
like floating orbs and stars

Each branch bears
a different memory
decorations of loved ones
pictures from past and present
figures of small hands
now grown big

Glass and crystal,
wooden and paper,
together dress
the tree for the season

From high above
the angels hark to all
the season is here.
Pierson Haines, Grade 6
Chapin Middle School, SC

Sorrow Screams
Sorrow is white.
It sounds like screaming.
It tastes like sea salt.
It smells like something rotten.
It looks like a child crying.
It makes me feel like just falling apart.
Houston Clifton, Grade 5
Salem Elementary School, AR

Basketball
Basketball Basketball
I love to play.
Basketball
Basketball of the day.
Basketball basketball
When I get the ball
I shrink very small.
Basketball basketball I like the ball.
Myles Chadwick, Grade 4
Lewis Vincent Elementary School, LA

Dark Nights
When nights as dark as velvet
fall upon me
I climb into bed and start to read
I feel my eyelids
getting heavy
my dreams start early
as my eyes
start to shut
Zoyie Walker, Grade 5
Walton Verona Elementary School, KY

Softball
Softball is a lot of fun.
Watch us hit it; watch us run.
Watch us dance and stomp our feet.
'Cause you know we can't be beat.
Chandler Masters, Grade 5
Midway Covenant Christian School, GA

A Miracle
I thought it was all over,
But then I picked a four leaf clover,
It brightened my day,
And I shouted hooray,
For today is the day!
Kara Kimple, Grade 4
St Thomas More School, NC

The Wrath of the Reaper
When you hear a thousand screams,
you see only a razor sharp scythe,
or you smell decaying blood,
you know your time has come.
You cannot run,
or neither hide,
he will give you fright,
he will scare you in the night,
never fear when he is here,
because you're next!
Zach Grainger, Grade 5
North Middle School, TN

Alison
Engines winding fast.
Mud, dirt, trailers, people here.
Winning all races.
Blake Guthrie, Grade 4
Briarwood Christian School, AL

Jesus
He died on the cross
And paid for all of our sins
Christians adore Him
Mary-Morgan Bullock, Grade 4
Briarwood Christian School, AL

Cheerleading

Down on the track screaming —
"Go Stangs, Go! make it to the endzone!"
The touchdown is made!
We scream, scream, and scream
We win the game!

Kayla Harris, Grade 6
Scotts Creek Elementary School, NC

Hospital Holiday

Three days off for Labor Day;
    I ended up in a hospital stay.

All I wanted to do was play,
    but the doctor had it her way.

Having pneumonia was not fun;
    When the needles came, I was ready to run.

The IV pole became my "Friend."
    When would all the commotion end?

X-rays, breathing treatments and such,
    the nurses sure made a big fuss.

Having a Gamecube in my room was fun,
    and playing games with Nurse Jamie, I liked tons.

Four days and I was on my way home,
    but the doctor said out of the house, I could not roam.

She said to take it easy and get plenty of rest,
    so I could get better and feel my best!

Alex Schmitt, Grade 5
Our Lady of Fatima School, MS

The Voice of Animals

I look outside the window,
I see all the beautiful life.
It seems that they are sad,
crying in the night.

They say they are depressed,
about their decreasing home.

Humanity was cruel to them,
taking all the land of their own.
Making room for our own living,
Why don't we move,
to a place with no life?

Humans do not care,
the animals monkeys, dogs, and hares,
will not be heard.
Their voices are purposely blurred.

Anna Birbiglia, Grade 6
Haynes Academy for Advanced Studies, LA

Rain

As the rain falls with a steady beat,
It reminds me of all the obstacles,
I have yet to defeat.
This makes me think in so many ways.
It makes me think of how far I've come.
It makes me think of how much further I'll fly.
It makes me wonder why.
For these reasons I love the rain,
For these reasons I feel the pain.
For these reasons I see how it can gain.
I love how it never changes, but is always different.
I love the way it is comforting, yet always surprising.
I love how people can generally predict it,
Yet it is so unpredictable.
I love the way the rain falls with a steady beat.

Sabrina Rice, Grade 6
Fairview Elementary School, MO

Life

Life is an adventure,
That takes you way up high.
Life is story,
That will make you cry.
Life is something that you need to understand.
Life is something in your hands.
Life is beautiful treasure,
And something that stays in your heart forever.

Sandy Alkoutami, Grade 6
Clyde Campbell Elementary School, NC

Fall

The school year is here and the season is fall,
The leaves are brown and not just one but all.
People say that it is hot or cold,
The leaves blow that's, What people are told.
Sometimes it is windy or not,
Mostly they say, that the weather is hot.
Fall is the beginning of a new school year,
It mostly gets windy when winter is near.
When it gets close to fall, the living plants turn brown.
Not just the trees, but the plants all around.
The animals in fall wait for the next season,
Because they get ready for winter, and here is the reason.
This season is in between winter and summer,
When the season comes, people wait for the other.
Fall is when all of the clouds become gray,
Fall lasts for a season and many a day.
Fall does not come to stay,
It does last longer than a day.
It changes your mood and the way you feel,
It makes you want to move and not be still.
Fall ushers in winter and that's how it ends.

Aubry Weatherly, Grade 6
Parkview School, OK

Space

Way, way deep in space
Many, many burning stars
We will never know
Landon Steeley, Grade 4
Briarwood Christian School, AL

Seasons

Summer
Relaxed, hot,
Exciting, playing, running,
Vacations, school, home, friends,
Dirt biking, four wheeling, jumping,
Cool, apples,
Fall

Winter
Cold, snow,
Sledding, playing, climbing,
Hunting hiking, snow, vacations,
Bobbing, freezing, cooking,
Cool, warm,
Fall

Summer
Awesome, fun,
Exciting, relaxing, blasting,
Summer break, bikes, schools, tasty,
Filling, blessing, falling,
Good, seeds,
Pumpkins
Robert Austin Johnson, Grade 6
Alvaton Elementary School, KY

My Hero

I have a hero;
He's not a zero.
His name is Leonard, he is not bad;
He is a veteran, and he is my dad!

He is still alive to this day;
And he sometimes plays.
Every day I love him;
And he used to go to the gym.

My dad's the best;
And he is not a pest.
Every day he loves me;
And he has lots of keys.

My dad never frowns;
And he never pounds.
He used to shoot a gun;
But now we have fun!
Austin Smith, Grade 4
North Elementary School, NC

Great Person

If I could change
one thing in the world
I would make everyone
a great person
people would not get killed
over things
like a "shoot out"
people could also
live their life
without fear
there would be no bad examples
set for children
a larger population
in the world
more buildings would be built
people would be hired
no terrorist attacks
if everyone was a great person
Patrick Henry, Grade 6
Beck Academy, SC

Swimming

Graceful, gliding swim
Kicking, stroking fast to win
Cross the finish first!
Morgan Sweere, Grade 6
Ruth Doyle Intermediate School, AR

Fall

Nuts drop to the ground
Pretty birds fly all around
Brown, yellow, orange, red
Miranda Shaffer, Grade 4
Briarwood Christian School, AL

Suddenly…

It is night, the stars shine,
the ladies twirl, the men drink wine.
Glasses clinking,
Jewels winking.

The bonfire burns,
the mood turns.
The glint of a sword,
held by a lord.

Clothes lie tattered,
Glasses shattered.
Wailing women crowd around,
finding bodies in a mound.

Oh! God I beg you please,
Why can't this bloodshed cease?
Udai Baisiwala, Grade 6
Dickerson Middle School, GA

Gabriella

Auburn hair, brown eyes, and tall
Shorts and T-shirts to volleyball
flip-flops to the pool
"Sup" and "Dude"
CYC Volleyball on Mondays
Go-Kart racing on Sundays
My sister, parents, and homework
drive me nuts.
Xbox 360 — awesome
iPod when I get in the car
Pizza from Papa John's — Yum
Gabriella Warden, Grade 5
Our Lady Catholic School, MO

Bad Kid

There once was a boy from Spain.
Who everyone thought was a pain.
He screamed and he kicked.
He bit and he licked.
Then went to play in the rain.
Alexus McCune, Grade 6
Martin Elementary School, WV

The Night Walk on the Beach

Ocean's big waves, sand
Between your toes, shells everywhere
Moonlight is shining.
Frannie Ware, Grade 4
Briarwood Christian School, AL

Farms

They are sweet and cool
They have all types of livestock
Some are big livestock
Others are very small now
Now you know more about farms
Jaron Walker Hendrix, Grade 6
Nodaway Holt Elementary School, MO

My Friend

I have a friend
who turns me mad.
I have a friend
who sometimes acts bad.
I have a friend
that is Chinese,
but that doesn't stop me from
being her friend if I please.
My friend is different.
My friend is smart.
My friend is nice.
But best of all,
my friend will ALWAYS be my friend.
Kainath Merchant, Grade 5
Evansdale Elementary School, GA

Saved the Day

Standing in the middle of the goal knees bent
ready for the ball to be kicked in the goal,
looking at the player that's getting ready to kick
player posed looking mad
seeing the ball coming straight at me
team saying, "Get ready Olivia you can do it"
my heart beating as fast as a jaguar sprinting to its prey
nervous breathing loud and heavy
happening so fast
quickly put my hands up in front of my tummy
ball flying straight to my hands
Boom!
hit my hands really hard
felt like I broke my hand OW,
pushing the ball out of the net
fans clapping, yelling
"Good job Olivia, great block!"
smiling and high fiving my team
knowing I saved the day
team won the game.

Olivia Montgomery, Grade 4
Roberta Tully Elementary School, KY

Diving

What is scuba diving?
Scuba diving is exploring an aquatic world
A world so different from ours
A world full of life
A world where sharks roam free
A world where plankton are consumed
A world where whales consume the plankton
A world where coral houses many things
A world where fish dart in and out of the coral
A world where sea horses cling to kelp
A world where dolphins chase boats
A world where jellyfish bobble by
A world where man soothes his curiosity
This is scuba diving!

Kelsey Wood, Grade 6
Southwest Middle School, AR

Justin

Short brown hair, brown eyes,
And medium height.
T-shirts, and Jean shorts,
And blue crocs.
"Whatever!"
Soccer and volleyball.
My brother and sirens annoy me.
Reading, listening to music
And legos in my room.
Mexican, Italian, and Chinese, my favorites.

Justin Wampler, Grade 5
Our Lady Catholic School, MO

Autumn

Autumn is fun —
Copying autumn can't be done
Because autumn is beautiful and colorful;
Autumn makes me feel cheerful,
Autumn means there will be more piles of leaves —
Piles of leaves to jump on,
A pile of leaves to stomp on.
It means winter's coming too!

Luminous leaves flying around without a sound.
Then they are still;
Wait for a few minutes and a gust of
Wind will pick them up into the sky —
And they will look like a million butterflies!

Meredith Tuck, Grade 5
Palmetto Christian Academy, SC

Crack

Walking up to bat slow as a sloth
Excitement building up
In my shivering cold body
Stepping into the box so nervous
Hoping to smack a homerun
Swing, swing, strike
So, so upset
getting set for the next pitch
cleats digging like a mole in the dirt
bat back ready to strongly swing
Swing, swing
CONTACT, a foul
So, so, upset
Thinking I am going to get out
prepared once again taking deep breaths
waiting in my mind for the next pitch
pitcher throws a speeding bullet curved ball
Swing, Swing, CRACK!
HOMERUN
Out of the Park!
So, So Exciting!

Steven Piepmeyer, Grade 4
Roberta Tully Elementary School, KY

Life

The world is a magical place
especially the seasons
first comes winter
with the wicked whoosh of the wind
Then comes spring
With the chirp of birds flying back from the south
Then comes old summer
When children play all day and night
finally fall when leaves look alike
the world is as magical as the seasons
but life is the most magical thing of all

Sam Decker, Grade 5
Greathouse Shryock Traditional Elementary School, KY

Dolphin

Sniff, sniff the ocean scent of a Dolphin delights my senses.
As the Dolphin swims by, I see that it is night sky blue, and is lustrous like the ocean's surface.
The Dolphin looks happy with its freedom and it swims with pride.
A Dolphin makes a heavenly, melodious sound, good enough for a song.
The Dolphin swims by fellow fish with no concern to the food chain.
I see the Dolphin jump above the water smiling full of joy.
Skin so slippery it reminds me of a towering water slide.
The Dolphin looks at me through the water while it is swimming and looks as if it would say,
"Come in, the water is fine."
As the Dolphin searches for lunch he looks at me to remember our fun day.
"Bye bye," I say as the Dolphin swims away.

Trace Salpietra, Grade 6
Haynes Academy for Advanced Studies, LA

Myrtle Beach

Watch worn out visitors from every country and state arrive for a merry and excited week,
Beautiful, amazing, rich and gigantic hotels that are filling up fast from reservations,
Loud and bare footsteps as people walk to jammed streets;
packed cars riding to the beach and all the amusement parks
Saving and collecting green cash being wasted on useless souvenirs they are
going to lose since they are dumps
Eat from twenty different delicious, mouthwatering and expensive
restaurants with all different foods that you have to reserve to feast
I hate gooey, rocky, brown, and black sand getting into my mouth
Catch water as it rains while the other drops jump on the old, red, wooden bench
Run to the waves that gallop around like ponies that ride up and down
Run about on hot, high, and happy concrete near the beach where the town is
I will always be cheery and excited to go lay down on the beach.

Jessica Taylor, Grade 6
College View Middle School, KY

My Mom

My mom brought me into this world. She took care of me from the start. She loves me very much, even when I try and act all tough. She can make the darkest storms turn calm; she can make me laugh when I want to cry. She is perfect in every way; I wouldn't change her for the world. I love her so very much, she's an angel, and she's my mom.

Angelina Chastain, Grade 6
Northside Middle School, SC

I Am From

I am from…a mom who went out partying too much.
A dad who was never there for me

I am from sharing a mom with 4 sisters and 1 brother…
Isabelle and Anna live with Mom in North Carolina
And are the youngest of us all. Soul lives with them, too, and has always been sweet to me.

I am from living with my two older sisters, "Bossy Jennifer" and "Straight-A Tessa."
The three of us live with Aunt Pebbles and Uncle Rich in Kentucky
And we all play basketball at Burgin Independent School.

I am from wanting to be an elementary school teacher
Or a librarian who loves to read books and help children.

This is who and what I am from.

Xena Baez, Grade 5
Burgin Independent School, KY

I Can't Write a Poem*

Forget it!
You must be kidding!
I am tired.
My hand hurts.
I am stupid.
I am distracted.
I am thinking.
I have no brain.
I have no pen.
I have no pencil.
I am sick.
My dad is here to pick me up.
My head hurts.
I am hungry.
I need help.
There is no time.
Time's up? Oh, no!
All I have are these really silly excuses.
You like it? Really? No way!
When can I write another one?

Charles Simmons, Grade 6
Lost River Elementary School, KY
*Patterned after "I Can't Write a Poem" by Bruce Lansky

Friends for Life

I have a hand and you have another
Put them together and we have each other

The golden circle last forever
That's how long I'd like us to be together

We've been through thick and thin
With all the strength you've given me
I've been able to get back up again

If the sun is you and the moon is me
as we constellate we'll still be

FRIENDS FOR LIFE!

Harley Bayne and Meagan Cartee, Grade 6
Beech Springs Intermediate School, SC

Monsters in the Closet

Monsters in the closet only come out at night.
And cause you to sleep with a night light.

They give children a terrible fright.
Because we all know they will give us a bite.

Moms say they're not real, but I know that is not right.
Because in the shadows they seem to take flight.

The Monsters in the closet have been a terrible sight.
Until I figured out, it was an old costume that was too tight!

Joshua Neumaier, Grade 5
Our Lady of Fatima School, MS

Birds

As I sit outside the birds chirp so lovely.
They fly around the house so peacefully.
I watch them build their nest so smoothly.
I love the color of them.
They're so beautiful.
Their beaks are so different.
I once saw a family of birds find a place to nest.
Their kids grew up differently than them.
Have you noticed how they are sized?
Soon they will grow up.
Next summer they will be back.

Brittany Coffman, Grade 5
North Middle School, TN

Joy Joy

Christmas is a time of Joy
When each special child gets a toy
When all are loving and caring
When everybody is lovingly sharing
Christmas is for us all
Christmas is always after fall
December represents the birth of the boy
Christmas is for us to celebrate his joy!

Chet Conatser, Grade 4
Hatfield Elementary School, AR

Flowers

Some flowers are red
Some flowers are blue
Don't get too close to a Venus flytrap
It might eat you
Tulips are pink and
Are nice to smell
Daisies are yellow and
You can put them in your hair
Sunflowers are pretty in the bright yellow sun
So be a good kid and
You might just get all four flowers

Linkal Edgeston, Grade 5
Contentnea Elementary School, NC

Dust

The dust from the bombs,
the blood from the men,
the evil problem of the world
may God forgive mankind
for breaking His law
of killing other people.
Because of our evil hearts,
we have destroyed trees,
animals, and the land of the wild.
The dark world of killing has to go.

William Keene, Grade 4
St Mary Cathedral Elementary School, MO

Dad

My dad works all day long,
driving cattle,
giving shots,
and tucking me in at night.
Cole Steinbecker, Grade 5
St Vincent Elementary School, MO

My Dragons

My dragons fly through
the night sky
singing their sweet melody
they guard through the day
their colorful clutch of eggs
the way they fly
it makes you sigh
if you approach them without fear
they will never do so much as leer.
Brianna Garcia, Grade 6
St Teresa's School, GA

A Brand New Day

You slowly walk up to the tree
Getting down on both hands and knee
Looking up into the sky
And say a prayer like a lullaby
Leaning against the tree like you do
Then hear God whisper, "I love you"
You get up and walk away
Then get ready for a brand new day
Ashlee Anderson, Grade 6
Chapin Middle School, SC

Good-bye Summer

Good-bye chirping birds
lovely flowers
sitting in the grass
for hours and hours
Good-bye such blue sky
and such green grass
sitting down
while the puffy clouds pass
Good-bye no school
and staying up late
Good-bye swimming
and fishing bait
Good-bye butterflies
with your pretty wings
Good-bye lovely trees
and high, high swings
Good-bye hotness
won't miss you at all
Good-bye summer
Hello fall!
Katie Holtmeyer, Grade 6
St Gertrude School, MO

Thanksgiving Traditions

T hanking God for our many blessing
H aving a great meal,
A nd eating with family
N ovember games
K ick back, and relax
S it and watch the parades
G ive thanks
I shop 'til I drop after Thanksgiving
V isit loved ones
I wave to people on the floats
N o school
G ive to the less fortunate
Erika Page, Grade 5
Sullivan Elementary School, TN

Deer

Hunting is near.
I will give a cheer.
The grass will sprout.
The deer will come out.

I will find a good gun.
And I will give a good run.
Bring home a big buck
In the back of my truck.

My family will give a cheer,
Cause hunting is near.
Kylene Pickett, Grade 4
Northeast Baptist School, LA

Ayana

A merican and a Mexican.
Y oung sweet little girl.
A ctive all the time.
N ice to all the teachers.
A good helper, sometimes.
Ayana Galbreath, Grade 4
Byrns L Darden Elementary School, TN

Bird

Bird
Pretty
It can fly
Feels wonderful
Chirp
Katie Hamilton, Grade 5
St Joseph Institute for the Deaf, MO

Blizzards

Snow fluffy white ice
Hot Cocoa with marshmallows
I can't wait for it.
Kaisey Jenkins, Grade 4
St Patrick's School, AL

My Black Cat

I have a black cat.
In the night she looks like a bat.
I wish she could fly.
Someday she might die.
Landon Foster, Grade 4
Horace Mann Elementary School, OK

Trees

Waving in the wind.
God's creation and man made
Please don't cut me down.
Robbin E. Reese, Grade 4
Briarwood Christian School, AL

The Surprises of Autumn

Free-falling from the sky,
the former summer leaves
change colors and fall to the ground.

The graceful geese,
flying south for the winter
are in their orderly form.

The fresh cool breeze
nipping at your skin,
grab a jacket quickly
before you catch a cold.

Go outside as much as you can,
the colorful autumn days
will soon become winter.
Logan Bates, Grade 6
Dyer Elementary & Jr High School, TN

Christmas Time

Can you hear the chimes?
Bells and elves at Christmas time
Singing and ringing.
Cameron Bruce, Grade 4
Briarwood Christian School, AL

Leah

A little girl born far away.
She joined my family on a special day.
In China we stayed for quite awhile
until the day we saw her smile.

It took 18 hours to fly her home.
Now she'll never be alone.
Family and friends were at the airport.
Balloons and signs showed support.
If she weren't here I'd really miss her.
I love her so much she's my little sister.
Mason Compton, Grade 5
Walton Verona Elementary School, KY

Black and White

Black and white, different but alike.
The white of an egg as it sizzles for breakfast.
The black unlucky cat as it crosses your path.
The dazzling white moon beams.
The sinister midnight eclipse.
The white stripes of a candy cane so sweet.
The devil's evil eye as he stares you down.
The snow white strands of hair from long ago.
The black pearl as it's swallowed by the sea.
The pristine snow as it drifts from the heavens.
The brand new Hershey bar as it melts in your mouth.
The snow fox as it chases its prey.
The berserker's eyes as he starts to go wild.
The angel's wing as it flies toward the light.
The black ink as it starts to dry.
The snow capped mountains that shoot through the sky.
The darkness of night that blankets all.
The blind man's eyes as he stares toward the light.
The black raven as it flies overhead.
The white dove as it sits perched on a tree.
Black and white reach far and wide.

David Doboszenski, Grade 6
Charleston County School of the Arts, SC

The Beach

Splashing waves chasing after me
Surfboards riding on waves like pelicans getting fish
Police cars zooming, dashing like a cheetah
People chattering loudly in the water
The scent of food makes me want to eat and eat
Sea water burning my nose
Snow cones melting in my hands
Crab legs steaming making smoke come out of my mouth
Jumping like a kangaroo over the waves
Shells scattered along the beach
I feel happy.

Javier Raya, Grade 4
Bailey Elementary School, NC

Eagles

Eagles fly, so brave, so bold
Beautiful is to eagles, as shiny is to gold
Bald Eagles symbolize our nation
These birds are the next sensation.

Eagles are so brave and strong
If you say otherwise, you must be wrong.

Crows watch eagles in vain
Eagles give hope, as vultures give pain
Eagles call out because they want to be heard
Eagles are truly a remarkable bird.

Matt Summers, Grade 4
Mylan Park Elementary School, WV

The Storm Above the Willow Tree

The leaves were rushing in a circle,
The lightning bolt went "BOOM!"
The stem broke
The squirrels went rushing,
"CRASH!"
Sticks and leaves were flying everywhere,
One hit the little brown house on the hill,
And shattered its window,
"Boom, crackle, snap, pop!"
We always thought the tree would fall,
and it did,
But then next spring we will plant,
another willow tree,
and it will probably fall again,
again, and again.

Kelly Kirkpatrick, Grade 5
Greathouse Shryock Traditional Elementary School, KY

My Sister

My sister is six, sometimes she gets us in a fix.
When she was five she always cried.

She likes pretty clothes and shoes
and if they don't match she gets the blues.

My sister can be a little stinker
but my family would not be the same without her.

Jacobe Lynn Jacobs, Grade 5
Pembroke Elementary School, NC

Fall

F iery colors take over trees
A lmost every leaf falls down
L eaves cover yards and some fields
L ime green grass become brown and dead

Jinesh Patel, Grade 5
Salisbury Academy, NC

Bad Day

I had a bad day
My dad burnt the eggs
My dog bit my leg.
I missed the bus and I was late today
So I had to sit out when I was supposed to play.
I dropped my homework in the dirt
And at lunch I spilled milk all down my shirt.
I'm having a bad day you can bet
And the day isn't even over yet.
My dad forgot to pick me up
My sister threw my favorite toy in the dump.
My shower water was freezing cold
And my sandwich bread was covered in mold.
My horrible day has made me mad
Maybe tomorrow won't be so bad.

Taylor Bass, Grade 6
Briarwood Christian School, AL

Oh Desk

Oh desk,
    I hope I don't hurt you when
      I write on you.
    Or when I put my books
      Upon you.
I hope people don't hurt you
    When they slam their books
      On you.
Please, forgive everyone!
Samantha DeHart, Grade 5
Cool Spring Elementary School, NC

The Lion

The lion is king
Lions can run like the wind
It likes to eat meat
Linley Splawn, Grade 4
Briarwood Christian School, AL

BFF

M y best friend
A wesome
D elightful
I like you as a friend
S o beautiful
O n top of my friend's list
N ice

Marybeth Privette, Grade 5
Cool Spring Elementary School, NC

The Pitcher

As I wind up for the pitch
The batter waits
The catcher signs
I throw the ball
Whoosh!
Strike one

As I wind up for the pitch
The sun beats down
My coach starts to clap
I throw the ball
POW!
Strike two

As I wind up for the pitch
The crowd starts to chant
The batter is getting nervous
I throw the ball
Zoom!
Right into the catcher's glove
Strike three

She's out! One down two to go!
Ashly Padgett, Grade 6
College View Middle School, KY

Mother Nature

She sheds her tears on the Earth
Her long fairy golden hair
Her smile as sweet as nectar
Her anger you can hear a long while away
Her flying messengers shake their feathery crowns
Her clear blue eyes as pure as day
Her green grass gown pinned down with flowers and showers of gems
Her heart in the land walkers
Her soul in the sea
Her passion in fruit on every tree

Yara Bauer, Grade 5
Endhaven Elementary School, NC

Going to the Beach

Salty water, delicious cherry Italian water ice,
hard seashells, hot sand,
HUMONGOUS salty waves,
and big AMAZING fun board walk!!!

Yellow sun like a banana, blue bathing suits, green palm trees,
tan and brown sand like german chocolate, white lifeguard chairs,
pink flip-flops like a watermelon, teal cotton candy,
purple boogie boards just like a plum, hot pink nails,
and tans as red as a tomato!!!
I hear the waves go swoosh, birds go squeak
people go chit chat, singing music notes like la la
car horns go beep beep, little kids go splash
as they jump into the deep end of the sea
teens on the rides go Woo hoo!!!

I wonder how many seashells were in the ocean?
I wonder how many people go there every day?
I wonder how wide the sea is?
I feel excited when I'm at the hot beach.
I feel hot and sweaty as a body builder!
I feel thirsty as a cactus!

Seashells!! Seashells!! Seashells!!

Denise Gulley, Grade 4
Price Elementary School, KY

Where I'm From

I am from markers, from sharpie and permanent marker.
I am from the grass in the backyard.
I am from the roses, the dandelions.
I am from barbecue and dark brown eyes, from Grace and Bill and the Browns.
I am from watching movies at home and watching football every Sunday.
From do your best and be the best of the best.
I am from a cross.
I'm from New Jersey and Georgia.
From the war my father moved from to come to America,
The mother that cared for me, and the sister that is very intelligent.
I am from the closet that is full of memories.

Brielle Brown, Grade 6
Lakeshore Middle School, NC

Unbelievable

Have you had an unbelievable day
when you get a new friend
or a pet snake
It is the greatest thing that you can feel
and then the door bell rings
ring, ring, ring
and then you get that feeling
that is unbelievable,
Unbelievable as a shining star
It feels like a flying fish
Those are some feelings in an
unbelievable day

Amy Morrison, Grade 5
Greathouse Shryock Traditional Elementary School, KY

Friendship

Friendship is…

Friendship is people caring,
When you fall off a swing and break your arm.

Friendship is a white shirt and chocolate
When you put them together you've got trouble.

Friendship is family,
Looking in closets and under beds so there are no monsters.

Friendship is a lightning bolt
Striking people together to play.

Sydney Pemberton, Grade 4
Plano Elementary School, KY

I Am

I am the massive waterfall,
always going and never dry.
Full and on a never ending journey,
mysterious and amazing at the same time.
I am the cactus, mean and helpful.
With roots that stretch through Germany and Wales.
I provide water for the lost,
and pricks for those who dare touch.
I am the towering building, bold but not very tall.
5 foot 1 inch and still growing,
in height and heart.
I am the African Elephant,
giving people the anxiety to say "OOH" and "AHH"
and giving others a frightening moment of terror.
I am the ring of fire,
always burning with a bright flame.
Amusing to those who watch,
and a dare some will not risk to take.
I am the ring of fire,
No, I am greater than the ring of fire,
I AM AUBREY!

Aubrey Jones, Grade 6
Beck Academy, SC

Wondrous

The laughing of children with presents,
The houses full of light, with deep snow falling outside
Glistening like crystals.

Outside you can hear jingling of bells,
Being run by carolers going door to door,
Presenting songs for the whole town to enjoy.

All ages can be seen sledding and ice skating,
When the day is over it is time to drink hot chocolate,
Eat popcorn and know that Christmas Day is over.

Mike Sizemore, Grade 5
East Bernstadt Elementary School, KY

Lion

With a golden mane, its power is irrepressible
It has the strength of ten men
When angered, escape is improbable.
While catching prey it moves like lightning
Powerful, sharp claws that could cut trees.
At sunset its gold body is bright like the blazing sun
Its mighty roar calls all animals
Roar! Fearless, strong, and destructive
Raised to be a king at a young age
He rules his kingdom with an iron paw

Huy Tran, Grade 6
Haynes Academy for Advanced Studies, LA

Olivia

Bright blue eyes and layered brown hair
Jeans, T-shirts, and tennis shoes anywhere
"Coolness!"
Soccer, volleyball, and basketball when I'm bored
My brother and my sister make me mad.
Playing sports and listening to music
Pink, orange, lime green and light blue,
French fries and ice cream,
Things that make me smile!

Olivia Basler, Grade 5
Our Lady Catholic School, MO

Basketball

Basketball is a game of fun
All you do is run, run, run.
The change of momentum can change the game
or it can just make your team look lame.
The ball goes to and fro
it all depends on where the players go.
The man at the top is the guard
while the centers drive it hard.
Win or lose you should always say,
Good game, let's play another day!

Jon Mark Petty, Grade 6
Salisbury Academy, NC

Summer and Winter

Summer
Hot sweaty
Melting dying sizzling
Sunny humid stormy gray
Snowing freezing blowing
Cold snowy
Winter
Mackenzie Reid, Grade 4
Tamassee-Salem Elementary School, SC

Lost Dog

When I lost my dog
I cried and wept
My dog was gone
I couldn't accept

Why did he go
I really don't know
There was food in his dish
And water in his bowl

When I woke up
I thought I was mad
Because I saw a dog
Who looked really glad

I ran outside
And to my surprise
Max had a girl
Then I saw little eyes

Max had a family
Puppies in all
I couldn't believe it
My mom I had to call
George Heath, Grade 6
Westchester Country Day School, NC

Ode to My Dog, Jack

Oh, sweet Jack,
You're my special friend.

Your eyes so blue, like a summer sky,
a broken heart you sure could mend.

Oh, you are one handsome canine,
you are so quick.

With your slobbery tongue
you like to lick.

You like to jump in my lap
then we take a long nap.
Adrian Lewis, Grade 4
Pines Elementary School, NC

The Day

The day is hot
the sun's heat is unbearable
causes me to sweat
the fun goes away
night comes
my brother gets in a scuffle
morning finally arrives
my cat awakens me
with its loud meowing
go away sun
I've had enough heat
to last me all summer
Tyler England, Grade 6
Ketchum Jr High School, OK

1955 Chevy

An American classic
From the 1950's
She may be old,
But she's still nifty.

Visions of poodle skirts
Duck tails, and loafers
Listening to Elvis, the Supremes,
And the Coasters.

Driving down the road
With the wind in my hair
I look so cool in my
'55 Chevy Bel Air.

I wash her and polish her
Until she will shine
I have so much pride in
This car of mine.
Caleb Crosby, Grade 6
Appling County Middle School, GA

The Boy That Could Fly

I wish I could fly.
High in the sky.
I saw a flying dog.
With a big fat frog.
Miguel Flores, Grade 4
Horace Mann Elementary School, OK

Summer

S ummer is great.
U mbrellas are no more.
M ost wonderful season.
M uch more sunshine.
E very day I go outside and play.
R un around and have fun.
Brooke Moore, Grade 5
North Middle School, TN

Be Careful What You Wish For

Here I am at my house
as quiet as a mouse
Laying on my big red couch
saying to myself
I wish I had a little brother
So I asked my mom
She said maybe
Then one day she gave me the news
It's a boy
After that day I regretted my wish
So this is my advice
Be careful what you wish for.
Vaughan Angelloz, Grade 4
Lewis Vincent Elementary School, LA

06 Mighty Mite

Sweat on my tongue
A slush from Sonic after the game
Nachos after the game
Putting a helmet on
Being tackled
Their chances of winning slipping away
The end zone inches away
Someone fumbling the ball
The buzzer going off
Us cheering after the game
The pads colliding
The onion sweat smell
The nachos
06 Mighty Mite
Tate Ferguson, Grade 5
Berryville Elementary School, AR

In Gymnastics

In gymnastics I flip, twirl, and turn,
I try hard to stick it.
In gymnastics I give it my all,
And still have fun with it.

In gymnastics I compete,
And medals I win.
In gymnastics I make new friends,
We are close as kin.

In gymnastics I soar through the air,
My flip was high as a mountain top.
In gymnastics I have a favorite event,
It is beam when I leap and hop.

In gymnastics the bars screech and ping,
It is hard to learn the first thing.
In gymnastics God gives me the talent,
To earn a thousand medals.
Laini Vermillion, Grade 5
Providence Academy, TN

When I Was Little

When I was in preschool
I lived with my grandma.
When we went tot eh store,
She bought me candy.
She had a bunch of cats.
I liked to eat Churches Fried Chicken,
And Chinese food,
especially the fortune cookies.

My grandma read me my fortunes.

Judonte Williams, Grade 5
Lee A Tolbert Community Academy, MO

Kittens

I adore kittens.
They are soft as a cloud.
And I like the way they feel.
They look so adorable and innocent.
They smell like the woods.
Where they play outside.
Their cute little crying they do is so precious.
They love to play with one another.
They may be black, orange, white,
gray, or all the colors mixed together!

Kaitlyn Nicole Gibson, Grade 5
North Middle School, TN

The Lioness

Tan and Gold,
Sleek and Smooth,
Nice and Bold,
On the move.

In the moonlight
she stalks the prey.
Ready to bite,
it's almost day.

Pounce, jump,
she has a grip.
She's falling down
about to slip.

Boom! Bam!
She's out of breath.
Breathing hard,
she's at her death.

A peaceful life
this lion has had.
Now it's gone,
it's so sad.

Hadley Rollins, Grade 5
Hunter GT Magnet Elementary School, NC

The Golf Game

Going to my first tournament is something I'll never forget.
My coach is my granddad he's real good.
Following my hero Tiger.
So three long hours have gone by.
I'm on hole 18, it's real difficult.
It's about two hundred yards till the hole.
Yes! My ball drops in, I won!
Golf is a great sport!

Skyler McGinnis, Grade 5
North Middle School, TN

The Shopping Mall

Looks like lovely stores
Sounds like people noisily talking
Tastes like luscious, sweet cotton candy from the candy stores
Smells like fresh food in the food court
Feels like silky clothes

Marianne Akins, Grade 5
Briarwood Christian School, AL

Our Family Tradition

Our family tradition is something so sweet and fun.
We put our tree up and then go run.
When the neighbors go caroling,
We play in the snow.
Then we go sledding on down the road.
Kids are laughing and singing with joy
As they wait for Santa Claus to pass by with toys.
We wake up and find all the presents,
Then we go to church
And celebrate Jesus' presence.
We have lunch with all the family.
Then we go home and play a little bit.
At night we blow them a kiss and say
Good night and thank you for all the presents!

Hope Johnson, Grade 6
St Teresa's School, GA

Have You Ever Seen the Stars

Have you ever seen the stars shining so bright
that you wished you could just fly away…
and pick one right out of the sky…
and keep it forever…
to remind you of the night you just…
flew away?

Jennifer Hatch, Grade 5
Clarksburg School, TN

The Old Man

They said the old man was quite strange
And some of us thought him deranged
Til he came to our school
And showed us he's cool
And now we don't want him to change

Jonathan May, Grade 6
Haynes Academy for Advanced Studies, LA

The Rain

Calm
Soothing
I curl up in a chair with a blanket
Soft
Sleepy
Quiet as if in church
Rain
Rain
I close my eyes
I see blue and red
I see circles and swirls
I see the sea and feel
Wind.

Elizabeth Dias, Grade 6
Prince of Peace Catholic School, SC

Football

Football is fun
I'll pass and run
Watch out for the sack
I'll hit you in the back
When I go offsides
I'll lose five
When I get a touchdown
I'll spike it on the ground

John Lewis, Grade 5
Midway Covenant Christian School, GA

Father

Strong,
Honest,
Joyful,
Kind
A father like you
Is hard
To find.

Tristan Hale, Grade 6
Rose Bud Elementary School, AR

Baseball

Baseball, baseball
I'm running over with glee.
Catching, catching
I hope they choose me.

Michael Rogers, Grade 4
Northeast Baptist School, LA

My Dad

Some dads are mean,
Some dads are clean,
Some dads are bad,
And get really mad,
But My Dad...
He's awesome!!!

Colton Sensabaugh, Grade 5
Paint Lick Elementary School, KY

Somewhere Else

The sun beat down on me,
Sweat trickled down my nose and neck,
The desert sand felt like fire against my bare feet,
As the sun danced across the sky,
My pants were ripped, my shirt was torn,
And my head bleeding in need of stitches,
My hands and feet were scratched, my elbows and knees scraped,
My legs shook and I fell,
I fell into fire, into heat,
My face was molten,
I writhed in pain, it felt like torture,
The sun was a small speck,
I was falling, falling into darkness,
Then I was nothingness, I had gone,
Gone from the Earth, Gone from life itself,
Then I felt cold hands, like ice,
I lay on something soft,
The thoughts of death were driven away,
It was over, I was alive,
I lay on my bed, looking up at my mother,
The dream was gone.

Griffin Hamstead, Grade 4
Nature's Way Montessori School, TN

My Motor Scooter

One memory from the summer that was fun
getting my motor scooter.
Waiting for my dad to come home.

Knowing what I wanted
I was wanting an izip motor scooter
He finally came home.

He said to go upstairs
looking it up on the computer again
so we knew if we wanted it and where to get it
we were thinking it would be at Dunham's.
Wasn't there but their was another one
better than the other one.
Buying it
I was happy that whole evening.

Jackson Ketchem, Grade 4
Briarwood Elementary School, KY

Deer Hunting

Climb up in a tree there's so much to see
Hoping you come back with more than cold toes and a wet nose
BANG! You got him from a tree.
Now you're filled with glee
Dragging him home on your four wheeler
Cut him open
Get the meat
Bring him in
So your whole family can eat.

Carl Klem, Grade 5
Wright City Middle School, MO

Band

Looks like gold, metal instruments
Sounds like trumpeting and beating the drum
Tastes like rusty metal
Feels like silky, smooth metal
Smells like wet, soft mouthpieces

Bentley King, Grade 5
Briarwood Christian School, AL

Weapons of War and Words of Peace

War
loud, pessimistic
fighting, killing, weeping
weapons, soldiers, civilians, words
living, loving, celebrating
quiet, optimistic
peace

Weapons
destructive, violent
hurting, exploding, firing
war, death, life, peace
speaking, writing, singing
kind, exciting
words

Thomas Wray, Grade 6
Haynes Academy for Advanced Studies, LA

Dollywood

The extraordinary smell of funnel cakes
The screeching sounds of Mystery Mine
The loud rumble of roller coasters
The warm water of River Rampage
The fretful feel of Thunderhead
The hovering feel of Tennessee Tornado
The proceeding feel of Mountain Slidewinder
The frigid water of Dare Devil Falls
What a blast!

Hayden Wiggins, Grade 5
North Middle School, TN

Autumn Leaves

A utumn leaves,
U nbelievably beautiful,
T he leaves are scattered in the yard,
U pon the ground they look so stunning,
M y brother is in the kitchen he is such a card,
N ew England Patriots are on TV.

L eaving the house we come to rake the leaves,
E verybody is working hard,
A lmost finished yes we are,
V ery close to finishing the stack which we will guard,
E verybody is done by a mile,
S o we jump in with a smile.

Jeff Gottesman, Grade 5
Palmetto Christian Academy, SC

Summer Games

Summer heat beating down on my teammates, and me
Sweat on my eyebrow trickling down,
Forcing my legs past their limits,
The speedy ball zigzagging between my cleats,
I dive through their defense with intense speed,
My heart pounding,
Suddenly I was surrounded like the prey of a loin,
My brain throbbing and heart pounding,
I kicked the ball and it flew a hundred miles an hour,
Time stopped as soccer ball flew past their defense,
GOAL!!!!

Alexander Xavier Harkins, Grade 6
Alvaton Elementary School, KY

Where I'm From

I am from a picture,
from the peach colored room in the hall.
I am from Glass-Plus and So Soft.
I am from the petals of a soft pink lily,
from the maple,
still growing and reaching far.

I am from chocolate and peppermints,
from know-it-alls.
I am from my parents, Nirav and Jagruti Pancholy.
I am from mangoes and ice cream.
I'm from "smile" and "be happy."

I am from the Hindu religion,
I'm from India.
From veggies and pizza.
From the journey to America,
the journey from India to here,
the journey made by my mom and my dad.

I am from the picture albums,
stored beneath my bed,
with all the pictures of my gleeful moments.

Niraja Pancholy, Grade 6
Lakeshore Middle School, NC

Me and My Happy Self on Christmas!

Happy, Happy, Happy,
That it is Christmas, yes I am,
My mom and dad gave me a necklace
That said Marie Ann!

I also got another gift,
From Aunt Sally and Uncle Lou,
It was a doll with long hair,
And I named her Marie too!
That's why I love Christmas, yes I do!

Jazmin White, Grade 4
E O Young Jr Elementary School, NC

Presents!

Under the tree waiting to be unwrapped
With paper shining like gold.
I start to tear as the paper over laps
The letters on the tag are very bold.

Ornaments hang from hooks on the tree
Shining brightly reflecting the light
All over the tree reds, yellows, and blues
Santa will visit when it becomes night.

Kali Wilson, Grade 6
Pleasants County Middle School, WV

Living Mathematics in a Circle

Mathematics is similar to life,
You subtract and add
Going up and back down again
Life is like mathematics
Every person, every thing is unique
Just as no two numbers are the same
Math and life is the same in a way
You use both every single day

Audrey Holds, Grade 5
Meramec Elementary School, MO

Helicopter

H igh tech
E dges closer to the enemy
L eft or right
I t's always loaded for war
C omes to help
O utstanding
P ositions to fight
T rooper's best transportation
E ven helps wounded
R ises so high

Ethan Mosko, Grade 5
Briarwood Christian School, AL

Backpack

I have a big purple backpack
Inside it is my sack
In it is a can
It holds a man
His full name is Mackalack

Victoria Anderson, Grade 6
Armorel Elementary School, AR

Thanksgiving

Thanksgiving
turkey, family
playing, celebrating, eating
giving thanks
holidays

Jorge Quezada, Grade 5
Westwood Elementary School, AR

Fall

Fall is cool
Fall is fun
Fall is when the leaves die young
Fall is very cold
Fall is very calm
Fall is when we go camping
Fall is very lovely
Fall is very colorful
Fall feels like winter
Fall has no snow
Fall is the be best
Fall is for you and me

Aubrey Earhart, Grade 6
Stuart Middle School, KY

Present

Red, blue, green, yellow.
Big and small I like them all.
You can buy them from the mall.
I like toys the best.
So don't give me a test.
Presents make me smile.
So go the extra mile.

Hannah Flynn, Grade 5
Walton Verona Elementary School, KY

Jellyfish and Starfish

Jellyfish are slow
Starfish are snail-paced moving
But they're majestic

Macy Tran, Grade 5
Duncan Chapel Elementary School, SC

That Gingerbread House

That gingerbread house,
With waffle crisps as doors,
Has one little tweak,
To its candy galore.

It's not just a house,
With a stump and a hatchet,
But a ginger bread house,
With a speck of white magic.

It's not only the door,
That has this sweet taste,
But the whole house does,
With even icing as paste.

It is far too big,
For only one mouse,
So hurry and get there,
To that gingerbread house.

Linsey Boerrigter, Grade 6
South Oldham Middle School, KY

My Mom Is Having a Baby!

My mom is having a baby!
May is when it is due.
I sure love babies
I do! I do!

I have a dog
He may have some
Jealousy, jealousy, jealousy
Watch out for his jealousy!

My mom is having a baby!
May is when it is due.
I sure love babies
I do! I do!

My mom is having a baby!
Woo-hoo! Woo-hoo!

Madeline Skaggs, Grade 4
Capshaw School, TN

The Year That Went too Fast

When St. E's closed
It was hard for everyone
not just me.

I thought Natalie would
take it harder
because she had been
there longer than me but she
didn't I did.

When we got home from the
last day of school, I dropped my
backpack ran upstairs locked
my door and cried like a fool.

That final Mass, the whole school
broke down, we all felt lost would we
ever be found?

Everyone finds it hard to look
back at that final year because we
lost something so dear.

Garrett Lipic, Grade 6
Annunciation Elementary School, MO

Bald Eagle

Bald eagle
symbolic, magnificent
soars, flies, nests,
hunting, nursing, feeding, clawing
Great bird of America
The grace bird

Micah Heathcock, Grade 4
East Jones Elementary School, MS

The Silent One

When I was little
I was quiet as a mouse.
My mom said I looked like an angel
Because I was so silent.
I took lots of baths
Because I was always dirty.
I loved to jump and roll in puddles,
Play in the basement,
And run around with the dogs.
Sometimes I felt like I was invisible.
I only go in trouble once
Because I was sneaky
And went to my uncle's house
without permission.
When my mom found out
I was grounded for weeks.

Darrean Godley, Grade 5
Lee A Tolbert Community Academy, MO

Friends

Laughing, cheering, secrets told…
Crying, sighing, being bold.

Lunches, dances, sleepovers, too!
Shopping 'til our feet turn blue!

Birthday parties, stay all night…
Confessing that you broke your diet!

Phone calls, boyfriends, and homework…
Telling him that he's a "jerk!"

Silent lunches, no phone calls!
My friends all know it's not my fault!

They still love me when I'm down;
Help to make my world turn 'round!!

Maleah Mathis, Grade 6
Scotts Creek Elementary School, NC

Water Country

Enormous water slides as tall as skyscrapers
Waves in the wave pool running after me
People splashing in the water
Kids yelling in the water wildly
Chlorine in the water fills the air
Popcorn popping in the popcorn stands
Burgers being flipped over on the grill
Pretzels make my mouth water
Hard cement under my feet
Water taking me deeper in the pool
I feel joyful.

Juanita Chavez, Grade 4
Bailey Elementary School, NC

A Pilgrim

A Pilgrim is a person who comes for religious life.
A Pilgrim is a person who is very, very nice.
A Pilgrim is a kind person who never, never fights.
A Pilgrim is a person who does good things right.
A Pilgrim is a person who rode on the May Flower.
A Pilgrim is a person who always has a good power.
A Pilgrim is a person who always thinks of an idea.
A Pilgrim is a person who always has a question.

Jameisha Thompson, Grade 5
Franklin Elementary School, OK

The Ocean

As the ocean comes upon my feet
I stand there watching my special friends.
All my cats surround me, meow, meow, meow,
While the ocean comes upon my feet.

I listen to the ocean waves
As they splash upon my legs,
It seems as if they are speaking to me
While the ocean comes upon my feet.

I looked as far as I could see
And saw the waves touch the sky.
I saw my cats catch the fish
While the ocean comes upon my feet.

At night the moon sparkles in the ocean,
When all my cats are asleep.
I stand and watch the calming waters
While the ocean comes upon my feet.

Candace Niermann, Grade 5
Providence Academy, TN

Grace

Strawberry-blonde curly hair, brown eyes, and skinny
Comfortable T-shirts and soft, warm slippers at bedtime
"Gosh!"
Camping and fishing with my family, riding my golf cart
My brother smacking when he eats really annoys me!
Read a magazine or do gymnastics on the floor
Yellow smiley faces and the sun

Grace Elbl, Grade 5
Our Lady Catholic School, MO

Sprayed by the Mist

The boat glides across the waves like riding on a horse.
Dolphins were dancers on the waves.
A wandering horse was like a lost hiker.
Waves were splashing on the boat like thunder cracking.
The salt tasted like pretzels.
Fish felt really slimy.

I was sprayed by the mist.

Amy Waguespack, Grade 6
Montessori Community School, NC

Head and Foot

Head
Oval, hairy
Moving, looking, breathing
hard, hair, toes, soft
Running, jumping, walking
Small, nails
Foot
Dylan Fretwell, Grade 4
Tamassee-Salem Elementary School, SC

United States Flag

our red, white and blue
fifty bright stars on the flag
stripes wave in the breeze
Ka'Nisha Stevens, Grade 4
Broadway Elementary School, NC

Rabbits

Funny in a way.
A rabbit hops all day long.
Big ears, small, and great.
Ann Kelly Patrick, Grade 4
Briarwood Christian School, AL

At Christmas Time

Sparkling lights on the Christmas tree,
All of the children were filled with glee.
Sweet smells of pumpkin pie.
So many presents, oh my! Oh my!

When it's time to open my gifts.
I wink and give my nanny a kiss.
She softly smiles at me,
And I smile back.

As my family begins to leave
I hear sleigh bells off in the distance.
Who could it be?
Ho! Ho! Ho!
Merry Christmas, it's Saint Nick!!
Amber Thomas, Grade 5
East Bernstadt Elementary School, KY

Butterfly

Oh, butterfly,
Oh, butterfly.
Why won't you leave?
Don't you want to live
In a happy family?

Over the mountains,
Over the rivers,
Over the glassy water,
There's a happy family just for you.
Braylin Russell, Grade 4
Hayes Elementary School, OK

True One

A best friend is like jewelry;
They would always want to hang on to you or me,
A friend may not always be free;
But a best friend will always be there for me,
A best friend knows how you really feel when you are down;
So they turn that sad frown around,
A friend is just a person you know for a couple of days;
But a best friend has been there through your whole entire maze,
He or she may not always agree with you;
Though, always remember that they try to see you through.
A best friend is jewelry;
They follow us everywhere we go and you not even know;
They were there to show,
Now that's a true one.

JaLyn Anderson, Grade 5
Smart Start Academy, MS

My Hideaway

"Drip-Drop!" sings the rain. The leaves fill the earth with a whispering sound.
A deer family hides from the shower under a ledge.
You sit up in a tree, letting the clear rain fall over you.
A quail coos and a rabbit leaps into his hole away from the rain.
You open your mouth allowing the smooth droplets to slide down your tongue.
Breathing in, you smell flowers.
As you close your eyes to rest, you listen to the lullaby of nature.
When the rain stops, you slide down from your hideaway.
Above you, a little group of birds fly, and a tulip smiles up at the brilliant sun.
As you walk down the path towards home, you smile and feel that all is well.

Hannah Pryor, Grade 6
Queen of Angels Catholic School, GA

Dale

He was a legend in his own time
Behind that legend he was one of us
The drivers were in fear when the black number 3 was near
He earned the nickname the Intimidator
Because he won, knocked drivers in the wall
Dale Earnhardt was number one racing meant more than money
Racing was his life
It took 20 years of frustration everyone waited
He won the Daytona 500 he finally made it
Dale Earnhardt was the new king of NASCAR
In 2001 he took his last ride
Dale Earnhardt was gone everyone cried NASCAR lost its greatest driver
He will be remembered as the intimidator
And The black number 3
After his death a new person took his place
His son Dale Earnhardt Jr
It was hard to race without his dad by his side
But the Earnhardt legend lives on
Gentlemen start your engines
There they go off…
Oh we forgot you too Dale

Billy Mitchell, Grade 6
Stuart Middle School, KY

Poems

After the bell rang
Poems, poems, poems
My mind would not rest
Poems, poems, poems
On the subject
Poems, poems, poems
That I had a poem due Thursday.
Poems, poems, poems
I spilled my head
Poems, poems, poems
Onto the paper
Poem, poems, poems
And this is what I got.
Poem, poems, poems
Now my mind
Poems, poems, poems
Can finally rest.
Poems, poems, poems

Haley Thompson, Grade 6
Haynes Academy for Advanced Studies, LA

Snow

Small, tiny flakes silently falling from the sky.
A white velvet blanket covering the Earth's face.

What is it?

Sledding down a hill as smooth as a river made of glass.
Skiing and snowboarding down tall towering pyramids
and catching glimpses of shadows cast by mighty evergreens.

What is it?

Building strong, sturdy forts
and pelting friends with moist, cold, firm balls of ice
and enjoying the day being out of school.
I wish this day would never end!

What is it?

I don't know when it will return,
but next time I hope it will stick around longer.

What is it?
SNOW

Paul Eldridge, Grade 4
Sequoyah Elementary School, TN

Fall Senses

Fall is colorful, and oh so bright
Smell the wonderful pumpkin pie
Hear leaves crackling on the ground
Taste the hot apple cider, and
Feel the slimy goo inside the pumpkin I will carve!

Hunter Blakley, Grade 5
Sullivan Elementary School, TN

What It's Like to Have Fun with Friends

Playing with friends
A burst of emotion,
A burst of happiness,
And most of all:
Fun

Playing with friends
A happy sanctuary
A secure freedom

Riding bikes,
Playing sports,
Watching TV,
Playing video games

Playing with friends
Enjoyable non-wasted time.

Nate Beckemeyer, Grade 6
Annunciation Elementary School, MO

My Dog

I love my dog and he loves me.
When people fight, he will bite or growl.
He sleeps with me and watches TV.
His favorite toys are cars.
He takes them from people
And chases them around the house.
He busts open the back door
If we don't let him in.
He likes to be rubbed
And can jump up to my head.
He has green eyes and his name is
Snickers Puppy Paw Williams.
We play hide-and-go-seek
And I put perfume on so he can find me.
Sometimes I sing him to sleep.

Cambrie Agee, Grade 5
Lee A Tolbert Community Academy, MO

My Family

My family is a horse,
Majestic, caring, watching
My mother is the legs,
Directing us all to the right spot.
My father is the body,
Strong and almost unreal.
My youngest sister is the ears,
Listening for danger.
My other sister is the feet,
Prepared to go wherever the legs may direct.
I am the tail,
On the lookout for little pests and trying to protect the family.

Becca Sellers, Grade 5
Bloomfield Elementary School, KY

There's No Reality Anymore
Here is a peek into my dreamland
It's a land where you can freeze time
A land where you can wake up as someone else
It's a land where you can walk into the city and not see a person hiding from you in a box
It's a dream where nobody is last pick
It's a dream where nobody watches from the sidelines
It's a dream where you can wish upon a star and not doubt for a single second that it won't come true

In my land everyone's king
In my land nobody feels the need to own a gun
In my land nobody owns land
In my dream a woman's opinion always counts
In my dream everyone considers everyone equal
In my dream the world really is a straight social hierarchy

I know that everyone is asking
"Where is this land and how can I get to it?"
I can't tell you how to get there
But I can tell you this
My land is here but we have to make it so

Taylor Hunt, Grade 6
Chapin Middle School, SC

My Fat Cat
I have a cat named Whisker. He likes to sleep in my shoes, but he doesn't like milk instead, he likes tea or water from the faucet. Yesterday I taught him how to answer questions like yes or no. Today I have taught him how to shake hands. This is my poem about my fat cat Whisker.

Lory Miller, Grade 5
West Marion Elementary School, MS

Head to Head
Dad and I excitedly on our way to Rupp Arena
Where the Kentucky Wildcats basketball team will go head to head with their opponents.
Walking in with dark blue Kentucky sweatshirts on looking everywhere seeing Royal Blue.
Sitting down with an ice cold dripping drink hoping the Cats will win!
Cheerleaders, Basketball players enter the court
Finally the game begins
crowd as loud as 20 revving motorcycle engines
bursting with excitement, anxious for game to start.
"SWISH" ball slams into the goal
Crowd goes wild like monkeys swinging from forest green vines
Orange, rubber basketball quickly bounces
up and down, up and down, up and down,
Players dashing towards the goal
back and forth, back and forth, back and forth.
UK score continues to go up like a thermometer hitting 100 degrees
While the opponent stays the same
I wonder if the Cats will win…
Can they make the winning shot?
"SWISH" UK scores the winning shot, crowd goes wild.
"SLAM" door shuts, gym quiet
fans eagerly waiting for the next game.

Alex Singer, Grade 4
Roberta Tully Elementary School, KY

In My Heart

"Ask her," my friends shouted. "Ask her."
My heart was pounding with fear.
I had never had the courage
To talk to my mom like I did on this day.
Here is where my heartfelt Moment began.

"Who's my father?" I ask my mom
As we drive home from school.
"What!?" she asks.
"I know I have a father," I pause.
"Who is he? What's his name?"
"His name is Jason and he is
Thirty five years old."

Questions filled my mind.
How did they meet?
What does he look like?
All I knew about him was his name and age.
I was happy Even though I knew
So little about him.
Not even a picture to look back on.
I don't know him, but I know him
In My Heart

Chloe Boldrick, Grade 6
East Oldham Middle School, KY

Winter

Most people think
winter is just cold, and dark,
but I think it's FUN!
You get to dress
with all the coolest winter wear
and your feet "squish, squash" in the snow,
the winding wind whispers in your face "come play,"
you feel so happy!
And when those snowflakes touch your tongue,
as hard and fast as dripping water,
it's spectacular!

Jennifer Mansfield, Grade 5
Greathouse Shryock Traditional Elementary School, KY

'Tis the Season

Christmas is a time to share
to give to the homeless something to wear
Praise the Lord Jesus who came to earth
who is way more than we are worth
Listen to carolers sing songs of joy
and watch children open their new toys
The smell of holly in the air
and see Christmas lights everywhere
So as the Christmas season draws near
remember those who are dear

Judith Hill, Grade 6
Briarwood Christian School, AL

Books

I am weak
I pick up a book
And the words just leak
I may read about a crook
Or maybe magic spells
I love when I've begun
Oh the stories I can tell!
I hate when I'm done
Oh books are the best
And I can't rest
With a book on my desk!

Emma Lampe, Grade 5
South Smithfield Elementary School, NC

My Mother the Marathon Runner

As she gets to the line she thinks of her plan
To run steady and on track
This is for the lymphoma and leukemia society she
remembers
She takes off and jogs as well as she can
She looks to her side
Seeing my family and I cheering
She feels great and set on track
And has no need to hide
From the glaring sun staring at her skin
Her heroes are Sean
And also Little Benjamin
This woman is my mother, my hero, and one of my kin
She is wonderful
Because she is running for my friends
And when she is all done we will hug and love her so much
I am so grateful to have her around

Devin Crandall, Grade 6
Queen of Angels Catholic School, GA

The Pine Tree

I am the little pine tree oh so small
In the years ahead I will grow very tall
With a lot of water, sun and air
I will soon be way high up there!!!

Deep inside the soil where my roots are found
Drinking the water from under the ground
Water from the roots that they send through me
Then my trunk starts the process of making me.

As I start to climb higher and higher up in the sky
Where the sky above, oh so blue,
And the clouds are waving at me and saying HI!!!

I am a little pine tree oh so small,
Waiting my turn to grow very tall
I may not be tall right now but come to be spring
I will not be small!!!

Marie Floyd, Grade 6
Chapin Middle School, SC

Yellow Happiness

Happiness is yellow.
It sounds like flutes.
It tastes like peaches.
It smells like cinnamon.
It looks like a meadow.
It makes me feel like smiling.

Mikayla Williams, Grade 5
Salem Elementary School, AR

Life

Life can be happy
Life can be sad
Life can be fun
Life slips away
That's the way it is
No one can change it
Life everyone lives it

Charlotte Overton, Grade 6
Greenville Montessori School, NC

Changing Form

From a tiny seed to a flower
It takes time, but more than an hour
They grow and grow
Until they have reached full grown.
The birds and bees are flying,
The flowers are crying
The flowers turn out to be beautiful,
And the swaying is graceful,
In winter it gets much colder,
The flowers shiver,
The icy mountain became white
The flowers sleep in sight
In the cool spring
The flowers dance and sing
She turns out to be a beautiful flower
Which will begin again.

Airada Damdee, Grade 5
G C Burkhead Elementary School, KY

Paul Revere

Paul Revere
Had no fear
He rode at night
By way of light
On a horse
He kept the course
He rode through town
"The British are here"
He yelled with no fear
The people to alarm
So there would come
No harm

Ashlyn Tucker, Grade 6
Clarksburg School, TN

Cats and Rats

I know a rat whose name is mat,
He likes to play with a cat named pat,
They like to play every day,
they like to run out in the sun,
They like to eat a lot of meat,
They also fight every night,
When you tell them to go to sleep,
They will stand there and weep.

Stephanie Dickerson, Grade 5
Graham Elementary School, AL

Poems and Flowers

Poems flutter by
Like a butterfly
They land on flowers
With magical powers
They never land on roses
Because it hurts their noses
They never fly around mice
Because they get head lice

Vitia Zamudio, Grade 5
Berryville Elementary School, AR

Little Girls and Big Boys

little girls dancing swiftly,
little girls prancing quickly,
big boys skating calmly,
big boys running softly,
everyone laughing hardly,
playing gladly all at once,
little girls singing joyfully,
big boys racing happily,
what a sight they made,
big boys petting dogs,
little girls slacking off,
little girls playing hard,
big boys studying calmly,
what a class they are,
big boys and little girls,
having fun all at once.

George Azar, Grade 5
Our Lady of Fatima School, MS

Black Cat

I had a black cat
Who was really quite fat
And there he just sat
On my favorite hat

I gave him a pat
And he said, "What's that?
Are you expecting me
To go chase a rat?"

Kevin Gregory, Grade 5
Herbert J Dexter Elementary School, GA

Basketball

I love basketball,
It's my favorite thing to do.
I recommend it,
You should try it too!
All you have to do,
Is keep the ball with your team.
So you can shoot,
And make the crowd scream.

Oliver Lynch-Daniels, Grade 4
St Thomas More School, NC

Mommy

M eaningful
O utstanding
M agnificent
M inds her own business
Y oung

Dontrell Lewis, Grade 5
Vernon Middle School, LA

Stormy Night

Boom! Boom! Boom!
Went the thunder above my head
While I was in bed
Clash! Clash! Clash!
The lightning so fierce
SPLASH!
The water hit the roof so hard
Suddenly I heard a Whoosh! Whoosh!
Whirl! Whirl!
I looked out the window
Coming toward us was a black object —
A tornado!
Bam went the door!
Clop! Clop!
The hail was hitting hard on our heads
As we went out to go to the basement.
Then it all stopped
Tornado vanished in the air
Rain and hail stopped
Thunder and lightning gone
The storm was over!

Danielle Maddox, Grade 6
College View Middle School, KY

My Dog Lady

Lady she is so fast.
She chased my uncle but not for the last
She died in the past
She is so fast on her feet.
She is so sweet.
We let her outside one day
She used to play every day

Matthew O'Dell, Grade 4
Brilliant Elementary School, AL

I Believe I Can Fly

I believe I can fly.
I believe I can touch the sky.

I believe I can go sing in the local talent shows and musicals.
I believe I can sing.

I believe I can have Dog Daycare.
I believe I can be a vet.

I believe I can be a cheerleader when I am little.
I believe I can be a great cheerleader.

I believe I can fly.
I believe I can touch the sky.

Madison Lucas, Grade 4
Center Elementary School, GA

Sports Math

What's your batting average?
How many minutes in a football game?
How many innings in a full baseball game?
If you lose, who's to blame?
How many RBIs did you have in your last baseball game?
How many points did you score in your last basketball game?
Did you par on your last hole?
Sports math is the name of the game.

Jake Brown, Grade 5
Meramec Elementary School, MO

Soccer

Three yellow cards equal one red card,
One red card ejected out of the game,
Three red cards,
Out for the season.

Score, score, score
Make that point.
Block, block, block,
Stop that goal.

Goal kicks,
Corner kicks,
Toe kicks,
Drop kicks.

In the sweltering hot sun,
Running down the long, green field.
Sweat dripping down exhausted faces,
Hot as a broiling oven.

Playing hard and so rough,
Slowly losing strength.
Trotting along using the last bit of energy.
The game is now done!

Brennan Curole, Grade 5
Larose Upper Elementary School, LA

My Parrot

I used to have a parrot who love to eat carrots
at night he would sound like a chariot
when I come down and see what's wrong
he will look at me and sing me a song
he will ask for a cracker every time
then he accidentally slips on slime
you know what happened he broke his spine
so we go to the doctors office and he said he had nothing to do
so me and my family started to say boo hoo.

Diri Ibeawuchi, Grade 4
Nesbit Elementary School, GA

Alexandra

Long, dark brown hair, blue eyes, average height
Athletic shorts when I'm hanging around
And long jeans shorts with novelty shirts in public
"So" and "Forget it"
Playing sports and eating
It angers me when I make a mistake in a sport.
Talking on the phone, imitations
Lime green butterflies
Chocolate milkshakes, cheese pizza

Alexandra Linderer, Grade 5
Our Lady Catholic School, MO

Halloween Candy

It's Halloween night it's pitched black
I'm going trick-or-treating with a witch and my white cat.
We run in the neighborhood from house to house
Until we reach a lady in a silky pink blouse.
We stared at the delicious candy that she had.
And even though I bumped my head, I felt glad.
She had the puffy, chewy, round and blue kinds
And I said to myself "It's all mine."
When I got home, my mom said I'd be bouncing off the walls
But I ignored her and quickly ate five gumballs.

Kristina Jordan, Grade 5
Fox Elementary School, MO

Thriller

The sky is oh so gray,
My smile has gone away,
The wind is so strong,
Brewing up a swirling storm,
Twirling black nightmare,
Dances in the sky,
Coming near us,
Run inside,
Picks us up and twirls round and round,
Lets us down unsafely,
Throws us to the ground,
Thriller

Laura Deckelmann, Grade 6
Haynes Academy for Advanced Studies, LA

Galloping Ride

I feel happy when I ride my pony
I gallop
In the grassy green fields, and smile
The wind whips back into my face
I hear hooves below me
Eating up ground
I hear Tango's deep breaths
Every stride he takes
The wind encourages his mane
To race backwards
Running towards me
The hot summer sun
Beams down on us
Like a spotlight on stage
As it follows everywhere we go
I give him rein
And encourage him on.
This is when, I feel happy.

Claire Miles, Grade 6
East Oldham Middle School, KY

Fall

As the leaves are falling down
And I'm amidst the red and brown
I know that fall has come around

As I rake the leaf piles
And I look around for miles
I know that fall's here all the while

As the birds are flying by
And the clouds scatter the sky
The sun looks like a golden pie

With Thanksgiving being near
Soon the family will be here
It's a time full of cheer

With our food on the table
We will eat till we are unable
At our cabin made of maple

With fall coming to a close
I will be cold from nose to toes
What will happen next year?
Who know!

Erin O'Leary, Grade 5
St Michael Parish School, WV

The Sun

I used to wonder how far is the sun
Now all I want is just some fun
I think the Earth is a very nice place
But now I need an extra shoelace

Alec Camacho, Grade 4
Horace Mann Elementary School, OK

Basketball

B right and
A thletic and
S kills no matter how good.
K indness is expected, but some
E xceptions are granted.
T ry hard and play hard or the
B ench you will sit.
A wesomeness and nothing but fun.
L eft-handers and right-handers, doesn't matter which, you should always
L ove your teammates no matter what.

Jerrica Horn, Grade 5
Grovespring Elementary School, MO

Westchester!

When I came to this school I was scared,
I thought I'd die,
With teachers all over me every day,
But once I got here I knew I'd love it,
And right now, since fourth grade, I've loved it ever since,
The teachers are awesome,
And I was happy Mr. Hamblet came to be the principal,
Another thing about middle school is that you have to be organized,
But it's cool too,
The day also goes by faster. Thank God!

Phillip Young, Grade 6
Westchester Country Day School, NC

I Am

I am a caring girl who likes art.
I wonder if the gazelles I paint will jump out of the frame and prance around.
I hear the blue jays chirping in the oak trees of my painting.
I see my painting coming to life with every stroke I make with my paint covered brush.
I want to climb into the artwork and run towards the orange painted sunset.
I am a caring girl who likes art.

I pretend I am the queen of art and that my pencil is my wand.
I feel my pencil leading me to success.
I worry if my art tools will ever mislead me.
I cry when my art tools lead me to an un-erasable mistake.
I am a caring girl who likes art.

I understand that rainbow is only a drawing.
I say I will never give up art.
I dream to see that painted waterfall surrounded in lights at a museum.
I try my hardest to reach that goal.
I hope one day my pictures will really come to life.
I am a caring girl who likes art.

Alyson Schwartz, Grade 6
R D and Euzelle P Smith Middle School, NC

Christmas Lights

They hang out with Mr. Claus when it's time to deck the halls.
They sit upon the Christmas tree to fill kids' hearts up with glee.
You may have guessed it, Christmas lights to blink all through the night.

Kason Wheeler, Grade 6
Appling County Middle School, GA

Bunny Rabbit

Watch the little bunny rabbit
Eating its great meal.
Watch him sniff his food and grab it,
Throwing one last peel.

Watch the happy, little twitching
On the rabbit's nose.
As time goes by, it starts switching
To his little toes.

But one day as he was hopping,
A man eventually showed up.
The human hated to go shopping
So he ate the rabbit for his sup.

Katie Hazel, Grade 5
Hunter GT Magnet Elementary School, NC

Riding Four-Wheelers

When it is cold outside
Four-wheelers I like to ride.
I go fast and sometimes do tricks.
Stopping and starting will make it kick.

Be careful, don't run up behind someone
Or you'll have a wreck.
My sister stopped in front of me
And almost broke my neck.

Austin Audirsch, Grade 4
Northeast Baptist School, LA

Up to Bat

You stand at the plate.
You know that you have to get a hit,
Or the game is over!
Your teammates are cheering for you,
But you do not hear them;
For all you are concentrating on
Is the pitcher and the ball!
The pitcher throws the ball,
And you swing,
But you miss!
The pitcher gets the ball again.
He throws it again,
Slow and in the middle,
But you still miss!
One more time the pitcher gets the ball.
He smiles, thinking the game is over!
He throws the ball for the last time;
You close your eyes and swing —
"Whack!" and then you start running...
You don't know if you are safe or out
Until you hear someone say "Home Run!"

Taylor Parks, Grade 6
Scotts Creek Elementary School, NC

Love

I love you, you love me,
You know that as much as me,
I love you, I love you, I love you,
Much and much more than you'll ever know.

Abigail Constant, Grade 4
Constant Learning Academy, LA

You'll Get Hungry

On an icy hot afternoon
Little Lizzie went out to play
And listened to her mother say:
"Take a snack you'll get hungry today."

Little Lizzie said, "Good bye"
And left the house for the day.
Of course she forgot the snack,
That snack her mother said to pack.

Soon she did get hungry,
As hungry as a bear.
All of a sudden she heard her stomach growl,
Pain was shooting everywhere.

She turned and saw her front door,
She ran in and ate an apple to the core,
She knew there would be more,
So there she stayed forever more.

Josie Rogers, Grade 5
Providence Academy, TN

Winter

Winter you are an ancient soul,
With your frost covered bones,
And your long white hair.
You reach up your hands for the warm sun,
Spring is coming and you have to leave.
Your frozen tears hang from roofs as you say good-bye,
With your cold winter wind softening up.

Devon Potter, Grade 5
Lynn Fanning Elementary School, AL

World War 2

Bomb and bullets come from above,
    attack on Pearl Harbor has just begun!
Everyone screaming, running,
    soldiers must protect, but most are hit.
Casualties are high,
    ones alive must keep pride.
They must keep fighting, keep moving,
    if not, they could get shot.
Last moments for some
    with children, daughters and sons.
They must keep hope and stride with pride,
    for loved ones fought for their country and died.

Malachi Glass, Grade 5
E O Young Jr Elementary School, NC

My Favorite Season

God created the seasons
Each one was made for a reason
I can't choose a favorite
For they all are so great…
In the fall, I think of football
In winter, a spirit of giving
In the spring, I think of softball
And in summer, lots of swimming!
They are ALL a favorite,
Make no mistake of it!

Colton Vaughn, Grade 4
Evangelical Christian School, TN

What Am I?

I am a wall,
I am very tall
I watch him crawl,
Then I watch him fall.

There is a mouse,
Wearing a blouse,
Waving me around in his house,
Looking at his spouse

I'm on the ground, then I'm found
Twirled around,
Some guy frowned,
Then I'm back on the ground

I'm sitting all quiet,
I begin to ring, then there's a riot
Then some girls sings, wearing a gown,
Then I'm put down.

The wall in HumptyDumptey
Mickey Mouse's wand
Stone from the story David and Goliath
A telephone

Walty Feisal, Grade 6
St Mary's School, SC

Dogs

Soft and cuddly,
Filled with kindness,
Dogs are always happy.
They are filled with energy.
Dogs like to play and run.
They like to chase balls.
They love to catch frisbees
Some are fat, some are skinny,
Some are in the middle.
But they are all the same,
No matter how they are!

McKayla Denny, Grade 5
Paint Lick Elementary School, KY

Baseball

Baseball is my favorite game
You hit you run
You have fun
The crowd is cheering run, run, run
Baseball is my favorite game
That's why it's my middle name
I love Baseball

Billy Carmouche, Grade 4
Lewis Vincent Elementary School, LA

The Hershey Kiss

The Hershey Kiss,
A chocolate candy nobody can miss.
All wrapped up in its silver sheet,
It seems like a miracle when we meet.
Such a wonderful taste to my lips,
It makes me want to shake my hips.
Pop it in your mouth, then it's gone,
That's the end of my poetry song.

Brittney Stubbs, Grade 4
Crossville Christian School, TN

Tena Dailey

T errific at reading
E xciting attitude
N ice smile
A dorable girl

D iva
A ble to do anything
I ntelligent in all my classes
L ovable to my family and friends
E ager to learn
Y outhful and lively

Tena Dailey, Grade 6
Mark Twain Elementary School, MO

Hello Changing Seasons

fall, spring
winter, summer
changes come every year
look around, you can see changes
seasons

Kamesha Chalmers, Grade 5
Broadway Elementary School, NC

The Sun

The sun is big
The sun is bright.
The sun has volcanoes.
All of the planets orbit the sun.
Everyone knows we can't live on the sun,
But we all consider it a part of life.

Dewayne Horn, Grade 5
Paint Lick Elementary School, KY

Think Twice

If you think
No one cares
You're in this world
On your own

Think twice
People love you
There are plenty of things
You could do

Go out
Live your life
You're not alone
Live your dreams

Laurie-Jewell White, Grade 6
Des Arc Elementary School, AR

Flowers

Flowers are sweet.
Flowers are neat.
They are very petite,
But they can't stand the heat.
They make me complete.
They also like the peace.

Brianna Radford, Grade 4
Contentnea Elementary School, NC

Dogs

They're man's best friend,
They'll stick by your side,
Their love is not pretend,
In your heart they will abide.

They love to go on walks,
They hate to be ignored,
They listen when you talk,
They're overjoyed when adored.

They bark all day,
They never get hoarse,
When tired they'll lay,
It's a dog of course!

Erin Willis, Grade 5
Midway Covenant Christian School, GA

The Worst Day Ever

I was coming home from school.
Everyone thought I was a fool.
I got something wrong in class.
Then I broke the teacher's glass.
It was a very annoying day.
The girls always get their way.
This is the worst day ever!

Cameron Cox, Grade 6
St Andrew's Episcopal School, LA

My Summer

Summer why did you have to go away
Summer summer come again another day
Why don't you say I will be back again another day
I want you to come back and stay
Come back and stay
Come back and let's play
Fall, winter, and spring will come
But you are my favorite #1

Seavy Lecota Locklear, Grade 5
Pembroke Elementary School, NC

Christmas

Christmas is a time for cheer,
It only comes once a year,

A time to celebrate many things,
Like family, peace, and the birth of the king.

You'll see gifts wrapped with bows,
And trees wrapped with lights,
This night Santa will take a long flight.

Leaving presents and gifts,
We soon forget what Christmas is all about.

It started so long ago in a manger with a tiny baby.

This baby would go on to do great things,
He would be the world's king.

So as we gather on this merry night,
Most think Santa is coming with my gifts,
But others think my gift has already come.

Rebekah Byrd, Grade 6
E Lawson Brown Middle School, NC

Cornbread

I smell it in the oven
I know what it is
It's nothing like
dancing chocolate
or parachuting marshmallows
or even gingerbread men shooting gumdrops
the smell is smelled from a mile
but if it burned
I think I'd lose my mind
It is a delicious bread
Ding Ding
oops there goes the smoke detector
I'm mad it's a false alarm
Bing Bong
It comes out as hot marching fireballs
Out comes some delicious
    Cornbread

Colin Barker, Grade 5
Greathouse Shryock Traditional Elementary School, KY

Valentine's Day

Love is something you can't get free.
It is something you have to earn happily.
Love is something that makes you smile.
It will last and last a while.

Valentine's Day is a treat.
On Valentine's Day you get a lot of treats.
On Valentine's Day your love can get stolen.
On Valentine's Day your heart can also get broken.
On Valentine's Day you can get a teddy bear.
And you also have someone who cares.

On Valentine's Day you get heart-shaped candy.
You also get flowers that smell so dandy.
On Valentine's Day you have a lover and friends.
On Valentine's Day is where your heart begins.
On Valentine's Day your heart is so warm inside.
On Valentine's Day you will make some else's heart shine.

On Valentine's Day there's joy and laughter.
On Valentine's Day there's that special someone you're after.

TeAsia Oden, Grade 5
Childersburg Middle School, AL

Shalonda

S ophisticated but the stylish person you will ever meet
H onest and memorable
A dorable and sweet
L ove I have for everyone
O rganize I'm an organized person who likes to be
N ever shy to tell a person how she feels.
D eals with problems easily
A lways encouraged to do something by my mom and dad

Shalonda T. Walker, Grade 5
Mark Twain Elementary School, MO

People in the World

People in the world may be special to you.
People in the world may not tell the truth.
People in the world are sometimes mean.
People in the world don't always smell clean.
People in the world aren't always nice.
People in the world may not except christ.
People in the world may smoke weed.
People in the world may take speed.
People in the world may be stressful.
People in the world may be successful.
People in the world may be crazy.
People in the world may be lazy.
That are some of the people in the world.
And there is nothing you can do, to change
peoples lives so they can be like you.

Ty'ren Fobbs, Grade 5
AJ Brown Elementary School, LA

Family Is Great

F un
A mazing
M akes you happy
I mportant
L ovable
Y ours forever

Jayne Birney, Grade 6
Martin Elementary School, WV

Santa Is Coming

Santa is coming
He brings presents and cool toys
For good girls and boys.

Sawyer Russell, Grade 4
Briarwood Christian School, AL

I Am Haunted

I am haunted, by storms
Scary, dreadful storms.
Daddy has to go out
And work, fixin' the wires
In the pouring rain.
I am haunted.

I was haunted,
By monsters,
They chased me and grabbed me
With their long claws,
And they ate me.
I am haunted.

I will be haunted
By someone in the family dying,
Papa T., Grandpa Dalton,
Even Mom or Dad.
I will be haunted.

Emma Dalton, Grade 5
Eminence Middle School, KY

Cat

Cat
So cute
Runs so fast
Feel so happy
Black

Michael Croghan, Grade 5
St Joseph Institute for the Deaf, MO

Fall Is Here

Crunch, Crunch
Squirrels find their nuts
colorful, wonderful
red, brown all on the ground, it's fall
fall's here!

MeKaila Holly, Grade 5
Broadway Elementary School, NC

What Is Black History?

Black history is when we celebrate
The black people we appreciate

When there were slaves
that had heartache and pain it was so hard it put us in our graves.
All the hatred and dread
On which our blood was shed

We should not only celebrate black history in February
But every month because what our ancestors went through was more than a month
We should remember about our people and what they overcame

Timothy Martin, Grade 6
Covenant Christian Ministries Academy - Middle/High, GA

Suffering with Pain

Pain is when
Children get their lives cut short by starvation.
They never have any time to feel elation.
Suffering

Pain is when
Women, men, wives, husbands, sons, daughters, fathers
and mothers die for us and die for each other.
Fighting wars they did not want; all they wanted was
Peace and forgiveness
Suffering

Pain is when
People get killed or kill themselves. Because people make
Fun of how they look or they feel out of place.
So they unhook the hook of life.
Suffering

Samantha Nicholson, Grade 5
Childersburg Middle School, AL

December

It is freezing in December.
There are jackets, sweaters, and even pants.
You can sometimes see your own breath.

There are lots of holidays in December.
Like Hanukkah, Christmas, and Kwanzaa.
Hanukkah is full of happiness, food, and gifts.
Christmas includes a tree, lights, and it's warm and wonderful.
Kwanzaa is beautiful with all their candles and lights.

There are also birthdays. Like mine.
I always have my birthday when it is cold.
I love my birthday and we always get hot chocolate.
The hot chocolate is hot, but when we have a sip, it warms us up.
During winter everything is so white.
Sometimes if we're lucky we get snow.
December is my favorite month!!!!!!!

Shelby Katz, Grade 6
Haynes Academy for Advanced Studies, LA

The Beach

I can smell the ocean air
The seagulls flying overhead
There is so much to see and do
I might not want to go to bed

I love to walk along the shore
And squish the sand between my toes
The sun is shining on my face
And I've got sunscreen on my nose

I like to watch the waves go by
And see the water's motion
It's so relaxing just to sit
And stare out at the ocean

LOOK OUT! It is a hermit crab!
He lives inside a shell
He almost pinched me on my foot
I jumped and then I fell

My sister built a sandcastle
It sparkles in the sun
The waves will wash it all away
When the day is done

Melanie Scott, Grade 4
Schaffner Traditional Elementary School, KY

Great Animals

I love Tiger,
She's a kitty.
I love Tiger,
She's so pretty.

I love Humphrey,
He's a hamster.
I love Humphrey,
He's a little gangster. (And a great dancer!)

I love Princess,
Oh yes I do.
I love princess,
How about you?

I love Mickey,
He's a dog.
I love Mickey,
Even when he's a hog!

All of these are animals,
And I want you to know,
That they are great,
And I love them so.

Ashten Estep, Grade 4
Northeast Baptist School, LA

New York City!

Wow!
Picture it,
the sky scraping buildings,
looking over you.
The smell
of hot dogs
from the hot dog stand.
the cars and trucks honking loudly.
Swoosh!
A taxi races by like a racecar driver!
Screech!
He slams on his breaks trying not to collide into cars.
Cars and trucks honking and crashing,
crashing and honking.
The wind was a soaring bird.
Across my face.
Crowds of people walking and crossing streets,
carrying briefcases full of who knows what,
wearing nice suits and lattes in their hands.
This place is what I call,
New York City!!

Dominique Williams, Grade 5
Greathouse Shryock Traditional Elementary School, KY

Jack o' Lantern

J umbo sized
A lot of work!
C arving is the hardest part.
K ind of tricky to make!

O utstanding.

L ooks very cool after being made.
A mazing to make.
N ot that many made.
T hicker than a leaf!
E asy to make.
R emarkable in a way.
N ot that much time left to carve the pumpkin.

Mason Gregory, Grade 5
First Flight Elementary School, NC

Friends

Friends stick together,
Not apart…forever.
The power of friendship will take us to the light,
Not into the darkness of the night.

The power of friendship makes every path.
At school, it let's us help with math.
Together with hope,
We can build a rope

of life.

Yetunde Ayinmide, Grade 5
St Patrick's School, AL

My Dad's Love

While I gaze across the pond,
I wait for fish.
I think about my dad,
And his love.
It is worth more than silver and gold,
More than I can hold.
And it never stops…

Drew Little, Grade 4
New Salem Elementary School, NC

Bubble, Bubble

Bubble, bubble in the sky.
Pretty and free all the time,
Until you pop.

Bubble, bubble in the sky.
You will not make that much of a sound.
When you pop.

Bubble, bubble in the sky.
You will just vanish and,
Your soap will fall to the ground.

Paige Christy, Grade 4
Hayes Elementary School, OK

Alissa

A lissa is my best friend
L istens to me when I'm sad.
I ncredibly good in school.
S weet as can be.
S mart at everything.
A wesome by being my best friend.

Alyssa Nichole Peña, Grade 5
Vernon Middle School, LA

Halloween

Halloween is fun,
But kind of spooky too.
Have your fun
But you might get scared
So have your mommy with you.

Alexis Braswell, Grade 4
Moyock Elementary School, NC

Moonlight Shadows

Moonlight shadows on the ground,
Shapes appear all around,
I shudder against the breezy night,
Trying to forget my growing fright,
Leaves rustle on the ground,
But there is no other sound,
Here, I enter my gate,
I hurry so I won't be late.

Karrie Hubbard, Grade 5
Sullivan Elementary School, TN

Come Back Rain

Come back rain
For you help us so
You water our crops
You give us drinking water
Come back rain
Come back

Cody Hartzell, Grade 5
Cool Spring Elementary School, NC

Water

Bubbles float beneath
The surface of the water
The breath of the fish.

Bailey Murphy, Grade 4
Briarwood Christian School, AL

Sweet Home

S weeter than candy
W ears a beautiful smile
E ntreats me to TV
E very door welcomes
T reats me with warmth and love

H appy place to be
O pen for others to share
M eets me daily with wide arms
E verything a home can be

Austin Mitchell, Grade 5
Vernon Middle School, LA

Quick Move

It makes me feel tickled inside.
To be moving in such a glorious way.
It makes me delighted every day.
By the end of the dance
your heart is pumping rapidly
and way too powerful.
All of this is the best hobby,
DANCE

Janella Beeler, Grade 5
North Middle School, TN

Hunting Early

I see a deer
Is it in fear?
I see the fawn
Right before Dawn
I see the doe
Now I see the bow
Shh
There is no breeze
Shh
Freeze…

Lake Lile, Grade 6
Ketchum Jr High School, OK

Baseball

B ase ball
A t the base ball game
S aying things that are insane
E ating junk
B aseball I love it the most at the game
A t the game
L iking it
L akers will win the game

Eli Beebe, Grade 4
Lewis Vincent Elementary School, LA

Where I'm From

I am free deep dark, blue of the water.
I am from bubbles
glistening in the tub.
I am from snow
crunching under my feet.
I am from golden earrings
sparkling on my ear lobes.
I am from oranges
turning into orange juice.
I am from the cold wind
whistling in the air.
I am from cold rain
dripping on my window,
drip, drop.

Brianna Hill, Grade 5
Tates Creek Elementary School, KY

Summer and Fall Fun

Summer
Hot, joyful
Relaxing, swimming, playing
Friends, parents, costumes, teachers
Studying, raking, screaming
Candy, cool
Fall

Pumpkins
Orange, smelly
Carving, smiling, frowning
Orchard, garden, Thanksgiving, family
Cooking, chewing, savoring
Crunchy, tasty
Turkey

Bonfires
Gleeful, exciting
Frying, making, cooking
Sticks, friends, footballs, athletes
Throwing, catching, tackling
Entertaining, awesome
Football games

Gerard Squeglia, Grade 6
Alvaton Elementary School, KY

Discipline
Discipline will contain your young.
It will sometimes make you hold your tongue.
It is very mysterious when you are serious.
Not everyone will use it, but it will come to you.
It will help you fight through.
Discipline can be mean, but if you don't
use it you will SCREAM!!!!!!!!!!!!

Crimson Halpin, Grade 5
Graham Elementary School, AL

Life Does Not Frighten Me*
Life does not frighten me
Neither does death
All my days living just like the rest
There is nothing to be scared of
Not in Heaven, nor on Earth
For life does not frighten me

I will not cower to a stranger in the dark of night
I will serve as a wall if the devil is ever to attack
Life does not frighten me

Weary sounds will not haunt me
And I have no more predators
Because life does not frighten me

Life does not frighten me
Death does not frighten me
Nothing will ever frighten me
Life does not frighten me

Kayleigh Thesenvitz, Grade 6
Inola Middle School, OK
*In response to Maya Angelou

The End
Walking in the door all happy
Girls I need to talk to you
A bomb was getting ready to go off
Tingling hands, sweating face
Nervous stomach, beating heart
Her lips were moving but I didn't believe them
He died this morning
Laying down on my bed looking at my grandfather's picture
Felt like I was floating
Blank brain
Hopeless heart
Red cheeks
Burning eyes
Eyes were like a volcano rushing its lava out
Heart broken
Without a goodbye
Up up up
Gone
In a better place

Lauren Frederick, Grade 4
Briarwood Elementary School, KY

Cleo the Cat
Soft pitter patter of tiny paws,
Dangerous looking sharp claws.
Likes to sleep and snuggle on my soft bed,
Fluffy fur on her delicate head.
The faint aroma of pet shampoo,
The smell makes my sister say "eww!"
When curled up she looks like a hat,
That is my treasured charcoal cat.
Cleo

Melissa Brooks, Grade 5
North Middle School, TN

Great Grandma's Sunset
I look up and see the sun once high in the sky,
Now low
I sit on the dew painted grass and gaze up at the
sunset's lavenders, pinks and oranges
as they paint the sky like a once blank canvas,
I picture your fragile hand reaching up and painting the sunset
as you make a smile cross my face.

Kate Dryden, Grade 4
Brookwood Elementary School, GA

October
O ctober's here don't you know,
C ome, there's no swimming, kites or boats to row.
T ime of fall,
O r play some ball!
B rrrr! It's getting colder now,
E asy summer has taken a bow.
R ed leaves are falling to the ground,

October's traveling round, round, round!

Kira Wulff, Grade 4
Wohlwend Elementary School, MO

Sitting in My Room
Sitting in my room I think about this world,
An imaginary place where I could be queen,
And do anything I wanted to do,
A world to be free,
Free from the big wide world,
A place to run wild and have no worries,
A place to have such a wonderful time,
A place to have a new start,
A place where anything can happen,
A wonderful place to have quiet,
A place where you have all the time in the world,
Think just think,
It will come to you,
You just have to imagine,
This world is a wonderful place to be.

Danielle Francis, Grade 6
Haynes Academy for Advanced Studies, LA

Trick or Treat

T he time has come to have fun
R ight on your trail
I f your house is haunted
C an we come in?
K eep an eye out for your candy

O r it will be gone!
R ather we pull pranks

T hen someone rang the doorbell
R eally quiet you open the door
E ven at night we will start yelling
A ll our costumes are scary to you
T his fun night has ended…for now!

Jessica Gill, Grade 5
First Flight Elementary School, NC

A Strange Monster

There's a monster
who has twelve weird eyes
on its flat face.

There's a monster who has
three arms that go
clockwise and never stops.

There's a monster
who's always hanging around
on the wall and that is…
a clock!

Minseok Kim, Grade 5
Estes Hills Elementary School, NC

Flip into Gymnastics!

I love my teachers,
I think it's loads of fun,
You also get to do back handsprings
and front handsprings
and all that other fun stuff.
I also don't worry about falling,
because there's always mats under me
I'm always glad to be at gymnastics.

Maggie Scarbrough, Grade 5
North Middle School, TN

If Only

If only, if only,
The woodpeckers sigh.
The bark on the tree was
as soft as the sky.
Woodpeckers below,
hungry and lonely,
He cries to the moon,
If only, if only.

Timothy Nicholas, Grade 4
Cool Spring Elementary School, NC

This Is Where I Am From

I am from going to King's Island on scorching summer days
And riding roller coasters with my mom…like the Son of the Beast.

I am from working the day away with my cousin, Jordan, building our tree house
To riding my bike up to the corner market to reward myself
with an Ale-8 for all of my hard work.

I am from having air-soft matches with my friends…
Shooting people and getting shot
Then running until I get steaming hot!

But most of all, I am from Lexington and Burgin, Kentucky,
And having fun with my friends and family.

This is where I am from.

Dustin Stewart, Grade 5
Burgin Independent School, KY

Start of a New Life

On March 3rd I was in school. I couldn't think straight. I was an eager beaver.
Every five seconds, seconds that felt like hours, I'd look at the cruel clock.
Today was a very unusual day.

Brrring!!
"Please send Tori down to the office for early dismissal."
I stopped in my tracks and packed up.
Once I was in the offices I saw Aunt Angie.
"Are you ready?" she asked. I replied, "Oh yeah."

We sat in the hospital for what seemed like a lifetime but was really only 3 hours
It smelled like the doctor's office.
Finally, Dad came out and said "One person can come and see."
All eyes spun to me, so I walked with him.
Once I was in the curtained part of a room,
I saw Mom and then the small soft newborn.

Pinkish cheeks with hair as curly as a twisty slide.
Her big blue eyes started to POP open.
She makes a sound similar to "eee" like she was saying Sissy.
She was as sweet as an angel; I wanted to hug her in my arms.
Yet, I still felt very special.
I was the first person to see her other than my parents.
She and I will be great sisters.

Tori Pettit, Grade 6
South Oldham Middle School, KY

Kendall

K ind kid that is very nice.
E ntertaining child that is very smart.
N ot a very needy boy.
D on't cheat on test or class work.
A lways focused on doing the best I can do in sports and in school.
L oves a lot of girls and games like Xbox 360 and PS2.
L ike to go to school and do work sometimes.

Kendall Durham, Grade 4
Byrns L Darden Elementary School, TN

Reminiscence

Walking through the long grass,
I stared at my kingdom,
my backyard,
a tangle of trees and grass
where anything could have happened
and possibilities were continual
and inspiration
and imagination
could have struck at any moment.
But I left this place,
in my backyard
and grew up.
I forgot the memories
of my friends and I
as we rushed through the long grass
and enjoyed the beautiful landscape.
But I will go back
and enjoy a long day
as a small child once again.

Cooper Donoho, Grade 6
Charleston County School of the Arts, SC

The Wet Nose!

I woke up this morning to a big wet nose on my arm
I push it away and go back to sleep.
Later something licks my face
but I push it away and go back to sleep.
All of a sudden something jumps on my bed
I sit up in bed and realize that it is my
dog that wanted to be LOVED!

Ashley Howard, Grade 6
Center Place Restoration School, MO

Baseball Player

I am a baseball player.
I wonder if I will hit a home run.
I hear the crowd yelling my name.
I see the big lights in the corner of my eye.
I want to make my friends and family proud.
I am a baseball player.
I pretend I'm going to the World Series.
I feel mad if I strikeout.
I touch the smooth wood of my bat.
I worry the coach might bench me.
I cry when I get hit by the pitch.
I am a baseball player.
I understand I might not be the best.
I say I can do anything.
I dream I am the league M.V.P.
I hope I win the World Series.
I try to get the victory.
I am a baseball player.

Joshua Kuntze, Grade 4
Wohlwend Elementary School, MO

Softball

Softball
One hot summer day
Bases are loaded.
There are two outs.
I'm up to bat.
No noises were made except the chattering of teeth.
Thump Thump my heart sings nervously.

I could hear my coach pulling her hair out.
My nervous teammates surrounded me.
As I got in the batters box.
Smiles appeared on the other teams faces.
Thump Thump my heart sings nervously.

I swung the bat.
As I swung I heard a thiiiing noise.
I looked up and ran to 1st base as the ball went over the fence.
Thump Thump my heart sings joyfully.

As I ran in I received the game ball.
Thump Thump my heart sings joyfully.

Chelsea Mowery, Grade 5
Childersburg Middle School, AL

Choice

Life is but a rolling starlight sky.
Or it can be desert wasteland.
It's your choice not mine.
It follows you,
Wherever you go.
The guilt of a lie is not all alone.
You know the truth.
But time seems to hold you back.
I want to tell.
B-L-A-C-K!
I want to live an abundant life.
Free of these haunting shadows that follow.
I want to do the right thing.
In my heart I am good.
But friends make you feel like a swirling pool of thought.
I will be good…
Someday I will live free.
Away from this dark shadow that haunts me.
I will prevail this hopeful dream.
Now is my time to make a choice.

Dylan Ward, Grade 6
Benton County School of the Arts, AR

That Old Stinky Box

Once there was a brown dingy old box,
It was filled with dirty smelly socks,
They did not smell very sweet,
They smelt like Granny's feet,
Don't worry it is covered with metal locks.

Walker Nugent, Grade 4
Eastside Elementary School, GA

Fall Wonders

F all is wonderful, the best time of the year —
A ll the children laughing and playing in the leaves
L oving all the wonders of those beautiful fall leaves,
L inking arm in arm back to school they go

W hisking away summer and plunging into snow,
O ff and on the wind will blow letting the leaves fall,
N oon is struck on the clock and everyone hurries inside —
D rinking apple cider puts summer memories aside
E arthly critters scurry knowing fall is here —
R ascally little squirrels gather nuts for winter —
S omething marvellous is happening because everything knows the fall wonders are here.

Mary Galey, Grade 5
Palmetto Christian Academy, SC

Thoughts

A thought spreads its wings and flies into your mind.
It sits on a perch and rests for a while with many others.
After some time it will spread its wings yet again and fly to another perch.
It will land on that perch only to rest there until it is ready to find another perch.

If written down or spoken aloud, a thought can travel to many different perches.
It can also create new, wonderful thoughts. Those new thoughts will sprout wings and fly to
many perches with the others.
Soon these new thoughts will create even newer thoughts.

Sometimes in one's mind there can be thoughts upon thoughts upon thoughts upon thoughts,
all spread out onto one very large perch.
Each thought must leave shortly after landing to make room for more.
But in some other minds, this is different.
In these minds, there are many perches, and there is enough room for many tired thoughts.
If a thought becomes an idea, it stays at its perch until it becomes a reality.
But when it is a reality it becomes more than what it used to be.
It becomes more agile, more graceful, and it can occupy many a perch.
And eventually that reality will spread its wings and fly to the perch in your mind.

Mary Alice Schultz, Grade 6
St Mary's School, SC

Autumn

Down come the leaves, down come the leaves.
All colorfully dressed and neatly pressed, twirling down from the bough of trees.

Gorgeous leaf women escorted by graceful leaf men marching down the wooded stair.
Stepping across the ballroom floor and sitting down in their own little chair.

Now the leaves shall drink, feast, and have all sorts of fun.

Tis now the time to dance and gracefully prance two by two about the room.
The leaves are tripping and tramping and whirling and swirling until their stems begin to ache.

The party is in full swing and the leaves are flying about,
but soon they all lay on the floor sleeping in silence with nary a whisper or shout about.

Never will the forest see so much cheer until come autumn next year.

Hannah Maeser, Grade 6
Mountain Gap Middle School, AL

Poetry

Poetry makes me mad it makes me strain,
It makes me hurt and feel the pain!
Some people might like it but,
Poetry kills my brain!

All the troops are coming to attack,
I feel them creeping up on my back!
Does anyone have a paper sack,
Poetry kills my brain!

When it comes to poetry, I'm dumb as a cow,
I belong on the farm with my plow,
I am sorry poetry is just not my game,
Poetry kills my brain!

Emily Hammes, Grade 5
Providence Academy, TN

Grace

Really tall, very thin, red hair
Basketball shorts and loves any tees,
"Y'all" and "IDK"
Round-off backhandsprings at Olympiad
Flipping on the trampoline
My brother and his friends, frozen water bottles
And too much homework all annoy me
iPod with me…
Everywhere I go and…
Video games — What fun!
Hot wings — Yum!

Grace Richmeyer, Grade 5
Our Lady Catholic School, MO

The Puffy Owl

He was fluffy and wary,
But who knew he was scary!
He had yellow eyes and yellow beak,
With silent brown feathers he could sneak.
He was the scariest thing
That the mice would ever see,
But it's a good thing
They chose to flee!

Zac Selvidge, Grade 4
Cleveland Elementary School, OK

My Mom

I love my mom she makes me feel very calm
My mom loves me too
and not very few.
She really does care
that's why she makes everything fair.
My mom is very pretty
But she always calls me needy,
She says I've got to eat my fruit
and then says I'm very cute.

Michael Thompson, Grade 5
Franklin Elementary School, OK

Things I'm Thankful For

I love my life, I love my school
I help my friends, and follow the rules
I take care of my cats, dogs, and more
Here are some more things I'm thankful for
My TV, my toys, my clock, my room
My gifts that I receive on my birthday in June
My bat, my glove, my home, my bed
My skateboard that is black and red
But the biggest thing I'm thankful for
Bigger than a toy, a clock and even more
Better than a plane that flies below and above
Is my family that I really love

Gage Bloomfield, Grade 6
Father McCartan Memorial School, MO

Christmas Tree

Christmas tree, standing tall
I see you in the middle of my living room
Christmas tree, you never fall
You stand to guard the gifts from anything
Christmas tree, you are St. Nick's call
Without you we would have no gifts at all

You are a wonder
With your smooth bark
And your green leaves
Christmas tree, Christmas tree, Oh Christmas tree

Jorge Garcia, Grade 6
Chapin Middle School, SC

Leaves

Leaves, leaves, leaves what wonderful leaves.
They swish they sway they twirl
And whirl and every once
In a while they even dip and dive.
Leaves, leaves, leaves,
what wonderful leaves.

John Heavner, Grade 4
First Wesleyan Christian School, NC

The Pamlico Sound

Foggy mornings like snow falling
Crab boats bringing in their catch
Pelicans gulping down their fish
Gas gurgling in the boat like a wave lapping at the shore
Salty air crisp and damp as it sprays from the ocean below
Dead fish floating on the top waiting for the crabs to take it
Crispy shrimp in my mouth
Fish as crunchy as French Fries
Slimy muddy nets full of fish
Cold mornings on the boat
I feel small and out ruled.

Laney Glover, Grade 4
Bailey Elementary School, NC

For a Dream

For a dream to come true
You have to have a dream.
Like you can't go somewhere
If you don't know where you'll go.
So first you've got to find a dream
And then a dream come true.
Once you have a dream then
You can find a path,
Anyone will do.
Just remember one more thing,
No one is in your way.
The last part to a dream come true
Is just to follow through.

Angelina Olson, Grade 4
St Thomas More School, NC

Hope

Hope is like a flower,
In the midst of a barren field,
Blooming small but powerful.

Hope is like a trickle of water,
Fighting to give what is good,
Slowly becoming a mighty river.

Hope is like a kitten,
Hunting its first mouse,
Imagining it's a tiger.

Bethany Cardenas, Grade 6
IA Lewis Elementary School, LA

Rain's Lullaby

The rain with it's melody
    The drip
        drip
    plop
        plop
As it pounds on my roof
I listen to the pitter patter
    drip drop
Ringing out in perfect harmony
    The beat of the thunder
As it claps to the rhythm of the rain
    It lulls me to sleep
    like a sweet lullaby
and soon the drip drip
    plop plop
        pitter patter
    drip drop
        clap clap

    STOPS
Leaving me to dream of beautiful things

Ashley LaFrance, Grade 6
St Mary's School, SC

Play

Today is an icy hot day;
A wonderful day to play!
I ask my mother all the time
Can we go outside and play?

I look at the sky above,
And love to twirl around,
And see and hear the birds that sing
And look at insects on the ground!

Today the leaves were falling,
And calling on my name;
They scrunch and they crunch
As I run around and play!

But now I am older,
I do not play as I did,
But I still go out and breathe the air,
That I used to play in.

Sierra Owens, Grade 5
Providence Academy, TN

Why Spiders Creep Me Out!

Spiders are creepy crawly bugs.
They like to crawl into caves.
It is a tiny little bug that crawls.
They have puny little eyes.
They have eight creepy legs.
That's why spiders creep me OUT!

Sarah Hurt, Grade 5
North Middle School, TN

Broadway

Broadway
is a nice town
always have fun around
Broadway School is top rate and great
always

Jacob Smith, Grade 5
Broadway Elementary School, NC

Snowflakes

White and pearly
Even sometimes curly
Falling down
Upon your crown
Everyone loves them, surely

Wet and cold
So unique they can't be sold
Never the same
Snowflakes the name
Make them out of a paper fold

Ciara Troitino, Grade 4
Moyock Elementary School, NC

Bad Weather

The day was hot but now it's not,
I feel a sudden temperature drop.
A storm is coming I can tell,
I know the signs by now, so well.
The wind will whip, the trees will bend
My outside fun will have to end.
It started to pour, I went indoors.
I like watching storms,
They're very entertaining,
It's also fun to sleep when it's raining.

Ben Dean, Grade 6
Seven Holy Founders School, MO

Candy

C hocolate covered
A lways delicious
N ever ever bad
D ecorated and
Y ummy

Hannah Meyer, Grade 5
First Flight Elementary School, NC

Spider

S pinning a little web of
P ure silk. I see a small spider
I n the window
D ew glistens in the web
E ating a small helpless fly
R epeating it over again.

Amanda Taylor, Grade 5
First Flight Elementary School, NC

Divorces

Sometimes it's hard,
You might want to send a card,
But if you're sad, don't be mad.
Because you're in a bad situation,
Don't be scared, even though
They're still fighting.
You will still be their baby.
Divorces

It can be rough,
But just be tough.
They brought you home,
And gave you a name.

Don't be ashamed,
Don't lose your attitude.
Divorces

They might tear the picture,
But they will not ever tear you apart.

Cassandra Griffin, Grade 4
A H Watwood Elementary School, AL

My Walls

My walls they're filled with writing
Everyone that stepped in
Wrote on my bedroom walls

They were filled with names, jokes, comments,
Signatures and drawings

Every time you walk in
There is something new to see

They were unique
Like no one else's

Background a bright sunny yellow
But the walls were filled with many different colors
From writing and drawings everywhere

Not plain
Not boring
They're exiting

But they're definitely my walls
Know why?
They're different

Anna Hall, Grade 6
East Oldham Middle School, KY

Megan

My sister is the best sister in the world,
You smell and taste the strawberry perfume she wears every day
Every morning I hear her radio blasting
Telling me to wake up.

If you look in her room you see
It looks like a tornado went by.
But I look in her room and feel my biggest fear
That she is gone forever
But then I see her walk across the street to our
Neighbor's house and get in the car with Lindsey.

Getting home from school,
Starts her homework
With her radio blasting and all you can hear
Is BOOM and BAM
Like we are getting shot at.

But I look at her smiling face and see
That she is a daisy that has just
Bloomed on the first day of spring.
I am proud to call her my sister
And love her very much and
Know she loves me too.

Makenzie Rae Engel, Grade 6
South Oldham Middle School, KY

The Lion's Mane Jellyfish

The Lion's Mane jellyfish is aptly named.
Just as the lion's mane is thick,
The jellyfish's tentacles are one hundred strings.
As the lion's mane blows in the wind,
The jellyfish's tentacles flow through the water.
The lion's weapons are its teeth,
While the jellyfish uses its stingers.
The lion's territory is the plains,
The jellyfish floats in the oceans.
The lion is the king of the beasts,
The jellyfish is a terror of the seas.

Luke Bledsoe, Grade 4
Sequoyah Elementary School, TN

Horses

Horses are a gift of life
They are always a wonderful sight.
I love to watch their graceful moves
As they gallop through the dunes.
Jumping fences is such a thrill
As you ride in the field.
You take many ups and downs
As you jump fences then you turn around.
The day will soon be over so you would have a frown.
But don't worry
Tomorrow your face would turn around.

Jordan Ricketts, Grade 4
Evangelical Christian School, TN

Fishing Life

When I go fishing I see trees and
I hear the bees buzzing above my head.
I see fish that I had on a dish.
I see boats that make people gloat.

I saw a squirrel that went inside its own burrow.
I saw a fish under water, but I didn't bother.
I heard boats churning while they were turning
I heard a fish splashing while they were dashing.

The sun helped me have fun.
The sun made me tired.
The wind on my skin made me grin.
When I went fishing the worm made me squirm.

When I went fishing I drank a Coke
and it almost made me choke.
I wish I could taste fish,
but it wasn't on my list.

When we went fishing the mosquitos would bite
and that's just not right.
Instead of putting a worm on a hook
I would rather be reading a book.

Logan Wyatt, Grade 4
Schaffner Traditional Elementary School, KY

Baseball

Seth is my name.
Baseball is my game.
I play first and pitch
That seems to be my niche
It's what I love,
That's why I have a golden glove!

Seth Murphy, Grade 5
Paint Lick Elementary School, KY

Shoulda, Woulda, Coulda

It's the night before it's due
I don't know what to do
I'm runnin' out of time
The blame is only mine
Shoulda, Woulda, Coulda

My brother made me mad
I'm feelin' kinda bad
I hit him on the head
And that is all I said
Shoulda, Woulda, Coulda

My mother told me "no"
And all I said was "so"
Then I said things I regret
I wish I could forget
Shoulda, Woulda, Coulda

People pass through our lives
And in spite of all we try
I regret things I didn't say
Now they are gone this very day
Shoulda, Woulda, Coulda
Have No Regrets

Madison Jones, Grade 6
Queen of Angels Catholic School, GA

Puppy Love

Oh, I love you puppy
Yes I do
I know you're gone
I'll always hold you true
I miss you so
I wish you didn't go
Your brown little tail
Your cute little wail
Oh, I love you puppy

Steven Miller, Grade 6
Ketchum Jr High School, OK

Wind

The wind is graceful,
It is peaceful and joyful,
It could be harmful.

Priscilla Hearn, Grade 5
EA Harrold Elementary School, TN

I the Red Tailed Hawk

I the red tailed hawk
I fly on the thermals that carry me up into the sky.
Their warm air ruffles the feathers on my wings.
And it makes me think of all the things, that make me, me and me only.
My dark brown feathers, my snow white chest,
and my blood red tail that shines like fire in the sun.
And with my golden yellow eyes and swift talons there is nowhere my prey can run.
I plunge to the earth, as it rushes up at me I extend my claws,
This is my territory my place my land and I rule,
I am a red tail hawk.

Jordan Williams, Grade 5
William Southern Elementary School, MO

Sunsets

Sunsets are like explosions of colorful fireworks.

They fill the cold dark night with colors that you could only see in a dream.
Sunsets are my favorite things to look at,

Every night I wait for the sun to slowly set into warm colors.

Sunsets are as colorful as rainbows only better.
They take your mind on a journey.

Sunsets, don't they just look amazing?

Jarren Thomas, Grade 5
Greathouse Shryock Traditional Elementary School, KY

The Day of the Scary Crocodiles

It was an incredibly brilliant day outside,
When thirsty, leathery, crocodiles with ripples, crawled out of a pond.

I let out an intense scream of fight,
I was terrified! They were fierce as a wolf, with teeth as white as chalk.
At first I was motionless, but then I became hysterical!
Their eyes were glowing and glistening, they looked like a slithering sea of green.
With my heart pounding and my fierce panting,
I rode the green sea like a boat.
I was running as fast as a tiger, their gigantic teeth tearing at my shoes,
My arms flailing in the wind.
But when I shuffled to the end of the crocodiles,
My never-ending path of fear had not ended.

I let out a hollow shrill but no help approached,
So I continued to dart off like an arrow.
I began to come to the end of the gurgling river of crocs
When an ocean of teeth had me motionless.

Then came a girl with straw-colored hair
By the name of Sandy, to the rescue.
She said without proper croc techniques
There is no royal road to success!
I was saved.

Lucas Pegram, Grade 4
Carver Elementary School, NC

Gentle Breeze (Childhood Memory)

A gentle breeze
Blows on my face
Making my hair dance
And my insides laugh!
I run with it, jump with it.
And then it's gone.
That's ok,
My mind will remember.

Chelsea Dunn, Grade 5
Francine Delany New School for Children, NC

Football in the Rain

Playing football in the rain.
Always gives me such a pain.

Slipping and falling on the grass so hard.
Then the safety acts like a guard.

The safety knocks over the guy with the ball.
He fumbles and tumbles and takes a fall.

Zachary Kaefer, Grade 4
Moyock Elementary School, NC

Junky Room

My room, my room
looks like a tornado hit with
everything crashing in all directions!

My room is a full load of laundry,
that smells 100 years old!

My room is covered in chocolate
with cockroaches crawling on it!

My room looks like a war field after
30 bombs hit!

My room is chaotic!

Chris Tipton, Grade 5
Greathouse Shryock Traditional Elementary School, KY

King Tut

My dog's name was King Tut.
My brothers and I play football
And King Tut tackles us when we run.
I was playing the game Desert Storm
And he jumped on my head.
He is big and strong.
He can pull my daddy's truck.
We put a rope around him
And goes for the food
And pulls the truck behind him.
He can jump to the top of our porch.
He can even bite holes in bones.

Denzel Rodgers, Grade 5
Lee A Tolbert Community Academy, MO

Grand Canyon

Over the summer
Me, and my family went to the Grand Canyon
Walking
Two and a half miles along the canyon
It was as hot as the sun there
Seeing the Colorado River
Flowing as fast as a jet plane
Going to the edge
Of the Grand Canyon
It is so deep, It is a little scary
Hearing echoes of my yells (Hello hello hello)
The trail from the top to the bottom
It was as long as a train
Seeing people ride donkeys
Up and down the trail like ants
The hotel
Is as tall as a T-Rex
Also you can eat breakfast, lunch, and dinner there
"Well" It's time to get back on the train
Hoping to come back soon
Bye-Bye Grand Canyon

Stone Passmore, Grade 4
Briarwood Elementary School, KY

Brothers

B rothers are always friends
R unning and jumping all over the beds.
O n everything they help each other.
T ime is over until the next day.
H a, ha, ha as we play.
E verywhere we go it's a lot of fun to play.
R unning to the playground to have a lot of fun today.
S ometimes you're tired but it's a blast when you play all day.

Alex Perez, Grade 4
Nesbit Elementary School, GA

King's Island

When I got to King's Island I rode all the rides
I rode all the rollercoasters, drop zones, and everything inside
But there was just this one ride
This one ride hidden inside
I had ridden other rides
I got in line,
    saw people getting off
    who couldn't even walk
    in a straight line
I buckled, I felt fine
Spinning, rocking how sublime
Back and forth higher, higher vomit flies
Right across the sky
Shoes flying, birds saying good-bye
I got a new favorite ride

Juan Arguelles, Grade 5
Cline Elementary School, KY

Skateboard

I have four wheels
And a flat top
With edges that curve so slightly
I can go down a hill
While a car goes by
As you can see I am a very slim thing
I can do an ollie
Or a kick flip
So can you guess what I could be…
A skateboard!

Madison Dingle, Grade 5
Woodland Elementary School, KY

Skateboarding

I like skateboarding
it is fun
you just push
then you're done

So much equipment
you have to wear
or if you get hurt
your mom won't care

To go down a half pipe
you must have good eyesight
so that you can see
where you are going

Zachary Moreland, Grade 5
Woodland Elementary School, KY

Dancer

Dancers spinning everywhere,
Turning all about,
Leaping so high,
As if into the clouds.
Then land gracefully,
Only to once again begin
To point, spin, and sashay
Into the wings,
Waiting for my cue,
Beginning to understand what I do.
I AM A DANCER!

Sarah O'Neal, Grade 5
Corinth-Holders Elementary School, NC

Where I Need to Be

The woods are full of wonder.
I feel so good outside,
Where the tall trees are.
In the fall I see the wonderful leaves.
That's where I feel I need to be,
With the leaves and trees.

Breanna Stovall, Grade 4
Ode Maddox Elementary School, AR

He Walks

He walks he passes many people

They ridicule him for his looks
He does not listen

He keeps on walking
People are calling him names

One stops him and says why do
you keep walking he says

Because if I don't keep walking
I will have to listen to you

Ridicule me and so he keeps
Walking

John Deitrick, Grade 6
Ketchum Jr High School, OK

Love Is Red

Love is red.
It smells like a rose bloom.
It tastes like dark chocolate.
It sounds like a singing bird.
It feels like a hug from your mom.
It looks like a rainbow in the sky.
Love is caring for someone.

Chris Kelly, Grade 4
Pines Elementary School, NC

Imagination

The hilly land
with trees so tall on top
Seems as though it is
a mountain
Towering above me.
My imagination runs wild.

The soft, green fields
rolling smooth like the sea.
As I stare off into the distance,
My imagination runs wild.

Emily Christisen, Grade 5
St Vincent Elementary School, MO

Freedom

F reedom in the USA.
R eturning from fighting.
E very day we fight.
E verlasting war.
D ying for our rights.
O thers coming.
M ore heroes every day.

Roger Goheen, Grade 6
Temple Hill Elementary School, KY

Spirit

Christmas
Happy joyful
Celebrating giving caring
Tree decorations church bible
Reading shouting praying
Generous thankful
Praise

Sal Hemingway, Grade 5
C. C. Spaulding Elementary School, NC

Ode to a Candle

Oh candle,
you complete me.
I love your smell.
It smells just like
strawberries and peaches.
When I smell you I
feel like I'm in paradise.
You smell so good,
I don't want you to end.
Compared to other candles
you are the best.
Oh candle,
You make my day.

Kennedy Garner, Grade 6
Dyer Elementary & Jr High School, TN

I Like Hockey

I like hockey,
When I get the puck,
You will run out of luck,
And you will never stop me.

Just give me a couple of years,
And you will see,
I just might grow up,
Like the Great Gretzky!

Pete Nahn, Grade 6
Seven Holy Founders School, MO

Oh Frog

I have a frog with two round eyes.
He has a big mouth for catching flies.
He once had a tail now a lump.
Four long legs so he can jump.
He's got a belly shaped like a jug.
I guess from eating all those bugs.
He likes to play and jump around
In the air up and down.
He seems to be a nice frog.
He lives in the woods in a hole on a log.
He doesn't come out till after dark.
If you want to see him, go to the park.

Brittany Parker, Grade 6
Appling County Middle School, GA

Where Am I From?

Where am I from?
I am from the place where the tea is sweet,
I walk gracefully and proud.

Trees are everywhere with colors by its side,
Lime green is very pretty in the summer,
There are many landscapes here,
Mountains are at the top,
Beaches are at the bottom,
And ponds are in the middle,
Yellow jasmine is our state flower.

There are different sized things where I am from,
We have a lot of different animals,
Monkeys are even in our zoo.

Where I am from people are proud to be here,
I am from the southern part of the United States,
South Carolina is where I was born and where my home is.

Mary Myers Clark, Grade 6
Beck Academy, SC

The Right Way

I think all organs should be,
Given to someone who is rightful.
Not given to someone who needs it,
Due to their bad choices.
That is the right way.
I think all ages of kids should be,
Adopted throughout the world.
Not babies and young kids because
People think they are cute and need most help.
But kids of all ages need help.
That is the right way.
I think that all world hunger should be ended.
Everyone should get food and be fed.
Not just kids that live alone,
But parents are just as important.
That is the right way.

Michael Jacobs, Grade 6
Discovery School @ Reeves Rogers, TN

Mice, Mice, Mice

Mice, mice, mice
I hate mice dancing
all night sleeping all day
I hate, hate, hate these mice, mice, mice

They keep me up, up.
Those mice, mice, mice
play all night and sleep all day
I do not like those mice

Caleb Yeary, Grade 4
Tazewell-New Tazewell Primary School, TN

Plant

A green plant
when it grows,
has roots and a stem.
Some have leaves, some have petals, some grow food
Some kill others, some eat flies
Some save lives

Chris Nicholas, Grade 4
E O Young Jr Elementary School, NC

I Am

I am a crazy girl who wants to fly.
I wonder how it would feel to soar over a grassy plain.
I hear the *whoosh* of the wind in my ears.
I see a city, a bird, a plane beneath me.
I want to feel the icy caress of a cloud on my face
I am a crazy girl who wants to fly.

I pretend that I am a bird or a plane.
I feel happy when the sun smiles.
I touch a star.
I worry about my friends and what they think of me.
I cry when I lose a loved one.
I am a crazy girl who wants to fly.

I understand that we don't always get what we want.
I say "I want life to be life"
I dream about flying
I try to love everything
I hope I will live forever
I am a crazy girl who wants to fly.

Oriana Messer, Grade 6
R D and Euzelle P Smith Middle School, NC

Artist

I am an artist and I love to draw.
I wonder if I'm ever going to be famous.
I hear cameras flashing at my side.
I see news reporters and famous actors.
I want to have artwork on the news.
I am an artist and I love to draw.

I pretend to be in a contest in Japan.
I feel happy when I win the contest.
I touch the paintbrushes in the art studio.
I worry that Japan will not like my art.
I cry if they do not like my art.
I am an artist and I love to draw.

I understand whether they like it or not.
I say my art is for Japan's minister.
I dream that Japan's minister will like my art.
I try to win the award at the contest.
I hope I win the contest in Japan.
I am an artist and I love to draw.

Courtney Bailey, Grade 5
Byrns L Darden Elementary School, TN

Skateboard Cool

I skateboard like a darted arrow
Flow like a river
With turbulent waves
Austin Roberson, Grade 5
Carver Elementary School, NC

May

There was a day in may.
When I went to the bay.
On a hot summer day.
Where I saw some hay.
And I saw a blue jay.
Going outside to play.
I saw it flying away.
In a way.
I said yay.
Kayla Morgan, Grade 6
Graham Elementary School, AL

My Sports

Baseball is at the top of my list
Tennis is lost in the midst
Football is cool
Volleyball drowned in the pool
Basketball is sweet
My sports and hockey don't meet
Soccer is great
Jousting is not very popular in this state
Sports and I are like peas and carrots
Someday I hope I will get lots of merits
Jacob Baird, Grade 5
Contentnea Elementary School, NC

Thanksgiving Adventure

Oh yes
That time
Visiting family
Rejoicing grace
Feasting greatly
Playing football
Watching too
Mosquitoes biting
Mountain climbing
Feet hurting
Camping trip
Wind whipping
Enormous forest
Cool weather
Rough ground
Birds chirping
Tired people
Cold people
Great day
Thanksgiving Day
Trey Shields, Grade 4
Center Elementary School, GA

When Autumn Comes

I watch as the green leaves change into red, yellow, orange, and brown,
The orange of the pumpkins color looks so bright against the green stem,
I watch as the tricker treater runs from house to house to get candy,
I gracefully take my knife and cut my pumpkin into a happy little face,
I can't wait for autumn!

Madison Gahafer, Grade 5
Palmetto Christian Academy, SC

A Mother's Love

A Mother's Love brought you into the world.
A Mother's Love you cannot resist.
A Mother's Love is as sweet as candy.
A Mother's Love carries you through your pain.
A Mother's Love is with you always.
A Mother's Love will follow you to the end of time.
I always have a love for my Mother, this is why I say Mother's Love.

Davion Rankins, Grade 6
Appling County Middle School, GA

Where I'm From

I am from peddling my red and white tricycle and cooking in my own wooden kitchen
I am from the dark green, four door garage and the old wooden barn
From sitting by the rocky, moist pond and smelling the fresh flower garden
I am from the big stone house and matching chairs
From the playhouse and all the cousins
I am from smelling sweet honey suckles and the fresh taste of steak off the grill
I am from paper making and turkey Thanksgiving dinners
From swimming in the pool and watching home videos
I am from bankers to travelers, decorators to sunbathers
From hotdog tongues and Italian accents to long lives, blue eyes and brown hair
I am from Eliza, Hugh and Mattie to Uncle John, Grandpa John, and Cousin John
From Lily x 3, Landon, and Lindsey
I am from big family partying and big vs. little sibling fights
From playing charades and piano to laughing oh so loud
I am from mac and cheese, pasta, pizza, milkshakes, and Koolaid popsicles
I am from St. James and St. Francis to Junior Daughters of the King
I am from "Deal with it!" "Suck it up!" and always our families' "That's not fair!"
I am from Louisville, Monteagle, Charlottesville, King George and New England
This is where I'm from

Eliza Hill, Grade 5
Kenwood Station Elementary School, KY

If I Were in Charge of the World

If I were in charge of the world, you would not have to pay for anything,
also ice cream would be your every meal.

If I were in charge of the world, you wouldn't have to eat any of your vegetables,
and you wouldn't have any sisters.

If I were in charge of the world, you could play any sport without messing up,
also all the movies would be rated G.

If I were in charge of the world, I would own every bank,
and I would have everything in the world.

Andrew Lentini, Grade 5
Eminence Middle School, KY

Giraffe

This beautiful
  Elegant, graceful animal,
    Is one of the tallest of them all

  Getting food from the huge, green trees,
    With its long spotted neck
      Slowly walking, chewing its meal

    Long necked
      Spotted creature,
        Gigantic as a building

      Its brown spots so stunning,
        Shining in the sun
          He is wandering around curiously,
          What an elegant creature he is.

Andrea Mariano, Grade 6
Haynes Academy for Advanced Studies, LA

White Snowflake

White is a cold snowflake,
It feels like an icicle numbing your hand,
It looks like soft, fluffy pillow in a field of snow,
It sounds like running water in a silent room,
It smells like thick, warm eggnog in a mug,
It tastes like vanilla ice cream in a giant bowl,
White is a cold snowflake

Levi Shouse, Grade 5
Eminence Middle School, KY

I Am Lost

I am the thunder amidst a bellowing storm.
I am shallow water trapped in the deep end. I am lost.

I am a silent cry for help.
I am the eerie feeling penetrating your skin. I am lost.

I am a single word in an endless story.
I am the wind on a freezing day. I am lost.

I am a speck of dirt in a desert.
I am a star amongst no others. I am lost.

I am the spark that lights a fire.
I am the star that lights the sky. I am found.

I am the thought that creates something new.
I am a line in a picture of great wonders. I am found.

I am a thread in the finest cloth.
I am a flower in a great field. I am found.

I am a tune in a beautiful song.
I am a jewel in a majestic crown. I am found.

Mackenzie Bailey, Grade 5
Springfield Elementary School, SC

Gertie

A white stripe on chest
Mickey Mouse collar
big brown eyes
rolling all around.

Begging for food
furry tail
little ears
black shiny coat.

Full of energy
licking my face
running sideways
huge paws.

Big sharp teeth
slimy big nose
playing with cat
sticking nose in couch.

Always following me
big feet and legs
long skinny tail
barking every night.

Allison Privette, Grade 4
Schaffner Traditional Elementary School, KY

Mystery

I am a tiger
that creeps through my maze.
The mystery of which path to take,
ancestors who surround me
in Sweden, Austria, and Ireland

My cries are like gusts of winds
that just disappear when out of my mouth.
The stream is near to my success
therefore, I stand proud with courage

I am the rock
that no one can move.
Now I will run with strength and dignity,
smooth sailing isn't life
I will survive that viscous wave

Sweet things surround me
and bitter things in disguise.
My friends will help me
ride that roller coaster ride.
I come out of the darkness
With better thoughts in my head
At home at last safe in bed.

Jeni Erickson, Grade 6
Beck Academy, SC

Cats/Dogs
Cats
fuzzy, adorable
running, climbing, meowing
predator, hunter, animal, friend
shedding, panting, barking
smart, fast
Dogs
Kat Smith, Grade 5
Briarwood Christian School, AL

Help!!!
I entered a poem contest,
My paper is blank,
I have a lot of trouble,
I can't even think.

I got a sharp pencil
I started to write
I was shaking so hard
It didn't seem right.

Should I write about animals,
Fruits or air,
Rainbows, school
Ice cream or hair?

Computers, chairs
Magnets too,
Or maybe I should write about
Kudzu!

I'm really stressed,
I got a little afraid,
I wondered when the poem's due,
IT'S TODAY!!!
Chelsea Patma, Grade 5
Nesbit Elementary School, GA

Getting Ready
Baseball is fun.

You need a glove, bat,
baseball field, a hat, cleats,
team jersey, batting gloves,
and a baseball bag.

First you try out
before you're placed for a team.

Practice, practice, practice
every single day.

Get ready set…play ball!
Wes Hutton, Grade 5
North Middle School, TN

Flying into Clouds
I peek out the window
A smile rises upon my face
We enter the clear pillow
Beautiful, white surroundings
Zooming, I can barely embrace
The excitement that
Keeps my heart pounding
Danielle Ferens, Grade 5
E O Young Jr Elementary School, NC

Rainbows
As I lay in my bed,
I think of colors in my head.
I think of colors like blue and green,
In all of the rainbows that I've seen.
Orange and yellow are so bright,
They make a rainbow look just right.
I had a thought and then I said,
"I think my favorite of all is red."
A rainbow's shape is a bend,
And a pot of gold waits at the end.
Lindsey Harris, Grade 5
EA Harrold Elementary School, TN

Friends
Friends like to be study-buddies
When homework comes around.
Friends try to cheer you up
When you are falling down.
Friends try not to get mad
When you change the plan.
Friends!
Mariana Rivera, Grade 6
St Patrick's School, AL

Whitetail Deer
Whitetail deer are on the move.
They are going to the hemlock grove.
The deer are cautious, very cautious.
They are ready to bolt,
If something or someone jolts.
The sound of a gun,
Will make them bolt.
finally they hear a twig break and then,
Bang!
The deer bolt,
They're faster than lightning.
Every deer is there in the group,
But they keep running.
They run until their muscles explode.
They look around,
The hunter has missed.
Then a fawn and a doe kissed
Derek Johnston, Grade 6
North Shelby Elementary School, MO

Toes
Toes are five tiny people
in a row,
Sneaking inside of a smelly cave!
Dalton Schnurbusch, Grade 5
St Vincent Elementary School, MO

Rainy Day
Rain, a name
Rain, a thought
Rain dripping from the ceiling into a pot
Rainy morning and rainy day
Drip, drip, dripping
Slip, slip, slipping
Rainy day stare
Rainy day glare
Rainy day tears
Rainy day fears
Rain all night and day
Rain, go away!
Rain, rain falling fast
Rain hits the window glass.
Oh, how I wish it would go away!
I want to go out to play.
I want to see the sun
And not the clouds.
Yet the sun won't come out
Of its rainy day shrouds.
Jennie Jumper, Grade 6
Blackmon Road Middle School, GA

Softball
Roses are red,
Violets are blue,
I like softball
How about you.

You get to swing the bat
and get people out.
It's really fun you should try.
I like softball I really do.
Peyton Nace, Grade 5
West Marion Elementary School, MS

My Dog: Jazzeppi
Jazzeppi is my dog.
I take him for a jog.
We walk up hills and down,
All around town.

When I sit down to eat,
He begs for tiny treats.
Jazzeppi is my dog you see,
And always a friend to me.
Michael J. Suarez, Grade 5
Our Lady of Fatima School, MS

Love Is a River

Love is a river
Rivers flow through nature
Love flows through your heart
Fish have a special place in rivers
Friends and family have a special place in your heart
Love is a river
Smooth and steady

Jordyan Watson, Grade 5
Des Arc Elementary School, AR

Ocean Shore

Waves splashing up on shore
going back down making arresting noises.
Shells all the way across the shore line
waiting to be washed back up.
A seagull flying in the sky
swooping down to get some fish.
The sun shining brightly
lighting up the middle of the ocean.
The back of the ocean very placid
like a dead lake as still as can be
waiting for the next day.

Kennedy Hopper, Grade 5
Rossville Elementary School, GA

Raindrops

Raindrops on my window pane
There's nothing that's been the same
Since the sun faded out and gray faded in
Nothing's been better than then
Rain keeps falling on me
Gray skies are all I see
The sun shines through
Nothing left but dew

Natalie Stewart, Grade 6
Woodland Presbyterian School, TN

NASCAR

The cars are a rainbow
Flashing every 10 seconds,
As they race to win the
Daytona 500!

The fans are a crowded city!
The cheering
Is the sound of a drag strip!
The color calibrates its win!

When the color pulls into the winner's circle,
The crowd cheers
As he pops open a Gatorade
And throws it all over the crowd!

Ryan Richeson, Grade 6
College View Middle School, KY

Grandma

The green freeze pops,
The hugs that never stop!
The games of baseball,
The light left on for me in the hall,
The trips out to the farm,
The times she kept me from harm,

Then came the hospital care,
You in a wheelchair,
The feeling that you weren't ok,
The days now you can't come play,
Now you only lay in bed,
Sometimes you look like you're even dead,
I know you still love me,
Although you don't know me,
But why did it have to be this way,
Grandma I love you still and miss
You to this day.

Brenton Badley, Grade 6
Ketchum Jr High School, OK

The Marines

When you're in the Marines they order you around
it's kind of like the dog pound,
When the drill instructor yells in your face
you feel like you want to get out of this place,
The sound of the gunfire fills you with fear,
going through your head is come on let's get out of here.
Finally when you get home and settle down
you say to yourself hallelujah I'm back in my home town,
The next morning when you hop out of bed
you feel like you're dead.
Your arms go limp and you feel like a wimp.
And you can't do anything about it.
That's what it's like to be a Marine
and all those different kinds of things.

Philip Perkey, Grade 5
North Middle School, TN

Madness

I got mad at my friend
so I go outside to look at the clouds.
I could still see him sitting inside
just doing nothing.
My friend just stared
like a statue
searching for me.
He sees me and goes outside.
He has something in his hand.
Then I try to see what it is and he shows me.
It feels weird.
My friend gives me ice cream to eat.
He knows me so well.
He knows I like ice cream.

Levi Wright, Grade 5
Fox Elementary School, MO

My Little Brother

He is standing on the chair
Red is the color of his hair
My Mom says to get down
Get down from that chair.

He gives us a sneaky little grin
As if he is going to commit a sin
But don't be fooled
By that sneaky little grin

He is no fool
He goes to preschool.
So he decides to sit
Because he is no fool.

I am reminded by my Mother
That there is no other
Little red headed boy
Like my little brother.

Madison Costanza, Grade 5
Our Lady of Fatima School, MS

Summer

Summer days burn the skin.
On summer days I like to swim.
Summer days are a break
from all those tests you have to take.
Go around the block once or twice.

Take my summer day advice.
Drink lemonade and have fun.
Shade yourself from the hot sun.
Wear the clothes you want.
No bullies to tease or taunt.
No work to do.
Fun awaits you.
Swing from trees and do this and that.
Wear your favorite summer hat.
Play with a ball.
Run in the halls.
No teaching allowed
You'll have to be proud.
This is how you spend
your summer days.

Bailey Shipp, Grade 5
Forest Avenue Elementary School, AL

Bouncy Ball

I went to the mall
I bought a bouncy ball
I took it to school
Everyone said it was cool

Sonja Mitch, Grade 4
Horace Mann Elementary School, OK

Corey

C aring for others
O n time for school
R ight in math
E nergy left to spare
Y our friend

Corey Brannock, Grade 4
Tamassee-Salem Elementary School, SC

Red

It's a rose in the spring,
and a fire truck that rings.

It's the color of the hogs,
and it's the siren lights in the fog.

It's a candy apple Corvette,
and a very nice looking jet.

It's the bow on my Christmas gift,
and the lipstick on my mom's lips.

What color can this be?
Red is the color for me.

Sam Baker, Grade 5
Salem Elementary School, AR

Coffee/Peanuts

Coffee
black, bitter
refreshing, warming, awakening
cream, sugar, nuts, shells
crunching, boiling, eating
grilled, tasty
Peanuts

Loveday Glandon, Grade 5
Briarwood Christian School, AL

Mother

Mother
Nice, loving
Buying, shopping, traveling
Hugs and kisses
Baby short cake

Charnice Ward, Grade 5
Lloyd-Kennedy Charter School, SC

Horses

Horses
Fast, cute
Cantering, neighing, petting
Lots of fun, yeah!
Shadow

Tori Nichols, Grade 5
Frankford Elementary School, MO

Ben

Ben
Nice, friendly, hopeful, and loving
Relative of Jonathan
I love sports, candy, and animals.
I need friends, family, and pets.
I give clothes, money and food.
I fear Hell, death and Satan.
I would like to see my grandpa,
Ozzie Smith and Heaven
I am a resident of peace
Linderer

Ben Linderer, Grade 6
Our Lady Catholic School, MO

Football

I am a football
I am shaped like a bullet
And I am thrown as fast as one too
I get thrown and I land
Safely in the wide receiver's arms
When I am put in the air I feel glad
God put me in this world
I am full of air
When I get dropped it hurts
Really bad
I love to get thrown
This is why I am a football

James "Tyler" Collison, Grade 5
Grovespring Elementary School, MO

Who Am I

I am a girl
Who loves friends
And teachers
I am a girl
That will
Do anything
To help a friend
Who just wants
To be there
I am a girl
Who loves
Animals
Family
Life
I am a girl
That wants people
To take care
Of the world
And if we don't,
We'll die sooner
Than God wants us to

Laurin Hunnicutt, Grade 6
Westchester Country Day School, NC

I Live on an Army Post

I live on an army post where I am safe.
I wonder if my dad is okay.
I hear my dad in my dreams.
I see shooting in my imagination.
I want my dad to come home.
I live on an army post because I'm safe.

I pretend that I'm happy.
I feel like I'm going to cry.
I touch my mom's hand when I'm sad.
I worry if my dad is hurt.
I cry when he leaves.
I live with my mom when he's gone.
I live on an army post because of my dad.

I understand when my dad leaves.
I say I miss my dad.
I dream of my dad.
I try not to cry when he leaves.
I hope he is having a good time.
I live on an army post because my dad fights for our country.

Sedric Kennedy, Grade 4
Walker Intermediate School, KY

A Very Bad Day

Me and my friend Kiresten
were in the back sitting on the floor
playing a game.
Suddenly ahhhh!!
Kiresten screamed
there was a piece of glass stuck in my foot
so I screamed
ahhhhhhh!!
My mom came out of National City Bank
and noticed that I was hurt
so she went rushing to the back
and saw my foot
so she screamed very loudly
help, nobody was helping her
so she got me out
and went to the front seat and raced to the hospital.
When I got there the doctors were surprised that
I was hurt that bad.
They made me feel much better.
They gave me a treat because it was my birthday.
That was the craziest birthday ever!!

Mylin Ackerman, Grade 5
Greathouse Shryock Traditional Elementary School, KY

A Summer Dance

The flowers danced with the breeze
The tree leaves swayed to the music of wind
The grass bent its waist gracefully
As the clouds passed by and looked at them wistfully

Christine Ong, Grade 4
Crossville Christian School, TN

The Ballpark

At the ballpark you can see
crazy costumes,
freaky fans,
beers crashing,
and more.
At the ball park you hear
ugly umpires,
salespeople screaming,
the announcer yelling the players' names,
the ballpark, louder than any storm.
Amazing.
People singing, "Take Me Out to the Ball Game,"
and of course the sound of the bat hitting the ball.
WHACK!

Loren Melton, Grade 5
Greathouse Shryock Traditional Elementary School, KY

Sadness

Sadness if a leaf, falling from a tree.
Like a tree
    Crying,
    Crying,
    Crying.

I hear a little thump as the leaf hits the ground.
I can still smell the bit of "oakness" as the leaves are
somewhat damp.

When I picked up the dry leaf in my fingers,
it crunched and crumbled in my hand.

The leaf is broken.
It
is
no more.

It's broken down into a million pieces.

It
is
no more.

Darby Adams, Grade 4
Endhaven Elementary School, NC

The South

People who live in the south have good days and bad days.
Usually it's just a good day and full of happiness.
But on a bad day it's full of madness, why does this happen?
We must be strong going through those days,
like the days when you just want to cry, write it down, let it out.
Don't let those people get to you.
Fight with power.

Meagan Blackwell, Grade 5
Vernon Middle School, LA

I Live on an Army Post

I live on an Army Post in Kentucky where it is cold.
I wonder if we will move again.
I hear the guns fire out at the range.
I want my dad to retire.
I live on an Army post in Kentucky where it is cold.

I pretend that I am in combat with my dad.
I feel sad when my dad leaves.
I touch my dad's dog tags before he leaves so
I can remember the sound that they make when he moves.
I worry if my dad is safe.
I cry when my dad has to leave.
I live on an Army Post in Kentucky where it is cold.

I understand that my dad protects the U.S.A.
I say the Pledge of Allegiance every day because I am an American.
I dream about the war being over.
I try to believe that the war will be over soon and no kid will have to lose their mom or dad.
I hope our soldiers will stay strong and safe.
I live on an Army post in Kentucky where it is cold.

Tristan Trujillo, Grade 6
Walker Intermediate School, KY

The Basketball Star and the Singing Star

When I grow up I want to be a basketball player and star singer,
I sing really good. I play basketball, I know how to shoot threes.
Swish in the net, there goes the ball; you are supposed to follow through, I love basketball.
now back to that singing part; that singing makes your throat hurt but if I am going to be a singer
I am going to do all that it takes, there goes my career.

Carlisha J. Allen, Grade 5
Evangel Christian Academy, AL

What if Dogs Knew

What if dogs knew when it was time to eat, when it was their birthday, or when they first walked on their feet.
What if dogs knew when to say good-bye, when to be sad, and when to sigh.
What if dogs knew when to rejoice, when to be sad, and when they have that choice.
What if dogs knew when it was their time, when they got too old, and had to die.

Mary-Danse Jarratt, Grade 6
Holy Ghost Catholic School, LA

Ode to Our 5th Grade Teacher

Ode to our teacher you inspire our days when we come in and when we leave.
You are like a butterfly beautiful and talented as you fill are minds with wonder and knowledge.
You always remind me of a beautiful rose when you smile at us.
You are like a small rabbit sniffling your nose looking for something to teach.
You smell of coffee every morning.
The soft summer rain matches your light brown eyes.
In the mornings I smell the sweet cherry pie and I walk in the room you smell the same.
The sweet smell of you makes me tingle.
You are like a fox, sneaky catching every move.
As long as you have this poem we will still be with you.
The teacher we will remember for life is you.

Ashlyn Stone, Kelli Pentecost, and Chloe Duncan, Grade 5
Tigerville Elementary School, SC

Halloween

Halloween is a special time,
It is the best time for a scary rhyme.
You get to go out and to trick-or-treat.
And pull a prank or two that really can't be beat.

There are goblins and ghouls to give you a fright.
When walking about on this creepy foggy night.
Look up in the sky to see a full moon,
Hear a wolf howl, but do not swoon.

The wolf that you heard is all hairy and gray.
It comes closer and closer and you're really afraid.
Now that you see it, you're not scared at all.
It's a toddler, a little guy, about three feet tall.

So, knock on that door and await what will be,
A treat or a scare? Be ready to flee!
Don't run, don't scream, don't have a fit.
Don't stomp on a pumpkin, if it is lit.

Just hold out your hand and say, "Trick or treat,"
The surprise you will get will surely be sweet.
So dress in your costume; pirate, goblin, or ghoul.
And go out with your friends, it'll be really cool!

Cole Sandford, Grade 6
St Francis Xavier School, AL

Pool/Water

Slowly
and then quickly
I ran and then jumped and plunged

Deeper and
              deeper
I opened my eyes and looked around
under the surface was where I lived
I was glad to see that I was home.

Bubbles
swirling water
around me
up and up but not away from home.

There
she was the person swimming and pulling
I reached her.

We went up
more air
after we had reached the surface
I knew I would never be home again
until once more I jumped and plunged

Erin Laliberty, Grade 6
St Mary's School, SC

Macaroni

A drop of warm, cheesy, food on my plate,
Then I ate and ate

Filling my stomach very fast
At last!

Darcie Gallagher, Grade 6
Nodaway Holt Elementary School, MO

Maggie

Fun, happy, energetic, athletic.
Relative of Richard and Diana.
Lover of soccer, volleyball, my dogs.
Who feels happy when I'm with my friends
Sad when I have to clean
Excited when I get to go to a soccer or volleyball game.
Who gives hugs, smiles, and help.
Who needs my parents, my friends, my dogs
Who fears drowning, spiders, and clowns.
Who would like to see Italy, my grandma, my old dog.
Resident of daydreaming.

Skidmore

Maggie Skidmore, Grade 6
Our Lady Catholic School, MO

Change

As I walked up the steps
Excitement rushed over me
Up at the top
I stopped in my tracks
I gazed up at the big yellow monster
I unknowingly stepped in the first car
I barely remembered where I was
Up and up I went
I shut my eyes
Suddenly
The car sped up
I opened my eyes I was smoothly going down
Drifting up and down
I didn't know what I was thinking just before
I didn't back out
And I was glad I didn't

Michael Billups, Grade 6
East Oldham Middle School, KY

Christmas

C atching beautiful snowflakes
H ugging people for your gifts
R acing to play outside in the snow
I cicles hanging from mailboxes
S inging Christmas songs
T hanking people for your gifts
M aking everyone's day special
A ll together celebrating Christmas
S ewing hats, and scarves for Christmas gifts.

Sydney Ward, Grade 5
Sullivan Elementary School, TN

Hugs

I am a hug
So loving
So kind
When hugged
You feel warm.
I am a hug
So cozy
So nice
But not always
When not hugged
You feel sad
And not warm
And you do not feel
Loved, kind, cozy or nice
So hug all day and feel warm.
Maranda Mae Payne, Grade 5
Grovespring Elementary School, MO

Holocaust

Once in a time when the world was lost
Something called the Holocaust
There was sadness pain and death
Because of Hitler's evil quest

The war was hard and long
While other nations grew strong
Soon the war would come to an end
Hitler's death might make amends
Margaux Neville, Grade 5
Pembroke Elementary School, NC

The Moon

God named his flashlight.
He lets everybody use it.
Gave it a face,
A job,
And a home.
Its job — lighting the night skies.
Its home — on the blanket of stars.
Its name — moon.
And it doesn't let us forget it's there.
Courtney Brown, Grade 5
St Vincent Elementary School, MO

Soccer

Soccer
Fun, easy
Crazy, windy, rainy
I enjoy playing soccer
Kicking, scoring, catching
Outstanding, cool
Football
Jordan Flowers, Grade 5
EA Harrold Elementary School, TN

Riding on a Roller Coaster

Going to an amusement park,
The fancy lights make it not dark.
There are many rides I go on,
In an instant we are gone.
Going up a very tall hill,
Never ride after eating your fill.
Zoom down a big, large drop,
Then you feel your belly flop.
Fly around the steep turns,
Little kids to ride they yearn.
Pull back into the station,
You feel a good sensation!
Now you're back where you began,
Say, "Let's go on it again!"
Patrick Koch, Grade 6
St Teresa's School, GA

Softball

At home in the summer
I like to play softball.
My coach made me pitcher.
Why she chose me I can't recall.

One night during a game
I caught a fly ball.
Yeah! Playing softball is much better
Than going to the mall.
Morgan Whitehead, Grade 4
Northeast Baptist School, LA

Brothers

B rothers are so annoying!
R ather to sleep then play.
O r bother me until I cannot take it.
T hey never leave me alone
H e always hogs the computer
E very girl likes him but not me
R ather play football than to relax
S ometimes funny, hardly ever
Breanne DiBernard, Grade 4
St Thomas More School, NC

Veterans

Going to war
missing family,
just had a baby,
proud, missing,
and ready.
Tasting sweat and sand,
Hearing screams of men in battle,
Feeling a gun by my side,
Looking at a picture of my loved ones.
Riley Henderson, Grade 6
Benton County School of the Arts, AR

How I Feel When It Snows

The snow is falling from the sky.
It looks like clouds from way up high.
The grass is covered on the ground,
You only see white all around.

I love to feel it on my tongue.
It makes me feel so very young.
It's so much fun to slide around.
Or make an angel on the ground.

Sometimes the snow can be a pest.
It's so much work I cannot rest.
Although it's cold the snow must stay.
So, do you want to come and play?
Haley Stallings, Grade 6
Providence Classical School, AL

Thanksgiving

Visiting grandma
Eating turkey
Silly jokes
Interesting stories
Warm jackets
Families together
Playing outside
Having fun
Watching TV
Colorful leaves
People talking
Very windy
Playing games
Seeing cousins
Leaves falling
Pretty trees
Birds flying
Some flowers
Exciting games
Nice family
Jessica Jones, Grade 4
Center Elementary School, GA

Nighttime

I am a mattress
And this is my story
I'm big and puffy
Square as can be.
I have sheets and blankets
Covering me,
Teddy's bears
Everywhere
Brown and orange
While the people are snoring.
Briana Berry, Grade 6
Benton County School of the Arts, AR

Kristen

I am a pet lover named Kristen
I live in a town called Disten
I have a cat very fat
Who is afraid of pink hats
Did I tell you I have a dog named Wisten?

Kristen Burt, Grade 4
Judsonia Elementary School, AR

Butterfly

Butterflies flutter through the sky
I look up and see it up high.
Then it flies down to the ground
I creep up slowly
but it always flies up again,
then lands back down.
I try to chase it as it goes back into the sky.
Jumping up and down I never catch it,
but when I get close to catching it
I always get butterflies in my stomach.
I look at the pretty color of it as it flies away.
I always say I wish I could have caught it
but maybe next time!

Whitney Burnett, Grade 6
St Teresa's School, GA

Here I Sit with a Pen and a Pad

Here I sit with a pen and a pad,
trying to recite poems but they're all bad,
what can I do I'm running out of time,
out of time to find a rhyme
one step at a time
then you'll find the perfect rhyme,
one step at a time then it'll all be fine,
one step at a time then my poem will shine,
now I know what to say,
to recite my poem in a marvelous way,
feel the rhyme in your soul,
start from your head and end at your toe,
I found out destiny will bring out the best rhyme in me,
step by step,
day by day,
may the sun shine all day and all night.

Kayla Simon, Grade 5
Keyser Primary/Middle School, WV

Thanksgiving Day

P lenty of delicious food,
I gnoring the cold,
L onging for the warmth of the fire,
G roaning because I ate too much food,
R egretting all the delicious pumpkin pie I ate,
I mitating the turkey I ate,
M om telling me that we have to leave,
S aying, "Thank you for all the food!"

Ryan Rutrough, Grade 5
Sullivan Elementary School, TN

Fall

No more T-shirts,
Shifting to sweatshirts,
Soon I'll be changing to jackets.
It's getting colder,
Waiting for the bust in the frosty morning air is getting older,
Homework getting harder, crammed in my folder.
Oak leaves are falling,
Bluebirds are calling,
No more people are yawning,
Because everything's perfect in fall.

Lucas Davidson, Grade 6
Alvaton Elementary School, KY

A Quiet Night

It's a quiet night
I can hear planes taking flight

I hear trains blow their horns
I can smell that sweet scent of growing corn

I look at the stars in the sky.
It forms a constellation that looks like a pie.

I look at the moon,
and I can tell that daylight is coming soon.

Ronald W. Randolph, Grade 6
Saint Paul School, TN

Wind in My Hair, Waves at My Feet

The sun, once glaring down at me,
Now fades away.

The sand, once burning under my feet,
Now cools down.

The wind, once a smooth and calm breeze,
Now whips around my hair.

The waves, once refreshing like a cool drink,
Now ripple like stones beating you.

The lighthouse, once bright and cheerful,
Now looks like a ghost hiding with a dim candle.

The people, once coming in large crowds,
Now walk away in despair.

I am the last to survive
Wind in my hair
And waves at my feet.

I am the last to survive.

Catherine Y. Li, Grade 5
Goshen Elementary School at Hillcrest, KY

Cat

There was once a cat from Germany.
Who was walking a beam that was sturdy
He fell off the beam
And into a stream
And now his really dirty.

Daniela Singleton, Grade 5
American Heritage Academy, GA

A New Year

Tick tock tick tock
There it is
12 o'clock
Then 12:01

Hooray Hooray
We hug and cheer
We'll soon experience
A new year

Riley Patterson, Grade 4
St Thomas More School, NC

Color of the Sunset

The sunset with color true.
I gaze up into the sky
As all the wonderful colors go by.
As they go I sigh.
I drop my head in sorrow
As all the wonderful colors have gone by.

Henry Collier, Grade 4
St Thomas More School, NC

Ocean Ingredients

Salt water, whales, and seashells, too
Sea slugs, and crabs like a shoe.
Hammerheads, and lots of seals,
Penguins, coral and all the krill.

Michael Nguyen, Grade 4
Nesbit Elementary School, GA

Candy

C andy is
A wesome
N othing like it
D ifferent and
Y ummy

Natasha H. Sablan, Grade 5
First Flight Elementary School, NC

Spring Thinking

The sun shines on me
As the flowers do in spring
They open their blooms.
Can you hear the wind moving
As I ponder on my thoughts?

Hope Walker, Grade 6
Hand Middle School, SC

If I Were a Fish

If I were a fish I would see…
The colorful rocks in my tank lying at the bottom
My large green rock I hide inside to get away from the other fish
Goldfish in my tank swimming around in circles

If I were a fish I would hear…
The buzzing of the filter as it runs day and night
The creaking of the lid as people feed me
The swishing of the goldfish when they swim by me

If I were a fish I would smell…
The smelly food we eat
The air I breathe
The new clean tank we're in

If I were a fish I would taste…
The pellets that we eat
The water we drink
The algae off the tank

If I were a fish I would touch…
The gravel on the bottom of the tank
The rock I hide in
The toys in my tank

Paige Coffey, Grade 6
Union Chapel Elementary School, KY

There Was a Time

There was a time, when slaves were part of our lives.
There was a time, when an African American boy
was separated from his caucasian friend.
There was a time, when a woman was
forced to give up her bus seat.
There was a time, when a great man
signed the Proclamation and set the slaves free.
There was a time, when people thought violence was the answer.
There was a time, when people wanted to make a difference.
This is the time, where we now can.

Precious Johnson, Grade 6
Clarksburg School, TN

Dreaming

I must be dreaming because everything in my life is going okay.
But I'm wondering will I be on this Earth another day.
I look around and I see trash on the ground.
I see houses torn down.
I dream that I can fix all of these things.
Maybe I do something instead of sitting not doing anything.
All this violence and crime, makes you want to stay in your house all the time.
I want to go to college and get a Masters degree.
I have dreams and lots of them.
So instead of dreaming I will go somewhere.
I will not stay around when no one cares.

Keanna Robinson, Grade 5
Bossier Elementary School, LA

Home

I've never lived long at home
2-3 years then its all
gone.
Nowhere
to call home
never learned what home feels like to me
it's just a house
maybe I'll know what it feels like to be
home. Never more
to roam in my new
home.

Don Stolz, Grade 6
Annunciation Elementary School, MO

I Am Haunted

I am haunted in the past
By the boogieman that
lived in my closet.
The movie *Boogieman*
Made me hide under the BIG blue blanket
Until midnight.
I was scared of the mean monster
Who lived under my bed.
I wouldn't look under my bed.

I am haunted in the present by my house
It has a ghost inside
The goofy ghost tries to spook and scare me
Until I finally faint.
The goofy ghost scares me at night.

I am haunted in the future because I'm afraid
I will die!!!!!!
I am scared of carnival clowns because
carnival clowns are enemies and evil.
Clowns will end the world.

James Byers, Grade 5
Eminence Middle School, KY

War

Escaping killing fields,
Wrongful death has happened,
Dangerous happenings all around,
Killing is encouraged,
War is wanted,
Freedom is needed,
Hope, wanted,
If the war keeps happening,
We will be Earth of the dead,
Goals will turn around,

When will these dreaded wars end.

Emery Staton, Grade 5
William Southern Elementary School, MO

Imagination

I see horses galloping across fields, and cars that never yield.
Do you see what I see?
I hear storms across the sea, and birds singing in harmony.
Do you hear what I hear?
I feel a breeze passing by, and rain falling from the sky.
Do you feel what I feel?
I taste soup that's nice and hot, like it's fresh from the pot.
Do you taste what I taste?
I smell spices in the air, as it blows through my hair.
Do you smell what I smell?

You can only imagine.

Keenah Mays, Grade 5
The Altamont School, AL

Depression

The sky is blue.
My hair is blue.
My eyes are blue.
My skin is blue.
The grass is blue.
My teacher's blue.
Everyone's blue.
Can't you see and tell that everything is turning blue?
Why is everything turning blue?
Maybe you should figure it out by yourself.
Answer: my sadness
Or my depression
Makes the world change.

Alayjah Marrow, Grade 6
Woodlawn Christian School, NC

Sammy

My dog Sammy likes to eat candies.
He has lots of toys.
He is a boy who will bite everything in sight.
When he gets up, he's not much!
When he's been up, YOU had better get up!

Kendra Calihan, Grade 5
Paint Lick Elementary School, KY

Thanksgiving

Here comes Thanksgiving here it comes
Here comes Thanksgiving everyone
With lots of cake and lots of pie
Please believe me, I don't lie

You don't need to ask me, there are more things to eat
Like turkey, cranberry sauce, and other better things

Today, Thanksgiving is a time to thank
Jesus, God, and all the saints
To thank them for this heavenly blessing
We praise and adore their sacred name

Iván Puello, Grade 5
St Marys School, AR

Praise

I am a sunflower always happy
My smile is as big as a halfmoon
I am tall, graceful, and always cheerful
But just a leaf growing on the family tree
I am a lollipop sweet as can be
I am the sun shining bright all day
I am myself, I am my own
I am Hannah

Hannah Hagood, Grade 6
Beck Academy, SC

Life

Life can be as fragile as a bubble,
or as tough as a diamond.

It goes through twists and turns,
and you control them.

At the end of Life,
there is Death,
waiting around the twist or turn.

In death there is much sadness,
yet the joy of knowing that that person
will have eternal happiness with God.

Jonah Sharkins, Grade 6
St Francis Xavier School, AL

Gabriel

G reat in school, but bad at home
A very nice person
B orn in a great place, Arizona
R eally good at sports
I sometimes have a bad attitude
E very day is a great day
L ittle but really strong

Gabriel Ybarra, Grade 4
Byrns L Darden Elementary School, TN

Raindrops

I hear the rain drops
falling on the street.
They make a song
with every beat.
I hear the raindrops
fall from the sky
Sometimes they make
me want to cry.
After the rain
in the puddles I jump.
I love to splash
and make a big thump.

Latiya Mays, Grade 6
Western Hills Elementary School, AR

Candy

C onsuming, delicious
A mazing
N utty
D elightful
Y ummy, candy

Wyatt Tucker, Grade 5
First Flight Elementary School, NC

Flowers by the Season

Spring, summer
Winter, fall
Sometimes they are a bummer
And that's because they fall.

Fall they sail, winter they sleep
Spring they sprout, summer they grow.
They sprout when birds peep
And their pace is sometimes slow.

In their second fall they die,
Right before they say bye-bye.
This continues forever and ever.

Kevin Reilly, Grade 5
G C Burkhead Elementary School, KY

Pug

There once was a little tan dog
Who sat on a very big log
Up came a big bug
Said, "Are you a pug"
Dog ran off to find his friend Frog

Kali Schmalzried, Grade 6
Armorel Elementary School, AR

Freedom

Nature all around me
The freshness of the water
The chirping of baby birds
Puddles at my feet
The sweetness of the air
The beauty of freedom.

Emily Payne, Grade 4
Cleveland Elementary School, OK

Horses/Cows

Horses
fun, graceful
trotting, exciting, loving
pony, steed, cattle, bull
eating, milking, charging
boring, frightening
Cows

Katy Broughton, Grade 5
Briarwood Christian School, AL

My Angel Mom

Lovely as a rose
Midnight black hair
and
Crystal clear eyes
Sounding like an angel
Caring
and
Supporting
Teaching me for what I am
and
Who I will be
My Angel Mom

McKenzie Strange, Grade 4
Briarwood Elementary School, KY

Math It

Think it
Write it
Say it

I am trying to rhyme,
Rhyme with prime
Is it even?
Is it odd?
Is it divisible by 9?

Know it
Rock it
You'll definitely show it

Cameron Freeman, Grade 5
Meramec Elementary School, MO

Autumn

Acorns on the ground
The big blue sky up so high
That's fall and that's all!

Molly McKenzie, Grade 4
Briarwood Christian School, AL

Thanksgiving

T hanking God for what we have
H aving a feast with your relatives
A t the airport waiting for your plane
N ot being selfish to others
K nowing God is there
S aving the food so the dog won't eat it
G iving to other people
I n the house on a cold day
V ery nice to others
I nteresting colors on the trees
N ot being rude to others
G iving praise to God

Forrest Dreher, Grade 5
Briarwood Christian School, AL

Where I'm From

I am from pillows from cotton and feathers
I am from the junk under my bed old, new, expensive
I am from the lilies and the bushes
I am from cookouts and presents from Kayla, Christy, and Judy
I am from sleeping, watching movies, and out of state trips
From never be mean and mind your manners
I am from the Baptist church
I am from NC asthma and bachalitos
From the frogs the green and the pink
I am from PA the park and lake

Breanna Cruse, Grade 6
Lakeshore Middle School, NC

The Fox and the Rocks

Once there was a fat fox,
He fell and landed in huge rocks,
He broke his hand,
Then he got ran over by the geeky marching band,
Now he lives alone in a cardboard box.

Jordan Metts, Grade 4
Eastside Elementary School, GA

Generous Mom

Smelling like chocolate mint
Her curly hair black as charcoal
Carmel eyes sparkling like stars in the sky
Her peaches'n cream skin soft as silk

My mom is so generous
Taking time from her own and giving it to us
Driving us to soccer
Strings, basketball
And more
She is amazing

Whenever I'm sick
Checking on me
Bringing me
Soup, sprite and blankets
Comforting me
Giving hugs and kisses while saying I love you
My mom is very generous

Abby Tuck, Grade 4
Briarwood Elementary School, KY

The Halloween Story!

When it's Halloween I go trick-or-treating.
I always wear a weird costume.
I like the costumes the families wear too.
I also see all kinds of coal-colored eerie spiders.
I love to carve scary pumpkins every year.
I always get lots of yummy candy.
It's so fun.
It gets better every year.

Jacquelyn Richmond, Grade 5
North Middle School, TN

The Night Hunt

The moon was bright; the wind was blowing.
I was ready to go; my excitement was growing!

My dogs were highly trained, and my gear was ready;
As I entered the woods, my gun was steady.

I looked all around and listened to my dogs;
There was total silence! Nothing could I see or hear!

Then from out of the dark and across my path,
There scurried a coon full of anger and wrath.

As the dogs got the scent, they barked and growled
At that big ole sow.

Never had I seen such a vicious sight,
Dog against coon on that moonlit night!

Jared Buchanan, Grade 6
Scotts Creek Elementary School, NC

My Pet Fish

I went to the store to find a new pet,
but all I could find was something real wet.

It was all cut up and missing an eye.
It had a bad fin and smelled like something had died.

I brought him back home and gave him a bath.
He watched me clean my room and then do my math.

He was quite boring so I taught him a trick,
how to back flip right over a stick.

I was very sorry I taught him that,
because he jumped right into the mouth of my cat.

I'm going to the store across the lake.
This time to buy a tailless black snake.

Jack Schoephoerster, Grade 5
Laurence J Daly Elementary School, MO

Matt's Life

Basketball is my sport,
that I dribble up and down the court
Baseball is the game,
that makes it look like it's claim
Chess is my hobby,
that I play in the lobby.
Everybody will be watching me play these games,
I won't disappoint them or put myself in shame.
So everyone will be screaming my little bitty name,
and I'll have everyone going insane.

Matt Blanchard, Grade 6
Haynes Academy for Advanced Studies, LA

Winter Flakes!

I went outside and looked around
All of those snowflakes on the ground.
It's so cold, my whole body could freeze
Then I grab a tissue, and I sneeze.
I go inside and stand by the fire.
I stand, and I think what would I desire?
I go make a cup of hot chocolate.
I sit, I sip, I sleep.

Kelsey Kirkpatrick, Grade 6
Pleasants County Middle School, WV

Veteran's Day

T hank you,
H eroes
A job to be proud of
N one selfish, all
K ind and brave

Y ou rock! And
O vercome things
U nimaginable.

Dalton Short, Grade 5
Sullivan Elementary School, TN

My Grandma

My grandma is nice
My grandma is cool
My grandma is sweet
and not a fool
My grandma is a friend
when you need help
My grandma is neat
My grandma is great
but most of all
My grandma is never late

Alice Whitson, Grade 5
Graham Elementary School, AL

I Want to Be

I want to be a teacher
and a photographer
But me
I am just honest, humble, Haleigh.

Haleigh Mitchell, Grade 5
Evangel Christian Academy, AL

Good or Bad

Hero
Good, strong
Protecting, saving, rescuing
Loyal, brave, sneaky, clever
Kidnapping, fighting, killing
Evil, smart
Villain

Randall Martin, Grade 4
Tamassee-Salem Elementary School, SC

By the Beach

You open your eyes to see the sun begin to hide behind the pure white clouds.
The sky is a shade of deep purple with pink mixed in.
The crystal clear water laps at your toes.
It sends shivers up your body.
The seagulls call to their young, and their young respond with hungry cries.
You hear far-off music, soft and sweet.
The aroma from the lit candles around you is soothing.
Are you alone?
You look beside you and see your family.
The only noise is the melody.
You do not know the song, but it floats through the air.
Kites fly and birds soar, weightless, in the sky.
You are completely relaxed.
Memories flash through your mind.
Remember the first time you saw a tide pool with its gleaming fish and pinching crabs?
You run your toes through the snow white sand.
You take in a deep breath of the salty air.
The palm trees rustle from the sea breeze.
Could anything be more relaxing?
All you feel is calmness and serenity...
Slowly, you drift away into the world of dreams.

Kyle Bundschuh, Grade 6
Queen of Angels Catholic School, GA

I Live on an Army Post

My name is Sarah and I was born in Livingston, Tennessee.
I get scared when my dad has to leave my family.
I say "I don't want him to go" in my prayers.
I am the only girl in my family, so it's kind of hard to get along with my brothers.
I think that a soldier is getting ready to leave to Iraq when I hear tanks.
My name is Sarah and I was born in Livingston, Tennessee.

My name is Sarah and I was born in Livingston, Tennessee.
I want all of the soldiers to come back safe from Iraq.
I will be so happy when the soldiers come back from Iraq.
My dad gave me a necklace when he left to Kuwait.
I wish soldiers would not ever have to go to Iraq.
My name is Sarah and I was born in Livingston, Tennessee.

My name is Sarah and I was born in Livingston, Tennessee.
My family travels a lot so I have to change schools all the time.
Sometimes it is hard to make friends.
My name is Sarah and I was born in Livingston, Tennessee.

Sarah Collier, Grade 6
Walker Intermediate School, KY

Veterans

Veterans are special to me because they made me free

Because of them I am here today doing the things I do.
Sometimes it makes me sad sometimes it makes me mad.
Some day I will be there too.

I thank you soldiers over in Iraq. Goodbye guys and I hope you make it back.

Tanner Stout, Grade 6
Temple Hill Elementary School, KY

All I Have to Say About "It"

My parents split
That's all I have to say about "it"
It was sad
Nothing was glad
Two years later my dad remarried
It was a burden I seemed to have carried
A year ago my mom did the same
To a guy I forgot his name
"It" wasn't fine
Nor divine
Not the remarriages but the split
That's all I have to say about "it"
I don't remember the divorce
It just seemed to be the force
My parents worked out a deal
And put on it the official seal
I'd get to see my dad every summer
This wasn't a bummer
This is fair
Beyond compare
That's all I have to say about "it."

Matthew Sullivan, Grade 6
Harding Academy of Memphis, TN

Daddy

D earest person I know.
A ctive and vigorous in everything he does.
D aring in swimming and sports.
D emanding for what he wants.
Y oung at heart and always smart.

Rachel Williams, Grade 5
Vernon Middle School, LA

The Fair

All the children's frowns are turning upside-down.
It is because the fair's coming round.

From entertainment, to concession stands.
The fair is a cheerful land.

Even though litter swallows the ground,
The giggling children think they have found,
Quite a rather attracting sound.

Although the fair is not very pretty.
It brings delightfulness to the children in our city.

They dash, they bolt, and they sprint,
To the entrance to candy, rides, and sugar mints.

The fair is always a wonderful thing,
Because look at all the joy it brings!

Elizabeth McClain, Grade 5
Center Elementary School, GA

Dance

D ancing is what I love
A fter we win we get gigantic trophies!
N icky the assistant was always a big help.
'C ause I couldn't do my step ball flat.
E lizabeth was my best friend in dance
　　She helped me through what I couldn't do.

Hailey Conboy, Grade 5
North Middle School, TN

When Push Comes to Shove

"Crack," "Bang," "Crack," "Kulush,"
That's what happens when he gave me a push.
"Ding," "Bang," and all the above.
That's what happens when I give him a shove.

Aaron Moore, Grade 6
Martin Elementary School, WV

Work It Out

The Lord can always work it out for you
If it's that you need help for a test.
You can call him
If your parents are fighting.
You don't want to hear it.
You can call him.
Some people have their friends on their speed dial.
I have the Lord on mine,
My mental phone.
You always have phone complications.
I don't ever!
One word that's it
So who are you calling?

Kiera Bastien, Grade 6
Blackmon Road Middle School, GA

Courage

Courage is gold.
It smells like an apple pie.
It sounds like country music.
It looks like a beautiful golden rose.
I feel courageous when I don't get bit by a snake.

Autumn Williamson, Grade 5
West Marion Elementary School, MS

Camp

Camp, camp, full of fun and friends.
Camp is bunk beds and posters taped to the wall.
Camp is homesickness and a counselor's comfort.
Camp is s'mores by a campfire singing lots of fun songs.
Camp is spiders in my bunk and swimming with snakes.
Camp is freezing cold showers and dirty hair.
Camp is tipping your canoe and then laughing real hard.
Camp is a second family with love and food.
Camp is a warmth that never dies.
Camp is like home but further away.

Catherine York, Grade 6
Westchester Country Day School, NC

Oak Tree

The cold wind blew
through the old oak tree.
Sitting motionless for hours
with a gun was me.
Hoping for a deer
I wished I could see,
but the day was late
— time well past three,
so I had to leave
my old oak tree.
I started down to climb
and thought to me,
what a wonderful day
it turned out to be.

Timothy Baxley, Grade 6
Chapin Middle School, SC

Teachers

Interjections and conjunctions;
Similes and metaphors;
Hyperboles and exaggerations;
English Teachers

Volcanoes and magma;
The crust and the core;
Climate and weather;
Science Teachers

Exponents and variables;
Multiplication and division;
Addition and subtraction;
Math Teachers

Inserting and typing;
Researching and power pointing;
Copying and pasting;
Computer Teachers

Red pens and homework;
Yelling and detention;
Compassion and caring;
ALL TEACHERS

Maggie DeWeese, Grade 6
Scotts Creek Elementary School, NC

All About Me

D aring at football
A real friend
R eally great at basketball
I ndividual personality
U nderstanding
S uper at science

Darius Smiley, Grade 6
Brogden Middle School, NC

Fall

Fall
cold, windy
falling, howling, whispering
lots of pretty leaves
rising, screeching, yelling
hot, sunny
Spring

Caroline Wallace, Grade 6
Stuart Middle School, KY

Thanksgiving Day

A chill fills the air.
The sun is high in the sky,
And a few clouds pass.

Colors touch the sky.
Leaves sparkle in the sunlight.
The wind makes them dance.

Food's on the table.
Turkey and ham cook slowly
On this great fall day!

Oh gosh! My brother
Has found his way to the pies!
But Grandma just laughs.

We sit down to pray
And give thanks for what we have
With the family.

Leah Bush, Grade 6
Midway Covenant Christian School, GA

A Pianist

What is piano?
 playing many songs
 learning many scales
 drilling fun music
 performing in recitals
 doing written theory
 memorizing many pages
 playing Hanon every morning
 pounding the keys
 pressing the pedals
 turning the music pages
 playing a duet
 having frequent lessons
 learning new songs
 composing a song
 playing varying etudes
 sight-reading music
This is piano!

Gareth Evans, Grade 6
Southwest Middle School, AR

Baseball

You throw me,
You catch me.
Watch where you throw me!
Ahhh! Ouch!
Broken window!

Charles Nenninger, Grade 5
St Vincent Elementary School, MO

Friends

When I was a child
I had a bunch of friends
That played with me
On the playground
Every day.

I loved having my friends
Right there next to me
When we skipped, played,
And got hurt.

If one of us got hurt
Or someone was being mean to us
We would be there for each other
Every time.

Gradually all my friends moved away
Or found new best friends
Now here I am
With all my new friends.

Taylor Coley, Grade 6
Advent Episcopal Day School, AL

Fire

The fire dances and laughs at you.
It dodges your water hose.
And the house pleads for water
And is burned down.

John Lipe, Grade 5
St Vincent Elementary School, MO

December

I always love,
the Christmas snow.
Why are the days shorter?
I don't know.
The days they love,
to zoom away.
I look at the sky,
the clouds are dark gray.
December is a race car,
on a big track.
When will it ever come back?

Gracie Riggs, Grade 6
Beck Academy, SC

Americans

A lways believe in our troops.
M ake great choices.
E njoy living free because you never know if we'll lose it.
R emember the great times we had as Americans.
I nfluence others to help save our freedom.
C arry out the promises we have made.
A lways tell the truth.
N ever back down from a fight for our freedom.
S tart something then finish it.

That is the American way.

Zachary Wilson, Grade 6
Stuart Middle School, KY

The Day My Grandpa Slipped Away

When my mom first told me,
all the color drained from my face.
Warm tears thundered down my cheeks.
I was mad.
Why did he have to go?
Why would God take him away from me?
Didn't he know how much I would miss him? Why?
But I can remember.
Remember his kind, gentle, eyes.
Remember his soft, sweet,
soothing voice.
I can remember his funny,
goofy, laugh.
But I can also remember that sad, sad day.
The day our visits,
little chats,
His funny jokes,
all of it. It all ended.
It was the day,
my Grandpa slipped away.

Sarah Blair, Grade 6
East Oldham Middle School, KY

A Taste of Freedom

Freedom
is it glory
is it happiness
is it free right?
It is all.
The salty sea is there to see.
The tall buildings are climbing proud.
There aren't any people demanding.
But long drives to tall orange rocks or hills.
A smile flashing and a chirp of blue jays singing
All the great glory and high happiness
I'm glad to call America, America
Shout it with me
The freedom country
AMERICA

Peyton Greenberg, Grade 5
Greathouse Shryock Traditional Elementary School, KY

Butterflies

Butterflies flicker, they flit they fly,
It's so amazing how many times they fly by.
Side to side, up and down,
over and over on the ground.
Do you ever ask yourself,
do I know why or how beautiful butterflies fly by.
It's nothing to be ashamed of,
if you really don't know why.
The truth is in your heart every single day,
by and by!

Brittany Colvin, Grade 5
Glen View Elementary School, LA

Lucille Ball

Who is Lucille Ball?

A model
A "Chesterfield Girl"
A gifted actress
A radio show host
A native New Yorker
A wife of a Cuban man
A person who married in 1940
A person who divorced in 1960
A kid lover
An excellent memorizer
A beautiful girl
A compassionate person
A person who has incredible schemes
A spoiled person
A troublemaker
A Christian
A truthful person
A lovable woman
A fabulous friend

That is Lucille Ball.

Sarah Davis, Grade 6
Southwest Middle School, AR

Mustangs Galloping

Mustangs galloping through the wind,
hoping that I will see them again.
Surely I will because everywhere they roam,
you just have to call in a soft, gentle tone.
They're free spirited and kind to be so wild,
you could call them gentle beasts or so mild.
They run like the wind and explore new places, and
Sometime you'll see a couple of new faces
So just let them be and they'll always find a way,
they'll survive forever, night and day.
Mustangs galloping through the wind.

Abbey Whaley, Grade 5
West Marion Elementary School, MS

It's Coming

No work, no school, *only fun*
No madness, no sadness
Only the happy faces
No teachers, no desks, no tests
So no stress
It's almost here
And I just can't wait
It's almost here
And I'm leaving this state
I have to go home
Gather all my things
First my clothes, then my toothbrush
Next a book
All in my backpack
Don't call me, I will not answer
Cause I won't be home
The only sound that will be there
Is my cat playing with her toys
My dog making a lot of noise
I might see you in 6 or 7 days
So I have to go for the time is here!

Ashlynn Wheeler, Grade 6
Benton County School of the Arts, AR

Nick

Nick Mckenzie
One earring
Reads books
Writes books
Church goer
Likes pizza
Repairs computers
Loves sports
Blue eyes
Brown hair
Rides bus
1 sister
loves money
likes school
likes home

Nicholas Mckenzie, Grade 4
Tamassee-Salem Elementary School, SC

Halloween Night

The smell and the sight,
It's a wonderful night!
The small colored treats,
no healthy beats.
The costume and masks,
carrying our lumpy sacks.
You may think this is fake
on Halloween I get a cake!
Yes it is my birthday on this holiday
and I wouldn't miss it any day!

Kiana Raby, Grade 5
North Middle School, TN

Halloween

Jack'O lanterns and jokers creeping through the night
You never will know what will scare you until they give you a fright
Parties and candy, costumes and pumpkins
Run they're coming to get you, don't worry it's just for fun
Trick or treat please, do I have to smell your feet
Decorations galore
Spaghetti is his brain
Go ride on the spooky train
Walk through the door of the haunted Mansion
Be aware there is something on the floor
Don't worry it's not real
have fun on a scary night!

Lauren James, Grade 6
Cathedral School, NC

Autumn Days

An autumn day is a wonderful thing —
When we bring out the turkey and sometimes sing,
As we pile up the leaves or sit on the hay,
Whatever we do, we mainly just play —
When it is night I go to my bedroom and turn out the light,
I say a prayer and brush my hair and hope soon it will be a beautiful sight,
I wake up the next morning, wake up shining and bright —
Going out to play and glad that it's not night,
I wish I would never have to say —
Soon autumn will be over, but that's ok

Grayson Mosteller, Grade 5
Palmetto Christian Academy, SC

Boom Boom

Boom Boom
The thunder crackled the storm got louder
Than a train coming off its tracks

Boom Boom
The thunder vibrated our little house the satellite flew off the roof
Like a Frisbee being thrown in the air

Boom Boom
The thunder repeated as a tornado whirled away all of the toys
Just like Scooter when he chases his tail

Boom Boom
The thunder quivered my window that would have sent pieces flying all over the place
Like the sprinkler that blasts water on the trampoline

Boom Boom
The thunder roared as rain hit the window making a loud noise
Like a jet hitting its maximum speed

Boom Boom
The storm is over it is calm as the flood rages outside
No more rain but instead there is sunlight beaming down

Jacob Appleby, Grade 6
Union Chapel Elementary School, KY

Where Am I From

I am from exploring and traveling the U.S.
From riding in the car and digging in dirt
I am from hiking in the mountains and
Adventures in the forest

I am from blistering feet,
From sweat and smelly body.
I am from nature,
From animals and bugs.

I am from picnics in the park during spring
And the haunted forest walks in the fall
I am tan from the sun's brightness in summer
And white from the moon's bright white light in the winter

But most of all
I am from exploring
And traveling this amazing world
And one day I want to be from
Traveling the outer space

Quincy Godfrey, Grade 4
Price Elementary School, KY

Spiders

As I walk around my huge house
I see all the creepy things they call spiders.
I see their scary webs
And their eight legs and six eyes.
I just run away in fear!
They could come into my house and bite me!
(I hope they aren't poisonous!)
The only good thing is they eat insects.
I'm glad bugs don't take over the world!
Sometimes I wish they were not here,
because they are annoying.
I don't like spiders!

Kaylee Roberts, Grade 5
North Middle School, TN

Eagle

Majestically, it glides high above the earth.
Nesting in the towering mountains in a soft well-built nest.
Its sharp beak clutches new material for its home.
Powerful, it swoops down and strikes its prey.
Grasping helpless woodland animals against their will.
Its chocolate brown wings gently highlight its soft features.
In a language unbeknownst to humans, it squawks its feelings to
The world.
It smells of light mountain mist and the forest tree bark.
No wonder such a unique creature was chosen to represent
America!
An eagle, what an exquisite sight!

Natalie Rine, Grade 6
Haynes Academy for Advanced Studies, LA

A Winter Day

I run outside and see a fresh white blanket covering the ground
As I walk off my front porch,
I can hear the crunch, crunch, crunch of snow.
When I walk into the wind,
the cold nips at my rosy red cheeks.
The first thing I wanted to do,
was build a snowman.
He had a red hat and a scarf to match.
His nose was a very bright orange,
and his eyes, buttons, and mouth,
were all a very deep shade of black.
Oh, he was a wonderful, whimsical, seemingly wise snowman.
He was like a beautiful sunset in the evening.
When I am all finished,
I go inside for some hot cocoa.
I say to my mom,
"I had the best day I could have possibly had."

Carter Bosse, Grade 5
Greathouse Shryock Traditional Elementary School, KY

It

What is *it* you might ask,
It's simply what I say.
For instance, *it* could be,
A cat, a lamp, a baseball tee.
It's also a bed, a picture of you,
Or simply number one or number two.
I'm telling you this so you can see,
It can be what you want *it* to be.

Blake Baker, Grade 5
Forest Avenue Academic Magnet School, AL

I Can't Write a Poem*

Forget it. You must be kidding.
Don't have a brain. I have to go to the doctor.
I can't write good. I don't have a led pencil.
I hate paper. I'm sick.
I have a big headache. I have to go somewhere.
I broke my bones. I have to go to the mall.
I don't have time. I can't see anything.
I don't have hands. I don't know anything.
I left my game on and have to go
Turn it off before it messes up.
I left the water on.
I don't even know how to write a poem.
I have to go to the nurse.
I'm blind. I'm stupid.
My brother took it.
A snake bit me.
Uh oh, time's up?
All I have is this dumb list of excuses.
You like it? Really, no kidding?
Would you like to see another?

Adis Grahovic, Grade 6
Lost River Elementary School, KY
*Patterned after "I Can't Write a Poem" by Bruce Lansky

Up in Alaska

I swim gracefully and I sing great, I jump high to make a show, up in Alaska eagles sing, deer listen, wolves creep, during the summer I love it there, it is warm and cold at the same time and I sing and sing till my voice goes dry. Up in Alaska, I feel free, from all war, all up there is peace.

Rio Gauthier, Grade 5
Runnels School, LA

The Painful War

Today I come to you telling you something time cannot erase. I have this memory in my head. I can see it like it was yesterday. It was hard to say goodbye, even though we did not see eye to eye. Now many people are in wheelchairs, some are using a cane. Through all the pain and suffering the War is still going on. I did not want to say goodbye even though we did not see eye to eye. I could see the sadness in the room when they left. I miss him and hold my head up high when I talk to him in heaven.

Janee Helmick, Grade 6
Mckinley Jr High School, WV

Sports Standards?

So I'm not
A Shaquille O'Neal
Or a Sammy Sosa
Why does everyone want
Me to be…them?
Why do high schools
Want me to play sports or I can't come?

It's not fair at all!!!
So I like other things, I'm smart
So I don't want to get hit by a linebacker,
So I do other things.
Well, if my "athletic ability" isn't great
Maybe your students aren't that smart!
Who knows?

JUST
TAKE
A
STAND!

Joe Ponzillo, Grade 6
Annunciation Elementary School, MO

Baseball

I play it outside with my friends and family.
I also watch it on TV as a Major League game.
It is America's greatest game and part of our proud history.
I go to the park and see it in person, boy is that a blast.
I have always loved baseball and this will never cease.
When the bat hits the ball and it makes that crack sound I just love it.
When you see or make a home run you know that it is going to be gone before it comes close.
When you are in the field with the wind in your hair and the grass moving slowly with the wind,
Those are the most memorable moments on a ball field.
It feels even better though when you jack the ball out of the park and you score the winning run to make your team win.
As a child when you play baseball you keep even the littlest thing that you can do well in your head.
When I get older I still want to be one of the players and no one can stop me.

Alex Leach, Grade 6
Queen of Angels Catholic School, GA

I Remember Grandpa

I remember Grandpa…
helping me when I'm scared, helping me when I'm confused, teaching me to ride a bike.

I remember Grandpa…
being in the hospital, dying, the cemetery.

I remember Grandpa.

Nick Lesmes, Grade 5
Sycamore Elementary School, GA

The Way to Win

You are a slave to the day
Going and doing a task
But it doesn't have to be that way
Are you yourself, or are you wearing a mask?
Sinning and not caring
Having lots of idols
Self-centered and not sharing
Living up to the wrong titles
Go to the Lord your God
He will forgive you of your sin
The Lord will never treat you like sod
This is the way to win

Chaffin Hart, Grade 6
Briarwood Christian School, AL

Getting on Base

Some people hit home runs
People hit doubles
You can hit triples
Then they hit singles
Players can hit pop flies
Even a lucky inside the park home run
The pitcher might walk you with bad pitches
Pitchers might hit you
Last resort — BUNT IT!

Matthew Mattox, Grade 4
Moyock Elementary School, NC

The Dreadful Room

You're in a dark, giant, cold room.
You are all alone and can see nothing.
You're confused, scared, and cold.
You see a small light; there is a figure you recognize.
Someone you love.
You run towards it, but slowly, it fades away
right as you reach it. It's gone.
The life slipped right through your hands.
You are once again in the dark room.
There was nothing you could've done, yet,
it feels like you could've done everything.
You cry out, but fear muffles the sound;
You try again, but the darkness swallows you.
I've seen death
Have you?

Erin Duffy, Grade 6
Woodland Presbyterian School, TN

Popcorn

Pop, Pop, Pop! What is that noise?
Is it something falling down a rocky hill? No,
Is it popping balloons? No.
Is it someone stomping on the floor! No.
Than what is it?
POPCORN!

Bradly Howard, Grade 4
Center Place Restoration School, MO

Christmas

C hristmas trees covered in ornaments
H undreds of presents to open
R iding a great bike
I cicles hanging form the roof
S now falling from the sky
T ying ribbons on the gifts
M ilk and cookies to give to Santa
A tasty and delicious dinner
S anta and the reindeer coming to my house

Tahlia Richardson, Grade 5
Sullivan Elementary School, TN

No One Can Escape

With the wind whistling on a dark, scary, moonless night.
With porches filled with jack-o'-lanterns.
Trick or treaters in costumes roaming the streets.
From goblins to ghosts, witches to warlocks
Hearing screams and squeals.
Trick or treaters trying to escape.
But no one can escape the fright of Halloween night!
With owls screeching and monsters roaring.
Witches casting spells upon trick or treaters.
Children shivering from the coldness.
With hovering ghosts frightening children.
Remember! Remember!
The 31st of October
with owls screeching
and monsters roaring…
No one can escape…the fright of Halloween night.

Michael Martin, Grade 5
Saffell Street Elementary School, KY

The Dance

She's up, she's down, she's all around,
Dancing on the tip of her toes.
It's beautiful you see, and it's lovely when she
Dances with grace it makes my heart grow.

Then she does an arabesque landing in a perfect pose!
She looks me straight in the eye,
And the twinkle in her eye
Glows as she swishes back up on her toes.

It's a question for all of us;
How does she do it?
To see her jump so gracefully.
As if there's nothing to it!

She looks like a swan
Dancing on the pond;
I don't know what to say;
I wish I could dance that way!

Abby Palmeter, Grade 5
Providence Academy, TN

I Like to Play with Babies

I like to play
with babies sometimes.
I like to hold
them and feed
them. But when
it comes to
changing their
diaper I don't
like it too
much, and when
they cry. But
I still like
to play with
babies.

BreAnna Yawn, Grade 5
West Marion Elementary School, MS

Time Waits for Nothing

Time waits for nothing,
Nothing slow nor fast,
Time waits for nothing,
Time is never first nor last.
Time waits for nothing,
Time will never stop,
Time waits for nothing,
For time, there is no top.
Time waits for someone,
For soon the time will come,
When Jesus descends from heaven,
To sit upon the throne.
Time waits for someone.

Jared Henson, Grade 5
Griffin Christian Academy, GA

Butterflies

Butterflies are so pretty
They come from caterpillars
They are great creatures.

Abby Reid, Grade 4
Briarwood Christian School, AL

The Right Time

You can always tell
when fall is coming
It's just the right temperature
and people start hunting
You know when
it is just the right time
when Mom and Dad
start saving every dime
Summer is dying
Autumn is trying

BJ Pinkston, Grade 6
Stuart Middle School, KY

I Am

I am curious and calm
I wonder about the world
I hear whispers in the world
I see the moon and stars
I want to know the future
I am curious and calm

I pretend to know
I feel the world holding me
I touch the moon and stars
I worry about what happens next
I cry because I don't know
I am curious and calm

I understand I can't know the future
I say the future will come
I dream about the moon and stars
I try to forget; but I can't
I hope to find the future
I am curious and calm

Maria Plummer, Grade 5
Berryville Elementary School, AR

Thanksgiving

Turkey in the oven,
Pumpkin pie, and biscuits too.
Relatives coming over.
Cousin sneaking food, dogs,
Aunts, and Uncles too.
Gathering around the table.
Time to eat!
Thanksgiving is here.

Devan Blevins, Grade 6
Rocky Comfort Elementary School, MO

Jessie*

Her nose is cold;
Her actions are bold;
Sometimes she sleeps with me.

She loves to lick,
Except when she's sick;
Her teeth are very small.

Her jingling collar
Makes me holler,
Especially when I'm asleep at night.

And when we awake
Her body does shake,
And then I get ready for school.

Donnie Elmore, Grade 5
The Village School of Gaffney, SC
*Dedicated to my dog Jessie

Matthew

M ake's people laugh most of the time
A cts really funny a lot
T hinks he's really funny
T hinks he has the greatest dad
H as three dogs at home
E ven thinks he's great
W ants to play a lot

Matthew Riggins, Grade 4
Byrns L Darden Elementary School, TN

Earth

E veryone
A ll oceans and land
R ound in a sphere
T o live on
H igh in space

Andrew Cuffe, Grade 4
St Thomas More School, NC

That Old, Rusty Wheelbarrow

In that old, rusty wheelbarrow,
Laid my friend,
My protector,
Someone
I cuddled with.
In that old, rusty wheelbarrow,
Lay memories of tears that fell
Like glistening raindrops.
In that old, rusty wheelbarrow,
There was once a hidden secret
That I loved and I knew
It was mine forever.
In that old, rusty wheelbarrow,
There lay no sparks
Of life.
In that old, rusty wheelbarrow,
Was my friend,
My protector,
Someone I cuddled with,
And someone
I would never see again.

Emily Smith, Grade 6
East Oldham Middle School, KY

Mahleek

M aster at drawing
A good student
H elpful
L eader
E njoyful
E xciteful
K eeps my grades up

Mahleek Dailey, Grade 5
Mark Twain Elementary School, MO

Autumn

Autumn is my favorite season
Let me tell you the first reason
It's not so hot, time to play
Outside is where I'll be today

Halloween is my favorite holiday
Trick or treaters hoping for candy
Kids are dressed up as ghosts
and I'm a really good host

The leaves will turn colors
This is a sign that autumn is here
The leaves will be green and gold
These pretty colors are very bold

The weather will be cooler here
This lets me know winter's near
It's a great time to walk
or just sit outside and talk

It's a good season to fish
or throw a rock and make a wish
It's the best season of all
Let's go outside and have a ball
Nicholas Ratchford, Grade 4
Schaffner Traditional Elementary School, KY

Be

Be the one,
those count upon.
Be compassionate and caring.
Be strong, be daring.

Be the one who fulfills their dreams.
Who does things that seem…
impossible!
And makes them probable.
Madison Kearschner, Grade 5
Greathouse Shryock Traditional Elementary School, KY

Life

Life is a flower
From the first seconds of it
When the flower bud is blooming
You can taste the sweetness and happiness of life
The perfect perfume
That clears my head of distasteful memories
I feel the softness of the petals and
Sometimes the stiffness of the stem
This is life
Sometimes happy
Sometimes sad
Amy DeCillis, Grade 4
Endhaven Elementary School, NC

Nature Yellow

Nature Yellow is…
glorious, bright goldenrod bought from the store
Nature Yellow is…
the beautiful, blinding sun huge red dot in the sky
Nature Yellow is…
good smelling, tall daffodils, ready to be picked from a field
Nature Yellow is…
sour, sweet, lemons, harvested from a farm
Nature Yellow is…
spectacular, great, goldfinch living in the trees
Nature Yellow is…
awesome, cool, gold in a gold mine
that's Nature Yellow
Zachary Williams, Grade 4
Spencer County Elementary School, KY

Major League Baseball

Every kid has a dream
to play on their favorite baseball team.
If you can make it to the big league
you will get fatigue.
A lot of players are big and strong,
and others just tag along.
It is exciting when they pull a double play,
so they usually show a replay.
Only the best get into the hall of fame,
and others nicknames get them their claim to fame.
I like it best when they hit a walk-off homerun,
but that means the game is done.
Brad Baker, Grade 6
Seven Holy Founders School, MO

Jefferson Davis Memorial

Towering, steps leading skyward
Riding elevator upward to the top
Looking out windows as high as the sky, it seems
Seeing the whole world

Hearing birds chirp as loud as a marching band
Feeling the wind whip through the air
Walking to the gift shop just ahead
Inside many things appear
Taking ticket from Grandpa's hand
Walking around seeing a museum in the very back
Looking on walls pictures appear

Seeing a feather, blank ink,
A Bible, and a clay man staring at me
Watching a video telling about how it was made
Walking back out from the gift shop we go
I dashed back out from our exciting trip
No gifts to show, but that's ok
Hearing the car zoom past the Memorial
Now it's time for lunch!
Elizabeth Cravens, Grade 4
Alvaton Elementary School, KY

What's Happening to Me?
What's happening to me?
I just want to be free.
I really want to get out.
I just want to shout.
Parker Parham, Grade 5
Duncan Chapel Elementary School, SC

Fall
Crispy, crunching leaves
Under my special, kind feet
Cold brisk wind, Brr!
Ashley Bichsel, Grade 6
North Shelby Elementary School, MO

Seasons
It all starts with winter,
It snows and it snows.
I'll build a snowman,
And then winter goes.

In dances spring,
Flowers come into bloom,
I'll pick them till they leave,
Which sends me into gloom.

But then creeps in summer,
Let's head to the sea!
I'll go swimming all day,
Until summer leaves me.

Then autumn slithers in,
Otherwise know as fall.
Then it rolls away,
Like a clumsy ball.

And alas here comes winter.
It starts and it ends.
And before you know it,
The cycle begins again.
Alicia Willard, Grade 5
Stoutland Elementary School, MO

My Colors
My colors
Red for the battles
Oh, white for the pure soldiers
Blue for the beauty
Lexi Whitley, Grade 6
Dyer Elementary & Jr High School, TN

Dolphins
Dolphins are pretty
Dolphins can jump in the air
Dolphins can sense things
Sydney Harrington, Grade 4
Briarwood Christian School, AL

The Friend-in-Ship
The friend-in-ship is about having a friend who is like a ship.
We can sail across seas safely or we can go on a bumpy ride.
But your relationship don't sail at all.
But all is to be loyal, nice, and to be trustworthy
to others that you love and give your heart to
then your ship will sail evenly to your heart.
But everything is not what it seems if you don't be respectful and
responsible for your actions then you can't be respected.
Zorea Marbury, Grade 6
Childersburg Middle School, AL

The Scorching Dust
Whoosh, Whoosh, Whoosh
I try to hold in sorrow, but can't take it anymore.
I can't feed my baby any milk.
I can't feed my son any food or water,
but
I am still fighting against the dust.

I touch my dry, sandy skin.
I feel the lice wriggle on my head.
I hear the wind speaking like the gods above are telling me it will be okay.
I smell the stench of sweat from my body and my children,
but
I am still fighting against the dust.

The sand storm swallows the hearts of the citizens of Oklahoma.
Our home is blowing away and soon we won't have shelter,
but
I am still fighting against the dust.
Alisha Chowdhury, Grade 6
Haynes Academy for Advanced Studies, LA

Football
Football is fun; football is cool.
But not when you get smashed by a player that's smaller than you.
He may be fast or he may be slow,
But that's kind of embarrassing if you have played three years in a row.
He's four feet tall and weighs only 60 pounds,
But when you are hit by this player you're sure to hit the ground.
Football, yes, I love the game,
But there is only one sport that has the name.
Kendarius Wells, Grade 5
Graham Elementary School, AL

The Fair
Shocked my eyes grew as people engulfed the grounds.
Screams filled the air, pops bursting everywhere as voices rang out.
Numerous games that made you a winner.
Speedy rides that make you want to puke.
Games that make you feel like the big cheese.
Eat the most delicious food on the planet.
Toys make you feel like you just became a king.
Anybody could make this the best weekend.
Max McHugh, Grade 5
Cline Elementary School, KY

Summer Skate Park

Over the summer going to the skate park was so fun
Wanted to try a huge bowl
Did not get it
Asking a stranger to help me was easy
Showing me took no time at all
Hearing myself saying take a deep breath
Flying in the bowl
When hitting the sides keep your legs bent
Hitting the back bam fall
Got out of the bowl and tried again
Going farther was fun but still fall
Getting up and going the next day was better
The next time I go the bowl will be the first thing I do

Aaron Smith, Grade 4
Briarwood Elementary School, KY

My Goats

I don't mean to boast
On any of my goats.
But they are just way too cool
I miss them every day while I'm at school.

I hear them talk
To each other.
I hear them ask about the weather
And wait 'til the other one answers.

I watch them graze grass.
I wonder if they ask,
"Why is this girl watching us
Like we are as beautiful as flowers?"

I think I might die of sadness,
If something happened to one of them.
Without at least a goodbye,
Without a final good-baaa!

Bethany Jewett, Grade 5
Providence Academy, TN

God

I want to be funny and holy, and I want God to be in my life.
I need God in my life and so do you.
I have God in my life and so do you.
I want you to know I love God and you do too.

Terra Pierce, Grade 5
Evangel Christian Academy, AL

Mighty God

I need a place to rest upon the tough ground
and no one is around
I have a place in God's arms to stay
and this is where all His children lay
I want you to know you can lay here with me
and we will lay here for eternity.

Rachel Baxley, Grade 5
Evangel Christian Academy, AL

Where I'm From

I am from shoe length lanyards that take all day to make.
I am from potholder looms everywhere I go.
I am from playing outside with all my friends
Chasing, tagging, slipping, and falling.

I am from piano practice every Monday, practicing, rehearsing,
And playing at the fancy recital in a fancy dress every year.
I am from Chinese School
Moon cakes, graduation fancy clothes and more.

I am from selling lemonade
On hot days, washing cars
Yard sales, and craft sales
All to buy slip'n slides and video games.

I am from yummy cookies
To sweet corn and juicy steak
I am from KFC chicken and biscuits
And grandma's chocolate and pound cake.

I am from book sales
From Scholastic and shhh we're in a library.
I am from video games that I can beat in one day.
But most of all that's where I'm from and I'm proud.

Milan Eldridge, Grade 4
Price Elementary School, KY

Purse

Purses are my life
they mean everything to me
I have red, black, yellow, and purple
all the colors of the world!

I got my purses at the mall
and every department store
you can think of, it's just
too much to write!

My mom says I have 1,000,000
purses, but I tell her mom
I do not, but then I look in
my closet and oops I lied!

I get purses for my birthday
and Christmas too
my closet is overflowing
I'm going to need more room!

Thank you Lord for purses
in my life even though I
sometimes don't carry
my purses I love them!

Kynnedy Nathan, Grade 4
Schaffner Traditional Elementary School, KY

Fall Is Here

F alling in leaves
A pple pie
L eaves changing colors
L ots of laughter

I ce tea
S quirrels gathering nuts

H alloween
E ating Halloween candy
R ain is gone
E verything is bright
Wilson Hudson, Grade 5
Palmetto Christian Academy, SC

Halloween

H aunted ghost
A cross the country.
L ots of monsters
L augh with evil,
"**O** h candy!"
W hining and moaning,
"**E** ek, your soul is
E scaping!"
N ever let fright inside.
Thorin Bein, Grade 5
First Flight Elementary School, NC

Fall

F un for kids
A wesome
L eaves crack loudly
L eaves fall from trees
Luke Mikszta, Grade 4
St Thomas More School, NC

Horses

Dogs are black,
Cats are white,
Will you buy me
A horse tonight?

Give me a pinto,
Or stallion,
Even a walker will do,
As long as it is not from the zoo.

Wild or tame
They're just
The same,
They're all as cute
As can be.
Ashlee Bone, Grade 5
EA Harrold Elementary School, TN

It Is Raining

It was raining out.
I looked around to see about,
And when it stopped raining,
I went outside for training.
Cameron Hamby, Grade 4
St Patrick's School, AL

Tim

There was a young man name of Tim
His favorite special was gym
He was playing dodge ball
His pants started to fall
And everyone yelled "Look at him!"
Timothy Harris, Grade 5
C. C. Spaulding Elementary School, NC

Sailing

Sailing on the ocean blue,
Sailing with who knows who.
Sailing is wet,
But in the tropics I sweat and sweat.
I love to sail
And I love to swim.
Fish and coral everywhere,
Now I have salt in my hair.
The taste is bad,
But the sight is good.
It's hot,
It's humid,
It's rainy and more.
I love to lie on the beach
And I love to play in the sand.
Sail in the North Pacific,
South Pacific,
Atlantic and more.
Play on rocks
And swim in water.
Man, sailing is not a bother!
Torrie Gurel, Grade 6
Benton County School of the Arts, AR

Basketball

B est thing to ever happen to earth
A mazing and awesome
S pecial and totally cool
K icking cool
E verlasting fun
T errific so not terrible
B est sport ever invented
A lways in my day
L ove it every day
L ove it you will
Ciera Foster, Grade 5
Berryville Elementary School, AR

Destruction

Dark clouds rush in
Covering the sky
Pouring rain
Hammers down
on our house
Bright lightning
Flickering in the sky
Giant booming thunder
Shakes the whole house
Speeding wind
Blowing trees and
Knocking them over
People's houses
Being destroyed
By the vicious tornado
Leaving as quickly as it came
now that it's gone
All that's left behind
Is destruction.
Harrison Black, Grade 4
Buckner Elementary School, KY

I Wonder

I wonder if the sun
Will ever shine,
Oh, do I wish it would
Be mine.
But, not as bright as a light
Just like the moon at night.
Oh, I wish it wasn't hot,
But, I don't care if you
Like it or not.
Erin Withey, Grade 6
Appling County Middle School, GA

Fall

Fall is just a season to some people,
To me it's much more.
The leaves change,
As people change,
Light jackets,
And piles of leaves,
Trick-or-Treat!
As some kids say,
So much candy,
And tooth decay
A walk in the park,
With leaves of all colors,
Charlie Brown special,
As families watch.
Fall is just a season to some people,
To me it's much more.
Olivia McCarthy, Grade 5
Woodland Elementary School, KY

Chunky and Barney vs the Mouse

Chunky and Barney came back from the store
And put the food in the house,
But they noticed a small problem,
Chunky had spotted a mouse!

Chunky was afraid of mice,
"Deadly creatures," he said
That eat all of your food
Chunky was not in a good mood

But Chunky changed his fear to rage
And set up traps and a cage
Barney asked if he could help
But Chunky said, "guard the cage."

The mouse had come near the trap.
Chunky was beginning to clap!
And when the mouse stepped in, snap!
The friends have caught the mouse.

Will Comire, Grade 6
Cathedral School, NC

Ghosts

Look here, Look there, there are ghosts everywhere.
Too many to count.
Big ghosts, little ghosts, frightened ghosts,
Happy ghosts, and sad ghosts.
There are all sorts of ghosts
blue, red, white, orange, yellow
and many other ghosts.
Some people are scared of ghosts
Others could care less.
Are you scared of ghosts?
Believe me,
Ghosts are everywhere.

Ashleigh Boss, Grade 5
Arnaudville Elementary School, LA

Autumn

I see the trees and hear the bees
And luckily there is a breeze
And I think I am about to sneeze

I see the dew on the ground
Sparkling like diamonds
And all the flowers are making me wheeze
And I say jeeze Who else has to sneeze

I see the birds flying in the clear blue sky
And as the year gets older
The weather gets colder
And before you know it's AUTUMN

Matt Sawyer, Grade 5
All Saints' Episcopal School, TN

Christmas Day

Christmas day
is a wonderful way,
to get together
and be warm forever
sing carols and eat
open presents and sleep
a lot of pets
and internets
watching the Grinch
Dad got a new wrench
Mom's new cookbook
Grandpa's new fish hook
Carson got some new crayons
while our cat meows
Christmas tree lights
my dog who fights
the crisp candles glowing
Grandpa rowing
Whoosh! Whoosh! Whoosh! the basketball star.
The crisp air is like a freezer
Oh yes it's Christmas day hey!

Hanna E. Hager, Grade 5
Greathouse Shryock Traditional Elementary School, KY

The School

There was a big school
That was really cool.
It had a computer lab,
And a mascot who was a crab.
They also had a gym,
And a church that sang hymns.
The kids are really great,
But none of them got dates.
Oh, how it made them crabby!
Just like the principal who was blabby.
Some say she's out of place,
And when she runs away, it's a wild goose chase!
So this school is really cool
Even though they don't have a pool!

Alex Erbs, Grade 6
Seven Holy Founders School, MO

Emerson Conner

Emerson
Artsy, caring, quiet, loving
Sister of Caroline
Lover of animals, art, nature
I feel helpful, scared, confident
Who needs friends, environment
Who gives love, advice, compliments
Who fears darkness, heights, storms
Who would like to travel, be a vet, have a pet
Resident of Bowling Green
Conner

Emerson McCall Conner, Grade 4
Plano Elementary School, KY

On the Beach

The ocean waves crash
I hear seagulls chirp above
Feel the blazing sun.

Banks Nash, Grade 4
Briarwood Christian School, AL

The Big Snow

The snow is falling swiftly,
It covers each and every tree.
The snow is getting very deep,
It makes the animals look like sheep!
I wonder when it's going to end?
Because you could get lost, my friend!

Anna Parish, Grade 5
Coram Deo Home School Academy, MO

Grandfathers

My grandfather is loving,
it is very true.
He would do anything for you.
He will hold you tight.
He will keep you warm at night.
This man will show you compassion.
He might be in pain,
but you can light his day.
I love him so and so should you.
So please, I beg of you,
show these men some respect,
like I do.

Jocelyn Leibovich, Grade 6
Harding Academy at White Station, TN

The Seed

One seed falls in the water
Then it starts to grow
But with too much water
It starts to drown.

Then along comes a boy
Who sees the seed
Pulls it from the water
Then plants it in the ground
So that it can grow
Finally it grows into
A tree

Jeffrey Craddock, Grade 5
G C Burkhead Elementary School, KY

Bike

I like to ride it every day,
But definitely not on the highway
With friends, family, or just me.
Red, orange, or blue it can be,
Any color, size, style just for me.

Damaris Lopez, Grade 4
Cleveland Elementary School, OK

A Walk in the Woods

While I walk in the woods,
I hear the wonderful chorus of birds singing as they fly through the atmosphere.
I hear the crunching and rustling of leaves as deer trot along.
I hear the sweet sound of crickets chirping to one another.
I hear the wind fighting the trees up above.

I smell the fresh scent of maple and oak.
I smell the clean earth aroma.
I smell the dark green, prickly pine needles on the pine trees.
I smell the Tennessee River located at the end of the woods.
I smell the water droplets that are clinging to all the leaves near my feet.

I see the different markings of each plant and vine.
I see the scrapings on the trees.
I see the spiders putting their final additions on their flawless, silk webs.

Those are the things I hear, smell, and see while I walk through the woods.

Ben Welsh, Grade 4
Sequoyah Elementary School, TN

The Fuzzy Ball

Once there was a fuzzy ball, he sat on his hind legs.
He could hop like lightning,
But he ate like a bear.
His name was Thumper.
He was a hare, he had lots of fur, but little hair.

He ran away but we found him eating as usual.
He has a big fat tummy and is very soft.
He looks like Santa because he has very long, white whiskers,
But he leaves a lot of messy presents.
He is a hare, he has lots of fur, but little hair.

We don't need a lawn mower, he gets the job done.
He doesn't need any gas, just grass,
But he does have a lot of gas.
He bounds all over the yard chasing the cats,
Running from the dogs and catching insects and squashing them.

I love it when he does tricks.
He jumps and plays.
He will fetch like a dog, mew like a cat, sleep all day, run all night.
He'll lie around when he's lazy, jump when he's hyper,
He's so cute!

Collin Eldridge, Grade 5
Providence Academy, TN

Green

Green is the color of my favorite thing, money.
It's what I feel after I eat cafeteria food.
Green is the color everybody feels when we step on the b-ball court.
It's the color of all the lovely leaves in the spring.
Best of all, green is my favorite color.

Hyatt Frost, Grade 6
Ketchum Jr High School, OK

The Moments of Your Life

Cameras can capture a moment,
Treasured and special in your life
Trap it into a beautiful picture.

It focuses on one thing at a time
A special time with friends and family.
As you press the button, the moment is captured,
The sacred moment in your life.

The photo is printed out and put in the photo album.
It shows us all of what we treasured at the time
And the meaning of it will always be with us.

When we look back at a photo album
To look at the captured moments,
We discover the love and happiness shown,
Which are the moments of your life.

Juliann Cho, Grade 5
Estes Hills Elementary School, NC

Autumn

A lways fun,
U nder the table my dog is waiting for left over turkey —
T he pumpkin pie and turkey, so good,
U me, and my family celebrating thankfulness
M y friends and I jumping in the leaves —
N ever say no to a homemade thanksgiving dinner!

Rob McAdams, Grade 5
Palmetto Christian Academy, SC

Where I'm From

I am from rusty mufflers,
clothes pin hangers.
I am from a cramped small, loving home.
I am from a mole
crawling under my porch.
I am from a city bus
to town.
I am from
basketball city.
I am from playing
sports, basketball, football.
I am from playing
a melody on the violin.
I am from learning
at school.

Matthew Houp, Grade 5
Tates Creek Elementary School, KY

Leaves

Leaves change just like we do.
I can hardly wait to jump into that colorful leaf pile.
The smell of my grandmother's pumpkin pie takes over the air.
All of us cuddled in our beds no one awake except the moon.

Alex O'Brien, Grade 4
First Wesleyan Christian School, NC

Summer Days

Not having to get up and go to school,
Working the cows in the blistering hot sun,
Laboring in the hay field, a long and tiring day,
Going to the lake; fishing and swimming,
Mowing yard to make money,
Bushogging and cutting hay for my uncle,
Helping my dad plumb a house,
Running a bulldozer and back hoe to clean out a pond,
Feeding eight hundred rabbits,
Swimming in our new pool every day,
When the day is over it is time to shoot clay pigeons for fun.

Colton Mathews, Grade 6
Alvaton Elementary School, KY

Madison

Short blondish-brown hair, green eyes, and tall.
Shorts and T-shirts I play in.
Ride my bike, swim, play outside are favorite things to do.
Things that make me angry are my sister,
And people being mean to me.
Listen to my iPod alone.
Green, blue, pink, orange are favorite colors.

Madison Proffer, Grade 5
Our Lady Catholic School, MO

Scorching, Burning, Bright Gold Sun*

Scorching, burning, bright gold sun
You made temperatures reach one hundred and one
Up above the brown, dead grasses
You made me have to wear sunglasses
Scorching, burning, bright gold sun
You made my summer lots of fun

Will Compton, Grade 5
Walton Verona Elementary School, KY
*To the tune of "Twinkle, Twinkle, Little Star."

Football

I love tackling a football player in football.
I enjoy running the ball.
I really love catching the ball.
I relish the sound when we hit each other.
I prefer kicking the football.
I enjoy doing a butt roll because it gets me in shape.

Sye Watson, Grade 5
North Middle School, TN

Skateboarding

Skateboarding is what I do best,
But when it comes time I have to rest.
I will play guitar with my brother Les,
But when it comes time, I will be skateboarding.
It's what I do best!

Hunter Lewis, Grade 6
Scotts Creek Elementary School, NC

The Tree House

A long time ago I did find
A tree house that was divine
It looked all beat up and ratty
But I believed that it could be mine.

With work it was
We sawed boards
We hammered nails
We did this all day and all night.

After all the work came the play
We climbed and hung
We swung on the swings
And played all day long.

Alex Reichenbach, Grade 5
American Heritage Academy, GA

Razor

My name is Razor.
I'm as sharp as a blazer.
I can cut through paper.
I'm like a laser.

Marshall Mulkey, Grade 4
Moyock Elementary School, NC

My Teacher

My teacher is the best
She is above all the rest
She is so nice
She does not like mice
But she gave us a test.

Natasha McFarland, Grade 6
Martin Elementary School, WV

Michael

M agnificent
I ncredible
C aring
H appy
A wesome
E njoy Math
L oving

Michael Sheridan, Grade 4
Wohlwend Elementary School, MO

Turkeys

Turkeys
pretty ugly
gobble, squeak, holler
hunting, fighting, breeding, hibernating
ugliest bird in Mississippi
Gobblers

Bailey Thornton, Grade 4
East Jones Elementary School, MS

Cafeteria

Parents think we're having fun,
But we're in the torture chamber.
Attacked by pizza,
Peas shooting and blasting us out.
Trays are our only protection.
Covered with scrapes and bruises,
We crawl home.

Bailey Weisler, Grade 5
St Vincent Elementary School, MO

Blanket

I would be a blanket
I wouldn't have to get eaten
Or stuck in a sealed tight container
I always wanted to know
What it was like
Taking a bath in a washer
Or getting dried by a dryer
If I was going to be a blanket
I would want to look like this
Gold trimming with solid black
A black diamond
Or red and blue
With a mithral diamond
Really fluffy
No one would use me
They would just look at me
If I had a speck of dust
They would clean me

Hayden Champlin, Grade 5
Berryville Elementary School, AR

I Love School

Math is fun
You get new ideas
You work work work
Till your problems are done

Recess is great
You hang out with your friends
You get to socialize
And that is fun

Writing is cool
You get brainstorms
You write write write
'Til your writing is done

When you go home
You get on the bus
You go zoom zoom zoom
And that is a laugh

Yasmine Langes, Grade 5
Woodland Elementary School, KY

Summer

Summer is fun.
You can run under the sun.
You can swim in a pool.
Some people think it's cool.
You can sit by a fire,
While it grows higher and higher.
You can roast s'mores
Then make more!

Calli Crawford, Grade 5
Lula Elementary School, GA

The Ocean

Looks like a pretty long, blue blanket
Sounds like loud crashing waves
Tastes like a fresh drink of salty water
Feels like cold refreshing water
Smells like a salty ocean

Amanda Bailey, Grade 5
Briarwood Christian School, AL

Scarecrow

S caring all the crows
C reepy at night
A lways looking straight
R ocking back and forth
E ager to stare
C rows on his shoulders
R unning a stick up his back
O n a tree like a bird
W ooden or stuffed.

Ashley Beardsley, Grade 5
First Flight Elementary School, NC

November Thanks

Almost forgot!
Freezing weather
Time changes
House cleaned
Family comes
Leaves fall
Delicious food
Family talking
Turkey ham
Pie dessert
Belching grandparents
Dirty dishes
Vacation comes
Relatives play
Animals hibernate
Crying goodbye
Everyone leaves
Parents tired

James Doyle, Grade 5
Center Elementary School, GA

I Live on an Army Post

I am a son of a soldier who's in Iraq.
I wonder if my dad will come home with pride.
I hear gun's go off and wonder if it's my dad.
I see the bus leave with my dad in it.
I want my dad to come home fast.
I am a son of a soldier who's in Iraq.

I pretend that my dad is there for me.
I feel that my dad is with me when I see his picture.
I touch my dad's picture when I'm sad.
I worry that my dad might get hurt.
I cry when my dad isn't home.
I am a son of a soldier who's in Iraq.

I understand that my dad has to leave.
I say my dad is a hero and brave.
I dream my dad will never come back.
I try not to give my mom a hard time.
I hope the entire dads and moms are safe.
I am a son of a soldier who's in Iraq.

Joshua Hernandez, Grade 6
Walker Intermediate School, KY

Life Is…

Life is about education.
It's about listening and paying attention in school.
It's about choosing the right friends.
It's about having good judgment.
It's about respecting your parents.
It's about being generous to people.
It's about standing up for what you believe in.
It's about being happy at bad times.
But most of all life's about family and friends.
Only you choose to do the right thing or not.

Sergio Ortega, Grade 6
Lost River Elementary School, KY

Ocean

The ocean is an aquarium
to all plants and fish
of all colors, shapes, sizes, and names
but you can just call them aqua life if you wish.

The ocean is just a blue screen
with little swimming fish puppets along the ground
with little plants moving
and with the water sounds in surround sound.

The ocean is an aquarium
to all plants and fish
but they are the big happy family
which is what makes the ocean a dream or a wish.

Caileigh Marshall, Grade 5
McKee Road Elementary School, NC

Scoring a Touchdown

We all get in the huddle,
And the quarterback calls the play.
I decide no one's going to tackle me today.
I hear the QB call, "Hut one, hut two, hut three."
The center snaps; the QB turns and hands the ball to me.
I take a glance behind to see
If anyone is going to catch me.
Then, I start to prance
And in the end zone I do a dance.

TJ Valenza, Grade 6
Seven Holy Founders School, MO

Palm Trees

Palm trees are tall,
Palm trees are brown,
Palm trees are from those southern towns,
Palm trees have coconuts on their crowns,
Palm trees are slanted on their side,
Palm trees touch the sky.

Cody Rebstock, Grade 5
Wright City Middle School, MO

Just Walk It

Talk, talk, talk that's what some girls do,
but I don't talk, talk, talk I walk, walk, walk alone
People may think I'm unusual for a girl,
I don't believe that, if people stop talking
and start walking we will all get along
And it will be peaceful

Jamilla Denny-Green, Grade 5
C. C. Spaulding Elementary School, NC

Purple

Purple is bruised from blue to purple.
Purple is school spirit that is good with yellow.
Yelling left yelling right! Then scream!
I see purple.
Purple is round and is something you eat.
Maybe grapes or plums, not my choice.
Purple is sky mixed with blue.
Purple is germs that spread from me to you.
Purple is me!
Purple is not just a color.
It is a feeling, a sad feeling.
Purple is fire just as it burnt out.
Purple! Purple! Purple!
Purple is a Gatorade that I drink during a game.
Purple is a juice pop that will be gone in seconds.
1, 2, 3 gone!
Purple is a store, Hollister or Vanity.
Purple is my family, we all like purple.
Purple is food. Grape pie! Yum!
Purple is a boarder around me to you.
Purple is friendship that will last between me and you. Forever!

Jharon Satterfield, Grade 6
Lost River Elementary School, KY

While I'm Asleep

While the birds sleep and crickets chirp
While the moon settles in the sky.
This happens all the time
but I can't go outside.
While dogs howl,
when they see owls.
While the owls hoo!
The cows say moo.

Tessa Ryan, Grade 4
St Michael School, TN

The Tic Tock Clocks

There is a house
Where you can find
A lot of clocks that tell time
But wait, they can do more
They tic tock, and even snore!
All through the days
And all through the nights
They tic tock and snore
Which gives me a fright
And when they all strike 12
They rattle my bedroom shelves
You can find them any day
You can find them any night
Just a tic tockin' away
And keeping me up throughout the night!

Caitlin Woods, Grade 5
Wynne Intermediate School, AR

My Angels

I look to the trees
and woods and the grass.
I see my angels.
I'm glad God gave me them.
Something hits me in the head.
I look in the sky.
I see clouds of white
and skies of blue.
Birds are flying.

Aaron Carmack, Grade 4
Ode Maddox Elementary School, AR

The Hummingbird

The ruby red under his chest
fills nature with all the best,
He sings a song
and all join along,
As he dips his nose in the nectar
his heart starts beating all the better,
His tender fingers grip with power
as he sips out of the flower,
His little wings zip away,
but don't worry he'll be back someday!

Ann Rollins Johnson, Grade 5
Salisbury Academy, NC

My Grandma's Farm

I see horses and cows up by the fence
The blooming flowers all around me
Fields of green where the cows roam free
Raccoon tracks down by the creek
I smell lovely dandelions as they grow all around me
The fresh water from the small waterfall down in the big woods
The manure from the fields after the cows do their business
A big dead deer that my dad shot in the woods
I hear wild turkeys in the back fields going gobble, gobble, gobble
Like they're trying to give me a headache
The crunch of leaves when deer pass by
Wood peckers pecking as hard as they can like at war in Vietnam
The call of coyotes in the woods where me and my dad go hunting
I taste the lovely mint that grows in patches that
Are wilder than the fireworks on the Fourth of July
Fried ham that my grandma cooks me for breakfast
Eggs to go with my ham
I feel bushes rubbing my skin like they're giving me a massage
The cold cream that helps my poison ivy
Water going down my throat as I drink from the creek
My grandma's farm

Cole Kreilein, Grade 4
Briarwood Elementary School, KY

One and Only!

She is very pretty, caring, and loyal.
She always makes me laugh with her funny comments,
She dances like a gazelle; soaring into leaps across the stage,
Constantly grabbing your attention, whichever way she moves so you don't look away.
Even though she is older than me, she continues till this day to keep me close by,
She's smart and she's a great role model that is no lie.
She even comes to my games whether it is in the blazing heat or freezing cold
She's my one and only sister who has a heart of gold.
I love you Michelle.

Gabby Scirica, Grade 6
Holy Trinity School, KY

Timeless Nothing

Tick tock, tick tock…
Is all I can hear, as I stand here in the middle of nothing.
I have no concept of time,
But do I ever?
There is no such thing as time.
You have no idea what darkness I am standing in.
It is nothing like the darkness you are used to,
Which compared to this…
Is as bright as a thousand suns.
This darkness is like a nightmare that you can't wake up from.
My heart is thumping wildly, and it seems as if I'm barely breathing.
To me it is like drowning in a pool of nothing.
I cannot see anything.
I cannot smell anything,
But I can hear one thing…
The possibility of where I am and how I got here.

Sarah Hamon, Grade 6
Montessori Community School, NC

Santa's Been Caught!

Snowflakes drifting gently
on a chilly Christmas night
settling on a holly wreath
under the soft moonlight.
At first I hear a jingle,
and then a "Ho ho ho!"
I tie up my last present
with a cheery Christmas bow.
His sleigh is fast approaching
with Rudolph right in front.
As Santa shifts his toy bag,
he gives a jolly grunt.
I place all of my presents
under the Christmas tree
and sit down on the couch and wait.
Santa's real, you'll see!
Soon, I hear hooves on the roof
and another "Ho ho ho!"
Santa slides on down the chimney,
turns around at me and says, "Oh!"
Santa has been caught

Rae Cross, Grade 6
Charleston County School of the Arts, SC

Winter Is the Time of Year

Winter is the time of year,
when everyone gets out to cheer.
The first snowflake comes, it comes and it goes,
nobody's going to walk with only toes.
Christmas is coming, it fills me with joys,
lots of children get bunches of toys.
The cheering gives me a cold chill that rushes through my body.
We build snowmen as if we've never before.
Sometimes, winter can be tragic,
it can freeze your tush.
And the wind is whistling,
"whoosh, whoosh, whoosh."
Winter has its good times
it has its bad.
But remember,
winter is the time of year.

O. Hunter Mayfield IV, Grade 5
Greathouse Shryock Traditional Elementary School, KY

Weather

Hurricanes, tornadoes
They don't look like potatoes.
Tsunamis, thunderstorms.
Good thing my house is not torn.
People getting ready for it to come.
Stores so full, all the water gone.
There's going to be a flood near the pond.
Different kind of storms,
I safely wake up in the morn.

Kendall Elmore, Grade 5
Hall Fletcher Elementary School, NC

My Grandma's House in the Morning

In the morning there's a nice smell of grass.
The stars vanish when the sun comes up.
The dew sparkles as the morning sun shines.
The birds chirp as they wake up.
Lizards come out when the dew is gone.
The sun is shining high in the sky.
Most of the soft bunnies come out and find breakfast.
The dogs bark when the sun comes up and wakes them.
When noon arrives everything becomes calm.

Gregory Carson, Grade 5
Cline Elementary School, KY

Christmas Time

On a cold winter's night
The snow was falling
It looked like icicles glistening in the light

Sleigh bells were ringing
I knew it must be Santa.
He couldn't be far from sight.

All the children were tucked in bed,
Everything was very quiet.
I could see Santa's sleight,
It was oh so bright.

We hopped out of bed
To see if Santa had been by,
The presents were there
Placed under the tree just right.

Mandy Irvin, Grade 5
East Bernstadt Elementary School, KY

Boys and Girls Ways

Give a game to a boy and he will play it for a day.
Teach a girl to shop and she will shop till she drops.
Boys like games, girls like shopping.
Put them together and girls will rule.
Those are the girls' and boys' ways.

Jamia Thomas, Grade 5
Romine Inter District Elementary School, AR

Unicorn Night

Unicorn, unicorn come out and play
It's unicorn night you've slept all day.
Where thou wander we will see
Unicorn, unicorn come to me.
Running, leaping through the mists
Galloping through the forests
That's where we wander the unicorns chorus.
Unicorn, unicorn come to me
It's unicorn night may I dance with thee.

Katelyn Kornegay, Grade 4
Washington Montessori Public Charter School, NC

Beauty

Beauty, the Irish hillside when the sun is just breaking the horizon. A light drizzle over the cool, wet air.

Beauty, the sound of Celtic bagpipes playing in the unknown distance. It is certain that the man who plays the instrument is Celtic as well.

Beauty, not only shown in magazines; a phase where your visual and spiritual senses tingle without the slightest regret, without stress, without disaster in mind, and without fear.

Beauty, not only a vision, but also a pause in the painful, mournful world. This fact is not a tease. It is a sudden freeze in your neck, a chill sent racing down your spine, a crack of thunder breaking the silence and drawing your face away from a soothing breeze. You wonder to yourself, "What will this all add up to? What is the best word to describe this moment?" Well, we have found an answer to this question.

The answer, Beauty.

Curran Greene, Grade 5
Madisonville Jr High School, LA

Me?

I am the music that runs through your veins,
I am a gorgeous flower blooming from a seed.
I will fight for myself because a competition is what I am.
Sometimes I am the sugar in your coffee and the pepper in your sauce,
I can take something's but don't push me over the limit because I will put my hand in your face.
I don't think I am the coolest person on Earth but I am not the ugliest, dumbest, or anything else.
But one thing is for sure I am me.

Ashley Hannah, Grade 6
Beck Academy, SC

Mad

I got mad at my teacher so I couldn't concentrate. I could still see in my head all the goofy and funny times she had with us. My teacher stood at her desk searching for me. She looked left and right, up and down. She said, "Where are you?" Then I gave her a present to say I was sorry. It feels good to give my teacher something. She made me happy by giving me a gold star. She knows me so well. She knows I like gold.

Lucy Cacioppo, Grade 5
Fox Elementary School, MO

Friendship

Friendship is like a cd.
You can use it over and over, until it gets a scratch.
You polish it a little and it becomes the same thing you used to love.
I can be something you never get tired of.

Friendship has a piano's highs and lows, but it always sounds beautiful.
It is the key to a happy life.
Friendship can strum the strings of laughter.
It can play the chords of liveliness.

Friendship can come in many different colorful combinations.
It is a wonderful link between two people, just as a rainbow links two places in a colorful bond.
It can symbolize strength.
It can tie you up with society.

Like a plant, friendship can become entangled with weeds.
But, it can grow and prosper and be trimmed to perfection.
It can creep up the most unlikely wall.
It can bloom into a beautiful thing.

Alix Griffin, Grade 6
St Mary's School, SC

My Pappy, the Veteran

I have a hero, who is brave,
When he was a teen he liked to save.
His name was Bobby, and he was a dancer,
Until his body encountered cancer.

He was in the Navy,
His hat was quite wavy.
He was like a rabbit when he was young,
When he was older, he had no tongue.

He loved to see us happy,
To us he was Pappy.
He liked to give us gum,
His favorite flower was a mum.

Mighty Mark Martin was his favorite racer,
Sometimes he was even a swift pacer.
He had a friend named Tim,
I really, really do miss him!

Layla Bolin, Grade 4
North Elementary School, NC

I Cannot Find My Shoes

I cannot find my shoes today
I had them on my floor.
I cannot find my shoes today
I have looked everywhere.
I checked in my room,
checked in the hall, checked in the kitchen,
checked in the bathroom, checked down the stairs,
checked in the garage.
But they aren't anywhere.
I asked my mom if she had them
but she said she didn't know.
I can't find…What?…
They're on my feet, Ah man…
I missed school!
Well, I'm going out to play.

Brittany Kohn, Grade 4
Lewis Vincent Elementary School, LA

Sports

Sports are the things I love to do
And I do quite a few.
They are so much fun
Because they can include anyone.
Some include baseball, golf, soccer, hockey, and tennis
But my favorite is basketball.
Sports are different in their own way
Because they can be played any day.
Whether it's winter, spring, summer, or fall
You can play them even if you're small.

Matthew Maddock, Grade 6
Woodland Presbyterian School, TN

Why I Like Math

addition, subtraction, multiplication, division
expanded notation, prime and composite numbers
I really like this kind of math

some facts are easy, some facts are hard,
but I like them all
just the same

I like solving problems fast
zoom

I like coming up with different ways
of solving a problem

and I really like
getting all my answers correct

Caleb Hayes, Grade 5
Meramec Elementary School, MO

Rebels Win

Robert struck out,
It was my turn,
I stepped into the box hoping to get a hit,
The pitcher wound up,
He fired it right past me,
"Strike one," the ump said,
I stepped back in
Here it comes,
 I swung,
"Strike two,"
This was it,
Either I get a big hit,
Or my team loses the championship,
Here comes the pitch,
I put my best swing on the ball,
There it goes,
Up, up, up,
And over the centerfielder's head,
All I hear is Rebels win, Rebels win,
And my cleats stomping on home plate.

Matt Weber, Grade 6
Annunciation Elementary School, MO

Summer's Here!

Insane friends with nothing to do.
Blurry late nights slowly drifting to sleep.
Annoying allergies and aggravating sniffles.
Heroic sports calls for bravery.
Swimming in a clear ice-cold pool on blazing hot days.
Mysterious sleepovers waking up to your biggest nightmares.
Wild injuries always costing money.
Holiday World, as crowded as the stars in the sky.
Grounded again, the madness never stops.
Remarkable freedom ending so soon.

Katherine Rector, Grade 6
Alvaton Elementary School, KY

Ode to the Sun

Up in the sky,
Shining ever so bright,
The sun smiles down at us all,
Day by day, giving off lots of light.

Helping plants grow,
Allowing us to see,
We have fun under the sun,
Playing, just you and me.

I get up in the morning,
To watch this big star rise,
Always in the same place,
The east of those great blue skies.

And when the sun sets,
It is quite a sight,
All those beautiful colors,
I can only say good night.
Sarika Sachdeva, Grade 6
River Trail Middle School, GA

Fourth of July

Fourth of July
Smoke
Popping
Meatloaf
Fireworks
Fourth of July
Tyler Cobb, Grade 4
Tamassee-Salem Elementary School, SC

The Soccer Ball

One day I found a soccer ball,
And it was like no other,
I used it every single day
And it was like a brother.

One day when I was kicking it,
It hit a big trash bin,
And then I heard ping, pop, clink
And out came a million hair pins.

One day I lost that soccer ball,
I looked just everywhere,
And every single place I looked,
It just wasn't there.

One day when I looked for it,
I found it in the shed!
I didn't want to make much noise
A solemn celebration I had!
Reid Smith, Grade 5
Providence Academy, TN

Thanksgiving

Thanksgiving is a
time of year for everyone
to be so thankful.
Haylee Dorrill, Grade 4
Briarwood Christian School, AL

My Dog Rosie

My dog Rosie is very sweet
But because she is so big,
She needs a lot to eat.
She is so much like a pig!

My dog Rosie is really weird.
She likes to bark at you.
But she is not to be feared.
And now I have told you about,
My dog Rosie.
Libby Andrews, Grade 6
Westwood Christian Academy, GA

Funny Dog

My dog is funny,
He chases after bunnies.
When he is done with his bone,
He will put it in his pail
And wag his tail.
He barks when
It starts to get dark.
Don't make a peep
After he falls asleep.
Nighty, night
Sleep tight,
Don't let the bed bugs bite.
Lacy Lamle, Grade 5
St Paul's Lutheran School, OK

In the Stew

Rocks, rocks in the stew,
Cook them up
And watch them brew.

Clover, clover in the stew,
Chop them up
And watch it brew.

Pine cones, Pine cones in the stew,
Cook them up
And eat the stew!

Yum, yum tasty stew,
Make some more
And have more stew!
Nicole Gouhin, Grade 4
St Thomas More School, NC

Boxer

A boxer is a great breed,
They are lovable and easy to feed.
They love to wrestle and play,
And take a nap on a long day.
Alyssa Hayes, Grade 5
Duncan Chapel Elementary School, SC

My Muddy Buddy

I have a good buddy,
Who loves to get down and muddy,
He loves to go bogg'n,
With his steel headed nogg'n,
And comes home all dirty and cruddy.
Nathan Erickson, Grade 4
Eastside Elementary School, GA

Flute and Clarinet

We're playing the flute,
and we're playing the clarinet.
Do it right and just don't fret.

We're playing the flute.
We're playing along.
We're playing some music.
We're playing a song.

We're playing the clarinet.
We're doing it right.
I just hope
we finish tonight!

You play A, I'll play B
You play C, and I'll play D
You play E, and I'll play F,
and then we'll play G,
on the end of the music staff,
on the end of the music staff!
Kristin Hand, Grade 6
Appling County Middle School, GA

I Love Baseball

Baseball is my favorite sport
I love it so much I could go to court.

I could play baseball all day
Actually I think I may.

Baseball is absolutely the best
But that is my guess.

I love to slide to first base
And that is the case.
Brianna Hackworth, Grade 5
North Middle School, TN

Summer/Winter

Summer
sunny, joyful
flowing, shining, laughing
friends, grandparents, Santa Claus, New Year's Eve
snowing, sledding, melting
chilly, peaceful
Winter

Hannah Hall, Grade 5
Briarwood Christian School, AL

I Am

I am a bookworm girl who loves to read
I wonder if I'll ever write books of my own
I hear the voice of a book waiting to be read
I see a character jumping out of a book
I want to be an author of poetry and stories
I am a bookworm girl that loves to read

I pretend I am the character of a book
I feel the power of words when I write
I touch the emotions of a character
I worry that no one will like my work
I cry that not everyone has the joy of reading
I am a bookworm girl who loves to read

I understand not everyone can read
I say, "Teach everyone to read and write"
I dream up ideas for poems and stories
I try very hard to get my work published
I hope one day everyone can read
I am a bookworm girl who loves to read

Natasha Anbalagan, Grade 6
R D and Euzelle P Smith Middle School, NC

My Dog

My dog is as white as snow
with black spotted ears.
She has a long, fluffy, white tail.
I will love her through the years.

She jumps on you when you come in,
it's like a kangaroo jump.
Her eyes are a light blue,
and her nose is long like Pinocchio too.

She loves to play outside,
in winter or summer or a hot day.
When you throw the ball she runs after it.
Her little heart loves to jump and play!

When you're lying down on the couch or bed
she jumps on you likes she's a little pup.
She licks you with her long tongue — slurp!
She is as sweet as sugar to love.

Erica Roller, Grade 5
Providence Academy, TN

The Dress

I started as nothing as mice got my things.
They took bows, lace, and many rings.
Some took needles and thread to get ahead.
While others took time to trace out my lace.
I knew I'd look great because of the mice.
They took time to create and make me look nice.
There came a big bow,
Which they made to show.
Now I know, that I can go,
And make it to the ball without a great fall.
Now I'm a dress, just like the rest.
I'm very beautiful and am not a mess.
As I was put on,
I knew all along,
No one can make me more than the mice.
As we were leaving I heard voices cry,
That's mine, and that's hers.
And now I'll say goodbye.

Becca Messer, Grade 6
St Mary's School, SC

Grandma's House

If you ask me, I believe
The busiest place is Grandma's house on Thanksgiving,
The busiest place in the house is the kitchen —
It's full of pies, turkey, and chicken!
Cousins are there, aunts, and uncles too —
Grandpas, grandmas, me and you!
Lunch is the best course of the day,
Then we go outside to romp and play —
We jump in the bright, colorful leaves and
We climb into the very tall trees,
When we get chilly we go back inside —
We warm by the fire as we shut our eyes,
The best time of the year is fall,
At Grandma's house, family and all!

Logan Denny, Grade 5
Palmetto Christian Academy, SC

The War

I try to go to sleep but
Just a thought scares me
The guns the blood in the air
Hatred and despair
Those who lost hope and
Those who gained hope

I try not to imagine,
The images going through my mind
Is this their torture for doing nothing wrong?
Just stop! Please stop.
Give me a peace of mind.

Morgan Stanford, Grade 6
St Francis Xavier School, AL

Pink

Pink is every girl's color
It's on their clothes
And on their toes
It's even on their nose
Boys may say Yuk
But girls say it will bring you luck
Some girls like pink cars
Who knows you might find pink on Mars
My room is pink and my blankets, too
So listen up 'cause pink rocks!

Katelyn Rudel, Grade 5
West Elementary School, MO

Pay Attention You

I walked off a sidewalk
Or so I thought.
But it was really a cliff
Leading to man-eating sharks!
I was beaten and eaten,
It was then when I knew
My mother's old saying,
"Pay Attention" is TRUE!!!

Hannah McClellan, Grade 4
Moyock Elementary School, NC

Taunting

I snickered
I taunted
I just had to prove myself superior
I won the video game
I laughed
Before he nailed me
A fist that came out of nowhere
A burning sensation
That hit my cheek
Disoriented for two seconds
A crimson red gash
Lay atop my cheek
A bruise forming
Like a bad infection
He backed away
As I came forward
He looked terrified
My Brother

Spencer Root, Grade 6
East Oldham Middle School, KY

Rachel

R adiant
A ctive
C heerful
H elpful
E xcellent
L oving

Rachel Addis, Grade 4
Tamassee-Salem Elementary School, SC

Adventures on the Open Seas

Adventures on the open seas
Is like a sea side jubilee.
"Hoist the anchor let's set sail!" said the captain to his parrot pal.
Unremitting fun for everyone!

Scruples are allowed,
Nudge your neighbors tell them proud!
Be tranquil, rejuvenate,
Have eccentric fun don't you wait!

Katy Phillips, Grade 5
Rossville Elementary School, GA

My Outside Days

I like to be outside morning, noon or night.
I like to hunt I have a 243.
I like to go hunting to see what I can see.
I like to fish I take my pole
To the nearest water hole.
I like to play ball
The best time is the spring and the fall.
In the summer when the days get lazy
I like to jump into the pool;, mom says I'm crazy.
I like the PlayStation and Xbox
But I'd rather be in the wood chasing a coon or a fox.
I play with my mom, I play with my dad.
I can play by myself but that makes me sad.
So if you haven't been outside stick your head out and have a peek
You might see me playing hide-n-seek.
Come on out and have some fun
We can play in the shade or the sun.

Anthony Sartin, Grade 4
Brilliant Elementary School, AL

I Am From

I am from being born in a Danville, Kentucky hospital
to living in a little white house on Herrington Lake
and moving to a bigger house up the road with lots of room!

I am from fighting with my older brother, Nate,
to retelling the events of what happened to my parents
and having both of them ordering us to stop and apologize to each other...
and having it start all over again.

I am from aggravating my five kittens: Callie, Prince, Puss-n-boot, Tom and Killer
to feeding mommy cat, Precious...
and coming inside to pet my two indoor fat cats: Bob and Spooky...
my two living and breathy fluffy carpets!

I am from playing catcher on my softball team,
competing in cross country meets as the only girl from my school
and making lay-ups for my basketball team.

THIS IS WHAT I AM FROM.

Mackenzie Kibler, Grade 5
Burgin Independent School, KY

Cool and Crisp Fall

When the leaves
Fall
To
The
Ground —
And the cool and crisp chill of the fall wind,
    And the pumpkins start to grow
With the yellow blossoms —
And of course, the tasty seed of pumpkins —
    Fall's Here!

Emma King, Grade 5
Palmetto Christian Academy, SC

Life's Journey

Life is very long, but only if you make it.
It's like a hard test, but only if you take it.
Sometimes you think it's hard, but you need to try,
    to believe in yourself, you could soar and fly.

It's like the internet, there's lots of firewalls,
It's like you're in school, "no running in the halls."
There are rules and regulations that you need to follow,
    You can be an angel, don't forget your halo.

So spread your wings and fly, you could touch the sky.
Everyone is special in their own unique way.
You'll learn new things each and every day.
You have to believe you can achieve in life's journey.

Dewayne Fowler, Grade 5
C. C. Spaulding Elementary School, NC

Fall Day

I woke up one morning.
It was a fall day.
I got my jacket and went outside.
It was colder than ice.

When I got to school, I got my stuff out.
We did millions of fall projects.
We went out to play that cold fall day.
Are we crazy or what?

I could feel the cold breeze going through my hair.
I saw all the colors of fall.
All the leaves were swirling through the air.
We jumped in a pile of leaves one hundred feet high.

We went into the school.
Our faces were red as tomatoes.
I heard the ringing of the bell.
I got home and went to bed;
I could not wait for another fall day.

Lily Hollandsworth, Grade 5
Providence Academy, TN

Land Run

There was a great race.
A long time ago, history was made.
The people claimed one hundred and sixty
Acres of land.

There was a great race.
The people had dugouts, not houses.
The people did not have cars.
They traveled by horseback, then.

There was a great race.
A race that showed the way.

Matt Ritchie, Grade 4
Hayes Elementary School, OK

If I Were in Charge of the World

If I were in charge of the world
    I would cancel out broccoli
    And fruit.

If I were in charge of the world
    I'd make every kid's parents
Let them have ice cream for breakfast, lunch and dinner
    I'd destroy the schools and make money
    Fall from the sky.

If I were in charge of the world I would cancel all wars
    And kids would never have to grow up,
    And no animals would ever become extinct.

Auston Graves, Grade 5
Eminence Middle School, KY

Good Ole Kentucky Home

I love my cozy home,
Where pine trees sway
Watching the sunset go down
Black shingles,
Brown chestnut wood,
Rose color bricks,

Coyotes softly howl under the moonlight,
Deer rustling in the leaves,
Turkeys joining the fun
What a happy place!

White, purple, and red flowers
Popping out from every corner
Like balloons in the landscape,
The pool with gleaming water,
Butterflies on the purple lilacs
The woods are warm and cozy like a baby in a blanket,
As we sit by the fireplace I feel so safe…

At my good ole Kentucky home.

Abby Prow, Grade 4
Alvaton Elementary School, KY

Butterfly

Colorful, little.
Flies around all night. Keeps the
Days all fresh and new.
Nicole Cabrera, Grade 4
Briarwood Christian School, AL

Butterfly

Butterfly, flutter by
The shining sun in the sky.
Butterfly, spread your wings
And listen to the birds sing.
Yellow, orange, black, blue,
Keep your colors shining too.
Flutter by the house on the hill,
And land on the windowsill.
Fly higher and higher into the sky,
Come on now, butterfly,
Flutter by!
Hannah McGuire, Grade 6
Heavenly Host Lutheran School, TN

Sheep

Sheep
Hairy, white
walk, snort, huddle
eating, resting, running, shaving
All sheep have hair.
Baby lamb
Jessica Satcher, Grade 4
East Jones Elementary School, MS

Bear

Bear
Big, Scary
Walk, sleep, hibernate
Killing, terrifying, roaring, horrifying
All bears eat meat.
Animal
Gabe Skipper, Grade 4
East Jones Elementary School, MS

The Song

A song can be a
Rock song,
Love song,
Hate song,
Or just a song.
Jazz,
Rock,
Slow music,
Or anything
You want.
Karlie Johnson, Grade 4
Contentnea Elementary School, NC

The School Day

Horray the teacher is here
We all shout for joy
Let's sing a little song
That will last all day long.

The school day has started
And we never want to go.
The school day has started
And we don't stare out the window.

The principal comes in
And tells us to sit down
But we were never still all day
Because the school day had begun!
Caroline Thompson, Grade 5
Midway Covenant Christian School, GA

Moon

The moon is our silent light,
The soft glow is comfort,
On a night of harsh black.
I stare at the moon
As snow sprinkles down
On a cold winter's night.
Claire Cahoon, Grade 6
Discovery School @ Reeves Rogers, TN

Silly Me

Flip, flop, flippity, flop
what was that?
I don't know!
It could be a boy or girl,
or an animal or…
Who knows what!
It could be big.
It could be small.
It could be…
I peeked from behind a tree
to see…
a frog!?
Silly me.
Trevor Padgett, Grade 5
Walton Verona Elementary School, KY

America the Free

V ictory
E lated
T ime that got hard for us
God s **E** eing us
R eminder to us
A merica the free
N ever gave up
Nick Nichols, Grade 5
Temple Hill Elementary School, KY

Christmas

Snow bells are ringing ahead
as you know far and near
to spread Christmas cheer

As you can see at night
there is all kinds of lights
as beautiful as can be

Lights on the Christmas tree
sparkles with glee
As you can see
its a wonderful sight on
Christmas Eve
Jalyssa Locklear, Grade 5
Pembroke Elementary School, NC

Maddy

There is this wonderful game.
If you're good, it could lead you to fame.
You have to be aggressive
Because it's competitive
Basketball is my game!
Madison Riley, Grade 4
Judsonia Elementary School, AR

Basketball

Ball, ball, ball I am round and tan
Run, run and stand tall
Hit me with your hand
Bounce me and bounce me and bounce
Throw me to the net
Look out! What a score!
Now you're all set
I can't do much more.
Christopher McKinney, Grade 5
Walton Verona Elementary School, KY

Sadness

Sadness is leaves falling
Down
Down
Down
The lake is low with
no water in it anymore.
Hear the trees shimmering.
Taste the rain falling down
on my face it's like tear drops.
Smell the damp rain.
See the trees blowing gently.
The clouds are dark.
Nature is crying too all alone
in this big open space.
Mia Dimartino, Grade 4
Endhaven Elementary School, NC

Mustangs

See the mustangs run and race
Across the plain, wind in their face
Like ghosts they come, like ghosts they go
One ivory coat, white like snow
And sleek, black coats of ebony
With chestnuts running, fast and free

Hooves a thunderin' upon the ground
As thy mustangs race around
Tails swing and manes flow
As they feel the wind blow
The mustangs' legs are lithe and strong
Muscles flex as they race along

The mustangs head to shady places
To keep the sun out of their faces
As the end of day comes to pass
The mustangs lay in the soft, green grass
As the sunset downs, in a flash of gold
We tell of the mustangs in tales of old
We tell of the mustangs that live in the sun
We tell of the mustangs that run, run, run!

Tascha Turvey, Grade 6
Senn Thomas Middle School, MO

The Flow of Music

The soft tunes ringing in my head,
The rock music sounding like birds flying in a furious storm.
The sound of country passing by,
Sadness passes by with tears along the way.
The rap, winds itself by and gifts of rhythm to who needs it.
The flow of music, travels and travels for miles,
Until it has done its job.

Wesley Good, Grade 5
North Middle School, TN

Daddy Come Home!

Why o' why did you leave us I cannot tell
I know you're doing your job but my heart still fell

I'm sorry to put all of this on your shoulders I'm just so sad
Why do we have to fight in wars it makes me so mad

I wait for you O sweet Dad
I send you my love until my love goes bad

So long for now
You're a great man I know you will make us proud

Come one, come all we have a hero in sight
He is brave and handsome along with all his might

I wait for you O sweet Dad
I send my love for you until my love goes bad

Gabrielle Coleman, Grade 6
Madison Elementary School, AL

Trick or Treat

T rick or treating is romping fun.
R ustling leaves as you move past swaying trees,
I tching for more candy and treats
C rossing roads and fields to get to spooky houses,
K icking leaves and pine cones as I march by.

O ctober is my favorite month of the year.
R aised voices echoing down the street.

T ossed candy heard rattling in the kids' bags,
R eady to stop at someone's doorstep for some goodies.
E xcited, but it is almost over. So the night will last longer
A ll of the kids are trying to go slower.
T onight is done. Can't wait until tomorrow to eat the candy!

Mandy Vignali, Grade 5
First Flight Elementary School, NC

Christmas Street

Though there is light,
The air is cold and dreary,
The lights are not bright,
But when I remember I feel cheery,
It is Christmas time,
There is lots of hustle,
Everyone is cheery,
Lots of bustle,
It is not so dreary,
Snowflakes,
A ton of gifts,
Icing, cookies, and cakes,
Everyone running for lifts,
Look at those ice-skates,
Watch the swirling snow,
Everyone buying first rates,
Holiday music on the radio,
Everyone running up and down the street,
Ginger bread, lollipops, and candy-canes,
What a sweet treat!
All of this on Christmas Street!

Rachel Starr, Grade 6
Duncan Middle School, OK

All the Great Sports

Baseballs are white.
Footballs are brown.
Basketballs are orange.
Baseballs are round.

When David Ortiz hits a home run,
Randy Moss catches a touchdown.
When Lebron James jumps up and dunks,
Jose Reyes steals a base.

Bradley Freitag, Grade 4
Moyock Elementary School, NC

Leaves

Leaves are green.
Leaves are brown.
Leaves are falling to the ground.
Leaves are orange.
Leaves are red.
Leaves are falling above my head.
Garrett Vaughan, Grade 5
Midway Covenant Christian School, GA

Autumn

Sweet apple cider
A sudden nip in the air
Smells of burning wood.
Kelsey Knowles, Grade 6
Musselman Middle School, WV

Louis Is a Robot

Louis is a Robot
He eats computers for lunch
He likes to do the robot dance
He likes to watch birds that fly
And get shot with a shotgun
He loves to watch girl robots dance
He loves to watch dogs run
He loves his dog lucky
He likes his teachers
He loves to ride the bus
Tamara Armer, Grade 5
Berryville Elementary School, AR

Where I'm From

I am from soft beds,
fluffy pillows touching my face.
I am from waking up every morning,
eggs sizzling in a pan.
I am from watching TV
every day.
I am from relaxing on the sofa,
holding my cat.
I am from home.
Michael Morris, Grade 5
Tates Creek Elementary School, KY

Fall

Fall is fun,
I play in the leaves,
Leaves fall off the trees,
And I can play football,
I can eat turkey.
Leaves change color,
A full moon might scare you,
The stars are pretty,
The moon is bright,
And I can climb up a tree.
Kade Litton, Grade 5
Trinity Day School, GA

Zoom Zoom

All of the cars speeding down the track at 200 M.P.H.
fans cheering for their favorite driver
jumping, screaming, and hollering
Jeff Gordon, Tony Stewart, Jimmie Johnson, and Dale Earnhardt Jr.
most popular drivers in the race.

Zooming fast engines blasting your eardrums unless you have ear plugs
lucky going to the restroom a place of quietness.

Vroom — vroom goes the cars breeze blowing on my face from speeding Nascars.
gas smelling like stink bug
burnt rubber on track, cars slamming brakes

Black and white checkered flag waving by the finish line
lets drivers know it's last lap
drivers speeding up to cross the finish line first

Finally winner passes the finish line so fast you can hardly see him
Winner spins around in circles happy to have won the Bristol Cup Race.
Daniel Nally, Grade 4
Roberta Tully Elementary School, KY

She's Here, She's Here

The wait is almost over my puppy has been born.
I received a long awaited call for old Californ!

August the twenty-seventh in the later afternoon,
A litter of five had finally arrived.
Oh what a joy three girls and two boys.
Garbo, the pup's mom gave birth in a blue kiddy pool laying on a blanket of fleece.
Hey Ella, you got a new niece!

She's scheduled to arrive in a few more weeks.
We have a new cage, and lots of treats.
Her name, for now is a mystery, and soon we will decide.
Mom wants "Pringle," and my dad calls her "Pride."
My sister likes the name "Jack," but I still can't decide.

No matter the name, how special she'll be.
Loved by all in my family.
So sweet little girl, the size of a Coke can,
So small for now you can fit in my hand.
Jordan G. Keller, Grade 6
Nativity School, SC

Lightning

When I hear an earsplitting sound outside I want to run to my mom's room and hide.
My mom comforts me and says, "It's just lightning."

While lying in my bed I jump up to scream. I am very scared
but, I know it's just lightning.

When I see a bluish streak in the sky and I think I am going to die,
I know it's just lightning.
Mollie McDonald, Grade 6
Wayne Country Day School, NC

Boom! Boom!

Boom! Boom!
Woke me up in the night
Slush went my feet as my family ran to the car
Whoosh went the window wipers as we drove to a safer place
Flash! Went the lightning
AHHHHH everyone screamed

Boom! Boom!
Woke me up in the night
Peck, Peck the rain went on the window
Rumbly, Tumbly, thunder let out a roar
Splashing mud came on our car as we hit a BUMP
I shut my eyes until…

BOOM! BOOM!
BOOM! BOOM!
BOOM! BOOM!
Went the thunder
The same that woke me up in the night

Chaley Trail, Grade 6
College View Middle School, KY

A Boy and His Flute*

A boy with a flute
had a silky white collar on his
velvety jacket.
He is very rich with a small room
with the instruments and an ornate chair.
His background wall is sea green with
a violin and a recorder
He does not have a great deal of negative in his room.
He has much positive space.
Not too much or his room will be packed.
Tinting in the background does so much to the wall,
especially on him.
He is very focused and thoughtful, but most of all he is calm.
He is very special; he cares for the instruments.
The boy seems to be playing the flute in deep thought.

Carrie Toepfert, Grade 5
Saffell Street Elementary School, KY
*Inspired by "A Boy Playing a Flute"

Arctic Winds

As the Arctic winds blow on my face,
The black penguins walk in a race.
With the blistering winds freezing the water,
The icy paradise begs for warmer weather.

When the winter wonderland gets too warm,
The icy winds freeze it into a storm.
As you see the birds come back from winter,
You wish the warm would never come nearer.

Adrian Speed, Grade 6
Pleasants County Middle School, WV

Where I'm From

I am from basketballs being dribbled down the court.
From traveling to Gatlinburg and seeing many bears.
From sitting around the Christmas tree singing Christmas carols.
From helping my mom and dad make our Thanksgiving dinner.

I am from vegetable soup and brownies.
From the best parents in the world, Carmen and Richard.
From the leaders and believers.
From John 3:16 that I know by heart.

I am from Bowling Green, KY.
From green beans and fruit.
From the thumb that my uncle lost in the war.
From the wreck that my mom had on the interstate.

I am from a box full of memories.
From pictures and pictures galore.
From the snap shot picture for every memory.
From memories gathering in the family tree.

Haylee Hazel, Grade 6
Lost River Elementary School, KY

Madeline

Light brown, straight long hair, blue eyes,
baggy pants and big jackets and my friends house
and around my house.
"Oops my bad!"
People are mean to me and ignore me like my brother.
Having a party at my house,
playing soccer and volleyball alone, and the blue sky.

Madeline Kassen, Grade 5
Our Lady Catholic School, MO

Universal Soul

Through faith you'll find one's destiny.
In a moment's notice, that a dream came true.
A test of your might tests courage, that
takes through time and space.

Zachery Colabaugh, Grade 4
Tazewell-New Tazewell Primary School, TN

Oceans

People lying on their beach towels,
Listening to their radios,
Reading their books.
Seagulls calling other seagulls.
Starfish washing up on the shore.
Children playing in the sand,
Making castles,
Walking in the water,
Playing in the water.
The sun shining bright —
Water sparkling when the sun shines on it.
Kids finding shells and crabs on the sand.

Jada Camp, Grade 6
Woodlawn Christian School, NC

Valleys/Nature

Valleys
Warm breezy
Flowers trees grass
A place of peace
Nature
Ashley Stalvey, Grade 6
Appling County Middle School, GA

Thanksgiving

T urkey is very yummy
H aving a full belly
A lways fun and filling
N ever boring but really fun
K illing the turkey so you can eat
S erving others with food
G iving God all the thanks
I nviting friends and family over
V ery exciting and quality time
I nteresting colors on the trees
N ever complaining about food
G od is very good to us
Jacob Shirley, Grade 5
Briarwood Christian School, AL

The Unknown

The unknown is the darkest place
The people there don't own a face.
It can be without a trace
Or even in the void of space.

It is what most men dread
Almost more than the poison of lead.
And three old fates, it is said
Control your life by a piece of thread.

The residents they are the worst of hosts
They're wicked spirits and evil ghosts.
Allie Phillips, Grade 6
Houston Middle School, TN

My Mom

Roses are red.
Violets are blue.
I think my mom is pretty.
I think you should think that too.

So she goes out
And has some fun
We have some too
I always make sure
That she is happy
While she makes sure I'm happy.
Ryan Norris Jr., Grade 5
Aulander Elementary School, NC

Vernetta Gabriel

V ery smart
E ager to learn
R espectful
N otice others
E xcellent attitude
T idy and clean
T rendy
A wesome

G reat sportsmanship
A n excellent reader
B right ideas
R easonable responses
I ntelligent girl
E asy-going
L oving life
Vernetta Gabriel, Grade 6
Mark Twain Elementary School, MO

Football Fans

Dear football fans
are you ready for football
Ya let's go fans
let's put some points on the board
and make some tackles
and watch me run the ball
and yell for me ok ok.
Jeremias Bivens, Grade 5
North Middle School, TN

My Color

It's the fire burning with rage,
and an angry rooster in a cage.

It's the churning engines of NASCAR,
and the nightly appearing new star.

It's the early morning sunrise,
and your lover's big surprise.

Just what color could this be?
Why it's red, the color for me!
Morgan Dreher, Grade 5
Salem Elementary School, AR

The Wall

There once was a kid
Whose dad had gone to war.
When he found out
That his dad had died,
He was happy that his dad's name
Was on the wall.
Colby Gerber, Grade 4
Parkview Elementary School, MO

Eagle

Eagle
brown, beautiful
flies, eats, drinks
soaring, walking, hunting, fishing
Eagles flap their wings
Golden eagle
Austin King, Grade 4
East Jones Elementary School, MS

The Eraser

Zooming across the paper
Determined to destroy
The dreaded mark!
There it goes!
Right and left!
Stop erasing!
That's my homework!
It's lost control!
I mean…
I've lost control of it.
Brett Schario, Grade 5
St Vincent Elementary School, MO

Villain or Hero

Villain
Mean, bad
Dangers, evil, crazy
Steal, kidnap, protective, fast,
Flying, saving, super
Cool, strong
Hero
Aaron McCoy, Grade 4
Tamassee-Salem Elementary School, SC

The Snow and the Moon

It is silent,
Then it starts snowing,
A snowflake falls on my shoulder,
Then another and another,
It starts to get dark,
Then the stars come out,
Goodnight, I say to the moon!
Eilish Burner, Grade 5
Keyser Primary/Middle School, WV

Horse

Horse
Fast, gentle
Run, gallop, nay
Nibbling, eating, drinking, sleeping
All ponies are cute.
Pony
Jade Padgett, Grade 4
East Jones Elementary School, MS

Lucas

There once was an old woman from France
Who didn't wear any pants
Her legs got cold
And then they got mold
Her legs, they didn't have a chance.

Lucas Ashworth, Grade 4
Judsonia Elementary School, AR

When Winter Comes

When winter comes, the windows get colder.
The kids are on their way to go play.
I sit down as the fireplace smolders.
We get ready to go down the hill.

The sun sets, and the sky gets gold.
As the cookies are warming, we all smell them.
We're all sad because the season is getting old.
The moon rises, and we all go to bed.

Luke Burkhammer, Grade 6
Pleasants County Middle School, WV

It's Madness

I got mad at my mom
so I went to my room to hit and
tackle my stuffed animals.
I could still see my mom
walking around looking for me.
My mom is crying
like a person without a home,
searching for me.
She screams my name.
She keeps on screaming my name.
Then I scream mom and she screams back.
I feel sad in my room.
My mom takes me hunting
for me to feel better.
She knows me so well.
She knows I like hunting.

Tony Francik, Grade 5
Fox Elementary School, MO

Football

Tackle, pass, block, shout
That's what football is all about
You try your hardest, to do your best
Because to give 100% effort is the ultimate test
You come to the field anxious to go
Because you want to put on a spectacular show
While you're waiting for your game to start
You feel the beating of your heart
The excitement is always the same
Because it is such a spectacular game
When you're facing the other team
You want to win to complete your scheme

Troy Diebolt, Grade 6
Cathedral School, NC

The Fair

Cotton Candy tastes so sweet,
and animals smell like stinky feet.
Ferris Wheel rides are extremely scary,
When you are high in the sky it's very airy.
Port-a-potties smell worse than molded liver
when you go in it makes you quiver.
The kids are running everywhere
and it's making me pull out my hair.
Balloons are always there in the air
and that's why I just love the fair!

Sarah Mackey, Grade 5
North Middle School, TN

Deer Hunting

Last Friday I went deer hunting.
I carried my Dad's 270 Remington;
I needed the sling because it weighed a ton!
I killed my first deer!
2007 was the year!!
We took it to the packing house.
On the way home I saw a great big mouse!
My first deer was a yearling doe.
That night I heard an old man say, "Ho! Ho! Ho!"

Seth Sloan, Grade 6
Scotts Creek Elementary School, NC

Proud to Be Me

I am a free dolphin swimming in the ocean.
I watch out for predators, and never get in the way.
I am the teddy bear sitting on my bed, sweet and gentle.
A fierce cheetah roaming in the jungle.
I have an attitude, don't be surprised.
I will pounce on you like a tiger if you make me mad.
Like a pack of wolves my family sticks together.
I am a lion, head held high.
I am proud to be me.

Amanda Raines, Grade 6
Beck Academy, SC

Crystal Heart

I loved you till the end, when the road gave away,
when I had nothing left to give but my heart.

I gave it all to you. Maybe I put too much into it,
but looking back reminds me that it was worth it.

I gave you my heart, but you took it and ran.
Just to leave me with memories and no more than friends.

When I gave you my heart, I had nothing left.
So I picked up where you left off,
with a new start and a crystal heart.

Jordan L. Suber, Grade 6
McIntosh County Middle School, GA

Kittens

Kittens drink warm milk.
Kittens feel soft and furry.
They hate to take baths.
Nicole Lim, Grade 5
St Joseph Institute for the Deaf, MO

Snow of Joy

I am snow of joy.
I am the reliever of your soul's draught.
I bring joy to those who see me.
They run through me all so freely.
I am the Love that shatters hurt.
I am the heart's most favorite dessert.
You will see me on Christmas day.
It will be a joyous time to play!
Takira McCoy, Grade 6
Blackmon Road Middle School, GA

Fun

I cannot describe fun
but it can be in the sun.

I cannot tell what fun is about
but you can scream and shout.

I cannot describe fun
but you can sure run.
Stacy Knott, Grade 5
Arnaudville Elementary School, LA

Wishing

Wishing at night
For a beautiful day
Tomorrow.

Wishing at Christmas
For wonderful presents
From Santa!

Wishing in June
For a long break
In summer.

Wishing in winter
For a snow day
To play.

Wishing every day
For a black and white dog
To be your friend.

Wishing over school break
For a fun sleepover
At a friend's or Grandma's.
Jacob Ragsdale, Grade 6
St Joseph Institute for the Deaf, MO

Be Yourself

Don't be a sad person and mad person either be a happy person.
Don't be something you don't want to be.
Be yourself.
Roger Munguia, Grade 5
South Smithfield Elementary School, NC

Highlights of Summer

Lying on my cottony sleek beach towel on the blistering grains of sand.
Watching the lightning bugs as they light the yard and kindle their paths.
Listening to the noisy, nonstop motion of the ocean.
Going on a lengthy road trip to grandma's house.
Becoming drenched as I get in my pool.
The red-hot engravement the sun has left on my arm
Reminds me it is there every time I go outside.
Getting grubby in the garden as I pull the extended grass.
Sunglasses act as a shield for my eyes, blocking the torches of the sun.
Tasting the barbecue as the smoky smell goes through the air.
Finally finding a lull, consoling place to relax.
Hollie Austin, Grade 6
Alvaton Elementary School, KY

Glorious Moment

October gymnastics meet
stomach feeling nervous with butterflies
hearing crowd cheering
"You can do it," "Point your toes."
Seeing judge write down notes about gymnast's performance
excited, smelling concession stand food,
tasting last sip of water before it's my turn.
Hearing judge call "Ali Terrell," saluting judge
spreading arms out like wings, right foot back ready to accelerate
sprinting on spring floor, arms going around in a circle, thinking point your toes
jumping on the spring board like a frog leaping over a rock "Boing"
legs flying in the air, hitting handstand
legs are an arrow in the air, slowly falling on my back, then sitting up.
Once again saluting judge eagerly waiting for my score
watching numbers rapidly flip to 9.4
crowd clapping cheerfully
mom yelling, "Way to go Ali!"
Feeling happy with myself at this Gymnastics meet
tasting victory,
walking with my head held high
wishing this glorious moment would never end.
Ali Terrell, Grade 4
Roberta Tully Elementary School, KY

The Great Things About Leaves

When I feel the leaf that's sitting on my hand, the texture is furry and smooth.
The odors of some leaves are blank, and some smell like a bakery or a trash pile.
The leaves sound crunchy when I stomp them. When I see the leaves, I see
colors of brown, red, orange, and yellow, and some — just green, but the one thing
that's the same is the one who created them —
God.
Victoria Justice, Grade 4
First Wesleyan Christian School, NC

True Friends

A true friend is kind to you,
They always stop when you tie your shoe,
If you're sad or full of doubt,
They'll always try to help you out,
They always stand up for you,
Especially when you feel sad and blue,
They say you're special and smart and true,
They always encourage you to try stuff that's new,
You'll always have a friend beside,
That you can always share your deep feelings inside.

Cate Joseph Rasco, Grade 6
Graham Elementary School, AL

My Basketball Story

My first game is scary,
when I get on the court everyone's staring,
But as we play offense the crowd is glaring.
When my team plays offense or defense
I play on the side
When the ball glides
I am ready and steady
Swish! Score!
The crowd gives us all the glory
That's the end of my basketball story.

Hannah Baker, Grade 5
North Middle School, TN

Baseball

Baseball, America's game
So much fun
You'll never be the same
Hoping the game is never done

Standing in the box
The crack of the bat
Rounding the bases like a fox
I'm home just like that

On the mound
There is no doubt
As he stares at the ground
Strike 1, 2, 3 he's out

Out of all the places
I like third the best
There's not much space
There's hardly time to rest

We won the game
Seven to five
I'll never be the same
I made the winning catch, with a dive

Dalton Brown, Grade 4
Schaffner Traditional Elementary School, KY

Morning Time

When I get up for school each morning
I can hear my dad still snoring.
My mom is feeding the babies tummy
she must think it is pretty yummy.
I hear the birds bold and clear
There must be one quite near.
I walk outside and feel the breeze
And sometimes I even sneeze.
I wait until it is time to go
And hear my brother say, "NO! NO!
Wait for me, I am not quite ready."
This is my morning, what do you think?
I do not even have time to blink.

Kaylinn Baker, Grade 5
Heartland High School and Academy, MO

I Can't Write a Poem*

Forget it. You must be kidding.
I can't think of anything. My cat ripped my paper.
It's too hard to do. My cousin wants to play with me.
I'm going to get a snack. I've got to watch my shows.
My pencil broke. I don't have the time.
I've got work to do. I'm going to clean my room.
I'm sick. I'm tired.
I don't want to write. I have to eat lunch.
I'm too busy. I hurt my arm.
I have spelling to do. I'm in trouble right now.
I don't have lead for my pencil. I'm too bored.
My allergies are messing up. I can't write a poem.
It fell in the fish tank. I'm getting beat up today!
I'm getting on Myspace.
Uh oh, time's up?
All I have is this dumb list of excuses.
You like it? Really? No kidding.
Would you like to see another one?

Timothy Stricklin, Grade 6
Lost River Elementary School, KY
Patterned after "I Can't Write a Poem" by Bruce Lansky

The Worst Day Ever

Today is a horrible day,
It's a bad day to play.
Here comes the bully Tarents,
Thank goodness, here are my parents.
The bully, Tarents, starts jumping and jumping
Like he was nice.
My parents leave, so he comes back to life uh, oh.
So, I hide with my bug
At least someone give me a hug.
The night came so it was always the same.
Me and my bug all snuggled in bed,
Many tales my mom has read.
The Three Little Pigs, The Little Red,
Those are the books my mom has read.

Melany Silvera, Grade 4
Nesbit Elementary School, GA

I Miss

I miss my mother, brother, and all the others. I miss my love who is now above. I cry at my window as people pass by. I miss my baby that I lost. Maybe, just maybe, I'll see my baby again. I miss everything I had. I was sad about what I lost. So now I lay here in my bed and put my hands over my head and cry, cry myself to sleep.

Sydney Settle, Grade 4
Thomas Edison Elementary School, TN

DECEMBER

Snowflakes falling from time to time.
Christmas air flowing just about the time of year when people visit their families.
Making snowmen, having snowball fights, telling Santa and family what we want for Christmas.
Beginning to bake with my mom and aunts.
Tasting the holiday treats made with lots of sugar and love, and our own little hands.
That makes the season so special for me.
It reminds me what is really important. Spending quality time with family.
Remembering that it is more important to give than ot receive. That is what December means to me.

Gabrielle Theodore Berberich, Grade 6
Annunciation Elementary School, MO

The Touchdown

Five seconds left in the championship game the ball was snapped to the quarterback
I ran down field to catch the ball the quarterback dropped back to get a clear pass
He realized that I was open I ran toward the touchdown line
I waved for the ball so he would see me the quarterback took position to throw the ball to me

As the ball spiraled through the air a defender attempted to intercept the pass
I watched as the ball glided in my direction I observed with grief as the defender's right hand tipped the ball
The defender's contact sent the ball flying through the air it wobbled back and forth
Hoping that I would still catch the ball, I dove for it in midair I stretched out both of my arms

Over my shoulder I noticed the defender heading my way I closed my eyes very tightly unsure of what was going to happen next
Within seconds I felt his shoulder pads hitting my legs I slowly opened my eyes to see a wonderful sight
I recognized the ball was in my hands I quickly looked around to find myself past the touchdown line
At that moment I heard the shrilling whistle sound of the referee that is when I knew the game was over

Chris Taylor, Grade 6
Union Chapel Elementary School, KY

Cuba

In Cuba they grow the good smelling tobacco, the cute livestock and, as Cubans say, *azucar* (sugar)!
The beautiful land of Cuba has blood of many wars including the Spanish American War.
Cuba sounds like a bad place but the many rich Cubans gave their gold
To the Americans to support America in the Revolutionary War.
The sights of Cuba are extraordinary!
They are full of life and color, and the buildings are truly awesome!
The palm trees are like giant beautiful umbrellas, but all of these things are blocked off
From the inhabitants, and only the tourists can see the sights.
The Cuban independence is on May twentieth.
The United States helped Cuba to gain its independence.
It began by the blowing of the US ship Maine in the Havana Harbor that is when the Spanish American war began.
After the independence Cuba was very close to the United States, but in 1959 a communist government was established.
Even though I was born here in the US, my family was born in Cuba, they left their homeland due to political persecution.
My father tells me stories about his childhood in Cuba and they are very fascinating.
My family wish to return someday to Cuba, but only after democracy is restored.
I wish to one day see the place where my family once called home.
'Till then I am trying to learn more about this beautiful place called Cuba.

Annaleah Fernandez, Grade 6
Queen of Angels Catholic School, GA

Fall Sunset

You see a sunset,
I see a masterpiece.
I see ribbons of color draped across the sky —
pink, purple, orange, blue —
drawn by Him.
But after He's through,
He starts to erase,
and I see the gray smudges take over our glimpse of heaven.
I watch it roll over the hills,
race across the horizon,
skip along the city.
Look at the sky one fall evening.
Take a few minutes to admire the wonderful masterpiece.

Hannah Witner, Grade 6
Providence Christian School, NC

Dreams*

If you came upon a dream,
what would be that dream?
Would it be sad or happy?

If it could be anything
what would it be?
Would it be long or short?
Would it be friendly or scary?

If you could see this dream,
would you see it or believe it?
Would there be images
of a person you knew?

Would that person
be happy or sad?
How would this make you feel?
Would you yearn to see this person again?

What would this person look like?
What would this person say?
Would this person be happy to see you or not?

Juan Pablo Gee, Grade 6
Providence Christian School, NC
*In honor of my grandfather

Kid President

If I were president,
I would be the first black kid president.
I would stop the war in Iraq
And fly all the troops back to America.
I would give poor people money
To buy houses and clothing,
And make a law that said all people
Have to finish school no matter what.
I would take the rich people's money for one week
And let them see how it feels to be poor.

Deonte Phillips, Grade 5
Lee A Tolbert Community Academy, MO

Colors of the Rainbow

Do you like rainbows? I do very much!
Let's start the colors one by one —
Red is the first one so hot and fire like.
Orange is like a pencil or a sunset, so nice.
Yellow is so happy and is usually used in smiley faces.
Green is used in grass, leaves, and is the color of growth.
Blue is sad, gloomy, or cool and like coldness.
Purple or Indigo are cheerful colors.
Pink is like roses and is calm and soft.
Brown is an easy color to make when you paint.
Black is a color that is the darkest and last color.
I wonder why colors are so beautiful?
Do you have a favorite color? I do!
The one I like the best, is pink!
When I see a rainbow, I smile!
I ask myself, could it be any prettier?
Colors are everywhere!
In your room, in your home. Everywhere!
Colors are sad, happy and lots of other feelings.
Can you see how happy you could be just looking at a rainbow?

Rachel Evans, Grade 4
JJ Jones Intermediate School, NC

My Little House

My little house, why are you moving away?
    What is that you say?
You cannot stay because I won't pay?
    Well, if you need my help, here's my pay.
Now can you stay?
    Yes, now you can stay because I gave you my pay.

Lauren Takewell, Grade 4
Northeast Baptist School, LA

Dreams

Dreams are wishes we follow
Dreams are like a day relived
Dreams are as easy as a piece of pie
"Whoosh" the time always flies by
Dreams dance in our head with creativity
Dreams always fill our minds with imagination!

Hunter Holtkamp, Grade 6
Beck Academy, SC

Mercy Said No

As they say "he won't make it to live a day"
Mercy said no.
As they say "he won't make it to live a week"
Mercy said no.
As they say "he will never walk"
Mercy said no.
Now he walks, talks, and lives and now he is
a star basketball player at Salisbury Academy.

Jarvis Miller, Grade 5
Salisbury Academy, NC

Who Am I

I am an apple tree
Swaying in the wind
Where the yellow jasmine grow
Growing fearlessly with pride
On hills or mountains
Or where my roots are planted

I am a palmetto tree
Growing with dignity
Holding back that hurricane
Straight or slumpy
Graceful or graceless
My roots will stay or they will go
But they'll stay in the palmetto state

I am a bridge
Crossing the U.S.
Spanning the Ready River
Or the salty waters of the south
Doing my job
To the people who cross
Christopher Nelon, Grade 6
Beck Academy, SC

My Mother Is a Bee

My mother is a bee.
She is always working
In the kitchen, in the dining room,
Even in my room.
I think she is a Swiffer Duster.
She thinks I'm a brat,
But my mom is a bee
And I can tell you that.
Ellie Hampton, Grade 5
Berryville Elementary School, AR

Camping Time

Mountains and trees,
The smell of a burning campfire,
Then complete silence.
The wind blows through my hair,
The taste of dust in the air,
The night sky is falling,
The stars are shining,
Now it is time for bed.
Casady Ball, Grade 4
Cleveland Elementary School, OK

Blue

As bright as the sky
As deep as the ocean
As sweet as a newborn baby's eyes.
Tyler Wilkerson, Grade 5
Bloomfield Elementary School, KY

Halloween

Halloween
Trick-or-treat
Boo! I'm scared
Halloween is in the air
Witches and Ghost
Zombies and Mummies
O how they scare me
I'm not a dummy
Hold out my sack
Drop in the loot
Or I give you a scare
So be aware!
Rachel Fylstra, Grade 4
Moyock Elementary School, NC

Joy

Joy is like a baby bird,
Gentle and kind,
Growing and flourishing over time.

Joy is like a snowflake,
Fragile and unique,
Coming in different shapes and sizes.

Joy is like a falling leaf,
Fluttering and flying,
Dancing through the air.
Anna Ryder, Grade 6
IA Lewis Elementary School, LA

Friends

Friends are always kind,
And also caring;
Friends are there for you,
And always sharing.
Rebecca Dow, Grade 5
Midway Covenant Christian School, GA

Puppies

Puppies
small, cute
playful, cuddly, and chews a lot
feels really soft and furry
Tucker
Katelyn Payne, Grade 6
Stuart Middle School, KY

My Mother

My mother is nice
Eeek she hates mice.
She lets us go play.
This is a good day.
Logan Brannan, Grade 6
Martin Elementary School, WV

Dear God

Dear God, let it snow.
Oh Lord, let it blow.
Let it blow through my hair.
Let it snow everywhere.
Oh Jesus, don't you know
I really want that snow.
Please send it down.
I'll be waiting around.
Shealyn DeLancey, Grade 6
Pleasants County Middle School, WV

The Love of My Family

It is intense, yet gentle.
It leaves me with a sense
of warm embrace.
When it is cold outside
I thank God for my family.
Chattia O. Evans, Grade 4
Carver Elementary School, NC

Beautiful Nature

Nature's power roaming around
Where animals and humans live as one
Humans roaming among the trees
With foxes, deer, and fish
Running along with each other
Battling and living side by side
Adam Welch, Grade 5
Wright City Middle School, MO

Baseball

Baseball
The smell of summer
Fresh cut grass, hot dogs, and peanuts
Warming up, the feel of excitement!
Lines being chalked
Brand new uniforms, black and red
Umpires in place
Taking the mound
"Play ball"
The catcher's sign
Gripping the laces
Fastball
"Strike"
Baseball
Michael Post, Grade 6
Mayflower Middle School, AR

My Dad

My dad is too cool
He is so fun to play with
I really love him
Xavier Graham, Grade 5
Sycamore Elementary School, GA

The Great Outdoors

God made the great outdoors.
he made it in seven days.
From the bird that says, "tweet, tweet"
To the horse that gallops and neighs.

I love the great outdoors.
It's my favorite place to be.
You can find me in the dirt; you can find me in a tree,
But the place you won't find me is in front of a big screen TV!

The great outdoors is a fun place to be.
It's as fun as playing with my friends.
My friends are the animals God has made.
They're really funny and they cause lots of grins.

Go visit the great outdoors.
I'll bet you'll love it too.
It's a great place to explore.
An adventure is waiting for you!

Ian Wilson, Grade 5
Providence Academy, TN

Mathematics

Mathematics can be fun but
Today I did not get my homework done.

Numbers, numbers, 1, 2, 3
All the numbers are surrounding me.

Numbers, numbers, 4, 5, 6, 7
What is 6 x 11?

Numbers, numbers 8, 9, 10
Oh no! Now we have to review again.

RING! Now I can start succeeding
Oh no! I forgot to finish my homework in reading!

Patty MgBodile, Grade 6
St Francis Xavier School, AL

Soccer

The game was new to me this year
I went at it showing no fear.

I learned the rules, positions too
No hands, just kicking can you do.
Our uniforms of blue and gold
Coaches watching, our moves so bold
Yelling, "What were you told!"

We practiced hard to win the games,
In the end, champion was our new name.

Oscar Spruill, Grade 6
St Teresa's School, GA

Abby

Abigail —
Athletic, hyper, funny, talkative.
Daughter of Benny and Brenda, sister of Ben and Lauren.
Lover of Guitar Hero, golf, and basketball.
Who is an excellent point guard in basketball!
Who fears tarantulas, rattlesnakes, and leopard seals.
Who was born in Birmingham.
Who lives in Shelby County.
— Abby or Abbs

Abigail Parks, Grade 5
Briarwood Christian School, AL

I Live on an Army Post

I am a wild nine year old.
I wonder where we will move next year.
I hear the soldiers shooting guns during practice.
I see soldiers at the PX.
I want to live with my father.
I am a wild nine year old child.

I pretend it is ok that my dad lives in another state.
I feel sad when I hang up on my dad.
I touch the rabbit my dad gave me for Christmas.
I worry that I'll move far and not see my dad.
I cry when I have to go.
I am a wild nine year old.

I understand I miss my dad.
I say my dad loves me very much.
I dream I will live with my dad but I can't.
I hope I will live with my dad one day.
I am a wild nine year old.

Anthony Haynes, Grade 4
Walker Intermediate School, KY

The Star

Early one morning she rose from her bed
And walked downstairs with a sleepy head
The little girl put on her coat and gloves
So she could play in the snow she loves
The little girl ventured, hat in hand
Into a winter wonderland
She scooped up a fistful of snow
And prepared herself, ready to throw
But the little girl stopped when she saw
An object on the ground, waiting to thaw
It was covered in ice and hard as a rock
So she placed it near the fire in a warm woolly sock
Inside, she found, hid a huge glowing star
That seemed to have traveled from afar
"This," said her mother, "is a sign from above,
A symbol of Christ's great, perfect love,
For He, like this star, melts the sin
That traps and conceals the good within."

MeMe Collier, Grade 6
Briarwood Christian School, AL

Kings Island

Screaming, yelling
loops and upside down
water rides hurray
a thirty one story high tower
all the excitement ends
we settle down to exploding fireworks

Morgan Lamkin, Grade 5
Bloomfield Elementary School, KY

Red

Red is…
As hot as peppers
As hard as bricks
As deep as love

Sydney King, Grade 5
Bloomfield Elementary School, KY

I Am a Baseball Player

I am a baseball player.
I wonder if I strikeout.
I hear this team is really good.
I see them warming up.
I want to win this really bad.
I am a baseball player.
I pretend I am not scared.
I feel the ball hit the bat.
I touch home plate as I am safe.
I worry if I get an out.
I cry when I get hit with the ball.
I am a baseball player.
I understand I do not always win.
I say my team is one of the best.
I dream I am the World Series M.V.P.
I hope for the best.
I try to hit the ball every time.
I am a baseball player.

Cole Wegmann, Grade 4
Wohlwend Elementary School, MO

Wolves

W ild animals
O ut at night.
L iving free
V icious and mean.
E nergetic,
S cary creatures.

Patty K. Beasley, Grade 5
First Flight Elementary School, NC

My Hamster

My hamster climbed on my back.
Then he went on the pillow sack.
One time he went in my mom's drawer.
He was really sore.

Arlene Ayala, Grade 4
Horace Mann Elementary School, OK

Ra and Gar!

Brown bear,
Brown bear,
Bear in the woods.
Big Bear you're so very brown you look like my favorite brownie

Bushy,
brown and big
you look so yummy.
You are the best brown bear I ever saw.

I'm positive your hugs are the warmest and softest.
I would have one if I wasn't so scared of you.
So for now I will like you just the way you are.
I would like to give you your very own name.

Ha! I got it! Big Brown Bushy Brown Bear should suit you fine.

Lucy Massengill, Grade 4
Tazewell-New Tazewell Primary School, TN

The Happiness of Nature

Happy is a forest full of playing deer
Crunch
Crunch
Crunch
Leaves that are crunchy as cookies and wind rushing through my hair
Deer jumping happily, leaves falling slowly
Crunch
Crunch
Crunch
Crackles of leaves and a crunch for every step
Crunch
Crunch
Crunch
Logs that have hollow noises like a good watermelon
Cold air with every breath
Smell of maple with every sniff

The forest is a beautiful place

Cameron Clark, Grade 4
Endhaven Elementary School, NC

The World of Dreams

Imagine a world where the borders of reality and impossibility don't exist
Where dogs live in tanks and goldfish live in the yard.
Where your ability to go places is only restricted by your mind.
This world is so strange to us and yet parts of us can be found in it.
It is the world of dreams
a world so bizarre yet so close
We visit it every night but yet so few of our visits are remembered
It is a world very bizarre yet it lies inside us.
It reveals our hopes our dreams and our fear.
Few people realize how much our dreams can teach us.
So when you visit there tonight try to hang on to the memory of your visit.
For it may hold the key to something more.

Jeffrey LaPorte, Grade 6
Discovery School @ Reeves Rogers, TN

Summer Nights

Summer nights are peaceful
I sit on the porch
In a trance
As ants crawl
I watch fireflies

The stars twinkle
I listen to the night owls
The smell of barbecue
Makes me hungry
My love for the outdoors
Joys me

But soon fall will come with its brown crunchy leaves
Then winter will come with its white crisp snow
Then spring will come with its warm and windy days
But I will wait for my summer nights
On my porch

Tyler Wallace, Grade 6
St Francis Xavier School, AL

The Beach

Children making sandcastles as beautiful as the queen's palace
Fish welcoming me to the seashore
The scratching of the broken shells coming in with the waves
like a dog scratching the door on a rainy day
Waves crashing loudly into the rocks
When I swim I can feel the salt getting in my mouth
I crunch the sand as it blows towards me
The sun block on peoples' backs reminds me
of the smell of the ocean touching the dry sand
The sweet aroma of watermelon tickles my nose
The seagulls brushing against my side
Slippery seashells slipping through my fingers
Seeing the waves coming in make me feel relaxed
like lying in my bed at bedtime.

Stephany Celaya, Grade 5
Bailey Elementary School, NC

Fall

The leaves are falling.
They color the ground bright red
And swirl, twirl, whirl down.

Addison Clark, Grade 5
Hunter GT Magnet Elementary School, NC

Ode to Sylvester

Dear Sylvester
When I am cold
you make me warm.
I pet you and you are my cat.
You will not let anybody else pet you.
When my brother brought you home you were small
and now after 4 years you look like a bear cat.

Ryan Martin, Grade 5
Walton Verona Elementary School, KY

Veteran's Day

V eteran's Day
E leventh month, day, hour
T eamwork
E veryone had to have bravery to fight and survive
R emember the soldiers that fought to serve and protect
A lways remembered them
N ever forgot them
S oldiers died, some unknown

D readful losses
A lways do good for a return of good
Y oung soldiers risked their lives for our freedom

Vanessa Begley, Grade 5
Sullivan Elementary School, TN

My Humorous Dog

I have a charming dog named Bella,
she is friendly and bright yella.
She sleeps in my bed,
knocks me in my head.

When storms come about,
you better watch out.
She will run and hide,
she will knock you in your side.

If you throw her a ball,
she might run into a wall.
She likes to lay in your lap,
while she takes her nap.

If you feed her a treat,
you'll get knocked off your feet.
When you scratch her ear,
she will linger for a year.

When she gets in the bath,
you get a big laugh.
She dives and she dips,
then she wiggles her hips.

Kaitlyn Siegrist, Grade 4
Schaffner Traditional Elementary School, KY

Little Siblings

Little siblings may break your toys
They could even make some noise
Your siblings may wake you when you're asleep
They always disturb you when you're counting sheep
Those little pests don't have chores
And you get yelled at for slamming doors
They're annoying all the time
And I hope you like my rhyme!

Matt Phimphavong, Grade 6
Seven Holy Founders School, MO

The Seasons

The snow falls
It's winter time
Children play
It's spring again
The flowers bloom
Summer has come
Stronger winds
Shorter days
Autumn starts today.

Hope Crim, Grade 5
G C Burkhead Elementary School, KY

Josh

I knew a young man who danced
He really liked to prance
He was in a big show
And stubbed his toe
This put us all in a trance.

Josh Mason, Grade 4
Judsonia Elementary School, AR

Enjoying Christmas

The snow is falling,
People caroling,
Roads are blocked with snow,
Ho Ho Ho.
Kids making cookies
For Old St. Nick,
Presents are being unwrapped,
They have mistletoe.
Every time it snows,
It is being enjoyed,
Catching snow on your tongue,
Making a snowman,
Everywhere that you go,
You can't stop the joy of Christmas.
You can't stop the beat of Christmas.
Where everyone is happy
When everyone is together.
Christmas, Christmas,
Christmas, Christmas,
Christmas, Christmas.

Sarah Formby, Grade 6
First Assembly Christian School, AL

The Scary Old People

It's scary at night
Please don't let the old ones bite

The old ones never come out
Unless you're in the hall
Of the scary hospital on Elms Street

Michael Moore, Grade 6
Ketchum Jr High School, OK

Where I'm From

I'm from soft, elegant beds
nestling me down.
I'm from warm hot chocolate
with tiny, little marshmallows.
I'm from kicking soccer balls,
and grass stains.
I am from hot
summer days.
The sweat dripping down my head.
I'm from dinners
big and lovely by candlelight.
I'm from making beautiful
Christmas decorations, gleaming lights.
I'm from blankets
soft and cuddly.
I'm from a big,
caring family
loving my always.

Journey Davis, Grade 5
Tates Creek Elementary School, KY

Clocks

Coo-Coo!
Coo-Coo!
The little birdie sings,
As the clocks all ding.
In my little playroom,
I hope that I'll be done soon.
BONG! BONG!
BONG! BONG!
Grandpa says it's three now.
Maybe I'll be done now.
Tick-tock
Tick-tock
I'm counting the hours,
No make that minutes
Until I'm finished.
Ding-dong!
Ding-dong!
The clock on the mantel,
Says that my homework is through.

Helen Michaux Dubois, Grade 5
Nativity School, SC

Night's Wind

Blowing, glowing
In the night's light
Carefree and calm
In the balm
Cool breeze
By moonshine
Away

Keith McCormack, Grade 6
Seven Holy Founders School, MO

Autumn Is Awesome

A dventures
U nbelievable weather
T otal fun jumping in leaves;
U nhealthy candy on Halloween
M arvelous food on Thanksgiving
N o green leaves!

I s a beautiful season
S parkling leaves

A wesome colors
W arm cozy fireplaces
E xtra cold weather
S weet songs, birds sing
O vens with good food in them
M agnificent memories of fall
E xperimenting with new things

Anna Westmoreland, Grade 5
Palmetto Christian Academy, SC

Sunny Days

S o hot it is to be out here
U nder some trees it's so cool
N o one should hate these sunny days
N ow go inside to grab a friend
Y ou need to play on these sunny days
or these sunny days will blow away

Ariana Jones, Grade 4
St Thomas More School, NC

Goes Boom

I am red and blue
I am bouncing down a hill
I sound like boom boom
Between two legs
I go up and down
I am round
What am I

Gavin Wood, Grade 5
Woodland Elementary School, KY

Angels in the Sky

Angels in the sky,
They fly up so very high.
They fly up and down,
They fly all around.
Angels are never sick or sad,
They are always happy and glad.
Angels like to float on a cloud,
When Jesus comes they sing aloud.
It's time for the angels to go to bed,
Shh! Little Angels, lay down your heads.

Adriana Pintilie, Grade 4
Evangelical Christian School, TN

Me

I come from rosy red lips
And soft baby pink
Fairy tale dreams and firefly wishes
Bleach blonde hair and rays of golden sunshine
Big wet slobbery dog kisses
Hugging my brother for a be careful tonight
I believe in so many things
Hope Love
Happiness Faith
Pride Passion
And second chances
I am a singer in the shower
A dreamer of fantasy worlds
A writer of words
And a believer of God
I have
Family Friends Life
And nothing but time
But most of all I am
Me
Me as in a story still being written

Gabrielle Davis, Grade 6
Westchester Country Day School, NC

Ghost of the Night

Ghost, oh ghost,
Oh ghost of the night,
Ghost, oh ghost,
You give me quite a fright!

You hide in the closet,
You jump out and say, "BOO!"
You scare me to death,
I hope I'm not like you!

It's hard to believe,
But it is true.
I saw it with my own eyes,
Through the window you flew!

Grant Powderly, Grade 4
St Mary Cathedral Elementary School, MO

Moonlight Night

The glassy reflection of the elegant moon
on the banks of a brook,
While little squirrels steal nuts and act as crooks,
the creaking creatures,
with beautiful features,
the snoozing cows
along with the full plump sows.
The beautiful night,
but it soon will be light.

Blake Christian, Grade 5
Sullivan Elementary School, TN

Soccer

I dribble down the field
Look for a pass and shield
I pass, and then run down the side
And call, "I'm open, pass wide!"
She passes and I get the ball
I'm up against a girl that is tall
I try hard to fake her out
I do, and all the fans shout
I move to the goalie box
I get past a girl with golden locks
I shoot and score, yippee!
The whistle blows, we win, 2 to 3!
Soccer's my favorite; I think it's the best
But for right now, I need a rest!

Anna Guercio, Grade 5
Hickory Grove Baptist Christian School, NC

Pretty Butterfly

Pretty butterfly
Flying in the breezy wind
He lands on flowers

He drinks his nectar
He flies away in the wind
He finds new flowers

Birds come to get him
He flies away just in time
The birds miss this one

Spring is wonderful
Butterflies are everywhere
I love the springtime

Chris Vincent, Grade 6
Haynes Academy for Advanced Studies, LA

Western and English Riding

Western
fast, wild
bucking, galloping, loping
barrels, horn saddles, short manes, no horn saddle
jumping, posting, cantering
graceful, fancy
English

Mary Davis Barber, Grade 5
Briarwood Christian School, AL

Friends

Friends are the ones who stick with you forever.
Friends are the ones who don't leave you behind.
They're always there to catch you when you fall.
Friends stick together forever and ever.
They call you to see if you're ok.
Because friends are forever and they stick together.

Kelsey Longworth, Grade 4
Tazewell-New Tazewell Primary School, TN

Fall/Summer

Fall
red, cold
crunching, falling, floating
getting close to winter
sticking, hanging, laying
green, hot
Summer

Jasmine Miller, Grade 6
Stuart Middle School, KY

Oranges

Every day I eat an orange
Oranges are
Good for everyone
I always eat
An orange a day.
It's very good for me,
Or so
They say!

Josie Kennedy, Grade 5
St Paul's Lutheran School, OK

Where I'm From

I am from a garage
building engines.
I am from oil on my hands
oil of the lifters.
I am from a monster garage
motors upside down.
I am from long cranks
with oil all over.

I am from making fudge
and cleaning rags.
I am from the know-it-alls
the pass-it-ons.
From perk up to perk down.
I am from working with tools.

I am from my granny's
visiting all the time.
I am from keeping my room clean.
I am from special moments.

Jarrett Hoskins, Grade 5
Tates Creek Elementary School, KY

What Time

Mom what time
Hello mom what time is it?
Mom I am hungry
Dad it's time for practice
Mom it's time for Katelyn to be quiet.

It's time to have fun.

Lane Finley, Grade 6
Armorel Elementary School, AR

Did You Know

The Holocaust is one of the world's worse sorrows.
Mostly done in the name of religious and political beliefs.
To a group of people who will be remembered for many tomorrows.
They did not deserve those cruel sad deaths!
But one day soon their persecutors will face their final test.

Destiny Malcolm, Grade 5
Pembroke Elementary School, NC

Victory!

CRACK! went the baseball bat,
The ball soared with a SWOOSH! through the big white fluffy clouds,
As the players scrambled like a pack of wild dogs
Hollering I've got it NO! I've got it.
Suddenly, I found the ball way above the clouds
BANG!
Two teammates collided in search of the ball.
I picked up the ball on a bounce and fired it to our third baseman.
POP! went the glove as he caught it,
SLAP! He had tagged the runner.
"He's out!" hollered the umpire,
That was our third out
We had won the game.

Tristan Durbin, Grade 6
College View Middle School, KY

India

Mountains, lakes and beaches
Located in South Asia
Neighbors to Nepal and Pakistan
Industry, agriculture and tourism its main economy
Known for the Himalayan Mountains, lowland plains of the Indus
Ganges and Brahmaputra Rivers
Known for its cultural diversity
Many languages such as Hindi, Tamil and Bengali
One of the world's earliest civilizations
The varied plant life includes bamboo, jasmine, henna and hemp
India is a home to Bengal tigers
In 1877, India became part of the British Empire
India became independent in 1947
In modern India, Mahatma Gandhi was an important leader
Mahatma means "great soul"
My dream is to explore India more
India

Georgina Johns, Grade 6
Houston Middle School, TN

Great Wind

W eather is whistling everywhere by the sweet smell of wind,
I try to get my bike up so I can ride with the wind in my face.
N ow, animals are coming out to feel the great breeze,
D eer hunt for food as they pause to feel the great breeze go through their fur,
Y ellow, orange, and red leaves fly through the air as the great wind goes by.

Tanner L. Brace, Grade 4
Oak Grove Elementary School, NC

Halloween Night

It is Halloween night
People are getting ready to go trick or treating.
Someone scares me…boo! boo! boo!
I jumped and ran away.

Nicole Nix, Grade 4
Brilliant Elementary School, AL

Leaves

Red, yellow and brown leaves in fall, falling out of trees.
And dancing in the breeze.
No leaves in the winter.
Fallen out of trees and will soon freeze.

Stems with green leaves in spring growing in the light.
And resting in the night.
Green leaves in the summer,
Makes all around nature seem calmer.

Amber Butler, Grade 6
Manning Elementary School, SC

Halloween

Halloween costumes are very fun
It's not done yet, it has just begun.
Just think about what I can be
Will I be a princess or a bumblebee?

I could be a soldier, sweet hearted bat too,
Or a super star or devil, wait ooohhh…
A French maid, good witch, or cheerleader
I wouldn't want to be a bird feeder.

I want to be a soldier because it has a dress
My mom says "STOP BEING A PEST."
I know why she says that, because…
I could wear it only once.

No, I really want it!
I won't leave it a bit
It's really pretty I tell you
If you don't someone's coming for you!

Katia Caballero, Grade 5
Nesbit Elementary School, GA

Birds

Bird, so majestic to life.
They are so magnificent with peace and grace,
So many shapes, so many sizes, so many colors; I love it all.
Yet, as spring passes and winter comes,
All the birds go "bye-bye," but I say why…oh why.
As spring comes once again, I'm happy but sad,
Because spring comes once a year and that brings me tears.
And as winter comes again,
I'm happy, because I know that when the birds go,
They will come back.

Iain Smith, Grade 6
Providence Christian School, NC

Military Child

I am a Military Child, born in Germany.
At night I hear guns and tanks shooting getting ready for Iraq.
I cry when my dad leaves.
But, I know he is coming back.
I am a Military Child, born in Germany.

I cry when people die.
I cry when people are alive.
I'm glad they come back.
I am a Military Child, born in Germany.

Soldiers risk there lives for the U.S.A.
They risk there lives for their family.
They cry when they leave.
They know that they are still in our hearts.
I am a Military Child, born in Germany.

They are brave to go to Iraq to fight for U.S.A.
We love that people are still alive when they are in Iraq.
I am a Military Child, born in Germany.

Salvatore Hrycych, Grade 6
Walker Intermediate School, KY

Blue

Blue is the color of a clear bright blue spring sky
the color that sucks away the darkness
blue is the color of the clear ocean with a blue tint
and the color of the fish that swim below its depths
The color of raindrops falling
sadly from the dark blue clouds of a rain storm
blue is also the color of an early morning sky
and the dark blue at night
the color of the pool in the summer
and the ice in the winter
the color of a blue bird soaring in the sky
the color of a blue flower sprouting from the ground
the color of the dark blue green Kentucky grass
that is the wonderful color of blue

Austin Horvat, Grade 6
East Oldham Middle School, KY

Alex

Like a carnation rose, I bloom in the Midwest.
A pioneer traveling to the south.
I am the wind that moves swiftly.
I can sweep you off your feet.
I'm not all sugar and spice with everything nice.
I am a spoiled, bad-tempered brat.
My roots go through South America, Africa and Europe.
I am a colorful rainbow of the Earth.

I am Alex.

Alexandra Cort, Grade 6
Beck Academy, SC

Ghost
G houlish
H aunting
O hhhhh
S pooky
T errifying
Justus Ammerman, Grade 5
First Flight Elementary School, NC

Corn
The food my grandma fixes
it is so pretty to see,
all the food sitting on the table.

It is so good
I hear the corn on a cob popping
like fireworks shooting up in the sky.

It tastes so delicious,
I think I am in heaven.

It feels so bumpy,
it is like I am on a dirt road.
Rosie-Marie Snider, Grade 5
Cool Spring Elementary School, NC

Steven
There is a girl next door
She really does like to snore
She keeps me awake
The house she does shake
I really can't take anymore!
Steven Danner, Grade 4
Judsonia Elementary School, AR

Skateboarding
I skate with my friends;
I skate for the fun;
I skate 'til you can't see the sun

I skate in the night.
Some people say skating
Gives them a fright!
My mom gets scared
When I do something big;
When I land it, I do a little jig!

I never get scared.
Sometimes I get dared.
I skate with my friends;
I skate for the fun!

I love skateboarding!!
Trevor Fos, Grade 6
Scotts Creek Elementary School, NC

A Day in Class
At morning when I sit in class,
I dream about fishing for bass.
My table becomes a beautiful sea,
My wheelchair a boat that carries me.

I float around for the perfect spot,
The wind is cool the sun is hot.
My pencil as a fishing pole,
I cast and wait for my goal.

As I wait for a bite,
Something strange comes into sight.
There's no more lake and no more bass,
Just me still sitting here in my class.
Joshua Killough, Grade 6
Providence Classical School, AL

Elephants/Giraffes
Elephants
large, gray
trumpeting, stomping, smashing
animal, male, animal, female
walking, running, outstanding
tall, beautiful
Giraffes
Sarah Burrow, Grade 5
Briarwood Christian School, AL

Bright Happiness
Happiness is bright yellow.
It sounds like birds chirping.
It tastes like sweet sugar cookies.
It smells like colorful flowers.
It looks like the sun beaming.
It makes you feel wonderful!
Megan Phillips, Grade 5
Salem Elementary School, AR

Friendship
Friendship is…

Friendship is a rainbow,
brightening your day.

Friendship is a tissue,
Wiping away tears on a bad day.

Friendship is a present,
It always brings you joy.

Friendship is like your birthday.
You always have fun together.
Allison Marie Parson, Grade 4
Plano Elementary School, KY

Why Pray?
Look around you!
Trees so fine, grass so green.
Who do you think put it this way?
God did! Lord of Lords, King of Kings,
Master of life and death.
He made this world for us today
Think of what He did.
Sent His son for our sin
for us to become the way we are now.
Praise the Lord for what He did
ask for forgiveness today
and live a life of joy and happiness
so get down and pray…today!
Bryan Landreth, Grade 6
Thomson Middle School, GA

The Circus
Looks like clowns doing tricks
Sounds like noisy elephants roaring
Tastes like soda and cotton candy
Feels like cold plastic
Smells like mixes of candy
Walker Wright, Grade 5
Briarwood Christian School, AL

Loving Father
Dark chocolate hair
Mustache as prickly as a porcupine
He's always saying
"Don't call people names"
and
"Try your best"
Looking up to him
Because he's
Hard working
and
Encouraging
Loving my dad
because he's
Loving towards me
That's my
"Try your best"
Encouraging
Loving
Dad
Darren Brown, Grade 4
Briarwood Elementary School, KY

Tar Heel State
old north state nickname
came from tar, pitch, turpentine
hooray tar heel boys
Spencer Faulk, Grade 4
Broadway Elementary School, NC

Baseball

Baseball is a wonderful sport.
The thing I like the most is when someone gets a hit.
I like to be on base, so I can score.
I like it when the coach waves me home,
I also like to make a strong accurate throw home,
Instead of a lousy one.

Charlie Lawson, Grade 5
North Middle School, TN

Vacation

It's vacation this time of year
Even though right now I'm standing here,
Soon I'll be on vacation
At my grandparents' plantation.
The air is warmer there,
But not enough to singe my hair.
Right here it's very cold,
Over there the weather gets bold.
At the plantation it gets hot,
Over here it does not.
We all sit down for dinner,
My grandmother's pie is a winner.
It comes out nice and hot,
It isn't just store bought.
We sit on that big tire,
Around the open fire.
The stars shine bright,
It takes away any fright.
Everything is fun,
It's very sad when it is done.

Reynaldo Uria, Grade 6
Victory Christian School, OK

When I Went to Coney Island

A rainbow of color sitting in front of me speeding
It went around and around to side to side.
I filled with excitement in the middle of the ride
When someone spit
It landed on me
EWE YUCK!

Robin Bowen, Grade 5
Cline Elementary School, KY

Love of Basketball

Basketball is my favorite thing.
I like the feel of the slick leather on the ball
I love the sound *swish* when I make it,
I feel excited when the crowd cheers.
I feel blissful when the ref blows his whistle for a charge.
I feel pleased when I make two pressure free throws.
I love compliments from my coach after the game,
and the smell of victory in the air.

Dylan Brewster, Grade 5
North Middle School, TN

Baseball

B aseball can become addictive.
A s you're playing, keep your head in the game.
S tart to play when the umpire yells, "Play Ball."
E xciting is when you get a hit.
B e ready to catch the ball when it's hit at you.
A wesome is when you hit a home run.
L osing is not an option.
L eaving the field after we win. Everybody is ecstatic.

Cory Mayfield, Grade 5
North Middle School, TN

The Holocaust

It is sad what the Nazis did
It is also horribly bad
Their lives were ripped and wiped out too
I know some kids wanted to be superheroes
Some wanted to smell beautiful Red Roses
But they will always live on in our minds and hearts

Blue Lowery, Grade 5
Pembroke Elementary School, NC

Cheetahs

Cheetah
Fast, strong
Eating, sleeping, hunting
Fastest of them all
Animal

Cheetah
Sneaky, majestic
Leaping, running, thinking
Chasing all their prey
Spotted

Matthew McKenzie, Grade 6
Haynes Academy for Advanced Studies, LA

A Shepherd

A Shepherd is a person who watches over his sheep
And in God's eyes, the sheep is you and me.
God watches over us and keeps us safe
And if one of us gets lost, He will look for us
Even if it takes three days.
God is my Shepherd, and He will always be,
And He will be yours if you just believe.

Katelyn Dewrell, Grade 5
First Assembly Christian School, AL

The Color Blue

Days pass and nights feel stronger
Trying to forget but emotions feel stronger
Looking out the window my heart starts to race
My thoughts start to picture a beautiful face
A smile so warm a moment to share
With love and hugs and lots of care

Katie Mitchell, Mara Huffman, and Elena Bagatelas, Grade 6
Houston Middle School, TN

Ella

Running after bouncy balls
Eating like a hog
I don't know what to do
Because she keeps chewing on logs.

Running across the street
Chewing on socks
Barking at your feet
Sly as a fox.

Chewing up flowers
Chasing cats
She is such a busy dog
Thinks she's all that.

This little white dog
All cute and frisky
Loves to play
But is very risky.

She runs like a jackrabbit
Tries to climb trees
She loves us so much
And so do we.

Jenna Montano, Grade 6
Holy Trinity School, KY

The Circus

Looks like clowns on unicycles
Sounds like really goofy music
Tastes like funnel cakes
Feels like hairy elephants
Smells like buttery popcorn
Isabella Powell, Grade 5
Briarwood Christian School, AL

Fall

Sprinting through the leaves
Hearing leaves crunch
Wearing warm sweatshirts
Going inside to watch TV
Watching the big game
Getting candy on Halloween
Scaring people with my costume
Eating most of my candy at once
Getting a belly ache from all my candy
Going back to school
Michael Hammock, Grade 6
Alvaton Elementary School, KY

Waterfall

Waterfalls falling
the sound goes pitter-patter
falling from high up.
Sarah Hunt, Grade 5
Duncan Chapel Elementary School, SC

Trail Blazer

My heart raced like a marathon runner
when I found out that I could ride the ATV ALONE!
I jumped up and down like a rabbit "Hooray" feeling like Mr. Fantastic
I stretched my legs across the black leathered seat
Quickly
        turned the key,
            flipped the switch,
                pressed the start button.
The engine roared like a hungry lion
Pressing the gauge, Off — I went "Zoom" Going down hills
Tickling in my stomach like a butterfly fluttering
Trying to get airborne as I go down the small hills
Seat vibrating between my legs
Wanting to sit down, but could not
My mouth and eyes bulge as I go zooming down the hills
"Ouch" the burn of the motor, like a match, hits my knee
Seeing my brother waving his arms like he wanted to fly telling me to come in
Returning to the porch I say
"Can I
    do that
      again!"

Jesse Borgmeier, Grade 4
Roberta Tully Elementary School, KY

Fall

I can hear the leaves crunch under my feet as I run to get the football.
"Crunch, crunch," as I throw the football back to my dad.
I can smell hot dogs on the grill. I can hear the football game on TV.
I see people burning leaves. I can feel the cool breeze that blows on my face.

Christian Stewart, Grade 4
First Wesleyan Christian School, NC

The Great Adventure

Crowds going to seat waiting for the circus to begin
Eating popcorn, nachos, hot pretzels or cotton candy.
All of a sudden the lights go out telling the crowd it is going to begin.
Then the lights flicker red, blue, and green spotlights going in every direction.

Tiger trainers walking to cage,
Crowd excitedly watching the tigers jump through the ring of fire,
Elephant rolling on metal cylinder
Can't believe an elephant can roll and not smash it.

Funny clowns making the crowd laugh hee, hee, hee.
Motorcycle man flipping on a skinny rope.
Acrobats swinging from bar triangular bar gripped in his mouth.
Many exciting tricks.

Lady's and gentlemen 2 more events.
More elephants, tigers, and ponies.
Crowd clapping as loud as an elephant stomping.
Arena lights come on sparkly American flag coming down
Lets everybody know circus is over.
Can't wait to go to another circus.

Tyler McNaughton, Grade 4
Roberta Tully Elementary School, KY

Lies in Your Eyes

You cannot run,
Nor can you hide.
For you know I am coming,
To look inside,
In your treasure chest or box.
Sneaky I am much like a fox.
I ask you questions,
And all you say is "no."
When I try to ask why,
You say "whatever" or "so."
Lies all lies,
That's why you never stare in my eyes.
Beneath the lids all I can see,
Is what I truly believe.
For it lies in your eyes.

Joshua Spann, Grade 5
Hunter GT Magnet Elementary School, NC

Maddy

Maddy
Small, funny, happy, shy
Who gives Jelly Bellies, smiles, pillows
Who needs family to visit, dogs to snuggle, friends to talk to
Relative of Cooper, Steve (Dad)
Lover of dogs, cats, and drawing squiggles
Who feels happy with my dog, sad when a relative dies,
bored when I'm at school
Who would like to see the Eiffel Tower, Paris, Mexico
Who fears snakes, sharks, when my brother scares me
Resident of the state of happiness
Bacon

Maddy Bacon, Grade 6
Our Lady Catholic School, MO

I Scream for Ice Cream

You know what's colorful and really sweet?
It's always a delicious treat.
Ice cream!
It comes in all kinds of flavors
And I really really crave 'em
There's chocolate, strawberry and rocky road.
Peanut pecan and chocolate marshmallow.
But on a very hot summer day,
Your ice cream drips and melts away.
When it is very hot,
Ice cream drips like a very sweet dot.
And when it finally drips and drops
You will hear a loud "PLOP"
Succulent sweet strawberry is my favorite
It makes me soar
how much I savor it.
So, when you go out to get ice cream
Make it so good that you will scream!
AAAHHHH!!!!!!

Andrew Doelling, Grade 5
Greathouse Shryock Traditional Elementary School, KY

Fall Leaves

Fall is a time to look and see —
The amazing things God has done for me —
The thought of turkey in my mouth
Makes me shout!
Fall leaves are beautiful, colorful and bright;
They shine in the sunlight.
The best part of fall is family coming to my home,
Fall leaves are colorful and bright — they show God's might

Kenton Holden, Grade 5
Palmetto Christian Academy, SC

Anything

I am anything I want to be
from happy to sad, to a wannabe,
I laugh at my friends
because they are funny
I cry at sad movies,
and act like a star on the red carpet

I am anything I want to be
from my head to my feet
I am a guitar player,
a singer,
and a chef at home, sizzle sizzle,

I am a night person
and like to party,
my family fights for my recipes, yum!
and my dad is teaching me
some great songs to play
but I am just a beginner
and I am getting there
so I am anything I want to be.

Caroline Elder, Grade 5
Greathouse Shryock Traditional Elementary School, KY

Who Must We All Know?

Who must we all know?
Who can it be?
Who is He we can't see?
Who made the stars?
Who made the planets?
Who made the moon?
Who made Mars?

For who is He we can't see?
For He is God He isn't odd for if you look hard
and read his book you'll see
who made you and who made me.

Take my choice and look really hard and read His book
and you'll see who He is that we can't see.

Margaret Len Lowery, Grade 5
Pembroke Elementary School, NC

Skater

S kates clicking together
K eeping everything in order
A ll skaters ready to skate
T oe picks hit the ice
E veryone making designs
R eady to hit the ice

Allyson Payne, Grade 5
Briarwood Christian School, AL

The Shooting Star

Roses are red, violets are blue.
I have a sweet poem for you.
Water is blue shining in the sun.
The sun is bright as a full moon.
As it brightens the sky.
A shooting star passes by.
And as I wish upon a star my
wish comes true as the shooting
star passes by.

Kia Magee, Grade 5
West Marion Elementary School, MS

Bad Kids

Running all around
Making teachers have a frown
When they're banging on the desk
and they're taking a spelling test
Teacher gives them a big fat F

Morgan Guillory, Grade 4
Lewis Vincent Elementary School, LA

Imagination

Take me far away.
Take me
where fairies roam,
where mermaids sing.
Lead me on an adventure.
Take me
where elves wander,
where unicorns run freely.
Take me
to a magical place
called my Imagination.

Celeste Fishback, Grade 6
Benton County School of the Arts, AR

Grenada Lake

Grenada Lake
dive, look, climb
swimming, fishing, jumping, eating
Always good for you.
Reservoir

Nichole McLaurin, Grade 4
East Jones Elementary School, MS

My Love

My love is so deep and true.
My love is all for you.
My love comes from my heart.
It has been there from the start.

I think my love is the best.
Yes! Better than the rest.
My love always comes through.
It comes through just for you.

Do you have love like me?
I think not.
My love never stops.
My love is for my mom.
Yes, it is.
It will always be yours till the end.

Raquel Metcalf, Grade 5
Bossier Elementary School, LA

Field Trip

I'm going on a field trip.
Weird field trip
Long field trip
Field trip, field trip, field trip.

Nice, fun, quiet field trip
Bad, mean, loud field trip
Very curious field trip
Field trip.

Justin Baker, Grade 5
Tates Creek Elementary School, KY

Ashlyn

There was an old man from Maine
Who thought he had a bad name
He went to his mother
To ask for another
She came up with old John Wayne

Ashlynn Wolfe, Grade 4
Judsonia Elementary School, AR

Skateboarding

I love to skateboard.
I love to skate on half pipes.
Skating is fun man.

William Gregurich, Grade 4
Moyock Elementary School, NC

The Beach

Such beautiful seas,
Children's laughter in the air,
The wind in your hair.

Adeline Ray, Grade 4
Briarwood Christian School, AL

Who I Am

I am a boy that works
On models
On rockets
On boats.
That's pretty much all I can do
Except for play
The violin.
I've taken for eight years
And play in an orchestra
With horns
Trumpets
And flutes.
With cellos
Violins
And even harps.
What a sound we make
All 60 of us doing what we do best.
The blare of the trumpet
The calm wind of the flutes
The steady stream of the violins
The calming melody of the cellos.

Andrew Foreman, Grade 6
Westchester Country Day School, NC

My Truck

I found a truck parked in the woods.
It was an old rusty one.
The tires were black, flat, and old,
And its usefulness was done.
On the seat there was green mold,
And the floor board was all dusty.
The brown metal was really cold,
And there was no engine at all.

Noah Shultz, Grade 6
Pleasants County Middle School, WV

The Treasure Chest

I'd like to go hunting
for a treasure chest;
That's filled with tiny
beads and things,
as breakable as glass.

I'd like to go hunting
for a treasure chest;
That's filled with Kings and Queens,
And be a noble guest

I'd like to go hunting
for a treasure chest;
That's filled with love and kindness,
that would be the best.

Rebecca Helton, Grade 6
Tri-County Christian School, MO

My Daddy

My daddy is smart
Yes, he is my loving daddy
He buys me stuff
He's a good father
He loves me
He does a marvelous job of taking care of me
Yeah, he's a good daddy.

Tau'Shell Rawls, Grade 5
Western Hills Elementary School, AR

He Was the One

He was the one who would always make me smile.
He was the one that made my life worthwhile.
He was the one who would make me jump with joy.
He was the one!

He was the one who filled me with butterflies.
He was the one who never told lies.
He was the one that was always funny.
He was the one!

Until one day he broke my heart.
On that day my real life began to start.
On that day my fantasy ended.
He was the one!

Taylor Simmons, Grade 6
Stuart Middle School, KY

Me and Jazz

Jasmine is my best friend.
She treats me with respect.
We have a lot in common.
We are silly,
Send each other e-mails,
Sell cookies for fundraisers,
And laugh together.
She is like a sister to me.
She is always on my side,
And often on my mind.

Diamond Campbell, Grade 5
Lee A Tolbert Community Academy, MO

Down in New Orleans

The south is so unlucky
It seems like hurricanes come all the time.
People have to heal their losses and build new houses
So be helpful
Donate a dollar or two
Then you will help a family in need.
If you go to New Orleans
Then you will see what I saw is true.
So please donate a dollar or two.

Kody Morgan, Grade 5
Wright City Middle School, MO

Did You Ever Wonder

Did you ever wonder
What's all around behind a white, fluffy cloud?
Is there a heaven in the sky?
Oh, how I wish I could fly.
Is there a whole other world
That we just don't know?
How do we get there?
Where do we go?
I truly do not know.
Oh, but I have wondered
What's high in the sky?
What's behind white, fluffy clouds?
I will find it, I truly will,
For there is not time to kill,
Our life is only so long.
I know I'm just a child, but my mind is very wild.
It wanders through the world like the wind,
Around every corner and every bend.
Do not doubt me because I'm a child,
Remember my mind is very wild,
Did you ever wonder? I have.

Caitlin Berry, Grade 6
IA Lewis Elementary School, LA

The Holocaust

The Holocaust was very sad.
The people who killed the Jews were very bad.
There were over six million deaths.
I could not imagine that being me.
Who could have done this? I plead.

Dylan Deal, Grade 5
Pembroke Elementary School, NC

Meaning of Christmas

Christmas means to be full of joy,
Not just to receive a lousy toy.
It means to be merry to all who are here,
To remember Christ at this special time of year.

Crunch, crunch, crunch…that's the sound of candy canes,
Christmas doesn't mean to be insane.
Christmas means to care for your life,
Not to carry a stupid knife.

BOOM! Christmas should be full of holly,
It means to soar, not to get a doll named Molly.
Christmas is like my favorite grandma,
She's joyful and always wears a shawl.

Christmas means to have fun,
Not to be selfish and have a gun.
It doesn't mean to be mean and pout,
So be happy, not down and out.

Bakari James, Grade 4
North Elementary School, NC

The Blindfolds
We think our world is perfect, or at least close to it,
but the truth is that we are blindfolded.
Around us, near us, everywhere, the real world happens.
Starvation.
Murder.
World Catastrophe.
We've built a shield, our own little world, where these things do not exist.
We need to face the truth,
that we are the ones who have created our blindfolds.
They mask us from what we do not want to see,
so that we do not have to face the harsh coldness of reality.
No one reaches out to stop injustice and harm in the world,
because the blindfold is too heavy.
But a few of us are finding the strength to lift our blindfolds,
and reach out to change reality, instead of cowering away from it.
What will you do?
Keep in mind:
If you do not reach out and lift your blindfold to help now,
what will happen when your blindfold is too torn and tattered to shield you any longer?
Who will be there to help you?

Aleah Kadry, Grade 5
American Heritage Academy, GA

My Dogs
I have nine dogs
They all eat like hogs
They all have a name
But none are the same
Some are tall
Some are small
Romeo is the biggest of all
Jewel was our first
Duke was our last
But they all are a blast
There names are Jewel, Romeo, Fifty, Buck, Banks, Carmen, Misty, Punisher, and Duke
If my parents buy one more dog, I think I will puke.
But at the end of the day
I would not want it any other way.

Victoria Castillo, Grade 5
Hatfield Elementary School, AR

Wild Rose Horse Bud
The beauty of her pale glow
Her soft velvety feel
She is always happy and loving
I can't wait till she blooms this year
Her legs are as long as stems shooting to the ground
But instead of standing still they move her all around
She always looks good in bunches out in the field
And every day she grows more and more beautiful than her real appeal
When she's out in the field she's reckless and wild but in the arena she's calm and mild
No matter how we show she is pleasing to me.
And whatever the judges say she's the perfect bud to me.

Hallie Harrison, Grade 5
Tuscaloosa Academy, AL

Changing

I'm changing. I'm changing —
orange, brown, and yellow.
I'm not so young anymore. As the wind blows me
I fall and I dance among the sky.
And then I fall gently
And lay on the cool soft ground.
I swell up and disintegrate
and start life all over again.

Anna Lineberger, Grade 4
First Wesleyan Christian School, NC

Son of a Soldier

I am the son of a soldier that blows stuff up for a living.
I wonder if my dad is having fun in Iraq?
I hear my dad talking to me.
I see my dad almost every day on the web cam.
I want my dad to come home very soon.
I am the son of a solder that blows stuff up for a living.

I pretend my dad never left.
I feel lonely when he is gone.
I touch his heart when he is home.
I worry about him when he is in Iraq.
I cry when he does not call for days.
I am the son of a soldier that blows stuff up for a living.

I understand why he cannot come home.
I say my dad has been in the Army fifteen years.
I dream he will come home soon.
I try to pretend my dad never left.
I hope he will come home safe.
I am, I am the son of a soldier that blows stuff up for a living.

Eric Holman, Grade 5
Byrns L Darden Elementary School, TN

My Mom

Always has special cologne
I know it from anywhere

Her hair is short
Once a month it gets cut
And her hair is fluffy

Her eyes are sea blue
With a little dab of green

She comes home tired after a long day of hard work
When she gets home she expects a happy family, with food

Her job is stressful, she whines
The whining really gets on our nerves
I remind them who gets us the money

Yup, that's my mom

Kirstin Wolgast, Grade 4
Briarwood Elementary School, KY

Forests

Next to you big trees
Upon big rocks and other things
In front of you who knows.
Regarding all the chirping and other things
Throughout your walk you hear crackles from the leaves.
Over you the bare trees
Onto different leaves colors of orange and brown.
Until we reach our destination, who knows.

Steven Nelson, Grade 5
Grovespring Elementary School, MO

If I Were President

If I were president
I would slow down all the poverty
By lowering food prices.
I would ban discrimination,
Install more security systems,
And place a policeman on every street.
Every school would have new supplies,
And lunches would include
Pizza and rotel and chips.
Gas would never be over $2.00 per gallon,
And I would bring most of our soldiers
Home from Iraq.

Trey Bradley, Grade 5
Lee A Tolbert Community Academy, MO

Winter

Winter is here
I am filled with joy and cheers,
winter is finally here!
holy moly I like it!

When I see the
beautiful crisp white snow
I go crazy, great
time of year is my time

I like opening presents
at Christmas, skating on
the clear, slippery
ice, throwing snowballs

When I wake up
in the morning and
look out the window I
see the snow, I dress warmly

When I ride my sled
down my big hill I
get a tickle in my tummy
that's what makes me crazy about winter!

Tiffany Ellis, Grade 4
Schaffner Traditional Elementary School, KY

Stone Compass
Shaped like a circle,
A stone compass points the way
Out of the forest
Jacob Hampton, Grade 6
St Joseph Institute for the Deaf, MO

Dogs in Heaven
Dogs in heaven, they
will not bite, they will play with
you but rest all night.
Kathleen Hooker, Grade 4
Briarwood Christian School, AL

Martin Luther King Jr.
If Martin Luther King
came back to life magically,
I bet he'd be astonished,
that he had made history.

If he came back magically,
he could ride a bus.
And he could sit where he wanted to
without any fuss.

If he came back magically,
he could go into any store.
That's something he couldn't do,
many years before.

If he came back magically,
I could talk to him,
because skin color wouldn't matter,
and we could be friends.
Jodie Ritter, Grade 5
Walton Verona Elementary School, KY

Candy
C hewy and sweet
A nd
N ever get enough
D ark chocolatey
Y ou'll love it!
Robin Hamm, Grade 5
First Flight Elementary School, NC

Martin
M any students
A fter schools programs
R ecess every day
T he teachers are nice
I n and out you go all day
N ice all day every day
Rickie Miller, Grade 6
Martin Elementary School, WV

Spring
Florescence's vigor's,
Emerald trees develop,
The gleaming sun glistens upon,
The sights of spring that are here.

Pollen flows throughout the blue,
Annotates carol in timely mornings.
The quarrel secretly sneaks behind,
Nothing will ruin this worthy spring.

Morning sunshine lights up swiftly.
Etiolate overcast clears from the sky.
Late at night, the sun's still up.
Look at all that spring can grant us.

Now you've seen how great spring is.
Let's describe what spring desires.
Beautiful, warm, and wonderful too.
This is all spring can give you.
Diana Dang, Grade 5
Nesbit Elementary School, GA

My Garden
My garden makes the world so bright.
Colorful daylilies reach for the light.
They smell so sweet.
I must confess.
My little garden is the best!
Tia Solomon, Grade 6
Appling County Middle School, GA

Chocolate Ice Cream
It is wonderful!
Yum! Chocolate is delicious!
Try it today now.
Camille Goldman, Grade 4
Briarwood Christian School, AL

Jasmine Bates
J oyful
A wesome
S mart
M agnificent
I nspiring
N ice
E nergetic

B eautiful
A dmiring
T alented
E xcellent
S pecial
Jasmine Bates, Grade 6
Mark Twain Elementary School, MO

Yellow Bee
Yellow black striped bee
sitting on a blue flower
buzzing around town.
Taylor Itschner, Grade 4
Moyock Elementary School, NC

The Frog King
Once there was a frog
Who went hopping around.
While he was sleeping
His brother got crowned.

He went to his brother
And disturbed his lunch.
He didn't mean
To spill his punch.

You better watch out
Or your brother will get mad.
Then he will say
"Off with your head!"
Chase Arant, Grade 4
Northeast Baptist School, LA

Leave
Leaves wait to leave on a tree
When the wind comes.
Kids wait to leave their home
When time comes.
Cruz Manrriquez, Grade 5
Westwood Elementary School, AR

The Big Outdoors
I like the big outdoors,
With green grass on the floor
Of the ground
Everything buzzing around,
When I sit down everything,
Flies around me
A tiny frog hops my way,
When it sees me it sits on a rock,
And stays
When I lay my head,
On a big oak tree,
I close my eyes and listen for the river,
I hear the leaves rustle
With leaves so green,
I feel like I am in a rainforest
Where it rains all the time,
Here comes the rain
Like big sparkles in the sky
Then I run home.
Takaya Harris, Grade 5
Wright City Middle School, MO

Recess

The swing set
swaying back and forth,
like a bird
flying north.

The tower
so tremendously tall,
sliding down slides
having a ball.

The field
was the place to play,
wishing we could stay there
all day.

The track
rapidly racing,
rooting for racers
as if you also are a racer.

Jaela Packer, Grade 5
Greathouse Shryock Traditional Elementary School, KY

Family

Stories are like family.
You can bring them together
and you can break them apart
but some can always stay together.
Stories and families can have generation.
Stories and families can end and some live on
but, both have to have a sad part.
Like when someone dies in the end.
But the end can always be happy and cheerful.
Some family and stories never end.
Its like a never ending story.

Kevin Scheidhauer, Grade 6
St Mary's School, SC

Christmas Night

The night was dark the snow was here
It was really cold when I heard a reindeer.

I jumped out of bed, I ran outside
I climbed on the roof, I tried to hide.

No one was in the sleigh, so I sat right down
The reindeer took off; they just about hit the ground.

We flew around all night long,
Then once again I was back at home.

Santa was waiting, he climbed in the sled
I said "Goodnight, everybody, I'm going back to bed."

Hannah Cribb, Grade 6
Beech Springs Intermediate School, SC

I Am

I am the daughter of a loving mother.
I wonder how much she loves me?
I hear her saying how much she loves me.
I see her writing, "I love you."
I want her to give me a hug.
I am the daughter of a loving mother.

I pretend not to care.
I feel her love in my heart.
I touch my mom's soft hands.
I worry about how much she cares.
I cry when she cries.
I am the daughter of a loving mother.

I understand that she cares a lot.
I say I don't care.
I dream that one day, I will say, "I love you too."
I try to listen, but I don't.
I hope she loves as much as she says she does.
I am the daughter of a loving mother.

Victoria Viernes, Grade 5
Byrns L Darden Elementary School, TN

Sad Summer

When I awoke this morning,
I knew today would not be boring.
The sun was shining,
There will be no whining
Coming from my mouth
Down here in the South.
I got on my clothes.
Already could I smell a rose.
Summer was here
I shall not make a sneer.
After my eggs and toast,
I went out to see what I love the most
    Summer.
But when I got outside, it was a sad sight,
There was not a wind for my new kite.
Where was the summer I love?
Why in the sky was there not a dove?
Maybe I should ask my mother.
Wait a minute!
All the leaves are different colors!
Silly me! It's only fall!

Jayden Saunders, Grade 4
Evangelical Christian School, TN

Spaghetti

A spaghetti smell filled the room
Until I heard the broom.

Then the sauce covered my mouth
Then I thought the smell was going south.

Tristlynn Jae Roberts, Grade 6
Nodaway Holt Elementary School, MO

Love

Love is violet
It tastes like a hot fudge sundae
It sounds like birds chirping
It smells like fresh baked cookies
It looks like fireworks
It feels like cotton

Skyla Parker, Grade 4
Cleveland Elementary School, OK

What's an Angel?

What's an angel?
Do you know?
Do they have halos and wings?
Do they look like us?
Do they have horses or dogs?
Do they have harps or horns?
The only way I'll find out is
When I die and go to Heaven.
Then I'll know what angels look like.

Destiny Stanley, Grade 5
Berryville Elementary School, AR

Super-man

Brave, heroic
Flying, saving, fighting
Powerful man of steel
Falling, killing, giving up.
Scared villain
Lex Luther

Hannah Wyman, Grade 6
Stuart Middle School, KY

Thunderbolt

Thunderbolt loves to fetch.
With a tennis ball, he does best.
On wood floor,
He slides into the door,
It is silliness galore!

Sadly, he will quickly grow,
And his silliness will quietly go.
But he will always be our pup,
Even if he is all grown up!

Jenn Ott, Grade 6
Seven Holy Founders School, MO

Courtney's Headbands

Courtney's headbands
Pink, blue, polka-dot,
Sparkly silver,
Stripes, butterflies.
Oh, I forgot…
Green,
And that purply-pink.

Emma Lundy, Grade 5
St Vincent Elementary School, MO

I Am a Military Brat

I am a Military Brat, born in Trier Germany; I am half German, half American.
I wonder where we will move next.
I hear tanks shooting.
I see airplanes flying over my house.
I want to move back to Germany.
I am a Military Brat, born in Trier Germany; I am half German, half American.

I pretend playing battle with my daddy.
I feel happy that my daddy is not getting deployed right now.
I touch my heart to say the pledge.
I worry that my daddy might get hurt.
I cry when we move because I will miss my friends.
I am a Military Brat, born in Trier Germany; I am half German, half American.

I understand that my daddy has to leave sometimes.
I say my daddy is my hero.
I dream that my daddy comes home safe.
I try to respect the flag by saying the pledge.
I hope for peace all around the world.
I am a Military Brat, born in Trier Germany; I am half German, half American.

Cassidy Brown, Grade 4
Walker Intermediate School, KY

Where I'm From

I'm from books,
from Kleenex and Timex.
I am from the cold smooth water by the dock.
I am from the pines, the daisies
I am from camping and blond hair,
from Allen and William and James.
I'm from the jokers and the droners,
From slept until your head was hairy and cute as a button.
I am from Williamson's Chapel Sunday school room and all the scriptures inside
I'm from Hickory and the farm, Candy and fruit.
From the cancer we lost my grandfather to,
the boats our foundation started on,
and the war torn skies my cousin fights under.
I am from photo books that bring back memories
like waves on a clear lake.

Amy Blew, Grade 6
Lakeshore Middle School, NC

Lukas

Juke —
Peppy, coordinated, athletic, creative.
Son of Paul and Kathleen.
Brother of Stephan, Nicholas, Andrew, and Maria.
Lover of music, basketball, and tennis.
Who fears big spiders, really tight spaces, and realizing very bad things.
Who was born in Baltimore, Maryland.
Who now lives in Birmingham, Alabama.
— Lukas

Lukas Castellanos, Grade 5
Briarwood Christian School, AL

Living Your Life

"Wah" "Wah"
That is the sound of a new baby.
Could be a girl or a boy
with red, orange, blond, gold, brown, or black hair,
short hair or long hair,
blue, green, brown, or black eyes,
freckles or no freckles,
dark skin or light skin,
but what matters most is that you are alive.
Now that everyone knows you are living
they can send you to school later on.
First elementary, then middle school, high school,
and finally college.
College is cool as a cat that can catch,
but work is like a whispering wind,
always saying things that turn out different.
"Who? What? When? Huh?"
That is what you ask.
Now, when you have done what was needed,
you act like a willow wilting in the world
with one place to go, Heaven.

Nann Webster, Grade 5
Greathouse Shryock Traditional Elementary School, KY

Life

Life is like a never-ending roller coaster,
Ups and downs all the time,
Never stopping and never knowing what's next,
Scary sometimes, but fun also,
Turns and curves all the time,
But when you get off,
You're glad you took chances and made it through okay.
So it turned out okay

Bridgett Gibbons, Grade 6
North Shelby Elementary School, MO

Golf

When I play golf, I like to play on the Par 3.
But I never have a tee.
Ahh — that's okay. I'll just use my pitching wedge
because I can hit the ball pretty hard.
Ooh! A par! The next hole isn't too far.
Oh my gosh — a hole in one!
This is getting to be quite some fun!
Splash! Aww…I hit it in the pond!
This counts for two strokes.
I need to choke up on my grip.
Wait…Wait…Yes! I made it on the green!
Isn't that a sight to be seen?
I believe I'm going to make some putts on the Par 3, but not all.
I hope I don't make any ruts on the green with my golf cleats.
Darn! I missed the putt!
Sigh. Oh well, I guess that double bogeys aren't horrible
(although the fact of getting a bogey isn't horrible either.)

Sam Thomas, Grade 6
Woodland Presbyterian School, TN

Old Muriel

Some trees are big, some trees are small.
Some trees are short, some trees are tall.
Some trees have leaves, some trees don't.
A lot of trees I like to climb, others I won't.
But there is one tree out there that I just adore.
She is twisted and has four trunks or more!
Old Muriel is her name, she is very rare.
As you can tell by her condition,
she deserves love and care.
She is big and huge,
and like my dream playground.
I have so much enjoyment
from this tree that I have found.
So when I am watching television,
and at the corner of my eye,
I see Old Muriel standing there,
alone and about to cry.
I turn off the television, run out the door,
and climb on Old Muriel just a little more.

Christine Herrington, Grade 6
Holy Trinity School, KY

Gracy My Cat

Gracy is very small
and loves to run down halls!
She's fast and cute
and loves fuzzy boots!
She is gray and fast
and she's a total blast!
She's happy and fat
and Gracy loves to kill rats!
She is cuddly and fuzzy
like a heating pad!
My kitten is sweet, and, fat and not neat!
She's #1 in my neighborhood!
My sweetie is like a zooming race car!
She's good and great too.
She is as sly as a fox
and she loves to climb into boxes!
My Gracy is #1 to me!

Dustine Bosco, Grade 5
Greathouse Shryock Traditional Elementary School, KY

Sarge and Major

Sarge and Major are boxers.
They like to run.
They like to sleep.
They like to play.
Sometimes they get tired and have to rest.
So do Morgan and Kelley.
That's okay because pretty soon…
We will play some more.

Kelley Eads, Grade 5
Paint Lick Elementary School, KY

Thanksgiving

T ogether with family
H appy people together
A ll of your family here
N o one is starving
K ids playing
S anctuary with everyone
G reat people everywhere
I nteresting conversations
V olume is loud at the table
I nteresting people
N ot a person hungry
G rateful for everyone

David Salchert, Grade 5
Briarwood Christian School, AL

An Ode to Scooter My Dog

Oh, Scooter you're one cuddly dog.
You're so cute
you make me mute.

You hate yucky fish
in your red dish.

Scooter you are very cuddly,
also a bit bubbly.

I love you!

Brenda Williams, Grade 5
West Liberty Elementary School, WV

Winter

Winter is my favorite time of year
Snow falls!
We get out of school
We wait for Christmas!
On Christmas
We open our presents
We play with our new toys
We remember the birth of Jesus Christ.
Six days after Christmas
We begin our New Year.

Joshua Huggins, Grade 6
Saint Paul School, TN

Mom/Dad

Mom
kind, sweet
playing, loving, cooking
house, dog, movies, coach
working, fishing, talking
fun, cool
Dad

Gabrielle Piwetz, Grade 5
Briarwood Christian School, AL

Squeak, My Hamster

My hamster's name is Squeak,
since that is how she speaks.

Squeak sleeps all day in her wheel,
then gets up at night for a meal.

Food bulging from her cheek,
she's on her wheel in a streak!

Tyler Daneault, Grade 5
Our Lady of Fatima School, MS

My Little Brother

I have a little brother
I love him like no other

We fuss and we fight
Sometimes we even bite

When he pulls my hair
I scream "Don't you dare"

He can be very sweet
But he has stinky feet

There will never be another
Like my dear baby brother

Abbie Carden, Grade 5
Clarksburg School, TN

Children

They are fun,
They like to run,
They are sweet,
They love to eat,
They can be happy,
But they need their nappy,
They are careless,
Sometimes they're hairless,
They can be grouchy,
They sit very slouchy,
They are shy,
They think they can fly,
They're calm or wild,
Chubby or mild,
That describes a child.

Hayden Culler, Grade 5
JJ Jones Intermediate School, NC

Rivers

Tombigbee River
Mobile and don't forget the
Tennessee River.

Will Halama, Grade 4
Briarwood Christian School, AL

My Family Is a Barnyard

My family is a barnyard
Smelly, big, and loud

My brother is a donkey,
Making noise nonstop

My dad is a bull,
Stomping around thinking he is the king

My mom is a horse,
Graceful and pretty

And I'm a sheep,
Always admiring my wool.

Rebecca Woford, Grade 5
Bloomfield Elementary School, KY

Being Drug Free

I'm Drug free,
some people don't want to be Drug Free,
But They Need to be Drug Free
just like me,
The Best Way to be,
Drug Free Just Like me.

So be all you can be!
And be Drug Free!

Destiny Lynn Campbell, Grade 6
Pembroke Elementary School, NC

Mrs. Raburn

Mrs. Raburn
Nice, fun
Teaching, reading, helping
She loves her children
Typing, learning, smiling
Smart, pretty
Teacher

Brinkley Ference, Grade 5
EA Harrold Elementary School, TN

Jazz

Piano in the background
Trumpets up close
I see happiness
Yet sadness
Then everything goes dark
A slight light appears
It's jazz
Piano in the background
Trumpets up close
All over again

Drew Lempesis, Grade 6
Prince of Peace Catholic School, SC

Dad

Dad I love you now and I always will.
If I have to, I'll pay for the house bill.
Love is very powerful but not for me,
I love you times 3.
When I grow up, I know what I want to do,
I want to be a great dad like you!

Zach Beld, Grade 6
Stuart Middle School, KY

The Heart of the Flute

This young man in this realistic painting
has a loving heart for the flute.
As he puts on his warm, gray velvet jacket,
he sets in his favorite ornate chair.
The young man plays a soft, slow tune on his lovely flute.

As he sits in his favorite ornate chair,
he thinks and plays a soothing tune on the flute.
I've always been a big fan of the flute, but yet
I've always wondered if I would have as many
fans for playing the flute as well as all the
other famous flute players.

Why he thinks and imagines of being a famous musician,
He still plays that lovely flute.
Why he's pretending to be a famous musician.
He flashes a big smile and ends it with a lovely bow.
He might of played three hundred and fifty years ago,
but he's still here.
So shhh…listen to him play that soft, slow and flowing music!

Keely Horn, Grade 5
Saffell Street Elementary School, KY

Fall Leaves

The fall leaves falling from up high
The trees above are wondering why?

It's time to start raking
And putting them into a stack.

The wait 'till next year, the time will come soon.
Then it will happen all over again!

Connor Simmons, Grade 6
Appling County Middle School, GA

New Falls and Triumphs

With new falls comes new triumphs,
Along with those triumphs comes new walls,
Those walls you have to climb,
They may be sour like lemons and lime,
When you reach the top rejoice,
For God has given us a new choice.

Adriana Lebron, Grade 6
East Hoke Middle School, NC

I Am Marissa

I am Marissa.
I wonder if I am good at soccer.
I hear people talk about me.
I see people prettier than me.
I want to be pretty.
I am Marissa.
I pretend that I am flying.
I feel God touching me.
I touch pretty things.
I worry if my family gets hurt.
I cry when someone yells at me.
I am Marissa.
I understand that people see me differently than I do.
I say that I am weird.
I dream that I will be loved.
I hope I am famous.
I try not to cry when people are around me.
I am Marissa.

Marissa Clodius, Grade 4
Wohlwend Elementary School, MO

Ghostly Ghost

How scary a ghostly ghost would be,
I could just imagine —
He would be 5 foot tall,
He would be so scary

His eye's would be green and at night they would glow
He would be green and have spikes at the end of his tail,
Man he would be so scary.
This is my imaginary ghostly ghost.

Kaylai Anderson, Grade 4
Tazewell-New Tazewell Primary School, TN

First Trick

One afternoon as I am skateboarding
on the rocky concrete I think…
Should I try a trick?
A kickflip maybe?
Getting ready to perform the trick
I stand with one foot under the board
and
with
one
foot
on top
kicking the board hard upwards board flips…
feeling the wind against my feet spinning a 180
Swish, swish
stopping the rotation by placing my feet back on the board
coming down faster than a Cheetah
wheels hitting the ground hard…
2 wheels then on all 4 wheels…
"I DID IT!"

Dylan Stallings, Grade 4
Roberta Tully Elementary School, KY

The Holidays

The holidays are so much fun,
Especially eating the cinnamon buns,
We eat all the food,
I get in a mood,
That I don't want the day to be done.

Kate Worley, Grade 5
Midway Covenant Christian School, GA

Who Am I

I am the bright, yellow sunshine
Sometimes the puffy white clouds!
 I am the leaves on a tree
My brothers, the bark
My parents the limbs, and
My Grandpa, Merritt, the roots.
He's passing down a legend.
 I'm a giant to my grandma,
But a midget to my friends!
With a swing and a step,
I walk with pride
Into the world
Where I won't hide!

Merritt Phillips, Grade 6
Beck Academy, SC

The Holocaust

There is Murder everywhere
They say it's not fair
They need help here and there
They need help everywhere

The Nazis are really not fair
They really didn't care
Do you?

Phoenix E. Maynor, Grade 5
Pembroke Elementary School, NC

Imagination

As I race into the woods
I feel the sun in my face.
It is almost four o'clock
In the afternoon.
They are waiting on me.
As I race over the bridge
I enter the land, the land
I like to call Serengeti!
Every day the land grows
Bigger with trees, people,
Trolls, and creatures of all kinds.
They are waiting for me.
For I am their Queen
Who created this land.
For this land shall live
Forever in peace!

Hayden Baucom, Grade 5
New Salem Elementary School, NC

Autumn

Pretty leaves fall and change colors too.
Beautiful leaves sway how about you?
It's Autumn time now.
That's when it smells good.
Thanksgiving is coming and Harvest too.
Football games are coming and parades and pumpkin pie.
Autumn is among us — you can't deny — now I need my Grandma's pie.

Destinee Hall, Grade 4
First Wesleyan Christian School, NC

Fun in the Country

Living in the country is "Oh, so awesome!"
But my allergies come back when the flowers blossom.

I get to ride horses all evening long,
And then grab my fiddle and play a song.

Working in the field is so hot and hard,
But if I want to rest, I just lay in the yard.

Cleaning up the barn can really start to stink,
But I'll be going in soon after the animals drink.

Well, it's getting dark and almost time to go in.
I hope I'll be able to come out tomorrow and do it all over again!

Ethan Pittman, Grade 5
Enon Elementary School, LA

I Remember Aunt Patty

I remember Aunt Patty…
watching her do flips everywhere, being scared she would fall,
seeing her do excellent gymnastics, being sad when she got sick.
I remember Aunt Patty.

I remember Aunt Patty…
listening to music with her, having lots of fun,
loving every minute with her, learning how to say goodbye.
I remember Aunt Patty.

I remember Aunt Patty…
being with her every minute, crying for a very long time,
going out of control when she was gone, saying goodbye for the last time.
I remember Aunt Patty.

Alexandria Reeves, Grade 5
Sycamore Elementary School, GA

Alexandria Fair

Dusty grass covers me as we meander forward
Miles away screaming and excited voices fill the air
Trotting hooves cover the ground as echoes and animals reek in the atmosphere
Scents on the filthy ground are everywhere
Anxiously waiting in long lines
Talkative groups all around
Memories are formed as darkness falls

Emily Hartig, Grade 5
Cline Elementary School, KY

When Fall Comes

Fall is a ball.
When fall comes the leaves are going to fall.
I call on a friend to play.
Then we will have a good day.

Grant Lester, Grade 5
EA Harrold Elementary School, TN

Starbucks

When I picked up
the white paper cup
and took a sip
it was like drinking the sun
then I heard a screech
I turned around
and it was the blenders
mixing up that rich dark chocolate
getting ready to be poured
over the scorching hot coffee
they started to pour the chocolate
over the coffee
I almost fainted
the chocolate was a mud puddle
it was about
to be served
but it needs
1 more thing
the whip cream
now it's ready to go!
Yum!

Devin Spratt, Grade 5
Greathouse Shryock Traditional Elementary School, KY

I Am

I am a quiet girl, who likes plants
I wonder what stories of their own do plants have
I hear pine trees whispering to each other
I see flowers dancing in mid air, holding hands
I want to dance around with the plants and have fun
I am a quiet girl, who likes plants.

I pretend to jump up and be carried away by the breeze
I feel the breeze swirling around me with cherry tree flowers
floating everywhere
I can touch the hot sun, while I am flying
I worry about pollution that kills the rich soil
I cry when a flower perishes
I am a quiet girl, who likes plants

I understand that plants aren't immortal
I say, "Let the life go on."
I dream to have a garden with beautiful plants in it
I try not to increase the pollution too much
I hope that someday people will start caring about our planet
I am a quiet girl, who likes plants.

Katherine Zeng, Grade 6
R D and Euzelle P Smith Middle School, NC

The Beginning of Horses

Horses running
Running from life
Afraid of their own shadow
Unwilling to live, or serve, or please

There is the thunder of hooves on grass
There is the scraping of hooves on sand
There is the crunching of hooves on leaves
There is the splashing of hooves on water.

Horses still running
Until something crosses their path
A child, nothing more
The horses stop, they seem frozen in time

All of a sudden
Horses aren't running from life
Aren't afraid of their own shadow
Are willing to live, to serve, to please

The child turns and starts walking
Stops and looks back
Smiles, turns, and walks on
As the horses willingly follow.

Elisa Daniel, Grade 6
Benton County School of the Arts, AR

Life in Middle School

Now that I'm in middle school
There are new things for me to learn
A whole new set of learning tools
Had me quite concerned.

The teachers will do their best for you
If you pay attention
Acting like you have no clue
Can land you in detention!

Study hard and do your best
And things will work out fine
Work real hard to pass your test
So please do not decline!

I learned these few studying rules
And now there is no fear
To be at Southlawn Middle School
In my six grade year.

Southlawn Middle School is so cool
If you do not get on task
You will go to summer school
And next year you will be in the same class.

Roderick Thornton, Grade 6
Southlawn Middle School, AL

Fall

I love fall,
The trees are so tall.
When the leaves fall,
They are so colorful and small!
That's why I love fall!

Lance Hubbard, Grade 4
First Assembly Christian School, AL

The World

The wind is blowing
The birds are chirping
The world is talking
So say hello to the world
Everything is talking
And everything is alive

Farris Bryant, Grade 5
Des Arc Elementary School, AR

My Dear Dog Maddie

Sad tears
Had been shoved in my heart
The minute I saw it
My dear dog friend had just died
Days had gone by
Without her
The fourth morning I woke up
What was that
I thought to myself
A brown and white speck
On the floor
It was a gift
From my old dog friend
It was my new dog friend
My dear dog Maddie

Tricia Hirchert, Grade 6
East Oldham Middle School, KY

Mommy

My mommy held
me close at night
and scared the monsters away.
Sometimes I wish
upon a shooting star
to bring her back to me.

But when she was with me
it was a dream
as if I was sitting with an angel
that fluttered its wings
in front of me
and that angel was…
Mommy.

Paige Murphy, Grade 6
Stuart Middle School, KY

I Am a Football Player

I am a football player.
I wonder if I'll get tackled hard.
I see guys on my team getting injured.
I want to play next year.
I am a football player.
I pretend I am scared.
I feel it when I get tackled.
I touch my ankle when it hurts.
I worry that I might get injured.
I cry when I get hurt.
I am a football player.
I understand I am going to get hurt.
I say I can do it.
I dream I can beat big people.
I hope that we can win all of our games.
I try not to make mistakes.
I am a football player.

Yusef Brown, Grade 4
Wohlwend Elementary School, MO

Math

How many inches to get to the store?
If you go to the bank, how many more?
How about time?
How long will it take?
How many steps will you make?
Is it far away?
Will it take a day?
How much water for the bath?
To figure it out, try doing math.
Math is simple, as you see,
Simple as can be.
It isn't all just to add.
It isn't all subtract.
It really is how these numbers
come together and interact.

Alex Maue, Grade 5
Meramec Elementary School, MO

My Closet

My closet's full of comfy clothes
Withered flowers
And gummy toes
Crunched up papers
And silky throws
A baby doll
With a squishy nose
And much more
But no one knows
How it all got there
So I'd better go clean it
And put it where it goes!

Rachel Moore, Grade 5
American Heritage Academy, GA

Roses

The tallest rose that you have seen
Was once a little tiny seed
In the dirt
It grows and grows
With a little help
From the hose
Through sun and through rain
In day and in night
That rose will grow
With all of it's might
Taller, taller every day
Until it grows old
And fades away
It lives a life of beauty
The rose that grows in the ground
We will see it forever and ever
It's cycle that goes around

Lydia Chappel, Grade 6
St John the Baptist Catholic School, AL

Bear

Bear
fast, mean
run, follow, sleep
chasing, hiding, biting, hibernating
All bears have claws
Big Bear

Ashley Maxcey, Grade 4
East Jones Elementary School, MS

My Thanksgiving Ways

Christmas shopping
Fresh turkey
Chasing chicken
Cold coming
Leaves falling
Mashed potatoes
My birthday
Holiday trip
Scrumpulous ham
School's out
Pilgrim hats
Heavy clothing
Camp fires
Tasty peas
Orange pumpkins
Variety feast
Ranch dressing
Brown trees
Season fall
Very hungry
Autumn's awesome!

Jacob Faubion, Grade 5
Center Elementary School, GA

I Am a Cup of Tea

I am a cup of tea.
I am comforting to some
and bitter to others.
My flavor varies
from calming herbal
to pleasurably fruity.
Add sugar and I become sweet.
Add lemon and I become sour.
Some people sit down with me
and slowly sip away
appreciating my flavor.
Others quickly gulp me down
ending with a grateful ahhhh.
Then swiftly hurry off.
Some enjoy me
and some don't.
Don't rely on other's opinions.
You must taste me
before you decide.
I am a cup of tea.

Sydney Cowart, Grade 6
Charleston County School of the Arts, SC

Mad

I got mad at my sister
so I moved to Pluto.
I could still see my sister
sitting on the ground.
My sister was sulking around
like a dog that had just gotten scolded.
Searching for me.
She watches Mars.
She searches Saturn.
Then I throw a rock and she looks at me.
It feels cold enough to freeze fire.
My sister sends up a golden dragon
for me to ride home.
She knows me so well.
She knows I like dragons.

Trey Davidson, Grade 5
Fox Elementary School, MO

Skateboarding

Skateboarding is the best thing in my life
But I don't know it is better than a wife.
I think it's easier to do an ollie
But when you get better you will learn a nollie.

Skateboarding is dangerous, cool and fun
If you finally do a trick you say "Yes I'm done."
But be careful why you're skating
Or you will end up fainting.

Chandler Threet, Grade 6
Ketchum Jr High School, OK

Gone*

Whose name I've kept in my heart all these years,
Longing to hear his little voice.
But nothing can change the fact,
That he is gone…
Gone to a better place.
Gone to a place unreachable.
Gone to a place where he can run, jump,
And play all he wants.
And in that place,
Is where I hope he finds great joy.
I would do anything to hold him in my arms,
Laughing while he licks my face.
But still,
Nothing can change the fact,
That he is gone.
Gone to a better place,
Forever and ever.

Caroline Kaltenborn, Grade 6
Woodland Presbyterian School, TN
*Dedicated to my dogs, Captain Jack and Ulfy.

Mouse in a Hole

There once was a mouse in a hole
He accidentally ran into a pole
"Ouch!" said the mouse
When he ran from his house
The silly old mouse in the hole

Stephanie Matute, Grade 5
South Smithfield Elementary School, NC

My Pit Bull

Very big and pretty, as hungry as a pig
Plays outside a lot, chases people around
Also as beautiful as a butterfly
Light comes from the sun outside when my dog is playing
Also the light comes from a bulb
When my dog stands under it

Bark Bark Bark
My dog barks a lot.
She barks at me also as people walk by
Barks at night too

I wonder why dogs don't talk
I wonder why dogs have four legs
I wonder why dogs have fun
When ever I am around my dog I feel happy
She makes me forget my problems
I'm happy when she is around
My dog makes me happy

Bark Bark Bark
Bark Bark Bark
Bark Bark Bark

Sasathia Roberson, Grade 4
Price Elementary School, KY

Christmas Is Here

Christmas!
Christmas!
It's finally near,
I can't wait until it's here!
I think Christmas candy,
Is so very dandy.
The Christmas tree is bright,
With red and white lights.

Emerie Allison Budder, Grade 5
Wickliffe Elementary School, OK

Halloween

You want to run you want to hide
from the ghost's deadly stride!

Pulling pranks is fun to do
except when one is pulled on you!

When you dress in a ghost's wear
you'll give the room a quite big scare!

Candy is quite fun to eat,
you get it when you trick-or-treat!

Candy, candy, candy galore
man I got a quite big score!

Masks are scary, masks are mean,
masks make me a pee machine!

Levi Landan Johnson, Grade 5
North Middle School, TN

The Beach

Crabs are in the sand
Shells are washed onto the shore
The ocean sparkles.

Hayden Dooley, Grade 4
Briarwood Christian School, AL

Soccer

Soccer is for fun.
Soccer is cool.
Soccer is not just about winning.
It's all about fun.

Coaches are fun.
Coaches are cool.
Coaches have good plays about soccer.
They help us all have fun.

If you ever lose, be happy.
Cheer for the other team,
If they ever make a goal.
That's what soccer is all about.

Suzanne Tosang, Grade 4
Hayes Elementary School, OK

My Nightmare

My bad day was a nightmare
I slept late last night
Dreamt of a knight
I woke at nine, now I am busted

I forgot my bus, my book bag and no correct uniform, and did not wash...
Everyone in the school stared at me with a disgusting face
Even the teacher stared at me

My teacher was very upset
Talk about upset makes me mad
I talked back to my teacher
Now she is more upset

I am going to the office
Now I am really sad
Because of the angry faces of my parents waiting
I got grounded for the rest of my life and a detention too!

I screamed and somebody yelled my name and shook me
It was mom, my unangry mom
And it was only six thirty
Just a nightmare

Christine Hong, Grade 5
Forest Avenue Academic Magnet School, AL

Wow, Saint Louis Is Amazing

Enjoying the tall, gorgeous arch;
Looking at many different kinds of people,
Listening to the loud sirens of the police cars
Lovely flowers; sniffing lots of wonderful smells
Delicious foods, that make your mouth water, just like back home;
Trying many different foods, from all over the place
Running on the dirty old ground;
Viewing the park's lovely, old trees
Being completely helpless in the city

Caitlin Cox, Grade 6
College View Middle School, KY

Disney's Private Island

I see beautiful waves of crystal clear ocean water,
I see grains of white sand that scorch my feet as I lightly tread upon it,
I hear the loud constant waves that sound like rolling thunder,
I hear the shrills of wind as they whisper to me,
I smell the salty sea air as it sails along the shore,
I smell the fragrance of sunscreen being spread over red burnt bodies,
I taste bitter salt water that tastes like my grandma's brine pickles,
I taste the pizza sold at the beach that is the color of the setting sun,
I touch my brightly colored beach towel that has been baked in the tropical sun,
I touch the seashells on the shore as I collect them by the dozen,
I feel as though I will never go home,
I feel relaxed and renewed.

Ali Lampert, Grade 6
College View Middle School, KY

Halloween

Scary, funny and pretty
sweet and imaginable
hairy, nasty and gross
    that's Halloween
Trick-or-treating
goodies galore
sweet and sour candy
    that's Halloween
Dracula, Frankenstein
The Goblin, the Boogie Man
Homer, Bart and Marge
    that's Halloween
Painting, dressing up
all preparing for Halloween
the Devil and Batman
    that's Halloween
Army guys, fake guns and knives
horns, sharp teeth
Sumo wrestlers and more
I almost forgot…
    BOO!

Jakob Morgan, Grade 4
Schaffner Traditional Elementary School, KY

Nine Eleven

American flags flying not so high
at half mass they honor our country
on this tragic day
America was sacrificed
to the jealousy of others
it was sad for those
who lost friends and family
not to mention their homes
it has been many years now
since that day of 2001
life has recovered
little by little
all is better now
since that dreadful day
that dreadful day of 9/11

Duncan Wood, Grade 5
Greathouse Shryock Traditional Elementary School, KY

The Eagle

The beautiful, elegant bird flies high in the sky
This bird stands tall in the highest green, leafy oak trees
Its eye sees every tiny creature that comes and goes
Giant wings help it fly gracefully
It soars across the deep blue sky as it looks down at us
Fast, strong, and deadly
The eagle hunts for prey with its sharp vision
It swoops down to catch it
Its tangerine, pointed beak captures delicious fish in the rivers
Soon it will rest and call it a day.

Megan Lombard, Grade 6
Haynes Academy for Advanced Studies, LA

My First Time Riding the Scrambler

Excitement runs through my veins as the bar is ticking,
Speed increases as we move forward gaining speed,
Jerks are felt that plunge me north and south,
Dizziness fills me, happiness consumes me,
People become a blur,
The feelings blend together that make me giggle, I can't stop,
The ride decreases, blended feelings and gigglings stop,
Unhappiness dumps into me as the ride ends,
Dizziness consumes me,
Body shakes as I tumble to the ground.

Mallory McGrath, Grade 5
Cline Elementary School, KY

Ashleigh

Her name is Ashleigh,
    She is a great friend,
    She likes to eat chocolate chip cookies,
      For that is her favorite dessert.

Her love for her family is unpredictable,
    Her feelings are like a variable,
    She could be mean like an ogre,
      Or nice like God.

You never know what to think of her,
    She could be a friend or a fiend,
    She has love, passion, and faith,
    Her heart is healthy as it can ever be.

Cindy Chen, Grade 5
Hunter GT Magnet Elementary School, NC

Your Typical School Morning

It's Monday morning at 7:01
You're half asleep, with your homework half done
You're all ready when your bus arrives
You get on the bus and get prepared for the 2 hour ride
You arrive at school
You walk into the cafeteria lunch room and
line up in the long line
impatiently waiting for the bell to ring "RING!"
the bell goes
"ZOOM" the kids go down the hall while the
principal's telling them to slow down you might fall
"BANG" the lockers go
You're writing in your agenda
at a steady pace
hoping that you will win 1st place
the principal's voice shows up on the intercom
you know what that means
It's time for the pledge to the flag, our state
Song, and of course the announcements
That's your typical school morning

Ra'Nesha Stroud, Grade 5
Greathouse Shryock Traditional Elementary School, KY

Jade

I read a big book that was scary
It was about a mean fairy
She was very fat
She ate a red cat
And that made her very hairy.

Jade Leonard, Grade 4
Judsonia Elementary School, AR

What I Want to Do

What I want to do
Is do something new
Maybe create something new.
That is what I will do,
Or create something unusual
Like paint a picture of Stan Musial.
Or maybe discover some knew dinosaur.
Or maybe learn about the Civil War,
Or even go visit Baltimore.
Ya! That is what I will do!

Kevin Dunn, Grade 6
Seven Holy Founders School, MO

Fall

Leaves fall down
To the ground.
Balls kicked up and around.

Breezes feel so delighting.
Snakes run into hiding.

Fall break is here,
Playing and fun is near.

We're so happy Yeep eee Yeep eee!!!

Eli Clarke, Grade 5
Childersburg Middle School, AL

Green Is the Color of Nature

Green, green,
The tall green soldiers
that you step on
when you play outside.

Green, green,
The tiny green things
that spread all over
the branches on trees.

Green, Green,
The huge bodies of water
that Spread
all over the Earth.

Green, Green.

Tristen Weller, Grade 6
East Oldham Middle School, KY

The Season of Fall

The birds start to migrate; the lovely colorful leaves start to change.
Are you ready for the sweet pumpkin pie?
I bet you can hardly wait as your mouth begins to water anticipating
that delicious taste.

Kirsten McConnell, Grade 4
First Wesleyan Christian School, NC

Disney World

It was so exciting!
I was going to Disney World and ride in a plane!
It was Mom, Dad, Aunt Ginnie, Amanda, and Logan.
I first drifted off into the sky like a helium balloon.
We finally landed I bounced right out of my seat!
I was extremely excited I was going to meet Mickey, Minnie, and Cinderella!

At the beginning my family and I went to the Magic Kingdom
and watched the thrilling 3D Bugs Life!
The next morning we had breakfast with Pooh, Tigger, and Piglet!
Then at Discovery Cove there were dolphins, fish, sharks, and stingrays!
Everyone went to go feed the stingrays, and fish!
Then Dad, Aunt Ginnie, and Amanda went to ride the dolphins!

On all the other days we went to M.G.M. studios, and Epcot!
My favorite was seeing Cinderella
in her long elegant sky blue dress as she signed my autograph book!
Finally we went to Universal Studios
and saw dinosaurs and many other prehistoric creatures.
We went on a terrifying ride Jurassic Park!
There was a huge dino right behind me!
After that I said my goodbyes to Mickey, Minnie, and Cinderella.
I drifted right back into the sky, and my journey was over.

Rachel Carr, Grade 6
South Oldham Middle School, KY

My Favorite Soldier

My favorite soldier is KC.
On January 9th he is leaving on order for Iraq.
He is going there to risk his life for us.
I believe that he will not die without a fight.
KC taught me to fish and to hunt. He also taught me how to mow and weed-eat.
I wish he did not have to go. I like him very much.
By going to Iraq he is going to make me proud.
I am going to watch him leave. I will not feel too great for a couple of days.
I feel that my heart is going to shatter into pieces.
He is the only man in the house so it's hard.
We are going to bring the soldiers and him food.
Their colors are dark and light green with brown.
He is the best soldier I have ever known.
The hat he gave to me is my very favorite hat because it brings memories.
Last time he was in Iraq; a piece of shrapnel hit him. Letting him go will be tough.
First he will take a bus to Mississippi, then he will get on a plane to Iraq.
He carries an M-4 and I believe he does an awesome job with it.
KC can do 50 pushups or more. He has to do a six mile march.
I will always have deep memories. KC is my favorite soldier.

Kaleb Dickason, Grade 5
Hatfield Elementary School, AR

Be Thankful

I am thankful for my friends
I am thankful for my family
I am also thankful for
everything that makes me happy
We're gathered here together
on this Thanksgiving day
to have a feast and share everything
that we would like to say
some of us are thankful for
delightful dancing daisies
Others were thankful for the moon
that shines like a darkened star
And as we end
this turkey day
we all are pretty sad
but after all there's still next year
and it won't be so bad.
There are lots of things to be thankful for
and I've only named a few
but if you think very hard
you'll find some things you're thankful for too.

Ellie Baker, Grade 5
Greathouse Shryock Traditional Elementary School, KY

The Perfect Shot

The whistle bowls; it's a foul,
All the fans scream and howl,
They were the first to score and went one ahead,
But then our striker sent a rocket over the keeper's head,
And with this free kick I could put it to bed,
I took a deep breath and stepped behind the ball,
I looked up and saw the five man wall,
I started my run and swung my foot,
I connected,
The ball flew through the air bending sharply,
Too much?
No, it was perfect,
Into the back of the net it sailed,
Our whole team screamed and the crowd hailed.

Austin Del Rosso, Grade 6
Holy Infant Elementary School, MO

Storm

There is a storm rolling through the shadows
Dripping and pouring as it goes by.
You can hear the roar of the streak of lightning,
like an African lion.

The lightning stings my shoulder as I run.
Muddy ground soaks through my shoes.
If you look outside, you will see me
in this dreadful storm.

Haylee Edwards, Grade 4
Alpena Elementary School, AR

Vacation

What are the elements of a great vacation?
    Warm days at the beach
    Tubing behind a boat
    Parasailing on a calm day
    Skiing down a freezing mountain
    A slow ocean cruise
    A long extraordinary day
    Luxurious first class plane ride
    Amazing sights to see
    Busy car rides
    Packing loads of clothes
    Tanning to the sound of waves
    Feeding the hovering seagulls
    Wading deep into the ocean
    Swimming to the dolphins
    Snorkeling to view the reefs
These are elements of a great vacation.

Que Wood, Grade 6
Southwest Middle School, AR

What Happens in Fall

Leaves turn different colors when fall is near,
They turn different colors every year.
Fall is a season to have fun,
Fall is a season to play in the sun.
When the leaves fall off the trees,
We have fun in the sun falling on our knees.
Before it gets cold,
Because we were told.
The leaves grow back on the trees,
In the spring when you see the bumble bees.
Leaves are all different colors.
Leaves can be yellow,
Leaves can be red,
Leaves sometimes can be blue,
Leaves can be green and brown too.
Every thing comes back to life in the fall,
It's a good time to go Christmas shopping at the mall.
It's always a pretty time of year,
A time to grab your coat and shout and cheer.
When fall comes around every year for sure,
I know we're about to start a new year.

Jennifer Ratliff, Grade 4
Parkview School, OK

Katrina Song

Let the water flood the city's streets
Let the water wash us into the tired arms of the weeping willows
Let the water leave its mark on the city's soul

The water drowns us in our dreams
The water trespasses into our homes and steals our possessions
The water swiftly throws us up and down, back and forth
And we defy the water

Daniel Amoss, Grade 6
St Andrew's Episcopal School, LA

I Am Haunted

I am haunted by the hideous hockey mask I see, as I inch slowly through the haunted house,
Not wanting to know what's going to pop out at me next, wondering if the man is in front of me or my mother,
I can't tell from the flash, blink, shine, of the blinking light,
Suddenly I hear a "get out" in a sharp shrieking voice and I couldn't agree more,
So I bolt out the door and back to my friends and then decide to get a face painting.

I am haunted by the thought of waking up laying in a coffin wondering where am I,
Then trying to open it but it won't budge. I then realize I have been buried ALIVE,
I scream to the top of my lungs but can't anymore because I'm crying so hard,
I can't even talk and all the sudden here come the creepy crawly ugly scary insects,
Pouring over me and that's it, I've choked on them and died, just laying there waiting for my body to decay,
As my soul slowly watches as I'm floating into the sky thinking I knew that would happen.

I am haunted by the scorching hot Christmas day that is soon to come,
Where I'm sitting on a boat where I live because ALL the ice has melted away,
Now it has flooded the Earth and everyone is forced to live on water drip, drop, drip
as the sweat is pouring off of me like rain falling from a cloud,
I try to think of something else, like what Christmas was like 20 years ago but it doesn't work,
all I wanted for Christmas was snow.

I am haunted by the fact that it is so hot my new born baby girl has just died,
And honestly I hope it's cool in heaven!!! Now instead of my seat it's the drip, drop, drip from my eyes,
Thinking I couldn't take care of my own child.

I am haunted

Renee Toole, Grade 5
Eminence Middle School, KY

The Truth Within You

The truth does not lie in a cold dark forest.
Only the wisest men and women, boys and girls, know that it rests within YOU.
The truth lies within your own thought, singing songs of love.
Sometimes it may appear to be gone. If only you look deep down, you will find the courage.
The courage to do a thing that can cause destruction not only to others, but to you.
You must let it out.
Let the truth be free!

Jessica Graves, Grade 6
Centennial Magnet Middle School, NC

I Am

I am the baby of a four-kid family.
I wonder how long will it take me to move out of my mom's house.
I hear thunder sometimes when I am sleep.
I see my dog get excited when he sees me.
I want to get a phone for my birthday.
I am the most playful person to my dog.

I pretend that I am an adult sometimes.
I feel sad when I am sick because I can't go around anyone.
I touch my dog when we play and I pet him.
I worry if my baby cousin will be ok.
I cry when someone in my family dies. I am the daughter of a man that works at Elextrolux.
I say I want everything to my dad.
I dream that one day I will be a beautician.

Kayla Bradley, Grade 5
Byrns L Darden Elementary School, TN

Favor

Everybody knows I want to be a rock star,
But without you Jesus I won't get very far.
If I find your favor and you shine on me,
Then without a doubt a rock star I'll be.

Jesus, you are the way, the truth and the light,
If you find favor in me then my life will be tight.
I've been praying for forgiveness, I've been praying all night,
Find favor in your eyes if you're hearing my cries,
And hurry Jesus hurry, be the Lord of my life.

We all know that every man has committed sins,
But do not worry, everybody wins,
Jesus' forgiveness goes to everyone,
Now hold on a second, I ain't done,
The one thing you want to do in your whole entire life,
Is to find favor in the Lord Jesus Christ.

Baylor Griffin, Grade 6
Victory Christian School, OK

How to Fly

I will learn to fly, OK here is how you do it.
Do not do this! Fall off the bed and hit your head!
Say ouch fall off the couch!
Scream loud get rained on by a cloud.

Fred Markham, Grade 4
Brilliant Elementary School, AL

Summer

Summer fun in the sun
the smell and taste so sweet.
Laying around in the grass
about to go to sleep.
Thinking that I once was in school
but not now, my freedom is here.
Running around in the warm sun.
Summer is when you can spend more time with
your family on vacation.
I don't ever want summer to end.

Lauren Johnson, Grade 4
Lewis Vincent Elementary School, LA

The Seasons

Winter is dark and dreary cold.
Then spring arrives, brilliant and bold.
After that is summer, a season in which some people like,
Then autumn, a good season to ride a bike.
The seasons, the seasons, the seasons!

The good friends of darkness and light.
The sisters and brothers of day and night.
The queens and kings of peace and war,
Our great authors of myth and lore.
The seasons, the seasons, the seasons!

Diane Kim, Grade 4
Sequoyah Elementary School, TN

Autumn

Autumn is when the leaves are beneath my swollen feet,
as I pass by the moon so deep.
I whistle a little song I make,
It sounds like this.
No band I have, so here I go.
I start with a beep
then make a silly sound,
So, it goes beep, tee, tee, diddle-dum, to-to.
Now I lay beneath the tree and through the trees
and past the clouds, lay the sun asleep.
Away I cannot tell you what it looks like
'cause if I do
I'll spoil the surprise for me and you.

Emma Airey, Grade 4
St Charles Homeschool Learning Center, MO

Bang

Lining up, ready to go
You hear a million girls' hearts pounding.
You see their butterflies on their faces.
Then when you're almost,
Not quite ready.
BANG!!!
You're off.

I feel the wind in my hair, on my face.
The sweet taste of sweat
When I open my mouth.

Sprinting.
Passing everyone
I can.
I finish
With a smile on my face,
And a medal on my chest.
Cross-country!

Sarah Mack, Grade 6
South Oldham Middle School, KY

A Girl's Best Friends

I know a girl whose best friend is not lipstick or blush.
It's a dog — not any of that stuff.
The dog's name is Beau.
He's cute, cuddly and puts on a very good show.
Beau skips and sings and whines "Mommy Mommy."
But he does not like salami.
He has blue checkered collar around his neck.
But sadly it is not high-tech.
He is a very friendly fellow.
But he is not very mellow.
So who's this girl who loves dogs best?
It's the author Eva — didn't you guess?

Eva Kropp, Grade 4
Sequoyah Elementary School, TN

The Sleep Over

My friends came over for a sleep-over.
We played tag and red rover.
We stayed up all night.
Until we saw the daylight.

Grant LeNeave, Grade 5
Ascension Elementary School, KY

The Legend of Jack

The Devil climbed up a tree
Jack played a trick he couldn't see
Jack carved a cross in the trunk
The Devil's pride went "kerplunk"
Jack went not to heaven or hell
But only to the darkness in which he fell
An ember in a turnip is what he took
So that in the darkness he could look
At all that lies ahead

Charles Gaylord, Grade 6
Benton County School of the Arts, AR

Winter and Summer

Winter
cold, snowy
skiing, shivering, sledding
snowballs, ice, pools, beaches
burning, swimming, cooking
hot, sunny
Summer

Ryan Murphy, Grade 5
Briarwood Christian School, AL

Candy

C andy is delicious
A nd it's not healthy
N utritious is a now
D ecay is a yes
Y ellow, green other colors too.

Matthew Gilbertson, Grade 5
First Flight Elementary School, NC

Wood Duck

Wood Duck
Wet, dry
Fly, walk, run
Chomping, swimming, sleeping, drinking
Ducks fly in flocks
State waterfowl

Brandon Rew, Grade 4
East Jones Elementary School, MS

Squirrels

Scampering up trees
Jumping along finding nuts
Winter's approaching.

Griffin Oaks, Grade 4
Briarwood Christian School, AL

Swim Meet

I stand on the block of cold, sandy, plastic,
I'm feeling the power shoot through my feet and up through my body,
I hear the crowd constantly repeating my name,
Then the buzzer sounds and I fire through the water like a rocket;
The cold water blankets my body in an instant,
The bubbles rush by me as I streamline through the fierce waters,
The strength of my arms and legs is rushing through my body,
Is the next swimmer quickly approaching to catch me?
I look at the dark blue line beneath me,
I see what demanding hurdles I must reach for a victory,
To finally grasp the edge of the wall and experience the success of the moment,
I feel the anticipation of complete satisfaction,
I look around me as I constantly swim at the same pace,
I'm going under the rainbow colors on the flags — almost there now;
In the shadow of the approaching block I see the wall,
I lift my head up to breathe and I know I'm in the lead:
I'm the winner!

Andrew Jones, Grade 5
JJ Jones Intermediate School, NC

I Am

I am a loud girl who loves cheerleading
I wonder if I will be cheering for the Chicago Bears some day
I hear the crowd cheering as they repeat after me
I see the entire stadium as I am thrown in the air doing a stunt
I am a loud girl who loves cheerleading

I pretend I am the head cheerleader of the Russell County Squad
I feel nervous about heading to Florida for state competition
I touch the shoulder of one of my girls as I encourage her to do her best
I worry that maybe we have not practiced enough for this meet
I cry when the announcer calls Russell County as the overall winner
I am a loud girl who loves cheerleading

I understand that it takes a lot of time, strength, and practice to be the best
I say I will achieve my goal which is to be a professional cheerleader
I dream that all my hard work will pay off someday as my mom watches with pride
I try my hardest with every routine to not miss a movement
I hope I have the strength to fulfill this dream
I am a loud girl who loves cheerleading

Jenifer Green, Grade 6
Union Chapel Elementary School, KY

Fall

Feeling crisp, cool wind slapping my face, making my cheeks rosy red,
Going on rugged hiking trips at Mammoth Cave,
Raking leaves, then tumbling into them afterwards,
Meeting new friends at the beginning of a new school year,
Studying for tests that are the hardest,
Going on vacations during the fall break,
Closing down the pool for winter,
Taking in some hot cocoa after being in the crisp outdoors.

Ethan Turley, Grade 6
Alvaton Elementary School, KY

Best Friends

Best friends are there for you when you get hurt,
Best friends are there when people call you names.
Best friends are there to cheer you on in games.
Best friends congratulate you when you win,
Best friends cheer you up when you lose.
Best friends are lots of fun!
Best friends are number one!

Hannah Day, Grade 5
Paint Lick Elementary School, KY

My Thanksgiving Dinner

I go in and get a plate.
Oh how this dinner is gonna be great!
I get in line, here I go
what's going to be on my plate?
No one knows.
I put on white turkey, non-smoked.
Then mashed potatoes, no chunks, it's not a joke
Some gravy, both brown and white.
I'm almost done, but not quite!
Next comes the drinks,
I get lemonade.
Then some pie and some cake.
You'd think I was done,
but there's more to come.
A helping of family and a helping of friends,
doesn't that sound like fun.

Bethany Young, Grade 4
Alpena Elementary School, AR

Paradise Vacation

Whoosh!
You can feel the warm breeze
Blowing your hair in circles
It's like a tiny tornado
Finally it's summer
And it's vacation time
Yeah!
It's as if you walk on the beach
of summer fun
Just walk on the summer sand at the beach
Go on ahead
dig your toes in the sand
Smell the sweet scent of
coconuts growing on the trees
Taste the yucky salt water
pouring in your mouth
Watch the surfers
Soar through a tunnel of waves
Jump over the waves
up and down
That's a Paradise Vacation

Katie Fallon, Grade 5
Greathouse Shryock Traditional Elementary School, KY

Titanic

One night it was cold when the Titanic shined bold
So tragic the ship had to sink
we lie in our beds remembering the dread of all the lives
that America left almost 100 years since the ship
had been lost but the people who were on it will not.

Bryce Mayers, Grade 4
Lewis Vincent Elementary School, LA

Christmas, Sshh!!!!!!!

Sshh, sshh, sshhhhhhhhhhhhh…
shush, listen I think it's Santa
Clop, Clunk
I think he's here, I think he's here shush now
Lets all go to bed before he catches us
Clop, clunk, clank
He's here, he's here
I wish I could see him I want to see Rudolph
Ssshhhhh…
Be quiet or we won't get any presents
I hope he likes our cookies and milk
Crunch, crunch, slurp, slurp, slurp
He drank the milk ate the cookies
Now he's leaving presents, now he's leaving presents
Ssshhhhh…
Lets go to bed before he leaves
Ssshhh, ssshhhhhhh…
Yawns all around now they are all sleeping
They'll be surprised when they awake
Santa is gone now, Santa is gone now
He won't return till next year!!!!!!!!!!!

Raven Ash, Grade 6
Ketchum Jr High School, OK

My Best Friend

My best friend is my cousin, Austin
Who lives far away,
He used to live down the street
So we would often play.
Our favorite game to play was Battleground
Where we would often do two-player play,
We never did fight because
We spent our time having fun all day.
Then something bad happened
his parents got divorced,
Austin moved to Texas because
His mom got married to a guy in the
Air Force.

Tyler Moss, Grade 5
American Heritage Academy, GA

Fall

Fall is the time of year the pumpkins start to grow,
cool, chilly winds set upon,
yet, the joy and merriment is still there.

Meghan Elzy, Grade 6
Stuart Middle School, KY

Butterflies

Bright spots in the sky
Munch on many yummy leaves
We soar over earth
Ansley Godwin, Grade 4
Briarwood Christian School, AL

God of Love

God of love,
High in the unending heavens,
In the mysterious sky above.
Reigns a glorious being,
Our awesome God of love.
Ryan Miller, Grade 4
Hayes Elementary School, OK

A Successful Girl

I am a daughter of school teachers.
I wonder if my friends like me.
I hear loud crying.
I see lots of candy.
I want to be a lawyer.
I am a success at school.

I feel happy.
I touch lots of stuff.
I worry about my granny.
I don't cry a lot.
I am 10 years old.
I pretend I'm sad.
Marissa Picquet, Grade 5
Byrns L Darden Elementary School, TN

Cotton Candy Blue

Blue,
The cotton candy,
I eat with a smile,
Smothered on my face,
The ocean waves,
As they crash over my feet
Taking the sand castles away,
Cheering on the team,
The Wildcats,
Yelling "Go team Go!"
Sky light bright with
The puffy white balls,
Letting through the golden rays
Blue,
The cotton candy,
The ocean waves,
The team,
The sky light,
What more
Could I say,
Blue all the way.
Mitch Port, Grade 6
East Oldham Middle School, KY

The Cat and the Rat

There lies that silly, old cat.
He is wearing a furry, small hat.

He is waiting for that tiny, innocent mouse.
The cat's owner told him, "You have to get that rat out of the house."

The cat gets a baseball bat.
Now, he is chasing that poor rat!

Then the owner comes home.
The rat returns to his dome,

And the cat returns to his mat.
Better luck next time you silly, old cat!

Amber Penton, Grade 5
Enon Elementary School, LA

My Grandma

My grandma constantly has soft silky skin
She's always smiling at me with excitement as soon as I walk in the door
Her hair is the color of chestnut brown
She smells like red roses
She has eyes the color of a blue jay

I love going to my grandma's house
She always makes me my favorite breakfast
Blueberry muffins
I love it when she takes me to my cousins house
I love it when my grandma takes me to my favorite restaurant
The China King
When it's Thanksgiving
She makes the best pumpkin pie
It's so funny when my grandma says dinosaur
It's fun when I stay the night at my grandma's house
Ethan Kennedy, Grade 4
Briarwood Elementary School, KY

Halloween, Oh Halloween

Halloween, Oh Halloween, your creepiness descends,
Children walking, talking, laughing with candy in their bags.
Witches, Wizards, Ogres, pirates, princesses, and animals,
Strutting the streets at midnight;
The doorbell rings, a smiling face,
The candy he brings is gone in the blink of an eye.
Jack-o-Lanterns glow to bring the dark night to life.
A ghost pops out, BOO! And startles a trick-or-treater,
A skeleton then alarms her with a sly, toothless smile;
Black cat on a fencepost tiptoes across it
With a full moon as the background;
Witches swoop down on their broomsticks and snort out a laugh
With their warty green noses;
And wizards cast enchanting spells with their crooked branch wands.
Bare, leafless trees blow howling in the wind,
Halloween, Oh Halloween is something I adore.

Mary Glen Hatcher, Grade 5
JJ Jones Intermediate School, NC

The Hunt of the Tiger

The tiger prowls through the jungle,
Searching for its prey,
Its eyes lash back and forth,
Up and down,
Finally after hours of searching,
Its eyes lock on,
After stalking the unsuspecting prey,
He pounced,
It dashed,
Too slowly
The tiger sank his white teeth into the animals back,
It heaved down to the ground with a THUMP,
Then he roared in triumph,
And that is the hunt,
Of the TIGER

Joshua Chappell, Grade 6
East Oldham Middle School, KY

The Dolphin

Dolphin! Dolphin! In the sea,
Why don't you come and play with me?
When you leap, oh, so high,
You almost nearly touch the sky.

Courtney Pelzer, Grade 5
Robert E Cashion Elementary School, SC

What Is Time?

What is time?
Is it like a colossal cat waiting to ambush?
Or maybe it's a caterpillar,
developing into a magnificent butterfly.
Is it a sound,
like a chime of church bell?
Does it stop like a complete
silence in thought?
Maybe it's an object,
like the frigid lamp posts during the winter.
Or perhaps it's invisible and untouchable,
like the oxygen surrounding us all.
In fact it might be nonexistent,
like a four year old's imaginary kingdom.
Or the moments might be counting down,
like a time bomb waiting to explode.

Conor Galton, Grade 6
Charleston County School of the Arts, SC

Cross Country

You have to run two miles extremely fast.
We run, run, run to beat the rest,
Ten minutes have definitely passed.
We always, always try our best,
You try to push through the pain.
Pushing myself makes me better at running,
Crossing the finish line first makes it all worthwhile.

Brooke Rokisky, Grade 5
North Middle School, TN

Things That You Need

A doctor for health,
A teacher for education,
Love and support,
Friends and family,
Shelter for protection,
I can name many more things that you need,
But you can explore your mind and think.

Anastasia Freedman, Grade 4
Montessori Community School, NC

They Say Love Is Forever

They say love is forever.
I think not.
It's just a little rope tied in a knot.
The love is fine as long as it is in a knot.
Then is the worst done?
Oh, I think not.
If the knot is undone, your heart will be broken.
It is like you are in an arcade with one little token.
There are no machines for one little token, except for one,
"Is Your Heart Broken?"
I put my little token in the slot.
The arrow turned onto "yes."
Oh, what am I to do now that my heart is broken?

Corrina Gonzales, Grade 5
Keyser Primary/Middle School, WV

A. J.'s Pets

I have many animals in my house.
Some are smaller than a mouse
They are all sizes small and big.
Most eat just like a pig.

I have a little white and black funny dog.
She jumps around just like a frog.
I have two big dogs named Zari and Zavier.
They are never on their best behavior.

I have two turtles that like to swim around.
One escaped and it was finally found.
Under a bean bag in my room.
With a pile of poop that I swept with a broom.

Two green lizards live in a tank.
I named the biggest one after my friend Hank.
They like to eat crickets and mealworms.
But always wash your hands because they have lots of germs.

Last but not least is my cat Luna.
She is so fat because she eats a lot of tuna.
I love my pets all the same.
That's why I give them all good names.

Angelo Lewis, Grade 4
Schaffner Traditional Elementary School, KY

Fires

Burning embers glow,
Like a mountain lion's eyes.
Boring deeper and deeper,
Keeping your mind mesmerized.

The crackling and popping sounds,
Like many tiny fireworks,
Exploding in the air,
Painting dramatic pictures in the sky.

Smoke filling the air,
Lingering around,
Like dark angry clouds,
Searching for its next victim.

The lit bonfire blazes,
Sharing and telling new stories,
Hearing us laugh,
Making a memorable night.
Melissa Dosher, Grade 6
IA Lewis Elementary School, LA

The Raining Day

The sun goes behind
the clouds as the rain falls.
The thunder
lights up the sky.
The day grows shorter
as the rain falls all day long.
Johnny Johnson, Grade 5
West Marion Elementary School, MS

Mom/Dad

Mom
busy, nice
loving, working, helping
boss, clothes, worker, sports
caring, cooking, hunting
young, kind
Dad
Thomas Jennings, Grade 5
Briarwood Christian School, AL

Rabbits

Soft-sleepers through the night
Flower-hoppers hold on tight
Carrot-nibblers for all days
Sun-bathers in warming rays
Speedy-runners hopping around
Patient-waiters without a sound
Cabbage-lovers munching away
Fluffy-snugglers in your arms they stay
Madeleine Clarke, Grade 5
Herbert J Dexter Elementary School, GA

Fall

Fall begins with leaves blowing
at night the moon is glowing
mornings are cold
winds are brisk
as days go on
the sun grows bold
growing bright
only to give way to night
soon fall will come to an end
only for winter to begin.
Tim Depoe, Grade 5
McEwen Elementary School, TN

Trick-or-Treaters, Jack-o-Lanterns

Trick-or-treaters, jack-o-lanterns,
All the fun is spread and shared.
A scary house on the corner,
Invites children if they dared.
Trick-or-treaters, jack-o-lanterns,
All the fun is spread and shared.
Mischief, joy, and laughter,
Happiness everywhere.
Emily Richardson, Grade 6
Houston Middle School, TN

Soccer

Soccer is fun.
Soccer is cool.
Soccer is awesome.
Soccer is really hot when you play.
I love soccer.
Soccer is lots of fun.
Soccer sometimes is boring.
It is lots of hard work.
In soccer you have lots of games.
You can get hit.
I love soccer.
Ashley Matus, Grade 5
Berryville Elementary School, AR

Spring

Breezy in the sky
Flowers blooming here and there
Can you hear the birds?
Genie Muir-Taylor, Grade 4
Briarwood Christian School, AL

Baby Blue

Baby blue is…
As light as the evening sky
As soft as clouds
As relaxing as the ripples on a pond.
Kaylen Runner, Grade 5
Bloomfield Elementary School, KY

My Angel

An angel who protects me
Through the night
Sleeps right on my pillow
Until the morning's Bright
Glittery blue eyes
Brown glowing hair
That sparkles in the sun
Cares about me
Keeps me safe
And
Gives me faith
My angel is always near
My mom
My angel
Ashley Schneller, Grade 4
Briarwood Elementary School, KY

Trees

A great big tree sways
A great tree soars in the sky
Canopy of leaves.
Madison Payne, Grade 4
Briarwood Christian School, AL

Christmas Day

Families are awaking,
Kids getting ready for presents,
Children are being impatient.
Family sitting in front of the tree,
Kids getting into their stockings,
Having a shock,
Christmas Day.
A.J. Overbey, Grade 6
Rocky Comfort Elementary School, MO

Winter

What joy.
The snow
Hot cocoa
Marshmallows
Warm blankets
and more.

It's winter,
What joy.
Snow angels
Stiff mittens
The songs
The snowmen
The snowball fights

Winter, what joy.
Juliana White, Grade 6
Annunciation Elementary School, MO

Me

Josh Ellis
Brother to none.
Son of Mark and Rachel.
Who loves sports, food, and my family.
Who needs food, Gatorade, and basketball.
Who gives love to family, laughter to others
and kindness to people.
Who fears spiders, snakes, and lizards.
Who'd like to see Jupiter.
Who dreams of being a lawyer.
A student of Mrs. Adkins.

Josh Ellis, Grade 5
Cool Spring Elementary School, NC

My Favorite Sport

I have the ball, what should I do?
I am caught in the intensity of the moment.
All I can take in are the yells of the crowd.
The smell of anxiety filling the air,
Shoes screeching everywhere,
Glares of light shining on me,
Faces all around.
All starts to fade away in my mind.
I make my leap toward victory.
Whoosh, the winning basket belongs to me.

Sara Jones, Grade 6
IA Lewis Elementary School, LA

Warm and Bubbly

Spying my favorite dinner in the oven.
An icy cold, hard pizza waiting to be cooked
hoping to won't take long.
I love pizza.

Bubbles and pops like a boiling spaghetti pot
cheese melting together crust rising and turning golden brown.
Watching, from the oven's window.
I love pizza

Patiently waiting for the oven to beep.
30…20…10…FINALLY!

Smelling the different spices —
parsley, onions, and pepper,
fresh cheese and apple red tomato sauce.
I love pizza.

A big triangular piece sitting on the table.
Stomach grumbling, taste buds watering.
Lifting it to my mouth not nutritious *but* delicious.
The squishy pizza hits my mouth Mmmm…
I love pizza!

Austin Kampschaefer, Grade 4
Roberta Tully Elementary School, KY

I Am a Military Child

I am a Military child who was born in Houston, Texas.
I see tanks all over post.
I try to get good grades.
I hear guns shooting in a field.
I try hard in school
Sometimes when I'm sad I talk to my friend Felizia.
I am a Military child who was born in Houston, Texas.

I am a Military child who was born in Houston, Texas.
I hear airplanes.
I see people jumping out of airplanes.
I wonder what my daddy does in the army.
I'm sad when I have to move to different houses.
I cry when I move.
I am a Military child who was born in Houston, Texas.

I am a Military child who was born in Houston, Texas.
I hope for peace.
I understand the soldiers die to protect our country.
I see the American Flag.
I touch my heart when I say the Pledge of Allegiance.
I'm proud to be an American.
I am a Military child who was born in Houston, Texas.

Elicia Bonilla, Grade 5
Walker Intermediate School, KY

The Peaceful Stream

I sat down to watch the stars.
All the water creatures are sleeping in the moist mud and sand.
I hear the peaceful stream.
The squirrels are asleep with their babies.
The cardinal is in her nest keeping her egg warm.
I hear the peaceful stream.
I feel the cool air blowing.
I see the trees swaying side to side.
I hear the crickets making music.
I walk home and get in my warm, soft bed.
In the morning, I will hear the peaceful stream once more.

Paige Hamrick, Grade 4
Liberty Christian Academy, MO

Murtle

Murtle was his name.
Soccer was his game.
He could run all day and night.
He could kick the ball out of sight.
But when he got the ball the other team would cheer.
For he was as small as a baby deer.
Everyone would laugh and joke.
One even said I'll buy you a Coke,
If you get out of here.
But even though he was small he knew what to do.
He won the game that day,
But no one knows how he learned to play that way.

Casey Graves, Grade 5
Wynne Intermediate School, AR

Soccer Rules

S uper fun game
O lder kids play
C ool
C razy
E veryone likes it
R ules

R eady to play
U ltimate game for
L onely and
E veryone thinks it is
S uper!!!

Logan Smith, Grade 5
Berryville Elementary School, AR

The Beach

The beach is cool,
different from a pool.
The waves make cool motion,
while you're sitting there,
with your tube of suntan lotion.

Ellie Brungardt, Grade 4
Sycamore Hills - IMPACT School, MO

Moving

Moving
My heart aching
My eyes fill with tears
Running after the moving truck
Going

Uma Kaladi, Grade 5
Nesbit Elementary School, GA

Christmas

The speckled donkey grey
Carried Mary all the way
And then was born the Savior
Who lay
In a manger of hay

Katy McNamara, Grade 4
St Thomas More School, NC

Black

A gloomy day is upon us
Not a cloud in the sky can be seen
My mouth stings when I say the word
My eyes burn when I see the color
Everyone suffers when the word is
spoken in the world
My heart bleeds when I touch the color
I scream when someone says it
Everyone screams when they see it
It is an evil color
BLACK

Kayla Wilson, Grade 5
Des Arc Elementary School, AR

Big Beautiful Black Bat

Big beautiful black bat, asleep in a cave.
Big beautiful black bat, when the night comes you will fly away.
Come back, come back, come back big beautiful black bat.
Please don't fly away.

Austin LaPrade, Grade 4
Tazewell-New Tazewell Primary School, TN

The Great Things I Did This Summer

I went to Gulf Shores Alabama
Playing in the blue like ocean
Getting stung by jellyfish
"Ouch!"
My mom and I went to Branson Missouri
Seeing lots of magic shows
Going to the Titanic museum
Seeing an amazing pet show
Seeing a monkey in the show He was cute!
Getting a video showing life with a monkey and he biting it for me
Traveling to the C.M.A. festival in Nashville
Seeing Sara Evans, Josh Turner, Reba
Seeing Little Richard in his limo
When we were riding in the Carriage
Riding the bull at the Hard Rock cafe
Going on a boat with my dad and Cathy and my friends Alicia and Tess
Finding a dead fish and sticking it on a stick
Going in a 3 people inner tube
Standing up on inner tube like it was a surf board
The things I did this summer were great
But I was glad to come back to school

Sarah Martin, Grade 4
Briarwood Elementary School, KY

I Am

I am a volleyball player who wants to play at Miami.
I wonder if I'll ever get to a cupstacking championship.
I hear a crowd cheering for me at the championship game in Miami.
I see the cupstacking clock say 4.45 seconds, which means that
I beat the all time cupstacking record.
I want to make the JV volleyball team next year.
I am a cool volleyball player who wants to play in Miami.

I pretend I made the perfect serve.
I feel like a million bucks when I get an A on my test.
I touch a cool volleyball on a hot summer day.
I worry that I may not make the JV volleyball team.
I cry when I get a C or lower on a test.
I am a cool volleyball player who wants to play at Miami.

I understand I won't win all the volleyball games.
I say, "I can be anything I want to be."
I dream that all my dream will come true.
I try to do my best in school.
I hope I will do well in school.
I am a volleyball player that wants to play in Miami.

Carey Kauffman, Grade 6
R D and Euzelle P Smith Middle School, NC

Soldiers at War

You are in your bunker and you hear gun shots.
You quickly raise up from your bed.
You grab your gun and wake up your platoon and leave thinking you will never come back.
You hear the desperate cries of soldiers being shot.
You will never know if your mother or father will get to see you again. You follow your father's footsteps.
You tried to save your friend but he died in your arms.
You were wounded in battle and came home to see your family members.
One day you get a phone call saying you need to come back.
You wrote your family, but you stop writing because the last letter was the day you died.

Ashley Haynes, Grade 6
Kitty Stone Elementary School, AL

Summer

Without a chance it was finally summer. During the next day my friend and I were very happy so we were jumping up and down. Soon we arrived at the beach. Before we unpacked the car we went straight to the shore. Later on we unpacked our clothes. Quickly after we finished we ran straight for the ocean. We were yelling happily with joy as we ran in. We were laughing nonstop. When the ocean was calm it felt like we were floating on air. We got out of the water to eat lunch. After that we made a huge sand castle with four big towers.

While we were swimming the waves crashed down on us. The waves felt like a huge building crashing down on us. Later on after repairing our sand castle that the tide destroyed we took a long walk. On our way we found beautiful shells. When we got back the tide had gone all the way up to the stairs. When we finally managed to escape the tide we went to the house and ate dinner. Unfortunately the next day our adventure to the beach had to end. We had to go back home.

Athena Conits, Grade 6
St Mary's School, SC

Just Dreaming

Walking through the room you could already hear the evil sound blurts through your ear.
No one was here but the evil and your fear but you wonder what is near until a voice cut your ear.
You and I have the same fear wondering why we are hear.
But don't worry just this minute I have a plan are you with it?
We'll get through it.
Ready set go but wait nothing happens what a disaster, what do we do now plan B what's plan B I thought very hard.
Going through my mind I felt a funny feeling that evil was near by.
But as soon as nothing crossed our minds we had no choice but to at least try to defeat evil.

Antonio Timpson, Grade 5
Hall Fletcher Elementary School, NC

So Hungry…

As I stepped into my car, I wondered what I was going to eat. As we drove to the restaurant, I observed the trees whistling in the wind and the sun going down to bed. As we reached the restaurant I ran as if I hadn't eaten in seven weeks. And when we got in I could smell the chicken grilling on the grill, and the pizza being taken out of the oven, the dressing being put on the salads, and barbecue sauce being put on the ribs. I was so hungry I thought I wasn't going to make it. But after what felt like four hours, the food was finally there. And I could almost taste the ribs jumping in my mouth and my milk swimming down my throat! It was so refreshing. But after the meal, I was so stuffed that I thought I swallowed an elephant! And on our way home I could hear the crickets chirping and then I began to fall slowly asleep and woke briefly to find myself in my comfortable and comfy bed…

Carter Hillyard, Grade 6
Queen of Angels Catholic School, GA

Tears

The tears go down my face. I try not to cry, I try not to speak, and I try not to show any emotion. I feel like a water balloon full of hot water about to burst. If I speak I will show emotion. And I don't want to lose my self respect I want to scream, yell, and just let it all out. My heart hasn't stopped beating fast yet. I'm hot all over. I can't think happy thoughts. Holding this pain in is making tears run down my ace back to back. In my eyes you see pure anger. And a girl that just wants to be FREE of MISERY.

Caneisha Jenkins, Grade 5
Bossier Elementary School, LA

Autumn

All the leaves are falling
The scarecrows are coming out
I smell the wind passing by
The sky is full of puffy clouds
There's only one season this can be,
Autumn!

Alissa Kindle, Grade 5
Sullivan Elementary School, TN

An Ode to My Brother, Jah'Barie

You keep me company
when I am bored.

Sometimes when you sleep
you've even snored.

You make me smile
when I am down and out.

When our mother starts to yell
and she begins to shout.

You like to
bounce your basketball.

When I'm asleep
you are in the hall.

You are happy when
I come home from school.

When you see me
you scream out "Cool!"

Tranasia Ford, Grade 4
Pines Elementary School, NC

Tennis/Swimming

Tennis
athletic, fierce
challenging, trying, running
Andre Agassi, rackets, pools, swimsuits
gliding, diving, rushing
vigorous, intense
Swimming

Luke McKay, Grade 5
Briarwood Christian School, AL

Jackson

Jackson
Beautiful, exciting
Elect, represent, build
Driving, lawmaking, building, living
I'm going there now!
Capital

Jedidiah Slover, Grade 4
East Jones Elementary School, MS

Antarctica's Glaciers

Thick sheets of ice towering high into the blue sky.
Looking like monuments way up high touching to the cloudy blue sky.
Melting quickly into the ocean like drizzling rain.

Amanda Rollins, Grade 5
Paint Lick Elementary School, KY

Wind

I am the wind.
Whistling in your ears.
I am the thing that moves the trees, I make the leaves dance.
I ripple the water as if I was wrinkling paper into a ball.
I make the leaves of all colors dance like girls in pretty dresses.
I am the thing that motivates you.
I play with you.
I play with your dog.
I whisk and steer the Frisbee away for you and your dog to play with.
You and your dog play and play and play some more.
I am the wind.

I am the wind.
I blow fire out like the flicker of a light bulb.
I create clouds; they are like explosions in the air.
I can destroy houses with the swirling, powerful winds of a tornado.
I make hair flap within me.
You inhale me, you exhale me.
I am here for your survival.
You are never out of my grasping reach.
I am the wind.

Connor Hays, Grade 6
East Oldham Middle School, KY

Why Do We Have to Go to School?

Why do I have to go to school?
Is a question I constantly ask.
My parents don't shy away.
They are up for the task.

I exclaim, "I don't like it so why do I have to go?"
"I really want to know!"

They say it is to know how to read and write
as well as to prepare me for life.

Aren't you curious about things around you?
Are do you want to know what colors make up blue?

What about knowing how to tell time?
Or how much to pay when you take someone out to dine?

Aren't you the least bit interested in the first man on the moon?
How about the effects of the stock market crash and the stock market boom?

They say school will finish as fast as I can turn my back.
And they guarantee that I will wish I were back!

April St. Pierre, Grade 4
Paulina Elementary School, LA

Skating

Round, rolls, turns, and twirls
Backward, forward, around and around
By myself, with a partner, or with a group
This is what I do when I go skating
Disco ball, colored lights
Flashing pink, yellow, green, blue, all kinds of lights
Sometimes even my eyes light up when a boy asks me to skate
This is what I do when I go skating

DJ's playing "Pop Lock and Drop It"
Speaker phones echoing like an owl
Microphones saying "Hey, this is a couple skate only"
I also hear the skates rolling swish, swish,

I wonder if my mom's sisters knew how to skate at my age?
I wonder how much it cost to skate when my mom was my age?
I wonder how much the DJ got paid?
Feeling good, look at me do extra skate moves,
Like skating backwards, twirling like a ballerina,
And stopping on my tippy toes

"Pop Lock and Drop It"
"Pop Lock and Drop It"
"Pop Lock and Drop It"

Janell Malone, Grade 4
Price Elementary School, KY

Autumn Leaves

The leaves change just like we do.
First they grow, and then they change.
They are all so unique.
No one is alike everyone is different.
I love the leaves when they change colors.
It is all so neat!
We are all unique and different and so are the leaves.

Emily Wilson, Grade 4
First Wesleyan Christian School, NC

The Ocean Waves

The Ocean Waves
Crash against the soft sand
Making rip roaring sounds
As each wave rolls in on
The rocky beach.

The Ocean Waves
Are so huge that a swimmer
Could go under the giant
Monster and get swallowed whole!

The Ocean Waves
Are so beautiful that I dance
As the sun goes down.
The Ocean Waves
Make me happy!
Splash, splash, splash!

Breauna Brown, Grade 4
Schaffner Traditional Elementary School, KY

My Cat

My cat means a lot to me.
She is furry and fat and has small green eyes.
There is no other cat in the world that is as special as mine
Because without my cat,
I would be lost.

My cat lies by me.
Sometimes she licks my fingers and other times she bites them.
My cat is really jealous.
She hisses at every cat she sees.

But, one thing that is most important —
I will always love my cat.

Paul Jernigan, Grade 4
A H Watwood Elementary School, AL

A Butterfly's Life

Teeny tiny egg,
Stuck onto a little leaf.
What time will you hatch?

Small caterpillar,
Feeding on a dark green leaf,
Growing as he goes.

The leaves are all gone.
Where'd you go caterpillar?
Did you go to bed?

I see antennae.
What colorful wings you have.
You are beautiful.

Little butterfly
Flowing in the gentle breeze.
God's peace given me.

Andrew Vaughn, Grade 6
Haynes Academy for Advanced Studies, LA

Seasons

We miss the blooms of flowers in the Spring.
We miss the snowfall of Winter.
We miss the colors of falling leaves in the Fall.
And we miss the birdsongs of the Summer.

When we are in the Year,
there is always something
to love, cherish, and care about.

But when we are at the end of a season,
we say goodbye to the old things
and hello to the new.

The Seasons are sometimes fun,
when happy times come,
but they have to leave, too.

Joshua Menard, Grade 6
Haynes Academy for Advanced Studies, LA

The Outdoors

Everyone loves the great outdoors
There are so many things to explore
You could run, jump and play
I'd stay outside all day
Go and see many animals outside
But there are different places where they can hide
There are grass, plants, and many trees
Beautiful skies and pretty seas
Birds chirping overhead
Leaves changing colors, green, orange, red
There are many flowers to be seen
With colorful petals and leaves of green
If you go outside, come prepared
Or you could get quite a scare
The outdoors is a wonderful place
It will put a smile on your face.

Tori Lambert, Grade 6
Haynes Academy for Advanced Studies, LA

Jesus Is Love

Jesus is love.
He will never let you down.
He will always be there.
He will always be around.
He will take care of you.
Jesus is love.

Jesus is love.
He will always provide.
If you do what he says.
You will never go astray.
He will always make a way.
Jesus is love.

Robert Sherrod, Grade 6
Appling County Middle School, GA

If Only

If only she were different
if only we were different.
Sometimes I wonder why she is ours,
but she is, and she's here to stay.
She's perfect in every which way,
But that's the trouble.
She won't change.
She is supposed to be my guide, but she's not.
She's mean sometimes, and nice others.
I love her.
I hate her.
If only she could see me…
really see me.
Then she might understand my position in this
never ending battle,
and how much she's hurting me.
In the end, I love her, she's my true best friend,
but if only she were different.

Michaela Patafio, Grade 6
Queen of Angels Catholic School, GA

Index

Aaserude, Logan 152
Abasi, Arin 35
Abercrombie, Taylor . . .220
Abu-Rimileh, Amein 116
Ackerman, Mylin 277
Adams, Cameron 195
Adams, Darby 277
Adams, Jake 203
Adams, Katie 197
Adcock, Kate 144
Adcock, Megan 160
Addis, Rachel 310
Adhia, Anushri 137
Agee, Cambrie 249
Agnew, Corey 141
Ahuja, Hayley 220
Airey, Emma 353
Akins, Marianne 243
Albright, Meredyth 61
Algren, Madilyn 154
Alikhani, Matthew 95
Alkire, Jaden 111
Alkoutami, Sandy 233
Allen, Artiahnna 222
Allen, Branson 184
Allen, Carley 66
Allen, Carlisha J. 278
Allen Hutton, Kayce 25
Allman, Tessa 48
Alsop, Jeremiah 199
Alvarez, Pedro 55
Alvey, Chris 101
Ambs, Josh 109
Amick, Courtney 12
Ammerman, Justus 330
Ammons, Parker 210
Amoss, Daniel 351
Anbalagan, Natasha . . .309
Anderson, Ashlee 238
Anderson, Ceaquanita . . .180
Anderson, Drew 90
Anderson, JaLyn 248
Anderson, Jaylene 198
Anderson, John Robert . . .52
Anderson, Katie 151
Anderson, Kaylai 343
Anderson, Rachel 103
Anderson, Victoria 246
Andrews, Libby 308
Angelloz, Vaughan 242
Anthony, Walter 82

Antony, Andrew 127
Appleby, Jacob 290
Arant, Chase 338
Archibald, Drew 46
Arguelles, Juan 269
Arledge, Emilee 28
Armer, Tamara 314
Armstrong, Connor 126
Armstrong, Tyler 85
Arndt, Danny 64
Arndt, Michaela 108
Arnold, Haley 212
Arrasmith, Layth 24
Arsenaux, Thomas 219
Arterburn, Alyssa 37
Arthur, Alex 91
Ash, Raven 355
Ashby, Rachael 229
Ashley 91
Ashworth, Lucas 317
Askonas, Elise 45
Assadnia, Xander 30
Astrike-Davis, Emma . . .162
Atwell, Kourtney 97
Audirsch, Austin 255
Austin, Hollie 318
Austin, Josh 104
Ayala, Arlene 324
Ayala, Lorenzo 38
Ayinmide, Yetunde 259
Azar, George 252
Babcock, Daniel 95
Bachman, Miranda 144
Bacon, Maddy 333
Badley, Brenton 275
Baez, Xena 236
Bagatelas, Elena 331
Bahret, Brandon 32
Bailey, Amanda 302
Bailey, Courtney 271
Bailey, Demarcus 118
Bailey, Jordan 212
Bailey, Mackenzie 273
Bailey, Micah 86
Bailey, Sydney 67
Bain, Laura Lane 72
Baird, Jacob 272
Baisiwala, Udai 234
Baker, Adara 36
Baker, Ally 79
Baker, Blake 291

Baker, Brad 295
Baker, Chelsey 173
Baker, Ellie 351
Baker, Emma Rose 155
Baker, Hannah 319
Baker, Jessica N. 187
Baker, Justin 334
Baker, Kaylinn 319
Baker, Roxanne 218
Baker, Sam 276
Balentine, Morgan 111
Ball, Casady 322
Ball, Stefan 231
Ball, Zack 78
Ballard, C.J. 161
Baller, Kelsey 128
Banania, Cassandra 60
Bandy, Virginia 208
Banerjee, Tia 82
Barber, Mary Davis 327
Bardowell, Rafael 44
Barker, Colin 257
Barker, Terisa 23
Barnett, Chaim 56
Barnhill, Christian 224
Barroso, Brenda 75
Basford, Shayna 174
Basler, Olivia 241
Bass, Chance 176
Bass, Jason Evan 82
Bass, Taylor 239
Bastien, Kiera 287
Bates, Jasmine 338
Bates, Logan 238
Battista, Dylan 41
Baucom, Hayden 344
Bauer, Yara 240
Bauman, Alex 33
Bauman, Charis 66
Bauman, Laura 117
Baxley, Jordyn 122
Baxley, Rachel 297
Baxley, Timothy 288
Baybrook, Tyler 136
Bayne, Harley 237
Bazemore, Lauren 161
Beardsley, Ashley 302
Beardsley, Evan 128
Beasley, Patty K. 324
Beasley, Sydni 115
Beauchamp, Blaire 208

Beaver, Braxton 70
Beaver, Joel 166
Beaver, Tyler 198
Beavers, Haley 118
Beckemeyer, Nate 249
Becker, Samantha 64
Beckley, Maya 67
Beebe, Eli 260
Beech, Hannah 26
Beehner, Michelle 68
Beeler, Janella 260
Begley, Vanessa 325
Bein, Thorin 298
Belcher, Lauren 209
Belcher, Paige 40
Beld, Zach 343
Belfield, QuaDaeja 29
Bell, Brooklyn 140
Bell, Gabby 32
Bell, Shaniqua 73
Bell, Tynecia 66
Belleau, Peter 63
Bemis, Kelly 104
Benge, Ashton 46
Bennett, Cody 60
Bennett, Marlee 147
Benton, Brayden 51
Berberich, Gabrielle
    Theodore 320
Bergman, Kirsten 75
Bergsma, Coleman 63
Berkemeyer, Molly 185
Bernard, Brittany 107
Berry, Briana 280
Berry, Caitlin 335
Berry, Charlie 212
Bertling, Ryan 204
Bhakta, Shiv 225
Bhutta, Affan 95
Bichsel, Ashley 296
Biggs, Lauren 114
Bilden, Teddy 153
Billings, Lake 30
Billups, Michael 279
Bing, Cheetara 123
Birbiglia, Anna 233
Birdsong, Bryant 155
Birney, Jayne 258
Bivens, Jeremias 316
Black, Harrison 298
Black, Kirsten 204

Blackmore, Averie 34
Blackwell, Meagan 277
Blackwell, Treyli 29
Blair, Nyla 45
Blair, Sarah 289
Blakely, Autumn 226
Blakley, Cody 181
Blakley, Hunter 249
Blanchard, Matt 285
Bledsoe, Luke 267
Blevins, Ashley 132
Blevins, Devan 294
Blevins, Tristan 64
Blew, Amy 340
Bloomfield, Gage 265
Boaz, Abby 208
Boerrigter, Linsey 246
Bohannon, Eli 138
Boldrick, Chloe 251
Bolin, Layla 307
Bolognini, Lea 204
Bond, Terrell 110
Bondura, Christopher . . .90
Bone, Ashlee 298
Bonham, Becca 162
Bonilla, Elicia 359
Bonilla, Martha 227
Bonner, Drew 224
Boole, Taylor 97
Borgmeier, Jesse 332
Bosco, Dustine 341
Boss, Ashleigh 299
Bosse, Carter 291
Bouknight, Jacob 163
Boutwell, Hannah 191
Bowen, Robin 331
Bowers, Kate 208
Bowers, Marty 166
Bowles, Ashlie 158
Bowles, Austin 139
Bowling, Ellis 94
Bowman, Darrell 159
Box, Angie 128
Boyd, Baylor 198
Boyette, Rebecca 176
Boyls, Stephanie 13
Bozeman, Alexandra 34
Brace, Tanner L. 328
Bradley, Jennifer 30
Bradley, Kayla 352
Bradley, Trey 337
Brady, Elias 125
Brady, Emily 218
Bragdon-Hall, Della 202
Brammer, Jennifer 155
Brannan, Logan 322
Brannock, Corey 276

Brantley, Jacob 102
Braswell, Alexis 260
Bray, Julia 78
Breaux, Brianna 139
Breaux, Gage 25
Breedlove, Rayanna 172
Breland, Anna 35
Brenner, Austin 212
Brewer, Hogan 68
Brewer, Shelby 36
Brewster, Dylan 331
Bridgewater, Bobbie Jo . .121
Briggs, Triston 160
Brissette, Freddie 180
Britt, Delicia 133
Broadnax, Shareba 126
Broadway, Breeanna 29
Brooks, Berry 127
Brooks, June 165
Brooks, Melissa 261
Broughton, Katy 284
Brown, Breauna 363
Brown, Brielle 240
Brown, Cassidy 340
Brown, Courtney 280
Brown, Dalton 319
Brown, Darren 330
Brown, Deion 54
Brown, Ebonee 227
Brown, Hannah 131
Brown, Ian 72
Brown, Jake 253
Brown, Jayla 73
Brown, Katherine 80
Brown, Maci 211
Brown, Megan 196
Brown, Peyton 90
Brown, Tia 191
Brown, Yusef 346
Brownell, Samantha 100
Bruce, Cameron 238
Bruce, Kaitlin 146
Brueckner, Nick 194
Brungardt, Ellie 360
Bruskotter, Emily 112
Bryant, Brittany 215
Bryant, Farris 346
Bryant, Taylor 103
Buchanan, Jared 285
Buchanan, Steven 151
Budder, Emerie Allison . .348
Buesinger, Caitlin 61
Buis, Syann 177
Bullard, Adam 231
Bullock, Mary-Morgan . .232
Bundschuh, Kyle 286
Bundy, Scout 209

Bunner, Dustin 170
Burgess, Colby 214
Burkhammer, Luke 317
Burlingame, Christian . . .168
Burner, Eilish 316
Burnett, Melanie 41
Burnett, Tim 194
Burnett, Whitney 281
Burnette, Kaley 92
Burns, Travis 208
Burrow, Sarah 330
Burt, Kristen 281
Bush, Leah 288
Butler, Amber 329
Butler, Johanna 187
Butler, Quinisha 229
Butterfield, Mary Carol . . .52
Buxton, Ramey 29
Bybee, Peyton 27
Byerly, Robert 58
Byers, James 283
Byrd, Anna 46
Byrd, Breanna 86
Byrd, Kaitlyn 52
Byrd, Kelsy 84
Byrd, Kymberlyn M. 129
Byrd, Rebekah 257
Byrum, Brooke 34
Caballero, Katia 329
Cabrera, Nicole 312
Cacioppo, Lucy 306
Cagle, Keslie 126
Cahoon, Claire 312
Cail, Christian 32
Cain, Caitlyn 105
Caldwell, Courtney 154
Calihan, Kendra 283
Calloway, Demarquis . . .167
Calvo, Sofia 87
Camacho, Alec 254
Cameron, Paul 193
Camp, Jada 315
Campbell, Anna 173
Campbell, Destiny Lynn .342
Campbell, Diamond 335
Campbell, Jennifer 203
Campbell, Jonah 225
Cannon, Tori 109
Canter, Elizabeth 73
Capps, Jace 221
Capps, Madison 168
Carden, Abbie 342
Cardenas, Bethany 266
Carey, Dezahn 180
Carlson, Hannah 143
Carlton, Kirsten 134
Carmack, Aaron 304

Carman, Machelle 84
Carmouche, Billy 256
Carpenter, Jolie 130
Carr, Nicole 215
Carr, Rachel 350
Carrillo, Amy 197
Carson, Gregory 305
Carswell, Ariana 179
Cartee, Meagan 237
Carter, Cecily 56
Carter, Dallas 27
Carter, Karlee 97
Carter, Kyra 64
Cary, Hope 168
Casaburo, Chase 23
Casey, Megan 94
Cason, Bryce Lane 102
Casos, Sienna 185
Castellanos, Lukas 340
Castillo, Victoria 336
Castro, Felipe 228
Caswell, Chris 223
Cato, Carley 194
Cato, Caroline 198
Caulder, Corey 49
Celaya, Stephany 325
Centilli, Jessica 195
Chadwick, Myles 232
Challa, Raja 205
Chalmers, Kamesha . . .256
Chamblee, Kel-Asia 47
Champlin, Hayden 302
Chandler, Elizabeth 82
Chapman, Aaron 222
Chapman, Christian 27
Chappel, Lydia 346
Chappell, Joshua 357
Charbonnet, Sara Inez . . .64
Chastain, Angelina 236
Chavez, Juanita 247
Chavez, Kevin 44
Chavis, Christian 229
Chavis, Krystyna 162
Chavis, Morgan 161
Chavis, Storm 188
Cheatham, Garrett 225
Cheatham, Georgianna . . .46
Chen, Cindy 207
Chen, Cindy 349
Chen, Michael 113
Childers, Emily 162
Chin, Jay 90
Cho, Juliann 301
Chowdhury, Alisha 296
Christian, Blake 327
Christisen, Emily 270
Christman, Micah 59

Christy, Paige 260
Clark, Addison 325
Clark, Bethany Nichole . .136
Clark, Cameron 324
Clark, Lora 49
Clark, MaKenzie 164
Clark, Mary Myers 271
Clark, Stewart 22
Clarke, Eli 350
Clarke, Madeleine 358
Clay, Lauren 211
Claypool, Jaret 64
Claypool, Kayde 180
Claypool, Kyndell 78
Clendenon, Kyle 160
Clermont, Matthew 164
Clifford, Madelyn 45
Clifton, Houston 232
Cline, Katie 176
Clodius, Marissa 343
Coats, Ashton 199
Cobb, Tyler 308
Cobble, Mariah 51
Coffey, Courtney 155
Coffey, Paige 282
Coffman, Brittany 237
Coffman, Keith 192
Cohen, Amy 41
Coker, Ashleigh Sierra . . .76
Coker, Nicholas 102
Colabaugh, Zachery 315
Cole, Ashlynn 96
Cole, Carmen 94
Cole, Jackson 72
Coleman, Gabrielle 313
Coleman, Mary Kate 50
Coley, Taylor 288
Collett, Jacob 153
Collier, Henry 282
Collier, Jason 94
Collier, MeMe 323
Collier, Sarah 286
Collier, Thomas 86
Collison, James "Tyler" . .276
Colvin, Brittany 289
Combs, Carla 89
Comire, Will 299
Compton, Leslie 172
Compton, Mason 238
Compton, Will 301
Comstock, Elizabeth 221
Conatser, Chet 237
Conaway, Jason 144
Conboy, Hailey 287
Conits, Athena 361
Conner, Emerson McCall 299
Conner, Kristin 101

Constans, Isaac 161
Constant, Abigail 255
Conway, Cody 153
Cook, Cecelia 70
Cook, Nicole 220
Cook, Ramie 165
Cooper, Conner 208
Corbin, Kenny 154
Cordero, Jacob 161
Cornish, Anna 50
Cornish, Olivia 44
Cort, Alexandra 329
Corwin, Kaylee 122
Cosby, Junicia 212
Costanza, Madison 276
Coulter, Mason 171
Cowart, Ainsley 39
Cowart, Sydney 347
Cox, Caitlin 348
Cox, Cameron 256
Cox, Jennifer 47
Cox, Jordan 224
Craddock, Jeffrey 300
Craine, Darien 176
Crandall, Devin 251
Crapps, Bailey 114
Cravens, Elizabeth 295
Crawford, Calli 302
Crawford, Savana 199
Creech, Andrew 29
Cressman, Sarah 94
Crews, Lynsey 119
Cribb, Hannah 339
Crim, Hope 326
Crisp, Virginia 24
Croghan, Michael 258
Crosby, Caleb 242
Cross, Adam 203
Cross, Jesse 56
Cross, Katlyn 26
Cross, Rae 305
Crossland, Isabel 98
Crouch, Taylor 138
Crousser, Jona 147
Crow, Matt 221
Cruey, Emily 206
Cruse, Breanna 285
Cuffe, Andrew 294
Culler, Hayden 342
Cullum, Caroline 47
Cumbee, Stacy 104
Cumbie, A'Lexus 141
Cummings, Bryce 82
Cummins, Michaela 188
Curl, Gabrielle 106
Curnutte, Anna 185
Curole, Brennan 253

Currier, Conner 201
Curry, Zakyia 86
Czajkoski, Cole 148
Czerwonka, Anne 163
D'Antoni, Jacob 70
Dabbous, Zach 110
Dabbs, Peyton 133
Dailey, Mahleek 294
Dailey, Tena 256
Dale, Leah 36
Dalton, Emma 258
Damdee, Airada 252
Damian, Karina 194
Daneault, Allison 154
Daneault, Tyler 342
Dang, Diana 338
Daniel, Elisa 345
Daniels, Jai 128
Danner, Steven 330
Darling, Max 198
Davidson, Lucas 281
Davidson, McKenzie 216
Davidson, Trey 347
Davis, Aubrey 179
Davis, Austin 133
Davis, Brittanee 98
Davis, Cheyenne 49
Davis, Dakota 90
Davis, Gabrielle 327
Davis, Haley 67
Davis, Jay 168
Davis, Journey 326
Davis, Pamela 201
Davis, Patrick 77
Davis, Ronald 22
Davis, Sarah 289
Davis, Tayler Kathryn . . .113
Davis, Tre 150
Dawson, A. J. 220
Day, Hannah 355
Day, Ricky 230
Deal, Dylan 335
Dean, Ben 266
deAngeli, Nicola 133
Dear, Allison 166
Dearmon, Cody 196
DeCillis, Amy 295
Deckelmann, Laura 253
Decker, Sam 235
Dedovic, Anisa 220
Deen, Emmett 204
Deere, Shae 149
Degner, James 181
DeHart, Samantha 240
DeHaven, Mikaela 105
Deitrick, John 270
DeJesus Flippen, Fanticé .151

Krystine 151
Del Castillo, Paula 143
Del Rosso, Austin 351
DeLancey, Shealyn 322
Delmestri, Emily 96
Demla, Sonali 222
Dennis, Diamond 146
Dennis, Emily 159
Dennis, Gabbie 216
Dennis, Keith 197
Denny, Logan 309
Denny, McKayla 256
Denny-Green, Jamilla . . .303
Densmore, Casey R. 68
DePergola, Garrett 144
Depoe, Tim 358
DesCoteaux, Alysia 87
deVeer, Nicholas 157
DeWeese, Maggie 288
Dewrell, Katelyn 331
Dias, Elizabeth 244
DiBernard, Breanne 280
Dickason, Kaleb 350
Dickerson, Cody 93
Dickerson, Jacob 147
Dickerson, Stephanie . . .252
Dicus, KD 153
Diebolt, Troy 317
Diefenderfer, Daniel 138
Dillion, Destiny 122
Dillon, Tyre 120
Dilworth, Emma 75
Dimartino, Mia 312
Dinger, Amanda 212
Dingle, Madison 270
Dinkins, John 111
Dixon, Joseph 184
Dixon, Tabbetha 126
Doboszenski, David 239
Dockery, Sydrena 221
Doelling, Andrew 333
Donoho, Cooper 263
Donovan, Parker 228
Dooley, Hayden 348
Dooley, Johnson Hayes . . .40
Dooley, Sarah 188
Dopheide, Caitlin 192
Dorr, Chaning 80
Dorrill, Haylee 308
Dorris, Julie Anne 82
Dosher, Melissa 358
Douglas, Harley 194
Dow, Rebecca 322
Doyle, Clare 24
Doyle, James 302
Dozer, Matthew 195
Draughn, Claire 123

Dreher, Forrest 284
Dreher, Morgan 316
Driscoll, Mark 211
Droge, Nicholas 174
Dryden, Kate 261
DuBois, Caitlin 28
Dubois, Helen Michaux .326
Duffy, Erin 293
Dugas, Hanna 42
Duke, Hannah 186
Dulinsky, Natasha 191
Dumanowsky, Benjamin .144
Duncan, Catherine 130
Duncan, Chloe 278
Duncan, Joshua 154
Duncanson, China 36
Dunn, Chelsea 269
Dunn, Kevin 350
Dunn, Sean 28
Durbin, Baylee 105
Durbin, Tristan 328
Durel, Katie 41
Durham, Kendall 262
Durrett, Anna 101
Dutton, Nick H. 200
DuVall, Hadley 71
Duvall, Trey 78
Dyches, Mary Margaret .230
Dyson, Luke 26
Eads, Kelley 341
Earhart, Aubrey 246
Easterwood, Gabby 212
Easton, Alex 60
Eaton, Elizabeth 169
Eaton, Matthew 114
Echternacht, Brandon . . .38
Eddy, Blake 130
Edens, Kerri 70
Edgeston, Linkal 237
Edwards, Haylee 351
Edwards, Madison 133
Edwin, Rafael 43
Eid, Joseph 132
Elam, Kylee 223
Elbl, Grace 247
Elbl, Kaitlin 66
Elder, Caroline 333
Eldridge, Collin 300
Eldridge, Milan 297
Eldridge, Paul 249
Elkins, Shianne 98
Ellis, Destinee 77
Ellis, Josh 359
Ellis, Tiffany 337
Elmore, Donnie 294
Elmore, Kendall 305
Elmore, Logan 30

Elzy, Meghan 355
Emerson, Hailey 26
Engel, Makenzie Rae . . .267
England, Tyler 242
English, Lauren 123
Epting, April 102
Erbs, Alex 299
Erickson, Jeni 273
Erickson, Nathan 308
Erikson, Zane 170
Estep, Ashten 259
Evans, Chattia O. 322
Evans, Colton 108
Evans, Gareth 288
Evans, Kaitlin 39
Evans, Rachel 321
Evatt, Rebecca 202
Evely, Nick 121
Ewing, Shane 223
Ezell, Jessica 219
Faccinetti, Bianca 219
Fairchild, Emily 161
Falconberry, Anthony . . .30
Fallon, Katie 355
Fanning, Kaylynn 22
Farley, Brittany 109
Farley, Jared 56
Farrell, Calli 38
Faubion, Jacob 346
Faulk, Spencer 330
Faust, Allison 68
Fearing, Jonathan 184
Featherstone, Ellen 152
Feisal, Walty 256
Feng, David 170
Fenwick, Bailey 193
Ference, Brinkley 342
Ferens, Danielle 274
Ferguson, Riley 115
Ferguson, Tate 242
Fernandez, Annaleah . . .320
Fetty, Sara 36
Fields, Trakia 188
Fights, Preston 193
Files, Austin 115
Fine, Benton 200
Fingers, Sydni 147
Finke, Marie-Caroline . . .122
Finley, Lane 328
Fischbach, Hope 73
Fishback, Celeste 334
Fisher, Christian 172
Fisk, Hannah 150
Fitzpatrick, Mollye 40
Fletcher, Preston 61
Flinn, Kristina 181
Flores, Karla 43

Flores, Miguel 242
Flowers, Jordan 280
Floyd, Abby 72
Floyd, Imani 28
Floyd, Marie 251
Flynn, Anna 232
Flynn, Hannah 246
Foard, Jacob 105
Foard, Meghan 68
Fobbs, Ty'ren 257
Fogarty, Kassie 129
Folds, Luke 32
Folse, Allison 65
Forbus, Brannon 163
Ford, LaJuané 104
Ford, Tranasia 362
Foreman, Andrew 334
Formby, Sarah 326
Fortenberry, Travis 68
Forwith, Marina 161
Fos, Trevor 330
Foster, Ciera 298
Foster, Landon 238
Foster, Zack 49
Fourqurean, Sam 74
Fowler, Alex 52
Fowler, Clay 218
Fowler, Dale 81
Fowler, Dewayne 311
Fox, Kasey 108
Fox, Lacey 52
Foxworth, Cameron 186
Foxworth, Candice 72
Frakes, Marriah 57
Fraley, Danielle 231
Francik, Tony 317
Francis, Danielle 261
Frank, Trevor 208
Franklin, Alex 99
Franklin, Courtney Nicole 159
Franklin, Lawson 108
Franklin, Michael 41
Frazier, Maclean 31
Frederick, Cayman 130
Frederick, Lauren 261
Freedman, Anastasia . . .357
Freeman, Cameron 284
Freitag, Bradley 313
Fretwell, Dylan 248
Fretwell, Jeremy 82
Fridley, Margaret 88
Frint, Shaniah 213
Fritz, Andy 140
Frost, Hyatt 300
Fuller, Julia 177
Fullmer, Peter 213
Fylstra, Rachel 322

Gabriel, Vernetta 316
Gahafer, Madison 272
Gahr, Dakota 68
Galbreath, Ayana 238
Galey, Mary 264
Gallagher, Darcie 279
Galloway, Jonathan 201
Galt, Zack 228
Galvan, Courtney 127
Gammons, Cortnee 130
Gandy, Anna 155
Garcia, Brianna 238
Garcia, Jorge 265
Garcia, Kristina 216
Garner, Kennedy 270
Garner, Shertia 143
Garrett, Daniel 63
Gatlin, Vanessa 195
Gatton, Conor 357
Gauthier, Rio 292
Gautier, Bailey 150
Gavrock, Erika 93
Gaylord, Charles 354
Gearhart, Colton 47
Gebo, Josh 51
Gee, Juan Pablo 321
Geier, Kristin 190
Genereaux, Nicholas . . .35
George, Sydney 59
Gerber, Colby 316
Gibbons, Bridgett 341
Gibson, Kaitlyn Nicole .243
Gibson, Rikki 95
Gifford, Kellen 58
Gifford, Madison 28
Gilbert, Haley 43
Gilbertson, Matthew 354
Giles, Bailey 26
Gill, Jessica 262
Gillam, Nicholas 175
Gillespie, Zoe 224
Gillich, Heather 148
Ginter, Jacob 231
Giordano, Morgan 152
Glandon, Loveday 276
Glasgow, Stephen 168
Glass, Malachi 255
Glass, Robert 163
Gleeson, Madeline 99
Glover, Chris 201
Glover, Laney 265
Goble, Noah 214
Godard, Elisa 133
Godfrey, Quincy 291
Godley, Darrean 247
Godwin, Ansley 356
Godwin, Nilyeah 226

Goheen, Roger 270
Goldman, Camille 338
Gomez, Suzanna 59
Gonzales, Corrina 357
Gonzalez, Abby 157
Gonzalez, Monica 78
Gonzalez, Sana 222
Good, Wesley 313
Goode, Kiaren 142
Goodman, Sarah 98
Goranflo, Eric 108
Gordon, Whitney 194
Gordy, Carl 90
Gorla, Maria 141
Gosser, Caroline 129
Gott, Hunter 137
Gottesman, Jeff 245
Goudy, Sarah 126
Gouhin, Nicole 308
Grady, Connor 61
Graham, Elton 224
Graham, Jaime 64
Graham, Jeffery Austin . .22
Graham, Xavier 322
Grahovic, Adis 291
Grainger, Zach 232
Granger, Katie 58
Graves, Auston 311
Graves, Casey 359
Graves, Jessica 352
Graves, Jonathan 47
Gray, David 184
Gray, Montressa 116
Grayson, Randy 107
Green, Adriana 81
Green, Desmond 60
Green, Jenifer 354
Green, Jeremiah 229
Greenberg, Peyton 289
Greene, Curran 306
Greene, Nathaniel 171
Greene, Paige 173
Greene, Tom 214
Greenway, Tristin 196
Gregory, Chad 51
Gregory, Kevin 252
Gregory, Mason 259
Gregson, Seth 111
Gregurich, William 334
Griffin, Alix 306
Griffin, Baylor 353
Griffin, Cassandra 266
Griffin, Elantra 114
Griffin, Elizabeth 36
Griffin, Sierra 63
Griffith, Mattie Clayre . . .189
Grigg, Trenton 36

Grimes, Hannah 87
Grogan, Tapanga 55
Grubbs, Tristan 194
Guercio, Anna 327
Guidry, Lindie 103
Guillory, Morgan 334
Gulledge, Hannah 131
Gulley, Denise 240
Gupta, Mallika 40
Gurel, Torrie 298
Guthrie, Aubri 22
Guthrie, Blake 232
Guthrie, Elizabeth 204
Guyer, Sherry 232
Hackworth, Brianna 308
Hadjri, Malik 117
Haff, Sunnye 229
Hageman, Katie 107
Hager, Hanna E. 299
Hagood, Hannah 284
Hagstrom, Luke 85
Haigwood, Nicole 40
Haim, Nicole 71
Haines, Pierson 232
Haitshan, Monti Lynn . . .174
Halama, Will 342
Hale, Tristan 244
Hall, Anna 267
Hall, Brandon 108
Hall, Brin 182
Hall, Destinee 344
Hall, Hannah 309
Hall, John 223
Hall, Jordan 55
Hall, Laura 27
Hall, Michael 216
Halpern, Keara 100
Halpin, Crimson 261
Halter, Trey 39
Hamby, Cameron 298
Hameed, Sara 109
Hamilton, Katie 238
Hamm, Cathryn 203
Hamm, Robin 338
Hammes, Emily 265
Hammock, Michael 332
Hammond, Megan 185
Hammonds, Travis 202
Hamon, Sarah 304
Hampton, Ellie 322
Hampton, Jacob 338
Hamric, Styver 63
Hamrick, Paige 359
Hamstead, Griffin 244
Hand, Kristin 308
Haney, Ben 28
Hanlon, Tyrei 121

Hanna, Kailee 205
Hannah, Ashley 306
Hardin, Becky 46
Hardin, Hailey 108
Hardin, Jacob 186
Harding, Jonathan 144
Hardy, John 70
Hargrave, Heather 110
Harkins, Alexander Xavier 245
Harper, Bailey 124
Harper, Brooke 89
Harper, Robbie 26
Harrell, Jake 100
Harrill, Macey 96
Harrington, Matt 179
Harrington, Mckayla 58
Harrington, Sydney 296
Harris, Ashley 176
Harris, Ashton 187
Harris, Jordan 174
Harris, Kayla 233
Harris, Lakeisha 190
Harris, Lindsey 274
Harris, Scotty 39
Harris, Takaya 338
Harris, Timothy 298
Harris, Tyler 129
Harrison, Hallie 336
Harrison, Zack 65
Hart, Chaffin 293
Hart, Thomas 67
Hartig, Emily 344
Hartley, Abby 154
Hartline, Jonah 157
Hartman, Gabriella 80
Harton, Mckenzie 189
Hartzell, Cody 260
Harvey, Lexi 226
Hass, Isaac 46
Hassel, Keith "KJ" 193
Hassen, Alex 212
Hatch, Jennifer 243
Hatcher, Lamont 56
Hatcher, Mary Glen 356
Hawk, Judson 126
Hawkins, Karis 14
Hawley, Dustin 26
Hayden, John 156
Hayes, Alyssa 308
Hayes, Caleb 307
Hayes, Emily 82
Hayes, Taylor 84
Haynes, Anthony 323
Haynes, Ashley 361
Haynes, Jesse 131
Hays, Connor 362
Hazel, Haylee 315

Hazel, Katie 255
Hearn, Logan 184
Hearn, Priscilla 268
Hearyman, Hannah Beth .231
Heath, George 242
Heath, Rebekah 173
Heathcock, Micah 246
Heavner, John 265
Hedges, Tristan 227
Helmick, Janee 292
Helton, Abigail 31
Helton, Rebecca 334
Hemingway, Sal 270
Henderson, Riley 280
Hendricks, Colton 175
Hendrickson, Kelsey 102
Hendrix, Jaron Walker . .234
Henry, Patrick 234
Henry, Ray 134
Hensley, Sara 122
Hensley, Timothy 136
Henson, Jared 294
Hernandez, Joshua 303
Herndon, Luke 230
Herrington, Christine . . .341
Herrmann, Parker 39
Hess, Andrew 40
Hess, Dayana 216
Hessler, Sean 152
Hester, Devin 40
Hicks, Joseph 51
Hill, Bailey 120
Hill, Brianna 260
Hill, Eliza 272
Hill, Jenna 91
Hill, Judith 251
Hill, Karl 124
Hill, Maya 42
Hill, Taylor 155
Hill, Vincent 189
Hillis, Kelley 220
Hillyard, Carter 361
Hineman, Carl 112
Hinson, Ashley Nicole . . .82
Hinton, Katelyn 132
Hipp, Savanah 98
Hirchert, Tricia 346
Hirshman, Cooper 23
Hite, Sara 201
Ho, Justin 230
Hobbs, Neil 147
Hoffmann, Sarah Jane . .190
Hogue, Michael 102
Holden, Kenton 333
Holdman, Ethan 146
Holds, Audrey 246
Holladay, James 66

Hollandsworth, Lily 311
Holleman, MJ 232
Hollis, Jaran 208
Holloway, Lacey 140
Hollowell, Hannah 69
Holly, MeKaila 258
Holman, Eric 337
Holt, Blake 130
Holtkamp, Hunter 321
Holtmeyer, Katie 238
Holtzclaw, Shanna 98
Homan, Sarah 53
Hong, Christine 348
Hoog, Anthony 91
Hook, Jacob 125
Hooker, Kathleen 338
Hopkins, Jessica 216
Hopkins, Jules Pierre 86
Hopkins, Kylie 24
Hopper, Kennedy 275
Horn, Dewayne 256
Horn, Jerrica 254
Horn, Keely 343
Hornaday, Kate 222
Hornick, Andrew 40
Horvat, Austin 329
Hoskins, Jarrett 328
Houck, Amanda 144
Houp, Matthew 301
House, Jadyn 182
House, Ra'Shawn 157
Howard, Ashley 263
Howard, Bradly 293
Hoxit, Coleman 221
Hoyle, Brandon 162
Hrycych, Salvatore 329
Hubbard, Karrie 260
Hubbard, Lance 346
Huddleston, Emily 130
Hudson, Frances 151
Hudson, Wilson 298
Huffman, Mara 331
Huggins, Joshua 342
Hughes, Dillon 66
Hughes, Gabrielle 31
Hughes, Kelsey 145
Hughes, Steven 153
Humes, Ashley 46
Hunnicutt, Laurin 276
Hunt, Cody 166
Hunt, Drew 40
Hunt, Kaitlynn 194
Hunt, Kara 94
Hunt, Sarah 332
Hunt, Taylor 250
Hunter, Haley 70
Hurley, Cailin 191

Hurt, Sarah 266
Hutchins, Claudia 84
Hutchinson, Hope 99
Hutson, Hannah 166
Hutton, Wes 274
Hyde, Ray 23
Hyder, Susan 226
Ibarra, Alejandro 26
Ibarra, Cristina 36
Ibeawuchi, Diri 253
Imbusch, John David . . .144
Ingram, Trevon 110
Inman, Quinton 158
Irby, Charity 212
Irvin, Mandy 305
Isbell, Lindsey 189
Isbill, Jacob 115
Itschner, Taylor 338
Ives, Kacy 210
Ivey, Karl 180
Ivy, Molly 138
Jackson, Demytria 103
Jackson, Harley 65
Jackson, Jacquelynn 158
Jackson, Luke 145
Jackson, NaTassja 200
Jackson Jr., Demytryk . . .102
Jacob, Daniel 121
Jacob, Sarah Elizabeth . .134
Jacobs, Jacobe Lynn 239
Jacobs, Michael 271
Jacobs, Natalie 55
Jaggers, Ben 153
James, Bakari 335
James, Lauren 290
James, Mary Catherine . . .99
James, Regina 72
Jang, Rickie 151
Jankowski, Avery 118
Jarratt, Mary-Danse 278
Jasso, Guadalupe 56
Jazwinski, Maria 69
Jeffers, Kirsten 158
Jeffries, Max 38
Jenkins, Caneisha 361
Jenkins, Kailey 112
Jenkins, Kaisey 238
Jennings, Logan 100
Jennings, Robert 98
Jennings, Thomas 358
Jernigan, Paul 363
Jessee, Cheyenne 23
Jeter, Sully 218
Jetter, Ember Renee 219
Jewett, Bethany 297
Jimenez, Crystal 208
Jimenez, Yesenia 78

Jinkins, Logan 24
Johns, Eric 188
Johns, Georgina 328
Johnson, Alexia 136
Johnson, Ann Rollins . . .304
Johnson, Brianna 64
Johnson, Chase 79
Johnson, Dan 86
Johnson, Devyn 201
Johnson, Hope 243
Johnson, Hunter 122
Johnson, Jaquan 59
Johnson, Johnny 358
Johnson, Justin 172
Johnson, Karlie 312
Johnson, Kayden 30
Johnson, Lauren 353
Johnson, Levi Landan . . .348
Johnson, Madison 122
Johnson, Precious 282
Johnson, Reilly 76
Johnson, Robert Austin . .234
Johnson, Shelley 138
Johnston, Ben 208
Johnston, Daniel 44
Johnston, Derek 274
Johnston, Elizabeth 85
Johnston, Idalis 117
Jones, Andrew 354
Jones, Ariana 326
Jones, Aubrey 241
Jones, Briana 103
Jones, Bryson 169
Jones, Destiny 99
Jones, Hannah 174
Jones, Jessica 280
Jones, Kaielynn 158
Jones, Lexie 178
Jones, Lurlethia 126
Jones, Madison 268
Jones, Rachel 183
Jones, Samuel 95
Jones, Sara 359
Jones, Taylor 22
Jordan, Kristina 253
Jordan, Sage 130
Juarez, Kateri H. 192
Jump, Reagan 134
Jumper, Jennie 274
Justice, Victoria 318
Kaczmarczyk, Michael . .217
Kadry, Aleah 336
Kaefer, Zachary 269
Kaisheva, Bogdana 111
Kaladi, Uma 360
Kaltenborn, Caroline . . .347
Kampschaefer, Austin . . .359

Kanyuh, Hannah 57
Kaplan, Alyssa 93
Kassen, Madeline 315
Kassouf, Katie 25
Katz, Morgan 166
Katz, Shelby 258
Kauffman, Carey 360
Kauffman, Katherine 26
Keables, Kathleen 120
Kearschner, Madison . . .295
Keating, MacKenzie 165
Keene, William 237
Keener, Dalton 33
Keller, Jordan G. 314
Kelley, Queen 46
Kelly, Chris 270
Kelty, Devan 170
Kendall, Shawn 210
Kendall, Tyrone 59
Kennedy, Carly 189
Kennedy, Christopher . . .131
Kennedy, Ethan 356
Kennedy, Josie 328
Kennedy, Ryan 83
Kennedy, Sedric 277
Kerlin, Lexi 32
Kersey, Recardo 57
Ketchem, Jackson 244
Keys, Addison 186
Keys, Diarius 126
Khera, Kalin 22
Kibler, Mackenzie 310
Killough, Joshua 330
Kilts, Jessie 169
Kim, Diane 353
Kim, Minseok 262
Kimbler, Brett 180
Kimple, Kara 232
Kindle, Alissa 362
King, Ashton 96
King, Austin 316
King, Bentley 245
King, Connor 130
King, Emma 311
King, Julia 71
King, Kaitlyn 132
King, Kay 200
King, Marly 187
King, Maya 183
King, Sydney 324
King, Tristan 93
Kinney, Brooke 156
Kinsey, Brianna 67
Kirby, Jacob 136
Kirkpatrick, Kelly 239
Kirkpatrick, Kelsey 286
Kirkpatrick, Sarah 145

Kirn, Taylor 184
Kirsch, Jacqueline 28
Kirton, Ashley 121
Kitzel, Patrick 180
Klamm, Havanna 166
Klem, Carl 244
Klem, Elizabeth 108
Kniery, Sam 71
Knott, Stacy 318
Knowles, Kelsey 314
Koch, Dalton 43
Koch, Patrick 280
Koepp, Britney 82
Koerner, Siori 138
Kohn, Brittany 307
Kolb, Steven 78
Kornegay, Katelyn 305
Kourlas, Ty 69
Krassowski, Maya 97
Kratzwald, Holly 221
Kreilein, Cole 304
Kremer, Tanner 105
Kropp, Eva 353
Krzyminski, Kristin 194
Kuhns, Lindsey 228
Kulus, Kirstin 122
Kuntze, Joshua 263
Kurz, Sean 199
Kvasnak, Julienne 149
Kynerd, Mariel 113
L'Hote, Kellie 68
Lababidi, Deanna 176
LaFrance, Ashley 266
Laliberty, Erin 279
Lamb, Nicholas 75
Lambert, Bobby 209
Lambert, Dustin 127
Lambert, Tori 364
Lamkin, Morgan 324
Lamle, Lacy 308
Lampe, Emma 251
Lampert, Ali 348
Lampkin, Courtney 158
Lance, Buffie 170
Landewee, Claire 79
Landreth, Bryan 330
Lane, Alex 64
Langel, Rhiannon 93
Langes, Yasmine 302
Langley, Dory 64
Langston, Harrison 166
Lankford, Austin 216
LaPasha, Michael 227
LaPorte, Jeffrey 324
LaPrade, Austin 360
Largent, Emily 154
Lassley, Taylor 132

Lathers, Jericka 80
Lattner, Molly 130
Lauderdale, Olivia B. . . .132
Law, Tanner Lee 167
Lawhead, Michael 110
Lawson, Charlie 331
Lawson, Eric 174
Lawson, Zachary 68
Layson, Chase 158
Leach, Alex 292
Leachman, Kacie 120
LeBlanc, Brittany 42
Lebron, Adriana 343
Ledford, Terry 90
Lee, David 158
Lee, Justin 212
Lee, Kyle 56
Lee, Rhonni 86
Lee, Tavijae 31
Lee, Taylor Jay 112
Lee, Tyler 23
Legette, Mark 223
Lehr, Rachel 124
Leibovich, Jocelyn 300
Lempesis, Drew 342
LeNeave, Grant 354
Lenhardt, Sara 141
Lentini, Andrew 272
Leonard, Jade 350
Leonard, Justin 156
Leonard, Sarah E. 136
Leonard, Zachary 89
Leposa, Zach 47
Leslie, Acacia 81
Lesmes, Nick 292
Lester, Grant 345
Lett, Natalie 156
Leviston, Lenard 103
Lewis, Adrian 242
Lewis, Angelo 357
Lewis, Dontrell 252
Lewis, Hunter 301
Lewis, John 244
Lewis, Keanna 108
Lewis, Kendra 157
Lewis, Kylie 100
Lewis, McKenna 76
Li, Catherine Y. 281
Licciardi, David 218
Lickenbrock, Madeline . . .40
Lightfoot, Chase 178
Lile, Lake 260
Lim, Nicole 318
Linderer, Alexandra 253
Linderer, Ben 276
Linebaugh, Blake 98
Lineberger, Anna 337

Link, Patrick 15
Lipe, John 288
Lipic, Garrett 246
Lipke, Andrew 62
Little, Donnesha 47
Little, Drew 260
Little, Shanya 56
Litton, Kade 314
Lloyd, Addie 138
Locklear, Jalyssa 312
Locklear, Seavy Lecota . .257
Logan, Caroline 190
Logunleko, Ashley 44
Lokey, Scarlett 45
Lombard, Megan 349
Long, Brian 119
Long, Courtney 204
Long, Micah 162
Longworth, Kelsey 327
Loos, Zachary 228
Lopez, Brandon 46
Lopez, Damaris 300
Lopez, Kenia 94
Lopez, Sarahi 97
Lorenz, Alexis 22
Loucks, Sydney 37
Loupe, Abby 85
Lowery, Blue 331
Lowery, Margaret Len . . .333
Lowry, Elizabeth 224
Lowry, Terry 221
Lucas, Hannah 135
Lucas, Jordan 24
Lucas, Madison 253
Lucas, Sarena 158
Ludlow, Jimmy 55
Lund, Gretchen 127
Lundy, Emma 340
Lusk, Jacob 52
Lutes, Coreyanne 118
Lutton, Michael 202
Luvine, Ciara 63
Lynch-Daniels, Oliver . . .252
Lynn, Tyler 199
Lyons, Jas 156
Lyster, Emily 218
Mack, Sarah 353
Mackey, Sarah 317
Maddock, Matthew 307
Maddox, Ashleigh 148
Maddox, Barrett 42
Maddox, Claire 176
Maddox, Danielle 252
Maeser, Hannah 264
Magee, Kia 334
Magee, Rick 33
Mahurin, Morgan 89

Mai, Anh-Tu 216
Majette, Jaylil 30
Malcolm, Destiny 328
Maldonado, Adriana 228
Maliszewski, Erika 170
Malone, Anna 189
Malone, Janell 363
Malone, Shaterian 132
Malueg, Madeline 74
Manke, Ethan 216
Manley, Samantha 110
Manrriquez, Cruz 338
Mansfield, Jennifer 251
Mansfield, Kylee 179
Mantooth, Hali 152
Mantyh, Jim 228
Marbury, Zorea 296
Mariano, Andrea 273
Markham, Fred 353
Marks, Alyssa 133
Marks, Jeannie 40
Marquez, Adriana 77
Marrow, Alayjah 283
Marsden, Alexander 178
Marshall, Caileigh 303
Marshall, KeyShawn 144
Martin, Leah 126
Martin, Michael 293
Martin, Randall 286
Martin, Ryan 325
Martin, Sarah 360
Martin, Timothy 258
Martinez, Keri 44
Martinez, William 232
Mason, Josh 326
Massenburg, Anthony . . .112
Massengill, Lucy 324
Massey, Sarah 230
Masters, Chandler 232
Matheson, Austin 150
Mathews, Colton 301
Mathis, Ashton 54
Mathis, Maleah 247
Mattingly, Cole 62
Mattingly, Davis 121
Mattison, Reed 83
Mattox, Matthew 293
Matus, Ashley 358
Matute, Stephanie 347
Matz, Ben 106
Matz, Jonathan 23
Mauck, Madison 180
Maue, Alex 346
Maxcey, Ashley 346
Maxcey, Hannah 202
Maxwell, Graham 116
May, Jonathan 243

Mayer, Matthew 210
Mayers, Bryce 355
Mayfield, Cory 331
Mayfield IV, O. Hunter . .305
Maynor, Phoenix E. . .344
Mayo, Avery 189
Mays, Keenah 283
Mays, Latiya 284
Mays, Remi 174
McAdams, Rob 301
McBride, Jessica 175
McCabe, Jason 130
McCain, Hunter 100
McCartha, Grace 119
McCarthy, Olivia 298
McClain, Arlandis 155
McClain, Elizabeth 287
McClellan, Hannah 310
McCollough, John . . .144
McConkey, Ansley 115
McConkey, Cassie 64
McConnell, Kirsten 350
McCord, Nicholas 87
McCormack, Christina . .220
McCormack, Keith 326
McCoy, Aaron 316
McCoy, Takira 318
McCreery, Jack 75
McCune, Alexus 234
McDavid, Maggie 158
McDearman, John 135
McDonald, Devin 26
McDonald, Mollie 314
McFarland, Margaret 51
McFarland, Natasha 302
McGahee, Kayla 40
McGarel, Erin 181
McGhee, Tyler 116
McGill, DeAndre 166
McGill, Jasmine 224
McGinnis, Skyler 243
McGowen, Meagan 71
McGrath, Mallory 349
McGucken, Patrick 166
McGuire, Fiona 230
McGuire, Hannah 312
McHugh, Max 296
McKay, Luke 362
McKenna, Grace D. 158
McKenzie, Bethany 163
McKenzie, Brendan 124
McKenzie, Matthew 331
McKenzie, Molly 284
Mckenzie, Nicholas 290
McKinney, Christopher . .312
McLain, Zachary 99
McLaren, Baylie 220

McLaurin, Nichole 334
McLelland, Madison 210
McMahon, Keely 54
McManus, Ali 123
McNamara, Katy 360
McNaughton, Tyler 332
McQuilkin, Natalie 69
McRae, Deja 117
McVey, Cora Breanne 39
McVey, Jakeb 90
Mealer, Will 61
Meek, Brooks 150
Meeker, Kristen 52
Melhado, Elise 86
Melton, Loren 277
Menard, Joshua 363
Mendez, Kameron 85
Menetre, Miller 103
Mercer, Abby 128
Mercer, Bradley 186
Merchant, Kainath 234
Merritt, Anna 71
Merritt, Meagan 142
Mershon, Matt 161
Mertz, Savannah 110
Messer, Becca 309
Messer, Ina 101
Messer, Oriana 271
Messerley, Camile 142
Metcalf, Raquel 334
Metts, Jordan 285
Metz, Kyle 81
Meyer, Hannah 266
MgBodile, Patty 323
Mikszta, Luke 298
Mildren, Marisa 184
Miles, Claire 254
Miles, Kelly 126
Miles, Madison 63
Milholen, Gala 132
Miller, Alicia 85
Miller, Casey 144
Miller, David 205
Miller, Jarvis 321
Miller, Jasmine 328
Miller, Lory 250
Miller, Olivia 42
Miller, Olivia 158
Miller, Rachel 210
Miller, Rickie 338
Miller, Ryan 356
Miller, Savannah 44
Miller, Scott 102
Miller, Shelby 224
Miller, Steven 268
Mitch, Sonja 276
Mitchell, Austin 260

Mitchell, Billy 248
Mitchell, Haleigh 286
Mitchell, Katie 331
Mittal, Sarang 202
Molina, Cassandra 22
Montano, Jenna 332
Monteith, Alex 207
Montgomery, Olivia 235
Moody, Morgan 82
Moore, Aaron 287
Moore, Brianna 196
Moore, Brooke 242
Moore, Caroline 72
Moore, Kaitlyn 224
Moore, Kenny 207
Moore, Michael 326
Moore, Rachel 346
Moore, Rebekah 217
Moore, Sawyer 79
Moore, Tanner 83
Moore, Victoria 78
Moore, Wesley 63
Mora, Diego 213
Moreland, Alexandra 85
Moreland, Zachary 270
Morello, Pete 44
Morelock, Sara 181
Morgan, Alyssa 144
Morgan, Gracie 225
Morgan, Jakob 349
Morgan, Kayla 272
Morgan, Kody 335
Morgenlander, Josh 176
Morningstar, Kristen 126
Morphis, Spencer Lee . .166
Morris, Drew 196
Morris, Jake 108
Morris, Michael 314
Morrison, Amber 28
Morrison, Amy 241
Morrison, Katherine 206
Morton, Olivia 135
Morvant, Meagan 179
Mosko, Ethan 246
Moss, Tyler 355
Mosteller, Grayson 290
Mott, Harley 86
Mourad, Maes 206
Mowery, Chelsea 263
Moye, Christina 208
Mreir, Shady 228
Mueller, Haley 160
Muir-Taylor, Genie 358
Mujic, Adisa 96
Mulcahy, Kaylee 52
Mulkey, Marshall 302
Mulkey, Tyler 56

Mullins, Sarah 141
Munday, Autumn 108
Munguia, Roger 318
Munoz, Luisa 180
Murillo, Victoria 53
Murphree, Ryan 56
Murphy, Bailey 260
Murphy, Layn 220
Murphy, Paige 346
Murphy, Ryan 354
Murphy, Seth 268
Murr, Savannah 68
Murrell, Olivia 152
Myers, Autumn 211
Myers, Danielle 99
Myers, Maggie 159
Mylchreest, Max Joseph .177
Nace, Peyton 274
Nadeau, Mollie 136
Nader, Summer 170
Naeger, Andrew 166
Nahn, Pete 270
Nally, Daniel 314
Nanan, John 225
Nash, Banks 300
Nash, Virdal 217
Nathan, Kynnedy 297
Nauert, Nick 177
Navarro, Lauren 122
Nelon, Christopher 322
Nelson, Hannah 77
Nelson, Lillianne 125
Nelson, Steven 337
Nenninger, Charles 288
Nesta, Amanda 215
Neumaier, Joshua 237
Neville, Margaux 280
Nevils, Timothy 136
Newman, Jacob 24
Newton, Emily 130
Nguyen, Michael 282
Ni, Haley 102
Nicholas, Chris 271
Nicholas, Timothy 262
Nichols, Nick 312
Nichols, Tori 276
Nicholson, Allie 205
Nicholson, Dallas 188
Nicholson, Drew 39
Nicholson, Samantha . . .258
Nickles, Sarah 52
Niermann, Candace 247
Nix, Nicole 329
Nixon, Raheem 26
Noah, Cheyenne 200
Noah, Sam 231
Noblet, Elisabeth 217

Noe, Wes 52
Nolting, Jessica 160
Norman, Brianna 44
Norman, Cheyenne 50
Norris Jr., Ryan 316
Norton, Josh D. 111
Norton, Kaylee 57
Nugent, Jasmine 95
Nugent, Walker 263
Nwokeji, Briana 231
Nwokeji, Brittany 123
O'Brien, Alex 301
O'Dell, Matthew 252
O'Dowd, Patricia 65
O'Kelley, Caitlin 98
O'Leary, Erin 254
O'Neal, Johnathan Xavier 197
O'Neal, Sarah 270
Oaks, Griffin 354
Oden, TeAsia 257
Oldfather, David 170
Olinger, Victoria 170
Olson, Angelina 266
Olson, Jasmine 198
Olson, Mike 64
Omar, Aya 95
Onesto, Maricruz 26
Ong, Christine 277
Orman, Molly 45
Ortega, Sergio 303
Ortiz, Jaida 212
Osborne, Jacob 200
Osvath, Nolan 142
Ott, Jenn 340
Overbey, A.J. 358
Overstreet, Micah 152
Overton, Charlotte 252
Owens, Josh 130
Owens, Marquese 165
Owens, Sierra 266
Owens, Taylor 54
Oyler, Christina 60
Packer, Jaela 339
Padgett, Ashly 240
Padgett, Jade 316
Padgett, Kelsy 219
Padgett, Trevor 312
Page, Erika 238
Painter, Jenna 27
Palazzo, Raymond 54
Palazzolo, Chiarra 80
Palmer, Jhane 78
Palmeter, Abby 293
Palms, Cannon 132
Palso, Ryan 149
Pancholy, Niraja 245
Panzeca, Amy 160

Paramore, Amanda 64
Parham, Parker 296
Parish, Anna 300
Parish, Luke 164
Parker, Amber 163
Parker, Brittany 270
Parker, Skyla 340
Parks, Abigail 323
Parks, Taylor 255
Parnell, Jacob 150
Parrish, Koty 72
Parson, Allison Marie . .330
Parson, Emily 16
Passmore, Stone 269
Patafio, Michaela 364
Patel, Jinesh 239
Patenaude, Hannah 172
Patma, Chelsea 274
Patri, Tanay 57
Patrick, Ann Kelly 248
Patterson, Gage 104
Patterson, Riley 282
Paul, Natania 114
Paxton, Asher 40
Payne, Allyson 334
Payne, Emily 284
Payne, Katelyn 322
Payne, Madison 358
Payne, Maranda Mae . .280
Payne, Ruthann 191
Pearce, Garrett 31
Pearman, Devin 55
Pearson, Aaliyah 62
Pecaut, Makayla 90
Peck, Tommy 73
Peeples, Alex 137
Pegram, Lucas 268
Pelzer, Courtney 357
Pemberton, Sarah 202
Pemberton, Sydney 241
Peña, Alyssa Nichole . . .260
Pennington, Sarah 187
Pentecost, Kelli 278
Penton, Amber 356
Percer, Spencer 44
Perez, Alex 269
Perkey, Philip 275
Peters, Kevin 116
Peters, Zachary 157
Peterson, Neil 135
Pettit, Tori 262
Petty, Jon Mark 241
Pham, Lena 32
Pham, Tiffany 215
Phelan, Ralph 36
Phillips, Allie 316
Phillips, Carolyn Grace . .162

Phillips, Deonte 321
Phillips, Garett 214
Phillips, Katy 310
Phillips, Kelsey 191
Phillips, Madi 74
Phillips, Madison 72
Phillips, Megan 330
Phillips, Merritt 344
Phillips, Rylee 185
Phimphavong, Matt 325
Piazza, Sydney 224
Pichea, Walker 143
Pickens, Collin 40
Pickett, Kylene 238
Picquet, Marissa 356
Piepmeyer, Steven 235
Pierce, Anna 126
Pierce, Austin 158
Pierce, Evan 96
Pierce, Kali 171
Pierce, Terra 297
Piesker, Melissa 32
Pilco, Juan Pablo 169
Pillow, Noah 98
Pimentel, Alex 79
Pinkston, BJ 294
Pintilie, Adriana 326
Pittman, Ethan 344
Pittman, Kylee 30
Piwetz, Gabrielle 342
Placht, Steven 86
Plott, Nicholas 194
Plummer, Maria 294
Poindexter, Tiajma 123
Pollard, Jada 154
Ponzillo, Joe 292
Pope, Morgan 92
Port, Mitch 356
Porter, Clayton 216
Porterfield, Rebecca C. . .108
Posey, Dustin 54
Post, Dalton 50
Post, Michael 322
Potter, Devon 255
Potter, James 152
Pounds, Hanna 81
Powderly, Grant 327
Powderly, Jake 70
Powell, DeMorie 35
Powell, Isabella 332
Powers, Gabrielle 159
Powers, Kendall 124
Poznanski, Abbey 70
Price, Dionte 177
Prince, Meranda 109
Privette, Allison 273
Privette, Marybeth 240

Proctor, Matthew 83
Proctor, Shelly Grace 94
Proffer, Madison 301
Prow, Abby 311
Pryor, Hannah 248
Pudlo, Matt 188
Puello, Iván 283
Pugh, Seth 168
Purner, Emily 224
Quach, Kaitlyn 78
Quatkemeyer, Emily 122
Queen, Justin 228
Quezada, Jorge 246
Quick, Chaz 195
Quiroz, Sandra 50
Raba, David 174
Raby, Kiana 290
Radford, Brianna 256
Ragland, Hayla 53
Ragsdale, Jacob 318
Ragsdale, Justis 163
Raidt, Colleen 180
Raimondi, Nichole 37
Raines, Amanda 317
Ramirez-Reyes, Alberto . .118
Ramos, Zenaida 130
Randall, Ethan 224
Randall, Jordan 183
Randall Pagan, Melissa . .193
Randolph, Ronald W. . . .281
Rankins, Davion 272
Rasco, Cate Joseph 319
Rasco, Jackson 74
Rascon, Alex 168
Ratchford, Nicholas 295
Ratliff, Jennifer 351
Ratliff, Minnie Lee 155
Rawls, Tau'Shell 335
Ray, Adeline 334
Ray, Carson 167
Ray, Jessie 89
Raya, Javier 239
Raymer, Noelle 137
Raynor, Sierra 188
Rebstock, Cody 303
Rector, Katherine 307
Redmon, Alex 50
Reese, Bobby 210
Reese, Jennie 140
Reese, Robbin E. 238
Reeves, Alexandria 344
Regalado, Sierra C. 98
Reichenbach, Alex 302
Reid, Abby 294
Reid, Mackenzie 242
Reilly, Kevin 284
Reiser, Sarah Katherine . .228

Renfro, Olivia 227
Rennie, Anna 226
Rew, Brandon 354
Reynolds, Logan 146
Rhodes, Dylan 44
Rice, Sabrina 233
Richard, Josh 143
Richard, Morgan 62
Richardson, Darrell 142
Richardson, Emily 358
Richardson, Tahlia 293
Richardson-Piche, Kayla .128
Richeson, Ryan 275
Richmeyer, Grace 265
Richmond, Jacquelyn . . .285
Richter, Alyssa 196
Ricketson, Lance 46
Ricketts, Jordan 267
Riddick, Alexandria 229
Rider, Tabitha 73
Riffe, Connor 142
Riggins, Matthew 294
Riggs, Gracie 288
Riggs, John 116
Riley, Greg 44
Riley, Madison 312
Rine, Natalie 291
Riney, Alek 144
Ring, Kera 49
Rios, Brenda 82
Ritchie, Matt 311
Ritter, Jodie 338
Rivera, Mariana 274
Robbins, Cassidy 159
Robbins, Lori 212
Roberson, Austin 272
Roberson, Sasathia 347
Roberts, Alex 182
Roberts, Hannah 174
Roberts, Kaylee 291
Roberts, Matt 122
Roberts, Nick 89
Roberts, Rhiannon 72
Roberts, Spencer 149
Roberts, Tristlynn Jae . . .339
Robertson, Christie 146
Robinson, Courtney 46
Robinson, Keanna 282
Rodgers, Denzel 269
Rodriguez, Christian 190
Rodriguez, Jesse 175
Roemen, Emma 167
Roethling, Meredith 130
Rogers, Allie 192
Rogers, Josie 255
Rogers, Kaitlyn 37
Rogers, Michael 244

Rogers, Natalie 94
Rogers, Nick 106
Rokisky, Brooke 357
Roller, Erica 309
Rollins, Amanda 362
Rollins, Hadley 243
Roman, Elliott 33
Romeo, Marissa 126
Root, Spencer 310
Roper, Baylee 38
Rosenbohm, Megan 202
Rosenstrom, Andrew . . .229
Rosenstrom, Erik 35
Rotz, Toby Keith 119
Rowe, D'Aisha 93
Rudd, Samantha 211
Ruddock, Cecily 112
Rudel, Katelyn 310
Rudisill, Nolan 113
Rueff, Sarah 53
Rule, Robert 36
Runnells, Jessica 68
Runner, Kaylen 358
Ruocco, Zach 35
Rusher, Isabella 218
Russell, Braylin 248
Russell, Drew 109
Russell, Sawyer 258
Rutledge, John 90
Rutrough, Ryan 281
Ryan, Lander 67
Ryan, Tessa 304
Ryder, Anna 322
Sablan, Natasha H. 282
Sacco, Emma 171
Sachdeva, Sarika 308
Sakthivel, Senthil 149
Salazar, Maria 182
Salchert, David 342
Salpietra, Trace 236
Salvadalena, Lindsay 125
Sanderlin, Carolyn 202
Sanders, Kareem 127
Sanders, Morgan 181
Sandford, Cole 279
Sands, Morgan 187
Sanso, Maggie 207
Sartin, Anthony 310
Sartin, Bailey 186
Sarvis, Cameron 150
Satcher, Jessica 312
Sato, Yukako 105
Sattaphan, Nattapon 84
Satterfield, Jharon 303
Satterly, Rebekkah Anne . .65
Saunders, Hunter 69
Saunders, Jayden 339

Saunders, Kimberly 198
Sawyer, Erica 131
Sawyer, Kaneesha 146
Sawyer, Matt 299
Scales, Antonio 188
Scalzo, Jacqui 200
Scarbrough, Maggie . . .262
Scarpill, Cierra 210
Schad, Weston 109
Scharf, Mary Glynn 162
Schario, Brett 316
Scheidhauer, Kevin 339
Schemel, Gabby 22
Schiavo, Jenna 169
Schlagle, Jesse 23
Schmalzried, Kali 284
Schmidt, Sophie 132
Schmidt, Tatijana 37
Schmitt, Alex 233
Schmitt, Zachary 184
Schnelle, Ian 193
Schneller, Ashley 358
Schnurbusch, Dalton . . .274
Schoephoerster, Jack . . .285
Schofield, Dakotah 112
Schott, Sarah Brooks . . .176
Schulte, Caroline 196
Schultz, Mary Alice 264
Schutz, Madison 60
Schwartz, Alyson 254
Scirica, Gabby 304
Sclafani, John M. 208
Scobee, Emma 209
Scott, Joseph 191
Scott, Julie Ann 94
Scott, Matthew 139
Scott, Melanie 259
Scott, Taylor 137
Scott, Wil 78
Scrogham, T.J. 72
Scully, Erin 115
Seagraves, Alley 56
Sears, Brooke 185
Sedoris, Emma 156
Seech, Hunter 22
Self, Terry 71
Sellers, Becca 249
Sellers, Johana 72
Selvidge, Zac 265
Sensabaugh, Colton 244
Settle, Sydney 320
Sexton, Sara 148
Seymore, Joselyn 226
Shafer, Anna 220
Shaffer, Michael 205
Shaffer, Miranda 234
Shamblin, Nick 202

Shane, Taylor 139
Shannon, Mary Kate 107
Shannon, Zoë 26
Sharkins, Jonah 284
Sharpe, Audrey 208
Shatwell, Michael 101
Shegog, Deshai 174
Shelton, Kourtney 207
Shelton, Micaiah 53
Sheridan, Michael 302
Sherman, Abbie 191
Sherrod, Robert 364
Shields, Trey 272
Shiflett, Austin 195
Shimakonis, Chase 131
Shipp, Bailey 276
Shirey, Abby 130
Shirey, Mariclare 124
Shirley, Jacob 316
Shoemaker, Brady 54
Shook, Hunter 194
Short, Brooke 146
Short, Dalton 286
Short, Olivia 87
Shotnik, Grant 136
Shouse, Levi 273
Shows, Anna 90
Shuler, Maya Mishel 129
Shultz, Noah 334
Shymlock, Bailey 49
Sichel, Jacob 33
Sides, David 133
Siebe, Josh 149
Siebeling, Anna 188
Siegrist, Kaitlyn 325
Sierakowski, Veronica . . .97
Sifford, Mason 165
Sigmon, Kylee 146
Sikes, Ashley 151
Silva, Terry 194
Silvera, Melany 319
Simmons, Alexa 225
Simmons, Aubrey 177
Simmons, Charles 237
Simmons, Connor 343
Simmons, Jacob 58
Simmons, Summer 58
Simmons, Taylor 335
Simon, Kayla 281
Simon, Nicole 183
Simpson, Madison 132
Simpson, Nathan 26
Sims, Kyle 179
Sinclair, Andrew 144
Sinclair, Sarah 226
Singer, Alex 250
Singleton, Daniela 282

Singleton, Tiffany 46
Singley, Allie 175
Singley, Hannah 218
Sistrunk, Diamond 59
Sivashanmugam, Arvind . .84
Sizemore, Mike 241
Skaggs, Madeline 246
Skanes, Sydney 125
Skidmore, Maggie 279
Skipper, Gabe 312
Slice, Mary-Mac 51
Sloan, Seth 317
Slover, Jedidiah 362
Smalley, Brandy 119
Smeltzer, Olivia Grace . .88
Smiley, Darius 288
Smith, Aaron 297
Smith, Audrey Jeanette . .165
Smith, Austin 234
Smith, Caitlyn 116
Smith, Caleb 51
Smith, Carly 227
Smith, Cole 77
Smith, Emily 294
Smith, Georgia 107
Smith, Grant 203
Smith, Hannah 173
Smith, Iain 329
Smith, Jacob 266
Smith, Jacque 142
Smith, Kaila 127
Smith, Kat 274
Smith, Keyontranay 88
Smith, Logan 360
Smith, Mackenzie 162
Smith, Madeline 194
Smith, Reid 308
Smith, Taylor 136
Smith, Tityeonna 91
Smoot, Charysma 41
Smoots, Ben 171
Snell, Alexis 79
Snelling, Timothy 202
Snider, Rosie-Marie 330
Snow, Nathaniel 173
Snowden, Chasity 183
Snyder, Logan 64
Snyder, Rebecca 128
Solinger, Jane 29
Solomon, Tia 338
Sona, Ellie 86
Sona, Emma 172
Sorey, Annie 224
Spain, Sara 112
Spann, Joshua 333
Sparks, Hannah 167
Sparrow, Parker 162

Speagle, Tylar 26
Speed, Adrian 315
Speller, Sara 68
Spivey, Reed 53
Splawn, Linley 240
Spratt, Devin 345
Spruill, Oscar 323
Squeglia, Gerard 260
Srikrishna, Meghana 33
St. Pierre, April 362
Stachulski, Cassidy 174
Stafford, Keeley 220
Stafford, Kinley 184
Stallings, Dylan 343
Stallings, Haley 280
Stalvey, Ashley 316
Stanberry, Shelby 74
Standley, Hannah Elizabeth 232
Stanford, Morgan 309
Stanley, Destiny 340
Stansberry, Sydney 36
Stansbury, Logan 38
Staples, Tré 94
Stark, Bailey 98
Starr, Rachel 313
Staton, Emery 283
Steele, Ethan 227
Steele, Rebekah 47
Steeley, Landon 234
Steinbecker, Cole 238
Steinman, Gabe 25
Stellmach, Kimberly 230
Stellwag, Alison 202
Stelly, Ava D. 80
Stephens, Faith 147
Stephens, Hailey 202
Stephens, Jana 136
Stephens, Paige 195
Stevens, Ka'Nisha 248
Stewart, Andrew 219
Stewart, Autumn 138
Stewart, Christian 332
Stewart, Dustin 262
Stewart, Helen 150
Stewart, Natalie 275
Stickle, Meghan 37
Stillwell, Emily 182
Stinchcomb, Jenna 129
Stokes, Hannah 178
Stolz, Don 283
Stone, Ashlyn 278
Stone, Taylor 48
Stoneking, Brianna 140
Stout, Tanner 286
Stovall, Breanna 270
Stover, Evasia 181
Strachan, Alec 98

Strange, McKenzie 284
Strause, Bailey 97
Street, Hannah 68
Strickland, Anna Lea . .211
Strickland, Kali 183
Strickland III, Thomas
    Newton 34
Stricklin, Timothy 319
Stringer, Abbie 140
Stroud, Ra'Nesha 349
Stubbs, Brittney 256
Suarez, Michael J. 274
Suber, Jordan L. 317
Suggs, Katherine 211
Sughrue, Lacey 60
Sullivan, Kelly 43
Sullivan, Matthew 287
Sullivan, Nikki 60
Summers, Matt 239
Summit, Katie 209
Sumner, Isaiah 102
Surdyke, Thomas 143
Sutherland, Hannah 116
Svendsen, John 100
Swain, Cheyenne 86
Swain, Kai 150
Swain, Kerstin 90
Swann, Andrew 99
Sweat, Tasha 58
Sweatt, Ciara 135
Sweere, Matthew 52
Sweere, Morgan 234
Swoish, Alison 91
Sykora, Sam 184
Sylvia, Hampton 42
Tackett, Lydia J. 125
Takewell, Lauren 321
Tallent, RaShawn 116
Tanas, Joseph 60
Tarence, Ellie 94
Tarwater, Brittney 145
Taylor, Abby 168
Taylor, Amanda 266
Taylor, Chris 320
Taylor, Jessica 236
Taylor, Jurnee 28
Taylor, Kalyn 84
Taylor, Tyler 87
Tegethoff, Kylie 215
Tejeda, Alicia 88
Tejero, Tania 207
Templeton, Caroline
    Elizabeth 114
Tequia-Lagunes, Valeria .176
Terhaar, Turney 158
Ternus, Payton 136

Terrell, Ali 318
Thames, Taylor 124
Thames, Trevor 116
Thebert, Nyssa 29
Thesenvitz, Kayleigh . . .261
Thibodeau, Christian . . .108
Thomas, Amber 248
Thomas, Braelin 205
Thomas, Brannen 198
Thomas, Charlotte 112
Thomas, Dustin 144
Thomas, Jamia 305
Thomas, Jarren 268
Thomas, Matthew 216
Thomas, Molly 145
Thomas, Sam 341
Thomas, Taylor 30
Thomas, Tre-Kwon 42
Thomas, Tyler 188
Thompson, Austin 159
Thompson, Caroline 312
Thompson, Dannion 37
Thompson, Emily 197
Thompson, Greg 212
Thompson, Haley 249
Thompson, Hunter 203
Thompson, Jameisha . . .247
Thompson, Michael 265
Thompson, Ross 22
Thompson, Wendell 75
Thornton, Bailey 302
Thornton, Roderick 345
Threatt, Kiara 41
Threet, Chandler 347
Timmons, Charlquetta . . .49
Timpe, Emily 73
Timpson, Antonio 361
Tinsley, Lydia Sue 203
Tinsley, Thomas 30
Tippett, Tori 104
Tipton, Chris 269
Tishma, Mariel 139
Titus, Maggie 220
Todd, Tyler 170
Toepfert, Carrie 315
Tomlinson, J.R. 102
Toole, Nich 24
Toole, Renee 352
Tooley, Ryan 170
Tosang, Suzanne 348
Totton, Alecia 221
Tovar, Alex 88
Trail, Chaley 315
Tran, Huy 241
Tran, Macy 246
Tran, Melissa 112
Trent, Bradford 165

Triplett Jr., Jerome 150
Troitino, Ciara 266
Trujillo, Tristan 278
Trulson, Donna 35
Trunnell, Ashton 190
Truong, Michael 68
Tuck, Abby 285
Tuck, Meredith 235
Tucker, Ashlyn 252
Tucker, Katherine 102
Tucker, Wyatt 284
Tuckman, Aliyah 38
Tuilagi, Derek 182
Turley, Ethan 354
Turnage, Hope 60
Turner, Brian J. 69
Turner, Dana 44
Turvey, Tascha 313
Tye, Joshua 124
Underwood, Christine . . .225
Underwood, Monica 55
Uria, Reynaldo 331
Valdez, Makayla 60
Valenza, TJ 303
Van Winkle, Devon 198
VanCamp, Andrew 171
Vance, Chayiesha 154
VanHoy, Carley 83
Varnado, Eric 46
Vaughan, Garrett 314
Vaughn, Andrew 363
Vaughn, Colton 256
Vaughn, Eric 229
Vaughn, Laura Catherine .108
Velinsky, Kyle 48
Vermillion, Laini 242
Verser, Nathan 140
VerSteeg, Jameson 193
Vestal, Kylee 17
Vidacovich, Jacob 214
Viernes, Victoria 339
Vignali, Mandy 313
Vincent, Chris 327
Volker, Shayla Nicole . . .117
Wadley, Adrian 214
Wagner, Keegan 143
Wagoner, Emma 115
Waguespack, Amy 247
Walden, Sara 167
Waldron, Ashley 65
Walker, Alden 199
Walker, Erin 88
Walker, Hope 282
Walker, Kelsey 91
Walker, Lydia 116
Walker, Shalonda T. 257
Walker, Zoyie 232

Wall, Shanan 116
Wallace, Andrew 36
Wallace, Caroline 288
Wallace, Shanika 122
Wallace, Tyler 325
Wallis, Benjamin 149
Walls, Raven 117
Walls, Tanner 30
Walsh, Ben 87
Walter, Ashley 128
Walters, Mackenzie Kay .208
Walters, Mark 184
Walz, Rachel 154
Wampler, Justin 235
Wang, Yushi 49
Ward, Charnice 276
Ward, Dylan 263
Ward, Presly 198
Ward, Sam 176
Ward, Sydney 279
Ward, Tiffany 157
Warden, Gabriella 234
Ware, Frannie 234
Ware, Nyjalik 107
Warren, Adam 145
Warren, Alexandra 223
Warren, Matthew 168
Washington, Jessica 140
Washington, Tyshon 224
Watkins, Elizabeth 189
Watson, Jazmine 90
Watson, Jordyan 275
Watson, Lydia 140
Watson, Marla 43
Watson, Sye 301
Watts, Alex 81
Weatherly, Aubry 233
Weber, Maria 228
Weber, Matt 307
Webster, Nann 341
Wedding, T. Blake 93
Wegmann, Cole 324
Wegrzyn, Tyler 198
Weimar, Jenni 85
Weisler, Bailey 302
Welch, Adam 322
Welch, Katie 31
Weldon, Coleman 135
Welker, Derek 214
Weller, Tristen 350
Wells, Ann Marie 213
Wells, Kendarius 296
Welsh, Ben 300
Wesson, Archie 102
West, Carter 209
West, Chris 190
Westmoreland, Anna . . .326

Wetherell, Casey 137
Wettstain, Ashley Marie . .188
Weyland, Graham 74
Whaley, Abbey 289
Wheatley, Sarah 187
Wheeler, Ashlynn 290
Wheeler, Kason 254
Wheeler, Kate 140
Wheeler, Mercedes 220
White, Aaliyah 143
White, Ashleigh 45
White, Ashley 217
White, Bradlee 57
White, Chantz 44
White, Jazmin 245
White, Juliana 358
White, Kallie 89
White, Laurie-Jewell 256
White, Norris 83
White, Tina 122
Whited, Emily 43
Whitehead, Meghan 66
Whitehead, Morgan 280
Whiters, Maurice 119
Whitley, Lexi 296
Whitmore, Hannah 223
Whitson, Alice 286
Wibbenmeyer, Veronica .180
Wicker, Madison 123
Wiggins, Hayden 245
Wigley, Alison 167
Wilbanks, Amber 190
Wilbanks, Lee 27
Wilkerson, Tyler 322
Wilkins, Chandler 174
Wilkinson, Charles Wayne 59
Willard, Alicia 296
Willhite, Makayla 118
Willhour, Rachel 104
Williams, Brenda 342
Williams, Dominique . . .259
Williams, Gavin 156
Williams, Jana 56
Williams, Jordan 268
Williams, Jordon 79
Williams, Judonte 243
Williams, Keith 77
Williams, Lucianna 197
Williams, Makenna 208
Williams, Mikayla 252
Williams, Nyera 186
Williams, Rachel 287
Williams, Ryan 30
Williams, Shaylin 107
Williams, Telvin 175
Williams, Zachary 295
Williamson, Autumn 287

Williamson, Megan 87
Williford, Justin 112
Williford, Tyler 208
Willis, Erin 256
Willis, Montana 224
Willoughby, Amy 30
Wilson, Bethany 217
Wilson, Caitlin 194
Wilson, Dakota 147
Wilson, Danielle 169
Wilson, Emily 363
Wilson, Hannah 92
Wilson, Ian 323
Wilson, J.T. 175
Wilson, Kali 246
Wilson, Kayla 360
Wilson, Leanna M. 90
Wilson, Marquisia 131
Wilson, McKenzie 27
Wilson, Tiffany 18
Wilson, Zachary 289
Wimmer, Arielle Marion .199
Wingenroth, Leah K. 177
Winkler, Kayla 98
Winn, Savannah 19
Witherspoon, Alycia 41
Witherspoon, Ta'Quanna 116
Withey, Erin 298
Witner, Hannah 321
Wofford, Chloe 205
Woford, Rebecca 342
Wolfe, Ashlynn 334
Wolfe, Dalton 213
Wolff, Devon 68
Wolgast, Kirstin 337
Wood, Austin 218
Wood, Duncan 349
Wood, Gavin 326
Wood, Kelsey 235
Wood, Makenzie 31
Wood, Que 351
Wood, Rocky 132
Woodle, Devyn 60
Woodliff, Alexander 117
Woods, Caitlin 304
Woods, Dajee 174
Woods, Ellie 170
Woods, Lance 150
Woods, Matt 180
Woodson, Kyla 86
Woolard, Cyrus 75
Woolbright, Haley Morgan .81
Worley, Brianna K. 114
Worley, Kate 344
Wray, Thomas 245
Wright, Audrey 102
Wright, Cameron 170

Wright, Joey 139
Wright, John-David 216
Wright, Levi 275
Wright, Nathan 141
Wright, Walker 330
Wrigley, Alexis 52
Wulff, Kira 261
Wyant, Patty 196
Wyatt, Amber 77
Wyatt, Logan 267
Wyman, Hannah 340
Yanez, Miriam V. 113
Yarborough, Grace 202
Yates, Grayson 86
Yates, Kacie 136
Yates, Nick 216
Yawn, BreAnna 294
Ybarra, Gabriel 284
Yeary, Caleb 271
Yocom, Kassidy 113
York, Catherine 287
York, Jason 121
Youmans, Alexis 112
Young, Adrianna Rose . .130
Young, Bethany 355
Young, Cierra 60
Young, Elizabeth 135
Young, Phillip 254
Young, Roman 213
Young, ShaTonya 230
Young, Shaunkeria 52
Young, Zack 101
Zalegowski, Nicole 118
Zamudio, Vitia 252
Zane, Olivia C. 215
Zeng, Katherine 345
Zheng, Caroline 61
Zheng, Yinan 214
Zimmel, Sam 20
Zimmerman, Victoria 21
Ziyadi, Jocelyn 140
Zobel, Katie 219